Cooperation

Cooperation

The Political Psychology of Effective Human Interaction

Edited by
Brandon A. Sullivan, Mark Snyder,
and John L. Sullivan

Blackwell Publishing

© 2008 by Blackwell Publishing Ltd

BLACKWELL PUBLISHING
350 Main Street, Malden, MA 02148-5020, USA
9600 Garsington Road, Oxford OX4 2DQ, UK
550 Swanston Street, Carlton, Victoria 3053, Australia

The right of Brandon A. Sullivan, Mark Snyder, and John L. Sullivan to be identified as the authors of the editorial material in this work has been asserted in accordance with the UK Copyright, Designs, and Patents Act 1988.

Designations used by companies to distinguish their products are often claimed as trademarks. All brand names and product names used in this book are trade names, service marks, trademarks, or registered trademarks of their respective owners. The publisher is not associated with any product or vendor mentioned in this book.

This publication is designed to provide accurate and authoritative information in regard to the subject matter covered. It is sold on the understanding that the publisher is not engaged in rendering professional services. If professional advice or other expert assistance is required, the services of a competent professional should be sought.

First published 2008 by Blackwell Publishing Ltd

1   2008

Library of Congress Cataloging-in-Publication Data

Cooperation : the political psychology of effective human interaction / edited by Brandon A. Sullivan, Mark Snyder, John L. Sullivan
p. cm.
Includes bibliographical references and index
ISBN 978-1-4051-5876-3 (hardcover : alk. paper)—ISBN 978-1-4051-5877-0 (paperback : alk. paper)
1. Social interaction. 2. Cooperativeness. I. Sullivan, Brandon A. II. Snyder, Mark.
III. Sullivan, John L.
HM1111.C669 2008
302′.14—dc22
2007027267

A catalogue record for this title is available from the British Library.

Set in 11/13 pt Minion
by The Running Head Limited, www.therunninghead.com
Printed and bound in Singapore
by Markono Print Media Pte Ltd

The publisher's policy is to use permanent paper from mills that operate a sustainable forestry policy, and which has been manufactured from pulp processed using acid-free and elementary chlorine-free practices. Furthermore, the publisher ensures that the text paper and cover board used have met acceptable environmental accreditation standards.

For further information on
Blackwell Publishing, visit our website at:
www.blackwellpublishing.com

Contents

Contributors

Joyce E. Bono, Department of Psychology, University of Minnesota, Minneapolis, Minnesota

Christopher Chapp, Department of Political Science, University of Minnesota, Minneapolis, Minnesota

Amy E. Colbert, Department of Management, University of Notre Dame, Notre Dame, Indiana

Ed Diener, Department of Psychology, University of Illinois, Champaign, Illinois

John F. Dovidio, Department of Psychology, University of Connecticut, Storrs, Connecticut

Natalie D. Eggum, Department of Psychology, Arizona State University, Tempe, Arizona

Nancy Eisenberg, Department of Psychology, Arizona State University, Tempe, Arizona

Victoria M. Esses, Department of Psychology, University of Western Ontario, London, Ontario, Canada

Alexis Etow, Princeton University, Princeton, New Jersey

Samuel L. Gaertner, Department of Psychology, University of Delaware, Newark, Delaware

Edward S. Greenberg, Department of Political Science, University of Colorado at Boulder, Boulder, Colorado

Shang E. Ha, Institution for Social and Policy Studies, Yale University, New Haven, Connecticut

James Hanley, Department of Political Science, Adrian College, Adrian, Michigan

Jason Hartwig, Department of Political Science, University of Oregon, Eugene, Oregon

John R. Hibbing, Department of Political Science, University of Nebraska at Lincoln, Lincoln, Nebraska

Jonathan Liss, Department of Psychology, University of Massachusetts at Boston, Boston, Massachusetts

Michael A. Milburn, Department of Psychology, University of Massachusetts at Boston, Boston, Massachusetts

Kristen Renwick Monroe, University of California at Irvine, Irvine, California

Tomonori Morikawa, School of International Liberal Studies, Waseda University (SILS), Tokyo, Japan

Kathleen M. O'Connor, Johnson Graduate School of Management, Cornell University, Ithaca, New York

J. Eric Oliver, Department of Political Science, University of Chicago, Chicago, Illinois

John Orbell, Department of Political Science, University of Oregon, Eugene, Oregon

Randall S. Peterson, London Business School, London, United Kingdom

Jane Allyn Piliavin, Department of Sociology, University of Wisconsin, Madison, Wisconsin

Radostina K. Purvanova, Department of Psychology, University of Minnesota, Minneapolis, Minnesota

Benjamin Radcliff, Department of Political Science, University of Notre Dame, Notre Dame, Indiana

Wendy M. Rahn, Department of Political Science, University of Minnesota, Minneapolis, Minnesota

Patrick M. Regan, Department of Political Science, Binghamton University, Binghamton, New York

Sarah Ronson, London Business School, London, United Kingdom

Mark Snyder, Department of Psychology, University of Minnesota, Minneapolis, Minnesota

Brandon A. Sullivan, Department of Psychology, University of Minnesota, Minneapolis, Minnesota

John L. Sullivan, Department of Political Science, University of Minnesota, Minneapolis, Minnesota

Elizabeth Theiss-Morse, Department of Political Science, University of Nebraska at Lincoln, Lincoln, Nebraska

William Tov, Department of Psychology, University of Illinois, Champaign, Illinois

Tom R. Tyler, Department of Psychology, New York University, New York, New York

Paul A. M. Van Lange, Department of Social Psychology, Free University, Amsterdam, the Netherlands

Preface

One day, the three of us were chatting about politics, and we wondered why so much public policy in the United States often seems to be at odds with central findings from social science research. Certainly, we agreed, much knowledge generated from social science research is inconclusive, controversial or ambiguous. Yet, as "practicing social scientists," it seemed to us that many of our public policies are not only uninformed by evolving knowledge in psychology, political science, sociology, and organizational behavior, but may even be contrary to the best conclusions social scientists might draw from various analyses of core topics in these disciplines. In other words, existing scientific evidence seemed to suggest that many of our public policies are based on incorrect or incomplete assumptions about human nature and about the factors that promote a happy, healthy, and productive society.

Nowhere did this disconnect between public policy and scientific knowledge seem more true than with regard to assumptions about the sources of human happiness and the power of cooperative behaviors to solve problems that confront and challenge society. It often seems that public policies are designed in such a way that they have the effect of impeding rather than maximizing human happiness, and of making cooperation both more difficult and less rewarding than narrow, self-interested activity. A simple case in point is the research on the sources of human happiness, where much evidence shows that increasing levels of income or wealth do not result in commensurate increases in levels of individual or collective happiness. Rather, factors such as satisfying and supportive interpersonal relationships and a significant measure of economic *security* (not wealth or level of income) have a much more powerful and direct impact on happiness. The findings on this topic are quite consistent. Yet, public policies often seem to be designed to maximize wealth and income, if not for the collective as a whole at least for significant sectors of society. That is, policies all too often are fashioned in such a way as to reduce the net amount of happiness, by making supportive relationships and access to the kinds of consistency and security that promote happiness more difficult to achieve. Other examples abound.

What seemed to us to tie together many examples such as the one just given is the power and potential of cooperation. We all know that cooperation is common at all levels of every society. Yet, however prevalent cooperation may be in our political culture, it does not receive the rhetorical acclaim or moral high ground accorded to competition or the myth of the self-sufficient individual. Certainly, cooperation has not been studied as widely or deeply nor has it penetrated as profoundly into the political or popular culture of the US as has the corpus of concepts related to economic competition. Our political elites are now fairly uniform in their belief that economists have shown without doubt that marketplace competition is more efficient and thus "better" than collective solutions to most human problems.

The three of us began to wonder whether there was an evolving body of social science knowledge about the nature, sources, and impact of cooperative behaviors in our society. Although understudied, the concept of cooperation is becoming more central to research in psychology and political science. We were curious about whether recent work would support common conclusions and whether we might begin to draw some inferences that could guide us toward public policies that would enhance cooperative behaviors and human happiness rather than maximize wealth or economic efficiency, neither of which do much to promote happiness once basic needs are met.

The result, of course, is this book. We asked leading social scientists who are working on topics related to cooperation to write chapters that would meet several criteria. One, they should try to provide an overview of their work and that of others who work on similar topics. Two, they should try to identify "what we know" or at least "what we think we know" from their research as it relates to cooperative behaviors. Our focus was to be on claims we believe we can make rather than mere critiques of extant work or suggestions of further work that is needed. Three, they should write their chapter for other experts who are working on similar topics, and for informed novices who could get a good sense of the kinds of claims that are now supported by research on cooperation, its sources, and its consequences. That is, the chapters should be cutting-edge but easily accessible to readers of this book. If we wish to build our public policies around the best current knowledge of what enhances human happiness, it appears that we must have a better widespread cultural understanding of human cooperation.

Frankly, we have been pleasantly surprised by the consistency and congruence of the varying streams of research reported in this volume. We probably know much more with greater certainty than the three of us expected, though much of that certainty will surely be modified significantly if this becomes a topic of greater scholarly attention in the years to come.

Finally, we dedicate this volume to our readers, who we hope will be inspired both to rethink the role of cooperation in promoting human happiness and also to make cooperation a focus of their ongoing research.

1

The Centrality of Cooperation in the Functioning of Individuals and Groups

BRANDON A. SULLIVAN, MARK SNYDER, AND JOHN L. SULLIVAN

Introduction

What are the key ingredients for a happy, meaningful, productive life? How can we create effective groups, productive organizations, and well-functioning societies? As we near the second decade of the twenty-first century, the answers that we find to these questions have implications for the future of humankind. For example, as internet and wireless technologies increasingly bring people together and allow for instant communications across the globe, simultaneously the challenges and problems faced by individuals and societies are increasing in magnitude and complexity. Globalization means that individual lives as well as groups and organizations are directly influenced by economic and political forces many thousands of miles away. How we design public policies, institutions, and organizations to capitalize on such forces and cope with the resulting change will influence the quality of life of individuals and societies around the world.

Although the scope and pace of change may be at historically high levels, certainly this is not the first time in history that humanity has faced sweeping technological, economic, political, and social change. However, even as we face such changes today, we have one important advantage over the past: a sophisticated and vigorous social science. This science is accumulating valuable empirical knowledge regarding how individuals and groups function. As a result, for the first time in history we are gaining a solid scientific understanding of how political, economic, and social forces affect individuals, groups, and societies as well as how such forces themselves operate and are, in turn, shaped by individuals, groups, and societies. We are now in a position to use this new science to enhance the quality of life and well-being of individuals, groups, and societies and allow us to deal more effectively with the complex, large-scale problems we increasingly face. In other words, while the world experiences rapidly accelerating change, we are simultaneously developing a sophisticated and vitally important science that allows us to understand and use such change to improve individual and group functioning. With the aid of social science, we may be facing a future in which individuals feel *more* in control of their lives and well-being, are *less* worried about unpredictable and sudden change, and have access to *greater* resources for coping with the difficulties and problems in life and achieving a high level of well-being. The research discussed in this book points the way toward just these sorts of outcomes even in the face of tremendous change.

Despite the maturing of social science, there are barriers to achieving the goal of a broad and truly comprehensive understanding of the social world and applications of such a scientific understanding to real-world problems and situations. Perhaps most prominent among such barriers is the often fragmented nature of the social sciences. Although psychologists, political scientists, sociologists, and others frequently study the same, or highly similar, phenomena, there is little integration across disciplines. Even within a single field, such as psychology or political science, there are many sub-disciplines which focus on self-contained research programs that may integrate research within, but seldom across, sub-disciplines (and very rarely across fields). The net result of such fragmentation is that any one line of research, although appearing to be largely self-contained, may provide only a small piece of a much larger body of research on a given phenomenon. Further, considered in isolation a stream of research may appear small in scope, with limited application, and providing tentative support for a set of hypotheses. However, if integrated across other lines of research, the picture may be quite different—the scope of a phenomenon or class of phenomena may be quite large, suggest broad-scale application, and provide quite robust support for a set of hypotheses.

In this book, we argue that social science research, when integrated across multiple disciplines and lines of research, provides a scientific understanding of the key ingredients for a happy, meaningful life, how to create effective groups, productive organizations, and well-functioning societies. We acknowledge that this understanding is partial and reflects the findings and theories of a relatively new science. However, we firmly believe that there is tremendous value to be gained in integrating across fields and sub-fields and there is now sufficient evidence to do so.

Research across the social sciences is converging on the conclusion that a key ingredient for happy, well-functioning, and productive individuals and groups involves strong connections (characterized by fair treatment, trust, and mutual support) with other individuals, groups, and institutions. This conclusion has proven to be robust across diverse lines of inquiry and across disciplines. The fundamental importance of strong, supportive interpersonal connections appears across the lifespan, having been revealed by research on infancy and childhood through old age, emerging at multiple levels of analysis from individuals and small groups to organizations and entire nations, and relating to outcomes ranging from individual happiness and health to group and organizational functioning to the vitality of communities. Although such connections do not tell the whole story of individual and group functioning, they clearly tell a very important part of that story.

At the heart of this convergence of research findings lies a deceptively simple, yet vitally important phenomenon—cooperation. Many social scientists have examined cooperation, and many more have studied phenomena directly related to cooperation. However, the true breadth and power of cooperation as a critical force in human affairs only emerges when viewed across multiple areas of research in multiple domains. Few other constructs so consistently emerge as important factors in so many different areas of inquiry. Accordingly, we have two main goals for this book. Our first goal is to present a sampling of the evidence supporting the importance of cooperation as a key factor in individual and social functioning. This evidence has been generated by many different lines of research from many different fields within the social sciences. Our second goal is to begin to integrate this large body of evidence and synthesize it into a more nuanced understanding of the nature of cooperation. This understanding includes how and why cooperation is so important as well as what can be done to capitalize on the existing research to improve individual quality of life and to create productive, effective groups, institutions, communities, and societies.

The Central Importance of Cooperation

For the purposes of this book, we define *cooperation* as behaviors undertaken by individuals and groups of individuals in the service of a shared and collective goal and to promote collective well-being. Typically, cooperative behaviors occur voluntarily and in the absence of duress. In other words, when an individual is coerced or forced into serving a collective goal, this would not be considered cooperation. *Cooperative processes* are defined in turn as phenomena that characterize the *implementation* of cooperative behavior, many of which are involved in promoting cooperative behavior and determining when and where it will occur—causing such behavior to increase or decrease over time in response to changes in goals and environmental factors.

Evidence for the importance of cooperation arises from many individual streams of research. For example, empirical studies have shown that individuals lead happier, more satisfying lives when unpredictable threats to well-being are minimized (e.g., through stable economic and political systems that respect human rights), basic needs are guaranteed, and social connections are strong and mutually supportive (Diener & Seligman, 2004; Radcliff, 2001). In other words cooperation, in various forms, is a key antecedent to human happiness. Such research also shows that happy individuals are active citizens, and productive employees, and enjoy good psychological and physical health (Diener & Seligman, 2004). Related research has found that volunteering, an altruistic form of cooperative behavior, promotes psychological adjustment and well-being (Piliavin, 2003). At the group level, empirical research has demonstrated that cooperative interpersonal interaction between members of different groups (e.g., racial, ethnic, religious groups) whether in the workplace, at school, or in the neighborhood, reduces intergroup conflict and prejudice and promotes tolerance and positive intergroup

attitudes (Gaertner & Dovidio, 2000; Oliver & Wong, 2003). Research on negotiation and group decision making has shown that cooperative behaviors are key
antecedents for high-quality negotiation outcomes and effective team decision
making (O'Connor & Tinsley, 2005; Peterson, 1997). Other research has shown
that cooperative processes within a society influence the well-being of that society,
including economic, political, and social health (Rahn, et al., 2003). As illustrated
above and throughout the chapters of this book, the list of benefits associated with
cooperation is quite lengthy and includes many factors critical to individual and
social functioning.

The convergence of such disparate lines of research on a common underpinning
of human happiness and well-being has serious implications for the health of economies, the strength and effectiveness of democracies, and our ability to successfully
deal with global challenges through collective action. One purpose of this book,
then, is to illuminate the tremendous importance of cooperation in promoting
healthy, well-functioning individuals, groups, and nations and address the question of how cooperation research can be applied toward addressing and solving
real-world problems.

Integrating Disparate Lines of Research on Cooperation

In editing this book, and in inviting authors to contribute chapters, we set out to
evaluate and answer three specific research questions regarding what social science
has learned about cooperation. Although these questions are beyond the reach of
any single line of research, we contend that they can be answered, with surprising clarity, through integrating the totality of work contained within this book.
These questions also form the first half of the framework around which this book is
organized.

Three key questions

One premise underlying this book is that there is sufficient scientific evidence to
conclude that cooperation is a key factor, and probably a necessary condition, for
individual and societal functioning. Evaluating this premise requires an answer to
the following question:

*Question 1: What are the specific effects of cooperation (and the lack thereof) on
the well-being and functioning of individuals and groups of various size, including
organizations and societies?*

The research presented in this book, backed by decades of laboratory and field
research, provides a remarkably consistent and relatively simple answer to this
question. The effects of cooperation are robust and positive, and observed at all

levels of analysis. Each chapter in this book fills in some details concerning the effects of cooperation and/or the costs of failures to cooperate.

Beyond assembling the available research to answer Question 1, a major goal of this book is to integrate findings from across the social sciences to formulate an understanding of the mechanisms that explain the power and importance of cooperation.

Question 2: How and why does cooperation influence individual and group functioning?

Although the answer to this question is more complex, and perhaps less complete, than the answer to Question 1, existing social science research does provide a provisional answer. A part of this answer lies within an understanding of how the human mind is wired emotionally, cognitively, and behaviorally. In other words, some of the mechanisms through which cooperation influences well-being involve intra-psychic processes such as the generation of positive emotions and interpersonal engagement. Further, a substantial part of the answer to Question 2 lies at the intersection of individuals and groups, and requires an understanding of the psychological functioning of individuals within groups as well as how this interrelates with group dynamics and group functioning. These mechanisms involve the interplay between individuals and groups, including factors such as leadership, policy making, and resource distribution.

The answer to Question 1 suggests that cooperation is a crucial factor in shaping highly functioning individuals and groups. The answer to Question 2 provides a conceptual understanding of *why* cooperation is so important and the myriad ways in which cooperation operates and links individuals and groups. A third question posed in this book concerns the application of this science in the service of improving the human condition. If cooperation is truly as powerful a force as we contend, and if the social sciences provide an understanding of the mechanisms through which cooperation exerts such power, then we have sufficient tools to apply this research in the service of improving individual lives through promoting various forms of cooperation. Accordingly, we posed the following research question:

Question 3: How can institutions, procedures, policies, groups, and societies be designed to facilitate cooperation and thereby increase the well-being and performance of individuals and groups?

Although this question has received somewhat less empirical attention compared to Questions 1 and 2, social science research provides an extensive, if tentative, answer.

In answering our three research questions, a number of broad themes emerge which provide conceptual guidance in constructing a deeper understanding of why cooperation is so important for individual and group well-being. These themes are reflected in multiple lines of research and represent the specific points of convergence across literatures. Further, consideration of these themes reveals a functional model of cooperation which illuminates the needs and motivations that underlie the various phenomena discussed in this book. Finally, these broad themes provide the second half of the framework around which this book is structured and the contents can be understood and organized.

Broad Themes: A Functional Understanding of Cooperation

1 Positive social connection as a source of emotional well-being

First, there is considerable evidence that feeling connected to others through a sense of group identity or shared humanity is a key component of cooperative processes. One theme running through much of the research presented here concerns how group identities are formed, the thoughts, feelings, and behaviors associated with having a sense of connection with others and groups, and what happens when such connections and group identities are not formed or are characterized by suspicion and distrust. Positive social connections serve a number of functions which center around emotional well-being and psychological adjustment. Specifically, positive social connections are a major source of happiness, life satisfaction, meaning, and other forms of positive affect, whereas poor social connections produce unhappiness, dissatisfaction with life, and other forms of negative affect. In other words, an important function of positive social connections is producing and maintaining positive emotional well-being and regulating emotions throughout the lifespan.

2 Fairness, justice, and trust as guidance for surviving and thriving in a complex social environment

Surviving and thriving as a human being requires participating in social, educational, economic, and political groups, among others. Investing time, energy, and other resources in groups that honor commitments, respect individual needs and interests, and provide justice when rules are violated is likely to reward individuals with higher-quality lives and the support necessary for coping with problems. On the other hand, investing resources in groups that do not honor commitments, do not respect individual needs and interests, and fail to correct injustice and unfairness is likely to prove detrimental to individual quality of life and deprive individuals of coping resources. As a result of the need to wisely invest personal resources in groups, the expectation of cooperation, as experienced through perceptions of fairness, justice, and trust, serve a critically important function for individuals. There is considerable evidence that a central component of cooperative processes involves ways in which groups communicate (intentionally and unintentionally) to individuals the extent to which they are valued and can expect to benefit from group support and shared resources.

It is worth noting the possibility that positive social connections, which result from participating in trustworthy, mutually supportive groups, play a key role in emotional regulation because such connections are tied to an individual's survival and level of functioning. In other words, positive social connections produce positive emotions and dampen negative affect because they indicate the individual is in a safe environment in which social support in various forms is available. However, a lack of social connections or poor connections may produce negative emotions and amplify negative affect because such a lack of positive connections indicates the individual is in an unsafe environment in which support is unavailable, threatening survival and well-being.

3 Cooperation as a foundation for group functioning and productive intergroup relations

From the perspective of groups, from small decision making groups to entire societies as well as relationships between nations, a key problem is forming a solid foundation on which such groups can function and interact productively. This task involves convincing individuals and groups to actively participate, share resources, knowledge, and expertise, respect one another, and perceive group leadership and group decisions as legitimate and, in the main, wise. Groups of all sizes and with various purposes depend upon individual participation, motivation, and investment for high-quality performance. Groups built upon a foundation of cooperation are uniquely capable of solving difficult social, political, and economic problems, generating creative, high-quality outcomes, and prove viable and robust in the face of setbacks and over time.

In sum, research on cooperation and cooperative processes can be integrated from a functional perspective in which specific constructs are connected with specific underlying needs and motivations of individuals and groups. This functional perspective is summarized in Table 1.1 and represents the heart of the conceptual model of cooperation underlying this book.

4 Cooperation as a multi-level, cross-domain phenomenon

The final piece of this conceptual puzzle involves an accounting of the multi-level nature of cooperation along with ways in which cooperation and cooperative processes cross domains. For example, cooperative processes in the workplace affect experiences at home (Bono et al., 2005) and in the political arena (Greenberg, 1986). Government economic and social policies that reflect group-level cooperation affect individual happiness and satisfaction with life (Radcliff, 2001), which in turn influence economic productivity and health (Diener & Seligman, 2004).

Table 1.1 A functional framework for understating and integrating cooperation research

Construct	Function
Positive social connection	Emotional well-being and adjustment: promotes happiness, satisfaction with life, a sense of meaning, dampens depression, anxiety, and other negative emotions; facilitates healthy affect regulation
Fairness, trust, justice	Facilitate surviving and thriving in a complex social environment; guides individuals toward a wise investment of personal resources (time, energy, knowledge, etc.) in groups
Cooperative behaviors	Facilitate group functioning and productive intergroup relations; allow for active engagement of individuals and groups in the task, sharing of knowledge and resources to solve group problems, promotes positive, tolerant attitudes within and between groups which result in creative, mutually beneficial problem-solving

Cooperative decision making influences individual behaviors as well as group functioning and the legitimacy of political leadership (Hibbing & Alford, 2004; Peterson, 1997; Tyler & Blader, 2003). Experiences with parents in early childhood influence adult political attitudes (Milburn, et al., 1995). These are just some of the most prominent examples of research showing that the effects of cooperation in one domain are interconnected with phenomena in other domains. Such interconnection suggests that a full portrait of cooperation would cross economic, political, educational, medical, and interpersonal domains (among others). An important corollary of this interdependence is that a lack of cooperation within one domain, such as mistrust in the workplace or with government, is likely to have a negative impact on other domains, such as interpersonal relationships and health.

Another way to look at the deep interconnection that characterizes cooperation is by *level of analysis*. For example, individuals who experience cooperative processes in their daily lives experience greater psychological well-being and less risk of various psychological and physical illnesses, are more motivated, productive, and committed at work, are more trusting of other people, are more supportive of leaders and group decisions, invest more of their resources in groups, communities, and politics, are less prejudiced and more tolerant toward others, are more likely to help other people, and are more effective at resolving conflicts (Bono, et al., 2005; Diener & Seligman, 2004; Eisenberg, Valiente, & Champion, 2004; Gaertner & Dovidio, 2000; Hibbing & Alford, 2004; Monroe, 1996; O'Connor & Tinsley, 2005; Oliver & Wong, 2003; Piliavin, 2003; Tyler & Blader, 2003). At the group level (e.g., small groups, organizations, communities, etc.), cooperation is associated with greater group cohesiveness, sharing of resources and knowledge, effective management of conflict, tension, and negative feedback, the ability to forge positive,

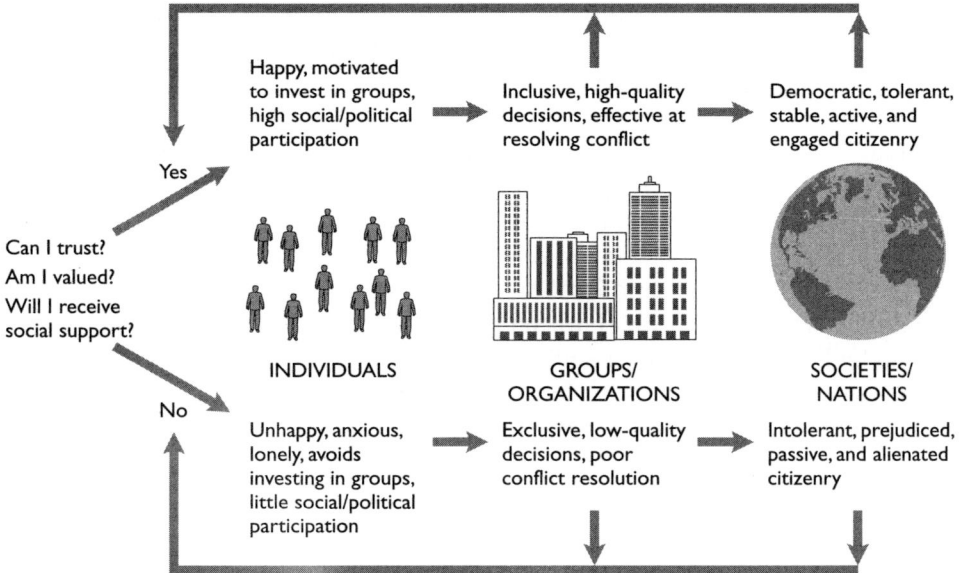

Figure 1.1 A multi-level model of cooperation and related processes

productive relationships with other groups, resolution of intergroup conflict, better leadership, and higher-quality group decisions (e.g., Gaertner & Dovidio, 2000; Peterson, 1997; Peterson & Behfar, 2003). Even among very large groups, such as entire nations and groups of nations, cooperation is related to the overall level of happiness and life satisfaction among the population, the strength and robustness of democracy and corporate profitability (through a more motivated and active citizenry), greater trust in government and support for public policies, the availability of various forms of help and support for people in distress, less intergroup conflict, including prejudice and violence, and more effective resolution and management of international conflicts (e.g., Oliver & Wong, 2003; Rahn, Yoon, Garet, Lipson, & Laflin, 2003).

From a conceptual point of view, the cross-level nature of cooperation means that cooperation involves complex, iterative processes in which individuals and groups continually influence one another in profound and important ways. Based upon evidence that individuals are active regulators of cooperative behavior, we propose a model of cooperation that captures the functional aspects of cooperation, the cross-level and cross-domain nature of cooperation, and the iterative processes that characterize changes in cooperation over time. This model, presented in Figure 1.1, begins with a set of questions individuals ask when deciding whether to cooperate. Specifically, individuals evaluate whether others can be trusted, whether they are valued by others, and whether others will provide various forms of support. To the extent that an individual answers "yes" to these questions, such a person will increase their level of cooperation with others, whereas answers of "no" will result in a decrease of cooperation. At any given point in time, every human being is engaged in this sort of evaluation and is deciding whether and how to cooperate with various individuals and groups.

When many individuals are inclined toward a high level of cooperation, groups and organizations are more likely to have active, engaged, and mutually supportive members. In turn, individuals will have increased access to more and better resources compared to those who do not belong to cooperative groups. This increased access to resources will raise those individuals' levels of happiness and satisfaction. In addition, groups will prove more robust and will be more effective at any given task or problem. When a society is characterized by a high level of cooperation, individuals will look out upon a social environment in which they can trust other people, depend upon groups and institutions to be receptive to individual needs, and in which resources and support are available to cope with problems that arise. Since this is an iterative process, individuals will respond to such an environment by increasing or maintaining their level of cooperation and will then enjoy the associated benefits. In contrast, when a society is characterized by exclusive, intolerant, and unresponsive groups, individuals will see a landscape in which cooperation is foolish at best and possibly dangerous. In this case, individuals are likely to become even less cooperative and suffer the associated consequences.

Individual Regulation of Cooperative Behavior

The cross-level and cross-domain perspective also supports the importance of cooperative processes, ancillary to cooperation itself, as a central component of understanding cooperation. Specifically, there is considerable evidence that individuals are often predisposed toward cooperation but actively monitor and regulate such behavior, taking account of circumstances that make cooperation a more or less appropriate action. Such active regulation of cooperative behavior is supported by a wide range of research from many different areas within the social sciences, including psychology, political science, sociology, and organizational behavior. Individual cooperation in groups (e.g., the extent to which individuals invest energy in a collective effort, willingness to abide by group decisions) is highly responsive to whether or not group processes are inclusive, just, and respectful of individual needs (Hibbing & Alford, 2004; Hibbing & Theiss-Morse, this volume; Tyler & Blader, 2003; Tyler & Lind, 1992). Even individuals who are strongly predisposed toward cooperative behavior tend to abandon cooperation when another person fails to reciprocate or when trust is breached (Van Lange, 1999; Van Lange, 2004). Cooperative, prosocial behaviors within teams, organizations, and societies are dependent upon the level of trust experienced within such groups (Greenberg, 1986; Peterson & Behfar, 2003; Rahn et al., 2003; Simons & Peterson, 2000). Similarly, negotiators regulate cooperative and competitive bargaining tactics depending upon how cooperative or competitive the other party is expected to be

(O'Connor & Tinsley, 2005; Tinsley, O'Connor, & Sullivan, 2002). Evolutionary models of human cognitive capacities predict that the ability to adjust cooperative behaviors to the situation is highly adaptive and functional (Orbell, Morikawa, Hartwig, Hanley, & Allen, 2004).

Taken as a whole, these lines of research suggest that people want to work together toward common goals, pool their resources and knowledge, and function as part of a larger community of other individuals with shared concerns. This tendency is a fortunate one, it would seem, as the viability and robustness of groups depend heavily upon such cooperation among individuals. However, when cooperation is unsafe, individuals tend to cease cooperating and working toward group goals and promoting collective well-being—which, although self-protective, also results in a lack of group resources, knowledge, and other forms of support. In other words, although failing to cooperate may help the individual under certain circumstances, a failure to cooperate can undermine the viability and functioning of groups and organizations, which may in turn often prove harmful to individuals. Alternatively, continuing to cooperate in the face of mistrust and deception represents one example of a situation in which cooperation is detrimental to individual well-being. In other words, a failure to actively regulate cooperation may cause an individual to be taken advantage of by others.

Beyond the Individual: Is Cooperation an Emergent or Aggregated Phenomenon?

One key question that arises when considering groups such as work teams, organizations, neighborhoods, and societies is whether cooperative behaviors at such levels of analysis are primarily the aggregated behaviors of individual group members or whether group-level cooperation also reflects emergent properties that cannot be reduced to individual behaviors. This question is actually quite profound from the standpoint of synthesizing a broad conceptual model of cooperation. If group-level cooperation is simply aggregated individual behavior, then research on groups can be understood and conceptualized as simply an extension of research on individuals applied to various social situations, such as work teams and political processes. As a result, it would be possible to predict what will happen to groups by knowing what is happening to individuals (e.g., whether trust in government is increasing or declining, the extent to which individuals are satisfied with life, etc.). However, if group-level cooperation reflects emergent properties, then research on groups, although not independent of individual-level phenomena, can be understood as exploring phenomena and processes that may be qualitatively different from those observed at the individual level of analysis. Further, emergent properties of groups would make it impossible to predict what will happen to groups even with a highly precise and sophisticated understanding of individuals.

To illustrate the importance of emergent properties, consider the following hypothetical scenario. Within a society, survey research has documented a small, consistent, linear decline in trust among individuals. When asked to indicate their level of trust in government institutions and corporations individuals have been reporting slightly lower levels each year for the past two decades. If group-level phenomena are simply aggregated phenomena, then we would predict that groups of various sizes within this society would experience a small, consistent, linear decline in cohesiveness, engagement, and effectiveness as individual group members reduce their level of cooperation. On the other hand, emergent properties would render group behavior fundamentally unpredictable based on knowledge of the decline in trust. For example, it is possible that group-level behavior would, in fact exhibit a slow, steady change until an unforeseen "tipping point" is reached, at which point group behavior may suddenly change exponentially and quite rapidly, with some groups becoming vastly more cohesive and active and others disintegrating. The reason for such a discontinuity in predicting group-level behavior from individual-level phenomena would be the operation of cooperative processes that are unique to groups and can only be observed by studying groups.

We argue, based on the available evidence, that cooperation at the group-level does reflect emergent properties. For example, the level of general social trust (i.e., the tendency to trust other people) within a society is heavily influenced by social-contextual factors and cannot be accounted for by aggregating individual experiences (Rahn, et al., 2003). The available evidence, however, is insufficient to detail exactly which properties are emergent versus aggregate or how such emergent properties arise. We propose that this is an important area for future research which concerns fundamental processes underlying group functioning.

Overview of Chapters

Because we contend that research from across the social sciences is converging on cooperation as a key factor in human functioning, we invited authors from various disciplines, including psychology, political science, organizational behavior, and sociology to contribute chapters. To further facilitate the integration of such diverse research, illustrate the multi-disciplinary nature of the convergence, and to specifically link different streams of research that reflect similar findings, we grouped authors into sections (each with two or three authors) according to underlying themes and findings, with the authors in each section approaching the subject matter of that section from a different disciplinary perspective. Taken as a whole, these eighteen chapters provide a truly comprehensive evaluation of the science of cooperation.

The first pair of chapters answers the question "What is it about people that leads them to cooperate?" A chapter by Paul Van Lange on individual differences in pro-social behavior and a chapter by James Hanley, Jason Hartwig, John Orbell, and Tomonori Morikawa, on evolutionary psychology document some of the more distal antecedents to cooperative behavior. The authors of both chapters argue that cooperative behaviors have tremendous functional value for individuals and groups. Their research describes some of the important processes underlying cooperation (and non-cooperation) and provides an understanding of why people are particularly sensitive to breaches of trust and being manipulated by others.

Next, a set of three chapters answers the question "What are the developmental precursors of cooperation and conflict?" A chapter by Nancy Eisenberg and Natalie Eggum on the development of prosocial behavior, a chapter by Michael Milburn and Jonathan Liss on the affective roots of cooperation, and a chapter by Kristen Monroe and Alexis Etow on altruism each illustrate the ways in which cognitive and affective factors importantly shape individuals' willingness to engage in cooperative, prosocial behaviors. This work also identifies key factors that may cause individuals to adopt a non-cooperative orientation. Together, this research shows how developmental processes play a key role in cooperative behaviors. It also documents important implications for social behavior, including the extent to which individuals offer help and support to others, and for political attitudes.

A third section answers the question "How and why do people cooperate within their group?" A chapter by Tom Tyler on group procedures and a chapter by John Hibbing and Elizabeth Theiss-Morse on group decision making explore the processes through which groups and those in positions of authority can facilitate or undermine cooperation on the part of group members. This research has important implications for understanding the conditions under which individuals are willing to invest personal resources in a group and to accept group decisions (even if the decision is costly to the self) as opposed to the conditions under which individuals may resist accepting such decisions. These authors also explore some of the individual cognitive processes that mediate the association between group processes and individuals' willingness to cooperate, which touches on certain aspects of the process of cooperation itself. Further, they delineate some of the key aspects of cooperative processes, such as critical factors that may cause someone to abruptly cease cooperating or that may enhance cooperation.

A fourth section answers the question "What conditions promote or impede cooperation between diverse groups?" A chapter by John Dovidio, Samuel Gaertner, and Victoria Esses on intergroup cooperation and a chapter by Eric Oliver and Shang Ha on relations between racial and ethnic groups identify critical aspects of intergroup relations and address the difficult and common problem of intergroup prejudice and conflict. From the perspective of cooperation, this problem reflects not only a situation in which individuals and groups actively resist cooperation, but they may also act in ways to harm members of an out-group. These authors have discovered very powerful forces acting on individuals and communities that can either exacerbate intergroup prejudice or alleviate such prejudice and promote intergroup cooperation. This research, although focused on antecedents to cooperation, also shows some important cross-level connections between social-contextual factors and individual cognitions that mediate cooperative behaviors.

A fifth section answers the question "What are the causes and consequences of cooperation and conflict in the workplace?" A chapter by Sarah Ronson and Randall Peterson on cooperation in work groups, a chapter by Amy Colbert, Joyce Bono, and Radostina Purvanova on leadership, and a chapter by Edward Greenberg on spillover effects from the workplace each discuss the importance of the workplace as both a key antecedent to cooperation and a key beneficiary of cooperative behaviors. Taken together, these lines of research show how organizational factors, such as group decision-making processes and leadership, can promote cooperative behaviors on the part of individual employees.

A sixth section answers the question "How does cooperation promote the health of individuals and communities?" A chapter by Jane Piliavin on volunteering and a chapter by Wendy Rahn on trust and political participation discuss powerful connections between cooperative processes and the well-being and functioning of individuals and communities. This research suggests some important antecedents to cooperative behaviors and processes through which such behaviors influence individual and community well-being. Jane Piliavin's research explores this question in terms of consequences for the individual whereas Wendy Rahn's work explores consequences for social and political functioning.

A seventh section answers the question "What is the role of cooperation in negotiation and conflict resolution?" A chapter by Kathleen O'Connor on negotiation and a chapter by Pat Regan on armed conflict each discuss how cooperative processes are central to conflict resolution ranging from negotiating business deals to bringing a halt to military conflicts and civil wars. This work informs a greater understanding of both cooperative processes and the central importance of such processes in managing and solving conflict.

A final pair of chapters addresses the question "How does cooperation promote the well-being and happiness of individuals and nations?" A chapter by Benjamin Radcliff on politics and happiness and a chapter by William Tov and Ed Diener on subjective well-being across nations each documents the important role of cooperative processes, at multiple levels of analysis, in promoting human happiness as well as the reciprocal relationship between happiness and individual and group-level functioning. When individuals and governments behave in ways aimed at promoting collective goals and ensuring collective well-being, individuals and nations are generally happy, satisfied with life, and achieve high levels of functioning.

Taken together, these eighteen chapters illustrate a wide range of social and political phenomena. We argue here that the research presented in each chapter illuminates an important component of a broad scientific understanding of cooperation and cooperative processes. We further delineate and describe key components of this broad understanding in the final chapter of the book. The final chapter revisits the scientific contributions of each of the previous eighteen chapters and provides added integration of these contributions as well as directions for future research.

References

Bono, J. E., Jackson, H. L., Vinson, G. A., & Muros, J. P. (in press). Workplace emotional regulation: The role of supervision and leadership. *Journal of Applied Psychology.*

Diener, E., & Seligman, M. (2004). Beyond money: Toward an economy of well-being. *Psychological Science in the Public Interest, 5,* 1–31.

Eisenberg, N., Valiente, C., & Champion, C. (2004). Empathy-related responding: Moral, social, and socialization correlates. In A. G. Miller (Ed.), *The social psychology of good and evil: Understanding our capacity for kindness and cruelty* (pp. 386–415). New York: Guilford Press.

Gaertner, S. L., & Dovidio, J. F. (2000). *Reducing intergroup bias: The common ingroup identity model.* Philadelphia: Taylor and Francis.

Greenberg, E. (1986). *Workplace democracy.* Ithaca, NY: Cornell University Press.

Hibbing, J. R., & Alford, J. R. (2004). Accepting authoritative decisions: Humans as wary cooperators. *American Journal of Political Science, 48,* 62–76.

Milburn, M. A., Conrad, S. D., Sala, F., & Carberry, S. (1995). Childhood punishment, denial, and political attitudes. *Political Psychology, 16,* 447–476.

Monroe, K. R. (1996). *The heart of altruism: Perceptions of a common humanity.* Princeton, NJ: Princeton University Press.

Oliver, J. E., & Wong, J. (2003). Intergroup prejudice in multi-ethnic settings. *American Journal of Political Science, 47,* 567–582.

Orbell, J., Morikawa, T., Hartwig, J., Hanley, J., & Allen, N. (2004). "Machiavellian" intelligence as a basis for the evolution of cooperative dispositions. *American Political Science Review, 98,* 1–15.

Peterson, R. S. (1997). A directive leadership style in group decision making can be both virtue and vice: Evidence from elite and experimental groups. *Journal of Personality and Social Psychology, 72,* 1107–1121.

Peterson, R. S., & Behfar, K. J. (2003) The dynamic relationship between performance feedback, trust, and conflict in groups: A longitudinal study. *Organizational Behavior & Human Decision Processes, 92,* 102–112.

Piliavin, J. A. (2003). Doing well by doing good: Benefits for the benefactor. In C. L. M. Keyes, & J. Haidt (Eds.), *Flourishing: Positive psychology and the life well-lived* (pp. 227–247). Washington, DC: American Psychological Association.

Radcliff, B. (2001). Politics, markets, and life satisfaction: The political economy of human happiness. *American Political Science Review, 95,* 939–952.

Rahn, W. M., Yoon, K. S., Garet, M., Lipson, S., & Loflin, K. (2003). *Geographies of trust: Explaining inter-community variation in general social trust using hierarchical linear modeling (HLM).* Paper presented at the 58th Annual Conference of the American Association for Public Opinion Research, Nashville, TN.

Simons, T., & Peterson, R. (2000). Task conflict and relationship conflict in top management teams: The pivotal role of intragroup trust. *Journal of Applied Psychology, 83,* 102–111.

Tinsley, C. H. & O'Connor, K. M. (2007). Looking for an edge? Cultivate an integrative reputation. *Negotiation,* Harvard Law School Program on Negotiation.

Tinsley, C. H., O'Connor, K. M., & Sullivan, B. A. (2002). Tough guys finish last: The perils of a distributive reputation. *Organizational Behavior and Human Decision Processes, 88,* 621–642.

Tyler, T. R., & Blader, S. L. (2003). The group engagement model: Procedural justice, social identity, and cooperative behavior. *Personality and Social Psychology Review, 7,* 349–361.

Tyler, T. R., & Lind, E. A. (1992). A relational model of authority in groups. *Advances in Experimental Social Psychology, 25*, 115–191.

Van Lange, P. A. M. (1999). The pursuit of joint outcomes and equality in outcomes: An integrative model of social value orientation. *Journal of Personality and Social Psychology, 77*, 337–349.

Van Lange, P. A. M. (2004). From generosity to aggression: Five interpersonal orientations relevant to social dilemmas. In R. Suleiman, D. V. Budescu, I. Fisher, & D. M. Messick (Eds.), *Contemporary psychological research on social dilemmas* (pp. 3–23). Cambridge, UK: Cambridge University Press.

2

Logical and Paradoxical Effects

Understanding Cooperation in Terms of Prosocial and Proself Orientations

PAUL A. M. VAN LANGE

Are people good or bad? Are people good *and* bad? Are people basically selfish, or would it be more accurate to characterize human nature by a broader set of interpersonal orientations? The dominating view in science on human nature has been that people primarily or exclusively pursue self-interest, with little or no regard for the well-being of others. Indeed, philosophers such as Thomas Hobbes or economists such as Adam Smith may easily come to mind, even though the assumption of rational self-interest is widespread among most or all scientific fields and disciplines. For example, within psychology, there are longstanding concepts such as the "pursuit of pleasure" in psychoanalytic theory, "utility" in models of social decision making, or "reinforcement" in theories of learning and behavior modification, which are rooted in the assumption of self-interest. And most nonscientists, too, tend to rely on a belief in "selfishness" when making judgments or when seeking to understand social behavior.

We suggest that the assumption of rational self-interest is too limited to account for interpersonal behavior. In fact, like Miller (1999), we suggest that people are inclined to use a biased framework for interpreting others' behavior, but not their own behavior or that of others close to them. Indeed, there is good deal of evidence indicating that people think of themselves as better than others, especially on attributes that are strongly linked to selfishness, such as being "good", being honest, and the like (e.g., Van Lange & Sedikides 1998). A more accurate representation of human nature can be derived from theorizing and research on interpersonal orientations (Kelley & Thibaut 1978; Van Lange 1999). In recent conceptualizations, a typology of five interpersonal orientations is advanced, designed to help us understand the basic decision rules (or motives) that people adopt in their interpersonal dealings. As can be seen in Table 2.1, the orientations include: (a) altruism, enhancement of other's outcomes; (b) cooperation, enhancement of own and other's outcomes (or joint outcomes); (c) equality, minimization of absolute differences between own and other's outcomes; (d) individualism, enhancement of own outcomes; (e) competition, enhancement of relative advantage over other's outcomes;

Table 2.1   An overview of five interpersonal orientations

1 Altruism	Enhancement of outcomes for others
2 Prosocial orientation	(a) Enhancement of joint outcomes (cooperation) (b) Enhancement of equality in outcomes (egalitarianism)
3 Individualism	Enhancement of outcomes for self
4 Competition	Enhancement of relative outcomes in favor of self
5 Aggression	Reduction of outcomes for other

Note: In this typology, prosocial orientation represents two conceptually distinct, but empirically interrelated orientations: cooperation and egalitarianism. These two orientations tend to go hand in hand (for empirical evidence, see Van Lange, 1999).

and (f) aggression, minimization of other's outcomes. However, prosocial orientation represents two specific decision rules—equality and cooperation—which tend to go hand in hand. Generally speaking, people who seek to enhance what is best for all (cooperation) also tend to value equality in outcomes (Van Lange 1999; Van Lange, De Cremer, Van Dijk, & Van Vugt, in press).

The major goal of the present chapter is to review evidence in support of six interpersonal orientations: Altruism, cooperation, equality, individualism, competition, and aggression. A secondary goal is to outline that each of these orientations can exert "logical effects" as well as "paradoxical effects" on behavior that supports collectively desired outcomes. Paradoxical effects imply that under some circumstances the activation of a given prosocial orientation may undermine collectively desired outcomes, and that the activation of proself orientations may support collectively desired outcomes. The implications of these effects for individuals and groups in society are outlined, with a strong emphasis on how we can promote collectively desired outcomes on the basis of these orientations.

A Social Interaction Analysis

What does it mean to adopt a social interaction analysis to interpersonal orientations? It means at least four things. First, it means that it conceptualizes these tendencies in terms of social interactions, which are defined in terms of persons and situations (see Kelley et al., 2003). Specifically, for a dyad, social interaction is defined as:

Social interaction = F (self, partner, and situation)

A key component of interaction is the situation, as it affords various orientations that people may take to these situations. For example, a social dilemma focuses on the conflict between self-interest and collective interest, thereby affording "selfishness" (such as the direct pursuit of one's own outcomes) and "cooperation" (such as the pursuit of collective outcomes). But importantly, by examining interactions, we also see that orientations such as equality become important. For example, equality as an instance of fairness may become important because of influences regarding the self (e.g., I hold a prosocial orientation, and thus wish to pursue equality in outcomes), because of partner influences (e.g., the partner holds a competitive orientation by which equality becomes very salient), or because the situation represents inequality (e.g., one has greater outcomes than the other when they initiated the interaction). Similarly, altruism is also activated by the self, the partner and the situation, as there is interindividual variability in empathy (e.g., dispositional empathy, Davis 1983), empathy may be more strongly activated by some partners than by others (e.g., one's child vs. a stranger), and some situational features are especially likely to call for empathy (e.g., when the partner is strongly dependent on your help).

Second, a social interaction analysis provides a fairly inclusive analysis, in that it allows us to focus on distal and proximal determinants of social interactions. Examples of distal determinants are personality variables (e.g., differences in prosocial, individualistic, and competitive orientations, Van Lange, Otten, De Bruin, & Joireman, 1997), relational variables (e.g., differences in trust in the partner; differences in relational commitment; Rusbult & Van Lange 2003), and situational variables (e.g., climates of trust versus distrust; group size). Examples of proximal mechanisms (which often are both a determinant and a consequence of social interactions) are emotions (e.g., feelings of guilt, feelings of shame), and cognitions (e.g., how the situation is "defined," especially in terms of norms and roles; Van Lange et al., in press). For example, prosocials may believe that others tend to be prosocial, individualistic or competitive, whereas competitors tend to believe that most or all others are competitive. Such beliefs may be rooted in social interaction experiences, with prosocials often developing interactions of mutual cooperation or mutual non-cooperation, and competitors often developing interactions of mutual non-cooperation. The latter experiences confirm their belief that "all people are competitive," even though in many cases it may have been the result of their own actions: indeed, a perfect example of a self-fulfilling prophecy (Kelley & Stahelski 1970). Thus, this example shows that beliefs can affect interaction outcomes, which in turn can affect beliefs.

Third, a social interaction analysis is also important from the perspective of observation and learning. Social interactions are largely observable to the self, to the other, as well as to third parties who may not be involved (e.g., observers). As such, the manner in which social interactions unfold (e.g., two people on the route to cooperation versus two people on the route to non-cooperation due to one person's lack of cooperation) serves important communicative purposes—both for the actors and for the observers. Actors may signal their boundaries of cooperation (e.g., by communicating threats and promises), and learn from their actions in their interactions (e.g., "Next time, I will more carefully examine his responses to my cooperative initiatives"). Observers may learn as well, an example being children copying and "learning from" interactions between their parents. The point is that social interaction experiences will often provide the basis for the development of a particular personality style. For example, people raised in larger families may be more likely to develop an orientation of equality because the situations that they enter are more likely to call for sharing (e.g., they learn quickly that not sharing is a dysfunctional way in which to solve social dilemmas; see Van Lange et al., 1997).

Finally, a social interaction analysis dictates the importance of interpersonal orientations; that is, the preferences that people have regarding the ways in which outcomes are allocated to themselves and others. We suggest that there are six important orientations, or decision rules, that can be meaningfully distinguished: Altruism, egalitarianism, cooperation, individualism, competition, and aggression, to which we turn our attention next.

Altruism

The claim that altruism should be considered an interpersonal orientation is rather controversial. Indeed, as most readers know, there has been a fair amount of debate about the existence of altruism both within and beyond psychology. Much of the controversy, however, deals with definitions of altruism, ranging from behavioral definitions (i.e., acts of costly helping are considered altruistic; Fehr & Gächter, 2002) to definitions that seek to exclude any possible mechanism that may be activated by some consideration that may not be free of self-interest (e.g., Cialdini, Brown, Lewis, Luce, & Neuberg, 1997). If we limit our discussion, for parsimony's sake, to research on cooperation and competition and to allocation measures, then we see that altruism is not very prominent. For example, in assessments of interpersonal orientations in a specific resource allocation task, the percentage of people who should be classified as altruistic (i.e. assigning no weight to their own outcomes while assigning substantial weight to other's outcomes) is close to zero (Liebrand & Van Run, 1985). Similarly, when people playing a single-choice prisoner's dilemma observe that the other makes a non-cooperative choice, the percentage of cooperation drops to 5% or less (Van Lange, 1999).

But this evidence should not be interpreted to mean altruism does not exist. In fact, what is more likely is that it does not exist under the (interpersonal) circumstances that are common in this tradition of research. People usually face a decision making task, be it a social dilemma task, a resource allocation task, or a negotiation task, in which they are interdependent with a "relative stranger" in that there is no history of social interaction or other form of relationship. Accordingly, there is no basis for feelings of interpersonal attachment, sympathy, or relational commitment.

We suggest that when such feelings are activated, altruism may very well exist. In fact, relative strangers (even animals) can elicit empathy, as we know from some movies (e.g., the killing of Bambi's mother in the movie *Bambi*).

As a case in point, Batson and Ahmad (2001) had participants play a single-trial prisoner's dilemma in which the other made the first choice. Before the social dilemma task, the other shared some personal information that her partner had ended the relationship with her, and that she finds it hard to think about anything else. Batson and Ahmad compared three conditions, one of which was a high-empathy condition in which participants were asked to imagine and adopt the other person's perspective. The other conditions were either a low-empathy condition, in which participants were instructed to take an objective perspective on the information shared by the other, or a condition in which no personal information was shared. After these instructions, participants were informed that the other makes a non-cooperative choice. Batson and Ahmad found that nearly half of the participants (45%) in the high-empathy condition made a cooperative choice, while the percentages in the other low empathy and control conditions were very low, as shown in earlier research (less than 5%, as in Van Lange, 1999). Hence, this study provides a powerful demonstration of the power of empathy in activating choices that can be understood in terms of altruism, in that high-empathy participants presumably assigned substantial weight to the outcomes for the other at the expense of their own outcomes. While altruism may serve more functions (e.g., generosity may be essential to dealing with misunderstanding; e.g., Van Lange, Ouwerkerk, & Tazelaar, 2002), one may speculate that, ultimately, the functional value of empathy derives from helping others in need. Indeed, if we were completely unable to empathize, then our children would be less likely to survive through important failures to help. However, the important point is that empathy can be a powerful motivator of behavior and interaction in social dilemmas.

Egalitarianism

The existence of egalitarianism or equality may be derived from various lines of research. To begin with, several experiments have been conducted within the realm of resource-sharing tasks to examine the factors that may determine different "rules of fairness." In these tasks, a group of people shares a resource and the problem that these decision makers are confronted with is how to optimally use the resource without overusing it. Research by Allison and Messick (1990) provided a powerful demonstration of what happens in such situations. Their results showed that when participants (in a group of six people) are asked to harvest first from the common resource, people almost without exception use the equal division rule. Individuals tend to favor equality in outcomes (rather than more complicated rules of fairness). Allison and Messick (1990) suggested that equality represents a decision heuristic that has the advantages of being simple, efficient, and fair. As such, equality has great potential to promote the quality and effectiveness of interpersonal relationships, and therefore can be considered as a "decision rule" that is deeply rooted in people's orientations toward others.

Another powerful illustration of equality in interdependence situations is when people have to negotiate allocations (e.g., how to allocate monetary outcomes). This problem is often addressed in research on ultimatum bargaining games, an exceedingly popular paradigm in experimental economics for over two decades (see Güth, Schmittberger, & Schwarze, 1982). In this negotiation setting, two players have to decide how to distribute a certain amount of money. One of the players, the allocator, offers a proportion of the money to the other player, the recipient. If the recipient accepts, the money will be distributed in agreement with the allocator's offer. If the recipient rejects the offer, both players get nothing. Some of the first studies using this research paradigm demonstrated that allocators generally proposed an equal distribution (i.e., a 50–50 split) of the money (for an overview, see Camerer & Thaler, 1995).

Although equality is in the eye of many the prime example of fairness, we already noted that fairness might also take different forms, independent of outcomes (at least tangible outcomes). More precisely, allocating outcomes is always accompanied by procedures guiding allocation decisions (Thibaut & Walker, 1975). The focus on procedural fairness was further inspired by research showing that when people are asked to talk about their personal experiences of injustice they are usually found to talk primarily about procedural issues, in particular about being treated with a lack of dignity and politeness when dealing with others (e.g., Mikula, Petri, & Tanzer, 1990). To conclude, egalitarianism has received attention in distinct literatures, often supporting the notion that equality in outcomes and treatment is deeply rooted in our system, in that equality often serves as a powerful, highly internalized norm as well as a heuristic for our own actions and expectations regarding other's actions.

Cooperation

There is a fair amount of research showing that the enhancement of joint outcomes, or cooperation, is an important consideration. People have a pronounced tendency to consider not only outcomes for themselves, but also outcomes for others. The enhancement of joint outcomes may sometimes take the form of self-interest and assigning positive weight to others' outcomes (or doing no harm to others). But perhaps just as often, or more often, the enhancement of joint outcomes takes the form of enhancing outcomes for the group as a whole (a tendency sometimes referred to as collectivism, see Batson, 1994). In terms of decision rules, in both cases, individuals tend to enhance joint outcomes (even though they may assign greater weight to outcomes for self than to outcomes for other).

Psychologically, the two types of cooperation are substantially different. The tendency to assign some positive weight to others' outcomes may be accompanied by a variety of mechanisms, such as wanting to act in line with the "no harm" principle (Batson, 1994), adopting a norm of social responsibility which dictates helping. The tendency to enhance group outcomes may readily be activated (e.g., at the very beginning of group formation), and is powerfully activated by identification with the group (e.g., Brewer & Kramer, 1986; Van Vugt & Hart, 2004). To the extent that a person feels more strongly part of, and valued by, the group, or the extent that a person derives self-definition and esteem from the group, individuals are more likely to behave cooperatively. A classic case in point is research by Brewer and Kramer (1986), in which participants were categorized as psychology students (i.e., the actual participants, hence strong group identity) or economics students (i.e., weak group identity). Using a specific resource dilemma, Brewer and Kramer showed that under conditions of strong identity, individuals were more likely to behave cooperatively when it was essential to the group (i.e., when the resources were near depletion). Such cooperative efforts were not observed when group identity was low. It has been suggested that under conditions of strong identity, there may be a blurring of the distinction between personal outcomes and collective outcomes—that is, me and mine become we and ours, just as we and ours become me and mine (e.g., Van Vugt & Hart, 2004).

Individualism

The fact that we suggest that "self-interest" alone is too limited to fully understand social interaction is not to deny the existence of individualism. Indeed, individualism, or the concern with own outcomes, as likely to be a very prominent orientation in a variety of different contexts. In fact, individualism may well be one of the primary anchors (or points of departure) that people use to interpret interpersonal situations. In many ways, people may approach an interpersonal problem as if it is an impersonal problem, and then "add" interpersonal preferences to it. For example, in deciding whether to go to a movie with a friend, people may first consider which movie they themselves would like to see, and later think about (or inquire about) the preferences that the friend may have, and then whether, how or even why they should take account of the friend's preferences. A concern with one's outcomes is an important orientation, and the literature documents numerous phenomena that align with an individualistic orientation.

Research on social dilemmas illustrates that individualism is an important orientation. For example, the success of tit-for-tat in dyadic interaction is arguably a consequence of the fact that individuals concerned with their own outcomes, now and in the future, should cooperate with a partner pursuing tit-for-tat (Kuhlman & Marshello, 1975; Van Lange & Visser, 1999). Variations in the so-called "payoff structure," by which one makes cooperation more appealing or non-cooperation less appealing, promote cooperation (see Komorita & Parks, 1995).

In fact, in social psychology alone, there are several empirically supported phenomena that suggest a strong concern with own "outcomes." Examples are the *self-serving bias*, by which people attribute success to internal causes and failure to external causes; and *self-enhancement*, the belief that one is superior to others on a number of attributes, or tendencies toward thinking and reasoning in terms of I, me, and mine (rather than we, us, and ours). The fact that each of these phenonema has also been demonstrated at collective levels (e.g., an ingroup or a relationship) once again illustrates that individualism alone is not enough.

Competition

There is also strong evidence in support of competition as an orientation quite distinct from self-interest. As noted earlier, the work by Messick and McClintock (1968) has inspired considerable research that reveals that not only cooperative orientations but also competitive orientations may underlie social interactions. For example, Kuhlman and Marshello (1975) have demonstrated that individuals with cooperative orientations do not tend to exploit others who exhibit cooperation at every interaction situation, irrespective of the individual's own behavior. They also showed that individuals with competitive orientations do not exhibit cooperation, even if cooperative behavior, rather than non-cooperative behavior, best serves their own personal outcomes (e.g., the tendency to compete with tit-for-tat partners, yielding bad outcomes; see Van Lange & Visser, 1999).

The importance of competition is even more directly shown in research on a decision making task that represents a conflict between, on the one hand, cooperation and individualism (Option A) and, on the other hand, competition (Option B). Hence, the only consideration to choose Option B is to receive better outcomes (or less worse outcomes) than the other, even though one could do better for oneself by choosing Option A. Research using this so-called Maximizing Difference Game has revealed that quite a few people choose the competitive alternative; it is also of some interest to note that among some (young) age groups competitive tendencies tend to be even more pronounced (McClintock & Moskowitz, 1976). Specifically, among very young children (3 years old) individualistic orientation dominates, after which competition becomes more pronounced (4–5 years), which is then followed by cooperative orientation (6–7 years).

Finally, one might wonder whether it is the aversion of "getting behind" or the temptation of "getting ahead" that underlies such competition. In a very nice study by Messick and Thorngate (1967), it was shown that the former tendency (aversive competition) is much more pronounced than the latter tendency (appetitive competition)—in other words, not losing seems a stronger motivation than winning. This early research was later extended and generalized by Kahneman and Tversky's (1979) gain and loss frames in their prospect theory, and by Higgins' (1998) distinction between prevention and promotion focus as two distinct self-regulatory systems. Recent research has also revealed that under conditions of uncertainty, competition may be especially pronounced, presumably because people really want to make sure that they do not get less than the other (Poppe & Valkenberg, 2003). Thus, there is little doubt that competition is an important orientation that needs to be carefully distinguished from self-interest.

Aggression

The orientation of aggression has received very little attention in research on social dilemmas. It is interesting to note that, especially in comparison to the orientation of altruism, much research on aggression focuses on genetic and biological factors. Examples are not only twin studies, but also studies focusing on associations of aggression with hormonal activity, such as variations in levels of testosterone. Generally, this body of research supports the view that aggressiveness, examined by self-report methodology, is substantially "influenced" by genetic factors and biological make-up. For example, there is research showing that manipulation of levels of testosterone, as part of a treatment for sexual transformation influences the proclivity to anger. There is an increase in the tendency toward anger among individuals who transform from woman to man, and a decrease in such tendency among individuals who transform from man to woman (Van Goozen, Frijda, & Van de Poll, 1995).

Importantly, the correlation between aggressiveness and testosterone is especially pronounced for scale items assessing aggressiveness in response to provocation (Olweus, 1979), suggesting that aggression needs to be considered in terms of anger that is interpersonally activated. Indeed, the methods typically used to study aggression consist of examining aggressiveness in response to provocation by another person. Hence, anger and aggressiveness should be easily aroused by those who fail to exhibit cooperative behavior. Indeed, the fact that there is not much systematic research on aggression in social dilemmas is not to imply that aggression is not an important orientation or motivation in the context of social dilemmas.

Because it is unlikely that aggression is a self-activated phenomenon in social dilemmas, people are unlikely to approach one another aggressively, with the primary goal in mind to reduce the outcomes for other(s). As noted earlier, aggression may be activated when others fail to cooperate. This interpersonal basis of aggression is important, and suggests several interesting phenomena. For example, it may well be that tendencies toward aggression are most pronounced among those who do not expect others to behave selfishly. As a case in point, Kelley and Stahelski (1970) provide some evidence for what they referred to as *overassimilation*, the tendency for cooperative individuals (at least, some cooperative individuals) to behave eventually even more non-cooperatively than the fairly non-cooperative partner with whom they interact (see also Liebrand, Jansen, Rijken, & Suhre, 1986). More generally, aggression may be activated by others' non-cooperative behavior, in dyads and groups, by violations of justice (broadly conceived), and perhaps by mis-perceiving or misunderstanding another person's intentions. Thus, it is surprising that aggression has received so little attention in social dilemmas, because—unless research suggests otherwise—aggression seems an important orientation in social dilemmas, albeit one that seems activated primarily by the behavior of others.

How to Promote Desirable Outcomes for the Collective

Solutions to social dilemmas and related situations are often categorized in terms of structural solutions and psychological solutions. The former type of solution emphasizes "structural" differences, by which people will be confronted with a different "game." Example are rewarding cooperation and punishing non-cooperation, by which cooperation is made attractive and/or non-cooperation is made unattract-ive. Both measures, alone or in combination, can be so strong that there is no longer a dilemma in a game theoretical sense. For example, one can make donat-ing blood so attractive by financial incentives that most people want to donate blood rather than not. Or one can make the overuse of water in times of a serious drought so unattractive (e.g., by making public the names of those who overuse) that virtually nobody would willingly and knowingly use more water than allowed. Weaker versions of reward and punishment by which the social dilemma still remains its key qualities (non-cooperation yielding greater individual outcomes, but poorer collective outcomes) have also been shown to be fairly effective in pro-moting cooperation. Another "structural solution" would be to remove or restrict individuals' freedom of choice. An example of the former is the implementation of energy-friendly lights in bathrooms, which automatically will switch off when nobody has been in the bathroom for some time. An example of the latter is to legally forbid certain actions, such as speeding on the highway. In these situations, the dilemma is "solved" in that people do not face a real(istic) choice, except for protesting or engaging in other forms of reaction. Generally, structural solutions can be quite effective, and once accepted, they often form stable solutions to social dilemmas.

At the same time, structural solutions are not without limitations. Indeed, some potential drawbacks are that (a) the repertoire of solutions is relatively limited, espe-cially because some solutions cannot be implemented (e.g., for legal reasons, for financial reasons); (b) people may not always accept certain measures (e.g., restrict-ing feelings of personal control); (c) the measures can be very costly (e.g., rewarding cooperation) so that they may be effective but not cost-effective; or (d) one often needs new systems (e.g., for monitoring and sanctioning non-cooperative behav-ior). From that perspective, it is societally desirable that policy can also use "psychological solutions," which capture the interpersonal orientations. And from a theoretical perspective, it is interesting to derive psychological solutions, which are based on the assumption that, in addition to individualism, altruism, cooperation, equality, competition, and aggression may underlie behavior in social dilemmas and related situations.

Psychological Solutions: Opportunities and Risks

The opportunities are there when one or more orientations support collectively desired outcomes, and the risks come into play when one or more orientations are conflicting with actions that support collectively undesirable outcomes. We review opportunities and risks for each orientation.

Altruism

As noted earlier, altruism may come into being when people empathize with another person. It should be clear that several media campaigns use empathy to promote donations to poor countries, to various health organizations, and to charity (e.g., helping the homeless after a natural disaster). These forms of public education may be especially effective when they include a "story" about a victim who is in serious need, often the victim is "individualized" by informing the public about some personal qualities. Such information may be especially likely to activate empathy, in turn, and helping. Activating empathy may thus be an important solution to various forms of helping, including donations, volunteering, and participation in some collective action (e.g., protesting against war).

It is interesting that empathy may not always yield benefits at the collective level. In fact, there is research indicating that feelings of empathy could promote choices that benefit one particular individual in a group—at the expense of outcomes for the entire group (Batson et al., 1995). Like selfishness, empathy can sometimes form a threat to cooperative interaction. That is, feelings of empathy may lead one to provide tremendous support to one particular person, thereby neglecting the well-being of the collective. For example, as noted by Batson et al. (1995, p. 621), an executive may retain an ineffective employee for whom he or she feels compassion, to the detriment of the organization. Another example is that parents may sometimes be so supportive of their children that it harms the collective interest (e.g., not making an attempt to stop their making noise in public situations).

Equality

Often equality supports collectively desirable actions. In fact, sometimes donations, volunteering, and related forms of helping may be rooted in "a sense of fairness": to enhance the situation of those who are worse off than oneself. Indeed, campaigns aimed at fostering helping behavior sometimes emphasize not only empathy but also feelings of justice—does it feel right when we do not stop the suffering? Also, when a majority of people make a cooperative choice (e.g., not overusing water) then policy makers could indeed make salient that important fact—because getting more than others for the wrong reasons simply does not feel good, and is very difficult to justify to oneself or to others.

Equality sometimes entails risks to collective outcomes. First, if individuals are primarily concerned about equality, then following "bad apples" seems "sensible." The realization that some others (perhaps even more so when the majority fails to cooperate) have greater outcomes than you have may lead many to also make a non-cooperative choice (e.g., Rutte & Wilke, 1992).

Second, a strong concern with equality may harm collective outcomes because people do not want unilaterally to invest in situations where such investing cannot occur simultaneously. Building exchange systems often takes time and unilateral actions—an example is the exchange of expertise among colleagues. If one (a statistics expert) is very seriously concerned about equality, then he or she may not want to invest too much time into conducting complex, time-consuming analyses, if there is a bit of uncertainty that the other (an expert in writing) is not going to reciprocate (e.g., will delay writing). Thus, the collectively desirable outcome (a joint high-quality product) is less likely to be obtained if it takes unilateral investment that challenges equality. And indeed, most situations of mutual helping are characterized by the very fact that one has to make a start in dyads (e.g., mutual baby-sitting among young parents) and groups (e.g., somebody has to initiate costly action to get organized for a joint activity); and so, a strong concern with equality (along with uncertainty) may undermine beneficial exchange.

Third, sometimes it may not be wise to emphasize equality in relationships, groups and organizations. For example, in marital relationships, a discussion about equity may well be an indicator that they are on their way to divorce, perhaps because it undermines propartner motivation (e.g., responding to the partner's needs; Clark & Mills, 1993). In groups and organizations, communicating equality may lead to social book-keeping that may undermine citizenship behavior, the more spontaneous forms of helping colleagues that are not really part of their job but essential to the group or organization.

Cooperation

A strong concern with collective well-being—cooperation—almost always supports actions that are collectively desirable. There is, however, one very important exception to this rule: that is, multi-layered social dilemmas in which "cooperation" is good for the own group, but bad for another group—and bad for the entire collectivity (see Bornstein, 1992). Consider, for example, the soldier fighting for his or her own country, but killing soldiers from the other country, thereby causing bad effects for the entire collective. It is this type of "cooperation action," often supported and respected by ingroup members, that threatens collective well-being (for evidence, see Insko & Schopler, 1998). In that sense, cooperation can be a risky orientation, especially because intergroup conflicts, once started, are often very hard to resolve.

Competition

A strong concern with receiving better outcomes—and not getting worse outcomes—than others often conflicts with good outcomes for the collective. In fact, there is some evidence indicating that it is exceptionally hard to induce individuals with competitive orientations to behave cooperatively. As noted earlier, they do not cooperate, even if the partner pursues tit-for-tat in an iterated social dilemma. At the same time, competition can sometimes be a powerful means to cooperation. Competition can have beneficial effects for cooperation in the multi-layered social dilemmas that we disucussed above for cooperation. When there are two (or more) well-defined groups who comprise the entire collective, then sometimes competition between the groups helps the entire collective. The competition should then deal with something desirable. For example, in the Netherlands, there is a contest between cities aiming for the award "Cleanest City." Two departments at a university may do better (yielding greater research output and enhanced teaching) if the university provides extra resources only for excellent departments. In fact, organizations often use competition as a means to promote functioning. Sometimes such practices take explicit forms, when, for example, competitive reward structures are being implemented: your evaluations and salary depend on your performance relative to others' performances. But even when not done explicitly, the performances of others typically matter in most organizations, because most jobs lack objective criteria, and so managers will often rely on social standards for evaluating individual performance.

Aggression

Of the orientations discussed here aggression would seem to be most susceptible to a partner's behavior (and perhaps other factors, such as earlier experiences of frustration). Indeed, as noted earlier, aggression may often be a response to something that does not go right. So, individuals are likely to act aggressively to another person in a dyad, or other people in the group, who fail to cooperate. As such, aggression, at least in genuine forms, may often serve to regulate fairness. Sometimes, aggression may lead to non-cooperative interaction: For example, cooperative individuals may start responding non-cooperatively in dyads or follow "bad apples" in groups. But as recent research has shown, aggression may restore fairness not only by eliciting non-cooperative interaction but also by eliciting cooperative interaction. The latter is especially likely to happen if people can use aggression as an instrument, by, for example, exhibiting instrumental cooperation or altruistic punishment. Instrumental cooperation refers to all behaviors by which individuals contribute to the quality of a system that rewards cooperators or punishes non-cooperators (Yamagishi, 1986). An example is a contribution to the maintenance of sanctioning systems such as monitoring devices needed for "publicizing" or punishing non-cooperators. Altruistic punishment refers to all behaviors in which individuals are willing to engage in costly acts by which non-cooperators are directly punished (Fehr & Gächter, 2002). Another tool that individuals and groups may use is social exclusion or forms of marginalization by which non-cooperators are in some way punished, in that they are not longer part of the group. This could mean that they no longer benefit from group outcomes, but we suspect that the social aspects of even very subtle forms of exclusion can yield powerful effects on the noncooperators' feelings and behavior. Indeed, there is evidence that very subtle forms of social exclusion may activate those regions of the brain that are associated with physical pain (Eisenberger, Lieberman, & Williams, 2003).

Concluding Remarks

This chapter reviewed evidence regarding the existence of six interpersonal orientations, or decision rules, which can be meaningfully distinguished: Altruism, cooperation, equality, individualism, competition, and aggression. The assumption of "rational self-interest" is limited for two important reasons. First, although behavior often makes sense when considered in "a larger scheme," not all behavior is "rational," as many forms of behavior may be quite heuristic, automatic, and/or unconscious. Apart from "bounded" forms of rationality, it is also important to note that often actions are fed by feelings and social emotions. As a case in point, guilt and shame are two powerful emotions, and it is plausible that the mere anticipation of such feelings may lead individuals to make a cooperative choice. As such, the term "rationality" captures connotations that do not do much service or justice to such affect-laden processes.

Second, there is more to social life than self-interest, as is increasingly recognized in various scientific disciplines such as psychology, biology, and economics (see Van Lange, 2006). Moreover, these orientations often serve "logical" effects—that is, effects that are to be predicted. The three prosocial orientations—cooperation, equality, and altruism—should often promote actions that serve the collective, whereas the three self-oriented (and antisocial) orientations should often promote actions that harm the collective. At the same time, each of these orientations may also exert paradoxical effects, with prosocial orientations inspiring actions that are harmful to collective interest, and the non-prosocial orientations inspiring actions that actually serve the collective interest. We suggest that the paradoxical effects are both inherently interesting and of great societal interest. Indeed, they may help us understand other "paradoxical" effects as well. For example, there is some evidence indicating that people with individualistic orientations serving as buddies for people with HIV may be more likely to persist in these activities than those with prosocial orientations—perhaps because in these demanding cirucumstances high levels of empathy, as part of prosocial orientation, can also lead to intolerable levels of fatigue and exhaustion (Snyder, 1993).

We think that the situations in which prosocial orientations may threaten collective interest are inherently interesting, and sometimes may represent "moral dilemmas" whereby caring-based norms (e.g., helping unfortunate people) may conflictwith justice-based norms (e.g., treating everybody equally). Given that conflicts between various forms of prosocial motivation are of great theoretical and societal interest, we suggest that researchers devote greater attention to such conflicts. Similarly, the situations in which proself/antisocial orientations, especially competition and aggression, can support collective interest are also of great scientific and societal interest. We suggest that not only individuals with competitive orientations, but also groups, may be triggered to compete for outcomes that are desirable from a collective perspective. Thus, the challenge is to exploit competition for the good of all.

Third, the question as to whether a particular social dilemma calls for a structural solution, a psychological solution (exploiting interpersonal orientations), or both will require careful analysis of the situation in light of interpersonal orientations. It is essential to analyze the situation in terms of its *affordances* (Kelley et al., 2003; Van Lange et al., in press)—what are the primary interpersonal orientations that a situation affords? What are the primary interpersonal orientations that a situation may activate in people? This focus on affordances follows from a social interaction analysis of interpersonal orientations and is consistent with other theorizing in social and personality psychology (e.g., Mischel, 2004; Penner, Dovidio, Piliavin, & Schroeder, 2005; Snyder & Cantor, 1998)—and we suggest that this type of theorizing is in fact very practical in generating solutions to social dilemmas and related situations. Social dilemmas represent a conflict between self-interest and collective interest, but often there is more to it. For example, a concern with equality may lead some people to behave non-cooperatively, because they hate to be exploited by some "bad apples." This may account for the individuals' initial reluctance to make very large contributions to a new collective task, because they want to ensure that most people do not free ride on their efforts. Also, sometimes a social dilemma may be altered in such a manner that a broader set of orientations may serve a collectively desirable action. For example, in the early nineties, the Dutch government decided to build a carpool lane—a less congested lane that only could be used by carpoolers—separated from the main highway by a wall low enough so that those who did not carpool would be able to see (and experience) that they were being overtaken by the carpoolers. This is a perfect example of a situation in which competitive orientations are activated to the benefit of all.

More generally, we speculate that the logical effects tend to come to mind more quickly and tend to be better understood than the paradoxical effects. However, we make a plea for the paradoxical effects, because new, creative solutions may be rooted in motivations such as individualism, competition, and even aggression—which typically have been labeled as bad. They may not always be bad, and it is up to visionary scientists and policy makers to use these orientations creatively to help us solve social dilemmas in everyday life.

References

Allison, S. T., & Messick, D. M. (1990). Social decision heuristics in the use of shared resources. *Journal of Behavioral Decision Making, 3,* 23–42.

Batson, C. D. (1994). Why act for the public good? *Personality and Social Psychology Bulletin, 20,* 603–610.

Batson, C. D., & Ahmad, N. (2001). Empathy-induced altruism in a prisoner's dilemma II: What if the target of empathy has defected? *European Journal of Social Psychology 31,* 25–36.

Batson, C. D., Batson, J. G., Todd, R. M., Brummett, B. H., Shaw, L. L., & Aldeguer, C. M. R. (1995). Empathy and collective good: Caring for one of the others in a social dilemma. *Journal of Personality and Social Psychology, 68,* 619–631.

Bornstein, G. (1992). The free-rider problem in intergroup conflicts over step-level and continuous public goods. *Journal of Personality and Social Psychology, 62,* 597–606.

Brewer, M. B., & Kramer, R. M. (1986). Choice behavior in social dilemmas: Effects of social identity, group size, and decision framing. *Journal of Personality and Social Psychology, 50,* 543–549.

Camerer, C., & Thaler, R. H. (1995). Anomalies: Ultimatums, dictators and manners. *Journal of Economic Perspectives, 9,* 209–219.

Cialdini, R. B., Brown, S. L., Lewis, B. P., Luce, C., & Neuberg, S. L. (1997). Reinterpreting the empathy–altruism relationship: When one into one equals oneness. *Journal of Personality and Social Psychology, 73,* 481–494.

Clark, M. S., & Mills, J. (1993). The difference between communal and exchange relationships: What it is and is not. *Personality and Social Psychology Bulletin, 19,* 684–691.

Davis, M. H. (1983). The effects of dispositional empathy on emotional reactions and helping—a multidimensional approach. *Journal of Personality, 51,* 167–184.

Eisenberger, N. I., Lieberman, M. L., & Williams, K. D. (2003). Does rejection hurt? An fMRI study of social exclusion. *Science, 302,* 290–292.

Fehr, E., & Gächter, S. (2002). Altruistic punishment in humans. *Nature, 415,* 137–140

Güth, W., Schmittberger, R., & Schwarze, B. (1982). An experimental analysis of ultimatum games. *Journal of Economic Behavior and Organization, 3,* 367–388.

Higgins, E. T. (1998). Promotion and prevention: Regulatory focus as a motivational principle. In M. P. Zanna (Ed.), *Advances in Experimental Social Psychology* (Vol. 30, pp. 1–46). New York: Academic Press.

Insko, C. A., & Schopler, J. (1998). Differential distrust of groups and individuals. In C. Sedikides, J. Schopler, & C. A. Insko (Eds.), *Intergroup cognition and intergroup behavior: Toward a closer union* (pp. 75–107). Hillsdale, NJ: Lawrence Erlbaum.

Kahneman, D., & Tversky, A. (1979). Prospect theory: An analysis of decision under risk. *Econometrica, 47,* 263–292.

Kelley, H. H., Holmes, J. W., Kerr, N. L., Reis, H. T., Rusbult, C. E., & Van Lange, P. A. M. (2003). *An atlas of interpersonal situations.* New York: Cambridge University Press.

Kelley, H. H., & Stahelski, A. J. (1970). Social interaction basis of cooperators' and competitors' beliefs about others. *Journal of Personality and Social Psychology, 16,* 66–91.

Kelley, H. H., & Thibaut, J. W. (1978). *Interpersonal relations: A theory of interdependence.* New York: Wiley.

Komorita, S. S., & Parks, C. D. (1995). Interpersonal relations: Mixed-motive interaction. *Annual Review of Psychology, 46,* 183–207.

Kuhlman, D. M., & Marshello, A. (1975). Individual differences in game motivation as moderators of preprogrammed strategic effects in prisoner's dilemma. *Journal of Personality and Social Psychology, 32,* 922-931.

Liebrand, W. B. G., & Van Run, G. J. (1985). The effects of social motives on behavior in social dilemmas in two cultures. *Journal of Experimental Social Psychology 21,* 86–102.

Liebrand, W. B. G., Jansen, R. W. T. L., Rijken, V. M., & Suhre, C. J. M. (1986). Might over morality: Social values and the perception of other players in experimental games. *Journal of Experimental Social Psychology, 22,* 203-215.

McClintock, C. G., & Moskowitz, J. M. (1976). Children's preference for individualistic, cooperative, and competitive outcomes. *Journal of Personality and Social Psychology, 34,* 543–555.

Messick, D. M., & McClintock, C. G. (1968). Motivational bases of choice in experimental games. *Journal of Experimental Social Psychology, 4,* 1–25.

Messick, D. M., & Thorngate, W. B. (1967). Relative gain maximization in experimental games. *Journal of Experimental Social Psychology, 3,* 85–101.

Mikula, G., Petri, B., & Tanzer, N. K. (1990). What people regard as unjust: Types and structures of everyday experiences of injustice. *European Journal of Social Psychology, 20,* 133–149.

Miller, D. T. (1999). The norm of self-interest. *American Psychologist, 54,* 1053–1060.

Mischel, W. (2004). Toward an integrative science of the person. *Annual Review of Psychology, 55,* 1–22.

Olweus, D. (1979). Stability of aggression patterns in males: A review. *Psychological Bulletin, 86,* 852–875.

Penner, L. A., Dovidio, J. F., Piliavin, J. A., & Schroeder, D. A. (2005). Prosocial behavior: Multilevel perspectives. *Annual Review of Psychology, 56,* 365–392.

Poppe, M., & Valkenberg, H. (2003). Effects of gain versus loss and certain versus probable outcomes on social value orientations. *European Journal of Social Psychology, 33,* 331–337.

Rusbult, C. E., & Van Lange, P. A. M. (2003). Interdependence, interaction, and relationships. *Annual Review of Psychology, 54,* 351–375.

Rutte, C. G., & Wilke, H. A. M. (1992). Goals, expectations and behavior in a social dilemma situation. In W. B. G. Liebrand, D. M. Messick, & H. A. M. Wilke (Eds.), *Social dilemmas* (pp. 289–305). Elmsford, NY: Pergamon Press.

Snyder, M. (1993). Basic research and practical problems: The promise of a functional personality and social psychology. *Personality and Social Psychology Bulletin, 19,* 251–264.

Snyder, M., & Cantor, N. (1998). Understanding personality and social behavior: A functionalist strategy. In D. T. Gilbert, S. T. Fiske, & G. Lindzey (Eds.), *The handbook of social psychology* (pp. 635–679). New York: McGraw-Hill.

Thibaut, J. W., & Walker, L. (1975). *Procedural justice: A psychological analysis.* Hillsdale, NJ: Lawrence Erlbaum.

Van Goozen, S. H. M., Frijda, N. H., Van de Poll, N. E. (1995). Anger and aggression during role playing: Gender differences between hormonally treated male and female transexuals and controls. *Aggressive Behavior, 21,* 257–273.

Van Lange, P. A. M. (1999). The pursuit of joint outcomes and equality in outcomes: An integrative model of social value orientation. *Journal of Personality and Social Psychology, 77,* 337–349.

Van Lange, P. A. M. (Ed.) (2006). *Bridging social psychology: The benefits of transdisciplinary approaches.* Mahwah, NJ: Lawrence Erlbaum.

Van Lange, P. A. M., De Cremer, D., Van Dijk, E., & Van Vugt, M. (in press). Self-interest and beyond: Basic principles of social interaction. In E. T. Higgins & A. W. Kruglanski (Eds.), *Social Psychology: Handbook of Basic Principles*. New York: Guilford Press.

Van Lange, P. A. M., Otten, W., De Bruin, E. N. M., & Joireman, J. A. (1997). Development of prosocial, individualistic, and competitive orientations: Theory and preliminary evidence. *Journal of Personality and Social Psychology, 73*, 733–746.

Van Lange, P. A. M., Ouwerkerk, J. W., & Tazelaar, M. J. A. (2002). How to overcome the detrimental effects of noise in social interaction: The benefits of generosity. *Journal of Personality & Social Psychology, 82*, 768–780.

Van Lange, P. A. M., & Sedikides, C. (1998). Being more honest but not necessarily more intelligent than others: Generality and explanations for the Muhammad Ali effect. *European Journal of Social Psychology, 28*, 675–680.

Van Lange, P. A. M., & Visser, K. (1999). Locomotion in social dilemmas: How we adapt to cooperative, Tit-For-Tat, and noncooperative partners. *Journal of Personality and Social Psychology, 77*, 762–773.

Van Vugt, M., & Hart, C. M. (2004). Social identity as social glue: The origins of group loyalty. *Journal of Personality and Social Psychology, 86*, 585–598.

Yamagishi, T. (1986). The provision of a sanctioning system as a public good. *Journal of Personality and Social Psychology, 51*, 110–116.

3

Evolutionary Psychology and a More Satisfactory Model of Human Agency

JAMES HANLEY, JASON HARTWIG, JOHN ORBELL,
AND TOMONORI MORIKAWA

In studying social behavior, many scholars assume that people behave rationally, assuming that they choose among alternative actions by comparing the value of the likely outcomes (taking account of how likely, or unlikely, they are), then selecting the one with the highest expected value. We call this approach "rationality in action." Although it is a commonly used, and valuable, starting point for deductive modeling, most scholars do not believe that it comes close to actually modeling the real cognitive processes at work in human decision making. Some argue that the truth value of the assumptions is not important, that their purpose is to produce testable predictions of social and economic outcomes (see Friedman, 1953). But that is not good enough for those of us who believe the social sciences should be integrated, rather than remaining apparently unrelated disciplines, and who want to develop empirically testable predictions that are based on *empirically defendable* assumptions about behavior. The problem is to find a "model of human agency" that is both defendable in light of actual human decision processes *and* simple enough to be a useful tool for building deductive models. Our goal is twofold: to have a better model of human behavior generally, and, more specifically, to understand *why* people cooperate and *how* they decide to do so.

Scholars differ on the trade-offs they are prepared to make between how simple their behavioral models are and how well the assumptions underlying those models fit the empirical data. Psychologists, whose business is to understand the bases of human behavior, will often insist that the assumptions fit the data, while economists and political scientists, whose business is to understand processes at the aggregate level, are often prepared to cut corners with respect to the truth value of assumptions, believing that what matters is that aggregate behavior can be understood *as if* the assumptions were true (Alchian, 1950).

Because we are trying to promote integration of the social sciences we believe in using models that are both simple *and* empirically defendable. From this perspective, there are several problems with rationality in action. The best known is that humans have difficulty estimating probabilities, as shown by extensive empirical research (Dawes, 1988; Kahneman, Slovic, & Tversky, 1985). Another problem, which we are more concerned about, is the auxiliary assumption (Simon, 1985) that people rationally maximize their *private* welfare (however each individual might define it). This is an assumption that is empirically unproven, hence problematic.

Much of the research in this area makes use of the prisoner's dilemma, as do we. The prisoner's dilemma (PD) is a game in which two individuals interact with each other, each having a choice of two strategies, cooperate or defect. The collective outcome is maximized if both individuals cooperate, with each receiving the mutual cooperation payoff (c). But the best individual outcome, greater than c, is gained by defecting when the other cooperates, which returns the free rider's payoff (t). This creates for the other player, who cooperated, the *worst* available payoff, the sucker's payoff (s). So both players, knowing that it pays more to defect if the other cooperates, and also that they can really be hurt by cooperating with a defector, rationally choose to defect, which results in both receiving the mutual defect payoff (d), which is better than s but worse than c.

Note what makes the prisoner's dilemma so interesting: *Both* players would be better off if they both cooperated rather than defected, but for each it *always* pays more to defect. In broader terms we have a *social* dilemma, where the collective good of everyone is undermined by each person's self-interest. Although studied most intensively in experimental conditions, such dilemmas are common outside the laboratory as well. Two people sharing a meal in which the check will be split evenly, for example, each have an incentive to order a more expensive item, knowing the other must pay part of the extra expense. But if both do, neither makes the hoped-for gain. Carpoolers face similar dilemmas, as each is better off if able to avoid paying a full share for gasoline. Even on the international scale, all countries would be collectively better off if they did not produce nuclear weapons, yet each is individually rational to do so, to be militarily superior to a nuclear-free opponent, or to be militarily equal to another nuclear equipped one.

Such mutual defection is what will happen *if* people in fact always maximize their private welfare, as is generally assumed. But people maximizing their own welfare can be led to cooperate in prisoner's dilemma circumstances by creating certain types of incentives. These include potential punishment by the state (Hobbes, 1651/1947), punishment by others who are negatively affected by a defecting choice (Fehr & Gachter, 2002), or punishment as a side-effect of egalitarian motivations (Fowler, Smirnov, & Johnson, 2004), as well as the threat of retaliatory defection in iterated sequences of games, the prospect of retaliatory defection in future encounters (Axelrod, 1981), and the threat of the risk of exclusion from future profitable relationships (Vanberg & Congleton, 1992). These collectively suggest people *will* maximize their private welfare by defecting *unless* the incentives are changed to make cooperation a better bet, and also that there is no natural disposition toward cooperativeness.

Yet it has also been well established, via a long tradition of laboratory research, that people often *do* cooperate even when these types of incentives are missing and cooperation does *not* maximize their private welfare (Caporael, Orbell, & van de Kragt, 1989; Ledyard, 1995; as well as others emphasized by Van Lange in this volume). Cooperative behavior, then, is a strong test of the empirical validity of "rationality in action" as a foundation from which to model social processes, and these empirical findings cast doubt on both its empirical validity and its value as a model used to predict behavior. Consequently we ask whether there is a "model of human agency" that is both consistent with these empirical facts and simple and predictively accurate *enough* to serve as a practical basis for modeling social behavior.

We believe there is, a model we call "rationality in design." This model requires an approach based in the theory of evolution. The tradition of political philosophy, out of which economics and sociology sprang during the eighteenth and nineteenth centuries, has been built from unproven "seat of the pants" assumptions about human nature that seemed reasonable at the time. But the escalating convergence of evolutionary theory and psychology during the past thirty years compels us to think of the brain as a product of eons of natural selection. So a defendable model of human agency must be compatible not only with observed behavior in the here-and-now, but also with a plausible evolutionary explanation for such behavior. This convergence is healthy for psychology, providing a unifying paradigm where none existed before and is a critical step toward unifying psychology with the life sciences. Extending that convergence to the social sciences will be an important further step toward such theoretical unification.

In pursuit of this goal we will summarize findings from an evolutionary computer simulation designed to address how cooperative *dispositions*—natural inclinations to cooperate, such as those documented in the laboratory literature mentioned above—might have evolved. But a satisfactory model of human agency must go beyond *simply* analyzing when people are disposed to play cooperatively in PD-type games. Because the interests of people who live in groups often *do* come into conflict, we must also ask how cooperative dispositions might have co-evolved side-by-side with the capacities for successfully playing conflictual games. People often do cooperate, but they also often compete with each other. This is different from defection in prisoner's dilemma games. Defection in the PD is a form of cheating when our interests are partly congruent but partly divergent, for example if we are working together on some project, and I shirk in my efforts, letting you do the brunt of the work in order to get a benefit that we can both share in. Competitive behavior occurs when our interests are wholly divergent, as when two teams compete for a victory that only one can achieve. Our simulation is an effort to understand how such seemingly disparate capacities might have co-evolved in the same species.

Rationality in Design

We propose the concept "rationality in design," following Dennett's (1995) emphasis on evolution as an engineering process. Natural selection (involving random variation, different rates of survival of variants, and genetic retention of successful variants through successive generations) is capable of constructing astonishingly complex structures, including the human brain. Natural selection, of course, cannot look forward and anticipate problems or their solutions. Instead it responds randomly to problems as they present themselves, "tinkering" with the design and creating solutions only from a basis of structures that already exist. Nevertheless natural selection often produces solutions so elegant that many people doubt that they could possibly have been designed by such a blind, decentralized process. In our terms, therefore, a "rational design" is an evolutionary response that solves an adaptive problem at least sufficiently well to let the animal in question survive and reproduce in the environment it inhabits (it may *not* be well suited to some different habitat).

This rational design may not in fact reflect the process assumed in the "rationality in action" model. The question is whether it is possible to identify a plausible evolutionary process that would make humans' empirically observed propensity for both cooperative behavior and competitiveness understandable as a rational design created by natural selection. If so, then we have a model of human agency that, in accordance with our goal, is (1) consistent with observed human behavior, (2) theoretically defendable in evolutionary terms, and (3) at least a candidate for being the model from which social scientists might go about their business of constructing theories about aggregate or social processes.

Constructing the Evolutionary Simulation

Simulation is a tool for discovery, not for proving things empirically. It is particularly useful when the processes being explored are (1) not observable as a practical matter, and (2) complex enough that they are difficult to analyze with standard methods. Since the evolutionary processes that interest us happened over many eons of humans' ancestral past, obviously we cannot observe them, thus meeting the first criterion; and since we are addressing the interaction among multiple cognitive processes and behavioral dispositions, the second criterion is also met.

Modeling cognitive evolution requires a complex simulation, with several crucial components. We must model (1) a "social structure" (a pattern of relationships among individuals); (2) multiple behavioral dispositions and cognitive capacities; (3) the relationship of those dispositions and capacities to individuals' decision making; (4) the relationship of such behaviors to the individuals' reproductive success; and (5) the way in which individuals' capacities and dispositions are transmitted to their offspring if they *do* reproduce. We will explain these components as succinctly as possible.

Social structure

The simulation has a population of 50 individuals, pairs of whom encounter each other in circumstances where they have a choice between entering a (potentially cooperative) PD game or rejecting that game and making a living by "going it alone," a strategy we call the alternative or ALT choice.

Behavioral dispositions (1): Cooperativeness

Each individual has a fixed *probability* of cooperating that is constant throughout its lifetime. In each encounter it is randomly determined—based on their probability of cooperating—whether the participants will cooperate or defect *if* a PD game ensues (which requires *both* individuals to agree to enter it).

Behavioral dispositions (2): Mistrust

Although any individual who expects another to defect can be said to "mistrust" that individual in this circumstance, we model mistrust as a generalized disposition—directed at *all* individuals—having a value between 0.0 and 1.0, with an individual at the lower end being disposed to trust everyone, and one at the higher end being disposed to trust no one.

Cognitive capacities (1): Manipulation

In the prisoner's dilemma it always pays more to play with a cooperator than with a defector, no matter what choice you make. So everyone, whether intending to defect or cooperate, will want cooperators to enter the game with them. Accordingly, we model individuals as sending the message "I will always cooperate" to potential partners, and sending it with varying degrees of *persuasiveness*, some being "naturally" more persuasive than others.

Cognitive capacities (2): Mindreading.

Given that cognitive capacities for manipulative persuasion are clearly adaptive, it follows that a defensive capacity for seeing through such persuasiveness will also be adaptive, allowing both intending cooperators and intending defectors to see through the lies of intending defectors. We use the standard terminology of ethology and call this capacity "mindreading." As with manipulation, we model individuals' mindreading capacities as varying between 0.0 and 1.0.

Decision making

The question now is how one individual makes the decision whether or not to enter a prisoner's dilemma game with a particular other individual. We model this in straightforward expected value (EV) terms, with the individual calculating the EV of entering, comparing that EV with the fixed value of ALT, and selecting the option that maximizes its well-being. To make that calculation the individual needs an estimate of the other's likelihood of cooperating, and *that* involves the interaction between the other's capacity to send a persuasive "I will cooperate" message, the decision maker's capacity to see through to the truth of that claim, and its level of mistrust. The specific modeling of that interaction is detailed enough that a technical explanation is inappropriate here (see Orbell, Morikawa, Hartwig, Hanley, & Allen, 2004), but in general, the greater the other individual's persuasiveness in manipulation the more likely the decision maker is to believe its message of cooperativeness, while the greater the decision maker's mindreading the less likely it is to be fooled by an other who is "lying." *After* the decision maker has exercised mindreading on the other individual's manipulated messages, mistrust comes into play. Mindreading determines a particular probability of the "I will cooperate" message's truthfulness. Then, the greater the decision maker's level of mistrust, the higher probability (greater certainty of the other's cooperation) it requires before agreeing to enter a prisoner's dilemma game. Two individuals equally good at mindreading might both conclude that some particular individual has a 70% likelihood of cooperating, but because one's mistrust threshold is at 65%, while the other's is at 75%, the first will enter a prisoner's dilemma game with that particular individual while the second will not.

Relative game success and relative reproductive success

Payoffs from an individual's encounters during its lifetime are treated as "units of reproductive fitness" that determine how many offspring an individual will pass on to the next generation. Two criteria bear on this: The *absolute* success of an individual and its *relative* success compared to others in its generation. Should an individual's absolute payoffs fall below zero, it is assumed to have died without reproducing (it is, therefore, possible for a population to die out altogether). But at the end of a generation, the surviving individuals are ranked according to how well they did in comparison to each other, with the more successful having more offspring (which populate the next generation) than those who are relatively less successful.

Transmission of attributes between generations

This is an *evolutionary* simulation, so it is crucial not only that a more successful individual have more offspring, but that its particular attributes, both its dispositions and its cognitive capacities, are likely to be passed on to those offspring. But mutation occurs between generations, so an individual's offspring inherits its parent's capacities with some *random* chance of change in the values of those capacities. In our simulation each capacity has a set probability (.05) of mutating, and the value mutates either up or down with equal probability. Those new values are then tested in interactions with other individuals, and mutations that reduce an individual's chances of success result in fewer offspring in the next generation, while mutations that enhance the chances of success are rewarded with more offspring. The randomness of mutations and their value is critical, because it allows success to be determined wholly by the interactions with other individuals in the simulation, rather than by the expectations of the researchers.

Method and Findings

We ran the simulation multiple times, each time varying the payoffs available to the agents. We looked for two types of results: (1) Regularities in the dispositions and cognitive capacities of the population under different payoffs after 20,000 generations of evolutionary change; (2) Regularities in the evolutionary processes that produced these outcomes. In particular, we were trying to uncover the possible evolutionary cause of humans' natural disposition to cooperate, which we believe is intertwined with our disposition to engage in competitive behavior.

We started each run of the simulation with a population of 50 individuals, each characterized by cognitive and dispositional attributes that made them very disinclined to enter prisoner's dilemma games. Essentially we created non-social individuals, with only a 10% probability of cooperating, a mistrust threshold so high they would need to be 90% sure of another's cooperation before entering a prisoner's dilemma game, a very low ability to successfully manipulate their message of cooperativeness so as to make it believable, and a very minimal mind-reading ability. In the early stages of each such run, therefore, agents' "I will always cooperate" messages were mostly lies; each had very high levels of mistrust in others in general; each was overwhelmingly unpersuasive sending lies as well as truths; and each had only limited capacity to penetrate to the (lack of) truth underlying most of the claims made by others in the population.

The payoffs of the prisoner's dilemma game remained the same in each run (t = 15; c = 5; d = –5 and s = –15) but the value of the alternative payoff (ALT, earned whenever a pair of individuals encountering each other did *not* enter a prisoner's dilemma game) varied in each run. This allowed us to observe how evolutionary pressures and their outcomes differed as entering a prisoner's dilemma game became more or less attractive compared to ALT. The question, then, was: How would the several individual-level attributes evolve from this initial (Hobbesian?) world through an extended sequence of generations?

An initial finding[1] was that sustained transitions to high levels of cooperative

Table 3.1 Cooperative transitions within the parameter range 0 <ALT <c. (based on 10 simulations for each value of ALT)

1 ALT values	2 Number of cooperative transitions	3 Mean generation where transition starts	4 Mean PC values after the transition	5 Predicted threshold PC
4.5	9/10	6535	0.981	0.975
4.0	10/10	5923	0.965	0.950
3.5	10/10	5983	0.940	0.925
3.0	9/10	5924	0.926	0.900
2.5	9/10	6046	0.898	0.875
2.0	10/10	4474	0.897	0.850
1.5	8/10	3398	0.858	0.825
1.0	8/10	4040	0.833	0.800
0.5	8/10	5566	0.815	0.775

dispositions happened only within a particular range of comparative values—when the value of ALT was greater than zero, but lower than the payoff for mutual cooperation. The reason is fairly simple. If the payoff from ALT is better than the payoff for mutual cooperation, then an individual must expect the higher free rider's payoff before joining the prisoner's dilemma game. But *both* individuals must expect that, meaning that both must intend to defect while expecting the other to cooperate. Therefore each must also be a good manipulator, but not a very good mindreader And since these types will suffer from their interaction with each other—getting only the mutual defect payoff, which is lower than ALT—evolutionary pressures will favor better mindreaders (whether they are likely cooperators *or* defectors), who avoid games with defectors and get the higher payoff of ALT.

But if the payoff from ALT is less than zero, even a low estimate of an other's probability of cooperating will usually make joining a PD game the more attractive alternative. This is particularly so for intending defectors, who, in these game parameters, will be disproportionately likely to enter PD games, returning them (when they play with each other) payoffs that are less than zero—and leading, sooner or later, to the death of the whole population. Accordingly: *Selection in favor of high cooperative dispositions can only happen when the payoff from "going it alone" is, simultaneously, greater than zero and less than the payoff from mutual cooperation.* In short, there *must* be a way to make gains other than playing prisoner's dilemmas, or the population will die out, but that other way must not be too good or individuals will never bother to enter games with each other.

That explains the outcomes, but exactly what evolutionary process has occurred? We conducted 90 simulation runs in which ALT was greater than 0 but less than the mutual cooperate payoff of 5. At each interval of 0.5 (0.5, 1, 1.5, etc.) we repeated the simulation ten times. Sudden transitions from very low to very high average cooperativeness did not happen every time, but did happen at least 8 out of 10 times at each value of ALT, as is shown by Table 3.1, column 2. The simulation contains many random elements, as previously noted, so these "cooperative transitions" happened at varying points in the 20,000 generations, sometimes as late as after 18,000 generations and sometimes as "early" as before 3,000 generations; column 3 of Table 3.1 reports the average generation at which such transitions happened across the nine values of ALT.

Of greatest interest, column 4 reports the average value of the populations' cooperative dispositions after the transition. There is, of course, variation within each category and we must remember that, for some runs, no such cooperative transition happened at all. Nevertheless, after a cooperative transition has happened, the characteristic pattern of behavior is for a population of individuals with very cooperative dispositions to enter prisoner's dilemma games and, usually, cooperate. They are not *perfect* cooperators, of course, but these high probabilities must be compared with the starting probability of .1. Second, their cooperativeness increases as the value of ALT increases. The pattern is consistent enough to suggest a systematic relationship between the various values of ALT and the values of the prisoner's dilemma outcomes. We will return to this regularity shortly.

The next question is: *How do such cooperative transitions happen—in particular, what (if any) is the role of selection on the mistrust capacity and on the capacities for manipulation and mindreading?* To answer this, we will look closely at one simulation run—where the value of ALT was 4—to illustrate the evolutionary trajectory of the successive populations' average dispositional and cognitive attributes, as well as the pattern of outcomes to joined prisoner's dilemma games. Following this we will report on the micro processes that produced such patterns.

First, the graph in Figure 3.1 shows evolution on the disposition to cooperate through 20,000 generations. Most obviously, after some false starts in an upward direction, the mean probability of cooperating moves rapidly to well above .90 where, after a period of substantial instability, it seems to settle to equilibrium. In this example, the cooperative transition gets under way at generation 5,319 and is well established within twenty subsequent generations. Clearly, something has happened at or shortly before generation 5,319 that provoked this change. We will return to that shortly.

Next, Figure 3.2 shows that this change in mean cooperative dispositions is matched by changes in behavior. Prior to the transition, very few prisoner's dilemma games were joined (and in these few games mutual defection was overwhelmingly the most frequent outcome), but after the transition prisoner's dilemmas dominate,

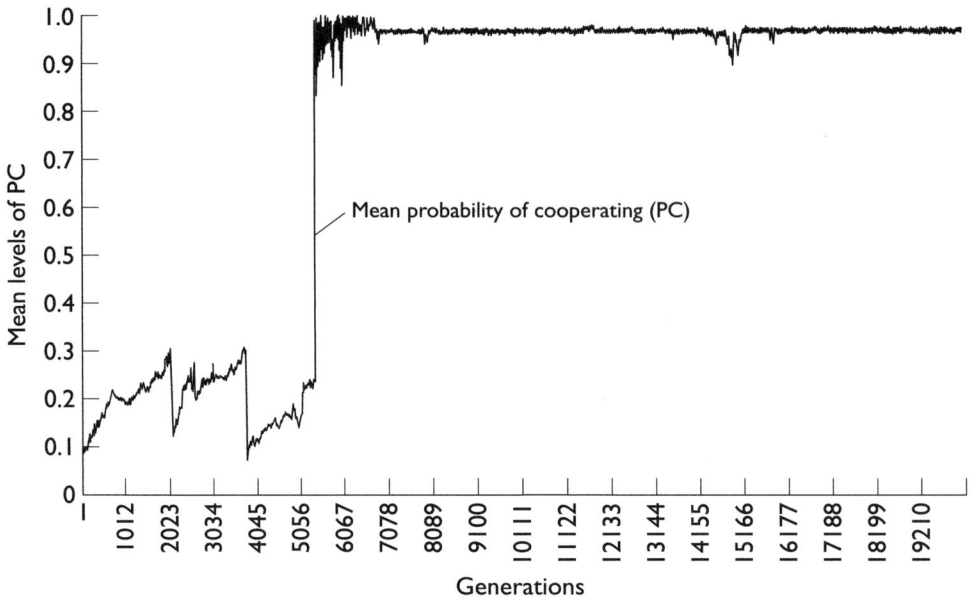

Figure 3.1 A cooperative transition when ALT = 4 – mean PC

and as the increase in cooperation would suggest, the overwhelming majority of outcomes were mutual cooperation, accounting for 2,000 of the 2,500 encounters in each generation.[2] There is *some* instability in this result—in direct association with the temporary downward movement in cooperative dispositions that is visible in Figure 3.1—but mutual cooperation is a notably reliable outcome.

The patterns of change in the disposition to cooperate, and the consequent behavioral changes, are unmistakable. The social interactions of the agents favored those who did *not* behave in a purely self-interested manner, but rather those who were more "naturally" inclined to be cooperative. But this despite the fact that the dominating strategy—the highest paying one, regardless of what the other player does—is defection. So the increase in cooperativeness is not the end of the story, but must itself be explained. And the explanation lies in the trajectories of the cognitive dispositions, mindreading and manipulation.[3]

There is, as would be predicted, strong selection on mindreading, which enables an individual to see through, to some extent, another individual's lies (manipulation) about its cooperativeness. High mindreading values allow an individual to avoid games with likely defectors, thus preventing the losses associated with either the mutual defect or sucker payoffs. But there is considerable instability in the trajectory of mindreading across generations. Beginning at .01 (ability to see through 10% of another individual's manipulation) it peaks at approximately .98 by generations in the 6,000 range, plunges to approximately .35 in the 14,000 generations range—coinciding with the much smaller decrease in cooperativeness seen in the

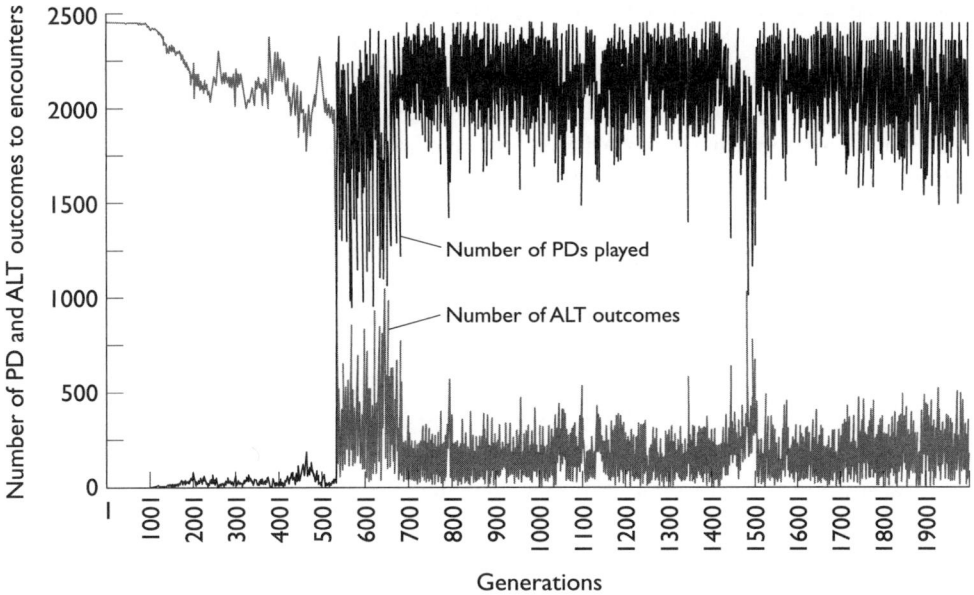

Figure 3.2 Number of ALT outcomes vs prisoner's dilemmas played.

first figure and the considerable drop in PDs played in the second figure—before rising back to .9 and ending—without appearing to have established an equilibrium—at .7. So on the whole, mindreading is favored by the evolutionary process, but not consistently so.

Mistrust, in contrast to mindreading, begins high but is selected by the evolutionary process for *lower* levels. That is, agents become *more* trusting as the generations pass. Although it eventually stabilizes, mistrust also passes through a period of instability. Beginning at .9 (an individual must be more than 90% certain of another individual's willingness to cooperate before it will enter a prisoner's dilemma game) it initially mirrors mindreading, falling as mindreading rises, so that in the early years of the simulation run, agents seemed to substitute mindreading for a generalized mistrust. Around the time mindreading is rising to its maximum—the time in which cooperativeness takes it upward jump, as seen in Figure 3.1—mistrust falls *below* 0.1, meaning agents need less than .10 certainty of the other's cooperation if they are to enter a prisoner's dilemma. Following this it rises to a rough equilibrium of about .4 (meaning, after using mindreading to see through to the truth of the other individual's claims of cooperativeness, the deciding individual must be 40% certain of the other's cooperativeness).

This means that in the "nasty" world preceding the cooperative transition, mistrust is adaptive, working to keep individuals out of PD games that would, most probably, return a lower payoff than ALT. In the far "nicer" world after that transition, however, such high levels of mistrust are *mal*adaptive, granted that the payoff from mutual cooperation (now the most likely outcome to a joined PD game) is higher than the payoff from ALT, and so there is rapid selection *against* such mistrust. But because defection in PD games pays more than cooperation, this happily cooperative and trusting world provides selective advantage for individuals with *less* cooperative dispositions, meaning some degree of mistrust becomes advantageous, thus is selected for by the evolutionary process.

Ideally, for the decision-making individual, mistrust will be high enough to help it avoid playing with defectors, but low enough to not cause it to avoid games with cooperators (this is true whether the deciding individual itself intends to cooperate or defect, as it always pays more to play with a cooperator). More specifically, given that the messages the individual receives from the other are first adjusted by mindreading, so that true messages of cooperation are, on the whole, more likely to be accepted and false ones less likely to be accepted, the optimal level of mistrust is high enough to prevent the individual from accepting false "I will cooperate" messages but low enough to ensure that it does accept the true "I will cooperate" messages. In short, mistrust is a balancing act between being too trustful and too mistrustful, resulting in a broadly stable evolutionary equilibrium with mistrust and mindreading, in combination, functioning to ensure that post-transition cooperative dispositions do, for the most part, result in consummated and mutually cooperative PD games.

So how does this all work together to so frequently create transitions to co-operativeness out of such initially nasty worlds? The first step was the evolution of significant mindreading capacities. The explanation for this is straightforward: While mean cooperativeness was very low in this initial world, individuals could occasionally be led into entering a PD game by a potential partner's exceptionally persuasive lies. In such a game, the overwhelming odds were that the individual would be playing with a defector, meaning that (regardless of whether it cooperates or defects)—it would end up taking a loss relative to ALT. Thus any attribute that served to keep individuals *out* of PD games under these circumstances would be highly adaptive. Mistrust, already high at the outset of our simulation runs, would contribute to that purpose, but mindreading would also do so, keeping people *out of* normally quite costly social interactions. Therefore we would expect the mindreading capacity to be favored by the evolutionary process, and in fact we did observe positive selection on it.

Yet high mindreading capacities can serve a second function—to *protect* individuals who happen to carry a random mutation that increases their probability of cooperating. In a nasty world where most have quite high mindreading capacities, more cooperative individuals will be recognized by the majority of more defection-inclined individuals as desirable targets for exploitation. But since such "mutant cooperators" are also likely to be mindreading-equipped, they will, sensibly, reject such offers. In itself, such rejection will not provoke cooperative transitions, but through time it will support "upward drift" on cooperative dispositions that would otherwise be selected against. "Drift" is a directional change in an attribute that is not caused by selective pressures. With the simulation's random mutations, an individual's offspring are equally likely to become more or less cooperative. Because so few PDs are being played in these beginning generations, there is no real selective pressure either favoring or disfavoring cooperation. If one individual has an offspring that is *more* cooperative, that offspring is equally likely to have its own offspring that is *less* cooperative, returning cooperativeness to what it was in the grandparent. But in the lack of pressure for or against cooperativeness, some lineages will chance to have a series of successive mutations toward more cooperatives, so that several generations down the line, a great-great-grandchild will be more cooperative than its ancestor, yet possibly without either having ever participated in a PD. And such upward drift on cooperative dispositions, coupled with well-developed mindreading, is precisely the basis from which cooperative transitions emerge.

Because drift is random with respect to selective pressures, it is unlikely that any *given* lineage will become highly cooperative. Granted mutation, there is a 50% chance of becoming more cooperative in one generation, a 20% chance in two successive generations ($.5 \times .5$), a 12% chance in three successive generations ($.5 \times .5 \times .5$), etc. It is still less likely that two different lineages will follow this path in the same set of generations. But with many lineages and with the passage of many generations, it is likely to happen sooner or later, and when it does happen the same mindreading capacity that had previously performed an essentially *defensive* function can now let two individuals of these respective lineages recognize each other as good bets for a joined and mutually cooperative PD game. If they do—and *that* is not inevitable, as column 2 of Table 3.1 shows—then, with a high probability, both will cooperate, winning the mutual cooperative payoff. Because in this simulation that is higher than the payoff for ALT, both will produce more offspring than the great majority of others in their generation who have chosen the latter option. The process will be repeated in the next generation, with the difference that that generation will be populated by a greater number of offspring of each of these successful "founding parents," providing still more potential for players to capture the profitable mutual cooperation payoff. In the case being followed, that is exactly what happened in the generations prior to, and immediately after, 5,319, with the cooperative transition being completed within 20 generations.

In summary: (1) Mindreading is initially selected in a "nasty" or generally uncooperative world because it serves the prophylactic function of preventing individuals from making the error of entering PD games that are highly likely to result in loss; (2) Once widespread in the population, mindreading permits upward drift—if it happens to occur—on cooperative dispositions that would otherwise be selected against in this nasty world; (3) With time, such drift makes it likely that two mindreading-equipped individuals with sufficiently high cooperative dispositions to make them attractive as partners for each other will encounter each other and enter a PD game accordingly; (4) As long as the ALT payoff is greater than zero, but less than the mutual cooperation payoff, such individuals will have a fitness advantage over those who have not entered such games, and will have dispropor-tionately more offspring as a consequence; (5) as the population is characterized by progressively higher mean cooperative dispositions, an equilibrium will emerge at which mindreading and mistrust combine to militate against invasion of the gener-ally cooperative world by individuals with less cooperative dispositions.

The evolutionary process described above did not produce a perfectly coopera-tive population, and most individuals had at least *some* probability of defecting in any given game. While we suspect this is broadly reflective of the imperfect world in which we live, the process by which such imperfect equilibria happen is sug-gested by the monotonic relationship between values of ALT and the level at which mean cooperative dispositions equilibrate (column 4 of Table 3.1 above). First, we must recognize that the most adaptive outcome of any particular PD game for any individual is to free ride on the other's cooperation. But this will seldom be possi-ble once mindreading has evolved to the generally high levels illustrated by Figure 3.2. Given that both must agree before a game is consummated, this means that, in order to enter a PD game at all, an individual must actually *be* sufficiently coopera-tive that a potential game partner, equipped with solid mindreading capacities, will expect that individual to cooperate, and consequently calculate an expected value of entering the game that is higher than the value of ALT. The optimal level of cooperativeness, therefore, is high *enough* to persuade a partner to enter, but no higher—because once a partner has entered, the best choice is to defect, captur-ing thereby the superior free rider's payoff. Since the individuals in the simulation sample their actual strategy choice randomly from within that range, they will in fact usually cooperate, but not always. This resembles a trap, but a peculiar kind of trap in which, because of the target individual's mindreading capacity, the bait— one's own cooperative dispositions—must be sufficiently real to make that target's entering the trap a well-informed and good bet. One *has* to be sufficiently coopera-tive *in fact* to spring that trap, but cooperative dispositions, if real, cannot simply be changed once the individual has taken the bait.

How cooperative one must be depends on the value of ALT compared to the expected value of entering the PD game being offered. The higher the value of ALT—the nearer it is to equaling the value of mutual cooperation—the more cooperative one must be to convince the other that it is worthwhile to enter the PD with its risk of being suckered rather than just take the sure payoff from ALT. The predicted selected (threshold) value of cooperation (PC) is shown in column 5 of Table 3.1,[4] with the actual mean value after the cooperative transition appearing in column 4.

The general rule is: *Within the specified parameter range, one only needs to be suf-ficiently cooperative—in fact—to persuade a skilled mindreader that entering a PD game with oneself represents a better bet than the known value of "going it alone."*

Implications

The evolutionary story told here does not deny other plausible evolutionary models that have been told about how cooperation could evolve. Kin selection, reciprocity, tit-for-tat in all its various forms, an evolved willingness to "altruistically punish" defectors, cultural evolution, and group selection are all, no doubt, part of the whole story. And of course the natural world—the real environment in which humans evolved—most certainly contained a variety of other types of opportunities for interaction, such as hawk–dove or coordination games.

Also, we have only looked at the ultimate selective pressures on the dispositions and capacities in question, and have ignored the immediate ways in which those pressures might have been expressed. We have worked from the assumption that understanding the ultimate selective pressures is the first order of business, one that sets up the search for proximate mechanisms in a systematic manner.

Returning to the interests we expressed in the beginning, we believe that the simulation results have implications for how scholars across all the social sciences should go about building "models of mind." First, we agree with Van Lange that "the assumption of rational self-interest is too limited to account for interpersonal behavior" (this volume, p. 17), but that self-interest at the genetic level must be the guiding principle in analyzing the evolution of cooperative dispositions, including the various types of dispositions which Van Lange catalogs. These cooperative dispositions must be addressed in the context of the evolution of various other dispositions and cognitive capacities that, most certainly, were co-evolving during the same extended period. Cooperative dispositions could not have evolved in a vacuum absent other interacting dispositions and associated cognitive mechanisms, and our findings show just one way by which their evolutionary trajectory could have developed from a basis in the co-evolution of other capacities, with the evolutionary trajectory of such other capacities being influenced, in turn, by evolving cooperative dispositions. Subsequent work might well show our model to be wide of the mark—in fact our understanding of the scientific process leads us to expect that to happen, given that these are the early stages of this approach—but we doubt very much that such subsequent work will be able to satisfactorily avoid addressing the co-evolution of cooperative dispositions and the wide range of other dispositions and capacities that influence our social behavior. In other words, it is our *approach*, rather than our specific findings, that is most important.

Second, the finding that cooperative dispositions evolve strongly only within a limited range of game parameters is provocative. While we believe that the reason why such dispositions do *not* evolve beyond those parameters is clear, it might seem paradoxical that, within them, they evolve to higher levels when the ALT alternative approaches more closely the payoff from mutual cooperation, rather than as it moves further below it. At first sight, one might expect such dispositions to evolve to *higher* levels as the relative advantage of mutual cooperation becomes *greater*, not less. As we have proposed above, however, there is a good evolutionary explanation for this in the twin facts (1) that actually *having* quite high cooperative dispositions is a prerequisite for persuading a potential partner to enter a game; and (2) the magnitude of the ALT payoff increases such an individual's scope for being picky with respect to the games he or she chooses to enter by making the choice *not* to enter comparatively more rewarding.

This granted, a further theoretical and empirical issue is to identify natural world circumstances that could plausibly have placed the payoff from mutual cooperation in such relatively close proximity with the ALT payoff (which we have conceptualized as "going it alone") or finding a means of survival and gain that does not require risky collaboration with other individuals, such as gathering roots and berries (in contrast, for example, to the need for collaboration in taking down large game). While we cannot here address the issue of how frequently such alternatives were simultaneously available, we do believe it is likely that such circumstances must have (1) arisen with sufficient frequency to have had the proposed consequences for human cooperative dispositions; and (2) done so where the slim difference between those payoffs was of real adaptive significance.

Third, while the model of human agency that emerges from this analysis is developed around a "selfish gene" framework, it is a substantially different model from the one we have called "rationality in action." Certainly, the humans (and perhaps the other similarly highly social animals, such as chimpanzees and perhaps wolves and dolphins) that are suggested by the simulation do calculate their own advantage when making decisions between entering and not entering particular social relationships, and the algorithm we have used to model that decision is, essentially, the same subjective expected utility algorithm that defines "rationality in action" as discussed above. But that algorithm is employed here to capture the hard fact that evolutionary logic *requires* it. Animals that do not act so as to maximize their fitness—even if they are not calculating precisely in the way we have modeled it— are probable losers in the evolutionary sweepstakes.

Of greater importance is the configuration of dispositions and capacities that emerges after an extended evolutionary sequence using this algorithm. These individuals do have conflicts of interest, and they do employ their evolved capacities for mindreading and manipulation in the working out of those conflicts. But they also have strong cooperative dispositions that are expressed in frequent cooperative *behavior*. While rationality in action predicts defection in *every* prisoner's dilemma game,[5] the cooperative dispositions that evolve in our simulated populations predict defection only infrequently—particularly so when individuals are also (1) very good at conveying their cooperative intentions to potential partners, who are likely to be similarly cooperative and (2) quite trusting that others *will* in fact cooperate, like themselves. Both of these dispositions, cooperativeness and trustingness, are ignored by the model of rationality-in-action. In the model of rationality-in-design, they are not assumed, but appear as natural developments *within* the model.

There remains the question of how *useful* this model of agency is as a basis for constructing models of broad social and economic processes, the peculiar subject matter of the social sciences proper. As indicated earlier, our preference is for theoretically and empirically defendable starting assumptions *in conjunction with* theoretically and empirically defendable deductions from those assumptions—leading us to prefer the rationality-in-design approach to the a priori assumption of rationality-in-action. Therefore we believe it will be useful given time—time in which many scholars participate in extending and evaluating the model, and piece by piece learn how to analyze the ways in which social outcomes in the present are related to evolutionary pressures in the past.

Notes

1 The findings have been reported extensively elsewhere (Orbell et al., 2004) and we only summarize them here.
2 Games in which one player cooperated and the other defected also occurred, but in a relatively small number of cases.
3 For graphs of these trajectories, see Orbell et al., 2004.
4 As predicted by $PC(c) + (1 - PC)(s) = ALT$.
5 In the absence of any of the incentives discussed in the introduction.

References

Alchian, A. (1950). Uncertainty, evolution and economic theory. *The Journal of Political Economy, 58 (June)*, 211–221.

Axelrod, R. (1981). The emergence of cooperation among egoists. *The American Political Science Review, 75 (June)*, 306–318.

Caporael, L., Dawes, R., Orbell, J., & van de Kragt, A. (1989). Selfishness examined: Cooperation in the absence of egoistic incentives. *Behavioral and Brain Science, 12 (December)*, 683–699.

Dawes, R. (1988). *Rational choice in an uncertain world*. San Diego: Harcourt, Brace, Jovanovich.

Dennett, D. (1995). *Darwin's dangerous idea: Evolution and the meanings of life*. New York: Simon & Schuster.

Fehr, E., & Gachter, S. (2002). Altruistic punishment in humans. *Nature, 415 (10 January)*, 137–140.

Fowler, J., Smirnov, O., & Johnson, T. (2004). Egalitarian motive and altruistic punishment. *Nature, 43316 (January)*, E1–E2.

Friedman, M. (1953). The methodology of positive economics. In M. Friedman (Ed.), *Essays in positive economics* (pp. 3–43). Chicago: University of Chicago Press.

Hobbes, T. (1651/1947). *Leviathan*. New York: E. P. Dutton & Co. Inc.

Kahneman, D., Slovic, P., & Tversky, A. (Eds.) (1985). *Judgment under uncertainty: Heuristics and biases*. Cambridge, UK: Cambridge University Press.

Ledyard, J. (1995). Public goods: A survey of experimental research. In J. H. Kagel and A. E. Roth (Eds.), *The handbook of experimental economics* (pp. 111–194). Princeton, NJ: Princeton University Press.

Orbell, J., Morikawa, T., Hartwig, J., Hanley, J., & Allen, N. (2004). "Machiavellian" intelligence and the evolution of cooperative dispositions. *American Political Science Review*, *98*(1), 1–15.

Simon, H. (1985). Human nature in politics: The dialogue of political science with psychology. *American Political Science Review*, *2 (June)*, 293–304.

Vanberg, V., & Congleton, R. (1992). Rationality, morality and exit. *American Political Science Review*, *86*, 418–443.

4

Empathy-Related and Prosocial Responding

Conceptions and Correlates During Development

NANCY EISENBERG AND NATALIE D. EGGUM

In the last five years, there has been increased interest in the topic of positive psychology—the study of human happiness and thriving (Seligman & Csikszentmihalyi, 2000). One of the foci that received increased attention as a consequence is the study of aspects of human responding that foster close, positive relationships with others and cooperative, prosocial behavior among people (Aspinwall & Staudinger, 2003). Similarly, in recent theory and research, caring is viewed as one component of positive youth development (Lerner et al., 2005). Thus, prosocial behavior—behavior intended to benefit another—generally is believed to provide benefits not only for other people, but also in regard to the well-being and psychological development of the benefactor. In addition, other-oriented emotion and behavior is likely to contribute to peace and cooperation on the societal level (Eisenberg & Ota Wang, 2003), especially if directed not only toward people similar to the self, but also toward those who are different or tend to be the object of prejudice and dehumanization.

In this chapter, we discuss some of the affective and cognitive bases of other-oriented responding. We argue that empathy-related emotions are an important source of motivation in regard to both prosocial and antisocial behaviors and that sympathy may counteract prejudice and the process of dehumanization. We also discuss sociocognitive factors such as moral reasoning, an understanding of emotion, and perspective taking are relevant to prosocial (and antisocial) development because they can have both direct and indirect effects (e.g., through empathy-related reactions) on morally relevant actions. We focus more on prosocial emotion and behavior in this chapter than on antisocial behavior, although the latter is discussed to a limited degree. In addition, our focus in this chapter is primarily on the developmental research involving children, although many of the findings are applicable to adults.

Conceptual Distinctions

Motivation is important to take into account when considering both other-oriented emotions and prosocial behavior. In regard to emotions, Batson (1991) made an important distinction between empathy and personal distress; we have built on his definitions and added a third distinction.

Specifically, it is useful to differentiate among empathy, sympathy, and personal distress. We define *empathy* as an affective response that stems from the apprehension or comprehension of another's emotional state or condition, and is similar to what the other person is feeling or would be expected to feel. Thus, if a person is watching a sad individual or views someone in a situation that is likely to induce sadness and consequently feels sad, the observer is experiencing empathy. However, we believe that in most contexts, especially after infancy when children can differentiate between their own and others' emotions, empathy usual evolves into, co-occurs with, or sequentially alternates with, sympathy and/or personal distress.

Sympathy is defined as an emotional response stemming from the apprehension of another's emotional state or condition, which is not the same as the other's state or condition, but consists of feelings of sorrow or concern for the other. This definition of sympathy is similar to both Batson's (1991) and Hoffman's (2000) definitions of empathy. Thus, if a girl sees a sad peer and feels concern for the peer, she is experiencing sympathy. In our view, such a sympathetic reaction often, but not always, is based upon empathic sadness. However, sympathy also may be based on cognitive perspective taking or accessing information from memory that is relevant to the other's experience (e.g., information regarding what emotion the other person is feeling or about the plight of a person) without the actual experience of empathy.

It is also likely that in many contexts, for some people more than others, empathy leads to personal distress. *Personal distress* is a self-focused, aversive affective reaction to the apprehension of another's emotion (e.g., discomfort, anxiety; Batson, 1991). Personal distress sometimes may stem directly from empathic arousal, primarily if the empathic response is experienced as overly arousing. However, it is likely that personal distress can be elicited by the experience of emotions other than sympathy (e.g., guilt) or through the retrieval of relevant and emotionally arousing information from mental storage. Thus, a person may never experience a dejected child's sadness (empathy) or concern for that child (sympathy), but may experience anxiety, discomfort, or aversive overarousal due to viewing the child.

It is also useful to differentiate among various modes of prosocial behavior (i.e., voluntary behavior intended to benefit another). Prosocial behaviors can be enacted for a variety of reasons, including to improve another's situation, to reap benefits for the self, to gain approval from others, and to avoid repercussions for not helping another. Altruism often is defined as those prosocial behaviors motivated by other-oriented or moral concerns/emotion rather than concrete or social rewards or the desire to reduce aversive affective states (Eisenberg, 1986). However, there is some debate regarding whether altruism ever really occurs (e.g., Maner et al., 2002) and if it can be motivated by values rather than empathy/sympathy (Batson, 1991; Eisenberg, 1986).

These conceptual nuances are important because sympathy and personal distress are believed to be linked with different motivational states and, consequently, with different likelihoods of behaving in ways that benefit or harm others. According to Batson (1991), experienced empathic emotion (what we label *sympathy*) leads to the altruistic desire of reducing the other's suffering. If the cost of helping does not exceed the benefit, altruistic motivation will manifest as helping behavior. Thus, sympathy is expected to predict other-oriented prosocial actions, but not prosocial behaviors motivated by factors such as personal gain or the desire to obtain social approval or alleviate one's own feelings of guilt, shame, or distress. Conversely, if the perception of need evokes personal distress, helping behavior will only occur if it is the easiest means of reducing internal distress. Therefore, if escape from the situation is an easy and viable option, helping is not likely to occur.

The Relation of Sympathy and Personal Distress to Prosocial and Antisocial Behavior

There is now considerable research supporting the assumption that sympathy fosters an other-orientation whereas personal distress undermines concern for others. In a series of studies with adults, Batson and his colleagues (see Batson, 1991) experimentally manipulated sympathy versus detachment or distress and found that adults who experience sympathy are relatively more likely to help others when it is easy not to do so (i.e., to escape) than are those who more detached or more likely to interpret their emotional arousal to distress. He has also provided evidence that sympathy is linked to greater helping when the likelihood of self-gain or approval for helping is minimized, and that the desire to reduce one's own distress does not seem to underlie altruism. Although there is debate about whether feeling oneness with others, for example, is other-oriented or selfish (e.g., Maner et al., 2002), Batson's work as a whole provides fairly strong support for the assumption that sympathy is at least partly other-oriented in motivation and increases the likelihood of individuals assisting the object of their sympathy.

Many of the methods used by Batson to study sympathy are not easily adapted for use with children. Thus, Eisenberg, Fabes, and colleagues (see Eisenberg & Fabes, 1990; Eisenberg, Valiente, & Champion, 2004) conducted a series of studies using a multi-method, albeit nonexperimental, approach in which they have shown that children who experience sympathy are relatively likely to assist the object of their sympathy (or others in a similar situation), whereas children who experience personal distress are relatively unlikely to assist.

As a first step, they constructed and validated measures that could differentiate between sympathy and personal distress. In several studies, adults and/or children viewed videotapes likely to induce either sympathy or personal distress or discussed real-life events that induced sympathy or distress (or discussed a neutral topic). During the procedures, their facial reactions were videotaped, their heart rate and/ or skin conductance was assessed, and immediately after the evocative event they reported how they felt during the film or discussion. Both child and adult participants tended to exhibit facial concerned attention in sympathy-inducing contexts and, especially for children, distress in situations believed to elicit personal distress. Moreover, older children's and adults' self-reports of emotion during these procedures tended to be consistent with the emotional context (Eisenberg, Fabes, Schaller, Miller, Carlo, et al., 1991; see Eisenberg, Valiente, et al., 2004, for a review). Younger children's self-reports of sympathy and personal distress were less differentiated and contextually appropriate, although they usually were better than chance levels (see Eisenberg & Fabes, 1990).

In addition, study participants exhibited higher heart rate (HR) and skin conductance (SC) in the distressing situations than in the baseline/neutral and/or sympathy conditions (Eisenberg, Fabes, Schaller, Carlo, & Miller, 1991; Eisenberg, Fabes, Schaller, Miller, et al., 1991; also see Zahn-Waxler, Cole, Welsh, & Fox, 1995). Both HR and SC, especially the latter, have been viewed as measures of emotional arousal (e.g., Lazarus, 1974; MacDowell & Mandler, 1989). Based on the physiological literature, we suggested that HR acceleration during and immediately after the onset of an evocative stimulus might reflect distress whereas HR deceleration likely reflects interest in, and processing of information, coming from external stimuli—in this case, the sympathy-inducing stimulus (Cacioppo & Sandman, 1978). HR acceleration has been linked to the processing of information that is internal rather than outside of the self and, thus, might tap a self-focus). SC is likely a purer measure of emotional arousal than HR; thus, when people are exposed to evocative empathy-inducing stimuli, high SC is likely to reflect distress or other arousing emotions (depending on the context) and is expected to result in an aversive state and the desire to avoid/reduce the situation rather than confront the other's distress (Eisenberg & Fabes, 1990; Fabes, Eisenberg, Karbon, Troyer, & Switzer, 1994).

After we had demonstrated that our facial, verbal, and physiological measures were useful in assessing sympathy versus personal distress, in a series of studies we examined the relations of these emotional reactions to prosocial behavior. In a typical study, children (and, in a few studies, adults) viewed an empathy-inducing film (e.g., about a child with spina bifida or children in the hospital who were very sad and bored [or, for adults, their mothers]) while their facial reactions were videotaped and their physiological responses (HR, SC) were obtained. Immediately after viewing the tape, study participants reported on their affect during the film using adjectives that tapped sympathy, personal distress, empathic sadness, and sometimes happiness. A little later, the children (or adults) were provided with an opportunity to assist the needed/distressed person in the film or others with a similar problem by donating part of their payment for participation in the study, donating time to help the person, or doing a boring task to help the needy or distressed children rather than playing with attractive toys.

Across several studies, Eisenberg, Fabes, and colleagues found that measures of sympathy tended to be correlated with higher levels of helping or sharing, whereas indices of personal distress tended to be negatively related or unrelated to prosocial behavior (e.g., Miller, Eisenberg, Fabes, & Shell, 1996; see Eisenberg, Valiente, et al., 2004). Specifically, HR deceleration (versus acceleration) during short evocative parts of the film enactments tended to be related to greater helping (e.g., Eisenberg & Fabes, 1990; Eisenberg, Fabes, et al., 1989; Fabes, Eisenberg, Karbon, Troyer, et al., 1994), whereas higher SC tended to be related to lower levels of prosocial behavior (e.g., Eisenberg & Fabes, 1990; Fabes, Eisenberg, & Eisenbud, 1993; Fabes, Eisenberg, Karbon, Bernzweig, et al., 1994). Children's reports of concern, empathic sadness, and/or low happiness sometimes predicted relations with prosocial behavior in the hypothesized manner (e.g., Miller et al., 1996; see Eisenberg, Valiente, et al., 2004), although such findings were relatively infrequent with younger children (Eisenberg, Fabes, et al., 1990; Fabes, Eisenberg, Karbon, Bernzweig, et al., 1994). It is likely that associations between verbal reports and prosocial behavior tend to be stronger and more consistent with age in childhood because reports of vicariously induced emotion become more differentiated and accurate as children's understanding of emotion increases. Unexpectedly, reports of personal distress sometimes have been positively related to prosocial behavior (helping), especially among adults, probably because of the difficulty in differentiating between distress for others or self-related distress with self-report measures (Batson, 1991; Eisenberg, Fabes, et al., 1989). Although positive relations between adults' reports of sympathy or personal distress and indices of social desirability suggest that self-reports of empathy-related responding sometimes may be contaminated by concerns about responding in a desirable manner (Eisenberg, Fabes, et al., 1989), social desirability generally has not been substantially related to younger children's reports of situational empathy-related responding (Eisenberg, Fabes, et al., 1989; Eisenberg, Fabes, Schaller, Carlo, et al., 1991).

In nearly all of the aforementioned studies, situationally induced vicarious responding was examined as a predictor of prosocial behavior directed toward the elicitor of the emotional response or similar individuals. There also is evidence that children who respond with sympathy in such situations are more helpful in general. For example, children prone to sympathy and/or low personal distress in such a laboratory context tend to be more prosocial with peers, as observed for preschoolers (for facial concern/sadness; Eisenberg, McCreath, & Ahn, 1988; Eisenberg, Fabes, et al., 1990) or as reported by teachers (for measures of schoolchildren's low SC; Holmgren, Eisenberg, & Fabes, 1998), and are viewed by parents as more prosocial (for low SC; Fabes et al., 1993). However, findings of relations between indices of empathy-related responding in a specific situation with prosocial behavior in another situation are much less consistent than when assessing prosocial behavior directed toward the target of empathy-related responding (or similar others). For example, facial measures of sympathy or distress in response to one specific film sometimes have not been related to measures of dispositional prosocial behavior outside of the empathy-inducing setting (e.g., Eisenberg, Fabes, et al., 1990; Fabes et al., 1993).

In a study using a somewhat different method, Zhou, Eisenberg, Losoya, Fabes, Reiser, et al. (2002) examined the relations of situationally induced mild empathy to children's dispositional aggression and socially competent responding. Children viewed static slides depicting people in positive or negative situations (based on their facial expressions and/or the context). Their facial reactions and self-reported reactions were assessed. Because the pictures were not presented as "real" and the children knew nothing about the people in the slides, their reactions might have reflected empathy and/or sympathy (due to their mild nature, personal distress reactions were not likely to have occurred). In mid-elementary school, higher levels of children's facial reactions to slides depicting negative emotions predicted low levels of externalizing problem behaviors (e.g., aggressive, defiance, as reported by teachers and parents). Two years later, empathy with negative emotions (based on both facial and self-reported reactions) predicted both relatively low levels of externalizing problems and high levels of teacher-reported socially appropriate behavior. Moreover empathy with negative slides was predictive of antisocial behavior, even when controlling for levels of empathy and problem behaviors two years before.

Other researchers have also found an association between situational (or combined dispositional and situational) measures of empathy or sympathy and externalizing problems (e.g., Zahn-Waxler et al., 1995; see Eisenberg, Fabes, & Spinrad, 2006), and children who exhibit concern for others tend to be less stable in the degree of their externalizing problems over time (Hastings, Zahn-Waxler, Robinson, Usher, & Bridges, 2000). Thus, situationally induced empathy/sympathy appears to predict low levels of antisocial behavior, as well as relatively high levels of prosocial behavior.

Interestingly, preschoolers' personal distress reactions to films of distressed peers have been related to the their tendencies to engage in compliant, requested prosocial behaviors in contexts such as the classroom (Eisenberg, Fabes, et al., 1990; Eisenberg, McCreath, et al., 1988). For example, Eisenberg, McCreath, et al. (1988) found that preschoolers' sadness/concern facial reactions to two videotapes of distressed children were positively related to their prosocial behavior that was spontaneously emitted during a peer interaction. In addition, for girls only, facial concern/sadness was positively related to requested prosocial behaviors. Anxious facial expressions in response to the films were positively related to frequency, but not proportion, of compliance with peers' requests for prosocial actions, perhaps because children high in frequency of performing compliant prosocial behaviors also were frequent targets of peers' requests for sharing or helping. Compliant prosocial behavior, in contrast to spontaneously emitted prosocial behavior, has been associated with low assertiveness, low levels of peer positive reinforcement, and lower levels of social interaction with peers. In fact, children high in compliant prosocial responding, especially boys, seem to be nonassertive and likely are viewed as easy targets by their peers (e.g., Eisenberg, Cameron, et al., 1981; Eisenberg, McCreath, et al., 1988; see Eisenberg, Fabes, et al., 2006). Moreover, young children's compliant prosocial behaviors are much less likely than spontaneous sharing behaviors to predict children's sympathy and prosocial tendencies at older ages (Eisenberg, Guthrie, et al., 1999, 2002), and, unlike spontaneous sharing, have not been associated with other-oriented moral reasoning (Eisenberg-Berg & Hand, 1979). Thus, it is likely that compliant prosocial behaviors do not reflect other-oriented motivations. Rather, it is likely that young children who exhibit high levels of compliant behavior with peers are relatively low in social competence and emotion regulation, and engage in requested prosocial behaviors as a means of curtailing unpleasant social interactions. Findings of this sort highlight the importance of considering the motivation behind behaviors when assessing relations between empathy-related reactions and prosocial behavior.

Relations of Dispositional Measures of Empathy-Related Responding to Prosocial Behavior and Aggression

There also is considerable evidence that dispositional sympathy (or sympathy combined with empathy) is related to higher levels of prosocial behavior and lower levels of aggression. In meta-analyses in the 1980s, Eisenberg and Miller (1987) found that that a variety of types of measures of empathy/sympathy—especially dispositional measures—predicted higher levels of prosocial behavior, whereas Miller and Eisenberg (1988) found modest relations between some measures of empathy-related responding (especially dispositional measures that did not involve picture methods with younger children) and low levels of antisocial behavior. Since the 1980s, these relations have been obtained in numerous studies, demonstrating that measures of dispositional sympathy (or sometimes empathy) are associated with, and predict, prosocial behavior, as well as low levels of antisocial behavior and high levels of socially appropriate behavior (e.g., Eisenberg, Fabes, et al., 1996; Murphy, Shepard, Eisenberg, Fabes, & Guthrie, 1999; see Eisenberg, Fabes, et al., 2006, for a review). Moreover, children's and adolescents' self-reported delinquency and externalizing problem behaviors also have been negatively related to their self-reported dispositional empathic efficacy (Bandura, Caprara, Barbaranelli, Gerbino, & Pastorelli, 2003). In contrast to findings for sympathy, children's self-reported dispositional personal distress on questionnaires tends not to be related to children's prosocial behavior (e.g., Eisenberg, Miller, Shell, McNalley, & Shea, 1991; Eisenberg, Carlo, Murphy, & Van Court, 1995; Litvack-Miller, Dougal, & Romney, 1997), although self-reported dispositional personal distress is a predictor of quality of social behavior, including low helping, in adults (Davis, 1994).

Dispositional Prosocial Tendencies: Consistency Over Time?

An important issue in regard to dispositional other-oriented responding is whether it is stable across time and predicts prosocial tendencies in the future. Evidence of consistency in empathy-related responding and prosocial behavior during childhood and into adulthood has been obtained. A number of investigators, but certainly not all, have found evidence of modest stability during childhood and adolescence (Hastings et al., 2000; see Eisenberg, Fabes, et al., 2006).

Moreover, we have obtained evidence of remarkable consistency across time for measures of prosocial dispositions that are most likely to tap altruistic, other-oriented tendencies. In a longitudinal study, we observed preschoolers' naturally occurring prosocial behaviors and coded them in regard to their spontaneity (if they were performed spontaneously or in response to a verbal or nonverbal request) and if they involved a cost such as giving up an object or space (sharing) or relatively low cost (helping, e.g., passing a toy that the child was not using or tying another child's apron; Eisenberg-Berg & Hand, 1979). We argued that costly, freely enacted prosocial actions (i.e., spontaneous sharing) are most likely to reflect sympathy, and, in fact, they were related to rudimentary other-oriented (likely empathic) prosocial moral reasoning in the preschool years (Eisenberg-Berg & Hand, 1979). Then, every two years, starting from age 9–10 years into early adulthood, we assessed a number of measures of prosocial orientation/behavior. Specifically, in late childhood and adolescence, behavioral measures of helping or sharing were obtained (e.g., donating money, doing additional questionnaires for free at a later time). Adolescents also reported on their prosocial behavior. Moreover, mothers' reports of children's prosocial behaviors were obtained in adolescence whereas friends reported on participants' sympathy and prosocial tendencies in early adulthood.

We (Eisenberg, Guthrie, et al., 1999) found that spontaneous sharing was at least marginally, positively correlated with costly donating at age 9–10 and 11–12, costly helping (giving of time) at 17–18, self-reported helping at age 15–16, self-reported consideration for others at 19–20, a self-report prosocial dispositional aggregate measure at ages 21–22 and 23–24, mothers' reports of helpfulness at ages 15–16 and 17–18, sympathy throughout adolescence and into adulthood, and friends' reports of sympathy at assessments in early adulthood. Early spontaneous sharing generally was unrelated to self-reported empathy (rather than sympathy) in childhood, self-reported personal distress in adolescence or adulthood, and low-cost helping (e.g., picking up dropped paper clips), as well as adult friends' reports of prosocial behavior (although it was related to reports of sympathy). Thus, spontaneous sharing in preschool was fairly consistently related to a variety of measures of other-oriented responding. In contrast, early compliant prosocial behaviors and spontaneous low-cost helping infrequently predicted prosocial responding across time, although preschoolers who were relatively high in compliant sharing sometimes reported being relatively helpful in adolescence and adulthood and were viewed by friends as more prosocial at age 25–26 (Eisenberg, Guthrie, et al., 1999, 2002).

Of particular note for this discussion, sympathy in adolescence generally tended to mediate the relations of preschoolers' spontaneous sharing and their prosocial tendencies in adulthood (Eisenberg, Guthrie, et al., 1999). In addition, there generally was moderate to substantial stability in self-reported prosocial behavior and sympathy across adolescence and into adulthood, as well as consistency between mother-reported adolescent prosocial behavior and adult self-reported prosocial behavior (Eisenberg, Guthrie, et al., 2002). Thus, there was strong evidence of intraindividual consistency in prosocial dispositions over time, including empathy-related responding. Moreover, across adolescence and into adulthood, measures of sympathy and prosocial tendencies often were related, supporting the notion that sympathetic tendencies may underlie a stable prosocial disposition (see Eisenberg, Miller, et al., 1991; Eisenberg, Carlo, et al., 1995).

In summary, evidence of a role of vicarious emotion, especially sympathy, in prosocial dispositions (and low antisocial tendencies) is substantial. Although empathy and sympathy involve some social cognition, by definition they involve affect. We now briefly turn to the role of social cognition per se in prosocial tendencies in children.

Social Cognition and Prosocial Tendencies

Sociocognitive capacities likely contribute to prosocial orientations and actions in a variety of ways (see Eisenberg, Fabes, et al., 2006). Most theorists have argued that true empathy and sympathy require some ability to identify others' likely emotional states (e.g., Eisenberg, 1986). Moreover, individuals who understand others' emotions and cognitions are likely to be higher in moral reasoning (see below), and may be more likely to feel a connection with others that seems to promote prosocial behavior.

Understanding emotions and perspective taking

Feshbach (1978), Roberts and Strayer (1996), and others have proposed that an understanding of one's own emotions facilitates an understanding of others and, hence, the capacity for experiencing empathy. Consistent with this view, emotional insight (Roberts & Strayer, 1996) and emotion knowledge has been linked to children's sympathy/empathy (see Eisenberg, Fabes, et al., 2006).

Perspective taking involves visualizing the impact a situation has on another person; it often is assumed to derive from the effort to put oneself in the other's place. Batson and Shaw (1991) suggested that the degree of empathic emotion due to perspective taking is determined by the perceived magnitude of another's need and the strength of the affective attachment felt towards the other. In a typical study, Batson and his colleagues (2003) manipulated perspective taking by assigning adults to one of three perspective taking conditions: *imagine-self, imagine-other,* or *no-perspective.* In the *imagine-self* condition, participants were told to imagine how they would feel if they were in the place of the other person. In the *imagine-other* condition, they were told to imagine how the other person likely feels. Theoretically, imagining yourself in the place of another should allow you to understand the interests and desires of another, which should promote moral behavior. In contrast, imagining how another feels should evoke empathic emotion, but not necessarily moral motivation. Results from Batson's previous work support this idea (Batson, 1991). In a situation that did not involve fairness, Batson found that participants in the *no-perspective* condition were primarily motivated by self-interest, whereas participants in the *imagine-other* condition were more altruistic than in the *imagine-self* and *no-perspective* conditions (which did not differ). Furthermore, the participants' reports of sympathy were significantly and positively correlated with their altruistic behavior. In a second study with a focus on fairness (morality), Batson and colleagues found that the *imagine-self* perspective promoted moral behavior when beginning with an initial advantage over the other person, albeit not if both people begin with an equal advantage/disadvantage (Batson et al., 2003).

Corresponding associations between perspective taking and sympathy or prosocial behavior have been found in children (see Eisenberg, Fabes, et al., 2006, for a review). For example, in a sample of second-, fourth-, and sixth-graders, Litvack-Miller et al. (1997) found that perspective taking accounted for a significant proportion of variance in teacher-reported comforting and altruistic monetary donations. FitzGerald and White (2003) found a similar relation between perspective taking and teacher/peer rated prosocial behavior in a sample of 6- to 13-year-old children and a negative relationship between perspective taking and teacher/peer rated aggressive behavior. Moreover, in our longitudinal study, adolescents' and young adults' reports of tending to try to take others' perspectives frequently were significantly positively related to self-reports of sympathy and prosocial behavior (see Eisenberg, Carlo, et al., 1995; Eisenberg, Guthrie, et al., 2002). Thus, perspective taking has been linked to sympathetic emotion and behavior in both adults and children.

One would not expect perspective taking to predict prosocial behavior in all situations (Eisenberg, 1986). Only very rudimentary perspective taking may be required for many everyday prosocial behaviors, so most individuals may have the requisite skills. Moreover, knowledge of another's emotional state can be used to manipulate or hurt other people as well as to help them. In addition, prosocial behaviors that are performed for motives such as avoidance of punishment or social disapproval would not be expected to related to perspective taking skills. We return to the issue of when perspective taking predicts other-oriented prosocial behavior shortly.

Moral reasoning

Investigators have argued that prosocial moral reasoning, as well as traditional measures of prohibition-oriented (i.e., Kohlbergian) moral reasoning, are associated with higher levels of both sympathy and prosocial behavior (e.g., Eisenberg, 1986). Prosocial moral reasoning is reasoning about moral dilemmas in which one person's needs or desires conflict with those of others in a context in which the role of prohibitions, authorities' dictates, and formal obligations is minimal. In Eisenberg's model (1986) of prosocial moral reasoning, lower level reasoning is based on hedonic, self-oriented, or external concerns, whereas at a higher level, reasoning is internalized and/or self-reflectively other-focused. Moreover, individuals may exhibit moral reasoning representing a range of reasoning levels at any point in time. According to both Kohlberg and Eisenberg, higher-level moral reasoning partly reflects advances in individuals' abilities to take the perspective of another, as well as an understanding of relatively abstract conceptions (Colby & Kohlberg, 1984; Eisenberg, 1986); thus, an individual's level of cognitive development imposes a cap on moral reasoning. According to Eisenberg (1986), personal factors (e.g., goals, needs, and preferences), often a product of socialization and contextual factors (e.g., cost/benefit of helping), also influence the type of moral reasoning one applies to moral dilemmas.

The relation between moral reasoning and sympathy/empathy may be complex and bi-directional. Hoffman (1987) hypothesized that sympathy/empathy stimulates the development of internalized moral reasoning reflecting concern for others' welfare. In addition, Eisenberg (1986) suggested that sympathy primes the use of pre-existing other-oriented moral cognitions in specific contexts. Conversely, the cognitive structures associated with higher-level, and especially other-oriented, moral reasoning may sometimes prime the experience of sympathy or stimulate moral evaluations that increase a person's tendency to focus on another's needs and experience sympathy in a given context.

In fact, there is considerable evidence that prosocial moral reasoning, as well as traditional measures of prohibition-oriented (i.e., Kohlbergian) moral reasoning, are related to both sympathy and prosocial behavior (see Eisenberg, 1986; Eisenberg, Fabes, et al., 2006, for reviews). For example, in the longitudinal investigation of prosocial moral reasoning already discussed, we have repeatedly found correlations between contemporaneous self-reported sympathy and youths' higher level prosocial moral reasoning and/or the greater use of empathy-relevant types of moral reasoning (e.g., reasoning focusing on others' needs) or lesser use of hedonistic reasoning, from early adolescence into adulthood (Eisenberg, Carlo, et al., 1995; Eisenberg, Guthrie, et al., 2002; Eisenberg, Miller, et al., 1991). A similar pattern of findings has been obtained in other samples in both the US (see Eisenberg, 1986) and Brazil (Eisenberg, Zhou, & Koller, 2001). Furthermore, in our longitudinal study, we have found numerous *across-time* correlations between measures of prosocial moral judgment in adulthood and measures of sympathy or empathy in late childhood and adolescence; Eisenberg, Guthrie, et al., 2002). These findings are consistent with the view that empathy-related responding contributes to moral reasoning (and perhaps vice versa).

Moreover, in another study, Skoe, Eisenberg, and Cumberland (2002) found an association between young adults' reports of experiencing sympathy when resolving moral conflicts and higher levels of their care-related moral reasoning, especially when discussing real-life dilemmas. Adults' reports of feelings of sympathy also were related to ratings of importance of a moral dilemma. Thus, sympathy may stimulate, or at least co-occur with, use of care-related moral reasoning.

Additionally, lower level moral reasoning has been associated with aggression and antisocial behavior (for review see Rest, Narvaez, Bebeau, & Thoma, 1999). Indeed, Arsenio and Lemerise (2001) contend that bullying (a form of aggression) "cannot be understood without reference to traditional moral issues involving fairness, other's welfare, and refraining from harming others for personal gain" (p. 62). When proactive aggressors, for example, aggress to obtain their social goals, the immoral behavior is rationalized. In support of an association, Raaijmakers, Engels, and Van Hoof (2005) found modest negative correlations between delinquency and moral reasoning and reciprocal relations between the two in a sample of Dutch adolescents and young adults.

Moral reasoning, as well as sympathy, might mediate some of the relation of perspective taking with altruistic and other moral behaviors. In a study conducted with Brazilian adolescents (Eisenberg, Zhou, et al., 2001), we obtained evidence that (a) moral reasoning mediates the relation of sympathy to prosocial behavior and (b) sympathy mediates the relation of cognitive perspective taking to moral reasoning and prosocial behavior. In a structural equation model, both sympathy and cognitive perspective taking predicted adolescents' level of prosocial moral reasoning, which in turn predicted their prosocial behavior. Perspective taking also predicted sympathy and the latter had a direct path to prosocial behavior. Thus, sympathy may contribute to prosocial behavior directly by affectively motivating the individual, as well as through its effects on prosocial moral reasoning. Consistent with the argument that perspective taking does not directly predict prosocial behavior but is related primarily when it affects moral cognitions or emotion, a model with a direct path added from perspective taking to prosocial behavior did not fit the data as well and this direct path was not significant. These findings suggest that it is important to foster the capacity for moral affect (such as sympathy) as well as moral values (as reflected in moral reasoning) rather than to merely try to stimulate perspective taking, at least for people with typical levels of sociocognitive skills. However, in young children who are just developing a rudimentary understanding of emotions, fostering such understanding may be an important first step to enhancing their capacity for sympathy and higher-level moral reasoning. In addition, for youth whose abilities to understand others' emotions are stunted, such as those with psychopathic tendencies (Blair, College, Murray, & Mitchell, 2001), it may be important to try to heighten their understanding and processing of others' emotional states.

Relations of self-regulation to an other-oriented emotional focus (sympathy) versus a self-focus (personal distress)

As our review thus far illustrates, it is likely that individual differences in both cognition and affect are related to differences among people in their prosocial behavior. However, we believe that even if people are relatively high in perspective taking and moral reasoning capacities when tested in nonevocative contexts, they are likely to be low in other-oriented prosocial behavior *if* they are prone to experience personal distress in real-life interactions. In other words, for people prone to personal distress, an affective self-focus is likely to overwhelm or undermine the tendency to cognitively focus on others' needs or on other-oriented or other moral values relevant in an evocative context. Thus, it is important to consider factors that may determine whether people are prone to empathy, sympathy, and personal distress.

In examining this issue, one can focus on biological factors such as genetics or on socialization/environmental factors—both have been linked with empathy, sympathy, and prosocial behavior in numerous studies (see Eisenberg, Fabes, et al., 2006 for a review of both bodies of literature). However, it may be useful to also consider more proximal causes; we suggest that an important mediating variable between hereditary endowment or socialization experiences and people's empathy-related responding is individuals' ability to regulate their emotional arousal, including their vicariously induced emotion. Emotion-related regulatory capacities appear to have both genetic (through temperament) and environmental bases (see Rothbart & Bates, 2006) and have been identified as possibly mediating between parenting and children's sympathy (Eisenberg, Liew, & Pidada, 2001), social competence, and adjustment (e.g., Eisenberg, Zhou, et al., 2005). Thus, the role of emotion-related regulation in empathy-related responding seems to be critical for conceptualizing ways to understand and alter individuals' empathy-related responding and altruistic behavior.

We have argued that there is an optimal level of vicarious arousal that focuses a person's attention on another's emotional state and needs and, simultaneously, does not overarouse the individual to the point that he or she becomes self-focused. This belief is based on the assumption that the experience of personal distress involves empathic overarousal (Eisenberg, Fabes, Murphy, et al., 1994), whereas the experience of sympathy involves moderate or well-regulated levels of vicariously induced emotional arousal. Support for this view comes from several lines of work. For example, negative emotional arousal is associated with a focus on the self (e.g., Wood, Saltzberg, & Goldsamt, 1990). In addition, as discussed briefly already, in our own research, people exhibited markers of relatively high emotional arousal (e.g., higher skin conductance and heart rate), and sometimes reported more distress, in situations likely to elicit personal distress, whereas sympathy tended to be associated with HR deceleration, a marker of an external attentional focus (Eisenberg, Fabes, Schaller, Carlo, et al., 1991; Eisenberg, Fabes, Schaller, Miller, et al., 1991). In addition, Bengtsson (2003) found that elementary schoolchildren who were high in self-reported empathy and teacher-reported prosocial behavior tended to experience moderate (rather than high) levels of threat and to modulate the emotional significance of empathy-eliciting stimuli through the use of cognitive restructuring (which can be viewed as a mode of emotion regulation).

In addition, in a series of studies, we often have found that individual differences in regulatory processes involved in emotion regulation (e.g., the abilities to shift and focus attention or inhibit behavior) have been positively related to sympathy and negatively related to personal distress. Among adults, for example, dispositional personal distress has been negatively related to both self-reported regulation and/or friends' reports of students' coping. Dispositional sympathy has been either positively correlated with indices of regulation or positively related to regulation once the effects of individual differences in negative emotional intensity were controlled (see Eisenberg, Fabes, Murphy, et al., 1994).

Similarly, in several studies we have found that children's sympathy is associated with measures of their dispositional self-regulation. In a study of 6- to 8-year-old schoolchildren, we obtained teachers' and children's reports of sympathy (on questionnaire measures) and parents' and teachers' reports of children's regulation (children's abilities to shift and focus attention and to inhibit and regulate their overt behavior; Eisenberg, Fabes, et al., 1996). In general, adults' reports of children's regulation were positively related to children's dispositional sympathy. Further, for boys, physiological arousal (heart rate, skin conductance) when exposed to a relatively distressing film clip was related to low dispositional sympathy. Thus, those boys who appeared to be prone to physiological overarousal were low on dispositional sympathy. In two- and four-year follow-up assessments of this sample, similar relations between were found, both within a given assessment time and often across two or four years (Eisenberg, Fabes, Shepard, Murphy, Jones, et al., 1998; Murphy et al., 1999). In addition, the concurrent association between dispositional sympathy and regulation was replicated in a sample of third graders in Indonesia (Eisenberg, Liew, et al., 2001), although three years later, this relation was found more consistently for boys than for girls (Eisenberg, Liew, & Pidada, 2001).

In summary, there is fairly consistent evidence that children who are high in dispositional sympathy (and in prosocial behavior) are well regulated (see Eisenberg, Fabes, et al., 2006, for a review of work in other laboratories). It should be noted, however, that findings in regard to situationally induced sympathy and personal distress are not as consistent. In adults, self-reported sympathy, sadness, and distress (and HR for men) in response to empathy-inducing films sometimes have been negatively related to a self-reported measure of emotion regulation, whereas facial reactions to the films were unrelated to measures of regulation (e.g., Eisenberg, Fabes, Murphy, et al., 1994). However, in a study of children aged 4 to 6 years, children's concerned facial reactions to the conflict film were positively related to teachers' reports of children's attentional control (Eisenberg & Fabes, 1995).

Moreover, in a study of children in kindergarten to third grade (Guthrie, Eisenberg, Fabes, Holmgren, et al., 1997), children who evidenced sympathy (e.g., facial sadness, mean heart rate decline, and self-reported sympathy) in response to an empathy-inducing film generally were rated higher in regulation and resiliency, although findings sometimes were obtained for only one sex and often were weak. In addition, higher sympathy (as indexed by facial concern) also has been correlated with high heart rate variability in studies with school-aged children (which is correlated with a measure of physiological regulation, vagal tone; see Fabes et al., 1993; also see Eisenberg, Fabes, et al., 1996). However, findings on vagal responding and concern are not consistent, especially for younger children (e.g., Hastings et al., 2000; Zahn-Waxler et al., 1995; see Eisenberg, Fabes, et al., 2006).

Thus, although situational measures of empathy-related responding tend to be related to children's regulation, the findings are relatively weak. The weak relations may be because emotional responding in any particular context may or may not be a very reliable index of general empathy-related dispositions. Moreover, in some situations, well-regulated people may be more likely to experience variously induced affect. For example, when the empathy-inducing stimulus is mild, one might expect better-regulated children to be those who react physiologically because they are likely to attend to the stimulus and, hence, take the other's perspective. In support of these ideas, in a study in which schoolchildren viewed mildly evocative empathy-inducing slides, those who exhibited a greater physiological reaction were viewed as well regulated by adults (Liew, Eisenberg, Losoya, Guthrie, & Murphy, 2003).

Prejudice

Prejudice is defined as "negative attitudes toward social groups, to create a psychological distance between the prejudiced person and the target of his or her prejudice" (Stephan & Finlay, 1999, p. 729). Understanding the effects of prejudicial attitudes on empathy, prosocial behavior, and aggression, and, most importantly, how to manipulate these attitudes, may prove to be a powerful tool in the quest to promote a cooperative and peaceful society.

Ingroup members harboring prejudice towards outgroup members often have exaggerated perceptions of homogeneity within outgroups, as well as inflated perceptions of differences between groups. Perceived dramatic differences, in concert with dislike, may avert empathic perspective taking. However, finding a common identity may blur harmful, dividing lines between ingroups and outgroups (Killen, Lee-Kim, McGlothlin, & Stangor, 2002). In fact, there is evidence supporting the notion that people experience more empathy towards others perceived as similar to the self (Schroeder, Penner, Dovidio, & Piliavin, 1995).

Stephan and Finlay (1999) suggested that inducing empathy towards dissimilar others may lead to a change of prejudicial attitudes. They distinguished *parallel empathy* (like Eisenberg's *empathy*) from *reactive empathy*. Reactive empathy is said to lead to *empathic concern* (Eisenberg's *sympathy*) or *personal distress*. When parallel empathy is experienced, experiencing an emotion similar to the other may arouse feelings of injustice, which in turn may counteract prejudice. Reactive empathy leads to cognitive dissonance and therefore a desire to change prejudicial attitudes to parallel the experience of compassionate feelings.

Like Stephan and Finlay, Batson and colleagues (1997, 2002) believe inducing empathy may alter negative attitudes towards stigmatized people and groups, although the mechanism of change differs between theories. Batson, Polycarpou, and Harmon-Jones (1997) asserted that taking the perspective of a stigmatized person increases empathy, as well as how much the empathizer values the stigmatized person's welfare. Furthermore, if membership in the stigmatized group is highly relevant and salient to the perceived need (e.g., the stigmatized person is the target of an ethnic slur), the increased value and changed attitude generalizes to the entire stigmatized group (Batson et al., 1997). In 2002, Batson and colleagues added an "action" step to their model, whereby increased motivation to help the stigmatized group follows from the improved attitude. In support of his ideas, Batson, Chang, Orr, and Rowland (2002) found undergraduates who were asked to imagine the other's feelings (high-empathy) when listening to an evocative audiotaped interview with a man convicted of the use and sale of heroin reported more positive attitudes toward drug users and were more inclined to help other drug users than were those who remained objective (the low-empathy condition). Path analyses indicated the relation between induced empathy and helping was mediated by the effect of empathy on attitudes.

Dehumanization/humanization

Bandura argued that moral conduct is regulated by social and internalized self-sanctions. He further proposed that moral conduct should be congruent with moral standards unless self-regulation is weakened by social circumstance or self-exonerative moral reasoning (Bandura, 2002, p.102). Bandura outlines a number of moral disengagement strategies including, but not limited to, dehumanization, euphemistic labeling, minimizing consequences, and diffusion of responsibility (Bandura, 2002; Bandura, Underwood, & Fromson, 1975).

Dehumanization has been linked to empathic responding and aggressive behaviors. Dehumanization divests people of human qualities or attributes bestial qualities to them (Bandura, Barbaranelli, Caprara, & Pastorelli, 1996). As a consequence, it serves to disengage self-sanctions prohibiting aggressive conduct. For example, Bandura et al. (1975) had college men allot punishment to a person (an actor) who was dehumanized, humanized, or neither by experimenters. Dehumanized actors received significantly more punishment than in the neutral condition and over twice as much punishment as the humanized actors.

Similar associations between dehumanization/moral disengagement and aggression have been found in younger children. In a longitudinal study of elementary and junior high students, Bandura et al. (1996) found children high in moral disengagement (including the use of dehumanization) to be less prosocial, to experience less guilt, and to be prone to aggression/ transgressive conduct. It is likely that level of sympathy partly mediates such a relation between level of moral disengagement and prosocial or aggressive behavior.

On the other hand, *humanization* can effectively counteract aggression (Bandura et al., 1975) and can promote empathy and altruism (Bandura, 2002; Monroe, 2004). Monroe conducted in-depth, qualitative interviews with rescuers of Jews during World War II, Carnegie Hero Commission Award recipients, and philanthropists (Monroe, 2004). Many interviewees had risked their lives for others they had never met before. A common theme emerged from these interviews: the altruists perceived themselves to have a strong, shared human connection with the person in need. Monroe concluded that altruists see strangers as fellow human beings.

Unfortunately, features of today's society often contribute to dehumanization. Advanced technology, increased mobility, and large city populations have increased anonymity and depersonalization. A society with characteristics such as these is likely to cultivate dehumanization (Bandura, 2002). Therefore, it is more important than ever for research to concentrate on the ways in which humanization can be fostered.

Conclusion

In summary, there is considerable evidence documenting the role of sympathy in prosocial behavior and aggression. In addition, associations of sympathy/empathy with moral reasoning, perspective taking, and an understanding of emotion have been demonstrated, although sometimes relations may be bidirectional. Research on the role of dehumanization in children's moral behavior is sparse, but research with adults as well as children attest to its importance in how people treat one another. In combination, these bodies of work indicate that the cultivation of sympathy—especially for individuals who are not connected to the self and may differ in ethnicity, race, nationality, or other ways—is critical for enhancing cooperation and altruistic behavior, as well as for inhibiting aggressive behavior. Batson's work, in particular, suggests that inducing people to perspective take and sympathize with stigmatized others leads to concern for the stigmatized group as a whole and a greater likelihood of helping members of the stigmatized group (Batson et al., 1997).

Although not reviewed in this chapter, there is a body of research linking sympathy and prosocial behavior to parents' behaviors and socialization practices (see Eisenberg, Fabes, et al., 2006). In addition, abuse and related trauma may bias a person to experience personal distress rather than sympathy (see Milburn, this volume). Prevention researchers have found that it is possible to enhance children's adjustment (including a reduction of externalizing problem behaviors) by promoting their understanding of emotion and their strategies for regulating emotion and for resolving conflicts (e.g., Greenberg, Kusche, Cook, & Quamma, 1995). Thus, it is important that investigators find ways to promote sympathy for others—especially those who differ from the self and/or are stigmatized and likely to be dehumanized.

Acknowledgment

Work on this chapter was supported by grants from the National Institutes of Mental Health, Fetzer Institute, and The Institute for Research on Unlimited Love—Altruism, Compassion, Service (located at the School of Medicine, Case Western Reserve University).

References

Arsenio, W. F., & Lemerise, E. A. (2001). Varieties of childhood bullying: Values, emotion processes, and social competence. *Social Development, 10*, 59–73.

Aspinwall, L. G., & Staudinger, U. M. (2003). Introduction. In L. G. Aspinwall & U. M. Staudinger (Eds.), *A psychology of human strengths: Fundamental questions and future directions for a positive psychology* (pp. 3–22). Washington DC: American Psychological Association.

Bandura, A. (2002). Selective moral disengagement in the exercise of moral agency. *Journal of Moral Education, 31*, 101–119.

Bandura, A., Barbaranelli, C., Caprara, G. V., & Pastorelli, C. (1996). Mechanisms of moral disengagement in the exercise of moral agency. *Journal of Personality and Social Psychology, 71*, 364–374.

Bandura, A., Caprara, G. V., Barbaranelli, C., Gerbino, M., & Pastorelli, C. (2003). Role of affective self-regulatory efficacy in diverse sphere of psychosocial functioning. *Child Development, 74*, 769–782.

Bandura, A., Underwood, B., & Fromson, M. E. (1975). Disinhibition of aggression through diffusion of responsibility and dehumanization of victims. *Journal of Research in Personality, 9*, 253–269.

Batson, C. D. (1991). *The altruism question: Toward a social-psychological answer.* Hillsdale, NJ: Lawrence Erlbaum.

Batson, C. D., Chang, J., Orr, R., & Rowland, J. (2002). Empathy, attitudes and action: Can feeling for a member of a stigmatized group motivate one to help the group? *Personality and Social Psychology Bulletin, 28*, 1656–1666.

Batson, C. D., Lishner, D. A., Carpenter, A., Dulin, L., Harjusola-Webb, S., Stocks, E. L., et al. (2003). ". . . As you would have them do unto you": Does imagining yourself in the other's place stimulate moral action? *Personality and Social Psychology Bulletin, 29*, 1190–1201.

Batson, C. D., Polycarpou, M. P., Harmon-Jones, E., Imhoff, H. J., Mitchener, E. C., Bednar, L. L., et al. (1997). Empathy and attitudes: Can feeling for a member of a stigmatized group improve feelings toward the group? *Journal of Personality and Social Psychology, 72*(1), 105–118.

Batson, C. D., & Shaw, L. L. (1991). Evidence for altruism: Toward a pluralism of prosocial motives. *Psychological Inquiry, 2*(2), 107–122.

Bengtsson, H. (2003). Children's cognitive appraisal of others' distressful and positive experiences. *International Journal of Behavioral Development, 27,* 457–466.

Blair, R. J. R., Colledge, E., Murray, L., & Mitchell, D. G. V. (2001). A selective impairment in the processing of sad and fearful expressions in children with psychopathic tendencies. *Journal of Abnormal Child Psychology, 29,* 491–498.

Cacioppo, J. T., & Sandman, C. A. (1978). Physiological differentiation of sensory and cognitive tasks as a function of warning processing demands and reported unpleasantness. *Biological Psychology, 6,* 181–192.

Colby, A., & Kohlberg, L. (1984). Invariant sequence and internal consistency in moral judgment stages. In W. M. Kurtines & J. L. Gewirtz (Eds.), *Morality, moral behavior and moral development* (pp. 41–51). NY: John Wiley & Sons.

Davis, M. H. (1994). *Empathy: A social psychological approach.* Madison, WI: Brown & Benchmark.

Eisenberg, N. (1986). *Altruistic emotion, cognition, and behavior.* Hillsdale, NJ: Erlbaum.

Eisenberg, N., Cameron, E., Tryon, K., & Dodez, R. (1981). Socialization of prosocial behavior in the preschool classroom. *Developmental Psychology, 17,* 773–782.

Eisenberg, N., Carlo, G., Murphy, B., & Van Court, P. (1995). Prosocial development in late adolescence: A longitudinal study. *Child Development, 66,* 1179–1197.

Eisenberg, N., & Fabes, R. A. (1990). Empathy: Conceptualization, assessment, and relation to prosocial behavior. *Motivation and Emotion, 14,* 131–149.

Eisenberg, N., & Fabes, R. A. (1995). The relation of young children's vicarious emotional responding to social competence, regulation, and emotionality. *Cognition and Emotion, 9,* 203–228.

Eisenberg, N., Fabes, R. A., Miller, P. A., Fultz, J., Mathy, R. M., Shell, R., et al. (1989). The relations of sympathy and personal distress to prosocial behavior: A multimethod study. *Journal of Personality and Social Psychology, 57,* 55–66.

Eisenberg, N., Fabes, R. A., Miller, P. A., Shell, C., Shea, R., & May-Plumlee, T. (1990). Preschoolers' vicarious emotional responding and their situational and dispositional prosocial behavior. *Merrill-Palmer Quarterly, 36,* 507–529.

Eisenberg, N., Fabes, R. A., Murphy, B., et al. (1994). The relations of emotionality and regulation to dispositional and situational empathy-related responding. *Journal of Personality and Social Psychology, 66,* 776–797.

Eisenberg, N., Fabes, R. A., Murphy, B. C., Karbon, M., Smith, M., & Maszk, P. (1996). The relations of children's dispositional empathy-related responding to their emotionality, regulation, and social functioning. *Developmental Psychology, 32,* 195–209.

Eisenberg, N., Fabes, R. A., Schaller, M., Carlo, G., & Miller, P. A. (1991). The relations of parental characteristics and practices to children's vicarious emotional responding. *Child Development, 62,* 1393–1408.

Eisenberg, N., Fabes, R. A., Schaller, M., Miller, P. A., Carlo, G., Poulin, R., et al. (1991). Personality and socialization correlates of vicarious emotional responding. *Journal of Personality and Social Psychology, 61,* 459–470.

Eisenberg, N., Fabes, R. A., Shepard, S. A., Murphy, B. C., Jones, J., & Guthrie, I. K. (1998). Contemporaneous and longitudinal prediction of children's sympathy from dispositional regulation and emotionality. *Developmental Psychology, 34,* 910–924.

Eisenberg, N., Fabes, R. A., & Spinrad, T. L. (2006). Prosocial behavior. In W. Damon & R. M. Lerner (Series Eds.) & N. Eisenberg (Vol. Ed.), *Handbook of child psychology: Vol. 3. Social, emotional, and personality development* (6th ed., pp. 646–718). New York: John Wiley.

Eisenberg, N., Guthrie, I., Cumberland, A., Murphy, B. C., Shepard, S. A., Zhou, Q., & Carlo, G. (2002). Prosocial development in early adulthood: A longitudinal study. *Journal of Personality and Social Psychology, 82*, 993–1006.

Eisenberg, N., Guthrie, I. K., Murphy, B. C., Shepard, S. A., Cumberland, A., & Carlo, G. (1999). Consistency and development of prosocial dispositions: A longitudinal study. *Child Development, 70*, 1360–1372.

Eisenberg, N., Liew, J., & Pidada, S. (2001). The relations of parental emotional expressivity with the quality of Indonesian children's social functioning. *Emotion, 1*, 107–115.

Eisenberg, N., McCreath, H., & Ahn, R. (1988). Vicarious emotional responsiveness and prosocial behavior: Their interrelations in young children. *Personality and Social Psychology Bulletin, 14*, 298–311.

Eisenberg, N., & Miller, P. (1987). The relation of empathy to prosocial and related behaviors. *Psychological Bulletin, 101*, 91-119.

Eisenberg, N., Miller, P. A., Shell, R., McNalley, S., & Shea, C. (1991). Prosocial development in adolescence: A longitudinal study. *Developmental Psychology, 27*, 849–857.

Eisenberg, N., & Ota Wang, V. (2003). Toward a positive psychology: Social developmental and cultural contributions. In L. G. Aspinwall & U. M. Staudinger (Eds.), *A psychology of human strengths: Fundamental questions and future directions for a positive psychology* (pp. 117–129). Washington, DC: American Psychological Association.

Eisenberg, N., Valiente, C., & Champion, C. (2004). Empathy-related responding: Moral, social, and socialization correlates. In A. G. Miller (Ed.), *The social psychology of good and evil* (pp. 386–415). New York: Guilford Press.

Eisenberg, N., Zhou, Q., & Koller, S. (2001). Brazilian adolescents' prosocial moral judgment and behavior: Relations to sympathy, perspective taking, gender-role orientation, and demographic characteristics. *Child Development, 72*, 518–534.

Eisenberg, N., Zhou, Q., Spinrad, T. L., Valiente, C., Fabes, R. A., & Liew, J. (2005). Relations among positive parenting, children's effortful control, and externalizing problems: A three-wave longitudinal study. *Child Development, 76*, 1055–1071.

Eisenberg-Berg, N., & Hand, M. (1979). The relationship of preschooler's reasoning about prosocial moral conflicts to prosocial behavior. *Child Development, 50*, 356-363.

Fabes, R. A., Eisenberg, N., & Eisenbud, L. (1993). Behavioral and physiological correlates of children's reactions to others' distress. *Developmental Psychology, 29*, 655–663.

Fabes, R. A., Eisenberg, N., Karbon, M., Bernzweig, J., Speer, A. L., & Carlo, G. (1994). Socialization of children's vicarious emotional responding and prosocial behavior: Relations with mothers' perceptions of children's emotional reactivity. *Developmental Psychology, 30*, 44–55.

Fabes, R. A., Eisenberg, N., Karbon, M., Troyer, D., & Switzer, G. (1994). The relations of children's emotion regulation to their vicarious emotional responses and comforting behavior. *Child Development, 65*, 1678–1693.

Feshbach, N. D. (1978). Studies of empathic behavior in children. In B. A. Maher (Ed.), *Progress in experimental personality research* (vol. 8, pp. 1–47). NY: Academic Press.

FitzGerald, D. P., & White, K. J. (2003). Linking children's social worlds: Perspective-taking in parent–child and peer contexts. *Social Behavior and Personality, 31*, 509–522.

Greenberg, M. T., Kusche, C. A., Cook, E. T., & Quamma, J. P. (1995). Promoting emotional competence in school-aged children: The effects of the PATHS curriculum. *Development and Psychopathology, 7*, 117–136.

Guthrie, I. K., Eisenberg, N., Fabes, R. A., Murphy, B. C., Holmgren, R., Maszk, P., & Suh, K.

(1997). The relations of regulation and emotionality to children's situational empathy-related responding. *Motivation and Emotion, 21*, 87–108.

Hastings, P. D., Zahn-Waxler, C., Robinson, J., Usher, B., & Bridges, D. (2000). The development of concern for others in children with behavior problems. *Developmental Psychology, 36*, 531–546.

Hoffman, M. L. (1987). The contribution of empathy to justice and moral judgment. In N. Eisenberg & J. Strayer (Eds.), *Empathy and its development* (pp. 47–80). Cambridge, UK: Cambridge University Press.

Hoffman, M. L. (2000). *Empathy and moral development: Implications for caring and justice.* New York: Cambridge University Press.

Holmgren, R. A., Eisenberg, N., & Fabes, R. A. (1998). The relations of children's situational empathy-related emotional to dispositional prosocial behaviour. *International Journal of Behavioral Development, 22*, 169–193.

Killen, M., Lee-Kim, J., McGlothlin, H., & Stangor, C. (2002). How children and adolescents evaluate gender and racial exclusion. *Monographs of the Society for Research in Child Development, 67*, vii.

Lazarus, R. S. (1974). A cognitively oriented psychologist looks at biofeedback. *American Psychologist, 30*, 553–561.

Lerner, R. M., Almerigi, J. B., Theokas, C., & Lerner, J. V. (2005). Positive youth development: A view of the issues. *Journal of Early Adolescence, 25*, 10–16.

Liew, J., Eisenberg, N., Losoya, S. H., Guthrie, I. K., & Murphy, B. C. (2003). Maternal expressivity as a moderator of the relations of children's vicarious emotional responses to their regulation, emotionality, and social functioning. *Journal of Family Psychology, 17*, 584–597.

Litvack-Miller, W., McDougall, D., & Romney, D. M. (1997). The structure of empathy during middle childhood and its relationship to prosocial behavior. *Genetic, Social, and General Psychology Monographs, 123*, 303–324.

MacDowell, K. A., & Mandler, G. (1989). Constructions of emotion: Discrepancy, arousal, and mood. *Motivation and Emotion, 13*, 105–124.

Maner, J. K., Luce, C. L., Neuberg, S. L., Cialdini, R. B., Brown, S., & Sagarin, B. J. (2002). The effects of perspective taking on motivations for helping: Still no evidence for altruism. *Personality and Social Psychology Bulletin, 28*, 1601–1610.

Miller, P., & Eisenberg, N. (1988). The relation of empathy to aggression and externalizing/antisocial behavior. *Psychological Bulletin, 103*, 324–344.

Miller, P. A., Eisenberg, N., Fabes, R. A., & Shell, R. (1996). Relations of moral reasoning and vicarious emotion to young children's prosocial behavior toward peers and adults. *Developmental Psychology, 32*, 210–219.

Monroe, K. R. (2004). *The hand of compassion: Portraits of moral choice during the Holocaust.* Princeton, NJ: Princeton University Press.

Murphy, B. C., Shepard, S. A., Eisenberg, N., Fabes, R. A., & Guthrie, I. K. (1999). Contemporaneous and longitudinal relations of dispositional sympathy to emotionality, regulation, and social functioning. *Journal of Early Adolescence, 19*, 66–97.

Raaijmakers, Q. A. W., Engels, R. C. M. E., & Van Hoof, A. (2005). Delinquency and moral reasoning in adolescence and young adulthood. *International Journal of Behavioral Development, 29*, 247–258.

Rest, J. R., Narvaez, D., Bebeau, M. J., & Thoma, S. J. (1999). *Postconventional moral thinking. A neo-Kohlbergian approach.* Mahwah, NJ: Lawrence Erlbaum Associates Inc.

Roberts, W., & Strayer, J. (1996). Empathy, emotional expressiveness, and prosocial behavior. *Child Development, 67,* 449–470.

Rothbart, M. K., & Bates, J. E. (2006). Temperament. In W. Damon & R. M. Lerner (Series Eds.) & N. Eisenberg (Vol. Ed.), *Handbook of child psychology: Vol. 3. Social, emotional, and personality development* (6th ed.; pp. 99–166). New York: Wiley.

Schroeder, D. A., Penner, L. A., Dovidio, J. F., & Piliavin, J. A. (1995). *The psychology of helping and altruism: Problems and puzzles.* New York: McGraw-Hill.

Seligman, M. E. P., & Csikszentmihalyi, M. (2000). Positive psychology: An introduction. *American Psychologist, 55,* 5–14.

Skoe, E., Eisenberg, N., & Cumberland, A. (2002). The role of reported emotion in real-life and hypothetical moral dilemmas. *Personality and Social Psychology Bulletin, 28,* 962–973.

Stephan, W. G., & Finlay, K. (1999). The role of empathy in improving intergroup relations. *Journal of Social Issues, 55*(4), 729–743.

Wood, J. V., Saltzberg, J. A., & Goldsamt, L. A. (1990). Does affect induce self-focused attention? *Journal of Personality and Social Psychology, 58,* 899–908.

Zahn-Waxler, C., Cole, P. M., Welsh, J. D., & Fox, N. A. (1995). Psychophysiological correlates of empathy and prosocial behaviors in preschool children with problem behaviors. *Development and Psychopathology, 7,* 27–48.

Zhou, Q., Eisenberg, N., Losoya, S. H., Fabes, R. A., Reiser, M., Guthrie, I. K., et al. (2002). The relations of parental warmth and positive expressiveness to children's empathy-related responding and social functioning: A longitudinal study. *Child Development, 73,* 893–915.

5

Emotion, Affect Displacement, Conflict, and Cooperation

MICHAEL A. MILBURN AND JONATHAN LISS

In a negotiation, particularly in a bitter dispute, feelings may be more important than talk. The parties may be more ready for battle than for cooperatively working out a solution to a common problem. People often come to a negotiation realizing that the stakes are high and feeling threatened. Emotions on one side will generate emotions on the other. Fear may breed anger, and anger, fear. Emotions may quickly bring a negotiation to an impasse or an end.

Roger Fisher and William Ury, *Getting to Yes* (p. 30)

In Roger Fisher and William Ury's (1981) best-selling book, *Getting to Yes*, generated from their work on the Harvard Negotiation Project, they devote several pages to the role of emotion in the negotiation process. In it they urge the negotiator to ask the question of what is producing the emotions that are affecting a negotiation. It may be that there is a great deal at stake in the negotiations, especially if the participants are nervous, anxious, even fearful. Fisher and Shapiro (2005) extend this analysis, emphasizing the important role emotions play in negotiation. Shapiro (2002) argues that as much as emotions are discouraged in the negotiation process, they are unavoidable, even if suppressed.

In addition to arguing for the importance of emotion in successful negotiations, however, Fisher and Ury (1981) identify several issues that reflect the process of *emotional displacement*, where parties in a negotiation may displace emotion from one situation onto a different, innocent target. A commonly used example of emotional displacement is an individual who, having been yelled at by his boss at work, comes home and kicks his dog. With their extensive experience in negotiation, Fisher and Ury argue that this process of emotional displacement can influence whether a negotiation can be successful or not. They consider a situation in which a person's negotiating partners are angry and ask, "Why are they angry? Are they responding to past grievances and looking for revenge? Are emotions spilling over from one issue to another? Are personal problems at home interfering with business?" (p. 31). It is this process of emotional displacement, transferring emotion that has arisen in one situation onto a different, sometimes unrelated target, that

I and my colleagues have addressed in our research program over the past decade and a half. In this chapter we will explore the role this process can play in facilitating, or more often, inhibiting cooperation.

Affect displacement can contribute to conflict between individuals, and this can in turn play a role in larger intergroup conflict. As Ronson and Peterson (this volume, p. 183) note in their discussion of trust and conflict in the workplace, "when conflict about ideas or opinions is misattributed as a personal conflict between individuals, this can have serious negative implications for both an individual group member's experience in the group, and consequently the performance of the group." When emotion from personal issues is displaced onto other areas, such as workplace issues, the emotional investment in the conflict generally increases, making the process of cooperation more difficult.

Colbert, Bono, and Purvanova (this volume) argue for the importance of "generative" leadership in promoting cooperation within organizations. The research discussed in this chapter strengthens the argument they make. They describe generative leadership as nurturing and focused on the well-being of their employees. In contrast, punitive leadership will likely trigger in employees negative emotional displacement from past experiences, particularly those whose childhoods were characterized by punishment, abuse, and humiliation, leading to increased workplace conflict.

O'Connor (this volume) makes a parallel argument in her discussion of integrative vs. distributive negotiation. Distributive negotiation favors shows of toughness in order to exact deep concessions, whereas integrative negotiation seeks a more cooperative solution and exchange of concessions. The distinction O'Connor draws, similar to that drawn by Colbert, Bono, and Purvanova, parallels the dichotomy suggested by Sylvan Tomkins (1963, 1965) in his Polarity Theory between left-wing (humanistic) and right-wing (normative) scripts. Tomkins links the emotional script a person experiences in childhood to their adult political ideology. It is instructive that both Colbert, Bono, and Purvanova and O'Connor report greater levels of cooperation when behaviors consistent with a left-wing script are employed.

An issue related to emotional displacement that can also affect cooperation is identified in Greenberg's (2004) Emotion-focused Therapy. Greenberg (2004) makes an important distinction between primary emotions and secondary emotions. Primary emotions are an individual's immediate and fundamental reactions to a situation, such as experiencing a loss and feeling sad. Secondary emotions are a learned reaction to these primary emotions and may be defenses against feeling the primary emotions, such as feeling hopeless when one feels angry (Greenberg, 2004). Emotional Awareness is the first stage of Greenberg's Emotion-focused therapy, and it should be a good place for individuals interested in facilitating cooperation to start as well.

Displaced Emotion and Conflict

When countries engage in military conflict, clearly efforts at cooperation have broken down. In Thomas Scheff's (1994) book, *Bloody Revenge: Emotions, Nationalism, and War*, he explores the causes of war. To do so, he applies a family systems model of understanding conflict (Bowen, 1978; Retzinger, 1991) to the broader issue of international conflict. Specifically, he argues that unacknowledged shame plays a central role in both interpersonal and international conflict, and it interferes with cooperation and conflict resolution between the parties involved in the conflict.

Scheff draws on Retzinger's (1991) analysis of emotional communication in marital conflict. Retzinger interviewed four married couples in a situation designed to evoke conflict. Following Gottman's (1979) research design, each couple was asked to discuss something neutral (the events of the day), something positive (activities they enjoyed doing together), and something negative (a "topic of frequent argument"). In her examination of videotapes of the negative interactions, she was able to identify both verbal and nonverbal indicators of shame, often masked by anger when couples engaged in a repetitive argument. The couples were often unaware of the anger and shame they were experiencing in the situation and could only identify it when subsequently viewing the videotape of their interaction.

Scheff (1994) applies this model to an understanding of international conflict. His model specifies that feelings of pride (i.e., high self-esteem) lead to and are enhanced by secure social bonds. These two elements lead to functional communication and cooperation on individual, societal, and international levels. In contrast, unacknowledged or denied shame contributes to insecure bonds, dysfunctional communication, and conflict.

In contrast to the typical explanations of the causes of war in terms of economic and territorial gain, Scheff examines personal exchanges between the rulers of Germany, Austria-Hungary, and Russia prior to the beginning of hostilities in World War I and identifies the operation of unacknowledged shame and the dysfunctional systems of relationships and communication tactics.

Scheff argues that World War II was just a continuation of the conflict in World War I. The humiliation of Germany following World War I has been well documented. These included most importantly the exclusion of Germany from the newly formed League of Nations, forcing Germany to accept sole responsibility for causing World War I, and the annexation of German territory by a number of countries. This general humiliation of Germany contributed to widespread dissatisfaction among the general German population.

This created a context in which Adolph Hitler gained power. Scheff (1994) explores in personal detail Adolph Hitler's life and makes clear how shame-based an individual he was, never being able to have an intimate relationship with anyone and constantly fearing rejection and humiliation. As a number of authors have demonstrated (e.g., Miller, 1983), Hitler's childhood was a daily hell of physical abuse and emotional humiliation from his father.

In more general terms, the widespread and normative use of violence towards children can have catastrophic yet subtle effects on emotional development. Alice Miller (1981, 1983) has written that a child experiencing harsh physical punishment has "no possibility of reacting appropriately to hurt, humiliation, and coercion," continuing, "these experiences cannot be integrated into the personality; the feelings they evoke are repressed, and the need to articulate them remains unsatisfied, without any hope of being fulfilled" (Miller, 1983, p. 7). She argues that this repressed anger that cannot be expressed toward parents is unconsciously displaced later in life. Under various conditions, it can be directed towards the self or towards others and may be the source of a variety of destructive or self-harming behaviors.

For Scheff's model to be correct, that hidden shame from an earlier time contributes to current conflict, it is necessary to posit a model of *emotional displacement*. Scheff makes explicit reference to Lasswell's (1930/1960) model of displacement offered in his pioneering volume in political psychology, *Psychopathology and Politics*. Lasswell offered an explanation for individuals whose lives revolve totally around politics, that driving this preoccupation are personal motives that are displaced and rationalized into publicly acceptable positions.

Family experiences are a major source of shame and other personal motives that individuals carry with them and displace onto others, contributing to intractable conflicts. Research on childrearing has identified physical punishment of children as a contributor to shame that adults carry with them. It is not always clear to children why they are being spanked, and even preschoolers can perceive the unfairness of harsh discipline (Konstantareas & Desbois, 2001). A comprehensive meta-analysis of 88 studies that investigated the effects of corporal punishment (Gershoff, 2002) examined 11 different outcomes, in both childhood and adulthood. This included immediate compliance, moral internalization, aggression (child and adult), antisocial behavior (child and adult), quality of parent–child relationship, mental health (child and adult), and being a victim of physical abuse. What is particularly important to recognize in Gershoff's findings are the negative effects of childhood punishment that are carried into adulthood, including adult antisocial behavior and adult mental health.

Gershoff's analyses revealed consistent negative effects across outcomes with the only positive outcome being immediate compliance. While there continues to be debate on the effects of corporal punishment (e.g., Larzelere, 2000), there is wide agreement that harsh and frequent corporal punishment has many negative side effects, with greater frequency of punishment leading to more negative outcomes both in the short and long terms (Baumrind, Larzelere, & Cowan, 2002; Benjet & Kazdin, 2003; Larzelere, 2000). In an emotionally invalidating environment, children learn to cope by suppressing their emotions. Research with adults has shown that unexpressed emotion stemming from stressful and traumatic experiences can have profound psychological and physiological consequences (Butler et al., 2003; Pennebaker, Kiecolt-Glaser, & Glaser, 1988; Petrie, Booth, & Pennebaker, 1998).

To argue that negative experiences in childhood, including physical punishment, physical and emotional abuse, and humiliation, play a role in adult behaviors that affect the likelihood of conflict or cooperation, it is first necessary to establish that the process of emotional displacement occurs. We first turn to evidence that experimentally demonstrates the process of emotional displacement. Following this discussion, we will address empirical evidence for long-term emotional displacement.

Experimental Demonstration of Displaced Emotion

Following publication of Dollard, Doob, Miller, Mowrer, and Sears' (1939) initial work on frustration and aggression, the topic of "displaced aggression" received considerable research attention. However, as Marcus-Newall, Pederson, Carlson, and Miller (2000) report, interest in the phenomenon declined, and social psychology textbooks have averaged only about five sentences devoted to the topic.

This lack of recognition by social psychologists of this process is striking, given that Marcus-Newall et al. (2000) demonstrate in their meta-analysis of studies of displaced aggression that the effect size is a robust +.54. Subjects who are provoked and unable to retaliate are significantly more likely to behave aggressively toward an innocent target than individuals who were not provoked. Marcus-Newall et al. (2000) also identify various moderator variables of displaced aggression, e.g., the greater the similarity between the source of the initial provocation and the innocent target, the greater the displaced aggression. In fact, a recent theoretical article investigating displaced aggression (Miller, Pedersen, Earleywine & Pollock, 2003) finds evidence for emotional displacement, particularly aggression, that greatly exceeds the initial triggering event. An incommensurate aggressive response, as a function of emotional displacement, may explain one of the obstacles to cooperative communication and exchange.

While clinical psychologists have long observed that emotion from childhood experience can be carried into adulthood and complicate adult behavior and emotional experience, social psychologists have given this hypothesized process little attention. Nevertheless, a number of studies have demonstrated this effect, often discussed in the context of scapegoating. Weatherley (1961) found that after being insulted, highly anti-Semitic subjects were more likely to include more fantasy aggression in a projective Thematic Apperception Test story toward characters with stereotypically Jewish names. Rogers and Prentice-Dunn (1981) found that white students at the University of Alabama behaved more aggressively after being shocked by a black confederate expressing what Rogers and Prentice-Dunn called "repressive racism." Meindl and Lerner (1984) found that after lowering subjects' self-esteem by inducing them to believe they had caused an accident, Anglo-Canadian subjects expressed public policy preferences less favorable to French-speaking Canadians.

More recently, Aviles, Earleywine, Pollock, Stratton, and Miller (2005) demonstrated that alcohol enhances the effect of displaced aggression. Their subjects received an initial provocation from the experimenter who insulted them for performing badly on what was a very difficult task, after which some subjects received a second provocation that was very mild, administered by a different experimenter. Aviles et al. (2005) found that subjects who received the second provocation exhibited higher levels of aggressive behavior, and those subjects who also had consumed alcohol prior to the second provocation showed even higher levels of aggressions.

These examples show the range of displaced emotion studies in social psychology. The dependent variables include aggression on a projective test (Weatherly, 1961), electric shock (Rogers & Prentice-Dunn, 1981), and public policy preferences (Meindl & Lerner, 1984). While Weatherly (1961) and Rogers and Prentice-Dunn (1981) both studied displaced aggression after being insulted, the Meindl and Lerner (1984) study shows a comparable displacement effect, but with a self-esteem manipulation. Taken together, they indicate a broader phenomenon than simply displaced aggression.

Now, it is important to acknowledge that the studies reviewed above are primarily experimental studies. Most experimental studies of displaced aggression only demonstrate a displaced aggression effect over the course of about 20 minutes. For displaced aggression to be relevant to the real world, it is necessary to identify a mechanism by which this displacement could take place over a longer period of time. Marcus-Newall et al. (2000) discuss two processes that could account for this, ruminative processes (e.g., Martin & Tesser, 1989) and cognitive neoassociationistic concepts (Berkowitz, 1989, 1990, 1993). Miller et al. (2003) develop a theoretical framework for their neoassociationist model of displaced aggression and identify social and personality factors that mediate and moderate this effect.

Miller et al. (2003) contrast "displaced aggression" with "triggered displaced aggression," which they define as, "circumstances in which a person experiences a strong initial provocation that precludes retaliation and then is exposed to a second provocation" (p. 76). When considering the possibility of displacement of affect from childhood mistreatment into adult situations, it should be obvious that children are unable to retaliate against a parent when they are mistreated. Abused children love their abusive parents and will go to great lengths to acquiesce to their demands. Thus, the use of corporal punishment against children creates a situation where triggered displaced affect can occur. We turn now to the evidence supporting the existence of long-term affect displacement.

Neurobiology

Abuse, neglect, and stress can exert significant neurohormonal, functional, and structural changes in the brain (Glaser, 2000) that are particularly influential in childhood (LeDoux, 1998). Perry (2000) reviews neurodevelopmental costs of childhood maltreatment, including both neglect and stressful events. He uses the term "neuroarcheology" to reference the adverse impact stress or trauma has on developing brain structures and the indelible effects of those events. In early childhood when most corporal punishment occurs, the limbic system, whose key functions relate to memory, affect regulation, and attachment, is at its period of greatest developmental activity. After early childhood, the next region of intense developmental activity in the brain is the neocortex, responsible for much of our higher-order functioning that includes reasoning, problem solving, and abstract thinking. Although Perry's (2000) research considers a variety of chronic stresses related to abuse and neglect, an environment that includes frequent physical punishment during developmentally sensitive periods will also activate a child's stress response. The child's brain in response to violence will develop in adaptive ways allowing the child to psychologically survive. When the child grows up, these emotional patterns engraved neurobiologically are no longer helpful and can influence emotional understanding, communication, and empathy—key components of cooperation and negotiation.

Long-Term Emotional Displacement

Our research program over the past decade has produced a number of research studies consistent with the hypothesis of long-term affect displacement (e.g., Milburn & Conrad, 1996; Milburn, Conrad, Sala, & Carberry, 1995). Since there is a long literature in psychology linking punitive parenting to adult political attitudes (e.g., Adorno, Frenkel-Brunswick, Levinson, & Sanford, 1950) we sought to investigate the relationship between childhood punishment and adult political attitudes.

While various studies of the relationship of physical punishment to authoritarianism (e.g., Altemeyer, 1988) have failed to find a link between childhood punishment, these past studies have neglected to include two important variables, gender and therapy. The differential emotional socialization of boys and girls encourages boys to acknowledge their anger, while girls are shaped to deny it (Fivush, 1989). Girls are socialized more toward empathy, resulting in males and females responding to internal cues of anger differently. Hokanson and Edelman (1966) gave electric shocks to male and female subjects, and both became physiologically aroused. The opportunity to express anger by retaliating produced a drop in arousal for men. In contrast, women tended to be generous and friendly toward their attacker rather than retaliating, and this response produced an arousal in females.

Miller (1983) has argued that childhood abuse, including childhood punishment, is an important contributor to violence in adulthood. Essential to the displacement of affect from childhood, she argues, is not only the abuse but the denial by the individual of the negative emotional consequences of that abuse. As a measure of denial, we asked respondents whether they had ever had psychotherapy. While an imperfect measure of denial, it seemed likely to tap into a willingness to examine the emotional consequences of childhood experiences.

In Study 1, we distributed questionnaires to college undergraduates, measuring their recalled childhood punishment experiences with a scale developed by Altemeyer (1988), as well as a range of political attitudes that contained a large symbolic component of power, toughness, and retribution. These included opposition to abortion, support for the death penalty, and support for the use of military force to protect US interests. We obtained two two-way interactions, Punishment by Therapy and Punishment by Gender. In the Punishment by Therapy interaction, individual with high levels of childhood punishment who had never had psychotherapy were significantly more punitive in their attitudes than were high punishment individuals who had received therapy. In the Punishment by Gender interaction, high punishment males were more punitive in their political attitudes than were low punishment males, although not significantly, while high punishment females were more liberal, consistent with the literature on differential gender socialization. These findings were obtained controlling for participants' parents' education (participants were all college students), and the extent to which their responses may be biased by their level of social desirability (Crowne & Marlowe, 1960) that could affect their responses.

In Study 2, we conducted a telephone survey of a probability sample of individuals living in eastern Massachusetts using the same measures of punishment, gender, therapy, and political attitudes. We obtained the same two-way interactions of Punishment by Therapy and Punishment by Gender. High punishment participants without therapy were significantly more punitive than were high punishment participants who had had therapy. Additionally, high punishment males were significantly more punitive than low punishment males, and high punishment females were less punitive than low punishment females, although not significantly. Our confidence in these Study 2 findings is strengthened by the fact that we statistically controlled for respondents' level of education, their parents' level of education, and their social desirability levels (Crowne & Marlowe, 1960).

So far, the findings we have discussed are correlational in nature. In addition, however, we have experimental findings that support the correlational results. Using a split-ballot design, we embedded an experiment into the survey in Study 2 using two different question orders. Respondents in the Control condition answered the political attitude questions first. In contrast, respondents in the Recall/Catharsis condition answered the childhood punishment questions first, then answered a projective sentence completion test (e.g., "My mother _____"; "My greatest fear _____") which some researchers have suggested has a short-term catharsis effect. Following this experimental manipulation, the treatment subjects then answered the political attitude questions.

Our results found that there was a significant difference in the pattern of responses between the respondents in the Control condition and those in the Recall/Catharsis condition. There were two significant three-way interactions, a

Punishment by Therapy by Treatment interaction, and a Punishment by Gender by Treatment interaction. In the Control condition, the pattern of means showed the same Punishment by Therapy and the Punishment by Gender two-way interactions that had been found in Study 1 and replicated in Study 2. In contrast, in the treatment condition, these two-way interactions disappeared. These results, again, were controlling for respondents' level of education, the level of education of respondents' parents, and social desirability.

While using one's power to compel another individual's cooperation can produce compliance, treating another individual badly will most often interfere with cooperation. Sexual harassment is such an abuse of power. As a test of the role that emotional displacement plays in contributing to the likelihood of sexual harassment, Begany and Milburn (2002) examined the relationship between authoritarianism and men's likelihood to engage in sexual harassment. Milburn and Ezzati (1998) found that childhood punishment predicted levels of authoritarianism, and they also found that subjects' anger, as measured by the Spielberger State-Trait Anger scale, and subjects' anxiety, as measured by the Manifest Anxiety Scale, predicted authoritarianism. Consistent with Adorno et al.'s (1950) argument that women are a potential target for authoritarian aggression, Begany and Milburn found that higher levels of authoritarianism predicted higher levels of men's likelihood to engage in sexual harassment, mediated by belief in rape myths (Burt, 1980) and hostile sexism (Glick & Fiske, 1996).

Using structural equation modeling, Liss (2005) tested an affect displacement model, replicating Begany and Milburn's (2002) findings that authoritarianism predicted higher likelihood of male sexual harassment, and also found support for long-term affect displacement. Males who reported higher levels of physical punishment in childhood were higher in authoritarianism, and higher levels of authoritarianism predicted higher likelihood of sexual harassment, mediated again by hostile sexism and belief in rape myths.

There is thus considerable evidence that emotional displacement appears to occur over a long period of time. While the ideal test of this hypothesis would be a longitudinal study, measuring childhood punishment at an early age, and then measuring political beliefs or other examples of emotional displacement in adulthood, most longitudinal studies have not asked the pertinent questions to address this issue. Nevertheless, we have seen that both survey and experimental studies provide evidence for the process of long-term emotional displacement.

Getting Beyond Trauma to Cooperation

Increasing cooperation by reducing intergroup conflict is discussed by Oliver and Ha (this volume). Arguing from a contact hypothesis perspective, they suggest that social contacts and participation in civic life can reduce intergroup conflict, although these contacts can be limited by racial segregation. These are useful ideas, but the research in this chapter suggests some significant potential limitations on these efforts to promote cooperation. As discussed above, the research by Rogers and Prentice-Dunn (1981) indicated that racial prejudice can reflect the process of affect displacement, and Meindl and Lerner (1984) demonstrated that affect displacement can play a role in intergroup attitudes. As we have demonstrated earlier using national survey data (Milburn & Conrad, 1996), physical punishment is related to authoritarianism and more negative racial attitudes, reflecting the process of affect displacement.

Ultimately, increasing cooperation in both the private and public spheres involves improving the treatment of children around the world, including the outlawing of corporal punishment, as has happened in 17 countries worldwide (Center for Effective Discipline, 2005). Long-term solutions toward building the capacity for more cooperative behavior should involve the positive socialization of children (Staub, 1992) to develop a greater capacity for altruistic behavior, as well as an understanding of their own current emotional functioning. The long-term positive benefits of altruistic behavior are noted in Piliavin (this volume).

The importance of situational factors in influencing altruism are noted in Van Lange (this volume), as are the limitations he also notes of rationality as an explanatory model for human behavior, or at least the inadequacy of the assumption of rational self-interest. These observations fit very well with the research presented in this chapter. Displaced emotion or displaced aggression is clearly not rational. It makes no sense to attack someone for a minor provocation when you have been upset by someone who behaved aggressively or insultingly to you at some previous time. But this is exactly what the literature on displaced aggression demonstrates that individuals do. This capacity for irrationality needs to be factored in to any model that seeks to maximize cooperative and prosocial behavior.

Monroe's work (this volume) explores the antecedents of altruistic behavior from the perspective of political science. A powerful source of altruistic behavior is identification with a broad, inclusive sense of a shared humanity. Such a cognitive framework seems to distinguish individuals who are truly altruistic from those who are not. A capacity for altruistic behavior obviously will facilitate cooperation on all levels. While an altruistic identity is arguably a central aspect of whether a person will behave in an altruistic way or not, this perspective can be enhanced by research in cognitive science that demonstrates the effects of schema activation (i.e., situational influences) on cognition about the self.

A model of the evolution of internal dispositions to cooperate is simulated in Hanley, Hartwig, Orbell, and Morikawa (this volume), and the importance of internal motivations for prosocial behavior is examined in Tyler's work (this volume). He notes that these internal influences can be more effective than external incentives or sanctions for cooperation. As we have seen in this chapter, however, in situations where negative affect is triggered by some perceived provocation, emotions from a different situation can be displaced onto the current situation and behavior inconsistent with a person's attitudes, values, or dispositions can result.

We have seen that, in addition to the cognitive contributors to altruism and cooperation, emotion plays a central role. Given the role that emotion plays in negotiation, conflict, and cooperation, an important developmental feature that will be central to enhancing cooperation is that of *empathy*, an "affective response that stems from the apprehension or comprehension of another's emotional state or condition, and is similar to what the other person is feeling or would be expected to feel." (Eisenberg & Eggum; this volume). Eisenberg and Eggum's work has focused on creating, testing, and elaborating on a model of the fundamental processes involved in empathic capacity and prosocial behavior. Their research has delineated important constructs, such as the crucial distinction between sympathy (which facilitates prosocial behavior and moral reasoning) and personal distress (which does not, and may be related to antisocial behaviors) as an outcome of observing others in distress.

This distinction between sympathy and personal distress is strongly related to the concept of triggered displaced emotion that we have discussed above. Whether someone's empathic reaction leads to positive cooperation or not may be largely influenced by the extent to which they are or are not triggered to negative emotional reactions that can be displaced onto other individuals. Consequently, the likelihood that a person is triggered to negative affect will be affected by the extent to which they have experienced trauma or abuse in childhood and have denied the negative emotional consequences of those experiences.

Eisenberg and Eggum's research has identified a strong dispositional component to empathic capacity and the tendency toward self-initiated prosocial behavior. This line of research has used a wide range of samples (e.g., children, adolescents, adults) and measures (e.g., self-report, psychophysiological, observational) to build a model of prosocial behavior intended to apply across contexts and situations. Because much social psychological work on prosocial behavior demonstrates situational influence, it is also possible that situational factors might differentially generate personal distress versus empathy, with obvious implications for cooperative behavior.

The work described in this chapter takes as a given that cooperation will contribute to the well-being of individuals and groups, given the obvious dysfunction of war and conflict for human societies. In this context, our work speaks strongly to the connections between cooperation and the well-being of individuals and/or groups.

In terms of the mechanisms through which cooperation influences individual and/or group functioning, the role of affect displacement is a key mechanism that can influence whether interaction will lead to cooperation or conflict.

When examined from the perspective of affect displacement theory, interpersonal conflict and cooperation, as well as national and international conflict and cooperation, become more understandable. While the cognitive perspective has dominated psychological thinking about conflict and cooperation during the past two decades, the central role that emotion plays in both conflict and cooperation has been identified by a small number of scholars from a variety of disciplines during this time (e.g., Fisher & Ury, 1981; Retzinger, 1991; Scheff, 1994). Affect displacement, while an explicit element of many clinical psychologists' understanding of human behavior, is beginning to be recognized more broadly as exerting an important influence upon individuals' behavior (e.g., Miller et al., 2003). Intractable conflicts that persist for decades, where negotiations go nowhere and cooperation seems impossible, appear from the perspective of affect displacement, comprehensible, and hopefully empowering to the parties and mediators involved in the conflicts.

References

Adorno, T. W., Frenkel-Brunswick, E., Levinson, D. L., & Sanford, R. N. (1950) *The authoritarian personality*. New York: Norton.

Altemeyer, R. (1988). *Enemies of freedom*. San Francico: Jossey-Bass.

Aviles, F., Earleywine, M., Pollock, V., Stratton, J., & Miller, N. (2005). Alcohol's effect on triggered displaced aggression. *Psychology of Addictive Behaviors, 19,* 108–111.

Baumrind, D., Larzelere, R. E., & Cowan, P. S. (2002). Ordinary physical punishment: Is it harmful? Comment on Gershoff (2002). *Psychological Bulletin, 128,* 580.

Begany, J. J., & Milburn, M. A. (2002). Psychological predictors of sexual harassment: authoritarianism, hostile sexism, and rape myths. *Psychology of Men and Masculinity, 3,* 119–126.

Benjet, C., & Kazdin, A. E. (2003). Spanking children: The controversies, findings and new directions. *Clinical Psychology Review, 23*(2), 197–224.

Berkowitz, L. (1989). Frustration-aggression hypothesis: Examination and reformulation. *Psychological Bulletin, 106,* 59–73.

Berkowitz, L. (1990). On the formation and regulation of anger and aggression: A cognitive-neoassociationistic analysis. *American Psychologist, 45,* 494–503.

Berkowitz, L. (1993). *Aggression: Its causes, consequences, and control.* New York: McGraw-Hill.

Bowen, M. (1978). *Family therapy in clinical practice.* New York : J. Aronson.

Burt, M. (1980). Cultural myths and support for rape. *Journal of Personality and Social Psychology, 38,* 217–230.

Butler, E. A., Egloff, B., Wilhelm, F. H., Smith, N. C., Erickson, E. A., & Gross, J. J. (2003). The social consequences of expressive suppression. *Emotion, 3*(1), 48–67.

Center for Effective Discipline (2005). http://www.stophitting.com/laws/legalReform.php

Crowne, D., & Marlowe, D. (1960). A new scale of social desirability independent of psychopathology. *Journal of Consulting Psychology, 4,* 349–354.

Dollard, J., Doob, L. W., Miller, N. E., Mowrer, O. H. & Sears, R. R. (1939). *Frustration and aggression.* New Haven, CT: Yale University Press.

Fisher, R., & Shapiro, D. (2005). *Beyond reason: Using emotions as you negotiate.* New York: Viking Press.

Fisher, R., & Ury, W. (1981). *Getting to yes.* New York: Viking Penguin.

Fivush, R. (1989). Exploring sex differences in the emotional context of mother–child conversations about the past. *Sex Roles, 20,* 675–691.

Gershoff, E. T. (2002). Corporal punishment by parents and associated child behaviors and experiences: A meta-analytic and theoretical review. *Psychological Bulletin, 128,* 539–579.

Glaser, D. (2000). Child abuse and neglect and the brain—A review. *Journal of Child Psychology & Psychiatry, 41*(1), 97.

Glick, P., & Fiske, S. (1996). The ambivalent sexism inventory: Differentiating hostile and benevolent sexism. *Journal of Personality and Social Psychology, 70,* 491–512.

Gottman, J. M. (1979). *Marital interaction: Experimental investigatons.* New York: Academic Press.

Greenberg, L. S. (2004). Emotion-focused therapy. *Clinical Psychology and Psychotherapy, 11,* 3–16.

Hokanson, J. E., & Edelman, R. (1966). Effects of three social responses on vascular processes. *Journal of Abnormal and Social Psychology, 3,* 442–447.

Konstantareas, M. M., & Desbois, N. (2001). Preschoolers' perceptions of the unfairness of maternal disciplinary practices. *Child Abuse & Neglect, 25*(4), 473–488.

Larzelere, R. E. (2000). Child outcomes of non-abusive and customary physical punishment by parents: An updated literature review. *Clinical Child & Family Psychology Review, 3,* 199–221.

Lasswell, H. D. (1930/1960). *Psychopathology and politics.* New York: Viking Press (originally published 1930).

LeDoux, J. E. (1998). *The emotional brain: The mysterious underpinnings of emotional life.* New York: Simon and Schuster.

Liss, J. (2005). *Affect displacement theory and sexual harassment: The role of childhood punishment.* Unpublished master's thesis, University of Massachusetts, Boston.

Marcus-Newall, A., Pedersen, W. C., Carlson, C., & Miller, N. (2000). Displaced aggression is alive and well: A meta-analytic review. *Journal of Personality and Social Psychology, 78*(4), 670–689.

Martin, L. L., & Tesser, A. (1989). Toward a motivational and structural theory of ruminative thought. In J. S. Uleman & J. A. Bargh (Eds.), *Unintended thought* (pp. 306–326). New York: Guilford Press.

Meindl, J. R., & Lerner, M. J. (1984). Exacerbation of extreme responses to an out-group. *Journal of Personality & Social Psychology, 47*(1), 71–84.

Milburn, M. A., & Conrad, S. D. (1996). *The politics of denial.* Cambridge, MA: MIT Press.

Milburn, M. A., Conrad, S. D., Sala, F., & Carberry, S. (1995). Childhood punishment, denial, and political attitudes. *Political Psychology, 16,* 447–478.

Milburn, M. A., & Ezzati, A. (1998). *Childhood punishment, anger, and authoritarianism.* Paper presented at the International Society of Political Psychology conference, Montreal, Quebec, Canada, July 1998.

Miller, A. (1981). *Prisoners of childhood.* New York: Basic Books.

Miller, A. (1983). *For your own good: Hidden cruelty in child-rearing and the roots of violence.* New York: Farrar, Straus and Giroux.

Miller, N., Pedersen, W. C., Earleywine, M., & Pollock, V. E. (2003). A theoretical model of triggered displaced aggression. *Personality and Social Psychology Review, 7,* 75–97.

Pennebaker, J. W., Kiecolt-Glaser, J. K., & Glaser, R. (1988). Disclosure of traumas and immune function: Health implications for psychotherapy. *Journal of Consulting & Clinical Psychology, 56*(2), 239–245.

Perry, B. D. (2000). The neuroarcheology of childhood maltreatment. In K. Franey, R. Geffner, & R. Falconer (Eds.), *The cost of child maltreatment: Who pays? We all do.* San Diego: Family Violence & Sexual Assault Institute. Retrieved from http://www.childtrauma.org/ctamaterials/Neuroarcheology.asp

Petrie, K. J., Booth, R. J., & Pennebaker, J. W. (1998). The immunological effects of thought suppression. *Journal of Personality & Social Psychology*, 75(5), 1264–1272.

Retzinger, S. M. (1991). *Violent emotions: Shame and rage in marital quarrels*. Newbury Park, CA: Sage.

Rogers, R. W., & Prentice-Dunn, S. (1981). Deindividuation and anger-mediated interracial aggression: Unmasking regressive racism. *Journal of Personality & Social Psychology*, 41, 63–73.

Scheff, T. J. (1994). *Bloody revenge: Emotions, nationalism, and war*. Boulder, CO: Westview Press.

Shapiro, D. L. (2002). Negotiating emotions. *Conflict Resolution Quarterly*, 20(1), 67–82.

Staub, E. (1992). The origins of aggression and the creation of positive relations among groups. In S. Staub & P. Green (Eds.), *Psychology and social responsibility: Facing global challenges* (pp. 89–120). New York: New York University Press.

Tomkins, S. S. (1963). Left and right: A basic dimension of ideology and personality. In R. W. White (Ed.), *The study of lives* (pp. 388–411). Chicago: Atherton.

Tomkins, S. S. (1965). Affect and the psychology of knowledge. In S. S. Tomkins & C. E. Izard (Eds.), *Affect, cognition, and personality: Empirical studies* (pp. 72–97). New York: Springer.

Weatherley, D. (1961). Anti-Semitism and the expression of fantasy aggression. *Journal of Abnormal and Social Psychology*, 62(2), 454–457.

6

Altruism and Cooperation

KRISTEN RENWICK MONROE AND ALEXIS ETOW

What is the relationship between altruism and cooperation? Does altruism foster cooperation? And how can our knowledge of the literature on altruism in everyday life—as opposed to experimental studies—inform us about cooperation? These are the questions underlying this chapter, questions with critical implications for the enhancement and growth of our society and common well-being.

To assess the relationship between altruism and cooperation, we must examine the conceptual definition of altruism as well as the criteria used to distinguish altruistic behavior from other forms of prosocial behavior. Altruism is discussed in many disciplines, from evolutionary biology to economics and psychology to political science. The most common conceptualization of altruism, however, begins by defining altruism as behavior intended to benefit the welfare of another, even at potential risk to one's own well-being. (See Monroe, 1996 for further details.) This definition entails several critical components. (1) It distinguishes altruism from other prosocial forms of behavior. Altruism is not helping, cooperation, sharing, or giving although it certainly does entail certain critical aspects of each of these behaviors. (2) Altruism involves action. It entails behavior. It cannot just be good thoughts or good intentions. We often intend to engage in altruistic behavior but this intention alone is not enough to constitute altruism. However, (3) altruism does have to be intended. In this sense, the motivation of the actor is critical. We may find what looks like an altruistic act that occurs as the unintended consequence of another's behavior. But this is not altruism. For example, if I dislike you and try to do something mean to you, but the effect on you actually is positive, would we consider my act altruistic? No. Similarly, if I try to do something to help you but it ends badly, that should not lessen the intention of my initial action. (4) The goal of the act must be intended to benefit the welfare of another, not just to further my own welfare or to promote our mutual welfare. This is perhaps the most important characteristic of altruism that distinguishes it from cooperation, which traditionally is defined as behavior designed to benefit everyone involved (see Sullivan, Snyder, & Sullivan's introductory chapter to this volume for a more complete definition). Indeed, cooperation is often urged for precisely that reason:

everyone benefits. (5) The most controversial aspects of the definition of altruism: Does altruism carry the potential of risk to the actor? Most analysts agree that altruism requires some potential for a diminution of the actor's well-being. While this is a gray area, certainly an act that improves both the agent's own welfare and that of another person would not qualify as altruistic. Instead, we should classify it in the category of collective well-being or collective welfare. Finally (6) altruism makes no conditions. Its purpose is to further the welfare of another group or individual, with no anticipation of reward for the altruist itself. This does not completely exclude rewards. An altruistic act may be rewarded while still remaining altruistic if the reward was not anticipated and was not part of the decision calculus. So altruistic acts may be rewarded but the reward must be the unplanned, unanticipated, and unintended consequence of the act.

We find this conceptualization of altruism the one that most accurately captures the central components of altruism as discussed in the literature, but as in any academic discussion, experts frequently disagree over minor points and readers will find different usages for altruism, both in general conceptual terms and in terms of how altruism is operationalized. So, for example, altruism might be operationalized by looking at how people share their food during famine (economics), or whether rabbits will cry out to alert other rabbits as a predator approaches (animal behavior), or whether a woman will forego having her own children in order to care for her sister's children (evolutionary biology). It is important to note this fact since much of the confusion in the literature on altruism relates to analysts operationalizing altruism in different ways. Our own perspective on altruism draws heavily on the work of the senior author (Monroe), which focuses not on experimental analysis but on behavior in the field and in a very limited context: the Holocaust and World War II. While this discussion will parallel the discussions of cooperation found in the other chapters in this book, at least insofar as all the chapters describe prosocial behavior and link an individual's moral duty with the prosperity of the community at large, the reader should note the important differences in approach and keep in mind the conceptual and empirical differences in the discussions of altruism and cooperation. For example, can we say cooperation always stems from a sense of moral duty? Not really. Cooperation may be caused by selfish concerns or by the desire to receive reciprocity, neither of which is a characteristic of altruism. This suggests, then, that cooperation would emerge under quite different conditions and for different reasons than altruism. Beyond this, analysts need to distinguish between different types of cooperative behavior. So while altruism and cooperation may be parallel or similar behaviors, and occasionally—or even frequently—may tap into the same emotions, analysts must take care to distinguish among the different varieties of prosocial behavior, especially when it comes to operationalizing their empirical work. This chapter is linked closely to the chapter by Eisenberg and Eggum in this volume. While this is appropriate, readers also should remember that whereas Eisenberg and Eggum examine prosocial behavior as it occurs for the individual and in the context of findings from their empirical research in psychology, our own chapter focuses on altruism as operationalized in a different context, with a focus on how altruism can play a role in counteracting potential threats such as prejudice and violence, and subsequently building more cooperative societies. So our focus is on asking what a heightened understanding of the causes of altruism can teach scholars and policy makers interested in building cooperative societies. Our analysis of the nature of altruism (1) supports other findings in the volume concerning the importance of cooperation as a critical tool for facilitating societal advancement and (2) offers additional insight into the nature of prosocial behavior.

This chapter thus surveys some recent literature in political science to ask what this approach to the topic has told us and also to identify what areas provide the richest potential for future work. It then suggests why further research on altruism is important in fostering a more harmonious political and social order.

Part 1 reviews the scientific literature and controversies most relevant for understanding what causes human altruism as defined by rescue behavior.[1] This literature suggests the critical motivating factor is psychological. More particularly, the key is identity, with an altruistic perspective emerging as the critical link between identity and moral action.[2] Part 2 places findings from the existing literature in the form of a theory of altruism and suggests the questions on which future work might most profitably focus in order to increase understanding of both altruism and its political significance. Part 3 suggests why such an understanding is important for social scientists. Though altruism and cooperation are inarguably recognized as crucial instruments for promoting prosocial behavior, the ways in which to instigate and integrate these ideals into more common social practices have yet to be discovered. Part of the problem stems from the long tradition of social and political theories which are based on the assumption of self-interest—such as rational choice theory and game theoretic models built on microeconomic assumptions. However, once we acknowledge altruism as an intrinsic part of our human nature that should be allowed for in our models of politics, we will begin to understand how to best facilitate cooperation and societal well-being.

1 Political Science and Altruism

The dominant tendency in early work in both biological and social science was to explain away altruism as a disguised form of self-interest.[3] Altruism was said to provide psychic gratification or to be instrumental behavior designed to encourage reciprocal altruism via mechanisms such as kin or group selection (see Becker, 1976; Dawkins, 1976 inter alia). Much of the best work that conceded the existence of human altruism was based on experimental laboratory work, such as Batson's (1991) work on empathic altruism. But experimental work cannot fully simulate the more complex interactions outside the laboratory, and the confounding conditions in political life are such that it is not clear how applicable are findings from a controlled laboratory experiment. This is where political analyses, even those based on small samples, provide rich insight.[4]

Once we move outside the laboratory, the best literature on human altruism often focuses on rescuers of Jews.[5] Much of the early work is autobiographical, by rescuers (Gies, 1987) or survivors (Levi, 1958/1961; Wiesel, 1960/1986), and consists of anecdotal portraits documenting rescue activity. There was little early work directly focused on rescuers' motivations until London's 1970 work. The early social science works on this topic were correlational and inquired about a wide variety of sociocultural influences, e.g., religion, social class, or gender. Such analyses proved inconclusive, and it now appears that the sociodemographic correlates of altruism serve as trigger mechanisms, stimulating what are the critical psychological forces driving altruism. This explains the variance and disagreement in early studies since one trigger mechanism (e.g., religion) could prompt altruism for one person while another trigger (e.g., duty) might activate altruism for another person, or for the same person at different points in time.

As analysts slowly came to appreciate the psychological aspects of rescue behavior, they tended initially to focus on general psychological factors, such as the thrill of adventure involved in rescuing or a sense of social marginality in which the rescuer felt an empathic bond with the persecuted because of the rescuer's own feeling of being an outsider (Ophuls, 1971). In 1986, a survivor named Nechama Tec (1986) first located what seems to be the critical personality factor, arguing that rescuers had a strong sense of individuality or separateness. Tec concluded that rescuers were motivated by moral values that did not depend on the support or approval of other people so much as on their own self-approval. That same year, a filmed documentary, interviewing survivors as well as rescuers, further documented this personality factor, arguing that rescuers "had to do it because that's the kind of people they were" (Rittener & Myers, 1986).[6]

The first important systematic analysis of rescuers supported these findings, establishing personality as the critical force driving rescue behavior. *The Altruistic Personality* (Oliner & Oliner, 1988) was the largest survey of rescuers ever conducted, including 406 rescuers, 126 non-rescuers, and 150 rescued survivors throughout the Third Reich. The Oliners' project was the first important work to scientifically isolate the importance of what we might think of as identity, and what the introductory chapter of this book refers to as a shared humanity, essential to engendering cooperation and strong communal connections. Oliner and Oliner (1988) found that an altruistic personality, in which habitual behavior, encouraged by parents or other significant role models, led to habits of caring that effectively became structured as an altruistic personality. These habits included tolerance for differences among people and a worldview characterized by the Oliners and their European collaborators as "extensivity" (Reykowski, 1987). Under this explanation, Oliner and Oliner found that in contrast to their non-rescuer counterparts, rescuers were likely to have a greater sense of attachment to family members and those close to them, and stronger inclinations of responsibility towards those with whom they may not have previously had personal ties. In contrast with non-rescuers and bystanders, the rescuers' propensity to help seemed to develop from natural dispositions of compassion. According to Oliner and Oliner (1988), 70% of the interviewees reportedly answered the call for help without hesitation, and 80% said they did so without first consulting someone else; this further suggests the innateness of caring as a common characteristic among altruistic individuals.

The psychological importance of reinforcing empathic and humane behavior was found by a generation of younger scholars, such as Fogelman (1994), whose parents were survivors. This work also stressed psychological factors related to the sense of self. In terms of identity, Fogelman found rescuers undergo a transformative encounter which effectively creates a different self, a rescuer self, which allows otherwise normal people to lie, cheat, or even kill if necessary. This transformed self is critical for Fogelman, providing rescuers with the ability to maintain a kind of double life. This transformation, however, while designed to help save life, often meant the rescuer engaged in what generally would be thought of as unethical behavior.[7]

Existing literature: Controversies and key concepts concerning the moral psychology

Existing scientific work on altruism thus has moved discussion into an area best described as the moral psychology. As with any other scientific field, however, the empirical literature on altruism is not free from controversy, with scholarly disagreements focusing on several critical issues. In enumerating these key issues, it is helpful to place our discussion of altruism in a broader context of behavior dealing with our treatment of others (see Eisenberg & Eggum, this volume, for a review). Doing so suggests how understanding altruism can help illuminate behavior along a more extensive ethical continuum, including ethnic, religious and sectarian prejudice, violence and even genocide on the one hand and other-directed and altruistic behaviors at other points along this moral continuum.

Character versus situation: What blend of influence?

The literature on helping and prosocial behavior tends to assume a character versus situation dichotomy. This seems a useful analytical tool, helpful in presenting various dimensions of the problem, but one that can distort reality, in which a more phenotypic approach more accurately captures political reality. The problem then becomes: How do we put together findings on the importance of the self with findings on the power of the external world to tap into critical aspects of a complex self, thus calling forth certain types of behavior, or even creating a transformative self?[8] Considering the rescuers—people who lived through the actual historical period, not a laboratory experiment or a computer simulation—yields particular insight about the relative power of the situation to influence behavior toward others, and about the complexities and variation in this psychological process.

At some level, the rescuers must be counted as illustrating the constancy of character, not the situation, since they were the ones who did, after all, withstand the incredible pressures of the political environment and the behavior of their fellow citizens. They acted out of their sense of self and refused to be people who were "just following orders." But, at least for the rescuers Monroe (1996, 2004) interviewed, it was not that their identities were transformed, as Fogelman seems to imply, so much as they were people whose core selves judged that lying or cheating immoral political authorities was less important than saving human life.

Yet even as the altruism of rescuers reinforces the importance of independent character it also reveals the extent to which altruists are influenced by critical others. This influences works through the altruists' initial acceptance of values of caring that then became ingrained into their character[9] or (less frequently) in terms of networks of people with whom they worked.[10] How do we evaluate this aspect of altruistic behavior? Is the answer to the debate over character versus situation more complicated than it first appears?

The altruistic perspective

Work by Monroe (1996, 2004) suggests that the explanatory blend between character and situation can be answered by *perspective*, a concept defined as our way of seeing the world and other people. How does perspective work to categorize and classify people into certain slots from which differential behavior then flows naturally? One important benefit from probing more deeply into altruism is the potential such an analysis provides for determining the nature of the stimulus from the external environment and to ask what part of identity is triggered by these external stimuli. Doing so focuses attention on the debate between explanations that stress the importance of the group (e.g., as emphasized by social psychologists such as Milgram, 1974) versus explanations that emphasize character (e.g., as favored by virtue ethicists such as Churchill and Street, 2002). The critical factor may be the power of the situation to shape both our perspective on the world and how we see ourselves at a particular moment in time, through calling forth different aspects of an identity that is complex and multifaceted.[11] Future analysis thus should focus not so much on the behavior of others but more precisely, if subtly, on how perspective works as the psychological factor that shifts our cognitive categorization and classification of people, in response to a wide variety of external, situational factors. Doing so allows culture to enter the equation in a more subtle way than is traditionally the case.

Categorization and the according of moral salience

We know that people have to use categories to organize reality and make sense of it. The vast literature in social identity theory (Tajfel, 1981; Turner, 1987; Turner & Hogg, 1987) and cognitive science (Lakoff & Johnson, 1999) makes it further clear that we categorize ourselves in relation to others and then compare ourselves with these critical others. But there are many ways in which we can compare ourselves to others. This means that scholars interested in moral questions must ask not just how people construct categories but how they accord moral salience to these categories.

Consider how this concerns altruism. Is it the recognition of common membership in a category that is ethically relevant, as social identity theory would seem to suggest? Or is it merely that shared membership in a category makes it more likely that one will treat other members of the same category well? While the cognitive recognition of a shared category may frequently accord moral salience, this need not necessarily be the case.

A consideration of altruism is important in suggesting a modification of social identity theory may be in order if we wish to build on it to explain ethical treatment of others. It is not enough to say that people divide the world into divisions of in-group/out-group. We have to ask how the categories are first constructed and then ask how the categories are accorded moral salience. We know rescuers, for example, did draw distinctions between Jews and Nazis. But they did not accord moral salience to these categories. Both Jews and Nazis were supposed to be treated as human beings. Instead, rescuers constructed a broader or an alternative category that conferred moral salience. For rescuers, the morally salient category was the human race, not ethnicity, religion, or even political affiliation. Other distinctions, while noted, were not judged relevant in a moral sense. The recognition of this common unifying bond that links all of humanity serves as a recurring theme throughout this book, underscoring its importance as the foundation of a society prospering with cooperation and a sense of kinship.

Relation of perspective to the according of moral salience

Monroe's (2004) analysis of rescuers found that how rescuers classified or categorized people carried tremendous moral implications for behavior. In part, rescuers seem to have adopted superordinate categories, thinking of all people as the same and thus deserving of equal treatment. This extensive categorization process searched for the common ties, not distinctions that separated people. The rescuers' categorization schema seemed to be one in which all people could exhibit individual and group differences but also could still be placed into the common category of human being. This common category took on a superordinate moral status in which all people deserve to be treated with respect and dignity.

The cognitive process by which altruists view others—their categorization and classification of others and their perspective on themselves in relation to these others—thus appears to play a critical role in identity's influence on moral action. This cognitive process apparently includes an affective component that serves as a powerful emotional reaction to another's need.[12] This reaction in turn provides the motive to work to effect change.

Tapping into a particular self-concept

A critical part of the process by which perspective influences moral choice involves the manner in which the external environment taps into altruists' core self-concept, a self-concept distinguished by its self-image as people who care for others. Perspective links the altruists' self-image to the circumstances of those in need by highlighting the needy person's situation in a way that then accords a moral imperative to the plight of others. By tapping into this particular self-concept, the suffering of others becomes morally salient for altruists, in the way that the plight of one's child or parent would be salient for most of the rest of us.

Because the values of caring for others are so deeply integrated into altruists' self concept, it forms a self-image that constitutes the underlying structure for altruists' identities. This is what causes the needs of others to be deemed morally salient. This self-concept translates and transforms altruists' knowledge of another's need into a moral imperative requiring them to take action. Their self-concept becomes so closely linked to what is acceptable behavior that rescuers—for example—did not just note the suffering of others; the others' suffering took on a moral salience. The suffering of Jews was felt as something that was relevant for the rescuers. It established a moral imperative that necessitated action.

Moral imperative and the lack of choice

The fact that altruists feel a moral imperative to help is evident most strikingly in statements that reveal altruists' implicit assumptions about what ordinary decent people should do. In *The Heart of Altruism* (1996), Monroe referred to these as canonical expectations about what is acceptable behavior. These unspoken expectations are embedded deep in an altruist's psyche, but are revealed in their description of what is—and what is not—in their repertoire of behavior. As one rescuer (Margot) said, "You don't walk away. You don't walk away from somebody who needs real help." Or Margot's statement that "[the] ability to help and alleviate the pain of fellow human beings . . . is the ultimate goal of our short existence on this earth."[13] Other rescuers expressed similar phrases, almost as if reading from a common menu of moral behavior available to them. Witness Madame Trocmé's question: "How can you refuse them?"[14] Or John Weidner's insistence that "when you have to do right, you do right." And all the rescuers' insistence that "there is no choice" (Monroe, 2004; 2006).

For altruists, all people within the boundaries of their community of concern are to be treated the same, and their circle of concern includes all human beings. This perception of a shared humanity triggers a sense of relationship to the other that then makes the suffering of another a concern for the altruists. Significantly, this extensivity included perpetrators, with the rescuers demonstrating extraordinary forgiveness of Nazis.[15]

It is this role of perspective to classify and categorize people and then to work through a cognitive process of salience that provides the link between the lack of choice and identity and the variation in our treatment of others. But more complete empirical evidence on this requires analyzing bystanders and perpetrators, and a full description of this psychological process should be a major focus of future work in this field.

2 A Theoretical Framework and Questions To Be Answered

The above gives us a general model of altruism in which altruists react to the situation of needy people from a sense of moral imperative because the critical part of their self-concept is as people who help. This particular self-concept constitutes the core or master identity for altruists. The altruist's perception of self in relation to others then delineates the domain of behavioral options open and choice becomes a function of identity, more particularly self-perceptions in relation to those around altruists. The altruistic perspective means altruists see categories of difference between people; but these categories do not carry moral significance for the altruist.

This provides us with a framework for understanding human social and political behavior that is grounded in empirical reality; but it still leaves certain problems that need to be addressed.[16] What are some of these problems?

Variance in altruism

By focusing on extreme instances of altruism the scholarly literature may present a skewed view of human nature, one that may encourages us to think in all-or-nothing terms. Is our only analytical choice altruism or the Hobbesian world of self-interest? As the literature on philanthropy and helping suggests, in everyday life, most of us engage in a wide variety of altruistic acts. (We give some but not all of our money. We can visit a needy person for one hour a week or have that person live with us.) Instead of juxtaposing altruism with self-interested models—a position in which the debate between rational choice theorists and their critics has too often been cast—we should instead focus on developing models that allow for finer differences in behavior along a continuum. Without moving to a self-interested model, we can acknowledge that there are "costs" to altruism, and differences in the range of altruistic values (Staub, 1989), just as we find limits to models based on self-interest (Monroe, 1991). Work designed to specify which conditions will encourage a self-interested approach and when external stimuli will evoke the more altruistic parts of human nature is preferable to more simplistic arguments about which approach is correct.

In shifting the debate, further questions involve asking to whom the altruism is directed. To those we love? To everyone? Can we be altruistic to one group but not to another? Some analysts have spoken of universal altruists—people who will help anyone in need—and particularistic altruists, those who will help only certain kinds/groups of people.[17] Future work should focus on asking how people draw the lines of the community of concern (Smiley, 1992), how these boundaries influence treatment of others, and how group variation enters the equation.

The self-concept

The self-concept is an important mechanism in short-circuiting critical behaviors. But is it the only concept? We need to both elaborate our understanding of the self-concept and refine our reservations about it as an explanatory concept. For example, the self is understood at the conscious level, expressed in semantic forms, and at an automatic non-conscious level. Subliminal priming studies (Bargh, Chen, & Burrows, 1996; Chartrand & Bargh, 2002) suggest our conscious judgments are primed by subconscious factors. But there probably are other things going on that psychologists do not yet fully understand. What part of the self-structure is (more) important for altruistic behavior? For self-interested behavior? The part that can be tapped into during an interview later, or the part the person is unaware of consciously, either during the altruistic act or afterwards? Clearly the self-concept as a factor in the altruistic process requires further elaboration.

It also requires some reservations. There are a number of studies on spontaneous behavior that reveal a direct link between emotional behavior and spontaneous behavior that is not conscious (McGaugh, 2003). This link has not yet been adequately explored although the Oliners found helping behavior was directly related to the altruist's emotional involvement with the other, e.g., crying by the needy person was important in encouraging helping by the altruist. The importance of the empathic or sympathetic reaction, noted in experimental work (Batson, 1991), may have an important role that we do not yet fully understand when analyzing altruism in the political world. At least on the individual level, higher levels of sympathy have been found to be correlative with a greater tendency towards helping behavior in both adults and children and lower levels of externalizing problems among children (see Eisenberg and Eggum's chapter in this volume for a review of these findings).

Similarly, we need to understand more about the boundaries between "the other" and my own self (Churchill & Street, 2002). Comparative analysis suggests such distinctions are critical for both altruism and behavior (such as genocide) at different points on the moral continuum. The distinction between us and them can be very useful but it also can be destructive. Staub's (1989) important work on genocide found people do not begin with sharp cognitive distinctions. People learn about differences and cognitively create differences by devaluing others. People who are "different" become further devalued, dehumanized, and eventually even killed because it is perceived to be the "right" thing to do, as with the public health officials during the Holocaust who acted to protect the good German body politic from the foreign vermin who infested it (Lerner, 1992). Some scholars working on altruism (Oliner & Oliner, 1988; Oliner, Oliner, & Baron, 1992; Staub, 1989) have now broadened the analytic context of their work by asking about cooperative learning after genocides to determine if and how this cognitive categorization process can be reversed, moving toward more positive views of "the other". One variable they focused on concerns the individual actor's embeddedness in the group. How do individuals separate from the group? Criticize it? Deviate from its behavior?[18] One key concept in this categorization process is the commitment to certain values. Staub's work on the prosocial values scale (1978) relates helping others to the positive evaluation of human beings, the concern for others' welfare, and—finally—the sense that one is responsible for another's well-being, a concept related to Monroe's recent work (2004) on moral salience. In this process, Staub found the embedded self was a relational self, with women and collectivist societies where people are closely tied to others, being more likely to be altruistic. While the importance of cultural and gender variation should be allowed for in future work, concepts such as culture and gender are far from uniform. There is tremendous individual variation within many of the analytical concepts—culture, gender, religion, ethnicity, etc.—said to affect norms.[19] Utilizing culture as an explanatory variable is a useful start; but social scientists' understanding of culture seems analogous to the surgeons performing surgery during the Napoleonic wars. Culture is more like a heavy meat cleaver than the fine scalpel we need to do the kind of careful cognitive analysis necessary to decipher how culture works, at least at the micro level.

We noted earlier that social identity theorists (Tajfel, 1981; Turner, 1987; Turner & Hogg, 1987) have focused attention on how the different parts of the self are activated by circumstances. For some people, the core identity is so broad that they are less affected by circumstances than are others. We need to know how this relates to values that are other-directed, and how strongly these values are held in an actor's hierarchy of goals and values. Work on genocide suggests identity evolves step by step and that we become different people as a result of our actions. The same is true of altruism. Any ethically tinged act (pro or con) carries the potential to change how we see ourselves and how we see others.

3 Why Altruism Matters for Social Scientists

Altruism matters for a variety of reasons beyond our basic intellectual desire to understand any aspect of human behavior. First, most of us agree that the world would be a happier place if we had more altruists. Encouraging altruism thus seems a worthy goal, something akin to fostering of world peace; both are equally vague and probably unattainable but nonetheless remain goals to which we should aspire. In this regard, altruism seems directly relevant for work on cooperation, conflict resolution, and social harmony, and hence speaks directly to fields such as international relations, psychology, social relations, etc.

Second, much social, economic, biological, psychological, and political theory is based on the assumption of self-interest.[20] The mere existence of altruism challenges the universality of this assumption and the validity of models—particularly rational choice or the cost/benefit model of decision making theory—premised on such self-interest based theories of human behavior. Understanding altruism can help us better understand the limitations of such models and theories, and determine when such theories will help us explain human behavior and when they will have limited utility. Determining the parameters of our social scientific models is as important as understanding the parameters of physical science.

Third, altruism is particularly helpful in revealing the limitations in the consequentialist logic which portrays ideas and identities as the outgrowth of self-interest. Once we incorporate an understanding of altruism into our models of political behavior, we can explain political action not just as an exercise in utility maximization but also as the product of a normative logic that is informed by the answers people give to fundamental questions: Who am I? How are people like me supposed to act in certain situations? Rational choice models and game theoretic models, based on traditional microeconomic assumptions, can undergo particularly significant and fruitful revisions by allowing for such factors. The value of introducing more sophisticated psychological assumptions into our political models is evident in the work of scholars who have done so in a wide range of fields, from studies of attribution and learning processes in international relations (Robert Jervis or Janice Gross Stein) to the underlying structure of public opinion (Robert Lane or Paul Sniderman).

Fourth, altruism creates what Tec (1986) called the light that pierces the darkness. In an age of continuing prejudice and ethnic, religious, racial, and sectarian violence, the value of placing findings on altruism into a comparative context cannot be overestimated. Altruism is an important normative behavior at one end of a moral continuum that includes intolerance, stereotyping, prejudice, discrimination, and racial, religious, ethnic, and sectarian violence, including genocide. The common normative theme is our treatment of others, arguably the foundation of all normative politics. Determining the cognitive and emotional constituents necessary for altruistic achievement allows us to conversely identify what would lead to adverse results. Ironically, a better understanding of altruism may subsequently increase knowledge of the psychological drives behind prejudice, racism, torture, and genocide. A crucial starting point rests in examining our other-oriented perceptions. The failure to move beyond the self in order to overcome stereotypical assumptions and generalizations forms the roots of hatred and violence. This chapter thus underlines one of the overarching themes in this book: the importance of recognizing the parallels between oneself and others in order to foster positive social networks and galvanize cooperation. In doing so, we should set work on cooperation and altruism in a comparative analysis—contrasting them with the impetus toward conflict or genocide, for example—since both immoral and moral behavior may come into sharper focus when analyzed in this comparative context.[21]

Finally, as we develop models of political behavior that allow for altruism's influence, political scientists in particular should follow the lead of behavioral economics, the field that grew out of the empirically based literature and theoretical insights of Kahneman, Slovic, and Tversky (1982) and which has recently been acknowledged in mainstream economics, as witnessed by Kahneman's Nobel Prize. Behavioral economics was successful because it offered clear theoretical alternatives to the prevailing rational choice ideology and because it did so via rigorous empirical demonstrations of the explanatory power of these alternative theories. The empirical work on altruism described in this chapter, while founded more in psychology than in political science, offers the rigorous empirical work on which future theorizing can be based. As noted by Sullivan, Snyder, and Sullivan in their introduction to this volume, the lack of synthesis between the fields which constitute the "social sciences" creates a substantial obstacle, hindering our ability to most effectively address the problems and issues facing society today. Adopting a more integrative and cohesive approach, which examines the nature and importance of altruism and cooperation from all angles—psychological, political, economic, sociological, etc.—is the first step towards a more thorough understanding of these phenomena, which are instrumental for the well-being of individuals as well as for the greater community. Therefore, the challenge for political scientists interested in developing richer models of political action is to incorporate these empirical findings into political models that more accurately allow for our complex psychological natures. A similar challenge exists for all social scientists interested in building models of human behavior that more fully capture our complex human identities. Further analysis of the relationship between altruism and cooperation is necessary to better understand how to engender greater unity, cohesion, and subsequent happiness within society. The pivotal point to recognize is that if as individuals we contain altruistic inclinations, then as a collective society we should be fully equipped with the necessary tools to build a more cooperative community.

Acknowledgment

We are grateful to Saba Ozyurt, Janusz Reykowski, and the editors for their comments on this chapter, first presented at the Annual Meeting of the International Society of Political Psychology in Toronto, Canada, July 2005.

Notes

1 In doing so, we cite only a few major works, and all on causation, not conceptualization. See Monroe (1996) for further details.
2 This link builds on three important psychological phenomena: (1) the human desire for self-esteem and the need for continuity of self-image; (2) core values stressing the sanctity of life and human well-being, values which then are integrated into our underlying concept of who we are; and (3) external stimuli that trigger critical aspects of our multifaceted and complex identity in such a way that we notice and accord moral salience to the suffering of others (Monroe, 2004).
3 Becker's (1976) work on altruism is perhaps the most extreme example of this type of work. See Monroe (1996) for a review.
4 Ironically, some real-world findings now are being tested and verified in experimental

laboratory work (McFarland, 2006 and McFarland & Webb, 2004; for work on *Gemein-schaftsgefuhl*, defined as identification with all humanity).

5 Because of their empirical prominence and to simplify discussion, I use rescuers as the empirical illustration. This focus on altruism in extreme situations, however, carries both theoretical advantages and disadvantages, as noted in Part 2.

6 The fact that both survivors and rescuers identify the same critical concept is significant, since a methodological concern when dealing with memories, especially of traumatic events, has been whether past action, caused by an unknown factor, may then lead to rescue activity that in turn engenders the set of attitudes, personality, or perspective noted years later by the analyst as explanatory.

7 See Monroe (2006) for a more extensive review of this literature, set in the context of work on genocide.

8 This transformative self need not be the kind noted by Fogelman (1994), although it seems clear that ethical acts both emanate from identity and in turn shape and modify identity, as noted in virtue ethics.

9 This process would correspond to that described by virtue ethicists.

10 This process corresponds to sociological theories of network behavior.

11 Churchill and Street (2002) suggest the lack of boundaries between the self and others is critical in times of danger.

12 See McGaugh (2003) on the importance of emotions for cognition.

13 Monroe (2004: chapter 1).

14 Rittener & Myers (1986; documentary).

15 This forgiveness was not universal but was significant. Recent work by Staub (2004) has built on this to develop a method of achieving broader forgiveness in communities where genocide has occurred.

16 See Monroe (2001) for a discussion of the philosophical foundations of this framework.

17 See Fogelman (1994) or Oliner and Oliner (1988) for discussion of this.

18 What Staub calls blind patriots, for example, say, "I love my group no matter what" while constructive patriots say, "Because I love my group, I will critique it so it will become even better."

19 Muslims can be Sunni, Shi'ite, Christians can be Protestant, Catholic, fundamentalists, etc. Cleavages overlap, further complicating any patterns of influence.

20 Mansbridge (1990).

21 Ironically, it was work with bystanders, Nazi sympathizers, and Nazis that more fully revealed what may be the critical factor in linking the lack of choice and identity to what we know is great variation in behavior toward others. Work by Glass (1997), Alford (1997), and Staub (1989) is particularly valuable in revealing the psychology underlying discrimination, prejudice, ethnic violence, and other forms of sectarian violence, including genocide.

References

Alford, F. (1997). The political psychology of evil. *Political Psychology, 18*(1), 1–15.

Bargh, J. A., Chen, M., & Burrows, L. (1996). Automaticity of social behavior: Direct effects of trait construct and stereotype priming on action. *Journal of Personality and Social Psychology, 71*, 230–244.

Batson, D. C. (1991). *The altruism question: Toward a social psychological answer*. Hillsdale, NJ: Lawrence Erlbaum.

Becker, G. (1976). *The economic approach to human behavior*. Chicago: University of Chicago Press.

Chartrand, T. L., & Bargh, J. A. (2002). Nonconscious motivations: Their activation, operation, and consequences. In A. Tesser, D. Stapel, & J. Woods (Eds.), *Self and motivation: Emerging psychological perspectives* (pp. 13–41). Washington DC: American Psychological Association Press.

Churchill, R. P., & Street, E. (2002). Is there a paradox of altruism? *Critical Review of International Social Philosophy and Policy*, 5(4), 87–105.

Dawkins, R. (1976). *The selfish gene*. New York: Oxford University Press.

Fogelman, E. (1994). *Conscience and courage*. New York: Anchor Books.

Gies, M. (1987). *Anne Frank remembered: The story of the woman who helped to hide the Frank family*. New York: Simon and Schuster

Glass, J. (1997). *Life unworthy of life: Racial phobia and mass murder in Hitler's Germany*. New York: Basic Books.

Kahneman, D., Slovic, P., & Tversky, A. (1982). *Judgment under uncertainty: Heuristics and biases*. New York: Cambridge University Press.

Lakoff, G., & Johnson, M. (1999). *Philosophy in the flesh: The embodied mind and its challenge to western thought*. New York: Basic Books.

Lerner, R. M. (1992). *Final Solutions: Biology, prejudice, and genocide*. University Park: Pennsylvania State University Press.

Levi, P. (1958/1961). *Survival in Auschwitz*. New York: Macmillan.

London, P. (1970). The rescuers: Motivational hypotheses about Christians who saved Jews from the Nazis. In J. Macaulay & L. Berkowitz (Eds.), *Altruism and helping behavior* (pp. 21–50). New York: Academic Press.

Mansbridge, J. (Ed.) (1990). *Beyond self-interest*. Chicago: University of Chicago Press.

McFarland, S. (2006, July). *A test of a Maslovian model of "oneness with all humanity."* Paper presented at the Annual Meetings of the International Society of Political Psychology. Barcelona.

McFarland, S., & Webb, M. (2004, July). *Measuring* Gemeinschaftsgefuhl: *Identification with all humanity*. Paper presented at the Annual Meetings of the International Society of Political Psychology. Lund, Sweden.

McGaugh, J. L. (2003). *Emotion and memory: The making of lasting memories (Maps of the mind)*. New York: Columbia University Press.

Milgram, S. (1974). *Obedience to authority: An experimental view*. New York: Harper and Row.

Monroe, K. R. (1991). John Donne's people: Explaining the differences between altruists through cognitive frameworks. *Journal of Politics*, 53, 394–433.

Monroe, K. R. (1996). *The heart of altruism: Perceptions of a common humanity*. Princeton, NJ: Princeton University Press.

Monroe, K. R. (2001). Moral action and a sense of self: The importance of categorization for moral action. *The American Journal of Political Science*, 45(3), 491–507.

Monroe, K. R. (2004). *The hand of compassion: Portraits of moral choice during the Holocaust*. Princeton, NJ: Princeton University Press.

Monroe, K. R. (2006, July). *Cracking the code of genocide: The moral psychology of rescuers, bystanders, and perpetrators during the Holocaust*. Paper presented at the Annual Meetings of the International Society of Political Psychology. Barcelona, Spain.

Oliner, P. M., & Oliner, S. P. (1988). *The altruistic personality: Rescuers of Jews in Nazi Europe*. New York: Free Press; London: Collier Macmillan.

Oliner, P., Oliner, S., & Baron, L. (1992). *Embracing the other: Philosophical, psychological, and historical perspectives on altruism*. New York: NYU Press.

Ophuls, M. (director), Harris, A., de Sedouy, A., Theile, W. (producers) (1971). *The sorrow and the pity* [documentary film].

Reykowski, J. (1987). *Activation of helping motivation: The role of extensivity*. Manuscript. Institute of Psychology, Polish Academy of Science. Warsaw.

Rittener, C., & Myers, S. (1986). *The courage to care* [documentary film and book]. New York: NYU Press.

Smiley, M. (1992). *Moral responsibility and the boundaries of community: Power and accountability from a pragmatic point of view*. Chicago: University of Chicago Press.

Staub, E. (1978). *Positive social behavior and morality: Vol. 1. Social and* Personal Influences. New York: Academic Press.

Staub, E. (1989). *The roots of evil: The origins of genocide and other group violence*. New York: Cambridge University Press.

Staub, E. (2004, August). The Sanford address. International Society of Political Psychology. Lund, Sweden.

Tajfel, H. (1981). *Human groups and social categories: Studies in social psychology*. Cambridge: Cambridge University Press.

Tec, N. (1986). *When light pierced the darkness: Christian rescue of Jews in Nazi-occupied Poland*. New York: Oxford University Press.

Turner, J. (1987). *The reemergence of the social group: A self categorization theory*. New York: Basil Blackwell.

Turner, J. C., & Hogg, M. A. (1987). *Rediscovering the social group: A self-categorization theory*. Oxford, UK: Basil Blackwell.

Wiesel, E. (1960/1986). *Night*. New York: Bantam.

7

The Psychology of Cooperation

TOM R. TYLER

The ability to gain cooperation from members is central to the viability and effectiveness of groups, organizations, and societies. This is true within animal groups, in both early and modern human communities, and in modern legal, political, and work organizations. As a consequence, understanding how cooperation can be motivated is a core concern of the social sciences, one addressed by anthropologists, psychologists, sociologists, economists, and political scientists, as well as by scholars in law, management, and public policy.

Social psychologists explore the psychological dynamics underlying cooperative behavior in a wide variety of situations ranging from dyadic bargaining (Rusbult & Van Lange, 2003; Thibaut & Kelley, 1959) to group and community level social dilemmas (see Kopelman, Weber, & Messick, 2002; Weber, Kopelman, & Messick, 2004).

The issue of cooperation is also central to many of the problems faced by real-world groups, organizations, and societies (De Cremer, Zeelenberg, & Murnighan, in press; Tyler, in press a; Van Lange, in press; VanVugt, Snyder, Tyler, & Biel, 2000). As a result, the fields of law, political science, and management all seek to understand how to most effectively design institutions to secure cooperation from those within groups. Their efforts to address these issues are informed by the findings of social psychological and economic research on dyads and small groups.

Law is concerned with how to effectively regulate behavior so as to prevent people from engaging in actions that are personally rewarding but destructive to others and to the group—actions ranging from illegally copying music and movies to robbing banks (Tyler, 1990; Tyler & Huo, 2002). In addition, the police and courts need the active cooperation of members of the community to control crime and urban disorder by reporting crimes and cooperating in policing neighborhoods (Tyler & Huo, 2002). Hence, an important aspect of the study of law involves seeking to understand the factors shaping cooperation with law and legal authorities.

Government also wants people to cooperate by participating in personally costly acts ranging from paying taxes to fighting in wars (Levi, 1988, 1997). Further, it is equally important for people to actively participate in society by voting, maintaining their communities by working together to deal with community problems, and otherwise helping the polity to thrive (Putnam, 2000). For these reasons, understanding how to motivate cooperation is central to political scientists.

Work organizations seek to prevent personally rewarding but destructive acts such as sabotage and stealing office supplies by creating and encouraging deference to rules and policies. They also encourage positive forms of cooperation like working hard at one's job and contributing extra-role and creative efforts to one's work performance (Tyler & Blader, 2000). For these reasons a central area of research in organizational behavior involves understanding how to motivate cooperation in work settings.

In all of these situations the interests of the group, organization, or society lie in motivating greater levels of cooperation from the individual. And, as in social dilemma situations, individuals have a mixed motive relationship to groups, organizations, and societies to which they belong. On the one hand, they benefit from the advantages they gain from cooperation with others. On the other hand, people pay significant costs when they cooperate with others. However, people would not join groups and cooperate with others, given the inherent problems of coordinating their actions with others, unless they judged such membership to be in their overall long-term advantage.

On the other hand, cooperation with others often interferes with the pursuit of short-term individual self-interest. This mixed motive character of cooperation is widely modeled in the framework of experimental games, such as the prisoner's dilemma game. The same mixed motive character of cooperation also emerges in real-world settings in the context of social dilemmas, such as the dilemma of the commons, in which people in communities have a short-term motivation to avoid helping their group, a motive that, if widely acted on, leads to long-term harm for everyone in the community. As Baron notes: "each person benefits by consuming the fruits of others' labor and laboring himself as little as possible—but if everyone behaved this way, there would be no fruits to enjoy" (Baron, 2000, p. 434). In groups the benefits of membership depend upon maintaining the efficiency and effectiveness of the group, which requires the cooperation of group members. Yet, each individual in the group can easily imagine that others would do the work needed, leading them free to pursue their own self-interest.

Because cooperation is central to this discussion, it is important to clarify what is meant by cooperation in this chapter. The term cooperation is used in various areas of psychology. In negotiation, for example, the idea of cooperation is opposed to the idea of competition (Pruitt & Carnevale, 1993). The relationship of people to groups does not involve cooperation versus competition. Instead, people have to make a decision about how actively to engage themselves in groups by taking actions that help the group to be effective and successful. This type of cooperation is what social psychologists have referred to as helping behavior or proactive behavior (Derlega & Grzelak, 1982). So here cooperation refers to the degree to which people act to promote the goals of the group. The alternative is not competition, but a lack of cooperation. Typically this lack of cooperation is motivated by a pursuit of self-interest.

Forms of cooperation

Two types of cooperation are central to the viability of groups. One type of cooperation involves following group rules, rules which limit the unrestrained pursuit of self interest (Tyler & Blader, 2000). The goal of these rules is to prevent people from engaging in behavior that would benefit their short-term self interest but which is contrary to the welfare of others and/or of their group. The area of study which focuses on how groups can limit rule breaking is referred to as the study of regulation. Regulation is the central focus of the law.

The other aspect of cooperation involves performance of behaviors that help the group (Tyler & Blader, 2000). Groups do not simply want their members to follow rules. They also want them to work actively on behalf of their group, engaging in tasks that effectively deal with group problems. In work institutions, for example, organizations want people to perform their jobs well. In communities, people who will work with neighborhood groups, meet about community problems, and otherwise help the community deal with its problems are desirable. And, governments rely upon their members to vote and otherwise participate in the political process.

Hence, there are two functions of cooperative behavior. The first is to limit behaviors that are obstacles to achieving group goals. The second is to promote behaviors that proactively advance group goals. So, for example, the ideal citizen both follows the law in their everyday life and works proactively to help their community deal with its problems.

Motivating cooperation

Within each of the forms of cooperation outlined, it is important to distinguish two reasons for cooperating. One reason is that people's self-interest is linked to cooperative behavior. Groups create organizational frameworks within which desired forms of cooperation are rewarded, so that cooperation is linked to incentives, and in which undesirable forms of cooperation are punished, so that the failure to cooperate is linked to sanctions.

The literature on cooperation suggests that the use of incentives and sanctions can effectively shape cooperative behavior. However, while effective, rewards and punishments are not a particularly efficient mechanism for shaping behavior. First, their impact on behavior is marginal. Further, these effects are costly to obtain, since organizations must commit considerable resources to the effective deployment of incentive and sanctioning systems. For these reasons, the adequacy of instrumental approaches to motivating cooperation has been questioned within law (Tyler, 1990; Tyler & Huo, 2002), political science (Green & Shapiro, 1994), and management (Pfeffer, 1994; Tyler & Blader, 2000).

A key contribution of social psychology is the suggestion that there are *social motivations* that can supplement instrumental motivations in securing cooperation within organizations. These social motivations link behavior to people's attitudes and values, leading behavior to be motivated by internal factors, rather than by incentives or sanctions. To the degree that behavior is internally motivated, cooperation is referred to as voluntary in nature. Voluntary behavior is behavior that is motivated by internal motivations, with the result that its occurrence is separate from variations in the external structure of the situation—i.e. distinct from the effects of variations in incentives or sanctions.

It is desirable for people to cooperate even when incentives and sanctions are not being effectively deployed. One reason is that organizations always find it difficult and inefficient to effectively deploy resources in ways that incentivize or sanction the behavior they are seeking to promote. Even when such systems shape behavior research suggests that they utilize large amounts of resources to achieve minimal behavioral changes. This is especially true for sanctioning systems, which require groups to create and maintain a credible system of punishment for undesirable behaviors. In addition, groups often find it difficult to specify in advance the behaviors that are desirable or undesirable for their members to engage in. Hence, they are more adaptive when their members are motivated to do whatever is appropriate within a particular setting for the good of the organization. In other words, there are many organizational settings in which groups benefit if they can give their members discretionary authority to do what is appropriate or reasonable in a given setting. To do so, they must have members who are motivated to act in the best interest of the group.

It is voluntary cooperation that is central to the viability and effectiveness of groups. Hence, the focus of this chapter is on why voluntary cooperation occurs. In particular, it presents and discusses the arguments of the group engagement model. The group engagement model addresses the question of why people willingly cooperate with groups, presenting a psychological framework within which to understand the motivations underlying voluntary cooperation (Tyler & Blader, 2000, 2003).

The Group Engagement Model

Attitudes and values as antecedents of cooperative behavior

There are three aspects of the group engagement model. The first focuses upon the important role of attitudes and values in shaping voluntary cooperative behavior in groups, organizations, and societies. In keeping with the focus on voluntary cooperation, the first issue addressed is an examination of the internal dynamics that can create and sustain voluntary cooperation with groups.

Legitimacy and compliance

One important example of the role of values is provided by the relationship between legitimacy and cooperation. As has been noted, one reason that people comply with laws is that they fear being caught and punished if they break the law. However, research suggests that people's views about responsibility and obligation to obey the law have a stronger influence upon their law-related behavior (Tyler, 1990; Tyler & Huo, 2002). If people feel that the law is legitimate, i.e. that they ought to obey the law, people comply with the law. Further, the key antecedent of voluntary obedience to the law is legitimacy.

Voluntary deference to the law (Tyler, 1990) flows from people's desire to do what they feel they ought to do in a particular situation. As a result, people follow rules even when the risk of being caught and punished for a transgression is low or nonexistent. In other words, they become self-regulatory, taking the responsibility for rule following onto themselves. In recent years there have been increasing articulations of the value of promoting self-regulatory approaches to rule following throughout the legal community as the limits of deterrence-based models have become more evident (Tyler, 2003; in press b).

One limitation of the original study described in *Why People Obey the Law* (Tyler, 1990) was that it did not focus on decision acceptance during personal encounters with police officers or judges. In this way, it did not directly follow from the earlier work of Thibaut and Walker (1975). This neglected issue was addressed by Tyler and Huo (2002) in a study of personal encounters with police officers and judges in Los Angeles and Oakland. Their study found that procedural justice was central to the willingness to defer to decisions. And their study measured both compliance and deference. It was further shown that procedural justice effects were strongest when the issue was deference. People complied in response to the threat or use of force, and deferred in response to procedural justice.

Additional support for the value of a legitimacy-based perspective is found in recent studies of employee rule-following behavior. Concerns about rule following have also become important in work organizations, in response to recent corporate ethics scandals. These have led to a focus on corporate governance. Within recent years a number of instances of corporate misconduct have come to public attention (Ivancevich, Duening, Gilbert, & Konopaske, 2003). These have raised the question of how to govern businesses so as to keep their conduct within the law. This recent concern highlights the enduring importance of the question of how to manage groups, organizations, and societies. In the case of managing business, both business and government are involved. Businesses might potentially manage themselves internally, or they might be externally regulated by government. In either case, the question is how to effectively bring conduct into line with rules.

Tyler and Blader (in press) explore this issue within two samples of employees. One is a sample of corporate employees, the other a random sample of American workers. In both they find that the legitimacy of corporate rules is a key antecedent of corporate conduct. Employees follow policies and obey rules when they view thc corporation as legitimate and entitled to be obeyed. This influence is distinct from that of sanction-related risks of rule breaking. Finally, employees are also influenced by their judgments about the degree to which the policies of their companies are consistent with their own moral values. In the work context, these findings point to the possibility of self-regulation, suggesting that businesses can effectively secure the deference of their employees to their policies and rules when they are viewed as legitimate authorities who are acting in ways consistent with their employee's moral values (also see Tyler, in press c).

Attitudes and helping behavior

It is also important to discuss the second aspect of cooperation—helping the group. Studies suggest that people are more highly motivated to work on behalf of groups to which they feel committed (Tyler & Blader, 2000). As was true with legitimacy, attitudes are especially important motivators of voluntary helping behavior. In work settings such behavior is described as extra-role behavior to distinguish it from in-role behavior, the work that is specified as part of job descriptions. Extra-role behavior is behavior that employees undertake voluntarily without expectation of reward because they are motivated to do what is needed to make the group succeed. Such behavior is found to be primarily responsive to attitudes such as commitment to the job, rather than to incentives or sanctions (Tyler & Blader, 2000).

While the study of voluntary behavior is most extensive within work settings, all types of organizations benefit from the willingness of their members to voluntarily act in ways that help the group. For example, while studies of legal authority have traditionally focused upon compliance with the law, communities are also heavily dependent upon their members to proactively cooperate with authorities in their efforts to fight crime (Sunshine & Tyler, 2003). Similarly, government relies upon citizens to voluntarily participate in the political process, not only by voting, but by working together to govern their communities.

Procedural justice as an antecedent of attitudes and values

Of course, knowing that attitudes and values encourage voluntary cooperative behavior is of little value unless the development of favorable attitudes and values can be linked to characteristics of groups. Fortunately, research consistently suggests that the way that groups are organized and managed shapes both attitudes and values.

One issue is the antecedents of legitimacy. Studies consistently find that the legitimacy of rules, policies, and decisions is consistently linked to the fairness of the procedures used by authorities to make and implement policies. Today, there is a large literature linking procedural justice to the legitimacy of authorities in legal, political, and managerial settings (Lind & Tyler, 1988; Tyler, 2000; Tyler & Blader, 2000; Tyler, Boeckmann, Smith, & Huo, 1997; Tyler & Smith, 1998). People are widely found to react to the fairness by which authorities and institutions make decisions and exercise authority, and these reactions shape both their willingness to accept decisions and their everyday rule-following behavior. And, these effects have been found to occur when substantial issues, such as personal freedom, are involved (Casper, Tyler, & Fisher, 1988; Tyler, Casper, & Fisher, 1989).

One important change within the procedural justice literature has been a broadened focus of concern. Early studies, such as *Why People Obey the Law* (Tyler, 1990), shaped their concerns in terms of the need to gain compliance, and focused on the role of legitimacy and procedural justice in shaping rule adherence. As has been noted, subsequent studies have strongly supported the argument that procedural justice shapes reactions to decisions (Tyler & Huo, 2002); to rules (Jackson & Fondacaro, 1999; Kim & Mauborgne, 1993; Sparks, Bottoms, & Hay, 1996; Tyler, 2004; Tyler & Degoey, 1995); and to policies (Smith & Tyler, 1996). This is true not only of legal authorities and institutions, but in the political arena as well (Farnsworth, 2003; Gangl, 2003; Hibbing & Theiss-Morse, 2002).

Beyond shaping orientations toward rules and authorities, procedural justice is also a key antecedent of voluntary helping behavior. Within work settings, extra-role behavior is found to be a response to fair procedures within the organization. More recent research moves beyond issues of deference to decisions and rules and recognizes that it is also important that people actively work on behalf of groups, organizations, and communities. This has led to attention to the facilitative influence of procedural justice on satisfaction, intrinsic motivation, commitment to groups, and the willingness to be creative and engage in voluntary behaviors to help those groups (Colquitt, Conlon, Wesson, Porter, & Ng, 2001). Interestingly, the research literature suggests that procedural justice is a key antecedent of both types of behavior. Through legitimacy procedural justice encourages deference. Procedural justice also leads to satisfaction, commitment and intrinsic motivation, and through them to efforts to be creative and to find voluntary actions that can help groups to be successful. Hence, subsequent research confirms the importance of exercising authority fairly.

One particularly valuable aspect of subsequent studies is the linkage of procedural justice and legitimacy to the maintenance of behavior over time. As already noted, one problem with compliance based upon deterrence is that changes in behavior are not maintained when the risk of punishment diminishes or disappears. In contrast, behavior linked to legitimacy, and hence to procedural justice, is expected to be better maintained over time. Studies have supported this argument. For example, research on adherence to mediation agreements over time indicates that people are more likely to adhere to agreements that are made using fair procedures (Pruitt, Peirce, McGillicuddy, Welton, & Castrianno, 1993). Further, those who experience fair procedures when dealing with the police are more likely to comply with the law in the future (Paternoster, Brame, Bachman, & Sherman, 1997). It is in the ability to encourage self-regulation that the potential gains of procedural justice and legitimacy are most clearly revealed, and studies support that argument made in *Why People Obey the Law* that such self-regulation was possible.

What is procedural justice?

Studies of procedural justice suggest that people have a multiattribute framework for assessing whether a procedure is fair or unfair (Tyler, 1988). Within that framework two aspects of procedures are found to shape judgments about their fairness: evaluations of the quality of decision making and evaluations of the quality of interpersonal treatment (Blader & Tyler, 2003). The importance of these issues varies across situations, with social context determining which procedural justice elements are particularly important.

The quality of decision making involves two issues. The first is the degree to which a procedure proves people with opportunities for participation or voice. People want to have the opportunity to present their arguments to the decision maker before decisions are made. For this reason people seek forums such as mediation, which provide greater opportunities for them to express their views. The quality of decision making also involves issues about the manner in which decisions are made, including consistency of rule application, the degree to which decisions are unbiased, neutral, and factual, and the transparency of rules.

The quality of interpersonal treatment also involves two issues. The first is the degree to which people are treated with dignity, politeness, and respect. The second involves inferences about trustworthiness. People are concerned that others, in particular third parties, are motivated to do what is right for everyone involved. Inferences about the benevolence of others are made based upon inferences about their character. As a result, when leaders explain and justify their actions, showing how they have considered the needs and concerns of the parties, there are judged to be more trustworthy.

Why Do People Voluntarily Cooperate with Groups?

The group engagement model argues that psychological engagement is the key antecedent of voluntary cooperation. When people expect to be treated justly by the group they are more willing to allow their sense of self to become intertwined with the group. This merger of self with the group—identification with the group (Hogg & Abrams, 1988; Tajfel & Turner, 1979, 1986)—leads to the willingness to engage on behalf of the group. People become engaged with the group, acting in ways that benefit the group. Another way of putting it is that the group and the individual become interrelated, so that the well-being of the group becomes the well-being of the individual, and self- and group-interest become indistinguishable. Hence, people become motivated to act in ways that benefit the group.

Identity moderation

There are two types of evidence that support this identity-based argument. One type of evidence comes from demonstrations of the *moderation* effect: that people care more about whether or not they receive just treatment when their identity is more heavily intertwined with that of the group. A number of experimental and nonexperimental studies demonstrate that people are more strongly influenced by the justice of a group's procedures when their identity is more intertwined with the group.

Experimental research demonstrates that the same fair or unfair treatment has distinct influences upon the self depending upon whether or not it is delivered by an ingroup or an outgroup authority. Smith, Tyler, Huo, Ortiz, and Lind (1998) had a confederate play the role of an authority. That authority was labeled as being within or outside of the participant's group. The study showed that variations in quality of treatment only shaped self-esteem when the authority was a within-group member. Similarly Tyler, Lind, Ohbuchi, Sugawara, and Huo (1998) demonstrated that disputants based their decisions about whether to accept or reject third-party dispute resolution based upon procedural justice criteria when the dispute was within group, and based upon outcome valence when the dispute was between groups. In both cases, people were more influenced by procedural justice when it was more identity relevant.

Nonexperimental studies also support the argument that people care more about procedural justice issues when their identity is linked to the group. Tyler and Degoey (1995) explored the willingness of people to voluntarily defer to rules enacted by a community authority to regulate water use based upon procedural justice criteria when they identified more strongly with the community. Similarly, Huo, Smith, Tyler and Lind (1996) found that people were more willing to accept third-party decisions from ingroup authorities based upon procedural justice criteria when they identified more strongly with the group, and Smith and Tyler (1996) found that white respondents were more willing to defer to decisions to redistribute resources to minorities based upon the procedural justice of the decision-making body (Congress) when they identified more strongly with America.

Recent studies also support the moderation finding. Tyler and De Cremer (in press a and b) and Van Vugt, Snyder, Tyler, and Biel (2000) explored the factors shaping the willingness of employees to cooperate with a new organizational entity following a merger in which the company being studied is taken over by another company. They found that the degree to which employees defer to their new leaders in procedural groups is greater when the employees identify more strongly with the new company. Similarly, Davis-Lipman, Tyler, and Andersen (in press) find that the more strongly students identify with their school, the more their decisions to seek help from faculty and deans are based upon their expectations about whether or not they will receive just and respectful treatment from those authorities. Again, procedural issues are more important when people's identities are more strongly linked to groups.

Recent studies have expanded the framework within which identity moderation effects are explored. De Cremer and Tyler (2005a, 2005b) demonstrate that similar moderation effects, i.e. increased concern about procedural justice when the self is more engaged in the group, occur with other factors that also reflect the degree to which people connect their identities to groups. Research demonstrates that people who have a greater need to belong to groups, who are more concerned about their social reputations, and whose self-construal is more strongly linked to groups, all demonstrate the same type of moderation effect already outlined. Similarly, De Cremer, Tyler, and den Ouden (2005) demonstrate that moderation effects are linked to direct measures of the degree to which people merge their sense of self with the group.

Identity mediation

Identity arguments are also supported by the finding of identity *mediation* (Tyler, Degoey, & Smith, 1996). In particular, identity can be measured using three constructs: pride, respect, and identification. Pride refers to the status of one's group. Respect refers to one's status in the group. These two status judgments shape the degree to which people identify with, i.e. merge their sense of self with, the group. That merger is referred to as identification. If these three indices are used to reflect the identity-based link between a person and the groups to which they belong, it is found that identity mediates the relationship between procedural justice and both voluntary cooperative behavior and self-esteem.

In the group engagement model, Tyler and Blader (2003) argue, the influence of both procedural justice and evaluations of outcome favorability and fairness can be understood through the mechanism of identity mediation. Using a sample of employees from various work organizations ranging from small companies to large organizations, Tyler and Blader (2000) show that identity mediates the impact of both procedures and outcomes on attitudes, values, and voluntary cooperative behaviors. They argue that both the procedural justice that people experience and the outcomes that they receive influence their engagement in the group to the degree that they communicate identity relevant information to other people within groups.

The arguments of the group engagement model have several broader implications for our understanding of why people cooperate. The first is that people's motivations for voluntary cooperation are linked to the psychological link that binds them to groups. It is the role of groups in creating and sustaining people's identities that leads people to act voluntarily on behalf of groups.

It is not obvious that the link between people and groups would be related to issues of identity. On the contrary, historically, social psychology has been dominated by a social exchange perspective, which argued that people are linked to groups because groups can more efficiently provide desired material resources (Thibaut & Kelley, 1959). Further, recent studies suggest that, if asked, most people would describe themselves as motivated to act based upon their material self-interest (the "myth of self-interest," Miller & Ratner, 1998). Further, the idea that people's actions are motivated by the desire to maximize material self-interest is widely articulate within the social sciences (Green & Shapiro, 1994). Hence, the findings here provide a different perspective upon the motivation underlying cooperation with others.

This different perspective is noninstrumental on several levels. First, it suggests that people are motivated by attitudes and values which are distinct from judgments about self-interest. Second, it argues that those attitudes and values are sustained by judgments about the justice of group procedures. And, third, it presents an identity-based model for why people care about procedural justice. On all of these levels, the model of the psychology of cooperation is noninstrumental. It suggests that the core issues for individuals are the motivation to be included within groups and to create and sustain a favorable sense of self at least in part by drawing upon group-based indices of status. These indices shape identification—the merger of self with the group—which is the root of the motivation to act voluntarily on behalf of the group.

Social Systems as a Dynamic Process

Social systems are dynamic and evolve over time. The model of social dynamics presented argues for the possibility of creating supportive attitudes and values through the use of fair procedures in groups, organizations, and societies. As people develop more supportive attitudes and values, their behavior becomes increasingly self-regulatory, and it is less and less necessary to provide incentives or threaten sanctions to gain compliance or performance. It is increasingly possible for groups to rely upon people to voluntarily defer to rules and to engage in extra-role actions designed to help the group. This frees up group resources to support the long-term goals of the group.

These dynamics are illustrated by the previously outlined discussion of the identity moderation effect. The more people identify with a group, the more they decide whether to accept decisions, to obey rules, and to work on behalf of that group based upon procedural justice criteria, rather than by considering the valence of the outcomes involved. Hence, they become more self-regulatory in the sense that they focus more on the manner in which authority is exercised, rather than upon outcomes. This facilitates the exercise of authority and makes groups more viable.

And, of course, the justice of the procedures involved shapes identification, so that the social dynamics involved go two ways. If people experience procedural justice, they identify more strongly with the groups that are exercising their authority fairly (Tyler & Blader, 2000; Tyler & Huo, 2002). If people identify with groups, then identity issues are more relevant, and they base their decisions about how much to cooperate more heavily upon procedural justice, and less heavily upon issues of outcome valence.

In addition, groups that are supported by the attitudes and values of their members, who are evaluating authorities procedurally, are more resilient and viable in the face of downturn, scarcity, and change. It is during periods of crisis and change that groups are most vulnerable. During such periods leaders are seldom able to offer immediate rewards to their members, or to maintain credible systems of surveillance and sanctioning. And they may not be able to offer assurances that change will lead to future success, since the viability of changed organizations itself depends upon future support from the members of the group. Hence, during such times the group depends heavily upon the willingness to its members to forego immediate rewards, to defer to rules when there is little credible threat of punishment for rule breaking, and to work for the group when the long-term prospects of success are uncertain. When groups have supportive attitudes and values they are more able to weather such periods, since people are motivated to work for the group for internal reasons that are not directly linked to immediate gains and loses. Instead, people are motivated to work for the group because their identity and sense of self is bound up in the viability of the group.

On the other hand, it is also possible to imagine the opposite social dynamic. That dynamic is, in fact, more characteristic of the existing American system of social control. In that system cooperation is managed via the application of incentives and sanctions. This focuses the attention of the people involved upon the degree to which their behavior will be rewarded or punished, and leads to increasing attention to the instrumental quality of actions, and less to acting in ways consistent with attitudes and values.

Psychologists (Deci, 1975, 1981) and economists (Frey, 1997) both point out that an increasing focus on the instrumental gains and losses has the effect of undermining intrinsic or internal motivations for behavior. An instrumental focus "crowds out" other motivations for action, such as attitudes and values. It has the effect of defining cooperative behaviors as being performed for rewards or because of the threat of punishment. If, in the future, incentives or sanctions are no longer available, other motivations for action are less likely to encourage cooperation. Hence, an instrumental focus leads to changes away from a self-regulatory approach and, over time, the use of instrumental approaches makes a self-regulatory model less viable.

Hence, once a group has moved in the direction of instrumentality, it spends increasing amounts of resources upon the motivation of its members. In particular, systems of sanctioning require increasing efforts at surveillance as group members develop more and more ingenious mechanisms for hiding their behavior. In the end, "instrumental means of producing compliance always depend on resource limits" (Meares, 2000, p. 401). As an example, consider the recent threats of the recording industry to sue those who illegally download music. Have these threats actually led to lower levels of rule-breaking behavior? Research suggests that they have not. Rather, people have worked harder to hide their behavior from surveillance (Karagiannis, Broida, & Brownlee, Claffy, & Faloutsos, 2004). This may lead to increasing efforts to find the illegal behavior, which will drive it further underground. Absent an alternative strategy, sanctioning models have only the possibility of increasing either efforts to detect illegal behavior or the level of sanctioning threatened.

The counterproductive effects of sanctioning models can be seen through the tendency to increase the seriousness of the sanction promised when illegal behavior is detected. Research shows that behavior is more strongly responsive to estimates of the likelihood of punishment than it is to the severity of punishment. However, sanctioning efforts seem inevitably drawn to increasingly severe punishments, as has been true with increasingly severe penalties for illegal music downloading, software piracy, and the copying of movies and books. This seems inevitable as policy makers rapidly confront the limits of their ability to sustain the more costly, but more effective, deployment of surveillance to increase the likelihood of detecting wrongdoing. Threatening ever-greater risks for illegal behavior becomes inevitable as a sanctioning strategy progressively undermines the other factors that might lead to compliance with the law. In this case people's views about obeying the law and doing what is morally right are crowded out by a heightened focus upon the risks associated with this illegal behavior.

Summary

The question of why people cooperate with others is a core social science issue. It is often answered instrumentally via the argument that groups can encourage cooperation via either the use of incentives or by the provision of sanctioning systems. Such approaches seek to change people's behavior by changing their estimate of the rewards and costs associated with various types of cooperative behavior in social settings.

This chapter outlines an alternative approach to encouraging cooperation. That approach builds upon the important role that internal motivations—attitudes and values—can have in encouraging people to cooperate in social settings. These motivations, when activated, have the advantage of leading to cooperation without an explicit link to either rewards or punishments. As a result, people act voluntarily, in response to their own internal motivations, and are not focused upon the immediate external environment.

A number of studies point to the viability of a self-regulatory approach of the type outlined. These studies demonstrate, first, that people can be motivated to cooperate based upon appeals to their attitudes and values. And, in fact, these approaches produce stronger influencing upon behavior than does the use of incentives and sanctions. This is especially true of influences upon voluntary or discretionary behavior, which is difficult to motivate via instrumental approaches. Hence, groups have a great deal to gain by focusing upon strategies that encourage people to act upon their attitudes and values.

The same research also indicates that the dynamics of groups clearly shape the degree to which people's attitudes and values become important in shaping their cooperative behavior. These studies suggest that people are strongly influenced by their judgments about the justice or injustice of group procedures. This includes both the quality of decision making and the quality of interpersonal treatment. Procedural justice judgments shape both attitudes and values and, through them, have an influence upon voluntary cooperation. The magnitude of that influence is typically much greater than is the influence of either incentives or sanctions upon voluntary cooperation.

Taken together these findings suggest that there is a viable alternative approach to gaining and retaining the cooperation of the members of groups, organizations, and societies. The use of this approach requires the development of attitudes and values over time through the use of just procedures for the exercise of authority. Once attitudes and values are engaged this approach has the virtue of being self-regulatory. Self-regulation allows groups to function without allocating large proportions of their resources to the maintenance of social order or the encouragement of productivity in group tasks. This strategy also helps societies to be more resilient in the face of downturns and periods of scarcity, since people have a non-instrumental basis upon which to maintain their loyalty to and cooperation with social institutions and authorities.

References

Baron, J. (2000). *Thinking and deciding* (3rd ed.). Cambridge, UK: Cambridge University Press.

Blader, S. L., & Tyler, T. R. (2003). A four component model of procedural justice. *Personality and Social Psychology Bulletin, 29,* 747–758.

Casper, J. D., Tyler, T. R., & Fisher, B. (1988). Procedural justice in felony cases. *Law and Society Review, 22,* 483–507.

Colquitt, J. A., Conlon, D. E., Wesson, M., Porter, C. O., & Ng, K. Y. (2001). Justice at the millennium: A meta-analytic review of 25 years of organizational justice research. *Journal of Applied Psychology, 86,* 425–445.

Davis-Lipman, A., Tyler, T. R., & Andersen, S. (in press). Building community one relationship at a time: The impact of personal relationships on help seeking and help acceptance. *Social Justice Research.*

Deci, E. L. (1975). *Intrinsic motivation.* New York: Plenum.

Deci, E. L. (1981). *The psychology of self-determination.* Lexington, MA: D. C. Heath

De Cremer, D., & Tyler, T. R. (2005a). Managing group behavior: The interplay between procedural justice, sense of self, and cooperation. *Advances in Experimental Social Psychology, 37,* 151–218.

De Cremer, D., & Tyler, T. R. (2005b). Am I respected or not?: Inclusion and reputation as issues in group membership. *Social Justice Research, 18,* 121–153.

De Cremer, D., Tyler, T. R., & den Ouden, N. (2005). Managing cooperation via procedural fairness: The mediating influence of self–other merging. *Journal of Economic Psychology, 26,* 393–406.

De Cremer, M. Zeelenberg, & J. K. Murnighan (Eds.) (2006). *Social psychology and economics.* Mahwah, NJ: Lawrence Erlbaum.

Derlega, V. J., & Grzelak, J. (1982). *Cooperation and helping behavior.* New York: Academic Press.

Farnsworth, S. J. (2003). Congress and citizen discontent: Public evaluations of the membership and one's own representative. *American Politics Research, 21*, 66–80.

Frey, B. (1997). *Not just for the money*. Cheltenham, England: Edward Elgar.

Gangl, A. (2003). Procedural justice theory and evaluations of the lawmaking process. *Political Behavior, 25*, 119–149.

Green, D. P., & Shapiro, I. (1994). *Pathologies of rational choice theory*. New Haven, CT: Yale University Press.

Hibbing, J. R., & Theiss-Morse, E. (2002). *Stealth democracy: Americans' beliefs about how government should work*. Cambridge, UK: Cambridge University Press.

Hogg, M. A., & Abrams, D. (1988). *Social identifications*. New York: Routledge.

Huo, Y. J., Smith, H. J., Tyler, T. R., and Lind, E. A. (1996). Superordinate identification, subgroup identification, and justice concerns: Is separatism the problem, is assimilation the answer? *Psychological Science, 7*, 40–45.

Ivancevich, J. M., Duening, T. N., Gilbert, J. A., & Konopaske, R. (2003). Deterring white-collar crime. *Academy of Management Executive, 17*, 114–127.

Jackson, S., & Fondacaro, M. (1999). Procedural justice in resolving family conflict. *Law and Policy, 21*, 101–127.

Karagiannis, T., Broido, A., Brownlee, N., Claffy, K. C., & Faloutsos, M. (2004). Is P2P dying or just hiding? Cooperative Association for Internet Data Analysis: http://www.caida.org/outreach/papers/2004/p2p-dying/index.xml.

Kim, W. Chan, and Mauborgne, Renée (1993). Procedural justice, attitudes and subsidiary top management compliance with multinational's corporate strategic decisions. *Academy of Management Journal, 36*, 502–526.

Kopelman, S., Weber, J. M., & Messick, D. M. (2002). Factors influencing cooperation in commons dilemmas: A review of experimental psychological research. In E. Ostrom, T. Dietz, N. Dolsak, P. C. Stern, S. Stonich, & E. U. Weber (Eds.), *The drama of the commons* (pp. 113–156). Washington, DC: National Academy Press.

Levi, M. (1988). *Of rule and revenue*. Cambridge, UK: Cambridge University Press.

Levi, M. (1997). *Consent, dissent, and patriotism*. Cambridge, UK: Cambridge University Press.

Lind, E. A., & Tyler, T. R. (1988). *The social psychology of procedural justice*. New York: Plenum.

Meares, T. L. (2000). Norms, legitimacy, and law enforcement. *Oregon Law Review, 79*, 391–415.

Miller, D. T., & Ratner, R. K. (1998). The disparity between the actual and assumed power of self-interest. *Journal of Personality and Social Psychology, 74*, 53–62.

Paternoster, R., Brame, R., Bachman, R., & Sherman, L. W. (1997). Do fair procedures matter? *Law and Society Review, 31*, 163–204.

Pfeffer, J. (1994). *Competitive advantage through people*. Cambridge, MA: Harvard University Press.

Pruitt, D., & Carnevale, P. (1993). *Negotiation in social conflict*. Pacific Grove, CA: Brooks/Cole.

Pruitt, D. G., Peirce, R. S., McGillicuddy, N. B., Welton, G. I., & Castrianno, L. M. (1993). Long-term success in mediation. *Law and Human Behavior, 17*, 313–330.

Putnam, R. D. (2000). *Bowling alone*. New York: Simon and Schuster.

Rusbult, C. E., & Van Lange, P. A. M. (2003). Interdependence, interaction, and relationships. *Annual Review of Psychology, 54*, 351–375.

Smith, H. J., & Tyler, T. R. (1996). Justice and power: Can justice motivations and superordinate categorizations encourage the advantaged to support policies which redistribute economic resources and encourage the disadvantaged to willingly obey the law? *European Journal of Social Psychology, 26*, 171–200.

Smith, H. J., Tyler, T. R., Huo, Y. J., Ortiz, D. J., and Lind, E. A. (1998). The self-relevant implications of the group value model: Group membership, self-worth, and procedural justice. *Journal of Experimental Social Psychology, 34*, 470–493.

Sparks, R., Bottoms, A., & Hay, W. (1996). *Prisons and the problem of order*. Oxford, UK: Clarendon Press.

Sunshine, J., & Tyler, T. R. (2003). The role of procedural justice and legitimacy in shaping public support for policing. *Law and Society Review, 37*(3), 555–589.

Tajfel, H., & Turner, J. C. (1979). An integrative theory of intergroup conflict. In W. G. Austin & S. Worchel (Eds.), *The social psychology of intergroup relations* (pp. 33–47). Monterey, CA: Brooks/Cole.

Tajfel, H., & Turner, J. C. (1986). The social identity theory of intergroup behavior. In S. Worchel (Ed.), *The psychology of intergroup relations*. Chicago: Nelson Hall.

Thibaut, J., & Kelley, H. H. (1959). *The social psychology of groups*. New York: Wiley.

Thibaut, J., & Walker, L. (1975). *Procedural justice*. Mahwah, NJ: Lawrence Erlbaum.

Tyler, T. R. (1988). What is procedural justice?: Criteria used by citizens to assess the fairness of legal procedures. *Law and Society Review, 22*, 103–135.

Tyler, T. R. (1990). *Why people obey the law: Procedural justice, legitimacy, and compliance*. New Haven, CT: Yale University Press.

Tyler, T. R. (2000). Social justice. *International Journal of Psychology, 35*, 117–125.

Tyler, T. R. (2003). Procedural justice, legitimacy, and the effectiveness of law. *Crime and Justice, 30*, 431–505.

Tyler, T. R. (2004). Affirmative action in an institutional context. *Social Justice Research, 17*, 5–24.

Tyler, T. R. (in press a). Social motives and institutional design. In G. V. Wangerheim (Ed.), *The evolution of designed institutions*. Malden, MA: Blackwell.

Tyler, T. R. (in press b). Legitimacy and legitimation. *Annual Review of Psychology*.

Tyler, T. R. (in press c). Promoting employee policy adherence and rule following in work settings: The value of self-regulatory approaches. *Brooklyn Law Review*.

Tyler, T. R., & Blader, S. (2000). *Cooperation in groups: Procedural justice, social identity, and behavioral engagement*. Philadelphia: Psychology Press.

Tyler, T. R., & Blader, S. (2003). The group engagement model: Procedural justice, social identity, and cooperative behavior. *Personality and Social Psychology Review, 7*, 349–361.

Tyler, T. R., and Blader, S. L. (in press). Can businesses effectively regulate employee conduct?: The antecedents of rule following in work settings. *Academy of Management Journal*.

Tyler, T. R., Boeckmann, R. J., Smith, H. J., & Huo, Y. J. (1997). *Social justice in a diverse society*. Boulder, CO: Westview.

Tyler, T. R., Casper, J. D., & Fisher, B. (1989). Maintaining allegiance toward political authorities: The role of prior attitudes and the use of fair procedures. *American Journal of Political Science, 33*, 629–652.

Tyler, T. R., & De Cremer, D. (in press a). How do we promote cooperation in groups, organizations, and societies? The interface of psychology and economics. In P. Van Lange (Ed.), *Bridging social psychology*. Philadelphia: Psychology Press.

Tyler, T. R., & De Cremer, D. (in press b). The psychology of cooperation in groups. In D. De Cremer, M. Zeelenberg, & J. K. Murnighan (Eds.), *Social psychology and economics*. Mahwah, NJ: Lawrence Erlbaum.

Tyler, T. R., & Degoey, P. (1995). Collective restraint in a social dilemma situation: The influence of procedural justice and community identification on the empowerment and legitimacy of authority. *Journal of Personality and Social Psychology, 69*, 482–497.

Tyler, T. R., Degoey, P., & Smith, H. (1996). Understanding why the justice of group procedures matters: A test of the psychological dynamics of the group-value model. *Journal of Personality and Social Psychology, 70*, 913–930.

Tyler, T. R., & Huo, Y. J. (2002). *Trust in the law: Encouraging public cooperation with the police and courts*. New York: Russell-Sage Foundation.

Tyler, T. R., Lind, E. A., Ohbuchi, J., Sugawara, I., and Huo, Y. J. (1998). Conflict with outsiders: Disputing within and across cultural boundaries. *Personality and Social Psychology Bulletin, 24*, 137–146.

Tyler, T. R., & Smith, H. (1998). Social justice and social movements. In D. Gilbert, S. Fiske, & G. Lindzey (Eds.), *Handbook of social psychology* (4th edition, Vol. 2, pp. 595–629). New York: McGraw-Hill.

Van Lange, P. (Ed.) (in press). *Bridging social psychology: Benefits of transdisciplinary approaches*. Mahwah, NJ: Lawrence Erlbaum.

Van Vugt, M., Snyder, M., Tyler, T. R., & Biel, A. (2000). *Cooperation in modern society: Promoting the welfare of communities, states and organizations*. New York: Routledge.

Weber, J. M., Kopelman, S., & Messick, D. M. (2004). A conceptual review of decision making in social dilemmas. *Personality and Social Psychology Review, 8*, 281–307.

8

Voice, Validation, and Legitimacy

JOHN R. HIBBING AND
ELIZABETH THEISS-MORSE

What gives decisions legitimacy? This question is vital for social structures of all kinds but especially for political institutions, since decision making is their *raison d'etre*. Not so long ago, political scientists' answer to this question was remarkably simplistic and incorrect. The assumption was that legitimacy derives primarily from the extent to which decision outcomes are consistent with people's policy desires, that those pleased with the substance of a given governmental decision will view the government as legitimate and those who are displeased will view it as less legitimate. The prevailing belief was that people "care about ends not means; they judge government by results and are . . . indifferent about the methods by which the results were obtained" (Popkin, 1991, p. 99). To understand perceptions of legitimacy, it was only necessary to measure the gap between an individual's policy preference and the actual policy output of the government.

But empirical evidence for the connection between dissatisfaction with policy outputs and dissatisfaction with government is weak (see, for example, Miller, 1974, pp. 952–957). A robust economy, to take one of the most desired political outputs, leads neither to greater approval of government nor to heightened perceptions of governmental legitimacy (Lawrence, 1997). After summarizing findings in the area, Pharr concludes that "policy performance . . . explains little when it comes to public trust" (2000, p. 199) and della Porta asks, "why do policy outputs . . . play such a minor role in shaping confidence in democratic institutions?" (2000, p. 202). Delli Carpini and Keeter (1996) as well as Hibbing and Theiss-Morse (2002) remind us that part of the answer to this question is that people are simply not aware of most governmental policy outputs. Surprise over policy outputs' lack of influence seems confined to academics and pundits who make their living following political events; ordinary people have no difficulty accepting the finding.

But if policy outputs only modestly influence popular support for government, what are other important factors? Thanks largely to the work of psychologists such as Tom Tyler, we now know that, contrary to Popkin's assertion, a key part of the story is indeed the process by which decisions are made. After all is said and done, people actually are quite attuned to the "methods by which results were obtained." More than anyone, Tyler has demonstrated the value people place on procedural justice as distinct from substantive justice by showing that people are not only concerned with what they receive but also with the manner in which they receive it. The relevance of procedural justice is now recognized in political science, though not nearly to the extent it should be. Old notions that people are nothing more than policy maximizers die hard.

Evidence for the relevance of procedural matters is irrefutable. In a study typical of Tyler's approach, he contacted 652 Chicago-area people with recent experience in the legal system to determine the influence of various factors on their evaluations of the legitimacy of the legal system. He found that assessments of the fairness of decision-making *procedures* were consistently more powerful in explaining perceived legitimacy than were assessments of the fairness and favorability of the *outcomes* (Tyler, 2001, p. 234). Similar findings have emerged in a variety of quite different settings (see, for example, Lind, Kulik, Ambrose, & Vera Park, 1993; Kitzmann & Emery, 1993). People are sensitive to procedures, and political scientists are indebted to psychologists such as Tom Tyler for driving this point home. It gives added importance to the institutions and political arrangements we spend so much time studying. Institutions matter not just because of the policies they produce but also because of the independent effect these institutions have on people's perceptions of and relations with the government.

Still, it is one thing to demonstrate the general relevance of procedures and it is another to identify (1) the specific procedural features that lead people to respond favorably and (2) the theoretical basis for procedures being so important to people. This is where we see a lack of clarity in previous research and these are our two primary goals in this chapter. Our analysis leads us to conclusions that will be viewed as more pessimistic than those of most contributors to this volume. We see personal interaction generally, and voice-to-power specifically, not as a universal enhancer of a contented social life but as something that raises the stakes, something that can lead to greater satisfaction but also to greater frustration depending upon the message people take from that interaction.

In so saying, we do not mean to imply cooperation and social involvement should be avoided; rather, we believe close attention to real theory and to real empirical evidence reveals participation to be a dual-edged sword. It does not automatically maximize happiness and human functioning. Under some circumstances, we will argue, participation significantly reduces happiness. Social scientists do society a disservice by issuing a universal request for everybody to get involved. Many people do not want to be involved (Hibbing & Theiss-Morse, 2002) and many types of involvement are inherently frustrating to people. We need to stop acting like naïve cheerleaders and become hard-headed analysts of the specific situations in which involvement increases or diminishes trust, legitimacy, and happiness.

Evolution and the Quest for Validation

Though there are lingering disputes over the specific procedures that are most satisfying to people, the evidence that process matters continues to grow (see, for example, Hibbing & Alford, 2004; Tyler, this volume). Often unspecified, however, is the theoretical basis for process being so important to people. Explaining why people value certain outcomes is almost unnecessary since people have long been assumed to value "more rather than less" (Buchanan & Tullock, 1962, p. 18); but explaining why people value certain processes raises exciting and provocative theoretical challenges.

To the extent social psychologists have attempted to provide a meaningful account of the importance to people of procedural justice (beyond the atheoretical assertion that people for unknown reasons value justice of all kinds), it is embodied in the dispute between Tyler and Thibaut. Though they agree on the importance of process, Thibaut and Tyler have disparate views of the reason process matters to people. Thibaut argues that certain procedures permit greater consideration of individualized arguments and that this in turn will lead to fairer outcomes. Hence, his position is that procedural fairness is important because it is intimately connected with specifics of the outcome (see especially Thibaut & Walker, 1975).

Tyler has a much different take, believing that process is important even in the absence of any connection with outcomes and, indeed, a growing body of evidence in psychology invites the conclusion that, with outcomes strictly controlled, procedures exert a strong effect on the degree to which people accept outcomes and approve of the decision-making system (see Lind & Tyler, 1988; Tyler, 1990; Tyler, 2001; Tyler & Blader, 2000). Tyler has won the empirical battle but there is no victor in the theoretical war. In fact, it appears not to have been fully joined yet. Quite apart from outcome, people clearly value particular procedures but the theoretical explanation for this empirical fact is poorly developed. Tyler is correct in saying that process is not valued simply because of its effects on policy, but his explanation for why it *is* valued is less satisfactory. The thrust seems to be that people derive a positive sense of self-worth from group interaction and from procedural justice but there is no explanation for why groups (and just procedures) would instill self-worth, or, more tellingly, for why certain types of involvement with others might lead to frustration rather than satisfaction.

Social psychologists are frequently accused (see Tooby & Cosmides, 1992) of creating impressive-sounding phrases that they then, without justification, refer to as theories. These "theories" generally turn out to be descriptions and unfortunately the same could be said for procedural justice theory as well. It is not enough to assert that, for unknown reasons, people crave process control (see Tyler, Rasinski, & Spodick, 1985). "That is just the way people are" is not a theory—and equating group interaction with enhanced feelings of self-worth is factually inaccurate.

But we believe procedural justice, appropriately conceived, is an important part of a larger theoretical edifice. Increasingly in the behavioral sciences, scholars are looking to evolutionary biology for explanations regarding the preferences, goals, and behavior of organisms.[1] For *homo sapiens*, the key evolutionary adaptation appears to be group living. Groups have long been vital to humans' ability to provision, protect, and procreate. They are the central organizing feature of human life and have been ever since *homo sapiens* became biologically distinct. Thinking and behaving in a socially sensitive fashion is necessary to make groups function properly, so from an evolutionary point of view social skills have value. People who are socially adroit have been selected for since they are more likely to prosper and proliferate and since individuals lacking the ability to form social bonds will derive none of the benefits of group life and will be at a disadvantage.

It is not surprising then that, with some exceptions, people today are highly social animals who care deeply about the judgments of those around them. They want to feel they have contributed to the group and that others in the group value (and respond to) their input. Research from psychology and across the social sciences stresses people's desire to be a valued part of a social unit.[2] It should be noted, however, that this socially sensitive behavior is not always desirable; it often leads to intergroup hostilities, not to mention intragroup jealousies, neuroses, and competition.

One of the outgrowths of humans' social nature is a powerful desire for validation, for assurance regarding worth and place within the group. People are neurotic about this. They want to know that others in the group, particularly powerful group members, view them and their needs with respect since losing a place within the group could be dangerous—or at least this was the case in humans' evolutionary past. Not surprisingly, then, psychological research has shown that when people are treated unfairly or with disrespect, it is tantamount to a personal attack on their sense of self-worth (Miller, 2001). This is especially true when disrespect seems connected to their performance. People who are made to feel they were ineffective in the performance of an action have been shown to display a decreased sense of self-esteem (Gecas, 1982), and frustration, resentment, and anger are common results of situations that diminish people's sense of self-worth (Miller, 2001). This stream of research provides an explanation for why individuals' evaluations of decision-making processes depend heavily on whether the process (and outcome) make them feel validated as members in good standing of a healthy group. Nonoutcome factors such as the process employed to make decisions are profoundly important because they reveal much about the group and about an individual's status within the group.

This rationale leads to the expectations that those processes bearing on people's feelings of validation are the ones that most clearly affect legitimacy. Voice should not be equated with validation. For this connection to apply, the person speaking must also have the feeling that the decision maker listened and responded favorably. Imagine three scenarios, one in which you offer your views to someone who listens and then responds positively, another in which you offer your views to someone who listens and then appears to ignore your requests, and a third in which you do not have an opportunity to express your views at all. Evolutionary theory suggests people will feel the most validated in the first scenario, the most invalidated in the second scenario, and have middling reactions when having no voice at all. In sum, this theory posits that people are eager to solidify their place in a group as well as to ascertain their place in the group and the orientations of others in that group.

Saying people are innately group oriented is not the same as saying they are innately cooperative. Evolution has selected for people who are group oriented and cooperative but also who are averse to being played for a sucker. Since the only place people can be played for a sucker is in a group, the dilemma is obvious. How can people behave in a cooperative fashion toward others without hurting their chances of fulfilling their individual needs and desires? Danger is present in tilting too far in either direction. This trade-off between a desire to treat others favorably and, at the same time, to receive a fair share constitutes the fundamental tension of the human condition and natural selection has rewarded a phenotype that is neither a selfish, individually absorbed egoist nor a completely self-sacrificing altruist. We call this phenotype the wary cooperator.

People want to be perceived as worthy and generous group members and so they have an instinct to contribute. But they also hate to be played for a sucker so they are tempted to refrain from contributing until they know others have contributed, or at least until they know that non-contributors are being punished. If this view is correct, it suggests a need to modify traditional perceptions of group membership, participation, involvement, and cooperation—the central topics of this volume. The good news for those hoping to increase levels of cooperation is that wary cooperators do not need a reason to cooperate. As is the case with the typically successful tit-for-tat strategy (see Axelrod, 1984), people's first move is to cooperate. No social learning is necessary because cooperative behavior is genetically programmed into most people. The bad news is that cooperation is extremely easy to drive out. The "wary" part of wary cooperation refers to the fact that people are vigilant in their search for free riders and other misanthropes. It does not take many non-cooperators or insensitive decision makers for a wary cooperator to cease cooperating. The implications for those promoting greater participation and cooperation should be obvious. Simply badgering people to participate is likely to be unproductive. A more promising strategy would be to reduce suspicions that others in the group are uncaring non-cooperators and, especially, to make certain that those who are non-cooperators are being punished for their degenerate behavior.

One way to do this is to form groups in which all members want exactly the same thing. If this is the case, it is very difficult for individuals in the group to feel they have been played for a sucker. But as Madison pointed out, this is clearly a cure worse than the disease. Homogeneous (or bonding) groups (see Putnam, 2000) produce few of the benefits that lead people to advocate increased levels of cooperation and group membership in the first place (see Eliasoph, 1999). A better bet is to accept wary cooperation as a core component of the human condition and to work from there. Exhortations are not the key to promoting participation and coopera-tion; protections against being played for a sucker are. People do not free ride whenever they get a chance, but they do hate it when others free ride and they will themselves free ride if it appears as though others are seen doing so without penalty.

Most people are wary cooperators and wary cooperators are highly sensitive to the actions of those around them and to the manner in which they are perceived by those around them, especially those in positions of authority within the group. Whether someone's generosity has been taken advantage of by free riders or their voice has been ignored, the message is trouble. Either the person's standing as a desirable group member is in question or the temperament of others in the group is suspect. The typical response to such a realization will generally be disappointment and frustration and that is precisely the result we expect to find in the empirical study we present here. Current thinking about evolution and group life is per-fectly consistent with ongoing work on procedural justice and, in fact, provides that work with the theoretical basis it has to this point lacked. It allows us to specify the precise procedural conditions likely to be pleasing or displeasing to people, as we document in the empirical portion of our chapter.

The Politics of Voice

Numerous features of a just and pleasing decision-making procedure have been advanced. The one we wish to focus on here is voice: the belief that people's views of decisions and decision making will be positively affected by "the degree to which people are given an opportunity to make arguments (voice)" (Tyler, 2001, p. 237). The ability of voice to enhance perceptions of government and political legitimacy has long been of interest to democratic theorists. Indeed, along with improving policy decisions themselves and improving people, it ranks as one of the core jus-tifications for democratic government. Democratic theorists believe that people will be more accepting of authoritative decisions if they have been afforded the opportunity to provide input into those decisions (see, for example, Gutmann & Thompson, 1996, pp. 41–42).

In spite of the initial appeal of the voice-legitimacy connection, empirical evi-dence for it is limited. Tyler (1990) does indeed find that people who believed they had a voice were much more accepting of being found guilty in a legal proceeding, ceteris paribus, but there are two features to note about this result. First, it does not tap the extent to which people *had* voice, only the extent to which they *felt* they had voice. Sometimes in a decision-making process those who had voice are actually less likely to feel as though they had a say. Second, legal settings are somewhat atyp-ical and questions arise over the extent to which Tyler's finding is generalizable to more democratic decision-making settings such as that found in legislatures or in New England town meetings.

With regard to this second point, Tyler's own results suggest legislative settings could be much different from legal settings. In multivariate models designed to show the factors affecting people's attitudes toward Congress, the "degree to which respondents believed they were allowed to make arguments" about their policy desires had no effect on the extent to which they trusted Congress and was actually negatively and significantly related to their expressed likelihood of obeying Congressional decisions. That is, the more voice people believed they had, the *less* likely they were to comply with Congressional decisions (Tyler, 1994).

Moreover, systematic research on participants in town meetings finds evidence that voice opportunities often lead to negative feelings. Mansbridge's interviews with town meeting attendees reveal a strong element of dissatisfaction. Reflecting the pervasive perception that a group of dominant decision makers calls the shots at these meetings, one attendee claimed, "If you don't say what they want to hear you're not even acknowledged. I had to ask four times on a question about the budget, but they'd rather not talk about it" (Mansbridge, 1983, p. 69). Many people feel uncomfortable speaking in public—several reported being "petrified" or "scared to death"—so they remain quiet (1983, p. 64). This finding connects with a major theme of research on deliberative democracy: voice opportunities often disempower the timid, quiet, and uneducated relative to the loquacious, extroverted, and well-schooled. For example, open voice opportunities appear to reduce the power of women and the less educated (see Fraser, 1989, 1992; Hansen, 1997; Sanders, 1997). In short, demands to give the people more voice ignore the fact that many people do not want voice and feel uncomfortable or worse when it is granted to them. As Russell Hardin points out, "deliberative democracy is the democracy of elite intellectuals" (1999, p. 112).

One aspect of the voice situation likely to decrease legitimacy is the perceived self-interest of the decision maker. Cohen expects that if people believe a decision maker has a personal stake in the decision rendered (unlike the perception of most legal settings where the decision maker's—i.e., the judge's—remuneration is not affected by whether the verdict is guilty or innocent) the salubrious effects of voice will be replaced by "frustration effects" (1985). If you make a plea to a self-interested decision maker who then decides to pursue his own self-interest at your expense, you are quite likely to feel worse than you would have if you had not had the opportunity to express yourself (see also Folger, 1977). Lind and Tyler try to pass off this challenge to voice by claiming that it would be "a very rare phenomenon indeed" (1988, p. 183) but this is surely not the case. People routinely believe members of Congress, for example, ignore the interests of the people so that they can line their own pockets with special interest largess (Hibbing & Theiss-Morse, 1995; 2002). It seems more the case that people's default is to believe decision makers are self-interested. Claims that politicians' motives are not self-interested are typically met with incredulity. So Cohen's alleged frustration effects are sensible, though as yet they are empirically unverified.

We will test for the possibility that voice under some circumstances increases frustration and diminishes legitimacy. To conduct such a test, we need to hold outcome (and other factors) constant so that we can isolate the effects of voice on people's attitudes toward the decision-making arrangement. Clearly, an experimental design is needed.

Research Design

We based our experiments on a variant of an extremely simple monetary payoff game that is widely employed in experimental economics (see Nowak, Page, & Sigmund, 2000; Van Dijk & Vermunt 2000). This game is not much of a game at all in that only one player has a decision to make. In the standard form, one subject, the divider, is asked to allocate a small amount of money between herself and another subject, the receiver. The receiver has no decision to make because the divider alone has the authority to select the specific allocation. Not surprisingly, this game has generally been used by economists and psychologists to determine the amount of money dividers provide to receivers. The answer to this empirical question is that, even in single-play games with anonymous partners, experimental subjects are surprisingly generous. Equal allocations are the modal decision with the mean being an allocation of a little less than 40% of the pot to the receiver.

Whereas economists are more likely to be interested in the precise nature of the decision made by the divider, as students of mass political behavior we are more interested in the reaction of people to authoritative decisions made by others. After all, citizens in a representative democracy typically do not make authoritative decisions themselves; they leave this for public officials. But their reactions to these decisions, including approval, perceptions of legitimacy, and the existence of diffuse support, are of paramount importance to political scientists. Our concern, therefore, is with the receiver in this simple game. The receiver has no decision to make with regard to the money, but he or she will have measurable reactions to the decision maker and to the decision made, just as citizens do in a representative democracy.

Subjects for our experiments were drawn from the population of Lincoln, Nebraska, a medium-sized (250,000 people) Midwestern city. They were recruited via an advertisement in the local newspaper, posters placed in a variety of locations around the city, and a letter sent to staff people (explicitly excluding faculty or students) at the University of Nebraska as well as at a local community college. Subjects were guaranteed $5 with the possibility of earning up to $25 total for their participation in the experiment and were told that the purpose of the study was to analyze how people allocated money in a decision-making situation. A total of 194 subjects participated in the experiments, which took no longer than 20 minutes.[3] Subjects were randomly assigned to either the voice or no voice condition (explained below) and participated in one of four decision-making processes, though in this chapter we will only be dealing with three of these four. The first experiment constitutes our baseline in which a self-interested, appointed, unresponsive decision maker selects how much money to keep and how much to give to the subject. The next experiment varies the institutional context by making the decision maker neutral, which, as discussed above, may very well affect the legitimating potential of voice. The final experiment directly addresses the possibility that the key to improving people's attitudes is to make them feel efficacious and validated, not just to give them voice.

Experiment 1 Unresponsive self-interested decision maker

Prior to commencing the experiment, subjects were always kept apart from an experimental confederate who was posing as another subject. When the two were brought together, the experimenter asked them briefly to introduce themselves. The confederate always introduced himself in the same way. The experimenter then explained that one of the subjects would be selected to divide $20 between the two of them and that the identity of the divider would be determined by a random process. Although the subject was led to believe the selection was random, in reality the confederate was always chosen to be the divider and the subject was always the receiver.[4] Subjects were randomly assigned to one of two conditions: voice or no-voice. In the voice condition, the receiver was given the opportunity to say whatever he or she wanted to the divider to try to influence how he divided the money. In the no-voice condition, the receiver was not given this opportunity. The experimenter then asked the divider (the confederate) to go to a separate room and write on a piece of paper how much of the $20 he would keep for himself and how much he would give to the receiver. After a minute, the experimenter fetched the piece of paper from the confederate, which always said that the divider kept $17 for himself and gave $3 to the receiver (the subject). The experimenter showed the decision to the subject and explained that this meant the subject would get a total of $8—the guaranteed $5 plus the $3 given to him or her by the divider.

The subject was then taken to a private room and asked to complete a short questionnaire, which included questions on his or her perception of the process and the outcome as well as basic demographic questions. After filling out the questionnaire, subjects were told to hand the piece of paper with the divider's decision to a clerk in the next room. The clerk, who had many pieces of paper with different amounts written on them strewn on her desk, acted confused for a moment and then said, "OK, so you get your guaranteed $5 plus the $7 the divider gave you, which means you get $12." In other words, the clerk tried to give the subject more than the divider had actually decided to give. The clerk subsequently recorded who corrected her on the amount owed and who did not. All subjects, before leaving the clerk's room, were given the full $25 for participating in the experiment and were debriefed.

Experiment 2 Neutral decision maker

In Experiment 2, we varied the decision maker's motivation by employing a neutral as opposed to a self-interested decision maker; thus, this arrangement serves as a rough parallel to the judicial decision-making settings that have figured so prominently in work on procedural justice. Three subjects (one of whom was a confederate) were brought to the experiment room, asked briefly to introduce themselves, and told that one of them would be randomly chosen to divide $20 between the other two. The divider's allocation between the other two subjects would determine how much money they each received and the divider would be given a set fee for participating in the experiment regardless of his decision. As such, unlike Experiment 1, the divider had no financial stake in the allocation decision. Through a seemingly random but actually rigged process, the confederate was again always chosen to be the divider, leaving the two subjects to be the receivers.

In the voice condition, the receivers were then told, just as they had been in Experiment 1, that they would each have an opportunity to talk to the divider to try to influence the division of the money. One receiver was taken to a separate room while the other talked to the neutral divider. They then switched places and the second receiver had a chance to talk. The receivers therefore did not hear what the other receiver said to the divider. In the no voice condition, neither receiver was given a chance to speak to the divider. One of the receivers was, however, brought to a separate room so the receivers would not be together when they received the divider's decision. The divider was told he had no more than one minute to write his allocation decision on two pieces of paper, one for each receiver, and was taken to a separate room. The experimenter then collected the pieces of paper and delivered them to each of the receivers. Both receivers were led to believe that they had received only $3 whereas the other receiver had received $17. The experimenter then explained, as in the first experiment, that including the $5 guaranteed, the receiver would get a total of $8 for participating in the experiment. The rest of the experiment was exactly the same as Experiment 1.

Experiment 3 Responsive self-interested decision maker

The third experiment was designed to attach apparent clout to voice while still keeping the outcome constant with that present in Experiments 1 and 2. It is similar to Experiment 1 in that there were only two subjects, one the confederate. After the initial introductions, the supposedly randomly selected divider (the confederate) was told to write on a sheet of paper an initial allocation of the $20 between himself and the receiver and to keep the decision secret. In the voice condition, the divider and receiver were then told that the divider would have a chance to reconsider his decision and that the receiver could say whatever he or she wanted to try to influence the final decision. In the no-voice condition, the divider and receiver were simply told that the divider would now have a chance to reconsider his decision. Just as in the first experiment, the divider was then ushered into a separate room. During the one minute the divider had to make his final decision, the experimenter handed the original decision to the receiver, reiterating that this was not the final decision. This first allocation was always $19 for the divider and $1 for the receiver. The experimenter then fetched the final decision from the divider and showed it to the receiver. The final decision was always $17 for the divider and $3 for the receiver, the same outcome as in all of the other experiments. The rest of the experiment was exactly the same as Experiment 1.

Expected Results From the Experiments

If deliberative theorists are correct regarding the satisfaction people feel whenever they have voice, those cells (in all three experiments) in which subjects had the chance to express their views to the decision maker should always display improved attitudes and enhanced perceived legitimacy. If voice always has a frustration effect, subjects in those same cells should always display more negative attitudes and should perceive the decision maker and the decision-making process as less legitimate. If the particulars of the decision-making context matter, then the effects of voice should be variable across the three different experiments.[5] For example, voice may have positive effects only when decision makers are neutral, as in Experiment 2. But our own belief, which we defend later in this chapter, is that the legitimizing effects of voice depend most upon whether getting involved makes the subject feel validated or invalidated. Accordingly, we believe voice will improve attitudes and perceptions in Experiment 3, where subjects are given the impression they made a positive difference in the money they received even though the decision maker was self-interested, but a negative effect in Experiment 1 where subjects are led to believe their input to a self-interested decision maker was immaterial. As such, we expect to find the biggest differences not between the voice and no-voice groups but between members of the group for whom voice mattered and members of the group for whom voice was apparently irrelevant, even as the final outcomes were always the same.

The Actual Consequences of Voice

The three major dependent variables we address are the receiver's perception of the fairness of the decision maker, the receiver's satisfaction with the decision itself, and the receiver's willingness to comply with the decision. The first two of these are measured by items contained in the brief post-test survey the subjects completed before they received their money and were dismissed. The "fairness of the decision maker" item reads: "Do you think the divider was fair, unfair, or somewhere in between?" Response options range from 1 (unfair) to 7 (fair). The "satisfaction with outcome" item asks, "How satisfied are you with the money you received from the divider?" Available answers again range from 1 (very unsatisfied) to 7 (very satisfied). The measure of compliance is slightly more complicated but constitutes a real behavioral measure as opposed to a paper and pencil survey response. Recall that at the completion of the experiment an apparently confused clerk attempted to give the subject $12 instead of the $8 he or she had "earned." To measure compliance, we simply note whether or not the subject complied with the actual decision by correcting the clerk's error and taking only $8. No measurement of a concept as hoary as legitimacy can hope to be complete, but it seems safe to say that political legitimacy is higher when people view decision makers as fair, when they are satisfied with decisions, and when they are willing to comply with those decisions.

Our presentation of the results will follow the pattern of graphically comparing mean responses of the no-voice group and the voice group on these three measures for each experiment. We begin with Experiment 1 in which the decision maker was selected supposedly randomly to divide the money, keeping whatever share of the $20 was not allocated to the receiver (the experimental subject). As seven-point survey items, the "divider fairness" and "allocation satisfaction" lines in Figure 8.1 are keyed to the axis on the left, with higher scores being more favorable perceptions. The compliance measure, on the other hand, records the percentage of subjects complying with the decision maker's actual decision, so works off the axis on the right side of the figure. Not surprisingly, given that the subjects received an allocation of only $3, perceptions of divider fairness and satisfaction with the money received tended toward the bottom half of the seven-point scale. Willingness to correct the clerk's error, however, was quite high with nearly two-thirds of all subjects reminding the clerk of the true nature of the divider's decision.

But the end goal of these procedures is a comparison of tendencies under the voice and no-voice interventions and on this point the results are clear. When the decision maker is self-interested and subjects receive no indication their input mattered, all three dependent variables—fairness of the divider, satisfaction with the $3 allocation, and willingness to comply with the actual decision—register a lower mean when subjects had a voice compared to when they did not. The raw substantive differences are not overpowering but this is to be expected since the actual outcome is always the same (disappointing) and since the rest of the process was also standardized. That these differences should appear at all in a negative direction and for all three variables of interest is quite noteworthy. Two of the three differences in means achieve statistical significance even though the Ns in experimental work are unavoidably small (in this case, 24 in both the voice and the no-voice groups). When decision makers are self-interested (that is, when they can personally benefit from their decision), voice is a detriment to the legitimacy of the decision-making process.

Turning to the neutral decision maker experiment, recall that here the decision maker was given a set fee for dividing $20 between two other individuals. Since the decision maker in this experiment does not get to keep a portion of the $20 for himself, he cannot take advantage of the situation for his own ends and this scenario is therefore somewhat similar to the judicial setting analyzed by Tyler in the research that generated positive effects for voice. Does voice create legitimacy if the listener is neutral rather than self-interested? When neutral third parties are

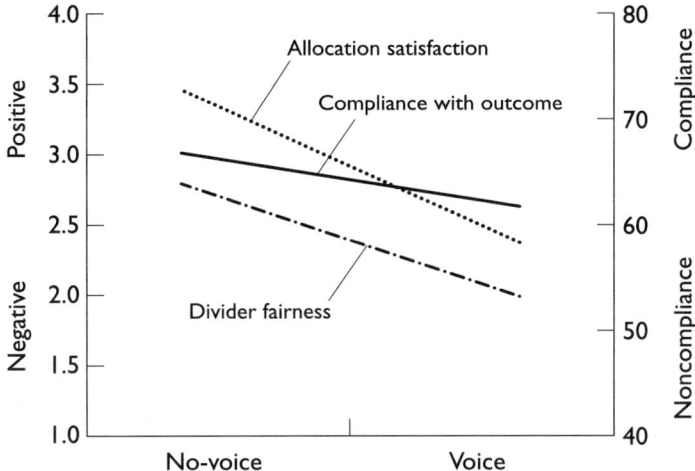

Figure 8.1 Voice lowers satisfaction and legitimacy when the decision maker is self-interested and non-responsive

Note: Divider fairness and Allocation satisfaction were coded so that 1 = unfair or dissatisfied and 7 = fair or satisfied. Compliance was coded as the percentage of people who complied with the decision maker's decision. N = 24 for both the voice and no-voice conditions. Using ANOVA, the significance levels of the differences between the no-voice and voice manipulations were as follows: Divider fairness p < .05, Allocation satisfaction p < .05, Compliance with outcome n.s.

making decisions, Figure 8.2 shows that perceived fairness of the decision maker and subject satisfaction with the $3 allocation are unaffected by voice. Compliance goes up a bit, but this relationship, like the others, does not come close to achieving statistical significance. All told, removing the decision maker's direct stake in the outcome of the decision does not permit voice to heighten legitimacy but does negate the frustration voice induces when the decision maker has a selfish reason to offer a paltry allocation.

The final decision-making process (Experiment 3) is similar to Experiment 1 except that subjects in the voice condition were given the impression that their voice had a role in convincing the decision maker to improve the allocation offered. The results are intriguing (see Figure 8.3). All three dependent variables—decision maker fairness, satisfaction with the $3, and compliance with the decision—are improved with voice. The improvement in satisfaction even reaches statistical significance and the other two do not miss by much in spite of the small numbers.

The central interpretation of these results is that satisfaction, perceived fairness, and compliance are determined neither by the favorability of the outcome (satisfaction varied markedly even though the outcome in all six cells was held constant at $3) nor the offering of input to decision makers (since voice produced

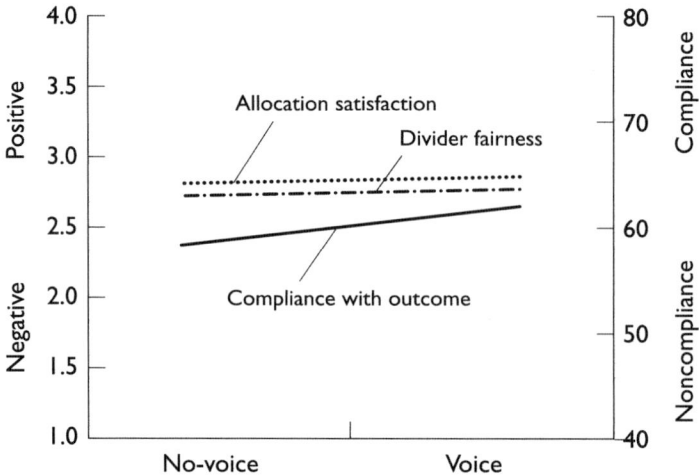

Figure 8.2 Voice is irrelevant when the decision maker is neutral (non-self-interested)

Note: Divider fairness and Allocation satisfaction were coded so that 1 = unfair or dissatisfied and 7 = fair or satisfied. Compliance was coded as the percentage of people who complied with the decision maker's decision. N = 24 for both the voice and no-voice conditions. Using ANOVA, the significance levels of the differences between the no-voice and voice manipulations were as follows: Divider fairness n.s., Allocation satisfaction n.s., Compliance with outcome n.s.

notably different responses depending upon the decision-making context). Rather, it seems people seek voice that matters. In fact, many times, especially when the stakes are not great (as is the case for most people in the political arena), outcome is important to people primarily for what they believe it says about them and their place in the social unit. Compared to no voice at all, voice is best seen as a feature of the process that increases the stakes. Voice with influence is beneficial. Voice without influence is not just neutral, it is deleterious. For voice to have a positive effect on legitimacy, then, people must have concrete evidence that their own voice made a difference in the outcome, but this is difficult in mass society. In large, heterogeneous, complex, democratic political systems, people seldom feel they have had a direct effect on improving outcomes, yet Experiment 3 clearly demonstrates that it is the validating effects of voice that matter.

The best way to illustrate this important point is to compare the post-experimental actions and responses of those subjects who had a voice that mattered (those in Experiment 3 who believed their intervention increased their allocation from $1 to $3) with the actions and responses of those subjects who probably felt their voice was ignored (those in Experiment 1 who talked to the allocator but still only received $3). This comparison is presented in Figure 8.4 and it shows the influence of the perceived responsiveness of the decision maker. Even though subjects

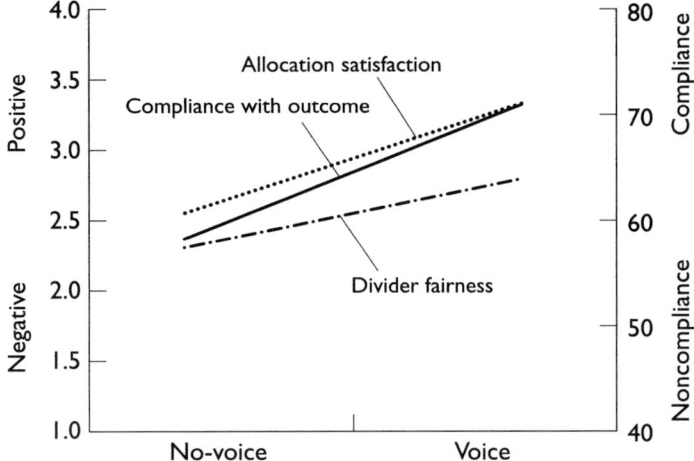

Figure 8.3 Voice increases satisfaction and legitimacy when the decision maker is self-interested and responsive

Note: Divider fairness and Allocation satisfaction were coded so that 1 = unfair or dissatisfied and 7 = fair or satisfied. Compliance was coded as the percentage of people who complied with the decision maker's decision. N = 24 for both the voice and no-voice conditions. Using ANOVA, the significance levels of the differences between the no-voice and voice manipulations were as follows: Divider fairness n.s., Allocation satisfaction p < .05, Compliance with outcome n.s.

in both groups ended up with just $3 of the $20, those who thought they talked the allocator up from $1 to $3 were nearly a full point (on a seven-point scale) higher for both perceived fairness of the decision maker and satisfaction with the amount received. Both of these relationships are statistically significant at the .05 level. Compliance with the outcome also goes up when subjects believe their voice mattered but this relationship is not significant.

Implications

Those who advocate additional cooperation and citizen involvement in society's decision-making contexts must become more sensitive to the differential effects of involvement by considering the message that involvement sends to participants regarding personal validation and group viability. While voice in conversational (non-decision-making) interpersonal settings may have generally positive effects (though even here voice carries a risk for the speaker) and while participatory theorists are correct about the potential for voice to increase legitimacy in decision-making arrangements, they have given short shrift to the real potential for

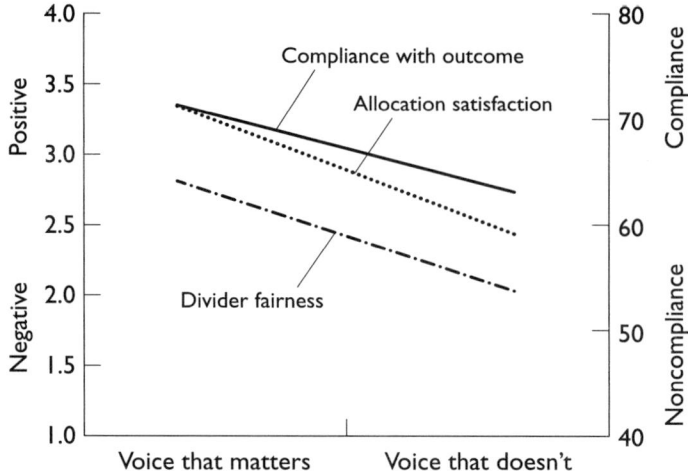

Figure 8.4 Comparing voice that matters to voice that doesn't matter

Note: Voice that matters refers to the results from Figure 8.3. Voice that doesn't matter refers to the results from Figure 8.1. For both the voice that matters and the voice that doesn't matter experiments, N = 24. Using ANOVA, the significance levels of the differences between voice that matters and voice that doesn't were as follows: Divider fairness $p < .05$; Allocation satisfaction $p < .05$; and Compliance with outcome n.s.

participation in certain contexts to damage a person's sense of self and sense of group.[6] Voice is not simply something that has more positive effects in some situations than in others. In the real world, voice sometimes has a negative effect on satisfaction, legitimacy, and compliance (see Figure 8.1). Voice is not a "no lose" proposition. And the dangers created by voice become more acute the more authority possessed by the individual to whom we are speaking, for decision makers are in positions to do greater and more rapid harm to group life and to the lives of individuals within the group. Our finding on the predictably varying consequences of voice could bring some order to the mixed, often disappointing, results generated by empirically oriented scholars working in the area. Mendelberg's (2002) conclusion, subsequent to a thorough review of the empirical literature, that "discussion sometimes meets the expectations of deliberative theorists . . . but attempts to deliberate can also backfire" remains dead on target and the theory and results presented here help to specify when voice will meet expectations and when it will make things worse.

This interpretation also fits with Tyler's attention to the motives of the decision maker. His work consistently finds that people's perceptions of the neutrality of decision makers, the trustworthiness of decision makers, the extent to which decision makers weighed pro and con arguments equally, the extent to which decision makers are concerned for others, and the general motives of decision makers, are crucial (2001). These results are exactly those that should obtain if people are at root concerned with being a valued part of a viable group. Voice is the one feature of the decision-making process that is misunderstood. People do not value voice in the same way they value decision makers who are not motivated by self-interest. Neutral, other-regarding decision makers are highly desirable in all circumstances. Voice is desirable only in particular circumstances, namely those in which it helps to convince the speaker that he or she is a valued part of the group and that the group itself is viable and not dominated by self-serving or callously uncooperative decision makers. Voice is not simply another feature of a just process.

Voice should not be seen as cooperation or as something everybody wants to do; rather, it should be recognized that voice entails risk—not in terms of potentially empowering the rabble-rousing masses to disturb societal order but in terms of raising the stakes for the individual doing the speaking. Voice creates a situation in which one's place in the group can be more clearly determined, and this raises the possibility that what is learned will not be favorable. For this and several other reasons, staying quiet is the preferred course of action for many people. Until political reformers more deeply appreciate and respect this situation, their well-intentioned prodding to expand participatory avenues at every turn will carry the potential for harm.

If the goal is for people to be happy, for cooperation to increase, and for entities designed for collective action, such as political institutions, to be perceived as legitimate, greater public involvement in the political arena should not be encouraged in the blanket fashion it often is. Rather, any enhanced involvement should be considered from the perspective of the message it is likely to communicate to the individual about his or her place in society. If heightened involvement decreases that person's sense of validity or harms perceptions of group viability, voice, participation, involvement, and cooperation will not be worth it.

Acknowledgment

This research was made possible by the financial support of the University of Nebraska Foundation Fund #1915. For their assistance in conducting the experiments described herein, the authors thank Scott Granberg-Rademacker, Elice Hubbert, Nathan Johnson, Chris Larimer, Nelson Okuku Miruka, and James T. Smith.

Notes

1 Compared to economists, psychologists, anthropologists, and even sociologists, political scientists have been less likely to adopt this strategy in their empirical work, but this may be changing. See Hibbing & Alford 2004; McDermott, 2004; Orbell, Morikawa, Hartwig, Hanley, & Allen, 2004.

2 See, for example, Boyd & Richerson, 1992; Cosmides & Tooby, 1992; Lind & Tyler, 1988: 236; Masters & Gruter, 1992; Masters, 1989; Monroe, 2002; Orbell, et al., 2004.; Putnam,

2000; Somit & Peterson, 1995; Thaler, 1992; Tooby & Cosmides, 1992; Trivers, 1971; Van Dijk & Vermunt, 2000.

3 The subjects were a demographically diverse group. The mean age was 36, with a range of 18 to 71. Males made up 43% of subjects, females 57%. Thirty percent of the subjects had a high school or technical school degree, 38% some college, and 32% a college degree. Income was broken down into three categories: under $20,000 (50%), $20,000 to $50,000 (39%), and over $50,000 (11%).

4 The two people who played the part of the divider in the experiments were very similar demographically (male, mid-20s, Midwestern) and were coached on how to respond in the experiment so they would behave in a consistent manner. The same confederate was always used for both the voice and no voice conditions within an experiment so variations cannot be attributable to divider characteristics.

5 Lind and Tyler (1988, p. 170) state that "one clear finding from research . . . is that people like to have an opportunity to present their views before policy decisions are made." Their reference to "opportunity" raises an interesting point. It may be that people like to know that the opportunity to participate is there even though they might be turned off when they do engage in actual participation. This is exactly the finding reported by Frey and Stutzer (2002) in their analysis of referenda in Switzerland. Individuals living in cantons with extensive opportunities for direct participation tend to be happier while no such relationship exists for individuals who actually participate in political decisions and in fact the sign is often negative. The *opportunity* to offer voice may increase satisfaction even as the act of providing voice in some circumstances decreases it.

6 Even the most forceful advocates of the ability of participation to enhance legitimacy have long recognized that not all speech situations will be "ideal" (Habermas, 1987) and that "actual deliberation is inevitably defective" (Gutmann & Thompson, 1996, p. 3), but rarely do they admit that the consequences of voice under some circumstances could be detrimental.

References

Axelrod, R. (1984). *The evolution of cooperation*. New York: Basic Books.

Boyd, R., & Richerson, P. J. (1992). Punishment allows the evolution of cooperation in sizable groups. *Ethology and Sociobiology, 13*, 171–195.

Buchanan, J. M., & Tullock, G. (1962). *The calculus of consent*. Ann Arbor: University of Michigan Press.

Cohen, R. L. (1985). Procedural justice and participation. *Human Relations, 38*, p. 643–663.

Cosmides, L., & Tooby, J. (1992). Cognitive adaptations for social exchange. In J. H. Barkow, L. Cosmides, & J. Tooby (Eds.), *The adapted mind* (pp. 163–228). New York: Oxford University Press.

Della Porta, D. (2000). Social capital, beliefs in government, and political corruption. In S. J. Pharr & R. D. Putnam (Eds.), *Disaffected democracies* (pp. 202–228). Princeton, NJ: Princeton University Press.

Delli Carpini, M. X., & Keeter, S. (1996). *What Americans know about politics and why it matters*. New Haven, CT: Yale University Press.

Eliasoph, N. (1999). *Avoiding politics*. Cambridge, UK: Cambridge University Press.

Folger, R. (1977). Distributive and procedural justice. *Journal of Personality and Social Psychology, 35*, 108–119.

Fraser, N. (1989). What's critical about critical theory? The cases of Habermas and gender. In N. Fraser (Ed.), *Unruly practices: Power, discourse, and gender in contemporary social theory* (pp. 113–143). Minneapolis: University of Minnesota Press.

Fraser, N. (1992). Rethinking the public sphere: A contribution to the critique of actually existing democracy. In C. Calhoun (Ed.), *Habermas and the public sphere* (pp. 109–142). Cambridge, MA: MIT Press.

Frey, B. S., & Stutzer, A. (2002). *Happiness and economics*. Princeton, NJ: Princeton University Press.

Gecas, V. (1982). The self-concept. *Annual Review of Sociology, 8,* 1–33.

Gutmann, A., & Thompson, D. (1996). *Democracy and disagreement*. Cambridge, MA: Harvard University Press.

Habermas, J. (1987). *A theory of communicative action*, Vol. II. Boston: Beacon Press.

Hansen, S. B. (1997). Talking about politics: Gender and contextual effects on political proselytizing. *Journal of Politics, 59,* 73–103.

Hardin, R. (1999). Deliberation: method, not theory. In S. Macedo (Ed.), *Deliberative politics: Essays on democracy and disagreement* (pp. 103–122). Oxford, UK: Oxford University Press.

Hibbing, J. R., & Alford, J. R. (2004). Accepting authoritative decisions: Humans as wary cooperators. *American Journal of Political Science, 48 (January),* 62–76.

Hibbing, J. R., & Theiss-Morse, E. (1995). *Congress as public enemy*. Cambridge, UK: Cambridge University Press.

Hibbing, J. R., & Theiss-Morse, E. (2002). *Stealth democracy*. Cambridge, UK: Cambridge University Press.

Kitzmann, K. M., & Emery, R. E. (1993). Procedural justice and parents' satisfaction in a field study of child custody dispute resolution. *Law and Human Behavior, 17,* 553–567.

Lawrence, R. Z. (1997). Is it really the economy, stupid? In J. S. Nye, P. D. Zelikow & D. C. King (Eds.), *Why people don't trust government* (pp. 111–132). Cambridge, MA: Harvard University Press.

Lind, E. A., Kulik, C. T, Ambrose, M., & Vera Park, M. (1993). Individual and corporate dispute resolution: Using procedural fairness as a decision heuristic. *Administrative Science Quarterly, 38,* 224–251.

Lind, E. A., & Tyler, T. R. (1988). *The social psychology of procedural justice*. New York: Plenum Press.

Mansbridge, J. J. (1983). *Beyond adversary democracy*. Chicago: University of Chicago Press.

Masters, R. D. (1989). *The nature of politics*. New Haven, CT: Yale University Press.

Masters, R. D., & Gruter, M. (1992). *The sense of justice*. Newbury Park, CA: Sage.

McDermott, R. (2004). The feeling of rationality: The meaning of neuroscientific advances for political science. *Perspectives on Politics, 2 (December),* 691–706.

Mendelberg, T. (2002). The deliberative citizen: Theory and evidence. In M. X. Delli Carpini, L. Huddy, & R. Y. Shapiro (Eds.), *Political decision making, deliberation and participation: research in micropolitics* (Vol. 6, pp. 151–193). Greenwich, CT: JAI Press.

Miller, A. H. (1974). Political issues and trust in government, 1964–70. *American Political Science Review, 68,* 951–972.

Miller, D. T. (2001). Disrespect and the experience of injustice. *Annual Review of Psychology, 52,* 527–553.

Monroe, K. R. (2002). Interdisciplinary work and a search for shared scientific standards. *PS: Political Science and Politics, 35,* 203–205.

Nowak, M. A., Page, K. M., & Sigmund, K. (2000). Fairness versus reason in the ultimatum game. *Science, 289,* 1773–1775.

Orbell, J., Morikawa, T., Hartwig, J., Hanley, J., & Allen, N. (2004). "Machiavellian" intelligence as a basis for the evolution of cooperative dispositions. *American Political Science Review, 98*(1), 1–16.

Pharr, S. J. (2000). Officials' misconduct and public distrust. In S. J. Pharr & R. D. Putnam (Eds.), *Disaffected democracies* (pp. 173–201). Princeton, NJ: Princeton University Press.

Popkin, S. L. (1991). *The reasoning voter.* Chicago: University of Chicago Press.

Putnam, R. D. (2000). *Bowling alone: The collapse and revival of American community.* New York: Simon and Schuster.

Sanders, L. M. (1997). Against deliberation. *Political Theory, 25,* 347–376.

Somit, A., & Peterson, S. A. (1995). *Research in biopolitics,* Vol. 3. Greenwich, CT: JAI Press.

Thaler, R. H. (1992). *The winner's curse.* New York: The Free Press.

Thibaut, J., & Walker, L. (1975). *Procedural justice: A psychological analysis.* Hillsdale, NJ: Lawrence Erlbaum.

Tooby, J., & Cosmides, L. (1992). The psychological foundations of culture. In J. H. Barkow, L. Cosmides, & J. Tooby (Eds.), *The adapted mind* (pp. 19–136). New York: Oxford University Press.

Trivers, R. L. (1971). The evolution of reciprocal altruism. *Quarterly Review of Biology, 46,* 35–57.

Tyler, T. R. (1990). *Why people obey the law.* New Haven, CT: Yale University Press.

Tyler, T. R. (1994). Psychological models of the justice motive: Antecedents of distributive and procedural justice. *Journal of Personality and Social Psychology, 67,* 850–863.

Tyler, T. R. (2001). The psychology of public dissatisfaction with government. In J. R. Hibbing & E. Theiss-Morse (Eds.), *What is it about government that Americans dislike?* (pp. 227–250). Cambridge, UK: Cambridge University Press.

Tyler, T. R., & Blader, S. (2000). *Cooperation in groups: Procedural justice, social identity, and behavioral engagement.* Philadelphia: Psychology Press.

Tyler, T. R., Rasinski, K., & Spodick, N. (1985). The influence of voice on satisfaction with leaders: Exploring the meaning of process control. *Journal of Personality and Social Psychology, 48,* 72–81.

Van Dijk, E., & Vermunt, R. (2000). Strategy and fairness in social decision making. *Journal of Experimental Social Psychology, 36,* 1–25.

9

Cooperation, Common Identity, and Intergroup Contact

JOHN F. DOVIDIO, SAMUEL L. GAERTNER, AND
VICTORIA M. ESSES

A fundamental paradox of human existence involves the importance of cooperation for survival, and the pervasiveness across time and across cultures of competition and conflict between groups. Nevertheless, these can also be recognized as complementary processes. Greater feelings of connection with others within one's own group produce greater bias toward other groups (Kessler & Mummendey, 2001); competition and conflict between groups reinforce cohesiveness and attraction within groups (Esses, Dovidio, Jackson, & Semenya, 2005). But this destructive cycle is not inevitable. In this chapter, we consider how the forces that create intergroup conflict can be redirected to enhance intergroup harmony and cooperation. First, we review the social and psychological processes that contribute to intergroup bias and conflict. Second, we propose a strategy, outlined in the Common Ingroup Identity Model, that redirects the processes that normally contribute to intergroup conflict to promote positive intergroup relations. Third, we discuss how the development of a common group identity while separate subgroup identities are also recognized can facilitate positive intergroup relations, encourage generosity and cooperation, and allow groups to benefit, without threat, from the unique qualities of the different groups.

Psychological and Social Foundations of Competition and Conflict

Group living, which requires cooperation of people identified as members of one's group, represents a fundamental survival strategy for humans. At the same time that individuals fundamentally depend upon cooperation with other members of their group for survival, they often perceive other groups and their members as a threat to their well-being. In a world of finite resources, people tend to perceive that their relations with other groups are competitive.

Competition between groups

Actual and perceived relations between groups are critical in determining inter-group attitudes. When groups are seen as in competition, positive outcomes for one group tend to be viewed as having negative consequences for the other group. This win–lose, zero-sum competitive relation between groups stimulates mutually neg-ative feelings toward and stereotypes of the members of the other group. Although competition often involves material resources (Sherif, Harvey, White, Hood, & Sherif, 1961), it can also be associated with the acquisition of intangible resources, such as prestige and group status (Blumer, 1958).

One reason why intergroup competition may be self-sustaining is that, as pro-posed by Social Dominance Theory, "complex human societies appear predisposed to organize themselves as group-based hierarchies" (Sidanius, Levin, & Pratto, 1998, p. 138). Social dominance theorists assume that hierarchical group organization served adaptive functions in human evolutionary history, and thus groups have a very basic motivational perspective to establish and maintain advantaged status in a hierarchy. Competition, bias, and individual and institutional discrimination help groups achieve and defend this advantaged position in a group hierarchy (Sidanius & Pratto, 1999). Thus categorization of people as members of one's own group or of other groups is a foundational process in determining cooperative or competitive orientations.

Categorization, Identity, and Intergroup Bias

In general, categorization enables people to make decisions quickly about incom-ing information. The instant an object is categorized, it is assigned the properties shared by other category members (Biernat & Dovidio, 2000). Moreover, social cat-egorization fundamentally involves a distinction between the group containing the self (the ingroup) and other groups (the outgroups)—between the "we's" and the "they's."

Social categorization and social identity

The essentially automatic process of distinguishing the group containing the self, the ingroup, from other groups, the outgroups, represents a foundational principle in some of the most prominent contemporary theories of intergroup behavior, such as Social Identity Theory (Tajfel & Turner, 1979) and Self-Categorization Theory (Turner, 1985; Turner, Hogg, Oakes, Reicher, & Wetherell, 1987).

In Social Identity Theory, Tajfel and Turner (1979) proposed that a person's need for positive self-identity can be satisfied by membership in prestigious social groups. This need motivates social comparisons that favorably differentiate ingroup from outgroup members. Although positive distinctiveness can be achieved by identifying dimensions by which the ingroup is already superior to the outgroup, needs for positive distinctiveness may also motivate actions (e.g., discrimination) that actively place the ingroup in a superior position. Although similar to Social Identity Theory, Self-Categorization Theory (Turner et al., 1987) puts greater emphasis on the cognitive processes involved in identification and on the continuum from personal to collective identity.

These theories of collective identity do not challenge the validity of instrumental theories of behavior, in which individual and group behavior are viewed as functional for obtaining resources and protecting self- and group-interest. Nevertheless, Social Identity Theory and Self-Categorization Theory emphasize how identification as a member of a social group is *sufficient* to shape how people respond to others and influence how people perceive themselves.

Social categorization and intergroup bias

Even when the basis for the categorization is quite trivial, such as when group membership is assigned randomly (Billig & Tajfel, 1973), the processes of social categorization and collective identity initiate a range of psychological processes that contribute to the development of intergroup bias and competition.

Perceptually, when people or objects are categorized into groups, actual differences between members of the same category tend to be minimized (Tajfel, 1969) and often ignored in making decisions or forming impressions. In addition, although members of a social category may be different in some ways from members of other categories, these differences tend to become exaggerated and overgeneralized. Thus, categorization enhances perceptions of similarities within groups and differences between groups—emphasizing social difference and group distinctiveness. Emotionally, people spontaneously experience more positive affect toward other members of the ingroup than toward members of the outgroup (Otten & Moskowitz, 2000). Cognitively, people retain more information in a more detailed fashion for ingroup members than for outgroup members (Park & Rothbart, 1982) and remember less positive information about outgroup members (Howard & Rothbart, 1980). And behaviorally, they work harder for groups identified as ingroups (Worchel, Rothgerber, Day, Hart, & Butemeyer, 1998).

Taken together, the arousal of ingroup favoritism and often outgroup derogation that accompanies the mere categorization of people as members of the ingroup or of outgroups (Tajfel & Turner, 1979), the motivation for humans to achieve advantaged status for their group (Sidanius & Pratto, 1999), and realistic threats and competition for scarce resources promote conflict between groups. As a consequence of both greater fear and greater greed between groups than between individuals, intergroup relations tend to be less positive and less cooperative than interpersonal relations. Insko, Schopler, and their colleagues have demonstrated a fundamental *individual–group discontinuity effect* in which groups are more greedy and less trustworthy than individuals (Insko et al., 2001). Thus, relations between groups tend to be more competitive and less cooperative than those between individuals.

Improving Intergroup Relations: The Common Ingroup Identity Model

Because identification with social groups is a basic process that is fundamental to intergroup bias, social psychologists have targeted this process as a starting point for improving intergroup relations (Brown & Hewstone, 2005; Miller, 2002). The approach we have employed, the Common Ingroup Identity Model (Gaertner & Dovidio, 2000), draws on the theoretical foundations of Social Identity Theory (Tajfel & Turner, 1979) and Self-Categorization Theory (Turner et al., 1987). This strategy emphasizes the process of recategorization, whereby members of different groups are induced to conceive of themselves as a single, more inclusive super-ordinate group rather than as two completely separate groups. As a consequence, attitudes toward former outgroup members become more positive through processes involving pro-ingroup bias.

Considerable empirical research, including studies in various cultures (e.g., Rebelo, Guerra, & Monteiro, 2004), provides support for the Common Ingroup Identity Model. Evidence for the model has been obtained in laboratory and field experiments involving temporary and enduring groups, as well as in cross-sectional and longitudinal field studies (see Gaertner & Dovidio, 2000). Moreover, the Common Ingroup Model has been applied to an integrative theoretical framework to explain how intergroup contact, along the lines outlined in the Contact Hypothesis (Allport, 1954), operates psychologically to reduce bias and improve intergroup relations.

Contact and Common Group Identity

Over the past half-century, Allport's (1954) revised Contact Hypothesis has been a guiding framework for strategies designed to reduce intergroup bias and conflict. This hypothesis proposes that simple contact between groups is not sufficient to improve intergroup relations. Contact must involve certain characteristics—equal status between the groups, cooperative (rather than competitive) intergroup inter-action, opportunities for personal acquaintance between the members, and norms supportive of equality—to reduce bias and conflict effectively. Although it is diffi-cult to establish all of these conditions in contact situations, this formula is effective when these conditions are met (Pettigrew & Tropp, 2006).

Structurally, however, the Contact Hypothesis has represented a list of loosely connected, diverse conditions rather than a unifying conceptual framework that explains how these prerequisite features achieve their effects. The Common

Ingroup Identity Model (Gaertner & Dovidio, 2000), however, suggests that representations of the groups are key mechanisms. Specifically, the model proposes that the development of a common group identity can be a common mediating factor for the effect of the conditions identified by Allport (1954) as necessary for contact to reduce intergroup bias.

A series of studies involving a range of different groups (racial groups and blended families) and contexts (e.g., schools and businesses) offer converging support for the hypothesis that the features specified by the Contact Hypothesis reduce intergroup bias, in part, because they transform members' representations of the memberships from separate groups to one more inclusive group (see Gaertner & Dovidio, 2000).

The work of Sherif et al. (1961) in the Robbers' Cave study implicated one particular element of intergroup contact, cooperation between groups to achieve a superordinate goal, as a particularly important factor. After competition between two groups of boys at a summer camp aroused intergroup conflict and hostility, which could not be allayed by mere contact, Sherif et al. presented the campers with a series of tasks that required both groups to cooperate to achieve. Consistent with the functional relations perspective, changing the nature of interdependence between members of different groups from perceived competition to cooperation significantly improves intergroup attitudes across a range of contexts. The success of cooperative learning techniques (Cooper & Slavin, 2004; see also Johnson & Johnson, 2000) and the jigsaw classroom intervention, in which students are interdependent on one another in problem-solving exercises (Aronson & Patnoe, 1997), implicate the importance of intergroup cooperation for improving intergroup relations.

We obtained direct evidence of the role of intergroup cooperation and its causal effects on group representations in reducing bias in a controlled experiment. Specifically, we brought two three-person laboratory groups together under conditions designed to vary independently (a) the members' representations of the aggregate as one group or two groups through manipulation of the contact situation and (b) the presence or absence of intergroup cooperative interaction (Gaertner, Mann, Dovidio, Murrell, & Pomare, 1990). The interventions designed to emphasize common group membership through structural changes in the contact situation (e.g., integrated vs. segregated seating; a new group name for all six participants vs. the original group names) and to encourage cooperative interaction (joint evaluation and reward vs. independent outcomes) both reduced intergroup bias. Moreover, they did so through the same mechanism. Contextual features emphasizing common "groupness" and joint outcomes each increased one-group representations (and reduced separate-group representations), which in turn related to more favorable attitudes toward original outgroup members and lower levels of bias. Consistent with the Common Ingroup Identity Model, one-group representations *mediated* the relationship between the interventions and the reduction of bias.

In general, then, there is convergent evidence across a range of paradigms and types of intergroup relations that one way that intergroup contact reduces bias is by creating or emphasizing a common ingroup identity. Research also shows that a common ingroup identity can promote positive intergroup behaviors that have consequence for individual and collective well-being, such as cooperation and prosocial behavior.

Common Identity and Cooperative Outcomes

Creating a common ingroup identity facilitates a variety of prosocially oriented behaviors besides more favorable attitudes, such as cooperative and socially responsible behavior in a commons dilemma. Commons dilemmas are situations in which it is in participants' short-term interests to compete and exploit the resources available while it is in the long-term collective interest for all participants to cooperate to conserve scarce resources. Kramer and Brewer (1984) led participants to focus either on their different group identity relative to others in the game (i.e., they were college students whereas other participants were not) or on a superordinate identity (i.e., participants were all residents of the same city). When resources became scarce, participants whose superordinate identity was emphasized conserved resources better than did those who saw themselves as members of different groups (see also De Cremer & van Vugt, 1998).

In work paralleling research on the Common Ingroup Identity Model, Wit and Kerr (2002) examined the choices people made in a commons dilemma when the experimenter emphasized that the person would be participating (a) as one of a group of six people in the session, (b) as a member of one of two different three-person groups in the same session, or (c) as one of six individuals performing the task. Later in the study, participants had the opportunity to allocate points, which could be redeemed for money, to their personal (individual) account, to an account for the three people in their group in the two subgroups condition, or to the collective account for all six people in the session. Participants allocated the most resources to the six-person collective account (a cooperative action) when the situation was framed so that players believed they shared one collective identity; they allocated the fewest resources to the six-person collective account when the subgroup social identity was salient and intergroup conflict was emphasized. Thus, collective identity instigated greater levels of cooperation and self-sacrifice for the collective good than did salient individual or subgroup identities.

We have also found evidence that developing a common ingroup identity can create a climate of trust that facilitates the exchange of personal, self-disclosing information and promotes helping members of other groups (Dovidio et al., 1997). Members of two different three-person laboratory groups (identified as overestimators and underestimators) were brought together under conditions that promoted a common group identity (e.g., integrated seating) or reinforced the different group memberships (e.g., segregated seating). To investigate self-disclosure, two pairs of participants were brought to separate cubicles. One dyad was composed of members from the two different original subgroups; the other was composed of two members from the same original subgroup. Dyad members were asked to discuss the topic, "What are you most afraid of?" These conversations were audio-recorded and subsequently coded for level of intimacy. To examine helping, the remaining two participants were escorted to separate rooms and informed that they had been chosen for the one-way communication condition and that they would be listening to a videotape of one of the previous participants in the study. One participant was informed that the person on the videotape was a member of his or her original subgroup category (e.g., an overestimator), whereas the other partici-pant was told that the other person was from the opposite group. The person on the audiotape explained that she was unable to complete an important project because of illness. At the conclusion of the session, each participant who heard the tape was given an opportunity to help by placing posters in various locations across campus.

Consistent with the Common Ingroup Identity Model, the One Group manipu-lation produced more inclusive, one-group representations than did the Two Group manipulation, as well as more positive outgroup evaluations and lower levels of bias. Furthermore this manipulation had the predicted effect on self-disclosure and helping. In the One Group condition, dyads composed of members of initially dif-ferent groups exhibited a level of intimacy in self-disclosure that was equivalent to that of dyads composed of members of the same original group, and significantly greater than that observed in the Two Groups condition. The pattern of results for intergroup helping paralleled those for self-disclosure. Moreover, the reductions in bias in self-disclosure and helping were mediated by more inclusive, one-group representations.

In summary, the findings related to the Common Ingroup Identity Model reveal that one fundamental way that intergroup contact operates to reduce bias and con-flict is by transforming people's representations from different groups ("us" and "them") to an inclusive, common identity ("we"). Cooperation is a particularly important element in this process. Inducing cooperative interdependence between members of different groups creates a common identity, which in turn mediates lower levels of bias (Gaertner et al., 1990). Creating a common group identity also facilitates more cooperation, more helpful behavior between members of originally different groups, and the exchange of more self-disclosing information (Dovidio et al., 1997; Wit & Kerr, 2002), as well as creating more generally a climate of for-giveness and trust (Wohl & Branscombe, 2005). These behaviors are particularly critical for sustaining positive intergroup relations because they all generate high levels of reciprocity, which can alter the trajectory for intergroup relations from spiraling conflict to sustained harmony.

Despite the evidence for the effectiveness of achieving a common group identity for improving intergroup relations, there may be limits to its effectiveness because of the difficulty in maintaining a common identity in the face of powerful social forces within naturalistic settings that emphasize group differences and reinforce separate group memberships. Hewstone (1996) has argued that, at a practical level, interventions designed to create a common, inclusive identity (such as equal status contact) may not be sufficiently potent to "overcome powerful ethnic and racial categorizations on more than a temporary basis" (p. 351). In addition, to the extent that identities associated with the original groups are important, it would be undesirable or impossible for people to relinquish this aspect of their self-concept completely. Indeed, demands to abandon these group identities would likely arouse strong reactance and exacerbate conflict. It is therefore important for practical as well as theoretical reasons to consider more complex forms of social identity in which more than one identity is salient at a time.

Within the context of the Common Ingroup Identity Model, the development of a common ingroup identity need not require each group to forsake its less inclusive group identity. In particular, the most recent developments in our work on the Common Ingroup Identity Model have focused on a second form of recategorization, the impact of a *dual identity* in which the superordinate identity is salient but in conjunction with a salient subgroup identity (a "different groups working together on the same team" representation). In this respect, the Common Ingroup Identity Model is aligned with bidimensional models of acculturation, in which cultural heritage and mainstream identities are relatively independent (Berry, 1997), not with unidimensional models, which posit that cultural identity is necessarily relinquished with adoption of mainstream cultural identity. We consider this development in the Common Ingroup Identity Model in the next section.

Dual Identity: Recognizing Difference and Similarity

Because individuals frequently belong to several groups simultaneously and possess multiple potential identities, it is possible to activate or introduce a shared identity even while separate group identities are salient. Within the Common Ingroup Identity Model, the dual identity approach is a particular form of crossed categorization (Brewer, 2000) in which the original group boundaries are maintained but within a salient superordinate group identity that represents a higher level of inclusiveness. Establishing a common superordinate identity while maintaining the salience of subgroup identities may be effective in reducing bias because it permits the benefits of a common ingroup identity to operate without arousing countervailing motivations to achieve positive intergroup distinctiveness. Moreover, this type of recategorization may be particularly effective when people have strong allegiances to their original groups. In this respect, the benefits of a dual identity may be especially relevant to interracial and interethnic group contexts.

Berry (1997) offered a framework to help understand the different types of consciousness and identity processes that immigrant groups can experience within the dominant culture of the host society. Specifically, Berry (1997) described four forms of cultural relations in pluralistic societies that represent the intersection of "yes–no" responses to two fundamental questions: (a) Are the original cultural identity and customs of value to be retained? and (b) Are positive relations with the larger society of value, and to be sought? These combinations reflect four adaptation strategies, identified by Berry, for intergroup relations: (a) integration, when cultural identities are retained and positive relations with the larger society are sought; (b) separatism, when original cultural identities are retained but positive relations with the larger society are not sought; (c) assimilation, when cultural identities are abandoned and positive relations with the larger society are desired; and (d) marginalization, when cultural identities are abandoned and are not replaced by positive identification with the larger society.

Although this framework was originally applied to the ways in which immigrants acclimate to a new society, we have adapted it to apply to intergroup relations between majority and minority groups more generally (see Dovidio, Gaertner, & Kafati, 2000). Substituting the separate strengths of the subgroup and subordinate group identities for the answers to Berry's (1997) two questions, the combinations map onto the four main representations considered in the Common Ingroup Identity Model: (a) dual identity (subgroup and superordinate group identities are high, such as feeling like different groups on the same team: which relates to Berry's adaptation strategy of integration); (b) different groups (subgroup identity is high and superordinate identity is low: separatism); (c) one group (subgroup identity is low and superordinate group identity is high: assimilation); and (d) separate individuals (subgroup and superordinate group identities are low relative to individual identity: which relates to Berry's adaptation strategy of marginalization). Within our conceptualization, the processes involved in the formation of a dual identity or one group identity represent recategorization, an emphasis on different group memberships reflects separatism, and perceptions of others as separate individuals rather than as group members represents decategorization. There is evidence that intergroup benefits of a strong superordinate identity can be achieved for both minority and majority group members when the strength of the subordinate identity is similarly high.

Consistent with our hypothesis that a dual identity represents a form of recategorization that can facilitate positive intergroup relations for minority group members, Huo, Smith, Tyler, and Lind (1996) found that even when racial or ethnic identity was strong for minority group members, perceptions of a superordinate connection enhanced interracial trust and acceptance of authority within an organization. Huo et al. (1996) concluded that having a strong identification with a superordinate group can redirect people from focusing on their personal outcomes to concerns about "achieving the greater good and maintaining social stability" (pp. 44–45), while also maintaining important racial and ethnic identities. We found converging evidence in a study of students in a multiethnic high school (Gaertner, Rust, Dovidio, Bachman, & Anastasio, 1996). Students who described themselves as *both* American and as a member of their racial or ethnic group showed less bias toward other groups in the school than did those who described themselves only in terms of their subgroup identity. Thus, even when subgroup identity is salient, the simultaneous salience of a common ingroup identity is associated with more positive orientations and lower levels of intergroup bias among minority group members.

As we noted earlier in our discussion of Social Dominance Theory (Sidanius & Pratto, 1999), groups that enjoy advantaged status in group hierarchies (i.e., majority groups) often resist the progress of minority groups because they perceive resources as zero-sum. The advancement of minority groups is thus perceived as a threat to majority group position. Nevertheless, recognition of a superordinate identity involving both the majority group and minority groups may facilitate majority group members' support for actions or policies that will benefit minority groups.

For instance, in a survey study of white adults, Smith and Tyler (1996) measured the strength of respondents' superordinate identity as "American" and also the strength of their identification as "white." Regardless of whether they strongly identified with being white, those respondents with a strong American identity were more likely to base their support for affirmative action policies that would benefit blacks and other minorities on relational concerns regarding the fairness of Congressional representatives than on whether these policies would increase or decrease their own well-being. However, for those who identified themselves more strongly with being white than with being American, their position on affirmative action was determined more strongly by concerns regarding the instrumental value of these policies for themselves. This pattern of findings suggests that a strong superordinate identity (such as being American) allows individuals to support policies that would benefit members of other racial subgroups without giving primary consideration to their own instrumental needs.

Indeed, creating or emphasizing a common identity between majority and minority groups may be a particularly effective way of increasing cooperation and support for minority groups among majority group members for whom group hierarchies are most important, people relatively high in the individual difference dimension of Social Dominance Orientation (Sidanius & Pratto, 1999). People high in Social Dominance Orientation believe that unequal social outcomes and social hierarchies are appropriate and therefore support an unequal distribution of resources among groups, in ways that usually benefit their own group. Individuals low in Social Dominance Orientation, in contrast, are generally concerned about others' welfare, empathic, and tolerant of other individuals and groups.

In a study of citizens of the United States and Canada, Esses, Dovidio, Jackson, and Armstrong (2001) investigated ways of increasing support for immigration in a series of experiments. In one experiment, compared to a control condition, persuasive messages that emphasized the benefits of immigrants produced more favorable attitudes toward immigration among people low in Social Dominance Orientation but *less* favorable attitudes among people high in Social Dominance Orientation who tend to see group relations in zero-sum terms. However, in a subsequent study in which the pro-immigrant message reminded participants of their common immigrant roots or emphasized the common national interest of citizens and immigrants, people high as well as those low in Social Dominance Orientation showed greater support for immigration. Thus, only when immigrants were incorporated as part of the ingroup did people high in Social Dominance Orientation exhibit support for them.

Emphasizing a common ingroup identity while maintaining recognition of different subgroup memberships also offers potential benefits for promoting intergroup harmony and cooperation beyond attempting to create a common ingroup identity through complete recategorization. First, as noted earlier, interventions designed to replace valued subgroup identities with a new superordinate identity can arouse identity threat, which can exacerbate rather than reduce bias (Brown & Hewstone, 2005; Hornsey & Hogg, 2000). Second, even when a common ingroup identity is successfully established entirely in place of subgroup identities, the benefits may be more limited than when subgroup identities are simultaneously maintained. Creating a common ingroup identity by itself enhances cooperation among those identified as members of the group, that is, *intragroup* cooperation (Dovidio et al., 1997; Wit & Kerr, 2002). In contrast, establishing a sense of dual identity promotes both *intragroup* and *intergroup* cooperation. As hypothesized by Social Identity Theory (Tajfel & Turner, 1979) and Self-Categorization Theory (Turner et al., 1987), members within each subgroup, who share identity on two dimensions (both subgroup and superordinate identities), will tend to be positively and cooperatively oriented toward each other. When a common superordinate identity is salient, these orientations will also extend across subgroup boundaries. Furthermore, generating a common connection between the subgroups with a common superordinate identity can encourage intergroup cooperation between the subgroups as they recognize and appreciate the novel contributions of each (see Brown & Hewstone, 2005). Thus, whereas complete recategorization within a superordinate group can promote intragroup cooperation often at the expense of stimulating competitive orientations toward members of other groups (Kessler & Mummendey, 2001), a dual identity can facilitate cooperation within and between groups (at least between the subgroups), which can operate in compatible and coordinated ways.

In this respect, the Common Ingroup Identity Model suggests that is possible to frame relations between groups, which are typically seen as zero-sum (Sidanius & Pratto, 1999), as mutually cooperative and beneficial. Group identity and its associated biases are often aroused to relieve personal or collective uncertainty (Grieve & Hogg, 1999) and to establish the group's positive distinctiveness (Tajfel & Turner, 1979). Within a common superordinate identity, subgroups may demonstrate their unique qualities, which may be superior to the other subgroup on some dimensions (but not others), in a relationship of positive interdependence. That is, the valued identity and qualities of subgroup identity can be reaffirmed in a context in which the different talents and resources of the subgroups are acknowledged but seen as complementary rather than competitive.

Recognition of the unique contributions of members of different groups can have further instrumental and social benefits, which can continue to enhance intragroup and intergroup cooperation. Instrumentally, seeing the talents of members of other groups as supportive rather than threatening is particularly valuable for benefiting from diversity in cooperation to solve complex problems requiring novel solutions. Antonio et al. (2004), for example, demonstrated that problem-solving groups showed greater differentiation and integration of multiple perspectives and dimensions when they included both black and white collaborators than when they were composed only of whites. Moreover, people are more likely to adopt the promising novel ideas of others when they share a superordinate identity with them than when they do not. For instance, Kane, Argote, and Levine (2005) rotated members across three-person work groups. For some groups, the rotator shared a superordinate identity with members of the group; for other groups the rotator did not. Kane et al. found that groups that did not share a superordinate identity with the rotator tended to dismiss the rotator's ideas even when the suggestions were superior to their own current ideas. In contrast, these superior ideas were readily adopted when the rotator shared a superordinate identity with the group members. Recognition and willingness to accept novel ideas can be a critical element of group success, which can have substantial impact on orientations toward others. Successful cooperation between members of different groups is particularly effective for promoting intergroup trust, reducing intergroup bias, and reinforcing future positive and cooperative relations.

In addition, socially, the benefits of positive contact and cooperation are more likely to generalize to other members of the subgroup who are not directly involved in the interaction when there are dual identities than when there is a single common group identity. When members are recategorized solely in terms of a superordinate identity, the associative links to other members of the subgroups are weakened. As a consequence, developing positive attitudes toward members of the other subgroup present will not necessarily extend to subgroup members not directly involved in the interaction (see Rothbart, 1996). In contrast, when members of the other subgroup are seen in the context of a dual identity, in which their qualities are valued, positive attitudes are likely to generalize to other subgroup members beyond the immediate contact situation.

Nevertheless, our recent review of the effects of the different types of recategorization revealed that, in contrast to the consistent finding that the strength of one-group identity relates to lower levels of intergroup bias, a dual identity can relate to either higher or lower levels of intergroup bias depending on the context (Gaertner, Riek, Mania, & Dovidio, 2007). We hypothesize that a critical factor moderating the impact of a dual identity is whether the components (subgroup and superordinate group identity) in combination signal inclusion or exclusion (Dovidio, Gaertner, Pearson, & Riek, 2005). For instance, when people are anticipating negative relations between groups, the salient common group component can indicate movement toward inclusion and intergroup integration; when people expect favorable relations between groups, the salient subgroup component can represent exclusion and discordance between groups. Consistent with this reasoning, in an experiment in which we varied whether groups were competitively or cooperatively interdependent (Gaertner et al., 2007), we found that when the groups were competing for influence the strength of the dual identity predicted lower levels of bias ($r = -.34$); when the groups were cooperating the strength of the dual identity predicted greater bias ($r = +.34$). Thus, a dual identity has some potential advantages over recategorization in the form of a one-group identity, but its effects are much more variable and it needs to be considered carefully in context.

Conclusion

In this chapter, we reviewed the factors that can contribute to intergroup bias, competition, and conflict and then described processes that can instead promote intergroup harmony and cooperation. Understanding the role of cooperation in intergroup relations is critical in these processes. For example, cooperation can help create a common ingroup identity. Once established, a sense of common identity can redirect the forces associated with social categorization to promote more positive intergroup attitudes and elicit positive intergroup relations that are reinforcing and potentially self-sustaining. Moreover, because this process, which is described in the Common Ingroup Identity Model, engages basic psychological processes, it can reduce bias even among younger children whose limited cognitive and social development might limit the effectiveness of knowledge-based or empathy-oriented approaches (Houlette et al., 2004).

In addition, the recognition of common identity while acknowledging one's own and others' subgroup identities allows groups to capitalize on the novel ideas and the various perspectives of members of different groups to enhance their effectiveness in achieving success in superordinate goals. These processes are important for realizing the potential benefits of diversity by encouraging the full participation of minority group members and leading majority group members to relinquish some of their advantages to pursue collective goals in which minority and majority group members benefit as one. Successful outcomes in these circumstances, in turn, facilitate intergroup trust, which increases the likelihood of cooperation in the future.

Thus, cooperation is central to the politics of intergroup relations for achieving justice and equity in a world in which resources are limited, in which these resources are distributed unequally among groups, and in which groups high in resources maintain their superior position through cultural mechanisms (e.g., legitimizing ideologies), institutional policies, and individual discrimination (Sidanius & Pratto, 1999). Majority group members are more likely to support policies (such as affirmative action) that benefit minorities directly but may be perceived to have costs for their subgroup (e.g., whites) when they recognize shared identity (e.g., as Americans) with the beneficiaries of these policies (Smith & Tyler, 1996). In addition, majority group members may be more likely to accept policies and practices that recognize group differences (such as bilingual education) when they perceive the connection between the subgroup and superordinate group identities as more complementary (Houvouras, 2001).

Improving intergroup relations involves the orientations and behaviors of minority groups, as well as majority groups. Developing a common identity helps in this aspect of the relations, too. Minority group members who identify more strongly with a superordinate identity will be more accepting of policies that are developed through fair procedures, even if the outcomes provide them fewer immediate benefits (Huo et al., 1996; Sunshine & Tyler, 2003). Also, minority group members will place more emphasis on learning the language of the majority group and become more actively interested in integration the more they identify with the superordinate group.

Taken together, these findings demonstrate that cooperation between groups can help create a sense of common group identity initially, which can then form a foundation for generating policies that are perceived to be fair and that effectively improve the status and well-being of disadvantaged groups. As Kelman (1999) noted in his analysis of Israeli–Palestinian conflict, "a long-term resolution of the conflict requires development of a transcendent identity for the 2 peoples that does not threaten the particularistic identity of each" (p. 581). To accomplish this, he proposes, it is essential first to reframe the longstanding negative interdependence between these groups in terms of "most notably the positive interdependence between the two groups that exists in reality" (p. 581; see also Bar-Tal, 2004). Cooperation is therefore a valuable prerequisite to the types of actions, formal and informal, that can lead to the reduction of intergroup conflict and progress toward fair and just intergroup relations.

In conclusion, although intergroup relations may be fragile in a world of historical conflict, separate identities and group allegiances, and scarce resources, intergroup conflict and competition are far from inevitable. Competition may breed more competition and conflict, but cooperation can contribute to shared identities that can promote even more effective cooperation in the future.

References

Allport, G. W. (1954). *The nature of prejudice*. New York: Addison-Wesley.

Antonio, A. L., Chang, M. J., Hakuta, K., Kenny, D. A., Levin, S., & Milem, J. F. (2004). Effects of racial diversity on complex thinking in college students. *Psychological Science*, *15*, 507–510.

Aronson, E., & Patnoe, S. (1997). *The jigsaw classroom*. New York: Longman.

Bar-Tal, D. (2004). Nature, rationale, and effectiveness of education for coexistence. *Journal of Social Issues*, *60*, 253–271.

Berry, J. W. (1997). Immigration, acculturation, and adaptation. *Applied Psychology: An International Review, 46*, 5–34.

Biernat, M., & Dovidio, J. F. (2000). Stigma and stereotypes. In T. F. Heatherton, R. E. Kleck, M. R. Hebl, & J. G. Hull (Eds.), *The social psychology of stigma* (pp. 88–125). New York: Guilford Press

Billig, M. G., & Tajfel, H. (1973). Social categorisation and similarity in intergroup behavior. *European Journal of Social Psychology, 3*, 27–52.

Blumer, H. (1958). Race prejudice as a sense of group position. *Pacific Sociological Review, 1*, 3–7.

Brewer, M. B. (2000). Reducing prejudice through cross-categorization: Effects of multiple social identities. In S. Oskamp (Ed.), *Reducing prejudice and discrimination: The Claremont Symposium on Applied Social Psychology* (pp. 165–183). Mahwah, NJ: Lawrence Erlbaum.

Brown, R., & Hewstone, M. (2005). An integrative theory of intergroup contact. In M. P. Zanna (Ed.), *Advances in experimental social psychology* (Vol. 37, pp. 255–343). San Diego: Academic Press.

Cooper, R., & Slavin, R. E. (2004). Cooperative learning: An instructional strategy to improve intergroup relations. In W. G. Stephan & W. Paul Vogt (Eds.), *Education programs for improving intergroup relations: Theory, research, and practice* (pp. 55–70). New York: Teacher's College Press.

De Cremer, D., & van Vugt, M. (1998). Collective identity and cooperation in a public goods dilemma: A matter of trust or self-efficacy? *Current Research in Social Psychology, 3*, 1–11.

Dovidio, J. F, Gaertner, S. L., & Kafati, G. (2000). Group identity and intergroup relations: The Common In-Group Identity Model. In S. R. Thye, E. J. Lawler, M. W. Macy, & H. A. Walker (Eds.), *Advances in group processes* (Vol. 17, pp. 1–34). Stamford, CT: JAI Press.

Dovidio, J. F., Gaertner, S. L., Pearson, A. R., & Riek, B. M. (2005). Social identities and social context: Attitudes and personal well-being. In S. R. Thye & E. J. Lawler (Eds.), *Advances in group processes: Social identification processes in groups* (pp. 231–260). Oxford, UK: Elsevier.

Dovidio, J. F., Gaertner, S. L., Validzic, A., Matoka, K., Johnson, B., & Frazier, S. (1997). Extending the benefits of re-categorization: Evaluations, self-disclosure and helping. *Journal of Experimental Social Psychology, 33*, 401–420.

Esses, V. M., Dovidio, J. F., Jackson, L. M., & Armstrong, T. M. (2001). The immigration dilemma: The role of perceived group competition, ethnic prejudice, and national identity. *Journal of Social Issue, 57*, 389–412.

Esses, V. M., Dovidio, J. F., Jackson, L. M., & Semenya, A. H. (2005). Attitudes toward immigrants and immigration: The role of national and international identities. In D. Abrams, M. A. Hogg, & J. M. Marques (Eds.), *The social psychology of inclusion and exclusion* (pp. 317–338). Philadelphia: Psychology Press.

Gaertner, S. L., & Dovidio, J. F. (2000). *Reducing intergroup bias: The Common Ingroup Identity Model*. Philadelphia: Psychology Press.

Gaertner, S. L., Mann, J. A., Dovidio, J. F., Murrell, A. J., & Pomare, M. (1990). How does cooperation reduce intergroup bias? *Journal of Personality and Social Psychology, 59*, 692–704.

Gaertner, S. L., Riek, B. M., Mania, E. W., & Dovidio, J. F. (2007). When does a dual identity reduce intergroup bias? To appear in R. Brown, D. Capozza, & O. Licciardello (Eds.), *Contact hypothesis and immigrant acculturation*. Rome: Franco Angeli Publisher.

Gaertner, S. L., Rust, M. C., Dovidio, J. F., Bachman, B. A., & Anastasio, P. A. (1996). The Contact Hypothesis: The role of a common ingroup identity on reducing intergroup bias among majority and minority group members. In J. L. Nye & A. M. Brower (Eds.), *What's social about social cognition?* (pp. 230–360). Newbury Park, CA: Sage.

Grieve, P. G., & Hogg, M. A. (1999). Subjective uncertainty and intergroup discrimination in the minimal group situation. *Personality and Social Psychology Bulletin, 25*, 184–198.

Hewstone, M. (1996). Contact and categorization: Social psychological interventions to change intergroup relations. In C. N. Macrae, M. Hewstone, & C. Stangor (Eds.), *Foundations of stereotypes and stereotyping* (pp. 323–368). New York: Guilford Press.

Hornsey, M. J., & Hogg, M. A. (2000). Subgroup relations: A comparison of mutual intergroup differentiation and common ingroup identity models of prejudice reduction. *Personality and Social Psychology Bulletin, 26*, 242–256.

Houlette, M., Gaertner, S. L., Johnson, K. M., Banker, B. S., Riek, B. M., & Dovidio, J. F. (2004). Developing a more inclusive social identity: An elementary school intervention. *Journal of Social Issues, 60*, 35–56.

Houvouras, S. K. (2001). The effects of demographic variables, ethnic prejudice, and attitudes toward immigration on opposition to bilingual education. *Hispanic Journal of the Behavioral Sciences, 23*, 136–152.

Howard, J. M., & Rothbart, M. (1980). Social categorization for in-group and out-group behavior. *Journal of Personality and Social Psychology, 38*, 301–310.

Huo, Y. J., Smith, H. H., Tyler, T. R., & Lind, A. E. (1996). Superordinate identification, subgroup identification, and justice concerns: Is separatism the problem? Is assimilation the answer? *Psychological Science, 7*, 40–45.

Insko, C. A., Schopler, J., Gaertner, L., Wildschut, T., Kozar, R., Pinter, B., et al. (2001). Interindividual–intergroup discontinuity reduction through the anticipation of future interaction. *Journal of Personality and Social Psychology, 80*, 95–111.

Johnson, D. W., & Johnson, R. T. (2000). The three Cs of reducing prejudice and discrimination. In S. Oskamp (Ed.), *Reducing prejudice and discrimination* (pp. 239–268). Hillsdale, NJ: Lawrence Erlbaum.

Kane, A. A., Argote, L., & Levine, J. M. (2005). Knowledge transfer between groups via personnel rotation: Effects of social identity and knowledge quality. *Organizational Behavior and Human Decision Processes, 96*, 56–71.

Kelman, H. C. (1999). The interdependence of Israeli and Palestinian national identities: The role of the other in existential conflicts. *Journal of Social Issues, 55*, 581–600.

Kessler, T., & Mummendey, A. (2001). Is there any scapegoat around? Determinants of intergroup conflicts at different categorization levels. *Journal of Personality and Social Psychology, 81*, 1090–1102.

Kramer, R. M., & Brewer, M. B. (1984). Effects of group identity on resource utilization in a simulated commons dilemma. *Journal of Personality and Social Psychology, 46*, 1044–1057.

Miller, N. (2002). Personalization and the promise of contact theory. *Journal of Social Issues, 58*, 29–44.

Otten, S., & Moskowitz, G. B. (2000). Evidence for implicit evaluative in-group bias: Affect-based spontaneous trait inference in a minimal group paradigm. *Journal of Experimental Social Psychology, 36*, 77–89.

Park, B., & Rothbart, M. (1982). Perception of out-group homogeneity and levels of social categorization: Memory for the subordinate attributes of in-group and out-group members. *Journal of Personality and Social Psychology, 42*, 1051–1068.

Pettigrew, T. F. (1998). Intergroup contact theory. *Annual Review of Psychology, 49*, 65–85.

Pettigrew, T. F., & Tropp, L. R. (2006). A meta-analytic test of intergroup contact theory. *Journal of Personality and Social Psychology, 90*, 751–783.

Rebelo, M., Guerra, R., & Monteiro, M. B. (2004, June 26–27). *Reducing prejudice: Comparative effects of three theoretical models*. Paper presented at the Fifth Biennial Convention of the Society for the Psychological Study of Social Issues, Washington, DC.

Rothbart, M. (1996). Category-exemplar dynamics and stereotype change. In Y. Amir & J. Schwarzwald (Eds.), *International Journal of Intercultural Relations* [Special issue], *20*, 305–321.

Sherif, M., Harvey, O. J., White, B. J., Hood, W. R., & Sherif, C. W. (1961). *Intergroup conflict and cooperation: The Robbers' Cave experiment*. Norman, OK: The University Book Exchange.

Sidanius, J., Levin, S., & Pratto, F. (1998). Hierarchical group relations, institutional terror, and the dynamics of the criminal justice system. In J. L. Eberhardt & S. T. Fiske (Eds.), *Confronting racism: The problem and the response* (pp. 136–165). Thousand Oaks, CA: Sage.

Sidanius, J., & Pratto, F. (1999). *Social dominance: An intergroup theory of social hierarchy and oppression*. New York: Cambridge University Press.

Smith, H. J., & Tyler, T. R. (1996). Justice and power: When will justice concerns encourage the advantaged to support policies which redistribute economic resources and the disadvantaged to willingly obey the law? *European Journal of Social Psychology, 26*, 171–200

Sunshine, J., & Tyler, T. R. (2003). Moral solidarity, identification with the community, and the importance of procedural justice: The police as prototypical representatives of a group's moral values. *Social Psychology Quarterly, 66*, 153–165.

Tajfel, H. (1969). Cognitive aspects of prejudice. *Journal of Social Issues, 25*(4), 79–97.

Tajfel, H., & Turner, J. C. (1979). An integrative theory of intergroup conflict. In W. G. Austin & S. Worchel (Eds.), *The social psychology of intergroup relations* (pp. 33–48). Monterey, CA: Brooks/Cole.

Turner, J. C. (1985). Social categorization and the self-concept: A social cognitive theory of group behavior. In E. J. Lawler (Ed.), *Advances in group processes* (Vol. 2, pp. 77–122). Greenwich, CT: JAI Press.

Turner, J. C., Hogg, M. A., Oakes, P. J., Reicher, S. D., & Wetherell, M. S. (1987). *Rediscovering the social group: A self-categorization theory*. Oxford, UK: Basil Blackwell.

Wit, A. P., & Kerr, N. L. (2002). "Me versus just us versus us all": Categorization and cooperation in nested social dilemmas. *Journal of Personality & Social Psychology, 83*, 616–637.

Wohl, M. J. A., & Branscombe, N. R. (2005). Forgiveness and collective guilt assignment to historical perpetrator groups depend on level of social category inclusiveness. *Journal of Personality and Social Psychology, 88*, 288–303.

Worchel, S., Rothgerber, H., Day, E. A., Hart, D., & Butemeyer, J. (1998). Social identity and individual productivity with groups. *British Journal of Social Psychology, 37*, 389–413.

10

The Segregation Paradox

Neighborhoods and Interracial Contact in Multiethnic America

J. ERIC OLIVER AND SHANG E. HA

The United States is in the midst of a massive racial transformation. Over the past three decades, large waves of immigration from Asia and Latin America have changed America from a country largely bifurcated between blacks and whites into a multiethnic society composed of at least four sizeable racial groups. Latinos and Asian Americans, already emerging as distinctive ethnic groups in American society, are expected to continue to grow in population size. Demographers predict that, by mid-century, whites will no longer be a majority of the American population and blacks will be one of its smaller minorities (Grieco & Cassidy, 2001; Schmidley, 2001).[1]

But while America's demographic destiny seems clear, the future of its race relations is not. Forty years after the passage of the Civil Rights Act, America remains a nation divided by color. Sharp racial and ethnic differences persist along nearly every marker of social and economic status. Race also remains the country's preeminent social issue, dividing Americans in their self-conception and their views of their fellow countrymen. And, most indicative of these racial divisions, America remains a highly segregated society. Across most neighborhoods, cities, and suburbs, America's ethnic and racial groups continue to live more apart than together (Logan, Stults, & Farley, 2004; Massey & Denton, 1993; Wilkes & Iceland, 2004).

Will America's growing diversity foster higher racial tension and conflict or can we, in Rodney King's oft-repeated phrase, "just learn to get along"? For social scientists, this question does not have a simple answer. On the one hand, most researchers find that racial diversity heightens racial tension. Numerous studies that compare people across large geographic areas, such as counties or metropolitan areas, have come to the same conclusion: the greater the level of racial diversity, the greater the level of intergroup tension and prejudice (Fossett & Kiecolt, 1989; Quillian, 1996; Taylor, 1998). On the other hand, other scholars looking at smaller contexts often find the opposite effect. When looking just at neighborhoods, researchers find that greater levels of racial diversity correspond with greater levels of racial tolerance (Dixon & Rosenbaum, 2004; Oliver & Wong, 2003; Welch, Siegelman, Bledsoe, & Combs, 2001). Thus the evidence suggests that diversity seems to both exacerbate and reduce intergroup hostility, depending on what level of geography is being considered.

The reason for this seeming contradiction is that the dynamics of intergroup conflict operate differently at different levels of geography. Larger areas, such as counties or metropolitan areas, are typically the places where people compete for jobs, resources, and political power. For example, almost no one vies with the people on their block for a job; almost always they are competing with people in their whole region. As a result, racial diversity in a county or metropolis means greater competition between groups for power and status. As more people of a minority group come into a larger context, there is greater pressure on a predominant group to share their privileges. The most vulnerable members of this predominant group are the ones most likely to feel threatened and most likely to express outgroup animosity. In smaller areas, the nature of interaction is more likely to be social. Rather than seeing other races as rivals or competitors, people in integrated micro-settings view others as neighbors or acquaintances. This is why the social contact provided by the integrated neighborhood offers more opportunities for positive interracial contact.

But while the "contact hypothesis" has intuitive appeal and some experimental studies have demonstrated its greater social potential (e.g., Gaertner, Mann, Dovidio, Murrell, & Pomare, 1990), the positive effects of social contact in real-world settings have been more difficult to establish. Part of the problem arises from the variety of social interactions that take place in a large and complex society. Most people have a wide variety of social interactions that can range from short and fleeting to complex and intimate. The greatest difficulty is to determine a threshold for which one might consider the social interaction to be meaningful enough to influence one's previously held perceptions and worldviews. As the previous chapter by Dovidio and Gaertner notes, social psychologists have specified a number of specific conditions under which social contact must occur for a transformative process to take place: Both parties must be of an equivalent social position, both parties must be working together in pursuit of a common end, the contact should be voluntary and long in duration, and the contact should be meaningful and extend beyond the immediate situation.

One of the primary places where positive contact effects might occur is voluntary civic association. Although scholars have been paying increased attention to voluntary associations in the past decade, few researchers have sought to examine the importance of civic associations for promoting interracial understanding in the United States. Yet civic associations may be the ideal location for fostering positive interracial contact. In fact, research on ethnic tension in India found that cities with integrated civic associations were far less prone to violence than those with segregated associations (Varshney, 2001). We believe that the same dynamics could be occurring in the United States and explain why people in integrated neighborhoods tend to be more racially tolerant. After all, the very traits that make voluntary organizations important for democratic functioning, i.e., equal status of members, shared goals, and cooperative work endeavors, also make them ideal sites for promoting interracial understanding. From this perspective, one of the best ways that America can overcome the inevitable racial tension that will accompany its growing racial diversity is by promoting participation in integrated civic associations.

This proposition, however, raises another, more complicated issue: How might the current patterns of segregation affect the nature of Americans' civic lives? Are people in integrated neighborhoods more or less likely to get involved in associations and clubs? How does the racial character of their surroundings affect the racial character of their civic experiences? These questions are crucial for understanding the potential of positive social contact in promoting racial harmony. Because most civic associations where people meet face to face will draw their memberships from their immediate surroundings, the impact of a neighborhood's racial composition will be a primary determinant of the racial character of their civic life. For instance, a Latino in a segregated barrio who belongs to a bridge club composed solely of Latinos will not have positive contact with people of other races, at least at the bridge table. If civic associations are the best mechanism for promoting positive interracial contact, then the key to unlocking the future of American race relations is in disentangling the relationship between the patterns of racial segregation and civic activities of the American public.

This chapter seeks to initiate this effort by analyzing the relationship between racial environments, civic activities, and social ties among America's four major racial groups. Analyzing the Census and survey data, we show that residential segregation presents paradox for the future of race relations in the United States. People in integrated neighborhoods, no matter what their race is, generally have more multiracial friendship and multiracial civic ties. Yet this same integration also seems to retard civic and community involvement. Much of this difference, we suggest, is related to a higher level of social alienation amongst people in integrated settings. People who live in integrated neighborhoods are less socially connected, which may limit their opportunities for involvement in the clubs and associations that could connect them with people of other races. Ironically, the civic life that could be so vital for redressing the challenges of America's growing racial heterogeneity may actually be undermined by the very integration that would be a hallmark of full racial equality. This segregation paradox highlights the significant challenges posed by America's growing racial diversity.

A Nation, Multiethnic and Segregated

To understand the dilemma of America's growing racial diversity, it may prove useful to first get a picture of the American racial landscape. The United States population can be divided roughly into four sizeable racial groups: non-Latino whites of European descent, who are roughly 69% of US residents; African Americans and Latinos, each approximately 12% of the American population; and Asian Americans, the fastest growing racial group, who comprise approximately 4% of the population.[2] If America were a fully integrated society, then the racial composition of most neighborhoods, cities, and states would reflect the racial distribution of these four major groups. In other words, most neighborhoods would be about 70% white, 13% black, 13% Latino, and 4% Asian American.

The actual patterns of residential segregation in the United States, however, reveal a far different arrangement. Figure 10.1 depicts the average dissimilarity scores for the four major racial groups in the United States across neighborhoods within metropolitan areas according to data from the 2000 Census. A dissimilarity score represents the proportion of people within a particular group who would have to change neighborhoods in order to have a proportionate distribution across a metropolitan area. It is a rough indicator of the proportionate spatial difference between groups in a metropolis.[3] For example, whites have an average dissimilarity score of 60 with respect to blacks. This means that in order to achieve a proportionate residential balance within the average metropolitan area, roughly 60 out of every 100 whites would have to change their neighborhood. The dissimilarity score thus provides a general barometer of the level of spatial distance among racial groups in America's metropolitan areas and a general indicator of the level of segregation among the four major racial groups.

There are four striking trends in the dissimilarity scores among the major racial groups in America. First, despite the modest increases in integration over the past several decades, America's racial groups continue to be highly segregated from each other. At the very least (i.e., the case of whites' segregation from Asians), four out of every ten Americans would need to change residences to achieve some proportionate level of integration. Second, African Americans are much more segregated from every other racial group, in terms of both their own residential patterns (i.e., how isolated blacks are from other groups) and the residential patterns of other groups (i.e., how many non-blacks would have to change neighborhoods to be integrated with blacks). In most instances, the dissimilarity scores between blacks and other racial groups exceed 55 and in some instance reach 60. Third, Latinos are also highly segregated from other groups, but the level of Latino segregation is lower than that of African Americans. Whereas three in five blacks would have to move to achieve proportionate integration with America's white majority, only one in two Latinos would have to move. Yet despite this higher level of integration, Latino rates of segregation are not decreasing over time—during the past thirty years Latinos' segregation rates have remained at the same level (Frey & Farley, 1996).[4] Lastly, Asian Americans are achieving comparatively high levels of integration with whites, but remain highly segregated from other groups. With an average dissimilarity score of only 42, Asians have the lowest levels of residential segregation from whites of all minority groups (i.e., only four in ten Asians would have to move to achieve proportional neighborhood integration with whites compared to five of ten Latinos and six of ten African Americans).

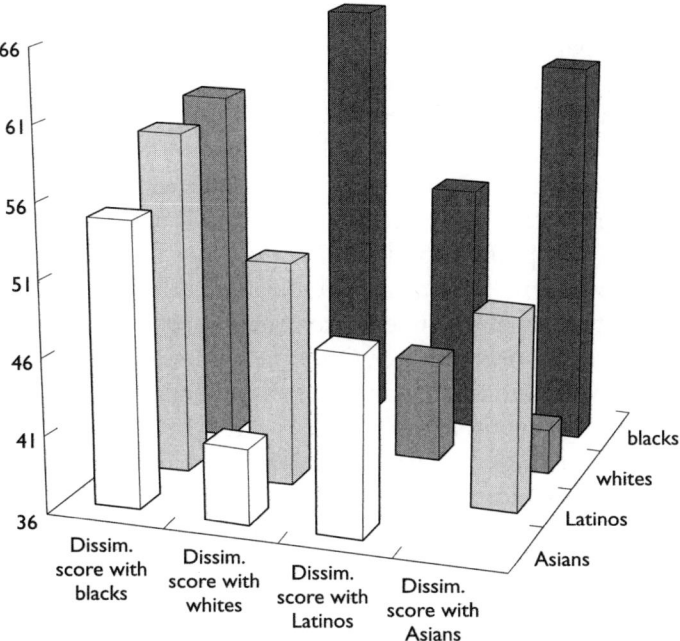

Figure 10.1 Neighborhood residential segration by race (source: The 2000 US Census (Logan, 2001).

How might these patterns of racial segregation affect people's racial attitudes? Adherents of Allport's (1954) hypotheses about racial contact may feel they have the answer: Racial prejudices acquired early in life can be corrected through repeated and positive social contact with people of other races. People who live in racially mixed neighborhoods may become more tolerant because their daily social experiences and interactions with people of other races rectify their socially learned prejudices. Although the contact hypothesis has been much criticized, recent studies have demonstrated positive effects of interracial contact on white attitudes towards minority groups, particularly when the conditions of equal status, goal sharing, and repeated interactions over time take place (see Dovidio, Gaertner, & Kawakami, 2003 and Pettigrew, 1998 for reviews). Despite many limitations, interracial contact, under the right circumstances, may be an important factor in alleviating racial misunderstanding.

In many ways, an integrated neighborhood could provide many of the conditions that facilitate the positive benefits of interracial contact. Living in close proximity with people of other races will mean that people have greater opportunities for social interactions with one another. With time, neighbors get a chance to know each other, develop friendships, and share an identity as residents of the same place. For example, residents of integrated neighborhoods such as Wicker Park in

Chicago or Fort Greene in New York may develop a common identity as neighbors in relation to other parts of the city which may transcend their previous ethnic or racial conceptions. And indeed, this is what other research suggests. In their study of whites' attitudes in Detroit, Welch et al. (2001) find that as the racial mix of a neighborhood increases, so does the likelihood that whites will have both casual interracial contact and close friends who are of different races. They also report that whites living in racially integrated neighborhoods are less likely to have negative stereotypes or be opposed to interracial marriage than those who live in all-white neighborhoods. Finally, and most importantly, they find that many of the differences in whites' racial attitudes across neighborhoods are attributable to their levels of interracial social contact. Once the higher level of interracial contact among whites in racially mixed neighborhoods is considered, the differences in levels of racial hostility across neighborhoods diminish significantly. If the same processes that work for whites in Detroit are applicable for all races, then the higher levels of racial tolerance in integrated neighborhoods for all racial groups may be the consequence of more integrated patterns of social contact. People in integrated neighborhoods may be more racially tolerant because they are more likely to have interracial social ties.

Yet, the Welch study did not specify *where* the contact within the residentially integrated neighborhood was occurring. Welch and her colleagues suggest that simple exposure to people of different races may be sufficient to alleviate biases, but according to other social psychologists (e.g., Pettigrew, 1998), contact needs to occur under very specific conditions for it to have its beneficial effects. For example, Varshney's (2001) study of Indian ethnic relations concluded that simply having high levels of interethnic socializing was not sufficient for reducing ethnic hostility; rather it was the participation in integrated civic associations that prevented ethnic strife. Simple exposure to people of other races may not, by itself, be sufficient for reducing racial hostility and may even lead to greater racial animosity. When testing for the positive effects that interracial social contact entails, it is therefore important to identify the varieties of community involvement that people have with neighbors.

This, however, raises another question: How might neighborhood segregation affect the likelihood that they get involved in civic activities and their racial experiences within theses groups? Past research on this question offers both incomplete and contradictory answers. Some studies demonstrate that social heterogeneity boosts civic participation. For example, Oliver (2001) finds that residents of racially mixed cities are more likely to contact officials, attend community board meetings, and work informally with neighbors than those in predominantly white cities. Other studies, however, find that, in heterogeneous metropolitan areas and counties, people participate less in civic associations, spend less time in voluntary activities, and show less willingness to help others (Alesina & Ferrara, 2000; Costa & Kahn, 2003).

These discrepancies arise partly from ill-specified explanations for how social environments affect the way people involve themselves in civic affairs. Most published research on the relationship between community heterogeneity and civic participation has come from economists using formal models to generate predictions about the relationships between social environments and individual behavior. Although such models offer strong predictions, they provide very little information about the causal mechanisms linking context and behavior. For instance, Alesina and Ferrara (2000) base their model on the assumption of homophily. In other words, social diversity imposes "costs" because individuals "prefer to interact with others like them because of shared interests, socialization to the same cultural norms, and greater empathy toward individuals who remind them of themselves" (Costa & Kahn, 2003, 104). Yet this research provides no detailed evidence to justify these assumptions. The fact that heterogeneity corresponds with less civic engagement is simply taken as proof that the operating mechanisms are at work. This approach is unsatisfactory. Not only does it preclude other explanations, but it is not grounded in any theory about civic participation.

To understand how the racial composition of a social environment might affect people's participation in civic organizations, we must determine why people become involved in civic affairs in the first place. In their authoritative study of civic participation in the United States, Verba, Schlozman, and Brady (1995) identify three factors that determine whether people get involved in local civic activities: resources, interest, and mobilization. People are far more likely to be civically active if they have more resources such as time and money, if they are interested in a particular set of issues, or if they are asked by others to get involved. According to Verba et al., most of the variation in rates of associational activity can ultimately be traced to these three determinants.

Two of these factors could be directly affected by the racial composition of their surroundings. First, people's interests in local organizations are likely to be shaped by their racial environment. Many people who get involved in politics do so from a feeling of "ethnic/racial community" (Bobo & Gilliam, 1990; Dawson, 1994). As people live amongst more people of their own ethnicity or race, particularly in contrast to neighboring different groups, they are likely to have a stronger sense of group affiliation. For example, a Latina may have little sense of ethnic community in her home country, but feel a strong sense of ethnicity in a barrio of Los Angeles (Jones-Correa & Leal, 1996). In a similar vein, Guterbock and London (1983) report that blacks who feel a greater sense of ethnic community are more likely to be active in voluntary organizations. Conversely, people who feel racially ostracized or alienated from their neighbors may withdraw socially and keep to themselves. Feeling less in common with her neighbors, the resident of a heterogeneous community would be less interested in local or community affairs, feel less bound by community norms that encourage civic involvement, and be less motivated to join a local organization (Campbell, 2006).

Racial heterogeneity may deter people's interest in joining local organizations by making these organizations more heterogeneous themselves. For example, an

African American woman living in a predominantly white neighborhood may feel less inclined to join an organization because its membership is likely to be mostly white as well. As Alesina and Ferrara (2000) deduce, the costs of finding and participating in local organizations that are of the same race or ethnicity may be so high for people in more integrated settings, that they simply choose not to get involved.

Second, racial diversity may affect associational participation by constraining the social connections between neighbors and thus limiting their opportunities to be mobilized. Given the high levels of racial mistrust in the United States, people living in integrated neighborhoods may have fewer social bonds with their neighbors, which can, in turn, reduce the opportunities to become recruited for a local group. The importance of these social networks cannot be overstated; after all, most people get involved in local voluntary organizations because they are asked at some point to do so (Verba et al., 1995). If people in integrated settings are less familiar with their neighbors, the likelihood they will join anything from a neighborhood association to the Rotary club will be significantly less. When looking at the impact of racial surroundings on local organizational involvement, it is essential, therefore, to also look at the informal social ties between its residents.

In sum, previous research suggests that voluntary organizations may be a key factor for alleviating racial tension in multiethnic areas, but the extent and nature of participation in such organizations may be affected by racial contexts as well. In particular, people in racially heterogeneous neighborhoods may be put off from participating in civic groups precisely because they are likely to be filled with people who are of other races. Ironically, civic life may be weakened by the very forces of racial mistrust and suspicion that it is so well suited for tackling. Of course, all of this remains in the realm of speculation. To examine whether segregation really affects racial contact and civic participation, we now turn to some actual data.

Examining Segregation and Civic Involvement With Surveys

We explore the relationship between segregation and Americans' civic and associational activities using two national surveys. The 2005 Citizenship, Involvement, Democracy Study (CIDS) consists of in-person interviews with a nation-wide, clustered sample Americans who answered an 80-minute questionnaire (n = 1,001). The CIDS contains extensive questions about civic engagement (both informal social activities and activities in formal clubs or organizations), social capital, democratic values, and diversity. This data set is complemented by the 2000 Social Capital Community Benchmark Survey (SCCBS), a phone survey made via two different processes: 26,230 clustered-sample respondents from 41 different areas and 3,003 additional respondents with an over-sampling of African Americans and Latinos from a separate national survey. Together, these two data sets represent the state of the art in surveys on Americans' civic activities. In order to examine the effects of people's racial surroundings, we merged data from the 2000 US Census that measured the racial composition of their neighborhoods and metropolitan areas.[5]

We start our analysis by examining the relationship between people's racial surroundings and the racial character of their social and civic contacts. As we would expect, people in more racially integrated surroundings are more likely to have interracial social experiences. Take, for example, people's friendship networks. Table 10.1 lists the percentage of whites, blacks, Latinos, and Asian Americans in the SCCBS data set claiming to have a "personal friend" of another race by the percentage of their own group in their neighborhood.[6]

For all four racial groups, significant differences exist in people's friendship patterns by the racial composition of their neighborhoods—people who live in more racially mixed neighborhoods tend to have more interracial friendship ties. Whites who live in neighborhoods that were under 80% white were nearly twice as likely in some instances to report having a friend of another race than those in neighborhoods over 95% white. Half of whites in a racially mixed neighborhood reported having an Asian friend compared to only 30% in a segregated neighborhood. For the friendship with Latinos, there was a similarly large difference (57 versus 33%). Whites' friendship patterns with blacks also vary by these patterns of segregation although the difference is not as great: 69% of whites in diverse neighborhoods report having a black friend versus only 55% of whites in predominantly white neighborhoods. Nor are these differences simply the result of regional differences in minority populations—very similar results (which are not listed here) occur when comparing interracial friendship patterns between racially diverse and predominantly white metropolitan areas.

The SCCBS data also show similar differences in blacks' interracial friendship patterns. Blacks who live in neighborhoods with a lower percentage of blacks (under 15% black) are much more likely, on average, to have interracial friendship ties. For example, in this group, 33% of blacks reported being friends with an Asian American, 52% reported a Latino friend, and 79% reported having a white friend. By contrast, among blacks in predominantly black neighborhoods (over 40% black), only 24% reported an Asian friend, 41% a Latino friend, and 70% a white friend.

There are notable differences between blacks' and whites' interracial friendship patterns. Whites are more likely to have Asian friends than blacks. In addition, blacks are more likely to have white friends than vice versa. These differences in friendship patterns make sense given the patterns of racial segregation between the groups. Whites and Asian Americans are both highly segregated from African Americans and are relatively integrated with each other—thus the differences in their friendships make sense. Similarly, the United States is nearly 70% white and only 13% black, thus blacks are going to have more opportunities for contact (and friendship) with whites. Indeed, this will be the case with all minorities in the United States: By virtue of the size of the white majority, Asians, Latinos, and

Table 10.1 Interracial friendship patterns by neighborhood racial composition (source: The 2000 Social Capital Community Benchmark Study and the 2000 US Census)

	% with Asian friend	% with black friend	% with Latino friend	% with white friend
Whites				
Neighborhood:				
<80% white	50	69	57	
80–95% white	41	66	49	
>95% white	30	55	33	
Blacks				
Neighborhood:				
<15% black	33		52	79
15–40% black	30		44	78
>40% black	24		41	70
Latinos (citizens)				
Neighborhood:				
<15% Latino	45	70		85
15–40% Latino	40	62		76
>40% Latino	38	60		73
Latinos (non-citizens)				
Neighborhood:				
<15% Latino	21	33		54
15–40% Latino	17	24		52
>40% Latino	18	22		50
Asians (citizens)				
Neighborhood:				
<5% Asian		62	53	83
5–20% Asian		53	56	81
>20% Asian		54	52	71
Asians (non-citizens)				
Neighborhood:				
<5% Asian		45	25	72
5–20% Asian		40	30	69
>20% Asian		46	33	67

Note: The number of cases is 28,440 in total (19,665 whites, 3,321 blacks, 2,284 Latinos, and 654 Asians). Neighborhood is measured at the zip code level.

Table 10.2 Percent of civic participants belonging to interracial associations by neighborhood racial composition (source: The 2000 Social Capital Community Benchmark Study and the 2000 US Census)

Whites	
Neighborhood:	
<80% white	40
80–95% white	29
>95% white	23
Blacks	
Neighborhood:	
<15% black	54
15–40% black	49
>40% black	43
Latinos	
Neighborhood:	
<15% Latino	62
15–40% Latino	63
>40% Latino	47
Asians	
Neighborhood:	
<5% Asian	
5–20% Asian	73
>20% Asian	64

Note: The number of cases is 28,440 in total (19,665 whites, 3,321 blacks, 2,284 Latinos, and 654 Asians). Neighborhood is measured at the zip code level.

blacks will all have more opportunities for interracial contact than does the white population.

Asian American and Latino friendship patterns also vary according to their racial surroundings, although, as one might expect, there are considerable differences by virtue of citizenship. Among Latino citizens who live in neighborhoods with fewer Latinos (under 15%), 45% report an Asian friend, 70% report a black friend, and 85% report a white friend; among Latino citizens in predominantly Latino neighborhoods, these percentages are 38, 60, and 73 respectively. However, among Latino non-citizens, the neighborhood differences are much smaller but, more importantly, the rates of interracial friendship are also much lower than among Latino citizens. Small differences exist in Asians' interracial friendship patterns by the percent Asian in their neighborhood. Among Asian citizens, those who live in neighborhoods with small percentages of Asians are more likely

Table 10.3 Whites' level of civic participation by the racial composition of their neighborhood and metropolitan area (source: The 2005 Citizenship, Involvement, and Democracy Study (CIDS) and the 2000 US Census)

Proportion of whites in area	% actively parcicipating in organization	% volunteering in organization
Metro area <70% white	29	19
Metro area >70% white	43	29
Neighborhood <60% white	27	21
Neighborhood 60–90% white	37	22
Neighborhood >90% white	38	28

Note: The number of cases is 725 whites. Neighborhood is measured at the census tract level.

to have interracial friendship ties across all groups than those who live in neighborhoods that are at least 20% Asian. Yet these differences pale in comparison to those between citizens and non-citizens. Asian citizens were nearly twice as likely to have Latino friends and much more likely to have black and white friends than non-citizens.

A similar pattern is also evident when the racial composition of people's civic life is considered. Table 10.2 reports, broken down by neighborhood racial boundaries, the percent of people who say their civic organization has an interracial membership.[7] Once again, people who live in more racially diverse neighborhoods are far more likely to belong to integrated civic associations. Forty percent of civically active whites in diverse neighborhoods belong to an integrated organization as opposed to only 23% in segregated neighborhoods. For blacks, these percentages are 54 to 43; for Latinos, they are 62 to 47; and, for Asian Americans, they are 73 to 64. There are also significant differences between Asian and Latino citizens and non-citizens (which are not listed here), with citizens being more likely to participate in integrated civic associations than non-citizens. Irrespective of the individual's race, thus, the pattern is remarkably similar—people who live in integrated neighborhoods are much more likely to have interracial civic ties than people who live in more segregated places.

So clearly people in integrated neighborhoods are more likely to have integrated civic and social experiences. But what effect do their surroundings have on their likelihood of engaging in such civic activities in the first place? To answer this question, we examine differences in the CIDS among different groups who reported "being active" or "volunteering in a civic association."[8] We chose these two measures of civic activity because they best represent the opportunities that most people would have for interracial contact in their organizations. Two other measures—

mere membership and donation—do not necessarily guarantee actual activities within civic organizations (Skocpol, 2003). Unfortunately, since the CIDS did not over-sample from minority communities, we limit our analysis to only the white portion of the study.[9] The results are listed in Table 10.3.

At the metropolitan level, racial diversity corresponds with less face-to-face civic activity. For example, comparing whites in predominantly white metropolitan areas (i.e., over 70% white) with whites in racially mixed ones, we see that the former are almost twice as likely to be active in their associations and volunteer at a rate 10 percentage points higher. At the neighborhood level, likewise, there are very significant differences in civic participation in relation to a person's racial surroundings. Whites in predominantly white neighborhoods are far more likely to participate and do volunteer works.[10] For example, only about a quarter of whites in racially mixed neighborhoods (i.e., a neighborhood under 60% white) were active in their organizations, compared to 38% of whites in predominantly white neighborhoods (i.e., a neighborhood over 90% white). Nor are these merely the consequence of different types of whites living in integrated and segregated areas. When other individual-level variables are taken into consideration with multivariate analysis, the same trends persist: Whites in integrated neighborhoods are less civically active than whites in segregated places.[11]

Thus, from the CIDS data, it appears that for whites, the more racially mixed their surroundings, the less civically active they tend to be. One might suspect that the causal relationship would be opposite: Instead of racial segregation increasing civic engagement (especially, for whites), civically engaged individuals may lead to segregation in some other way. For example, people in civically engaged contexts are less likely to move, and thus there is less opportunity for other racial groups to diversify the neighborhood. This is a weak argument because it is reasonable to assume that residential segregation precedes civic engagement: people choose where to live before deciding where to be civically affiliated and involved. In addition, exclusion of other racial groups from membership or civic activities, if any, does not always relate to neighborhood segregation.

The next question we address is *why* neighborhood racial integration corresponds to civic inactivity. According to our hypotheses, the lower levels of civic engagement in heterogeneous contexts should be attributable to either higher levels of social alienation or lower levels of social contact amongst neighbors. Table 10.4 presents the percentages on two items measuring people's feelings about how much they trust their neighbors and whether they feel a sense of belonging in their communities. Because we have data from the SCCBS on these items, we can examine patterns of neighborhood trust and alienation across all four racial groups.[12]

Once again, the racial composition of people's surroundings greatly affects their feelings about their neighbors. Whites in racially mixed neighborhoods reported lower levels of neighborly trust and less feeling of belonging. For instance, in racially mixed neighborhoods, only 47% of whites say they trust their neighbors compared to 65% of whites in predominantly white neighborhoods. Among minorities, the

Table 10.4 Feelings of neighborhood trust and belonging by percent of racial group in neighborhood. Source: The 2000 Social Capital Community Benchmark Study (SCCBS) and the 2000 US Census

	% who trust their neighbors "a lot"	% who say they get a sense of community from their neighborhood
Whites		
Neighborhood:		
<80% white	47	77
80–95% white	59	82
>95% white	65	83
Blacks		
Neighborhood:		
<15% black	25	73
15–40% black	22	71
>40% black	18	78
Latinos		
Neighborhood:		
<15% Latino	28	71
15–40% Latino	18	79
>40% Latino	13	78
Asians		
Neighborhood:		
<5% Asian	34	74
5–20% Asian	31	84
>20% Asian	28	73

Note: The number of cases is 28,440 in total (19,665 whites, 3,321 blacks, 2,284 Latinos, and 654 Asians) for neighborhood trust and 14,389 in total for the sense of belonging to community. Neighborhood is measured at the census tract level.

relationship between their neighborhood's racial composition and their feelings of social alienation are mixed. On the one hand, Asians, blacks, and Latinos who live in neighborhoods with a higher percentage of their own race report lower levels of trust in their neighbors, although much of this is related to social class, i.e., neighborhoods with higher proportions of minorities tend to be poorer, on average, and have higher levels of crime (e.g., Cohen & Dawson 1993). When the income level of the neighborhood is taken into account using multivariate analyses, these differences disappear. On the other hand, minorities who live in neighborhoods with more of their own race report higher feelings of a sense of belonging. For example,

78% of blacks in neighborhoods with a high percentage of blacks report feelings of belonging compared to only 71% of blacks in neighborhoods with few blacks. When higher levels of poverty in these neighborhoods are taken into account using multivariate analyses, these differences become much greater.

In short, from these simple data we see a mixed effect of neighborhood racial diversity on people's civic and social experiences. On the one hand, people in racially mixed neighborhoods tend to have more friends of other races and more racially integrated civic experiences. In the large SCCBS sample, the more people lived among those of other races and ethnicities, the more diverse their friendship and civic ties. This would bolster the idea that residential integration is important for promoting positive interracial contact. On the other hand, people in integrated neighborhoods, particularly whites, tend to be much more socially and emotionally isolated. For whites, living amongst people of other races tended to depress their rates of civic participation, heighten their feelings of mistrust, and lower their feelings of belonging. A similar, albeit more erratic, pattern also existed for minorities. Neighborhood integration may correspond with more interracial experiences but it also corresponds with greater levels of social alienation.

Conclusion

The relationship between social contact, civic life, and racial segregation presents a paradox for those concerned with social equality and the vitality of American democracy. The survey results above indicate that racial segregation, at least for the white majority, corresponds with higher levels of civic engagement. Whites who live in predominantly white neighborhoods and metropolitan areas are generally more active in their voluntary organizations than those in integrated contexts. Such higher levels of participation may be attributable to the correspondingly higher levels of social connection that whites feel in such settings. Whites in predominantly white contexts demonstrate higher levels of social trust, have more social acquaintances, and report a greater feeling of belonging in their communities. These results yield the uncomfortable conclusion that, for whites at least, racial segregation enhances their civic engagement. For other groups, the results are less consistent: African Americans and Latinos living in predominantly white neighborhoods tend to feel socially alienated, but we do not have sufficient data to test whether this social disconnectedness is linked to lower levels of civic engagement. Assuming these patterns are the same for minorities as they are for whites, we can only conclude that the difficult social reality of living in an integrated neighborhood diminishes the opportunities for positive interracial social contact, even though people in these settings do have more interracial social experiences.

Of course, segregation does not provide a good alternative either. Although people in segregated places may be more civically active and socially connected—a putative prerequisite for promoting interracial understanding—their civic activities and social networks tend to be more segregated. People in predominantly white neighborhoods are less likely to have friends of other races and less likely to belong to multiethnic civic associations. Whatever enhanced possibilities that this increased civic involvement provides for people in segregated neighborhoods are undercut by the racial isolation in which it takes place.

These findings highlight the challenges of building social capital in multiracial and multiethnic societies, which have been ignored in the previous social capital literature (e.g., Putnam, 2000). As America becomes more racially heterogeneous, the demands for increasing social capital and fostering interracial understanding will become more pressing. Voluntary civic organizations should be a crucial instrument in achieving both of these goals: Not only can they promote social capital and generalized trust, they are ideal settings for fostering positive interracial contact. The problem is that enhanced participation tends to occur in segregated contexts. Ironically, the people who are most active (i.e., people in segregated neighborhoods) are less likely to interact with people of other races. As long as integration stifles civic participation and segregation leads to segregated civic and social experiences, the challenges for creating sites for positive interracial contact become all the greater. Genuine social integration (especially, racial desegregation) may be the ultimate expression of American aspirations toward true equality, but achieving this integration may come at a cost to America's stock of social capital, at least in the short run.

The implications of these findings on group cooperation are abundant. Particularly, this study confirms the trade-off relationship between intragroup cooperation and intergroup cooperation. As Dovidio, Gaertner, and Esses point out in the previous chapter, racial categorization in American society dovetails with the emergence of ingroup favoritism and outgroup derogation: greater feelings of connection with others within one's own group entail greater bias toward outgroups. The segregation paradox—more civic activities in racially segregated neighborhoods—exemplifies this underlying dilemma in more general intergroup relations.

Also, this study addresses how intergroup cooperative behavior in multiracial America can be fostered. As we see above, Americans, especially whites, in racially integrated areas tend to be less civically active, but they are more likely to have multiracial social ties. Furthermore, once people in racially diverse neighborhoods participate in voluntary civic associations, they are more likely to contact their fellow members of other racial groups. It is thus the promotion of civic activities in racially integrated areas that is critical to cooperative race relations. Policy makers who are interested in American race relations and democratic practices should pay more attention to multiracial civic engagement—via reduction of interracial distrust and social alienation—rather than civic engagement in general.

Acknowledgment

Thanks to the people who made geo-codes available.

Notes

1 Throughout this chapter, the terms "white" and "black" will refer primarily to non-Latino whites and blacks, respectively. Latinos will generally refer to those Americans who have immigrated or whose families migrated from Latin America. Asian Americans will refer to those Americans who have immigrated or whose forebears migrated from Asia.

2 About 1.5% of Americans identified themselves as having multiple races in the 2000 Census and a little more than 1% of Americans identified with indigenous peoples of North America or the Pacific Islands (Grieco & Cassidy, 2001). While these groups also are part of multiethnic America, they will not be included in this analysis because multi-racialism is itself a complicated and deep topic beyond the scope of this analysis (see Perlmann & Waters, 2002 for details) and because most indigenous peoples are so geographically isolated from continental America.

3 The dissimilarity index is just one specific measure of racial segregation. Usually, segregation has been conceptualized as consisting of five dimensions: evenness (the distribution of each group across neighborhoods); exposure (the probability of interaction between different groups); concentration (the amount of physical space occupied by different groups, especially minorities); centralization (the distance to the urban center); and clustering (the degree to which minority groups live in areas that adjoin one another) (see Massey & Denton, 1988 for details). The dissimilarity index belongs to the category of evenness. Depending on the dimensions, the degree of residential segregation between two groups may be higher or lower. When segregation is high across all five dimensions, we call it "hypersegregation" (Wilkes & Iceland, 2004).

4 The relatively constant segregation rates do not mean that Latinos' integration patterns are holding constant. Some Latinos are integrating into American society, but the high level of immigration and great population increase are creating larger pockets of heavily Latino areas. As the Latino population grows so quickly, more Latinos are living in integrated settings, but more, particularly new immigrants, are moving into segregated ethnic communities. Therefore, Latino rates of segregation have slightly increased in regions where Latinos are relatively poorer than whites and include a growing share of new Latino immigrants (Logan et al., 2004).

5 Contextual variables are extracted from Summary File 3 (SF3), available at the Inter-University Consortium for Political and Social Research (ICPSR) data archive (Study No. 13402). Since neighborhood is always subjectively perceived, it is impossible to define it in an objective way (Sampson, Morenoff, & Gannon-Rowley, 2002). For the purpose of data analysis, neighborhoods mean the areas demarcated by the five-digit zip code tabulation areas (ZCTAs) or the census tracts. Census tracts, generally smaller than the zip code areas and a subdivision of counties and states, have on average about 4,000 inhabitants, usually between 2,500 and 8,000. Both census tracts and zip code areas are much smaller than the metropolitan areas, which require the presence of a city with at least 50,000 or more inhabitants. However, the size of the zip code areas varies; it can be as small as a few city blocks or cover many square miles.

6 Because minorities groups have differing portions of the population, the neighborhood racial percentages are not identically scaled. In addition, because of the heavy immigrant portion of the Latino and Asian populations, they are divided among citizens and non-citizens.

 7 Respondents in SCCBS were asked whether they participate in any civic organiza-
    tions among the following: religious organizations (besides the local place of worship),
    outdoor activity clubs, youth organizations, parents' associations, veteran's groups,
    neighborhood associations, clubs for senior citizens, charity or welfare organizations,
    labor unions, professional associations, fraternal organizations, ethnic or civil rights
    groups, political clubs, art or culture clubs, hobby clubs, self-help programs, inter-
    net-based groups, or any other kinds of organizations. Among those who said they
    participated in such organizations, a follow-up question was posed on whether the other
    members of the group were of the same race as the respondent (the respondent could
    answer all, most, some, few, or none). Those who said that some, few, or none of their
    fellow group members were of their race were counted as belonging to an interracial
    group. This measure did not include church membership, which was asked separately.

 8 Civic associations in CIDS are as follows: sports clubs, hobby clubs, trade unions,
    professional associations, consumer organizations, organizations for human rights,
    environmental associations, religious organizations, political parties, organizations for
    education, social clubs (for the elderly, the retired, or fraternal organizations), neigh-
    borhood associations, veteran's organizations, self-help groups, welfare organizations,
    and any other voluntary civic associations. By seeing the list of civic groups, respond-
    ents were asked to report whether they have (1) formally been affiliated, (2) actively
    participated, (3) donated money or (4) done any voluntary works in those associations
    in the past twelve months.

 9 Of the 1,001 respondents in the CIDS 725 were white, 157 were black, and 96 identified
    as Latino. Because of the clustered sampling frame of the study and the small number
    of cases for blacks and Latinos, the CIDS does not provide an adequate basis for geo-
    graphic comparison among minority groups.

10 Of course, race is not the only contextual determinant of American associational life.
    Community size and affluence are also negatively associated with most civic activities
    (Oliver 2001).

11 Although not listed in this chapter, in a separate publication, we conducted multivariate
    analysis using negative binomial regressions examining the likelihood of participating
    in organizations or volunteering by the racial and class composition of people's neigh-
    borhoods, their race, and a host of individual controls, including their education, age,
    sex, length of residence, and homeownership. The results from the multivariate ana-
    lysis are largely similar to the cross-tabulations, at least for whites: Whites who live in
    racially mixed areas, even when their individual factors are controlled for, are less civi-
    cally active (Ha & Oliver, 2006).

12 The variable of trust in neighbors was coded in a four-point scale (trust a lot, a fair
    amount, somewhat, and not at all) and the sense of belonging variable was originally a
    dummy variable, although respondents could voluntarily choose "it depends." The latter
    question was asked to randomly chosen half of the total respondents.

References

Alesina, A., & Ferrara, E. (2000). Participation in heterogeneous communities. *Quarterly
    Journal of Economics*, *115*(3), 847–904.

Allport, G. W. (1954). *The nature of prejudice*. Cambridge, MA: Addison-Wesley.

Bobo, L., & Gilliam, F. (1990). Race, sociopolitical participation, and black empowerment. *American Political Science Review, 84*(2), 377–394.

Campbell, D. E. (2006). *Why we vote: How schools and communities shape our civic life.* Princeton, NJ: Princeton University Press.

Cohen, C. J., & Dawson, M. C. (1993). Neighborhood poverty and African American politics. *American Political Science Review, 87*(3), 286–302.

Costa, D. L., & Kahn, M. E. (2003). Civic engagement and community heterogeneity: An economist's perspective. *Perspectives on Politics, 1*(1), 103–111.

Dawson, M. C. (1994). *Behind the mule: Race, class, and African American politics.* Princeton, NJ: Princeton University Press.

Dixon, J. C., & Rosenbaum, M. S. (2004). Nice to know you? Testing contact, cultural, and group threat theories of anti-black and anti-Hispanic stereotypes. *Social Science Quarterly, 85*(2), 257–280.

Dovidio, J. F., Gaertner, S. L., & Kawakami, K. (2003). Intergroup contact: The past, present, and future. *Group Processes and Intergroup Relations, 6*(1), 5–21.

Fossett, M. A., & Kiecolt, K. J. (1989). The relative size of minority populations and white racial attitudes. *Social Science Quarterly, 70*(4), 820–835.

Frey, W., & Farley, R. (1996). Latino, Asian, and Black segregation in the US metropolitan areas: Are multiethnic metros different? *Demography, 33*(1), 35–50.

Gaertner, S. L., Mann, J. A., Dovidio, J. F., Murrell, A. J., & Pomare, M. (1990). How does cooperation reduce intergroup bias? *Journal of Personality and Social Psychology, 59*(4), 692–704.

Grieco, E. M., & Cassidy, R. C. (2001). *Overview of race and Hispanic origin: 2000.* US Census Bureau Census 2000 Brief, C2KBR/01-1. Washington, DC: US Government Printing Office.

Guterbock, T. M., & London, B. (1983). Race, political orientation, and participation: An empirical test of four competing theories. *American Sociological Review. 48*(4), 439–453.

Ha, S. E., & Oliver, J. E. (2006). *The civic cost of integration: Racial heterogeneity and associational life in the United States.* Unpublished manuscript.

Jones-Correa, M., & Leal, D. (1996). Becoming "Hispanic": Secondary pan-ethnic identification among Latin American-origin populations in the United States. *Hispanic Journal of Behavioral Sciences, 18*(2), 214–255.

Logan, J. R. (2001, December 18). *Ethnic diversity grows, neighborhood integration lags behind.* Report to the Lewis Mumford Center. Available at http://mumford1.dyndns.org/cen2000/.

Logan, J. R., Stults, B. J., & Farley, R. (2004). Segregation of minorities in the metropolis: Two decades of change. *Demography, 41*(1), 1–22.

Massey, D. S., & Denton, N. A. (1988). The dimensions of residential segregation. *Social Forces, 67*(3), 281–315.

Massey, D. S., & Denton, N. A. (1993). *American apartheid: Segregation and the making of the underclass.* Cambridge, MA: Harvard University Press.

Oliver, J. E. (2001). *Democracy in suburbia.* Princeton, NJ: Princeton University Press.

Oliver, J. E., & Wong, J. (2003). Intergroup prejudice in multiethnic settings. *American Journal of Political Science, 47*(4), 567–582.

Perlmann, J., & Waters, M. C. (Eds.). (2002). *The new race question: How the census counts multi-racial individuals.* New York: Russell Sage Foundation.

Pettigrew, T. F. (1998). Intergroup contact theory. *Annual Review of Psychology, 49,* 65–85.

Putnam, R. D. (2000). *Bowling alone: The collapse and revival of American community*. New York: Simon and Schuster.

Quillian, L. (1996). Group threat and regional change in attitudes toward African Americans. *American Journal of Sociology, 102*(3), 816–860.

Sampson, R. J., Morenoff, J. D., & Gannon-Rowley, T. (2002). Assessing "neighborhood effects": Social processes and new directions in research. *Annual Review of Sociology, 28*, 443–478.

Schmidley, A. D. (2001). *Profile of the foreign-born population in the United States: 2000*. US Census Bureau Current Population Reports, Series P23–206. Washington, DC: US Government Printing Office.

Skocpol, T. (2003). *Diminishing democracy: From membership to management in American civic life*. Norman: University of Oklahoma Press.

Taylor, M. C. (1998). How white attitudes vary with the racial composition of local populations: Numbers count. *American Sociological Review, 63*(4), 512–535.

Varshney, A. (2001). Ethnic conflict and civil society: India and beyond. *World Politics, 53*(3), 362–398.

Verba, S., Schlozman, K. L., & Brady, H. E. (1995). *Voice and equality: Civic voluntarism in American politics*. Cambridge, MA: Harvard University Press.

Welch, S., Sigelman, L., Bledsoe, T., & Combs, M. (2001). *Race and place: Race relations in an American city*. New York: Cambridge University Press.

Wilkes, R., & Iceland, J. (2004). Hypersegregation in the twenty-first century. *Demography, 41*(1), 23–36.

11

The Paradox of Conflict in Groups

Conflict With Trust Is the Basis for Deep-Level Cooperation in Work Groups

SARAH RONSON AND RANDALL S. PETERSON

Conflict is an Essential Ingredient for Effective Cooperation and Superior Performance in Work Groups

It may seem odd to begin a book chapter on the importance of cooperation in work groups by suggesting that conflict is the key—after all, conflict and cooperation often appear to pull in opposite directions. However, the research we have been engaged in over the past decade continues to point to the notion that deep-level intragroup cooperation is achieved only in the context of effective conflict resolution that comes as a result of team leadership and/or conflict resolution strategies. In other words, the key to achieving the benefits of cooperation is actually conflict resolution. When the conflict that pervades group life is resolved amicably and respectfully, this sets the foundation for strong intragroup trust and encourages a virtuous cycle through which continuing conflict is resolved in an atmosphere of psychological safety and effective problem solving (cf. Edmondson, 1999; Simons & Peterson, 2000). The virtuous cycle can only begin, however, when initial group conflicts are successfully resolved (see Behfar, Peterson, Mannix, & Trochim, 2005; Peterson & Behfar, 2003).

We argue that conflict is key in part because it pervades life as a group member. As the workplace becomes increasingly diverse and teams are formed with the expressed intent of harnessing this diversity of backgrounds, beliefs, and perspectives, conflict is inevitable. Group members disagree over how to approach tasks, who they like and dislike, what the correct answer to a problem is, and many other issues. The key question is *not* how to avoid conflict since this is impossible, but rather how to *manage* the conflict within work groups. Unfortunately, conflict creates a paradox for groups. On the one hand, conflict feels uncomfortable for individual group members. When people disagree over substantive issues related to their work, it can easily transform into negative interpersonal relationships (Simons

& Peterson, 2000). It is easy to feel irritated when someone disagrees with you, or to take a heated debate about one of your ideas as a personal attack. As a result, group members can come to feel suspicious of one another's motives and generally fail to trust one another. On the other hand, conflict is actually necessary for the development of deep-level and effective cooperation in groups. Without conflict, group members cannot uncover and come to understand one another's perspectives, motivations, and goals, and use one another's unique perspective and information in service of the group. In short, conflict provides an opportunity for members to learn about one another and to demonstrate their trust of each other and their own trustworthiness as a group member. Thus, conflict can lead to the erosion of trust in groups, but ironically is also the foundation of trust building in groups that enables true cooperation to occur.

In this chapter, we explore this paradox and its resolution. We begin by defining what we will call fundamental or deep-level cooperation that emphasizes both trust and conflict. That is, we suggest that groups only truly act cooperatively when they achieve both trust *and* conflict simultaneously. We also suggest that the effective management of group processes facilitates the development of trust. We then tackle two of the primary goals of this book. First, we review the benefits of fundamental cooperation for individual group members and group performance. Second, we suggest ways to promote group cooperation by examining ways in which team leaders can facilitate cooperation and trust simultaneously, through both group process and structural interventions.

The Paradox of How Conflict Leads to Cooperation in Work Groups

Trust, conflict, and cooperation are intertwined. Scholars have long suggested, for example, that trust is the basis for cooperation (e.g. Blau, 1964), and the underpinning of successful interpersonal relationships (Rempel, Holmes, & Zanna, 1985). Trust is a belief that others will not act in a way that is against your best interests when they have the opportunity to do so (Mayer, Davis, & Schoorman, 1995; Zand, 1972). The essence of trust, therefore, is an expression of confidence that others have positive motives towards you (Mellinger, 1956), and that other group members will act cooperatively. By tradition, cooperation and conflict are perceived as opposites—conflict is typically described as occurring when people have opposing interests (Deutsch, 1973), which suggests limited opportunity for cooperation. However, our work suggests a somewhat different story, which we share here.

Conflict between work group colleagues is typically uncomfortable and disruptive. Conflict involves disagreement and argument that can be taken personally, particularly when people do not know each other well. It is easy for group members to misinterpret a heated debate over an idea or opinion as a clash of personalities (i.e., relationship conflict). Particularly when one group member strongly disagrees with another's position, it is hard to see how his or her argument can be based on the facts. The causes of differences of opinion can therefore appear ambiguous, and people may attribute the behavior to a sinister motive, such as a personal attack. This can easily devolve into dislike and personality conflicts between group members (Simons & Peterson, 2000).

When conflict about ideas or opinions is misattributed as a personal conflict between individuals, this can have serious negative implications for both an individual group member's experience in the group, and consequently the performance of the group. Specific individuals involved in a conflict can feel suspicious of and mistrustful towards one another, irritated and annoyed with one another, or alienated from the group (Simons & Peterson, 2000). This makes for an uncomfortable atmosphere and personal dissatisfaction with life as a group member, even for those not involved in the conflict. Conflict can also lead to a lack of communication between team members, preventing them from being willing to understand one another's point of view, and distracting group members away from the task and towards building their own power within the group (Jehn 1997). Ultimately, these processes harm group performance.

However, conflict is also at the heart of why work can be accomplished effectively by groups. Groups are useful not only because they have many members amongst whom work can be divided, but also because the interaction of these members creates something greater than any of the individual members could produce alone. Groups necessarily have more information, perspectives, and resources than any one individual member can possess (Davis, 1973), and it is likely that much of each individuals' knowledge will be unique. Except in situations with the most clearly demonstrable solutions, therefore, members are likely to disagree. From a decision-making perspective, some level of disagreement is good. It means that individuals are challenged to defend their opinions, think through their positions, and incorporate new information into their ideas. Groups in which a minority of members consistently advocate for an idea that is different to that favored by the majority of the group tend to more fully question their views, and to be more divergent in considering alternatives (Nemeth 1986). Group members with different perspectives also trigger unusual associations in others that help members to generate more creative ideas (Nemeth, 1986). This sort of beneficial conflict, which is related to the content of the group's work, ensures that group members consider all of the relevant information and are vigilant in thinking through the issues so that they can come to the best decision (Fiol, 1994; Janssen, Van de Vliert, & Veenstra, 1999). The problem, however, is that the negative interpersonal effects described above often accompany task conflict. The role and coexistence of task conflict and interpersonal conflict have long been established in the groups literature (e.g. Amason, 1996; Guetzkow & Gyr, 1954; Simons & Peterson, 2000).

What we suggest in this chapter is that, paradoxically, while conflict can lead to negative interpersonal consequences in groups, it can also strengthen interpersonal relationships between group members. Specifically, we propose that conflict is essential to the development of trust in groups in three interrelated ways: (1) conflict helps group members to uncover and understand one another's perspectives, and, importantly, motivations, so that they can bring their interests closer into alignment; (2) conflict gives members the opportunity to display and test whether or not they trust others in the group and demonstrate their own trustworthiness; and (3) conflict improves group output and therefore reduces the extent to which the group receives negative feedback.

Conflict aids the development of trust by uncovering and aligning incentives

One of the most hotly debated issues in the groups literature is the groupthink phenomenon (Janis, 1982). In a group characterized by groupthink, members are likely to agree with one another on the best course of action. This appears to be cooperative—everyone is going along with what other group members want. However, what is the motivation for their agreement? We follow the guiding premise of this book that cooperation involves actions taken for the benefit of a *shared and collective* goal (see Sullivan, Snyder, & Sullivan, this volume). Groupthink occurs because of pressure to suppress dissent in order to remain in favor with the group (Janis, 1982). Thus, group members agree on the surface in order to pursue the strictly *individual* agenda to remain within the group. Key group members assert this pressure in subtle ways, and thereby are also pursuing their own agenda by advocating a particular alternative. While group members share the same individual goal, these goals come into conflict with what is best for the quality of the group decision. Moreover, each individual's goals could also be met by doing something that is beneficial for the group—i.e., disagreeing with (for example) the leader. In a situation where the leader exerts pressure on the group, and group members bow to this pressure in order to remain in the group while realizing that they are going to take the wrong course of action, an individual group member is likely to win the favor of other group members by voicing her concerns rather than be shunned by them. In other words, it may be possible for group members to serve both the interests of the group and their own personal agendas in this situation. However, members are not aware that their interests are aligned, because no one voices their honest opinion. Thus, we would not define this as true cooperation.

When group members disagree with one another, their disagreement also communicates valuable information about their motivations. Conflict gives group members the opportunity to learn about one another's perspectives, and consequently, their underlying goals. Through debate and discussion, individuals can uncover possibilities for integrative solutions and joint gains in the space where their interests overlap (Johnson & Johnson, 1997). Moreover, in groups with no conflict, group members will not have the opportunity to do this. Colbert, Bono, and Purvanova (in this volume), suggest that by exhibiting unconventional behaviors and taking risks, leader's demonstrate their commitment to their goals, which builds trust. When one person has a poor understanding of how another sees a problem and what that person is trying to accomplish, his attributions about that individual's behavior are less likely to be correct. Thus, by helping group members learn about each other, conflict improves their ability to understand one another, and therefore enables them to see where their interests overlap. They can, therefore, correctly attribute behaviors that are counter to their own interests where their interests do not overlap.

In addition, group members can try to bring their interests into alignment through conflict. By advocating for their own perspective, individuals can help their group members to see their point of view, and may be able to convert others to supporting their position. This is particularly important in groups that are diverse in terms of characteristics such as functional background, where individuals are likely to be entrenched in a functional perspective on the problem that gives different factors greater priority than others would attribute to them. In support of this, Chatman, Polzer, Barsade, & Neale (1998) found that groups are better able to use the conflict created by diversity when the organizational culture emphasizes that members share common interests. Consistent minorities in groups are often able to convince the majority of different ways of looking at issues (Nemeth, 1986). Thus, in addition to helping group members to understand one another's perspectives, conflict can bring their goals into closer alignment.

Conflict aids the development of trust by allowing trust to be displayed and assessed

Task conflict gives group members the opportunity to voice their opinions about the task and therefore to feel that they have some control over the decision-making process—this increases satisfaction with the decision (Amason, 1996; Peterson, 1999; Thibaut & Walker, 1975). When group members voice their opinion about tasks, they are displaying a belief that the other members of the group will not hold these opinions against them and an expectation that the group will attempt to incorporate their ideas or concerns into the group decision. Without this trust, there would be no point in communicating one's ideas with others in the group. While this may not be a conscious effort, it reflects an underlying assumption about the group and its members. Approaching others with the assumption of complete trust, and acting in accordance with this, can lead to reciprocity from other team members (Pillutla, Malhotra, & Murnighan, 2003), which will ultimately build trust between group members. Moreover, if group members act in initial meetings as if they expect others in the group to respect their opinions and ideas, a norm for trust is more likely to develop, setting a pattern for subsequent group interactions (Bettenhausen & Murnighan, 1991).

In addition to communicating a sense of trust, sharing one's opinions with other group members tests the extent to which they can be trusted. If group members do indeed give sufficient consideration to one another's ideas and attempt to use each other's information for the benefit of the group task, they demonstrate that they can be trusted not to act against one another's best interests. This will also give group members greater confidence that they will be able to resolve disagreements in satisfactory ways in the future (Johnson & Johnson, 1997), and therefore they will feel more optimistic about the group.

Finally, conflict allows individuals to express their feelings instead of keeping them contained. Since it is stressful for organizational members to display feelings they do not feel (Hoschild, 1983), it will be taxing for group members to suppress their true opinions. When people keep their concerns to themselves, frustration, irritation, and resentment can build (Johnson & Johnson, 1997) that can result in a much greater conflict than if the disagreement had been aired sooner. Thus, conflict provides an opportunity for catharsis that prevents greater, more damaging conflicts from occurring.

In contrast, in groups that lack conflict, the development of trust will be problematic. If group members do not express their true opinions to one another, they may maintain a façade of friendliness and camaraderie, but based on a limited understanding of one another. Since it is unrealistic to expect that group members will always agree on everything, a lack of conflict can only be temporary and superficial, and as conflict does emerge, it is more likely to be misattributed. Thus, where groups do not experience some conflict in their early group life, they may come to live in an artificially harmonious state that hides tension that becomes difficult to resolve because intragroup trust did not develop.

Conflict aids the development of trust by improving group performance and reducing negative feedback

Members of groups are likely to have a complex web of opposing and overlapping interests, and it is in fact this characteristic that often makes group work worthwhile. In groups, people's conflicting goals lead to disagreements that can improve the group's output through discussion and debate—it helps group members to consider the full range of information that is relevant to their decision, double check what they think they know, and fully think through their ideas (e.g. Ely & Thomas, 2001; Jehn, 1997). By improving group output, conflict fulfils another function for groups. Peterson and Behfar (2003) have recently demonstrated that conflict is a reaction to, as well as cause of, feedback about group performance. In fact, when groups receive initial negative feedback about their performance, levels of both task and relationship conflict increase (Peterson & Behfar, 2003). Negative feedback reduces group efficacy, threatens group cohesion (Staw, Sandelands, & Dutton, 1981), increases interpersonal tension, and decreases the willingness of group members to entertain one another's ideas and consider other points of view (Peterson & Behfar, 2003). In addition to these direct effects, research also suggests that people use information about group outcomes to retrospectively infer the degree of task and relationship conflict—when people believe that a team has been more successful, they attribute greater task conflict and cohesiveness to the group (Staw, 1975). Similarly, when group members receive negative feedback, they may retrospectively interpret their previous group processes as being characterized by less task and more relationship conflict than they experienced at the time.

This suggests a circular process for groups. If group members initially lack conflict, they will have lower levels of performance, and this will result in subsequently higher levels of conflict. However, if group members initially have a controlled amount of conflict related to their task, they will have better outcomes, and therefore limited subsequent negative conflict—and consequently, higher levels of trust.

In sum, conflict creates a paradox for groups. Conflict can negatively affect the individual experiences of, and interpersonal relationships between, group members, and in this way, can disrupt the development of trust between group members. However, at the same time, conflict is actually *necessary* to facilitate the development of trust in groups, and therefore, ultimately, aids group performance by improving both group output *and* group processes. We argue that real cooperation in groups occurs only when the group has *both* trust and conflict. Several empirical studies of diversity in groups support this notion. For example, Polzer, Milton, & Swann (2002) find that groups in which members are perceived accurately by other members are able to capitalize on the conflict created by diversity. In part, these accurate perceptions facilitate the development of trust, as "the knowledge will facilitate smooth social interaction and enhance the chances that people will achieve the goals that brought them to the interaction" (Polzer et al., p. 299). Ely & Thomas (2001) similarly found that in diverse groups with an attitude that differences should be valued, group members felt safer revealing more about themselves and their true opinions, and therefore achieved higher levels of performance.

This culture of cooperation and trust can be seen in contrast to our earlier example of groupthink. If a group has conflict but no trust, then the conflict will degenerate into interpersonal issues that distract the group and make members resentful of and angry with one another (à la Simons & Peterson, 2000). In contrast, if a group has trust but no conflict, group members are not doing what is best for the group, which is to question and challenge one another to ensure that the group is considering all information and using its full range of resources. In such a group, members are more focused on their own personal concern for maintaining positive interpersonal relationships than what is best for the group. Just as we may gently challenge a friend who we believe to be making a bad decision, if we are committed to a group's goals, we will challenge the opinions and ideas of our fellow group members.

When a group is truly cooperative, the relationship between members changes from one of weak or conditional trust to one of strong trust, in which small breaches of trust will be more easily attributed to benign causes, and therefore more easily forgiven (Jones & George, 1998). When strong trust develops between individuals, the affective experience of their relationship changes, as they come to view each other as friends rather than colleagues (Jones & George, 1998). Thus, in cooperative groups, the experiences of group members are more positive, and the interpersonal relationships between members deeper. In the following section, we suggest that this sort of fundamental cooperation in groups has many benefits both for the psychological state of group members, as well as for group outcomes.

The Benefits of Deep-Level Cooperation in Groups

One of the primary goals of this book is to specify the effects of cooperation on the well-being and functioning of individuals and groups. In the context of small groups, cooperation benefits both the well-being of individuals and the functioning of groups. The most fundamental benefits of cooperation are to the psychological states and interpersonal relationships among group members. Highly cooperative groups can provide the strong interpersonal connections and mutual support that lead individuals to happier, more meaningful, more productive lives (see Sullivan, Snyder, & Sullivan, introduction to this book). In addition, members get along with each other, and are free from the stress of interpersonal strife. These improved psychological states and interpersonal relationships can have profound effects on group performance. Thus, cooperation can lead to higher-quality decisions, generative behaviors, and can promote team survival.

Psychological benefits of cooperation to individual group members

Improved emotional state of team members

The psychological benefits to individuals of working in a cooperative environment have been elaborated in other chapters of this book, but they apply equally to members of groups. Groups often constitute the primary environmental influence in which people work, and as such, the interpersonal atmosphere of the group has a major impact on an individual's psychological well-being. Conflict is stressful. When conflict occurs in groups, it can make people feel undervalued or unappreciated, irritated, angry, frustrated, and lacking in confidence (e.g. Jehn, 1997). As Greenberg suggests (in this volume), stress caused by working in a negative environment may also spill over into one's personal life. Members of cooperative groups can share the burden of the task with others, get support, and empathize with one another.

Interpersonal relationships

Damage to interpersonal relationships is the primary negative effect of conflict in groups. Trust between group members mitigates this damage (see Kramer & Tyler, 1996; Simons & Peterson, 2000). When group members have a cooperative spirit, they are better able to correctly attribute the otherwise ambiguous signals sent during discussions about the task. This improves relationships not only between those individuals who would otherwise be involved in personality conflicts, but also other bystanders on the team who no longer have to live in an environment with interpersonal conflicts.

Benefits of cooperation to group outcomes and performance

Open information exchange and decision making

One of the factors that limits effective group decision making is the tendency for group members to discuss information that is commonly held between them, and ignore information that only one group member knows (Stasser & Titus, 1985). In part, this tendency occurs because people are sometimes strategic in the way that they share information (Wittenbaum & Hollingshead, 2003).

When group members are cooperative and have a sense of trust for one another, the information sharing bias can be reduced. Trust facilitates the open exchange of information, ideas, and knowledge (Jones & George, 1998; Zand, 1972). When group members share a common goal, they look past their personal needs for the benefit of the group and believe that others will do the same (e.g., such as to promote their own preferred alternative or suggestion). This cooperation removes the incentive and motivation for individuals to hoard information or be strategic in not sharing it with one another. Gruenfeld, Mannix, Williams, and Neale (1996) support the idea that trust leads to more open sharing of information with the finding that groups of friends tend to be less subject to the information sharing bias than groups of strangers. When members openly share information, the group is able to make more informed and considered decisions, and consequently, improve decision quality.

Confidence and decision acceptance

For teams to work effectively, team members must have the confidence in others on the team to allocate work to them and allow them to carry out this work. In effective teams, members develop a sense of who knows what in the group, and rely on those individuals to fulfil that part of the task related to their area of expertise (Moreland, Argote, & Krishnan, 1998; Wegner, Erber, & Raymond, 1991). Moreover, once members have completed their portion of the task, others must trust that they have done their best, and that the quality of their work is good. This is not to say that team members cannot challenge ideas or question one another—vigilant consideration of all information involving all team members is an essential aspect of good group decision making (e.g. Janis & Mann, 1992). However, this questioning must be based on the assumption that having multiple heads working on a problem is better than one, rather than suggesting that the person tasked with that work may not have done the best job.

When team members have a fundamental attitude of cooperation and trust, they will have greater confidence in the ability of their fellow members (Jones &

George, 1998). This confidence means that members do not have to second-guess one another and prevents members from duplicating effort because each can rely on others to get their job done. Failing to trust even a single group member can disrupt group functioning if a norm develops for mistrust and double-checking. Cooperative group members are also more likely to come to agreement on alternatives or solutions because their joint commitment to the group's goal will make them more persistent at achieving consensus. Team members will, therefore, be more committed to the group's solution, which facilitates the implementation of the group's decision (Amason, 1996). Thus, cooperative groups are more efficient in their approach to work, and more effective at implementing their ideas.

Help seeking and learning

Part of the value of groups comes from the ability of group members to learn from and help one another. Cooperation between team members is essential for learning. When group members trust each other, they are more willing to ask one another for help (Jones & George, 1998), feel safe sharing new information, suggesting potentially silly or risky ideas, making mistakes, and asking questions (Edmondson, 1999). In addition, group members can feel free to offer their help to others or question one another in the presence of trust, because they will not fear that their actions will be misinterpreted as an intrusion or a lack of confidence in others. Group members learn by engaging in this help-seeking behavior.

Positive affect and creativity

In addition to improving the decision quality of groups, cooperation can aid the creation of new and novel solutions. As discussed above, members of cooperative teams will feel more relaxed, less stressed, and generally better about their work experience—that is, they experience higher levels of positive affect. Positive affect is a powerful enabler of individual creativity. Positive affect promotes variety seeking, so people are more likely to explore novel ideas in this state, while when people feel threatened, they use more rigid, narrow thought processes that inhibit creativity (Isen, 1999). Under threat, attention to information becomes limited and routine responses are dominant (Staw et al., 1981). This prevents divergent thinking and the generation of novel ideas.

Compliance with team rules and team survival

Group success cannot be measured by performance alone—in order to succeed, groups must first survive and function as a unit (Hackman, 1987). In order for a group to survive, its members must want to continue group membership—they must find value in being part of the group and be motivated to continue participation. In other words, the psychological experience of team members is essential to the survival of the team. In cooperative groups, where members have a more positive experience, they will be more satisfied with the team, and therefore more likely to want to remain on it. Moreover, groups often develop rules that govern the behavior of their members and enable the effective functioning of the group (Bettenhausen & Murnighan, 1984; Feldman, 1984). As Tyler suggests (this volume), people are more likely to comply with groups that they view as legitimate. Where group members believe that they will be treated fairly by the group, they will be more willing to comply with the rules that govern group life, promoting the survival of the group.

Resolving the Paradox: Lessons on Managing Conflict in Groups

Given the fundamental importance of conflict as a way to develop trust in groups, it is essential that conflict is managed effectively to produce positive outcomes. The literature suggests two interrelated ways in which conflict can be managed effectively. The first way is through the management of group processes, particularly by the group leader. The second way is structural—the team can be designed such that individual member incentives are aligned and cooperation is therefore promoted.

Group process solutions to managing conflict

Group processes have a major influence on how members experience life in the group. The perceptions and experiences of group members determine whether or not conflict will lead to the development of trust between group members: If members experience group life as negative, competitive, and stressful, conflict will lead to mistrust and interpersonal problems, while if they experience group life as positive, cooperative, and supportive, conflict can build this positive experience to help members develop trust. One of the key considerations is whether members feel included in the group. Inclusive processes make group members feel that they have a voice in what happens in the group and in group outputs (Hirschman, 1970), and therefore make them feel more positive about their experience. This makes them more willing to accept group decisions (Amason, 1996), and leads to higher levels of individual well-being (Sullivan & Peterson, 2005).

Peterson & colleagues suggest that the leader has a primary role in shaping the dynamics of the group (e.g., Peterson, 1997; Peterson, Smith, Martorana, & Owens, 2003; Sullivan & Peterson, 2005). When leaders are highly process directive, they take a major role in shaping the interactions of the group by facilitating the inclusion of group members (Peterson, 1997). The personality of the leader is one factor responsible for this (Sullivan & Peterson, 2005). Importantly, however, it is the fact that personality influences a leader's behaviors that leads to different perceptions for group members. For example, conscientiousness is associated with a desire for structure and order, and consequently, leaders who are high in this trait are likely to attempt to impose a structure on group processes. Similarly, leaders who are high in agreeableness are more likely to use process directive behaviors as a way to manage the interpersonal relationships of group members. In contrast, leaders who have high levels of neuroticism are more likely to try to ignore problems in the group (Sullivan & Peterson, 2005). These behaviors in turn shape how individuals perceive their group life. Members of groups with leaders who are high in conscientiousness, extraversion, and agreeableness, and low in neuroticism, are generally more likely to perceive the group as efficacious, cohesive, and committed, and to be more satisfied with group membership (Sullivan & Peterson, 2005). Importantly, these leaders are also more likely to create perceptions of trust and low levels of conflict amongst group members (see Sullivan & Peterson, 2005 for a full review).

Colbert, Bono, and Purvanova (in this volume) highlight the importance of leadership to the perceptions and actions of employees. They suggest that generative leadership fosters high-quality relationships with employees that improves cooperation and employee well-being. In large part, the benefits of generative leadership stem from the fact that generative leaders promote employee participation and autonomy. As we have also discussed, when people participate in decisions, they have an opportunity to voice their opinions, which increases their satisfaction and makes them feel more positive about their experience. We would suggest that leader personality and behavior can foster this participation. However, Colbert et al. go beyond participation, and identify a set of benefits of leadership to cooperation that result from the more underlying value of a desire to contribute to society.

By influencing the perceptions of individual members of the group and by managing group processes, these leader behaviors also influence the overall dynamic of the group (Peterson et al. 2003). For example, highly conscientious CEOs who are focused on structure and maintaining order also tend to lead teams that have a more centralized power structure and prefer to have a sense of control over their environment. CEOs who are low in terms of emotional stability tend to have teams that are less cohesive, and think in more rigid ways. In contrast, teams that are led by CEOs who are very open to experience are more likely to be flexible and think in multi-dimensional ways, as well as to be more willing to take risks (see Peterson et al. 2003 for a full review). In other words, group leaders not only shape the way that members experience group life, but also how these experiences combine into a group dynamic. In sum, by actively managing group dynamics, leaders can ensure that conflict occurs on the team—by encouraging people to speak their minds and by facilitating debate—and ensure that when it does occur, it is constructive and builds trust—by helping the group to see mutual points of understanding, coming to closure on issues, and reducing interpersonal tension.

Colbert et al. (this volume) allude to an alternative function of leadership. They suggest that generative leadership leads to high-quality relationships that are built on foundations of shared goals. For example, generative leaders provide compelling visions of the future of the organization, which allows them to "connect the values and goals of the organization with employees' self concepts, increasing the degree to which employees share leaders' goals" (Colbert et al., p. 204). If leader's can help to align the goals of organizational members, they provide a structural solution to the development of cooperation. We discuss these structural solutions in the following section.

Structural solutions to managing conflict

An alternative way to gain the benefits of conflict while minimizing its negative effects is by structuring the group so that members' incentives are aligned, and an overarching goal drives their behaviors. When individuals have interdependent goals, such that when one person achieves his or her goals, all others also achieve their goals (Deutsch, 1949), they can be confident that others will not act against their interests, and can therefore rationally develop a sense of "trust" in the other members of the group. In groups, this type of interdependence can be achieved in several ways. For example, when each group member must depend on others performing tasks in order to complete their own part of the work, they have task interdependence (Johnson & Johnson, 1997; Wageman, 1995). This may occur, for example, because one member must wait until another has completed their work before starting on their own part of the task (Van de Ven & Ferry, 1980), such as when several group members make components that are then assembled by another group member. Or it may occur because the information necessary to complete the task is distributed throughout the members of the group (Johnson & Johnson, 1989; Wageman, 1995).

Alternatively, rewards can create interdependence. Rewards may mean actual financial or other material rewards given to group members, or it may simply mean the achievement of goals, which are another major outcome of the task (Wageman, 1995). Reward or outcome interdependence exists in a group when one member's rewards depend on the performance of the rest of the group (Johnson & Johnson, 1989; Wageman, 1995).

Interdependence influences the way that group members experience their work. By promoting the feeling that one depends on others, interdependence leads to cooperative actions. When interdependence exists, group members can trust that others in the group will not act in a way to harm their own interests, because doing so would harm that person's interests as well. This provides a framework for interpreting the behavior of other group members, so that even when apparently ambiguous actions are taken by other group members, people are more likely to attribute the cause to something that will benefit the group, and this can reduce the misinterpretation of task-related conflicts as personal issues (à la Simons & Peterson, 2000). Thus, conflict can emerge in the group—and in fact, will emerge, because individuals' incentives will make them primarily concerned about doing what is best for the group. By structuring the group in a way that maximizes interdependence between members, conflict can promote the development of trust.

While structural solutions can aid the constructive emergence of conflict, as a complete solution, we argue that they are very difficult to achieve for at least three reasons. First, as Tyler (in this volume) observes, rewards and punishments have a marginal effect on behavior. People gain various social rewards through interpersonal interaction (Allen & Hecht, 2004) that cannot be controlled by structuring the task or reward system—for example, as people gain esteem from affiliation with the group (e.g. Tajfel & Turner, 1979). These social rewards may create individual incentives that are not aligned with group goals. Secondly, in an organizational setting, membership in a given group is unlikely to be an individual's only role, and people therefore have other personal and professional agendas. For example, while all group members may want the group as a whole to succeed, each individual may also want to be the highest performer in the group because that person is likely to get the most credit, best reputation, greatest share of organizational rewards, or simply the greatest sense of self-esteem. Finally, people may not accurately perceive the structure of the task or the rewards. For example, even in organizations truly unconcerned with individual performance, employees' socialization in other work environments will make it difficult for them to believe this. Tyler (this volume) further suggests that it is costly for organizations to put the necessary resources into structures that will promote cooperation. Fortunately, even in the absence of complete structural solutions, conflict can also be promoted in a way that helps to build trust by managing group processes effectively.

Teams in Context: The Broader Implications of Cooperation in Groups

In this chapter, we have reviewed the paradox of conflict that exists for groups. We acknowledge that conflict can destroy the relationships between group members, but also argue that it is a key foundation stone upon which deep-level trust is built in groups. In fact, we propose, only when groups have both trust *and* conflict are they truly cooperative. This type of deep-level cooperation provides numerous benefits for groups and their members. We argue that leaders have a significant role to play in managing conflicts effectively to ensure the development of trust and cooperation.

The pervasive use of teams to conduct the core work of many organizations suggests that teams constitute the primary work environment for many workers. For individuals, this means that what occurs in their work teams has a major effect on their day-to-day work lives. When teams are riddled with unresolved conflict and uncooperative conflict resolution behaviors, workers tend to experience less affiliation and more stress. In contrast, when teams are cooperative, workers find a more supportive environment, more interpersonal friendships, and in general are more successful at accomplishing work. In other words, people are happier in cooperative teams. The implication for organizations is that the team environment can have a major impact on the productivity of its workforce. Thus, managing to ensure cooperation on teams can improve not only the experiences of team members in interacting with the team and group outputs, but can also provide a foundation for overall organizational improvement.

References

Allen, N. J., & Hecht, T. D. (2004). The "romance of teams": Toward an understanding of its psychological underpinnings and implications. *Journal of Occupational and Organizational Psychology, 77*, 439–461.

Amason, A. (1996). Distinguishing the effects of functional and dysfunctional conflict on strategic decision making: Resolving a paradox for top management teams. *Academy of Management Journal, 39*, 123–148.

Behfar, K. J., Peterson, R. S., Mannix, E. A., & Trochim, W. M. K. (2005). *Conflict resolution strategies in autonomous work groups: identifying process indicators associated with group viability*. Unpublished manuscript. University of California, Irvine.

Bettenhausen, K. L., & Murnighan, K. (1991). The development of an intragroup norm and the effects of interpersonal and structural challenges. *Administrative Science Quarterly, 36*, 20–35.

Blau, P. (1964). *Exchange and power in social life*. New York: John Wiley.

Chatman, J. A., Polzer, J. T., Barsade, S., & Neale, M. A. (1998). Being different yet feeling similar: The influence of demographic composition and organizational culture on work processes and outcomes. *Administrative Science Quarterly, 43*, 749–780.

Davis, J. H. (1973). Group decision and social interaction: A theory of social decision schemes. *Psychological Review, 80*, 97–125.

Deutsch, M. (1949). A theory of cooperation and competition. *Human Relations, 2*, 129–152.

Deutsch, M. (1973). *The resolution of conflict: Constructive and destructive processes*. New Haven, CT: Yale University Press.

Edmondson, A. C. (1999). Psychological safety and learning behaviour in work teams. *Administrative Science Quarterly, 44*, 350–383.

Ely, R. J., & Thomas, D. A. (2001). Cultural diversity at work: The effects of diversity perspectives on work group processes and outcomes. *Administrative Science Quarterly, 46*, 229–273.

Feldman, D. (1984). The development and enforcement of group norms. *Academy of Management Review, 9*, 47–53.

Fiol, C. M. (1994). Consensus, diversity, and learning in organizations. *Organization Science, 5*, 403–420.

Gruenfeld, D. H, Mannix, E. A., Williams, K. Y., & Neale, M. A. (1996). Group composition and decision making: How member familiarity and information distribution affect process and performance. *Organizational Behaviour and Human Decision Processes, 67*, 1–15.

Guetzkow, H., & Gyr, J. (1954). An analysis of conflcit in decision making groups. *Human Relations, 7*, 367–381.

Hackman, J. R. (1987). The design of work teams. In J. W. Lorsch (ed.), *Handbook of organizational behavior* (pp. 315–342). Englewood Cliffs. NJ: Prentice-Hall.

Hirschman, A. O. (1970). *Exit, voice, and loyalty.* Cambridge, MA: Harvard University Press.

Hoschild, A. (1983). *The managed heart.* Berkeley, University of California Press.

Isen, A. M. (1999). On the relationship between affect and creative problem solving. In S. W. Russ (Ed.), *Affect, creative experience, and psychological adjustment* (pp. 3–17). Philadelphia: Brunner/Mazel.

Janis, I. (1982). *Groupthink* (2nd edition). Boston: Houghton Mifflin.

Janis, I. L., & Mann, L. (1992). Cognitive complexity in international decision making. In P. Suedfeld & P. E. Tetlock (Eds.), *Psychology and Social Policy (*pp. 33–49). Washington, DC: Hemisphere.

Janssen, O., Van de Vliert, E., & Veenstra, C. (1999). How task and person conflict shape the role of positive interdependence in management teams. *Journal of Conflict Management, 25,* 117–142.

Jehn, K. A. (1997). A qualitative analysis of conflict types and dimensions in organizational groups. *Administrative Science Quarterly, 42,* 530–557.

Johnson, D. W., & Johnson, R. (1989). *Cooperation and competition: Theory and research.* Edina, MN: Interaction.

Johnson, D. W., & Johnson, F. P. (1997). *Joining together: group theory and group skills.* Needham Heights, MA: Allyn & Bacon.

Jones, G. R., & George, J. M. (1998). The experience and evolution of trust: Implications for cooperation and teamwork. *Academy of Management Review, 23,* 531–546.

Kramer, R., & Tyler, T. R. (1996). *Trust in organizations: frontiers of theory and research.* Thousand Oaks, CA: Sage.

Mayer, R. C., Davis, J. H., & Schoorman, F. D. (1995). An integrative model of organizational trust. *Academy of Management Review, 20,* 709–734.

Mellinger, G. D. (1956). Interpersonal trust as a factor in communication. *Journal of Abnormal and Social Psychology, 52,* 304–309.

Moreland, R., Argote, L, & Krishnan, R. (1998). Training people to work in groups. In L. H. R. S. Tindale, J. Edwards, E. J. Posvac, F. B. Brant, Y. Sharex-Balcazar, E. Henderson-Kind, et al. (Eds.). *Theory and research on small groups* (pp. 37–60). New York: Plenum.

Nemeth, C. (1986). Differential contributions of majority and minority influence. *Psychological Review, 93,* 23–32

Peterson, R. S. (1997). A directive leadership style in group decision making can be both virtue and vice: Evidence from elite and experimental groups. *Journal of Personality and Social Psychology, 72,* 1107–1121.

Peterson, R. S. (1999). Can you have too much of a good thing? The limits of voice in improving satisfaction with leaders. *Personality and Social Psychology Bulletin, 25,* 313–324.

Peterson, R. S., & Behfar, K. J. (2003). The dynamic relationship between performance feedback, trust, and conflict in groups: A longitudinal study. *Organizational Behavior and Human Decision Processes, 92,* 102–112.

Peterson, R. S., Smith, D. B., Martorana, P. V., & Owens, P. D. (2003) The impact of chief executive officer personality on top management team dynamics: One mechanism by which leadership affects organizational performance. *Journal of Applied Psychology, 88,* 795–808.

Pillutla, M. M., Malhotra, D., & Murnighan, J. K. (2003). Attributions of trust and the calculus of reciprocity. *Journal of Experimental Social Psychology, 39,* 448–455.

Polzer, J. T., Milton, L. P., & Swann, W. B. (2002). Capitalizing on diversity: Interpersonal congruence in small work groups. *Administrative Science Quarterly*, *47*, 296–324.

Rempel, J. K., Holmes, J. G., & Zanna, M. P. (1985). Trust in close relationships. *Journal of Personality and Social Psychology*, *49*, 95–112.

Simons, T. L., & Peterson, R. S. (2000). Task conflict and relationship conflict in top management teams: The pivotal role of intragroup trust. *Journal of Applied Psychology*, *85*, 102–111.

Stasser, G., & Titus, W. (1985). Pooling of unshared information in group decision making: biased information sampling during discussion. *Journal of Personality and Social Psychology*, *48*, 1467–1478.

Staw, B. M. (1975). Attributions of "causes" of performance: A general alternative interpretation of non-sectional research on organizations. *Organizational Behavior and Human Performance*, *13*, 414–432.

Staw, B. M., Sandelands, L. E., & Dutton, J. E. (1981). Threat-rigidity effect: A multilevel analysis. *Administrative Science Quarterly*, *26*, 501–524.

Sullivan, B. A., & Peterson, R. S. (2005). *Linking leader personality with group dynamics: Leader process directiveness as mediator and performance feedback as moderator* (working paper).

Tajfel, H., & Turner, J. C. (1979). An integrative theory of intergroup conflict. In. W. G. Austin & S. Worschel (Eds.), *The social psychology of intergroup relations*. Monterey, CA: Brooks/Cole.

Thibaut, J., & Walker, L. (1975). *Procedural justice: A psychological analysis*. Hillsdale, NJ: Lawrence Erlbaum.

Van de Ven, A., & Ferry, D. (1980). *Measuring and assessing organizations*. New York: Wiley.

Wageman, R. (1995). Interdependence and group effectiveness. *Administrative Science Quarterly*, *40*, 145–180.

Wegner, D. M., Erber, R., & Raymond, P. (1991). Transactive memory in close relationships. *Journal of Personality and Social Psychology*, *61*, 923–929.

Wittenbaum, G. M., & Hollingshead, A. (2003). *From cooperative to motivated information sharing in groups: Moving beyond the hidden profile paradigm*. Presentation at Small Groups Meeting, Amsterdam.

Zand, D. E. (1972). Trust and managerial problem solving. *Administrative Science Quarterly*, *17*, 229–239.

12

Generative Leadership in Business Organizations

Enhancing Employee Cooperation and Well-Being Through High-Quality Relationships

AMY E. COLBERT, JOYCE E. BONO, AND
RADOSTINA K. PURVANOVA

Throughout this book, the role of interpersonal relationships in enhancing cooperation and well-being is emphasized. Consistent with findings from multiple disciplines, high-quality interpersonal relationships in the workplace have also been found to be vital in encouraging employee cooperation and enhancing employee well-being (e.g., Dutton & Heaphy, 2003; Gittell, 2003). However, organizations often struggle to create environments that support interpersonal relationships, encourage cooperative behavior, and enhance the psychosocial health of employees. Our primary aim in this chapter is to highlight the important role that organizational leadership plays in achieving these goals. Specifically, we introduce the concept of *generative leadership*. We suggest that generative leadership in work organizations creates an environment in which high-quality relationships between leaders and employees are formed and high-quality relationships among employees are nurtured. These high-quality work relationships lead to increased cooperation between individuals at work and ultimately enhance well-being for employees. Furthermore, we argue that generative leadership is necessary for long-term organizational sustainability. We believe this to be especially true for organizations (e.g., service organizations, caregiving organizations, knowledge organizations) that depend primarily on the engagement and commitment of employees for their success.

Generative Leadership

The *American Heritage Dictionary* (third edition) defines the term generative as "having the ability to originate, produce, or procreate." In psychology the use of the term generative stems from Erikson's (1950) psychosocial theory of development, which suggests that in midlife, individuals become concerned with having an impact reaching beyond the self. Recently, there has been a surge of interest in the psychosocial construct of generativity and the role that it plays in human well-being and thriving (Grossbaum & Bates, 2002), and volunteerism, civic engagement, and community involvement (Snyder & Clary, 2004). To date, however, there has been very little focus on generative leadership, especially in work organizations. This gap in the literature is curious given McAdams and de St. Aubin's (1998) observation that, "It seems intuitively right that some kinds of highly effective leaders owe their success to their generative capacities and inclinations" (p. 489).

In this chapter, we define generative leadership, provide examples of behaviors and characteristics of generative leaders, and discuss the impact of generative leadership on employee cooperation and well-being. Our focus is on work organizations, encompassing leadership at two levels—individual leader behavior and leadership culture. In the first instance, we are concerned with direct interactions between managers and employees. Thus, leadership refers to the behaviors that managers use to influence employee attitudes and behaviors. However, we also use the term leadership to refer to the more amorphous concept of a culture or environment created by organizational leaders. Used in this way, leadership refers to the norms and expectations established by top management, which guide the attitudes, behaviors, and experiences of individual employees.

In defining generative leadership, we draw from the extensive literature on the psychosocial construct of generativity as represented in the work of McAdams, de St. Aubin, and colleagues (see de St. Aubin, McAdams, & Kim, 2004; McAdams & de St. Aubin, 1992; McAdams & de St. Aubin, 1998), Peterson (2004), and Kotre (1984). Building on Erikson (1950), these scholars have identified three components of generativity: (a) creative or productive activities; (b) activities aimed at maintaining the positive or good aspects of a culture; and (c) giving up control and passing along the creative product to the next generation, empowering them, and offering them autonomy. The first component of generativity—creative and productive activities—is not hard to find among organizational leaders. Managers and executives typically attain their positions based on their creative and productive capacities, including their ability to have and implement new and creative ideas, produce new products, design new systems, or achieve new levels of productivity or profitability. However, merely creating or producing does not make a generative leader. Generative leadership also includes maintaining that which is good in an organizational culture and making it better, with the goal of enhancing the welfare of employees and other organizational stakeholders. Additionally, to ensure the organization's contribution to future generations, generative leaders empower employees, offer them voice and autonomy, and develop them into future leaders of the organization. To achieve these goals of positively influencing the long-term growth and development of both organizations and employees, generative leaders exhibit several types of behaviors.

First, generative leaders have a vision of the future that focuses on the long-term sustainability of their organizations (de St. Aubin et al., 2004). Although much has been written about the importance of a compelling, optimistic vision of the future as a key ingredient of leadership success (e.g., Bass, 1985), less attention has been paid by leadership scholars to concerns for long-term sustainability. By definition, the vision of generative leaders must include a concern for the long-term health and success of the organization. Yet, in the same way that generativity is about more than the mere survival of the species (de St. Aubin et al., 2004), generative leaders are concerned with more than the mere existence of the organization. The vision of a generative leader must extend beyond current quarterly returns to shareholders, reaching out to include attending to the long-term welfare of employees, consumers, and even society, as well as the organization itself.

Generative leaders also strive to engage employees in the work of the organization, including maintaining positive aspects of the organization's culture and implementing changes that will move the organization closer to the realization of its vision. Generative leaders engage employees, in part by linking employees to both the history of the organization and its future. For example, by telling stories and using metaphors and symbols, generative leaders emphasize the role that employees play in maintaining and improving the organization. Generative adults tend to tell stories that are optimistic and include redemption sequences (McAdams, Diamond, de St. Aubin, & Mansfield, 1997), in which bad events result in good outcomes. Other consistent themes in the narratives of generative adults are those that involve caring for others and establishing a legacy. Thus, the stories of generative leaders differ from those of non-generative leaders in that they tend to focus on the impact that employees and the organization will have on the future, as well as on the ways employees and the organization became stronger after encountering hardship and obstacles.

A third characteristic of generative leaders is their focus on the growth and development of employees. In this way, generative leaders enable employees to not only contribute to the future of the organization, but also develop in ways that enable them to lead fulfilling lives. For generative leaders, employees are whole human beings who play an important role in the future of the organization, not only human "resources." In their vision for the organization, in their policies and day-to-day practices, and in their dealings with employees, generative leaders consider and attend to the growth and development of individual employees in ways that benefit both employees and the organization. They develop, mentor, train, and socialize employees so that they can become the stewards of the organization in the future and so that they can pursue fulfilling lives and careers.

Considered as a whole, generative leadership behaviors are characterized by a spirit of caregiving. Generative leaders differ from non-generative leaders in that they are driven by communal motives (McAdams, Hart, & Maruna, 1998). Individuals with communal motives are primarily concerned with the welfare of other people and have attributes such as compassion and generosity. Because of their communal nature with its emphasis on caregiving, generative leaders are concerned with understanding and meeting the needs of others (Bell & Richard, 2000). Generative leaders exhibit care both through building and maintaining sustainable organizations that have a positive impact on society and by developing and caring for the employees within these organizations. In summary, generative leadership behaviors involve (a) communicating a clear vision of the future that focuses on the long-term sustainability of the organization, (b) engaging employees in the work of the organization by linking them to the organization's history and future, and (c) creating a culture of care, which supports employee growth and development, empowerment, and autonomy.

Generative leadership, as we have described it, is not inconsistent with several existing models of leadership. For example, many aspects of generative leadership are found in transformational leadership theory (Bass, 1985), which suggests that effective leadership involves having a compelling vision, communicating it with enthusiasm, improving the organization by challenging the status quo, acting as a positive role model for employees, and considering employees' individual needs. Similarly, the self-concept-based theory of charismatic leadership (Shamir, House, & Arthur, 1993) suggests that charismatic leaders link work to valued aspects of employees' self-concepts. Aspects of generative leadership can also be found in writings on empowerment and empowering leadership (e.g., Thomas & Velthouse, 1990). What is missing to varying degrees in these popular models of leadership, however, is a focus on the long-term health and well-being of employees and the long-term sustainability and social responsibility of organizations. The most immediate concern of many organizational leaders is the productivity or financial performance of the organization. Although we recognize that performance is an important, even essential, outcome of effective leadership, we also recognize that organizational leadership has powerful effects on the lives of employees. Unfortunately, immediate and pressing concerns for productivity and performance, especially in the short run, may lead to neglect of employee health and happiness. It is for this reason that we believe an explicit focus on the generative elements of leadership is important.

There are many ways that generative leaders may positively impact individual, organizational, and societal functioning. However, our primary focus is to link generative leadership with employee cooperation and well-being at work. We propose that generative leaders promote both well-being and cooperation at work by building and promoting high-quality interpersonal relationships (see Figure 12.1). In the next section, we define high-quality relationships and describe the mechanisms by which generative leaders form these relationships with employees and enable the formation of such relationships between employees. We then link high-quality relationships to employee cooperation and well-being.

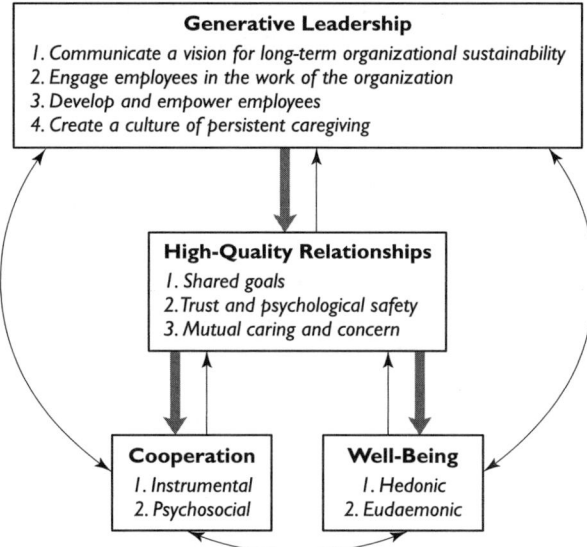

Figure 12.1 Relationships among generative leadership, high-quality relationships, cooperation, and well-being

Note: Bold arrows represent key associations between generative leadership, high-quality relationships, employee cooperation, and employee well-being, which are the focus of this chapter. However, there are many other associations (represented by thin arrows), including reciprocal effects, which are important to employee cooperation and well-being, but beyond the scope of this chapter.

High-Quality Relationships

Research on organizations has begun to recognize the importance of high-quality interpersonal relationships in the workplace (e.g., Dutton & Heaphy, 2003; Gittell, 2003). We propose that high-quality relationships in the workplace serve two primary purposes. First, they satisfy humans' fundamental need to belong, or "to form and maintain at least a minimum quantity of lasting, positive, and significant interpersonal relationships" (Baumeister & Leary, 1995, p. 497). As a result, such relationships are "life-giving" for individuals, resulting in feelings of vitality and experiences of thriving at work (Dutton & Heaphy, 2003). Additionally, high-quality relationships facilitate the accomplishment of interdependent work (Gittell, 2003) enabling the achievement of goals that could not be accomplished alone.

Relationships that fulfill individuals' need to belong and enable the accomplishment of interdependent goals share three primary characteristics. First, such relationships are built on a foundation of shared goals (Gittell, 2003). A long history of goal setting research confirms that specific, difficult goals to which individuals are committed positively impact individual performance by directing individual effort (Locke & Latham, 2002). The importance of goals increases when individuals are working together to accomplish a highly interdependent task. In situations of reciprocal interdependence, shared goals provide direction for both parties in the relationship, allowing them to coordinate their efforts and make decisions that will ultimately contribute to an effective outcome (Gittell, 2003).

Second, high-quality relationships are characterized by high levels of trust between the parties. As noted in the introduction to this book, research from many social science disciplines has identified trust as a necessary component of strong connections between individuals. To achieve interdependent outcomes, individuals must often rely on others to provide ideas, support, or other resources. Thus, it is important that the parties in interdependent relationships are willing to trust one another to perform in ways that best contribute to the achievement of shared goals. Trust also contributes to a climate of psychological safety, or the perception that risks may be taken without fear of adverse consequences (Kahn, 1990). In relationships characterized by psychological safety, individuals are more likely to raise questions, ask for help, and suggest ideas and solutions that may be counter to prevailing wisdom.

Finally, high-quality relationships involve frequent, positive interactions that reflect persistent caring and concern for one another (Baumeister & Leary, 1995). According to Bell and Richard (2000), individuals who care are empathetic (i.e., they want to know the other) and responsive (i.e., they want to help and meet the other's needs). Thus, within high-quality relationships, individuals not only attempt to understand and empathize with others, but also offer support and compassion in response to the needs of others (Kahn, 1993). Attempts to meet the needs of others may take the form of instrumental support (e.g., advice, mentoring, material assistance) or emotional support (e.g., reassurance of worth, friendship, affection; Gersick, Bartunek, & Dutton, 2000; Berscheid & Reis, 1998). Relationships may be most effective when caregiving is reciprocal (Baumeister & Leary, 1995). When frequent interactions are built on a foundation of mutual caring, individuals feel "seen ... known, and not alone in the context of their work lives" (Kahn, 1998, p. 41). The care and concern that characterize high-quality relationships also facilitate the achievement of interdependent goals.

Leader–employee relationship

Generative leaders enhance employee cooperation and well-being, in part, by developing high-quality relationships with employees. As noted above, generative leaders communicate a compelling vision of the future of the organization that focuses on long-term organizational sustainability. The vision "presents goals in terms of the values they represent" (Shamir et al., 1993, p. 583). In this way, generative leaders are able to connect the values and goals of the organization with employees' self-concepts, increasing the degree to which employees share leaders' goals. Additionally, by telling stories that link employees with the past and the future of the organization, generative leaders further emphasize the role of employees in the organization's history and increase the meaningfulness of organizational goals for employees (Shamir et al., 1993). Thus, relationships between generative leaders and employees are built on a foundation of shared goals.

Generative leadership also increases the likelihood that trusting relationships develop between leaders and employees. Generative leaders may exhibit unconventional behaviors and take risks (e.g., risking short-term profit for the long-term goal of building a strong employee base in the organization; Conger & Kanungo, 1998), modeling behaviors that are consistent with the goals and values they espouse (Bass, 1985). They also act authentically, in ways that are consistent with their true selves (Luthans & Avolio, 2003). Authentic actions increase the predictability of leaders' future behavior and increase employees' willingness to trust their leaders.

Finally, generative leaders are generous, compassionate individuals who exhibit persistent caregiving toward employees. Because care is the central, overriding motive behind the actions of generative leaders, they are likely to empathize with their employees and strive to meet their needs. Generative leaders may naturally assume the role of the caregiver in the leader–employee relationship. However, employees who interact with generative leaders may also reciprocate the caregiving behaviors exhibited by the leader. Generative leaders serve as a model of caregiving and create a culture in which such behaviors are the norm (Bass, 1985).

Relationships between employees

In addition to developing high-quality relationships with employees, generative leaders also create an environment that supports and encourages the development of high-quality relationships among employees. Generative leaders enhance group identification, encourage employees to form lateral developmental relationships, and provide a model of caregiving which provides employees with the motivation and the resources to form high-quality relationships with their peers.

Generative leadership behaviors increase employees' sense of group identification by emphasizing the distinctiveness and prestige of the group (Shamir et al., 1993). Because they have a unique focus on both long-term organizational sustainability and employee welfare, generative leaders help members identify with these distinctive goals and with their work group or the organization. Moreover, by emphasizing the values to which the organization has dedicated itself and by linking employees to the organization's history through the use of stories, generative leaders increase the salience of the work group in employees' self-concepts (Shamir et al., 1993). Under conditions of high group identification, psychological distance between group members is decreased and group members perceive others to be more similar to themselves (De Cremer & Van Vugt, 1999), leading to more positive, high-quality relationships among employees (Gibbons & Olk, 2003).

Additionally, generative leaders develop employees through mentoring and nurturing. As suggested previously, generative leaders create trusting relationships and psychologically safe conditions (Kahn, 1990) in which intellectual and professional growth and development may occur. This enables the creation of quality leader–employee relationships through which knowledge can be shared. However, the psychological safety created by generative leaders also facilitates the formation of lateral developmental relationships. In a climate in which the focus is on developing workers to carry on the work of the organization into the future, employees are encouraged to use all resources possible to build the capabilities they need. Thus, they are likely to seek knowledge and support not only from their leaders, but also from their co-workers.

Finally, the caring behaviors exhibited by generative leaders may provide employees with the resources that they need to form caring relationships with their peers. In his study of a social service agency, Kahn (1993) found that caregiving by leaders served to build employees' emotional resources and allowed them to extend care to the clients of the agency. Similarly, care received from a generative leader may provide employees with emotional resources and a model of caregiving that can be extended to their co-workers. Generative leaders' own caring relationships also provide a signal to employees that this type of relating is valued within the organization. Over time, the norm of caring will become engrained in the culture of the organization.

Cooperation

The high-quality relationships formed and supported by generative leaders can be characterized as cooperative relationships. Because these relationships are strong connections built on shared goals, trust, and mutual caring, they may encourage employees to engage in cooperative behaviors. In work organizations, cooperative behaviors tend to cluster into two broad categories: instrumental cooperation and psychosocial cooperation. Instrumental cooperation includes behaviors that help a group advance its thinking (Kahai, Sosik, & Avolio, 2003) and accomplish its goals. This includes seeking help from others by asking questions, helping others by clarifying problems or a range of solutions, and assessing the quality of peer input. Instrumental cooperation also includes sharing information with others, talking about objectives, and working together to solve problems (Lester, Meglino, & Korsgaard, 2002).

In contrast, psychosocial cooperation includes behaviors aimed at reinforcing a positive social climate within a group, such as supporting fellow team members and wanting others to succeed (Tjosvold & Yu, 2004). Psychosocial cooperation includes assisting co-workers, spontaneous helping (Wright, George, Farnsworth, & McMahan, 1993), and prosocial behaviors such as setting aside self-interest to contribute to the group (De Cremer & Van Vugt, 1999). We propose that the shared goals, trust, and caring that characterize high-quality relationships will serve to increase the prevalence of both instrumental and psychosocial cooperation.

Shared goals and cooperation

The primary way that shared goals affect cooperation is by creating interdependencies between employees. According to Deutsch (1973), the way goals are structured affects the extent to which group members will obstruct or promote the success of others. Cooperation theory suggests that people's beliefs about how their goals are related (i.e., whether or not they are mutual, shared goals), affects the "course and outcome of their interactions" (Tjosvold, Hui, & Law, 1998, p. 624).

Goal interdependence may encourage both instrumental and psychosocial cooperation. With respect to instrumental cooperation, Tjosvold and colleagues (1998) report that employees with interdependent goals are more likely to discuss problems, examine each others' perspectives, integrate their ideas, and apply their abilities to the task at hand. Furthermore, one study extended these results, showing that increased instrumental cooperation (due to interdependent goals) was a direct predictor of organizational citizenship behaviors (i.e., psychosocial cooperation) at the team level (Tjosvold & Yu, 2004). Furthermore, research by Wright et al. (1993) demonstrated that non-interdependent (i.e., individual) goals reduced spontaneous helping behaviors such as providing important job-related information to a colleague.

Trust and cooperation

It is broadly recognized by organizational scholars that trust may lead to cooperative behaviors (e.g., McAllister, 1995). One precursor to cooperative behavior is the expectation that others will act in kind, or reciprocate the efforts put forth. Employees may hesitate to cooperate if they feel others will take advantage of their prosocial behaviors by free riding (De Cremer & Van Vugt, 1999). However, in conditions of high trust, employees have greater confidence that others will act in good faith and treat them justly. As a result, they are more likely to identify with the group and to set aside self-interest for the greater good (see Tyler, this volume). High levels of trust also facilitate the effective management of conflict in groups, allowing cooperation to continue even when employees bring different perspectives to the workplace (see Ronson & Peterson, this volume). Jones and George (1998) also suggested that instrumental cooperation (e.g., free exchange of information) will be more likely to occur under conditions of unconditional trust because employees acknowledge that the knowledge and information they share will be used for the greater good.

McAllister's (1995) study of managers provided direct support for a link between trust and both instrumental and psychosocial cooperation. He found that both affective- and cognitive-based trust predicted organizational citizenship behaviors, although the link between trust and affiliative behaviors (i.e., psychosocial cooperation) was stronger than the link between trust and assistance behaviors (i.e., instrumental cooperation). McAllister's results were particularly interesting in that they suggest the links between trust and cooperation are reciprocal and self-sustaining, as peer citizenship behaviors predicted manager's level of trust, which in turn predicted the manager's own citizenship behaviors.

Mutual caring and cooperation

The high-quality relationships encouraged by generative leaders are characterized by care and concern for the welfare of others. De Cremer and Van Vugt (1999) suggested that when employees decide whether to cooperate, they often ask themselves the question, "Does the leader treat members with dignity and respect?" (p. 588). If they feel that the leader is respectful and caring, then employees' relational needs are met, and their willingness to cooperate with the leader and fellow group members increases. Further, Tjosvold and Yu (2004) stated that when leaders and employees support each other, they interact more effectively and tend to cooperate more.

Another benefit of the mutual caring that characterizes high-quality work relationships is its influence on conflict. In a study of Chinese workers, Tjosvold, Poon, and Yu (2005) linked quality relationships to the way employees approached conflict. When relationship quality was high, employees approached conflict in a cooperative manner, working to seek a mutually beneficial solution. However, when relationship quality was low, employees were more likely to adopt a competitive approach to conflict, leading them to be less likely to engage in instrumental cooperation behaviors, such as sharing ideas or clarifying problems.

In addition to the direct effects of caring on cooperation, mutual respect and caring also influence cooperation through trust. For example, Korsgaard, Brodt, and Whitener (2002) found that when managers demonstrated concern for employees, employees were more likely to trust the manager and to engage in cooperative behaviors (e.g., organizational citizenship behaviors). Similarly, in a longitudinal study of employees new on the job, Robinson and Morrison (1995) found that when employee expectations were violated, trust in managers was reduced, leading to a subsequent reduction in civic virtue, a form of psychosocial cooperation.

In summary, we conclude that the high-quality relationships formed and nurtured by generative leaders affect the extent to which employees engage in both instrumental and psychosocial cooperation. Employee cooperation is directly influenced by the extent to which employees share mutual goals and perceive themselves to be in trusting, caring relationships at work.

Employee Well-Being

In addition to increasing employee cooperation, we also propose that the high-quality relationships generative leaders build enhance employee well-being. Well-being is defined as "optimal psychological functioning and experience" (Ryan & Deci, 2001, p. 142) and has been studied from two perspectives: hedonic well-being and eudaemonic well-being. Research on hedonic well-being proposes that "well-being consists of pleasure or happiness" (Ryan & Deci, 2001, p. 143). Within the current research literature, hedonic well-being is most closely related to the concept of subjective well-being, "a broad category of phenomena that includes people's emotional responses, domain satisfactions, and global judgments of life satisfaction" (Diener, Suh, Lucas, & Smith, 1999, p. 277). Research on subjective well-being has focused on external life circumstances that may affect happiness and individual differences that influence the interpretation of these life events (e.g., Brief, Butcher, George, & Link, 1993).

The second perspective on well-being draws from Aristotle's concept of eudaemonia. Theories of eudaemonic well-being propose that well-being comes from "fulfilling or realizing one's daemon or true nature" (Ryan & Deci, 2001, p. 143). Thus, eudaemonic well-being is achieved through engaging in activities that are consistent with life values and support the realization of one's full potential (Ryff, 1989). Drawing from psychological perspectives consistent with the eudaemonic perspective Ryff proposed that psychological well-being is characterized by six dimensions: (a) self-acceptance; (b) positive relations with others; (c) environmental mastery; (d) autonomy; (e) purpose in life; and (f) personal growth. We propose that the relationships formed and facilitated by generative leaders impact both the hedonic and the eudaemonic well-being of employees.

First, a large body of literature suggests that social relationships are essential for both hedonic and eudaemonic well-being. As Baumeister and Leary (1995) noted, humans have a need to belong, or to form relationships characterized by frequent interactions and persistent caring. These characteristics are found in the high-quality relationships fostered by generative leaders. If the need to belong is a fundamental human motive, satisfaction of this need enhances happiness and well-being (Berscheid & Reis, 1998). Thus, generative leadership affects hedonic well-being through the formation of high-quality relationships.

In addition to the strong link between interpersonal relationships and hedonic well-being, high-quality interpersonal relationships increase eudaemonic well-being as well. Research on meaningfulness in life suggests that four categories of experiences characterize a meaningful life. These categories include relationships/intimacy, achievements/work, religion/spirituality, and self-transcendence/generativity (Emmons, 2003). Thus, experiences that involve high-quality relationships, or "relating well to others, trusting others, and being altruistic and helpful" (Emmons, 2003, p. 108), are linked to the perception of a meaningful life.

The importance of high-quality relationships for eudaemonic well-being is also emphasized in the literature on psychological well-being (Ryff, 1989). Psychological well-being, a construct designed to capture the experience of eudaemonic well-being, includes positive relations with others as one of its six components. Thus, according to Ryff, relationships are not merely predictors of eudaemonic well-being, but a core element of positive psychological functioning. Consistent with research by Emmons (2003), Ryff suggested that warm, trusting interpersonal relationships are an essential component of a meaningful life.

Given strong support for the link between interpersonal relationships and well-being within social psychological research, organizational researchers have begun to examine the impact of relationships in the workplace. Dutton and Heaphy (2003) theorized that high-quality connections at work may lead to feelings of vitality and aliveness, a heightened sense of positive regard between the participants in the connection, and felt mutuality, or "the sense that both people in a connection are engaged and actively participating" (p. 267). Further, empirical research has begun to provide support for the positive impact of high-quality relationships in work organizations. For example, in a study of relationships in academia, Gersick et al. (2000) observed that relationships often define the environment in which we work and that "such environments can be nurturant sources of learning, inspiration, and enjoyment, or they can be destructive sources of frustration and injury" (p. 1026).

Second, the relationships fostered by generative leaders possess an additional quality that may further enhance the well-being of employees; they are formed for the purpose of "caring for and contributing to the next generation" (McAdams & de St. Aubin, 1998, p. xix). Generative leaders mentor and empower employees, providing them with the knowledge and skills that will enable them to thrive within and contribute to the organization. They also provide emotional support and care for employees in ways that enhance their psychological well-being. Additionally, relationships among employees may provide further instrumental and emotional support that enhances employee well-being.

Finally, generative leaders may increase the well-being of employees by encouraging them to exhibit generative behaviors as well. In the course of building high-quality relationships with their followers, generative leaders perpetuate a culture of generativity by modeling generative behaviors (Bass, 1985). As employees observe the generativity expressed by leaders and operate within a culture of generativity, they may begin to exhibit generative behaviors themselves. Generativity allows employees to satisfy their need for communion, leading them to feel "needed by others and capable of creating positive results for others" (Keyes & Ryff, 1998, p. 230). Given the role that generativity plays in satisfying this fundamental human need, it is not surprising that generativity has been found to be positively related to the well-being of the generative individual, including increased life satisfaction, happiness, sense of coherence in life, and psychological well-being (e.g., Keyes & Ryff, 1998; McAdams, de St. Aubin, & Logan, 1993). As Keyes and Ryff (1998) observed, "generativity is fundamental to individuals feeling good about themselves and for judging their lives as worthwhile and meaningful" (p. 254).

Reciprocal Relationships

While we have argued that generative leadership enhances employee cooperation and well-being through high-quality relationships, it is also possible that heightened levels of cooperation and well-being within the organization increase the likelihood that generative leadership will be exhibited. That is, generative leadership in work organizations may create a self-reinforcing cycle. For example, research has shown that when individuals are more satisfied in a specific role (i.e., when they experience a higher level of hedonic well-being), they are more likely to express generative behaviors in that role (MacDermid, Franz, & De Reus, 1998). Similarly, increased levels of eudaemonic well-being, or a sense that one's life has purpose, may also encourage generativity directed toward sharing that purpose with the next generation. Furthermore, as generative leaders build high-quality relationships throughout the organization, these relationships may provide resources that build generative capacity for future generations of leaders. Over time, the high-quality relationships, cooperation, and well-being that result from generative leadership may also encourage the expression of generative leadership behaviors and the formation of a generative culture.

Other Outcomes of Generative Leadership

Our primary focus has been on the impact of generative leadership on employee cooperation and well-being through the formation of high-quality relationships. However, generative leadership may also enhance individual performance and organizational effectiveness, and may even impact the broader society as well. First, it is likely that the support and mentoring provided by generative leaders not only enhance employees' well-being, but also increase individual performance levels. When employees are engaged in supportive, caring relationships, social exchange theory (Levinson, 1965) suggests that they will be motivated to reciprocate by exhibiting behaviors that are beneficial to the organization. Thus, employees may reciprocate the care and concern provided by generative leaders with higher performance levels.

Second, although we have focused on the role of generative leadership in enhancing connections to others at work (e.g., high-quality relationships), it is worth noting that generative leadership should also strengthen the connections individuals have with the work itself. Generative leadership is expected to increase employees' intrinsic engagement with their work, including viewing work as more important, meaningful, satisfying, and self-concordant (e.g., Kahn, 1990; Ryan & Deci, 2000). Because generative leaders enable employees to see their job duties as part of a larger vision for the future, employees are more likely to internalize work goals (Bono & Judge, 2003) and see their work as representing important aspects of the self (Shamir et al., 1993). Internalized goals lead to feelings of self-determination and increased goal-directed effort and goal attainment (Judge, Bono, Erez, & Locke, 2005).

The benefits of generative leadership may also extend to organizational effectiveness. A key element of generative leadership is a concern for the long-term sustainability of the organization. Thus, generative leaders are not only motivated to develop and nurture individual employees, but also to make sound business decisions that will maximize the long-term effectiveness of the organization. Additionally, increases in employee well-being and productivity that result from generative leadership may increase organizational effectiveness when the efforts of all employees are aligned toward achieving a creative and productive future for the organization. Moreover, as we noted earlier, generative leaders perpetuate a generative culture, establishing norms of generativity throughout the organization. As employees develop their own generative capacity and model the generative acts expressed by their leaders, the impact of each leader's generativity is amplified throughout the organization.

It is also possible that generative leadership expressed in business organizations may spill over to positively impact communities and society. Scholars (e.g., Keyes & Ryff, 1998; McAdams & de St. Aubin, 1998) have highlighted the importance of generativity for communities and society, stating that "generativity is a critical resource that may undergird social institutions, encourage citizens' contributions and commitments to the public good, motivate efforts to sustain continuity from one generation to the next, and initiate social change" (Mc Adams & de St. Aubin, 1998, p. xx). The capacity for generativity developed in one role (e.g., parent, employee) may, over time, be expressed in broader society (Stewart & Vandewater, 1998). For example, Snarey and Clark (1998) found a positive correlation between the generativity expressed by fathers in their parental role and generativity targeted to benefit society. Thus, emphasizing the importance of and developing the capacity for generativity in business organizations may result in increased generativity focused on societal concerns.

When generative leadership is expressed in communities, we expect outcomes similar to those we posit for work organizations. For example, generative leadership may aid in the development of strong social networks, characterized by shared values, mutual trust, and cooperation. When members of a community work together for the long-term good of their community, the expected result is high-quality relationships, strong social connections, high levels of trust, and strong norms for cooperation. Thus, generative community leaders can strengthen and build the social fabric of their communities, which has been linked to economic prosperity (Putnam, 1995).

The term generativity is rarely used in the political arena, but Peterson (2004) suggests that generative imagery can readily be found in the rhetoric of US presidents, especially in inaugural speeches. Truly generative political leadership, however, may be harder to find. Peterson argues that truly generative political leaders are those who focus on the long-term thriving of a society and thus must address issues such as the health and welfare of children, care for the elderly, and concern for the environment.

Generative leaders in work organizations, communities, and societies share a focus on engaging, developing, and empowering individuals as well as creating a sustainable future. The processes by which these outcomes are achieved, however, may vary across domains. Specifically, a business or community leader may build social capital by fostering the development of high-quality relationships (as suggested by our model), whereas a political leader may improve the long-term health and welfare of a society through formal policy and law.

Encouraging and Supporting Generative Leadership

Given the role of generative leadership in enhancing employee cooperation and well-being, increasing individual performance and organizational effectiveness, and creating a high functioning society, both leaders and organizations must do all they can to exhibit and encourage generative leadership. However, in work organizations, several barriers exist. Although research on life stage and generativity has not been entirely conclusive, there is some evidence that—especially for men, who make up the bulk of top level organizational leaders—generative concerns emerge in mid to late adulthood after the establishment of identity and career (McAdams et al., 1998). Thus, many organizational leaders, especially early in their careers, may not have generative desires. Additionally, pressures to meet short-term financial goals may supersede concerns about the long-term sustainability of the organization and the psychosocial health of employees. Furthermore, there is little in business school curricula—even in leadership classes—that serves to build generative capacity and raise generative concerns for new managers. Thus, leaders in business organizations may possess neither the ability nor the motivation to exhibit generative leadership.

Nonetheless, we are optimistic regarding the future of generative leadership for several reasons. First, much of current leadership research and practice is based on transformational, empowering, and authentic leadership theories (e.g., Bass, 1985; Luthans & Avolio, 2003; Thomas & Velthouse, 1990), all of which include some generative behaviors. As these theories increasingly become the basis for leadership development efforts in management development programs and in work organizations, the capacity for generativity in organizational leaders may expand.

In addition to encouraging generative leadership through formal development, organizations may encourage and support generative actions among leaders in several ways. The creation and maintenance of a culture of generativity begins with the selection process. Although it is possible that the capability to be truly generative does not develop until mid-life, the desire to be generative may emerge by early adulthood (Stewart & Vandewater, 1998). Organizations may be able to identify applicants with a strong desire to be generative early in their careers. Likewise, promotion decisions should be based, in part, on the degree to which generative desires have been transformed into generative capacity (Stewart & Vandewater, 1998).

A generative culture, however, requires more than individual generative leaders. The organization must also ensure that employees are provided with the opportunities and resources needed to support and encourage generative behaviors throughout the organization. Research by McAdams and colleagues (e.g., McAdams & de St. Aubin, 1992; McAdams et al., 1998) suggests that generative behavior is influenced not only by individual motives, but also by cultural demands. Thus, organizational climate and culture have the potential to motivate or deter generative behaviors. Building a culture that supports generative leadership is a major undertaking that requires that policies, procedures, and informal norms are all aligned to communicate the importance of generative behaviors.

Conclusion

As a long history of research has shown, leaders in business organizations have the potential to positively influence individual attitudes and performance, group functioning, and organizational effectiveness. However, existing research has placed too little emphasis on strategies to enhance the long-term health of employees and organizations. In this chapter, we have suggested that generative leadership—behaviors focused on the long-term development and growth of individuals, organizations, and societies—plays an essential role in promoting employee cooperation and well-being through the formation of high-quality relationships throughout the organization. By creating a generative culture, business organizations can support and nurture generative leadership, encourage high-quality interpersonal relationships, enhance employee cooperation and well-being, and build an organization that will positively impact individuals and society well into the future.

References

Bass, B. M. (1985). *Leadership and performance beyond expectations*. New York: The Free Press.

Baumeister, R. F., & Leary, M. R. (1995). The need to belong: Desire for interpersonal attachment as a fundamental human motivation. *Psychological Bulletin, 117*, 497–529.

Bell, D. C., & Richard, A. J. (2000). Caregiving: The forgotten element in attachment. *Psychological Inquiry, 11*, 69–83.

Berscheid, E., & Reis, H. T. (1998). Attraction and close relationships. In D. T. Gilbert, S. T. Fiske, & G. Lindzey (Eds.), *The handbook of social psychology* (4th ed., Vol. 2, pp. 193–281). New York: McGraw-Hill.

Bono, J. E., & Judge, T. A. (2003). Self-concordance at work: Toward understanding the motivational effects of transformational leaders. *Academy of Management Journal, 46*, 554–571.

Brief, A. P., Butcher, A. H., George, J. M., & Link, K. E. (1993). Integrating bottom-up and top-down theories of subjective well-being: The case of health. *Journal of Personality and Social Psychology, 64*, 646–653.

Conger, J. A., & Kanungo, R. N. (1998). *Charismatic leadership in organizations.* Thousand Oaks, CA: Sage.

De Cremer, D., & Van Vugt, M. (1999). Social identification effects in social dilemmas: A transformation of motives. *European Journal of Social Psychology, 29,* 871–893.

de St Aubin, E., McAdams, D. P., & Kim, T. (2004). The generative society: An introduction. In E. de St Aubin, D. P. McAdams, & T. Kim (Eds.), *The generative society* (pp. 3–14). Washington, DC: American Psychological Association.

Deutsch, M. (1973). *The resolution of conflict.* New Haven, CT: Yale University Press.

Diener, E., Suh, E. M., Lucas, R. E., & Smith, H. L. (1999). Subjective well-being: Three decades of progress. *Psychological Bulletin, 125,* 276–302.

Dutton, J. E., & Heaphy, E. D. (2003). The power of high quality connections. In K. S. Cameron, J. E. Dutton, & R. E. Quinn (Eds.), *Positive organizational scholarship: Foundations of a new discipline* (pp. 263–278). San Francisco: Berrett-Koehler Publishers, Inc.

Emmons, R. A. (2003). Personal goals, life meaning, and virtue: Wellsprings of a positive life. In C. L. M. Keyes & J. Haidt (Eds.), *Flourishing: Positive psychology and the life well-lived* (pp. 105–128). Washington, DC: American Psychological Association.

Erikson, E. H. (1950). *Childhood and society.* New York: Norton.

Gersick, C. J. G., Bartunek, J. M., & Dutton, J. E. (2000). Learning from academia: The importance of relationships in professional life. *Academy of Management Journal, 43,* 1026–1044.

Gibbons, D., & Olk, P. M. (2003). Individual and structural origins of friendship and social positioning among professionals. *Journal of Personality and Social Psychology, 84,* 340–351.

Gittell, J. H. (2003). A theory of relational coordination. In K. S. Cameron, J. E. Dutton, & R. E. Quinn (Eds.), *Positive organizational scholarship: Foundations of a new discipline* (pp. 279–295). San Francisco: Berrett-Koehler Publishers, Inc.

Grossbaum, M. F., & Bates, G. W. (2002). Correlates of psychological well-being at midlife: The role of generativity, agency and communion, and narrative themes. *International Journal of Behavioral Development, 26,* 120–127.

Jones, G. R., & George, J. M. (1998). The experience and evolution of trust: Implications for cooperation and teamwork. *Academy of Management Review, 23,* 531–546.

Judge, T. A., Bono, J. E., Erez, A., & Locke, E. A. (2005). Core self-evaluations and job and life satisfaction: The role of self-concordance and goal attainment. *Journal of Applied Psychology, 90,* 257–268.

Kahai, S. S., Sosik, J. J., & Avolio, B. J. (2003). Effects of leadership style, anonymity, and rewards on creativity-relevant processes and outcomes in an electronic meeting system. *Leadership Quarterly, 14,* 499–524.

Kahn, W. A. (1990). Psychological conditions of personal engagement and disengagement at work. *Academy of Management Journal, 33,* 692–724.

Kahn, W. A. (1993). Caring for the caregivers: Patterns of organizational caregiving. *Administrative Science Quarterly, 38,* 539–563.

Kahn, W. A. (1998). Relational systems at work. *Research in Organizational Behavior, 20,* 39–76.

Keyes, C. L. M., & Ryff, C. D. (1998). Generativity in adult lives: Social structural contours and quality of life consequences. In D. P. McAdams & E. de St Aubin (Eds.), *Generativity and adult development: How and why we care for the next generation* (pp. 227–263). Washington, DC: American Psychological Association.

Korsgaard, M. A., Brodt, S. E., & Whitener, E. M. (2002). Trust in the face of conflict: The role of managerial trustworthy behavior and organizational context. *Journal of Applied Psychology, 87*, 312–319.

Kotre, J. N. (1984). *Outliving the self: Generativity and the interpretation of lives*. Baltimore, MD: Johns Hopkins University Press.

Lester, S. W., Meglino, B. M., & Korsgaard, M. A. (2002). The antecedents and consequences of group potency: A longitudinal investigation of newly formed work groups. *Academy of Management Journal, 45*, 352–368.

Levinson, H. (1965). Reciprocation: The relationship between man and organization. *Administrative Science Quarterly, 9*, 370–390.

Locke, E. A., & Latham, G. P. (2002). Building a practically useful theory of goal setting and task motivation: A 35-year odyssey. *American Psychologist, 57*, 705–717.

Luthans, F., & Avolio, B. (2003). Authentic leadership development. In K. S. Cameron, J. E. Dutton, & R. E. Quinn (Eds.), *Positive organizational scholarship: Foundations of a new discipline* (pp. 241–258). San Francisco: Berrett-Koehler Publishers, Inc.

MacDermid, S. M., Franz, C. E., & De Reus, L. A. (1998). Generativity: At the crossroads of social roles and personality. In D. P. McAdams & E. de St Aubin (Eds.), *Generativity and adult development: How and why we care for the next generation* (pp. 181–226). Washington, DC: American Psychological Association.

McAdams, D. P., & de St Aubin, E. (1992). A theory of generativity and its assessment through self-report, behavioral acts, and narrative themes in autobiography. *Journal of Personality and Social Psychology, 62*, 1003–1015.

McAdams, D. P., & de St Aubin, E. (Eds.). (1998). *Generativity and adult development: How and why we care for the next generation*. Washington, DC: American Psychological Association.

McAdams, D. P., de St Aubin, E., & Logan, R. L. (1993) Generativity among young, midlife, and older adults. *Psychology and Aging, 8*, 221–230.

McAdams, D. P., Diamond, A., de St Aubin, E., & Mansfield, E. (1997). Stories of commitment: The psychosocial construction of generative lives. *Journal of Personality & Social Psychology, 72*, 678–694.

McAdams, D. P., Hart, H. M., & Maruna, S. (1998). The anatomy of generativity. In D. P. McAdams & E. de St Aubin (Eds.), *Generativity and adult development: How and why we care for the next generation* (pp. 7–43). Washington, DC: American Psychological Association.

McAllister, D. J. (1995). Affect- and cognition-based trust as foundations for interpersonal cooperation in organizations. *Academy of Management Journal, 38*, 24–59.

Peterson, B. E. (2004). Guarding the next generation: The politics of generativity. In E. de St Aubin, D. P. McAdams, & T. Kim (Eds.), *The generative society* (pp. 195–210). Washington, DC: American Psychological Association.

Putnam, R. D. (1995). Bowling alone: America's declining social capital. *Journal of Democracy, 6*, 65–78.

Robinson, S. L., & Morrison, E. W. (1995). Psychological contracts and OCB: The effect of unfulfilled obligations on civic virtue behavior. *Journal of Organizational Behavior, 16*, 289–298.

Ryan, R. M., & Deci, E. L. (2000). Self-determination theory and the facilitation of intrinsic motivation, social development, and well-being. *American Psychologist, 55*, 68–78.

Ryan, R. M., & Deci, E. L. (2001). On happiness and human potentials: A review of research on hedonic and eudaimonic well-being. *Annual Review of Psychology, 52*, 141–166.

Ryff, C. D. (1989). Happiness is everything, or is it? Explorations on the meaning of psychological well-being. *Journal of Personality and Social Psychology, 57,* 1069–1081.

Shamir, B., House, R. J., & Arthur, M. B. (1993). The motivational effects of charismatic leadership: A self-concept based theory. *Organization Science, 4,* 577–594.

Snarey, J., & Clark, P. Y. (1998). A generative drama: Scenes from a father–son relationship. In D. P. McAdams & E. de St Aubin (Eds.), *Generativity and adult development: How and why we care for the next generation* (pp. 45–74). Washington, DC: American Psychological Association.

Snyder, M., & Clary, E. G. (2004). Volunteerism and the generative society. In E. de St Aubin, D. P. McAdams, & T. Kim (Eds.), *The generative society* (pp. 221–237). Washington, DC: American Psychological Association.

Stewart, A. J., & Vandewater, E. A. (1998). The course of generativity. In D. P. McAdams & E. de St Aubin (Eds.), *Generativity and adult development: How and why we care for the next generation* (pp. 75–100). Washington, DC: American Psychological Association.

Thomas, K. W., & Velthouse, B. A. (1990). Cognitive elements of empowerment: An "interpretive" model of intrinsic task motivation. *Academy of Management Review, 15, 666–681.*

Tjosvold, D., Hui, C., & Law, K. S. (1998). Empowerment in the manager–employee relationship in Hong Kong: Interdependence and controversy. *Journal of Social Psychology, 138,* 624–636.

Tjosvold, D., Poon, M., & Yu, Z(2005). Team effectiveness in China: Cooperative conflict for relationship building. *Human Relations, 58,* 341–367.

Tjosvold, D., & Yu, Z. (2004). Goal interdependence and applying abilities for team in-role and extra-role performance in China. *Group Dynamics: Theory, Research and Practice, 8,* 98–111.

Wright, P. M., George, J. M., Farnsworth, S. R., & McMahan, G. C. (1993). Productivity and extra-role behavior: The effects of goals and incentives on spontaneous helping. *Journal of Applied Psychology, 78,* 374–381.

13

Spillovers From Cooperative and Democratic Workplaces

Have the Benefits Been Oversold?

EDWARD S. GREENBERG

Scholars and practitioners generally agree that employee cooperation in the workplace is beneficial for both employees and their companies. Employees in cooperative settings tend to report higher levels of morale, job satisfaction, organizational citizenship, commitment to the organization, and trust in organizational leaders, as well as lower absenteeism, tardiness, and intention to quit, all of which contribute to better organizational performance. Research regarding the degree to which these cooperative arrangements in the workplace spill over into employees' lives outside of work is less clear, however. In this chapter, I will examine spillover effects on employees who are involved in a subset of cooperative workplace arrangements, namely those related to decision making on the job. I am particularly interested in examining possible spillover effects among employees in worker-owned and/or worker-run companies (namely, producer cooperatives and employee stock ownership firms or ESOPs) where employee-owners meet, deliberate, and decide both broad and specific company policies, and in workplace teams in conventional firms where employees are responsible for deliberating and deciding certain questions related to production or delivery of a service. If cooperation in the workplace produces spillover effects, one ought to see such effects in these two types of cooperative decision-making settings.

One cannot examine all possible spillover effects, of course. My focus in this chapter will be on those areas of potential spillover effects of cooperative decision making most often cited by advocates for worker-owned and worker-managed companies, and for teams in conventional workplaces. For the former, enhancement of democratic citizenship has been the possible spillover effect that has received the most attention; for the latter, employee well-being, defined mostly in terms of mental and physical health, and work–family conflict, has garnered the most attention. I will ask, then, whether participation in decision making by employees in worker-owned and worker-run companies has important spillover effects on their roles as citizens in the larger society and whether being on work teams in conventional companies positively or negatively affects employees' well-being outside the workplace. I focus on empirical research that addresses these questions, some from secondary sources and some from my own several research studies devoted to these topics. Though I find some empirical evidence of positive spillovers to both citizenship and well-being, there is less than might be supposed, given the enthusiastic literature that extols the positive benefits of workplace democracy and work teams. I find this conclusion both troubling and unavoidable.

Workplace Spillover in General

Jobs and a range of workplace practices have substantial spillover effects on employees. It is well established, for example, that the sorts of jobs people do and the kinds of workplaces where they do their jobs have consequences for them off the job. Researchers have demonstrated, for example, that jobs and workplaces that are highly stressful or that lack the opportunity for people to use their capacities or exercise autonomy on the job have adverse effects on a wide range of physical and mental health outcomes, ranging from increased cardiovascular disease and mortality, to increased depressive symptoms and personality disorders, including powerlessness, anxiety, and depression (Cappelli et al., 1997). Kohn and Schooler show that jobs with low complexity and latitude adversely affect both job attitudes (like satisfaction) and a generalized sense of personal distress, including a sense of powerlessness and anxiety (Kohn & Schooler, 1983). Karasek and Theorell report that high job stress and worry about job loss have important negative mental health outcomes, including depression and heightened feelings of anxiety (Karasek & Theorell, 1990).[1] Work stress and strain have been shown to contribute to feelings of emotional exhaustion, cynicism, and depersonalization (Taris, Schreurs, & Van-Iersel-Van Silfhout, 2001). Long-term work stress, moreover, has been shown to be associated with depression and physical disorders (Aneshensel, 1985; Kandel, Davies, & Raveis, 1985; LaRocco, House, & French, 1980; Pearlin & Radabaugh, 1976; Phelan et al., 1991). Several researchers have shown that feelings of job insecurity and job dissatisfaction increase the sense of powerlessness among employees (Greenhalgh & Rosenblatt, 1987). Persistent feelings of job insecurity are strongly associated with a range of mental and physical health problems (Ferrie, Shipley, Marmot, Stansfield, & Davey, 1998a; 1998b; Greenhalgh & Rosenblatt, 1987; Wilkinson, 1996). And Marmot and his associates have shown that status inequality in a hierarchical organization, all other things being equal, has strong effects on mental and physical health (Marmot, Bosma, Hemingway, Brunner, & Stansfield, 1997; Marmot, Siegrest, Theorell, & Feeney, 1999; Marmot & Wilkinson, 1999).

Considering positive workplace spillover effects, job satisfaction has been shown to enhance a range of well-being indicators (Diener & Seligman, 2004). Several studies show, for example, that job satisfaction is positively associated with general life satisfaction (Diener & Seligman, 2004; Heller, Judge, & Watson, 2002; Near, Smith,

Rice, & Hunt, 1983; Rice, Near, & Hunt, 1980), good marital relations (Doumas, Margolin, & John, 2003; Rogers & May, 2003), and overall sense of personal well-being (Diener & Seligman, 2004; Warr, 1999).

Askenazy's meta-analysis of empirical studies on the effects of innovative work practices in the United States—including total quality management, flexible workplace practices, job rotation, and autonomous work teams—reports a mix of positive and negative spillover effects. While innovative work practices improve efficiencies and profits for business firms, and enhance employee job interest and involvement, they have also diminished workplace health and safety, primarily because many of these innovations bring increased time and turnaround pressures, more decisional responsibilities, and more social pressures from other employees to perform at consistently higher levels (Askenazy & Cepremap, 2001).

This brief review—a look at the proverbial tip of the iceberg, as it were—demonstrates that jobs and workplaces have multiple and important spillover effects on people's lives outside the immediate work-setting, some being good for employees, some not so good. What we know less about, however, and what is at stake in this chapter, is whether innovations in the workplace designed to increase cooperation in decision making among employees have spillover effects, and if so, of what sort and to what degree?

Spillover From Participation in Cooperative and Democratic Arrangements at Work

In the next sections of this chapter, I examine the empirical standing of claims about the positive effects on employees of participation in cooperative workplace decision making, focusing on the effects of such participation on citizenship and on personal well-being, examining both the secondary literature and results from several of my own empirical studies.

Spillovers in worker-owned and worker-operated companies

There is a workplace spillover tradition that assumes the existence of a strong association between participation in decision making at the workplace and participation and civic-mindedness in conventional politics in the larger democratic society.

Theories of democratic spillover

Participatory democratic theorists believe that participatory practices within social institutions are rational for society, good for the development of human capacities, and a moral right in any society that advertises itself as a democracy. It is widely believed among these thinkers that democracy begets more democracy, that practicing participation in one social institution provides the learning necessary for practicing participation in other social realms (Pateman, 1970).[2] Among participatory democratic theorists, the workplace represents the most important setting for the education of democratic citizens primarily because of the presumed centrality of work in shaping people's outlooks, the tendency of workplaces to draw together large numbers of people who might be persuaded to act together in decision-making units, and the well-known influence of workplaces in shaping people's psychosocial outlooks. The idea here is that if workplace arrangements encourage democratic participation within the walls of the firm, workers in such settings are more likely to be participatory and civic-minded citizens outside; workplace arrangements that discourage participation or fail to teach democratic skills or nurture democratic aspirations are likely to depress participation in other social institutions, especially in the world of conventional politics (Pateman, 1970; Dahl, 1985; 1989).

Citizenship education in participatory workplaces might happen in a number of ways. Several scholars have suggested that the workplace and the larger political sphere share, as it were, similar authority patterns, so that lessons learned in the one sphere easily can transfer to others (Almond & Verba, 1963; Mason, 1982; Sigel & Hoskins, 1977; Sobel, 1993). Other scholars suggest that practicing democracy increases employees' sense of personal efficacy which they carry with them to other social institutions; thus, personal efficacy developed in democratic workplaces helps nurture feelings of political efficacy, an orientation that has long been associated with the propensity to participate in politics (Elden, 1981; Greenberg & Grunberg, 1999; Lafferty, 1989). Still others believe that practicing and learning civic activities in the work setting creates a set of skills—such as organizing meetings, speaking in public, deliberating with others, and so on—that is transferable to other settings (Verba, Schlozman, & Brady, 1995). The most optimistic participatory democratic theorists suggest that the experience of working together to reach decisions, especially in settings where democratic discourse is part and parcel of the working environment, encourages people to take into account the views and interests of others, to see beyond their own self-interest, and to gain a sense of commonality, and, as a result, to become more public-spirited (Cole, 1919; Greenberg, 1986; Mill, 1991; Pateman, 1970).

Empirical research on political spillover

While there is some support in the research literature for the existence of some of the democratic spillover effects specified above, the research leaves much to be desired, either because of the methods used or because of the mixed results that have been reported. It is probably fair to say that the definitive test of the theory has not yet been done.

Much of the research examines the citizenship spillover issue indirectly, inferring a relationship but not examining it directly. One indirect approach to the assessment of the political spillover question has been to demonstrate the existence of an association between some degree of job autonomy in the workplace and political participation outside of it, the argument being that those with some degree of control over their jobs are more likely to develop the skills and confidence to act as citizens. This view is supported by research showing, for example, that people in low-status, non-supervisory, and repetitive unskilled jobs (i.e. low autonomy jobs) are less likely to participate in conventional politics than people in high-status, supervisory, and/or highly skilled (i.e. high autonomy jobs) jobs (Sobel, 1993; Verba, et al., 1995).

Another indirect approach to the political spillover question has been to examine whether an association exists between participatory workplace democratic arrangements and the development of personal and political efficacy, political efficacy having been shown to be associated with political participation (Almond & Verba, 1963; Barnes & Kasse, 1979; Campbell, Converse, Miller, & Stokes, 1960; Elden, 1981; Milbraith & Goel, 1971; Rosenstone & Hanson, 1993; Schur, Eaton, & Rubinstein, 2004; Sigleman & Feldman, 1983; Verba & Nie, 1972; Verba, et al., 1995).[3] One of the first to make the claim about forms of workplace participation and political efficacy were Almond and Verba in their classic work *The Civic Culture* (1963) where they reported that "being consulted on the job" and "feeling free to protest management decisions at work" are associated with "feelings of subjective political competence," the feeling that individuals could influence the action of government and government officials. Unfortunately, *The Civic Culture* did not include very many specific questions about the many possible forms of participation in decision making on the job; questions that asked respondents if they were consulted on the job by supervisors, or if they felt free to protest management decisions, do not represent much of a basis for making broad claims about the impact of workplace participation on feelings of political efficacy.

As to direct assessments of the simple spillover thesis—that is, the purported association between participation in decision making on the job and political participation in the larger society—there is little to report. As I suggested in an earlier article, "studies that empirically investigate the link between participation in workplace decision making and participation in politics outside the walls of the enterprise are relatively rare" (Greenberg, Grunberg, & Daniel, 1996, p. 305; see also Carter, 2003). The few studies that address the issue are typically marred by small sample sizes, non-random sampling, and/or case-study approaches. Having said that, there is some, but not overwhelming support for the political spillover thesis. Menachem Rosner has shown, for example, that it is precisely those who participate in kibbutz-governing institutions who are most likely to participate in the governing affairs of the larger kibbutz movement and in Israeli politics (Rosner, 1976). Vicki Smith, in a study of 1,400 workers in 55 US firms characterized by a wide range of decision-making environments, reported that those most involved in decision making within their firms are somewhat more likely to be active in the affairs of their communities than others (Smith, 1996). A study by Peterson in several firms in upstate New York showed a similar result, though the study involved only a very small sample and a very low response rate (Peterson, 1992). A study of a worker-co-managed Canadian steel firm with 6,000 employees offered anecdotal evidence that, in the period after the co-management system was introduced, employees increased their activities in voluntary organizations in the community and did so with new sets of skills and a sense of confidence learned in the workplace (Savory-Gordon, 2003).

Two studies using national random samples also have confirmed the existence of a small but statistically significant spillover between participation in decision making in firms and political participation outside the firm. William Lafferty's Norwegian democracy project surveys found such a relationship (Lafferty, 1989), as did a study by Richard Sobel using data from the 1985 National Election Study pilot survey (Sobel, 1993). In both cases, the spillover effects were statistically significant but modest in scale.

My own research on this question shows mixed and weak results. In a study comparing workers in US producer cooperative firms—where worker/owners run all the affairs of the company—with workers in closely matched conventional firms in the wood products industry in the Pacific Northwest, I reported the following (Greenberg, 1986):

- Workers in democratically-run producer cooperatives were no more politically efficacious than workers in conventional firms.
- Workers in democratically-run producer cooperatives were slightly more likely to be involved in community affairs (contacted a public official, written a letter to the editor, or worked with others to solve some community problem) and in attending government meetings and hearings than workers in conventional firms (though levels of involvement for both groups was extremely low), but they were no more likely to participate in election campaigns or vote.
- In a supplemental panel survey of the same respondents done five years after the first survey, workers in the co-ops were more likely than workers in the conventional firms to be more involved in campaign activities, community affairs, and attending meetings (though not on voting), though overall levels of activity in all areas of political participation were extremely low for both groups.
- Perhaps most striking of all, workers in the more democratic producer cooperatives were significantly more likely than workers in conventional firms to describe their involvement in politics in terms of self-interest rather than in terms of the general good, suggesting that the slight gain in participation from workplace cooperation did not lead to gains in civic-mindedness. Interestingly, co-op workers became less civic-minded over time, while conventional workers did not change at all on this dimension.
- In a follow-up study done 10 years later comparing workers in democratically-run firms (producer cooperatives and employee-stock ownership firms) with workers in matched conventional union and non-union firms in the wood products industry, my colleagues and I were rather startled to discover that workers

in the more democratically-run firms were much less likely than workers in conventional firms to be active in politics (voting, campaign activities, community involvement). The surprising result, we found, could not be explained by a drop off in participation in the democratically run firms but seemed best explained by the economic troubles these firms were experiencing at the time (Greenberg et al. 1996).

So where does this leave us on the question of the potency of participation in decision making in the workplace for encouraging positive spillovers on democratic citizenship? One must conclude, I believe, that while much has been made about this dynamic in the theoretical literature, the empirical evidence for its existence is not strong. The empirical evidence suggests either mixed outcomes—spillover occurs in some cases and settings and not others—or fairly modest spillover effects.

Well-being spillovers from work teams

Many companies have introduced one form or another of teams in the workplace in hopes of improving their performance. Work teams generally are made up of a small number of employees who take on many responsibilities customarily done by supervisors. The most effective teams, according to the management literature, are granted a great deal of autonomy in achieving goals set by upper management. Typically, team members direct their own work, set their own schedules and work assignments, and coordinate with other teams and divisions within the company. The most effective teams are granted the necessary authority to make decisions that are essential to their area of responsibility, and take collective credit or blame for their performance. In their most highly developed form, the self-managed work team "is a group of individuals who have been given the responsibility to complete a whole task and to make the decision as to how to complete it" (Elloy & Terpening, 2001, p. 322). Of course, few teams reach this level of autonomy in American firms, though teams of one kind or another have become common.

Many claims have been made about the positive benefits of work teams for organizations, particularly for teams of the semi-autonomous variety, though the empirical evidence in support of these claims is meager. The evidence that teams have a positive impact on organizational performance and on the development of positive employee attitudes is mixed; what little empirical research exists shows positive results only some of the time, and these tend to be quite modest.[4] After reviewing this research, Glassop reached the following conclusion about the status of team effects: "In sum, while many benefits [of teams] have been cited for organizations and employees alike, the literature lacks consistent empirical evidence to support their widespread adoption" (Glassop, 2002, pp. 227–228).

My main concern in this chapter, however, is not with team impacts on organizational performance per se, or on the development of more positive work-related employee attitudes, but on their possible spillover effects. Here I want to examine the question of whether involvement in work teams affects employees in their lives away from the job, to see whether this form of small group participation in workplace decision making has positive or negative benefits (or some combination) for employees outside the walls of the firm.

There are only a few studies that look directly at team spillover effects on employee well-being. Again, as with employee participation in running producer cooperatives and ESOP firms, the results on spillover are mixed. While investigators have long believed that being on a work team will have beneficial mental health outcomes, only a few empirical studies support this position. Wall and Clegg found higher levels of psychological well-being among employees on autonomous work (Wall & Clegg, 1981). Van Mierlo and her colleagues reported that employees who say they are members of highly autonomous work teams show less psychological fatigue than their peers (van Mierlo, Rutte, Seinen, & Kompier, 2001), while Froiland reports that work team membership helps reduce feelings of burnout (Froiland, 1993). Elloy and his colleagues report that participation in the activities of semi-autonomous work teams tends to moderate feelings of emotional exhaustion (Elloy & Terpening 2001). Greenberg and his colleagues report that members of work teams have a stronger sense of mastery than non-team colleagues in a down-sizing firm (Greenberg & Grunberg, 2004). Another study by Friedman and Casner-Lotto found that being a member of an effective work team contributed to a general sense of self-confidence (Friedman & Casner-Lotto, 2002). On the other hand, van Mierlo reports that several researchers have found a number of negative mental health spillovers as a result of intense demands on time and effort placed on employees by virtue of being on teams (van Mierlo, et al., 2001).[5]

Empirical studies that link participation on work teams to physical health are rare, and those that do exist, oddly enough, show negative spillover effects. Askenazy summarizes literature on high-performance workplaces, one component of which involves participation on teams, and finds associations with heightened levels of occupational stress and injuries (Askenazy & Cepremap, 2001) and speculates that the high-pressure environment in high-performance workplaces may be to blame. Anderson-Connolly and his colleagues found that being on teams decreased satisfaction and increased reports of bad health symptoms among non-managerial employees in a large manufacturing company, for reasons that are not entirely clear (Anderson-Connolly, et al., 2002).

Preliminary Report on Well-Being Spillovers From Work Teams

Because the literature on team spillover effects is so underdeveloped and because the research that exists shows very mixed results, I will take the liberty of using data on teams (as-yet-unreported) from a research project my colleagues and I are conducting in a large American manufacturing firm.[6] The project looks at the impact of corporate downsizing, job re-engineering, and teaming on employee well-being over time. Information on teams and employee involvement in team activities were collected in two waves, two years apart, using a longitudinal-panel design.[7] In the project, we define well-being primarily in terms of mental and physical health, though we also pay attention to the issue of work–family conflict.

The company in our study does not keep records on teams, per se, so we depend upon individual-level, self-reports from employees on their team experiences. While this may represent a problem from one point of view, it represents a real advantage in another sense, given our belief that a team is not fully a team unless it is perceived as such by employees. Belanger, Edwards, and Wright (2003) note that relatively few studies examine workers' own reports of how teamwork impacts their attitudes toward their job or company and the same must be said about possible spillover effects. Other investigators have found that internal subjective experiences, more than external objective assessments, create the link between job redesign or enrichment (teams being one example) and employees' attitudes toward their work and company, and again, the same may be the case when it comes to spillover effects (Niehoff, Moorman, Blakely, & Fuller, 2001; Sikora, 2002).

Teams come in a variety of forms. Some are given more responsibilities than others. Some have more information related to their projects. Some but not others have access to an independent budget to accomplish team goals. Some are relatively free from direct supervision by supervisors, while others work on a shorter leash, as it were. Teams also vary in what might be called their "social atmospherics." Some teams, for example, are more cooperative in their activities than others; some teams are better than other teams in achieving their objectives. Some teams provide social support and affirmation for their members, while others are filled with social conflict and tension. Members in some teams are able to actively participate in team decisions, while on others, decisions are made in practice by one or a handful of others. Most existing empirical research on teams does not take account of the wide variability of teams, particularly in the variability of the experiences of members on teams. I will focus here on these latter aspects, partly out of necessity, partly out of theoretical importance.

We are interested, then, in the subjective aspects of team functioning, viewed from the perspective of the individual employee, that might be associated with spillover effects. But what aspects of team functioning should be of primary interest? Based in part on our own in-depth interviews and focus groups with employees and managers of the company in question, and based in part on the extant literature on work teams, we have identified four aspects of the team experience for examination of possible team spillover effects.

Team membership

There is some evidence that simply being in an environment where workers participate in decision making has modest spillover effects on social attitudes and political participation (Almond & Verba, 1963; Verba, et al., 1995) so it is not unreasonable to assume that the more intensely participatory environment of a small work team may have spillover effects as well. On the other hand, being on a team may also contribute, as we have shown, to higher time and effort demands on employees. These pressures may well contribute to negative spillovers in the areas of mental and physical health and may also create more work–family conflict as overburdened employees try to balance work and family obligations.

Participation in team decision making

The research literature supports the notion that employees in work organizations seek more participation in decision making, generally like the experience of playing such a role, and report a wide range of positive outcomes from the experience, including greater commitment to the work organization (Applebaum, Bailey, Berg, & Kalleberg, 2000; Elden, 1981; Freeman & Rogers, 1999; Greenberg & Grunberg, 1994; Greenberg, 1986; Levine, 1995; Mason, 1982; Pateman, 1970; Shadur, Kienzle, & Rodwell, 1999). Kirkman and Rosen (2000) note that "winning" teams are characterized by employees who can exercise freedom and discretion in decisions. These "winning" teams spur on employees to put in the extra effort to be more innovative and boost quality and production levels (i.e., these employees are more committed to helping their organization succeed). Given evidence of these strong effects within organizations and on basic outlooks, spillovers may well exist across a wide range of well-being outcomes, particularly those involving mental and physical health.

Harmonious and supportive teams

Here we refer to aspects of the team experience that are perceived to provide social support, harmony, cohesion, and positive social relations: being respected by other team members, feeling free to communicate ideas, working easily and well with others on the team, and so on. This social dimension of teams, rather than the task collaboration nature of teams, may serve as the foundation for employee evaluation of their relationship with the organization, their attitudes towards their jobs, and their general outlooks. Costa (2003) notes that team trust and cooperation are positively related to attitudinal commitment, for example. Perceptions of social support or coworker solidarity in the workplace have also been shown to be positively associated with organizational commitment (Cohen & Bailey, 1997; Cordery, et al., 1991; Parris, 2003) and job satisfaction and morale (Belanger, et al., 2003). Diener's review of the research literature leads him to conclude that close cooperation and social support in general and in the workplace are associated with various dimensions of well-being, including better mental health (Diener & Seligman, 2004). Dovey and Onyx report that membership of teams with high levels of team spirit encourages members to be more involved in community organizations and to be more skilled in organizational affairs (Dovey & Onyx, 2001). Spillover effects to mental and physical health seem plausible, then, and it may well be the case that working in a supportive work team environment causes members to take fewer negative aspects of their jobs home with them.

Team effectiveness

Teams in organizations vary widely in their effectiveness in carrying out team missions and meeting objectives defined by the team itself and by the organization. Lester, Meglino, and Korsgaard (2002) found that team member beliefs in team effectiveness were related to higher levels of motivation and satisfaction. Kirkman and Rosen (2000) include employee confidence in their collective effectiveness as one feature of a "winning team." Bayazit and Mannix (2003) also note that member beliefs in the team's effectiveness can be a key factor in turnover intentions. In general then, research supports the idea that employees who believe they are members of teams that perform at high levels of effectiveness are more positive about organizations that provide opportunities to feel a sense of accomplishment and to be a part of group that is respected by other employees, supervisors, and top management. It is not unreasonable to expect that these positive outcomes, to the degree that they contribute to job satisfaction and higher levels of work morale, may spill over into the mental and physical health parts of employees' lives.

Having identified four important aspects of the team experience,[8] I turn to a brief examination of their relationship to the following well-being outcomes: mental health (depression and mastery or self-efficacy), physical health (bad health symptoms and alcohol dependency), negative health behaviors (bad outcomes from drinking), and work-to-family conflict. In Table 13.1, I report the results of a series of regression equations that examine these relationships over time. In each equation, I am interested in the impact of Time 1 team experience variables on Time 2 well-being outcomes (roughly two years later), taking into account a range of control variables.[9] Time 1 scores for each of the spillover dependent variables and Time 2 scores for the team variables also are included as a way to partial out their effects in equations that are designed to examine the over-time effects of team experiences on important well-being outcomes.

The story conveyed by the summary table is very straightforward. Team experiences at Time 1 have very few effects on well-being outcomes at Time 2. Only three of the twenty-four cells show a significant result—the quality of team social relations decreases depression scores and increases work–family conflict, while having a say in team decision making decreases scores on the bad health measure. Though not reported in the table—my aim here is simply to determine if team experiences have any spillover impact at all on well-being—the effects in all three cases are quite small.[10] The implications of these results is quite clear: employee experiences on teams have little or no impact on a wide range of well-being outcomes. To be sure, they might well have an impact on other indicators of well-being not examined here, but in terms of the outcomes examined in the studies my colleagues and I have been conducting, the results are quite disappointing.

Table 13.1 Impact of team experiences at Time 1 on well-being outcome variables at Time 2

	(1) Mastery	(2) Depression	(3) Bad health symptoms	(4) Alcohol dependency	(5) Negative outcomes from drinking	(6) Work–family conflict
Member of a workplace team or not	ns	ns	ns	ns	ns	ns
Degree of say in work team decision making	ns	ns	*	ns	ns	ns
Perceived team effectiveness	ns	ns	ns	ns	ns	ns
Degree of team harmony and support	ns	*	ns	ns	ns	*

Notes

1. Columns 1–6 report the statistical significance of team variables at Time 1 for equations in which the spillover dependent variables at Time 2 are regressed on team independent variables at Time 1. Time 1 scores for the spillover dependent variables and Time 2 team variables are included in each equation.[11]
2. Because each has been shown to affect one aspect or another of the well-being outcomes under consideration, the following controls are included (T2): age, sex, tenure in the company, job rank, job stress, sense of security, perceived organizational support, and trust in top management.
3. * indicates statistical significance at 0.05 or better; ns indicates "not significant."

Observations About Disappointing Empirical Findings

It is well established that employee participation in cooperative decision making within firms has many benefits for individual employees and the firms for which they work. For the most part, however, these mostly beneficial outcomes—whether from participation in democratic decision-making arrangements at the level of the firm, division, or section, or in workplace teams of one kind or another—seem to stay mostly inside the walls of the organization. Contrary to the hopes and expectations of many theorists and practitioners, the available empirical research on these cooperative decision-making arrangements in the workplace does not support claims about spillovers into the lives of employees outside the organization. While there are compelling theoretical arguments to suggest that such spillovers should exist, researchers who have examined the question empirically report mixed and disappointing results. Some researchers report weak positive spillovers; others report weak negative spillovers; still others report no effects at all.

The question that immediately jumps to mind is why the results look like they do. One possibility is that the participation-cooperation treatments we encounter in the real world of work organizations are not very substantial. The treatments, that is to say, are not very strong in most cases. I suspect that a wide range of positive experiences at work, including participation in workplace decision making, while having good outcomes in terms of employee attitudes about the job and the work organization, may not be of sufficient magnitude to matter much for individual well-being when set against other possible influences such as family and friends, health and safety, and income and economic stability, among other things. In fact, it is hard to imagine what might go on in the workplace of a positive nature that might compete with these other life domains to significantly influence citizenship and well-being on a sustained basis.

The notion that weak treatments may be relevant to the weak spillover effects found in the research literature is the finding in my own earlier research that only intense and sustained face-to-face cooperative decision making seems to matter. I found that it was only in producer co-operatives and ESOPs where decision making was closest to what is typically called "direct democracy"—where decisions about everyday production issues, as well as longer-term planning, are done in face-to-face settings, with full information available to employees—that a small but significant spillover from cooperative decision making to political participation occurred (though political participation remained quite low even in these cases). Where decision making was indirect and distant—that is, when employee decision-making participation was confined to periodic election of a board of directors or a leadership team that made day-to-day and long-term decisions—positive spillover did not occur at all. This suggests that spillover is most likely to occur in what one might call "rich" participatory environments but not in firms where cooperative decision making is intermittent, relatively uninformed, and confined to indirect/representative forms of democracy (Greenberg, 1986). I need hardly remind the reader that such intense and long-duration direct democratic arrangements are rare in the United States and are unlikely to become much more common in the near future.

Regarding citizenship spillover effects, it may be, as Hibbing and Theiss-Moore suggest in their chapter for this book, that many people do not find participation in decision making intrinsically satisfying or beneficial to them, so that even if cooperation in the workplace happens, this may not result in spillovers to political participation (Hibbing & Theiss-Morse, this volume). Not everyone wants an increased "voice" in public affairs, that is to say, an orientation that is unlikely to be changed by participation in cooperative decision making at work, especially if, as in many instances, participation in workplace decision making is itself grudging or episodic.

At a more general level, it may be that scholars, practitioners, and activists have over-emphasized the importance of jobs and workplaces in the larger scheme of things. Could it be that ideological commitments and/or long-held beliefs in the social sciences about the centrality of work have caused many of us to have pre-judged the issue? Perhaps scholars, practitioners, and activists, expecting and assuming that what goes on at work has profound effects on individuals, have seized upon compelling anecdotes, supportive but narrow case studies, empirical but unsystematic studies, and weak results in well-designed studies, as evidentiary con-firmation of their preconceptions. I have no doubt, to be sure, that some aspects of work, broadly defined, have significant spillover effects. For example, there is a considerable body of literature showing that being unemployed—being without a job, that is to say—has profound effects on people, given the centrality of employ-ment for income, self-regard, and social interaction, among other things. There is also a considerable body of research showing that occupations matter to people in important ways and affect their well-being across a broad range, no doubt because occupations are tied to things such as income, social networks, training experiences, and social identities, among other things. But there is less reason to suppose that the everyday routines of working—things such as work pace, autonomy, mild stress, mild social conflict, relationships with supervisors, and so on—have much spillover associated with them.

Let's Not Throw Away the Baby With the Bathwater

Despite these disappointing findings about citizenship and well-being spillovers, there is no reason for people and organizations to abandon efforts to enhance cooperative and democratic decision making in workplaces. Perhaps most impor-tantly, even without very many positive spillover effects, we know from a massive research literature that cooperation and collaboration in work organizations con-tributes to the improvement of a broad range of employee job-related attitudes and behaviors and to better organizational performance. We should not allow dis-appointment about spillover effects to diminish the significance of these very real achievements of workplace cooperation and participation in decision making.

Nor do we need to abandon entirely the hypothesis that cooperative decision making in work organizations may have positive spillovers to citizenship and well-being. Spillover might occur under certain circumstances, with specific populations. For example, it could be that positive spillover effects for citizenship and well-being are more likely to occur among people with little experience in democratic prac-tices in the larger society, whose habits of participation have not yet set, and for whom cooperative democratic practices at work represent relatively new and significant experiences; young people and people in newly emerging democracies come to mind.[12]

Cooperative decision making may also have more spillover effects in more economically successful firms where the benefits of cooperation are clear. As my colleagues and I have shown, in economically troubled firms, where decisions made by employees or employee-owners are about cuts in pay and benefit, or about putting off plans to upgrade plant and equipment, the participatory experience is unlikely to be a positive one that encourages further participation either inside or outside the firm (Greenberg, et al., 1996).

Certain occupations may also be more open to the salutary effects of participatory decision making in work organizations than those who have been studied by social scientists so far. High end occupations, including software engineers, university professors, and health care professionals, are well studied, for example. So too are assembly line workers in routinized work settings. The former already enjoy a substantial voice in decisions about their day-to-day work, so additional participatory opportunities may fall under the category of diminishing returns. The latter have little opportunity to participate in meaningful cooperative decision making, even in firms where teams and consultative arrangements exist, because they are not invited to decide the most important matters associated with the work they do and how they carry it out. This leaves a range of "in-between" occupations where expectations about high involvement are not well established and where rigid hierarchical controls are less evident. Retail sales, financial services, and technical services delivery, to take but a few examples, fit such a profile. There may well be others.

It appears, then, that schemes for participatory democracy in work organizations are still worth pursuing. Employees and firms would be best served, however, given the evidence, if proponents would make more modest claims about the spillover benefits of such arrangements.

Acknowledgment

Special thanks to my collaborators on several of the projects reported in this chapter, Leon Grunberg and Sara Moore of the University of Puget Sound, and Pat Sikora of Sikora and Associates, LLC. This chapter is as much theirs as mine.

Notes

1 Also see Price, Van Ryn, & Vinokur, 1992.
2 The notion that workplaces might be schools for democracy where people are educated for participation has an impressive pedigree. Rousseau, J. S. Mill, G. D. H. Cole, John Dewey, Robert Dahl, Carole Pateman, and others, for example, have suggested that employees who are involved in democratic forms of activity within firms are likely to gain the skills, confidence, and knowledge that equip them for participation in normal politics, as well as a taste for the joys of democratic life (Bachrach, 1967; Barber, 1984;

Blumberg, 1968; Cole, 1919; Dahl, 1985, 1989; Dewey, 1927; Elden, 1981; Greenberg, 1986; Mason, 1982; Mill, 1991; Pateman, 1970; Peterson, 1992; Rousseau, 1987).

3 My own research in worker-owned and -run producer cooperatives showed no such connection, however. See Greenberg, 1986.

4 The purported benefits of teams to organizational performance are tied by most analysts to improvements in employee job- and work-related attitudes. It has been shown, for example, that involvement in work teams contributes to better morale and job satisfaction among employees (Cohen, 1994; Cordery, Mueller, & Smith, 1991; Dumaine, 1990; Goodman, Davadas, & Hughson, 1988; Hackman, 1987; Lewis, 1990; Stewart, Manz, & Sims, 2000) as well as improvements in trust of and commitment to the organization (Goodman, et al. 1988; Levine & D'Andrea, 1990; Mitchell, Holtom, Lee, Sablynski, & Erez, 2001; Osburn, Moran, Musselwhite, & Zenger, 1990; Wellins, Byham, & Wilson, 1991). There is also a body of research which suggests that membership on work teams reduces employee stress and burnout, which presumably adds to their productivity and commitment (Froiland, 1993). My colleagues and I found, however, that being on a work team reduced job satisfaction among non-supervisory workers, probably because of the increased work load and conflicting responsibilities involved in team membership (Anderson-Connolly, Grunberg, Greenberg, & Moore, 2002).

5 Also see Barker (1993) on this point.

6 My co-PIs on this project are Leon Grunberg and Sarah Moore of the University of Puget Sound. Our consultant and frequent co-author is Patricia Sikora.

7 The overall study involves four survey waves, over nine years, using a longitudinal panel design. Published papers, working and conference papers, and details of the study design and analysis strategies can be found on the project web page at www.colorado.edu/ibs/PEC/workplacechange.

8 Definitions and measurement of these four aspects of the team experience, as well as for measures of depression, mastery, physical health, alcohol dependency, negative outcomes from drinking, and family–work conflict are described in detail in Greenberg, Sikora, et al., 2005.

For each team measure, we performed a combination of item and scale analyses, including item-to-total correlations, exploratory factor analysis, and Cronbach's (1951) internal consistency analysis.

9 Complete results of the regression analysis are available upon request.

10 In each case the coefficients are quite small: the coefficient in the team social relations–depression equation is only –1.96 on a 49-point depression scale; the coefficient in the team social relations–work-to-family conflict is only .30 on a 30-point conflict scale; and the coefficient in the say in team decision making–bad health equation is –.05 on a 14-point bad health scale.

11 With the exception of having a say in team decisions. Questions for this scale were not included in the Time 2 survey questionnaire.

12 Thanks to Pat Sikora for this idea.

References

Almond, G., & Verba, S. (1963). *The civic culture: Political attitudes and democracy in five nations.* Princeton NJ: Princeton University Press.

Anderson-Connolly, R., Grunberg, L., Greenberg, E. S., & Moore, S. (2002). Is lean mean? Workplace transformation and employee well-being. *Work, Employment and Society, 27*(1), 7–31.

Aneshensel, C. S. (1985). The natural history of depression symptoms. *Research in Community and Mental Health 5*, 45–75.

Applebaum, E., Bailey, T., Berg, P., & Kalleberg, A. L. (2000). *Manufacturing advantage: Why higher performance work systems pay off.* Ithaca, NY: Cornell University Press.

Askenazy, P., & Cepremap (2001). Innovative workplace practices and occupational injuries and illnesses in the United States. *Economic and Industrial Democracy, 22*(4), 485–516.

Bachrach, P. (1967). *The theory of democratic elitism.* Boston: Little Brown.

Barber, B. (1984). *Strong democracy.* Berkeley, CA: University of California Press.

Barker, J. R. (1993). Tightening the iron cage: Concertive control in self-managing teams. *Administrative Science Quarterly, 38*, 408–437.

Barnes, S., & Kasse, M. (1979). *Political action: Mass participation in five western democracies.* Beverly Hills: Sage.

Bayazit, M., & Mannix, E. A. (2003). Should I stay or should I go? Predicting team members intent to remain in the team. *Small Group Research, 34*(3), 290–321.

Belanger, J., Edwards, P. K., & Wright, M. (2003). Commitment at work and independence from management: A study of advanced team-working. *Work and Occupations, 30*(2), 234–252.

Blumberg, P. (1968). *Industrial democracy.* New York: Schocken.

Campbell, A., Converse, P., Miller, W. E., & Stokes, D. E. (1960). *The American voter.* New York: John Wiley and Sons.

Cappelli, P., Bassi, L., Katz, H., Knoke, D., Osterman, P., & Useem, M. (1997). *Change at work.* New York: Oxford University Press.

Carter, N. (2003). *Workplace democracy: Turning workers into citizens?* European Consortium for Political Research, Joint Sessions, Edinburgh, Scotland.

Cohen, S. G. (1994). Designing effective self-managing work teams. *Advances in Interdisciplinary Studies of Work Teams, 1*, 67–102.

Cohen, S. G., & Bailey, D. E. (1997). What makes teams work: Group effectiveness research from the shop floor to the executive suite. *Journal of Management, 23*(3), 239–290.

Cole, G. D. H. (1919). *Self government in industry.* London: Bell.

Cordery, J. L., Mueller, W. S., & Smith, L. M. (1991). Attitudinal and behavioral effects of autonomous group working: A longitudinal field study. *Academy of Management Journal, 34*(2), 464.

Costa, C. C. (2003). Work team trust and effectiveness. *Personnel Review, 32*(5), 605–623.

Cronbach, L. J. (1951). Coefficient alpha and the internal consistency of tests. *Psychometrika, 16*(3), 297–334.

Dahl, R. A. (1985). *A preface to economic democracy.* Berkeley: University of California Press.

Dahl, R. A. (1989). *Democracy and its critics.* New Haven, CT: Yale University Press.

Dewey, J. (1927). *The public and its problems.* New York: Holt.

Diener, E., & Seligman, M. E. P. (2004). Beyond money: Toward an economy of well-being. *Psychological Science in the Public Interest, 5*(1), 1–31.

Doumas, D. M., Margolin, G., & John, R. S. (2003). The relationship between daily marital interaction, work, and health-promoting behaviors in dual-earner couples: An extension of the work–family spillover model. *Journal of Family Issues, 24*, 3–20.

Dovey, K., & Onyx, J. (2001). Generating social capital at the workplace: A South African case of inside-out renewal. *International Journal of Lifelong Education, 20*(3), 151–168.

Dumaine, B. (1990). Who needs a boss? *Fortune, 121*(10), 52–60.

Elden, M. (1981). Political efficacy at work: The connection between more autonomous forms of workplace organization and a more participatory politics. *The American Political Science Review, 75*(1), 43–58.

Elloy, D. F., & Terpening, W. (2001). A causal model of burnout among self-managed work team members. *Journal of Psychology, 135*(3), 321–334.

Ferrie, J. E., Shipley, M. J., Marmot, M. G., Stansfeld, S., & Davey, S. G. (1998a). The health effects of major organizational change and job insecurity. *Social Science Medicine, 46*, 243–254.

Ferrie, J. E., Shipley, M. J., Marmot, M. G., Stansfeld, S., & Davey, S. G. (1998b). An uncertain future: The health effects of threats to employment security in white-collar men and women. *American Journal of Public Health, 88*(7), 1030–1036.

Freeman, R. B., & Rogers, J. (1999). *What workers want.* Ithaca, NY: ILR Press Russell Sage Foundation.

Friedman, W., & Casner-Lotto, J. (2002). The power of teamwork. *Worklife Report, 14*(1), 8–9.

Froiland, P. (1993). What cures job stress? (a) Wellness programs; (b) Brown-bag stress seminars; c) Less work and more control over the job. *Training, 30*(12), 32.

Glassop, L. (2002). The organizational benefits of teams. *Human Relations, 55*(2), 225–249.

Goodman, P. S., Davadas, S., & Hughson, T. L. G. (1988). Groups and productivity. In J. P. Campbell (Ed.), *Productivity in organizations* (pp. 158–167). San Francisco: Jossey-Bass and Associates.

Greenberg, E. S. (1986). *Workplace democracy: The political effects of participation.* Ithaca, NY: Cornell University Press.

Greenberg, E. S., & Grunberg, L. (1994). *The exercise of power and influence in the workplace and the sense of powerlessness* (working paper). Institute of Behavioral Science, University of Colorado, Boulder.

Greenberg, E. S., & Grunberg, L. (1999). *The changing American workplace and the sense of mastery: Assessing the impact of downsizing, job reengineering and teaming* (working paper). Institute of Behavioral Science, University of Colorado, Boulder. (www.colorado.edu/ibs/pec/workplacechange).

Greenberg, E. S., & Grunberg, L. (2004). *The changing American workplace and the sense of mastery: Assessing the impacts of downsizing, job redesign and teaming.* From www.colorado.edu/ibs/PEC/workplacechange/papers/.

Greenberg, E. S., Grunberg, L., & Daniel, K. (1996). Industrial work and political participation: Beyond "simple spillover." *Political Research Quarterly, 49*(2), 305–330.

Greenberg, E. S., Sikora, P., Grunberg, L., & Moore, S. (2005). *Work teams and organizational commitment: The influence of the team experience on employee attitudes* (working paper). Institute of Behavioral Science, University of Colorado, Boulder (www.colorado.edu/ibs/pec/workplacechange).

Greenhalgh, L., & Rosenblatt, Z. (1987). Job insecurity: Toward conceptual clarity. *Academy of Management Review, 9*, 438–448.

Hackman, J. R. (1987). The design of work teams. In J. W. Lorsch (Ed.), *Handbook of organizational behavior* (315–342). Englewood Cliffs, NJ: Prentice Hall.

Heller, D., Judge, T. A., & Watson, D. (2002). The confounding role of personality and trait affectivity in the relationship between job and life satisfaction. *Journal of Organizational Behavior, 23*, 815–835.

Kandel, D. B., Davies, M., & Raveis, V. H. (1985). The stressfulness of daily social roles for women. *Journal of Health and Social Behavior, 21*, 202–218.

Karasek, R. A. J., & Theorell, T. (1990). *Healthy work: Stress, productivity and the reconstruction of working life.* New York: Basic Books.

Kirkman, B. L., & Rosen, B. (2000). Powering up teams. *Organizational Dynamics, 28*(3), 48–65.

Kohn, M. L., & Schooler, C. (1983). *Work and personality: An inquiry into the impact of social stratification.* Norwood, NJ: Ablex Publishing.

Lafferty, W. M. (1989). Work as a source of political learning among wage-laborers and lower-level employees. In R. S. Sigel (Ed.), *Political learning in adulthood: a sourcebook of theory and research* (pp. 890–101). Chicago: University of Chicago Press.

LaRocco, J. M., House, J. S., & French, J. R., Jr. (1980). Social support, occupational stress, and health. *Journal of Health and Social Behavior, 21*, 202–218.

Lester, S. W., Meglino, B. M., & Korsgaard, M. A. (2002). The antecedents and consequences of group potency: A longitudinal investigation of new formed work groups. *Academy of Management Journal, 45*(2), 352–368.

Levine, D., & D'Andrea, T. L. (1990). Participation, productivity, and the firm's environment. In A. S. Blinder (Ed.), *Paying for productivity* (pp. 183–237). Washington DC: Brookings Institution.

Lewis, B. (1990). Team directed workforces from a worker's view. *Target, 23*–29.

Marmot, M. G., Bosma, H., Hemingway, H., Brunner, E., & Stansfeld, S. (1997). Contributions of job control and other risk factors to social variations in coronary heart disease incidence. *The Lancet, 350*, 235–239.

Marmot, M., Siegrest, J., Theorell, T., & Feeney, A. (1999). Health and the psychosocial environment at work. In M. Marmot & R. Wilkinson (Eds.), *Social determinants of health* (pp. 105–131). Oxford, UK: Oxford University Press.

Marmot, M., & Wilkinson, R. (Eds.) (1999). *Social determinants of health.* Oxford, UK: Oxford University Press.

Mason, R. (1982). *Participatory and workplace democracy.* Carbondale: Southern Illinois University Press.

Milbraith, L., & Goel, M. L. (1971). *Political participation.* Chicago: Rand McNally.

Mill, J. S. (1991). *On liberty and other essays.* New York: Oxford University Press.

Mitchell, T. R., Holtom, B. C., Lee, T. W., Sablynski, C. J., & Erez, M. (2001). Why people stay: Using job embeddedness to predict voluntary turnover. *Academy of Management Journal, 44*(6), 1102–1123.

Near, J. P., Smith, C. A., Rice, R. W., & Hunt, R. G. (1983). Job satisfaction and non-work satisfaction as components of life satisfaction. *Journal of Applied Social Psychology, 13*, 126–144.

Niehoff, B. P., Moorman, R. H., Blakely, G., & Fuller, J. (2001). The influence of empowerment and job enrichment on employee loyalty in a downsizing environment. *Group and Organizational Management, 26*(1), 93–113.

Osburn, J. D., Moran, L., Musselwhite, E., & Zenger, J. H. (1990). *Self-directed work teams.* Homewood, IL: Irwin.

Parris, M. A. (2003). Work teams: Perceptions of a ready-made support system? *Employee Responsibilities and Rights Journal 15*(2), 71–83.

Pateman, C. (1970). *Participation and democratic theory.* Cambridge, UK: Cambridge University Press.

Pearlin, L. I., & Schooler, C. (1978). The structure of coping. *Journal of Health and Social Behavior, 19*(1), 2–21.

Peterson, S. (1992). Workplace politicization and its political spillovers. *Economic and Industrial Democracy, 13*, 511–524.

Phelan, J., Schwartz, J. E., Bromet, E. J., Dew, M. A., Parkinson, D. K., Schulberg, H. C., et al. (1991). Work stress, family stress and depression in professional and managerial employees. *Psychological Medicine, 21*, 999–1012.

Price, R. H., Van Ryn, M., & Vinokur, A. D. (1992). Impact of a preventive job search intervention on the likelihood of depression among the unemployed. *Journal of Health and Social Behavior, 3*, pp. 158–167.

Rice, R. W., Near, J. P., & Hunt, R. G. (1980). The job-satisfaction/life-satisfaction relationship: A review of empirical research. *Basic and Applied Social Psychology, 1*, 37–64.

Rogers, S. J., & May, D. C. (2003). Spillover between marital quality and job satisfaction: Long-term patterns and gender differences. *Journal of Marriage and the Family, 65*, 482–495.

Rosenstone, S. J., & Hanson, J. M. (1993). *Mobilization, participation, and democracy in America*. New York: Macmillan.

Rosner, M. (1976). *The kibbutz as a way of life in modern society*. Cambridge, MA: Institute for Cooperative Community.

Rousseau, J.-J. (1987). *The basic political writings*. Indianapolis: Hackett Publishing Co.

Savory-Gordon, L. (2003). *Spillover effects of increased workplace democracy at Algoma Steel on personal, family and community life*. Bristol: University of Bristol.

Schur, L., Eaton, A., & Rubenstein, S. (2004). Industrial democracy and political participation. *Proceedings of the Industrial Relations Research Association*, San Diego, CA: The Industrial Relations Research Association.

Shadur, M. A., Kienzle, R., & Rodwell, J. J. (1999). The relationship between organizational climate and employee perceptions of involvement: The importance of support. *Group & Organization Management 24*(4), 479–503.

Sigel, R. S., & Hoskins, M. B. (1977). Perspectives on adult political socialization. In S. A. Renshon (Ed.), *Handbook of political socialization* (pp. 43–61). New York: The Free Press.

Sigleman, L., & Feldman, S. (1983). Efficacy, mistrust, and political mobilization. *Comparative Political Studies, 16*, 118–143.

Sikora, P. B. (2002). Enlarging the view of participation in organizations: A proposed framework and anaysis via structural equation modeling. *Dissertation Abstracts International*, Section B: The Sciences and Engineering (63(2-B)).

Smith, V. (1996). Employee involvement, involved employees: Participative work arrangements in a white-collar service occupation. *Social Problems, 43*, 166–179.

Sobel, R. (1993). From occupational involvement to political participation: An exploratory analysis. *Political Behavior, 15*(4), 339–353.

Stewart, G. L., Manz, C. C., & Sims, H. P. (2000). *Team work and group dynamics*. New York: John Wiley.

Taris, T. W., Schreurs, P. J., & Van Iersel-Van Silfhout, I. J. (2001). Job stress, job strain, and psychological withdrawal among Dutch university staff: Towards a dual-process model of the effects of occupational stress. *Work and Stress, 15*, 283–296.

van Mierlo, H., Rutte, C., Seinen, B., & Kompier, M. (2001). Autonomous teamwork and psychological well-being. *European Journal of Work and Organizational Psychology, 10*(3), 291–301.

Verba, S. S., & Nie, N. H. (1972). *Participation in America: Political democracy and social equality.* New York: Harper and Row.

Verba, S., Schlozman, K. L., & Brady, H. E. (1995). *Voice and equality.* Cambridge, MA: Harvard University Press.

Wall, T. D., & Clegg, C. W. (1981). A longitudinal study of group work redesign. *Journal of Occupational Behavior, 2*, 31–49.

Warr, P. (1999). Well-being and the workplace. In D. Kahneman, E. Diener and N. Schwarz (Eds.), *Well-being: The foundations of hedonic psychology* (pp. 392–412). New York: Russell Sage Foundation.

Wellins, R. S., Byham, W. C., & Wilson, J. M. (1991). *Empowered teams.* San Francisco: Jossey-Bass.

Wilkinson, R. G. (1996). *Unhealthy societies: The affliction of inequality.* London: Routledge.

14

Long-Term Benefits of Habitual Helping

Doing Well by Doing Good

JANE ALLYN PILIAVIN

The literature on prosocial behavior has had a lot to say about the potential short-term benefits of helping behavior for both the victim and the helper. Batson (1991; 1998) argues that when the help is altruistically motivated, the helper's satisfaction is that the victim—for whom the helper experienced empathy—is no longer suffering or in need. Thus the helper has that warm glow of knowing that he or she has helped—has done the right thing. In the arousal/cost–reward model (Piliavin, Dovidio, Gaertner, & Clark, 1981; Piliavin, Rodin, & Piliavin, 1969), an individual who helps has reduced the unpleasant arousal experienced because of observing the distress of another. Cialdini and his colleagues (Cialdini & Fultz, 1990; Cialdini, Kenrick, & Baumann, 1982) have shown that helping another person can relieve sadness or guilt being experienced because of some other life experience. Clary, et al. (1998) imply that volunteers experience satisfaction from their community engagement. Except for work by the Snyder group, the literature has not actually focused on these benefits, but rather on the motivations for helping that are satisfied when the action is performed.

Taking a much longer range view, evolutionary psychologists have also discussed the benefits of helping behavior. The long-term benefits they claim do not accrue to the helper—who has usually died while saving the lives of friends and relatives—but rather to the helper's genes (Sober & Wilson, 2000). Through the mechanism of kin selection, more of an altruist's genes may be saved by saving several close relatives than the altruist could have promulgated through procreation. Similarly, through the mechanism of reciprocal altruism, even saving unrelated others who have genes for "tit-for-tat" helping tendencies can benefit the group in the long run.

If there are immediate benefits for helping for the individual, and benefits over generations for the group, might there also be long-term benefits for habitual helpers during their lifetime? What is the evidence for such effects? How are these effects obtained? Are there individual differences in the strengths of these effects? In this chapter, I will selectively review the literature, and then present an analysis of a data set—the Wisconsin Longitudinal Study—that has followed a cohort of individuals from high school graduation through the cusp of retirement.

Why Should We Expect to Find Positive Long-Term Effects of Prosocial Behavior?

There are a number of theoretical approaches that have been taken to explain why one might expect to find positive outcomes for individuals who engage in pro-social behavior such as volunteering, community activism, and informal helping of friends and neighbors. I will briefly sketch those that have received the most support and that I have been able to test with my data.

Alienation vs. social integration

Sociologists have proposed for many years that there are benefits of social participation. In the nineteenth century, Durkheim (1951/1898) argued for the importance of group ties, norms, and social expectations in protecting individuals from suicide. Van Willigen (2000, p. S2) states, "Beginning with Durkheim (1951) . . . sociologists have argued that some positions in society foster a subjective sense of alienation . . . while others promote a sense of attachment or integration (Mirowsky & Ross, 1986; Seeman, 1959)." Referring to Seeman's five types of alienation,[1] she goes on to suggest that, "the extent to which individuals feel they control the outcomes of their lives, believe they are part of a supportive community, find their daily work rewarding, have a sense of purpose to their lives, and expect that rewards can be achieved through socially normative means affects their psychological well-being" (p. S2). Volunteering, she suggests, can facilitate the development of these "psychosocial resources" and thus lead to positive effects on well-being.

This approach is consistent with a long tradition of research on social roles. The role accumulation approach (Marks, 1977; Sieber, 1974; Thoits, 1986) assumes that social roles provide status, role-related privileges, and ego-gratification, as well as identities that provide meaning and purpose. In general, the literature provides support for it: More is usually better in terms of roles. Thoits (1992; 1995), however, suggests that voluntary roles, such as friend or group member, may be more responsible for the positive effects of multiple roles than are obligatory roles such as parent or spouse. Keyes (1995) tested this suggestion, and found that, indeed, voluntary social roles predicted higher levels of social and psychological well-being. The relevance of these results for our concerns here is that four (half) of the voluntary roles he asked about are clearly helping roles: community activist, blood donor, volunteer, and caregiver.

Identity Theory, Group Identity Theory, Volunteer Motives, and Mattering

Psychologists have taken somewhat complementary approaches that emphasize the individual more than his/her connection to the community. Identity theory (Stryker, 1980; McCall & Simmons, 1978) suggests that our *self* is made up of a hierarchy of identities tied to our social roles, based on how much time we spend in them and the number of our relationships that depend upon the performance of those roles. Group identity theory (Tajfel, 1970; Tajfel & Turner, 1979) suggests that we obtain some of our sense of self—our self-esteem—from the groups and organizations to which we belong. It is not much of a leap to think that we may also obtain self- esteem from engaging in participatory roles in society. To the extent that one's identities are visible and held in high esteem in society—as is the case for volunteering—individuals holding such identities may come to feel that they *matter* in society. This sense of mattering (Elliott, Kao, & Grant, 2004; Rosenberg & McCullough,1981) can help combat alienation and anomie and lead to psychological well-being. In a recent paper, Elliott, Colangelo, and Gelles (2005) have found that mattering is protective against suicide. Further, as is discussed elsewhere in this volume (see Sullivan, Snyder & Sullivan, this volume), volunteers have a variety of motives for engaging in their unpaid activities. Two of these in particular: value-expression and enhancement should, when satisfied, lead individuals to feel better about themselves.

The literature on this question of the long-term impact of volunteering is largely focused on two age groups: adolescents and the elderly. The reason for this has to do with the two approaches described above. Adolescents are just beginning to develop their sense of self and their role-relations with others. A central issue for the elderly is the loss of many important social roles. Retirement, the "empty nest," and decreasing physical vigor take away many prior sources of a positive sense of self. Thus volunteering potentially could step in and fill that void. In contrast, midlife adults have many roles—sometimes too many—from which they can obtain self-esteem and a sense of mattering to society. Thus the benefits of adding volunteering and other prosocial activities may not contribute much to their sense of self, and could potentially even add stress to their lives.

Effects of habitual helping on adolescents

There is considerable evidence for positive effects on adolescents in terms of steering them away from "bad" activities, as well as some evidence for positive effects on self-esteem (e.g., Uggen & Janikula, 1999). There is also evidence that both participation in high school extra-curricular activities and volunteering in the community develop habits that carry over into adulthood (e.g., Astin & Sax, 1998). That is, teenagers who participate in their communities—in their schools, churches, or the community at large—grow up to be adults who do the same. On all counts, it is clearly beneficial *to the community* for a teenager to be active in this way. However, in this chapter we are focused on benefits *to the helper in the long run*, and thus we will not discuss this research further here.

Effects of habitual helping on the elderly

What sort of personal benefits are we talking about? There have been two major foci of this research: (1) positive emotions, life satisfaction, and psychological well-being and (2) physical health and mortality. With regard to the former, Van Willigen (1998) found effects of both attending voluntary association meetings and hours of volunteer work on life satisfaction and depression. Thoits and Hewitt (2001) used the first two waves of the national sample of adults collected by House and reported in Americans' Changing Lives (House, 1995) to study this question. They find that the number of volunteer hours at time one and the change in volunteer hours between the waves are both significantly related to all six measures of well-being examined, and controls for other forms of community participation do not eliminate these effects. The most highly significant effects are on life satisfaction and feelings of mastery.

There has been more research on physical health and mortality. Young and Glasgow (1998) found that self-reported health status increased as instrumental social participation increased for both men and women, using a longitudinal sample of 629 non-metropolitan elderly. Moen, Dempster-McClain, and Williams (1989), studying a sample of women who had been between the ages of 25 and 50 when interviewed in 1956, found that participation in clubs and volunteer activities had a significant protective effect on mortality. The analysis controlled for many other relevant factors, including the number of other roles and health in 1956, and the article makes clear that the activities were indeed largely community-oriented (PTA, scouting, book drives, etc.). In a second more complex analysis based on interviews done in 1986 with the 313 surviving women, Moen, Dempster-McClain, and Williams (1992) found effects on three measures of health: self-appraised health, time to serious illness, and functional ability. Oman, Thoresen, and McMahon (1999) also examined volunteering and mortality in a 1990–91 prospective study of 2,025 community-dwelling elderly aged 55 and older in Marin County, California. Mortality was assessed through November, 1995. Controlling for health habits, physical functioning, religious attendance, social support, and many other factors, high volunteers (two organizations) had 44% lower mortality than non-volunteers.

Because these are not experiments—and it is difficult to see how controlled experiments could be done—we cannot be certain that the effects are indeed causal. Assuming for now that effects are real, further questions arise. What are the mechanisms by which they are obtained? For whom is the effect of volunteering most beneficial? How much participation is optimal"?

Moderating Effects

For whom?

Van Willigen (2000) found that the benefits of volunteering were greater for the well-being of the elderly than for younger adults, again using the first two waves of the Americans' Changing Lives data (1986, 1989). Oman et al. (1999) also found—and report on studies by others—that the impact of volunteering on *mortality* increases with increasing age; that is, those most at risk are helped the most. Musick, Herzog, and House (1999) tracked respondents aged 65 and older at the first wave of the Americans' Changing Lives (House, 1995) data set, using the National Death Index, from the year of the survey (1986) through March, 1994. The protective effect of volunteering was found only among those with low informal social interaction (measured by how often they talk on the telephone with friends, neighbors, or relatives in the typical week and how often they get together with them). This seems to show that those who are less socially integrated benefit more, as would be expected by the Durkheimian analysis discussed above.

How much helping is best?

Friedland, et al.(2001) make the useful distinction between diversity and intensity of involvement in activities. Intensity is the extent to which one is involved, in terms of hours or commitment of effort; diversity is the breadth of involvement, in different organizations or tasks. They find that the number of different activities engaged in during midlife in three categories, passive, intellectual, and physical, is protective against Alzheimer's disease at age 70. Intensity of intellectual activities at midlife distinguished between the control-group members and the Alzheimer's patients.

Controlling for health, race, age, income, physical activity, and initial health and impairment, Musick, et al. (1999) found that moderate volunteering (<40 hours per year or for only one organization) had a protective effect against mortality. Luoh and Herzog find that volunteering leads to better health and lower mortality but that "the quantity of volunteer and paid work beyond 100 annual hours is not related to health outcomes" (2002, p. 490). Musick and Wilson (2003), using all three waves of the House data set, find positive effects of volunteering on depression (mainly in the over 65 group, consistent with van Willigen's findings with different dependant variables) and a consistency effect over time: volunteering in only one wave has no effect, in two it has some, and in three has a large positive effect.

Why? How does it work?

Musick, et al. (1999) suggest that one mechanism by which their finding that volunteering led to better physical and mental health among those with low social interaction could have been through preventing alienation and anomie, since the index measures social integration. Musick and Wilson (2003) also find very small mediating effects of psychological and social resources on the relationship between volunteering and depression. This is an area in which very little work has actually been done.

Implications for Research to be Presented

My expectations, based both on theory and on the research just presented, is that the route by which volunteering and other forms of community service lead to improved psychological well-being and health begins with the structural connections to others and to society as a whole, developed in the course of the activity. Social contacts per se provide rewards, so any kind of social activity could provide this positive outcome. However volunteering and other forms of service, in addition to involving social contact and the performance of social roles, can lead to the development of volunteer motives and identities that are highly valued in society. This in turn can lead to a sense of personal worth based on having contributed to society and to having *mattered*. Psychological well-being, including self-acceptance and a sense of purpose in life would be expected to follow. Positive emotions can lead to better physical health, both through psychosomatic connections but also through leading to better self-care. Thus the path from volunteering to health I propose to be as follows:

Volunteering → social integration → volunteer motives and identity → mattering → psychological well-being → physical health

The research reviewed above *suggests* that a lifelong habit of contributing to one's community through volunteer work and civic life may be protective of health and well-being. However, the most studied group of individuals—House's (1995) Americans' Changing Lives data set—has followed these individuals over less than a decade. The only data set that covered more time (Moen et al.,1989; 1992) was small and included only women in one locality. The research on which I report here, in contrast, follows a large sample for 40 years. Social participation information is available from the 1975, 1992, and 2004 waves. In both 1992 and 2004, information was obtained about psychological well-being and physical health. Thus both an analysis of the impact of volunteering on well-being and an analysis of the mediating role of "psychological resources" on perceived and actual health can be carried out. For a large subset of these individuals, we have information on the activities they engaged in during high school, coded from their high school yearbooks. Thus we can truly examine "lifelong" social participation with these data.

A problem for any causal analysis, unless repeated measures of the dependent variables are available, is attempting to demonstrate that the effects are not simply the result of a continuing state that existed prior to the purported effect. The earlier waves of the WLS did not include mental health or well-being measures. We can thus do only a short-term analysis of the impact of volunteering on well-being between 1992 and 2004, controlling stringently with *the same* well-being measures taken in 1992 in 2004. But here we are again back to a rather short period of time. However, a few items from the 1957 high school surveys can be employed as proxies for positive and negative psychological states at that time to obtain a longer-term control. Many other variables, including IQ, education, income, marital status, and other factors known both to predict volunteering and to contribute to mental health are employed as controls.

Although the data on social participation do not include a measure of the number of hours contributed, the question of "how much is best?" can be explored in relationship to diversity, that is, the number of organizations, as well as consistency over time. With regard to moderating effects, it is possible to test whether the positive effects of volunteering are the strongest where they are most needed: among those who are least well integrated into the society through other social ties. I am defining volunteering in these analyses as *taking actions, within an institutional framework, that potentially provide some service to one or more other people, or to the community at large.* It is my contention that it is this focus outside oneself that provides the greatest benefit to mental and physical health. Thus a measure of more "social" participation is included as a stringent control, as are participation in church-related groups and church attendance. The sociological approach that emphasizes avoiding alienation would not necessarily distinguish between different *forms* of social participation. Just getting out and about, making connections, should suffice.

As laid out above, I will argue that an important mediating mechanism lies in the development of a volunteer identity (see Grube & Piliavin, 2000) along with volunteer motives (see Clary et al., 1998; Sullivan, Snyder, & Sullivan, this volume) and in the sense of *mattering* (Elliot et al., 2004; Rosenberg & McCullough, 1981) that such an identity gives to the volunteer. The more diverse, intense, and consistent is one's volunteering and other community participation over time, the more of a volunteer identity and the more motives one will develop, and thus the more one will feel that one matters in the world. Although volunteer motives, volunteer identity, and mattering are measured only in 2004, I will attempt to show that the path to psychological well-being runs through the sense of mattering. Although there are measures of depression in the data set, in the interests of a simpler presentation I do not extend the analyses to that variable. And I discuss physical health only when attempting to answer the first question below.

Basic Questions to be Asked

1 Is volunteering positively related to psychological well-being and physical health?
2 What aspects of volunteering relate to health and well-being? Do diversity—volunteering for several organizations—and consistency—volunteering regularly over time—lead to more positive effects than less involvement?

3 Will volunteering have more positive effects for some people—those who are less well integrated—than for others?
4 What are the processes by which volunteering influences health and well-being? I expect that volunteering will lead to psychological well-being because of the development of a volunteer identity and volunteer motives, which then lead to a sense of mattering.

How the Longitudinal Study Was Conducted

The Wisconsin Longitudinal Study (WLS) began with a 1/3 random sample (N = 10,317) of women and men who graduated from Wisconsin high schools in 1957. The next two waves of survey data were collected from the graduates or their parents in 1964 and 1975; further telephone and mail surveys were conducted in 1992 and again in 2004. A random sibling was picked up in 1977 and also followed for the last two waves, although I will not be analyzing their data.[2] Major strengths of the data set are that retention has been excellent and a great deal of information has been obtained. A major weakness is that the sample reflects the Wisconsin of the late 1950s, in that very few minority group individuals are included, and, because the sample members are all high school graduates, the level of education, occupational status, and income are above average (see Sewell, Hauser, Springer, & Hauser, 2004).

In the interest of letting the chapter flow more easily, details of all measures are omitted. These can be obtained from the author or from the article "Health benefits of volunteering in the Wisconsin Longitudinal Study" (Piliavin & Siegl, under review). Social participation variables include a measure of high school extracurricular activities as well as diversity and consistency of adult volunteering from 1975 through 2004. Dependent variables include psychological well-being (Ryff, 1989)[3] in 1992 and 2004, and self-reported health in the same years. Intervening variables include volunteer motives (Clary, et al., 1998), volunteer identity (Grube & Piliavin, 2000), and mattering (Elliot et al., 2004).

The most important control variable, social participation in 1975, is a measure of more self-oriented activities, in contrast to "other-oriented" volunteering. Other controls for social involvement in 1975 include participation in church-related groups and church attendance. The number of children aged 6–12 in 1975 is included, because some volunteering is related to having children. Perceived social support,[4] marital status, and work status are included as other measures of social integration in 1975. Three dummy variables are used as proxies for psychological well-being in high school: interest and disinterest in school, and certainty with regard to the future. A fourth variable, perceived support, is based on two items concerning the encouragement of significant others—parents and teachers—for college studies. Many other variables that predict volunteering, psychological well-being, or physical health are included as controls.

What the Analysis of the WLS Reveals

We assume that family background factors and demographic and personal factors predict high school extracurricular participation, which leads to later life volunteer participation, and that those factors, plus social integration in 1992 and the interaction of integration and volunteer service, predict psychological well-being (and physical health) in 1992. Similarly, psychological well-being in 2004 will be predicted by all of the previous factors, plus psychological well-being, health habits such as smoking, weight control, and exercise, and physical health in 1992, volunteer motives, volunteer identity, and mattering. I will not deal with the relationships at the beginning of this model. Suffice it to say that there is indeed a consistency in individuals' tendencies to participate in society, beginning with extra-curricular activities in high school and extending to volunteering in what has been called young old age. We will begin our analysis with attempts to answer the first question: Is volunteering positively related to psychological well-being and physical health?

Table 14.1 shows the correlations of self-reported health and psychological well-being with measures of high school activities as well as volunteering in the three subsequent waves. The basic answer to the first question thus appears to be yes: community participation is related to later psychological well-being and physical health.

The table also shows the *partial* correlation of 2004 health and well-being with recent volunteering, holding constant the level of the health measure in 1992. What this correlation actually shows is the relationship of volunteering in 2004 to the *change* in well-being from 1992 to 2004. It also shows that the relationship doesn't go the other way. That is, the initial correlation *could* be interpreted to show that healthier people volunteer rather than that volunteering leads to better health. When you hold 1992 health constant and the relationship remains, this interpretation in ruled out. Thus, the relationship of volunteering to well-being is potentially causal. Of course, all sorts of other influences that may be the causes of *both* variables have not yet been eliminated. That is the next step.

For this step, regression analyses of both 1992 and 2004 health and well-being were carried out, in which a large number of variables known to predict both volunteering and psychological well-being and health were controlled.[5] Table 14.2 shows the impact of volunteering in 1975 and 1992 on well-being and health in 1992 and 2004, controlling for these factors. For the analysis of the 2004 measures, volunteering in 2004 is added, along with the measure of health in 1992.

What does this analysis tell us? Of course it is impossible to hold *everything* constant, but the control variables used cover the major social-structural factors that are usually mentioned in connection with the prediction of volunteering and psychological and physical well-being. What this table tells *me* is that for psychological well-being, volunteering within the last 15 years is related to current well-being. Looking at the 2004 analysis, it is clear that recent volunteering contributes to well-being over and above the level of well-being tapped in the 1992 wave. Volunteering before that, since it presumably contributed to well-being in 1992, no

Table 14.1 First-order correlations of volunteering measures with health and well-being measures, and partial correlations in 2004 controlling for health measure in 1992. All correlations significant at p < .001. Ns vary.

	Dependent variable					
Independent variables	Self-reported health in 1992	Self-reported health in 2004	Self-reported health in 2004, partialing 1992 health	Psychological well-being in 1992	Psychological well-being in 2004	Psychological well-being in 2004, partialing 1992 psychological well-being
High school activities	.103	.117	—	.102	.125	—
Volunteering in 1975	.050	.067	—	.107	.126	—
Volunteering in 1992	.074	.066	—	.165	.155	—
Volunteering in 2004	.078	.100	.071	.129	.164	.113

longer has a direct effect on well-being in 2004. Results are similar for self-reported health, but the effects are not as strong. This analysis supports a causal interpretation even more strongly than those reported in Table 14.1.

How much? What kind?

The second question asks, "Do diversity and consistency of volunteering relate to health and well-being?" Does working for more organizations lead to better outcomes than working just with one?[6] To what extent does consistent volunteering, as compared to more sporadic work, lead to positive health outcomes?[7] First I looked at well-being and self-reported health in 1992. Analyses show significant relationships for both diversity and consistency of volunteering with both measures. The stronger relationships are with the measure of consistency of volunteering over time. The findings are the same—or stronger—if current volunteering is used instead of volunteering at the previous wave. To provide better evidence for causation, I carried out other analyses on the 2004 wave, so I could control for 1992 well-being and health.

Table 14.2 Unstandardized regression coefficients for the regression of 1992 and 2004 measures of health and well-being on volunteering. Control variables are not shown.

Independent variables	*Psychological well-being in 1992*	*Self-reported health in 1992*	*Psychological well-being in 2004*	*Psychological well-being in 2004 (expanded model)*	*Self-reported health in 2004*	*Self-reported health in 2004 (expanded model)*
			Dependent variable			
1975 Volunteering	.394*	−.001	.166	.011	.005	.003
	(.181)	(.002)	(.157)	(.126)	(.008)	(.007)
1992 Volunteering	.940***	.003**	.475***	.056	.006	−.001
	(.111)	(.001)	(.103)	(.084)	(.005)	(.005)
2004 Volunteering	—	—	.436***	.338***	.118**	.015**
			(.120)	(.097)	(.006)	(.005)
1992 Health/well-being measure	—	—	—	.455***	—	1.948***
				(.011)		(.064)

Indicators of significance: *** = $p < .001$; ** = $p < .01$; * = $p < .05$

How much? Diversity

Volunteering for two organizations appears to contribute somewhat more to psychological well-being than volunteering for only one. Beyond that, there seems to be little further contribution. This holds true whether the volunteering measure is lagged (from 1992) or relatively recent (reported in 2004). The results remain when 1992 well-being is controlled—that is, when we look at the *change* in well-being. The effects on self-reported health are much weaker, in general, and show a different pattern. There are no interpretable effects using the 1992 measure of volunteering. Only those who volunteered for three or more organizations recently show positive effects using the 2004 volunteering measure and controlling for 1992 reported health.

How much? Consistency

The results for the consistency analysis are different. For both psychological well-being and self-reported health, the effect of volunteering in one wave is significant and remains at least marginally so with the introduction of the 1992 health measure. Second, the effects of volunteering over two waves appear to be additive: that is, the effect of volunteering in two waves is about twice that of volunteering in one wave for psychological well-being and about 50% greater for self-reported health. Those who have volunteered consistently in all three waves show similar increases. There is no evidence in these findings that one can get too much of a good thing. That is, there is never a decrease in the impact of volunteering as the amount increases. The introduction of the relevant past health control does not eliminate the differential effects.

At this point what do we know? Volunteering—at least in this cohort of Wisconsin high school graduates—appears to lead to better psychological well-being, and to a slight degree to better self-reported health. Volunteering for more rather than fewer organizations seems to make only a minor contribution to this effect. However, having consistently volunteered across one's life provides a major boost to psychological well-being as compared to more episodic participation. Effects on self-reported health are similar, although weaker. The effects remain after controlling for prior well-being.

For whom?

The third question is, "Does volunteering have more positive effects for some people than for others?" For the answer to this question I look only at psychological well-being.[8] I expect that volunteering will do more for the psychological well-being of people who are otherwise *less integrated in society*. People who are not married, for example, are consistently shown to be more at risk for depression. People who do not work—especially once children are out of the house—lack that source of support for a positive sense of contribution to society. People in rural areas have less overall social contact. I measure social integration with an index made up of five items measured in 1992: marital status, work status, rural–urban residence, visits with friends and perceived social support.[9]

Here I measure volunteering with the use of two variables. One is a measure that represents both diversity and consistency of volunteering in the first two waves.[10] For analyses of well-being in 2004, I add the overall measure of current volunteering. I also calculate an interaction term by multiplying the measures of diversity/consistency of volunteering by the integration measure. Table 14.3 presents the regression of psychological well-being in 1992 and 2004 on these variables and the usual controls, which are not shown for simplicity of presentation.[11]

The first step of the regression included all the control variables mentioned above, plus the measure of diversity/consistency of volunteering. On the second step, integration and the interaction of volunteering and integration are added. The addition of these variables increases the predictive ability of volunteering and the overall R^2. The fact that the coefficent for the interaction term is *negative* supports our expectation that the positive effect of volunteering is *greatest* for those who are *least* integrated in society. When we analyze well-being in 2004, all of these relationships are still found. Adding the measure of volunteering in 2004 increases R^2 but has no impact on the coefficients for 1992 volunteering. Finally, when the measure of psychological well-being in 1992 is introduced, it has—of course—a very large effect on the same measure taken in 2004. Also, the coefficients for all of the

Table 14.3 Regressions of psychological well-being in 1992 and 2004 on control variables, diversity/consistency of volunteering, integration, and their interaction. Well-being in 1992 and 2004 volunteering are added for 2004 well-being analysis. Entries are unstandardized coefficients (standardized errors) [a]

	Dependent variable: psychological well-being 1992	
Variables	*Step 1*	*Step 2*
Diversity/consistency of volunteering 1975–92	1.447*** (.217)	3.400** (1.146)
Integration 1992		3.189*** (.293)
Integration X div/ cons of volunteering		−.324* (.152)
Adjusted R^2	.067***	.103***
df	18/4880	20/4878

	Dependent variable: psychological well-being 2004			
Variables	*Step 1*	*Step 2*	*Step 3*	*Step 4*
Diversity/consistency of volunteering 1975–92	.836*** (.185)	3.486*** (.985)	3.368*** (.983)	1.591* (.805)
Integration 1992		2.341*** (.257)	2.314*** (.256)	.904*** (.212)
Integration X div/ cons of volunteering		−.394** (.131)	−.416*** (.131)	−.232* (.107)
Volunteering 2004			.520*** (.106)	.366*** (.087)
Psychological well-being 1992				.442*** (.010)
Adjusted R^2	.089***	.115***	.120***	.412***
df	18/3830	20/3828	21/3827	22/3826

[a] Indicators of significance: *** = $p < .001$; ** = $p < .01$; * = $p < .05$
Significance indicated for R^2 is for significance of change

Table 14.4 Regressions of psychological well-being in 2004 on control variables, diversity/consistency of volunteering, integration, their interaction, volunteer identity, 2004 volunteering, mattering and 1992 well-being. Entries are unstandardized coefficients (standardized errors) [a]

	Dependent variable: psychological well-being 2004			
Variables	Step 1	Step 2	Step 3	Step 4
Diversity/consistency of volunteering 1975–92	3.087** (.995)	2.935** (.997)	1.312@ (.818)	.874 (.771)
Integration 1992	2.261*** (.256)	2.225*** (.212)	.846*** (.217)	.587** (.205)
Integration X div/cons of volunteering	−.384** (.133)	−.368** (.133)	−.205@ (.109)	−.158 (.102)
Volunteering 2004	.504*** (.107)	.417*** (.113)	.335*** (.093)	.204* (.102)
Volunteer identity 2004		.103* (.044)	.040 (.036)	.017 (.034)
Psychological well-being 1992			.440*** (.010)	.376*** (.010)
Mattering 2004				1.315*** (.061)
Adjusted R	.123***	.124*	.411***	.475***
df	21/3673	22/3672	23/3671	24/36720

[a] Indicators of significance: *** = p < .001; ** = p < .01; * = p < .05; @ = p < .10
Significance indicated for R^2 is for significance of change.

volunteering variables decrease. However, they are all still significant, indicating that the effect is in all likelihood causal. Thus, volunteering leads to improved psychological well-being, especially among those who are least well integrated into society.

Do volunteer identity and mattering mediate these effects?

Our last question has to do with the *process* by which volunteering affects psychological well-being. I proposed that the effect of volunteering on well-being would be mediated by volunteer identity and mattering. That is, people who volunteer have a better sense of self because they have developed a positive identity as a volunteer that makes them feel that they matter in society. Table 14.4 shows the model presented in Table 14.3 with the addition of measures of volunteer identity and mattering. Step 1 in Table 14.4 is the equivalent of Step 3 in Table 14.3. The numbers are slightly different because of missing data on the new variables that have been added.

Note that when volunteer identity is added on Step 2 it has a small significant effect on well-being. This disappears when 1992 well-being is entered, indicating that it is correlated with well-being rather than a cause.[12] All of the coefficients for volunteering drop on this step, as in Table 14.3, indicating as before that *part* of their impact on 2004 well-being is because of either their effect on 1992 well-being or the reverse—a selection effect. The effect on 2004 volunteering is very small as one would expect.

The effect in which we are most interested, however, is the impact on all of the volunteering measures when we introduce the measure of mattering. What is expected when testing a mediation effect is that the effect of the causal variables will decrease or disappear when the mediator is entered into the model. This is exactly what happens to the coefficients for the volunteering variables; when mattering is entered, the remaining effects of the 1975–1992 volunteering measures disappear. The size of the coefficient for 2004 volunteering is greatly reduced. Thus, as predicted, mattering appears to mediate the effects of volunteering on psychological well-being.

Conclusions

We have once again confirmed the hypothesis that volunteering—defined in this research as doing other-oriented community participation—is positively related to psychological well-being and self-reported health. We can conclude with some confidence that the first relationship is causal, based on controls for psychological well-being measured in 1992 that were used in the analysis of the 2004 data. In addition, controls for more self-focused social participation and participation in church-related groups indicate that the effect is specific to the more altruistic form of social engagement. Our second hypothesis, that volunteering for more organizations, and more continuous involvement in those organizations, will lead to more positive effects, was also borne out. There was evidence that working for two or more organizations provided more benefit than working for one or none; only participation beyond two conveyed benefits for self-reported physical health. This replicates the research of Luoh and Herzog (2002). The relationship of continuity of involvement, on the other hand, appears to be linear for both outcome variables, at least over the range we tested. Participation in both 1975 and 1992 leads to greater benefit than participation in one wave or not at all, and volunteering in 2004 provides yet more benefit. This is consistent with the research of Musick and Wilson (2003) using the House (1995) data set.

The third hypothesis, that the relationship of volunteering to psychological well-being will be moderated by level of social integration, with those who are less well integrated benefiting the most, was also confirmed. This result is consistent with the findings of Musick et al. (1999). In analyses of the 2004 measure of psychological well-being, these results are maintained even when 1992 well-being is introduced. This provides evidence that the effect of volunteering on well-being is not simply a selection of healthier individuals into volunteering but rather that there is indeed some causal relationship of volunteering to well-being. Finally, we found, using the 2004 wave of the WLS, in which the 1957 cohort are in their mid-sixties, that one process by which volunteering has a positive impact on psychological well-being appears to be through the mediation of the sense of mattering. Volunteering makes one feel better psychologically *because it contributes to the sense that one matters in the world.*

Acknowledgment

The research reported in this chapter was supported by a grant from the National Institute on Aging (1-R03-AG21526) and from the author's Conway-Bascom Professorship from the University of Wisconsin.

Notes

1 Powerlessness, isolation, self-estrangement, meaninglessness, and normlessness.
2 Data for both grads and siblings are available for public use at http://www.ssc.wisc.edu/wlsresearch/
3 The measure used here combines the four scales of mastery, personal growth, purpose in life, and self-acceptance.
4 The sum of yes–no responses to the two questions, "Is there a person in your family (a friend outside your family) with whom you can really share your very private feelings and concerns?"
5 Sex, socioeconomic status of parental household, IQ, high school grades and school track, interest in school, years of education, earnings and occupational status in the 1970s, number of children, frequency of church attendance, and a measure of social participation that is more self-oriented than volunteering.
6 The measure of diversity of volunteering is a simple count of the number of organizations (out of the five) with which the respondent was involved, at the previous wave.
7 The measure of consistency of volunteering is the number of waves in which the respondent indicated that s/he did volunteering.
8 I have done the analyses for self-reported health and, as usual, the effects are much weaker and are very sensitive to adding and removing variables from the equations.
9 The index has a range of 2–10. A score of 2 reflects an unmarried, non-working individual living in a rural area who has no kin or friends they can count on for support and few social visits.
10 The reason for this is that consistency and diversity as measured before are rather highly correlated, and thus should not be used in the same analysis. It is the simple sum of the number of organizations worked for in waves one and two, using a three-category measure (0, 1, and 2 or more organizations) at each wave. The measure thus has a range from 0 to 4: a score of 4 can be obtained only by working for two or more organizations in both waves, a score of 3 must involve some volunteering at both waves, and a score of 0 means no volunteering in either wave.

11 Analyses are available on request.
12 Measures of volunteer motives were included as well and suffered the same fate.

References

Astin, A. W., & Sax, L. J. (1998). How undergraduates are affected by service participation. *Journal of College Student Development*, *39*, 251–262.

Batson, C. D. (1991). *The altruism question: Toward a social-psychological answer*. Hillsdale, NJ: Lawrence Erlbaum Associates.

Batson, C. D. (1998). Altruism and prosocial behavior. In D. T. Gilbert & S. T. Fiske, *The handbook of social psychology*, Vol. 2 (4th ed.) (pp. 282–316). New York: McGraw-Hill.

Cialdini, R. B., & Fultz, J. (1990). Interpreting the negative mood/helping literature via *Mega*-analysis. *Psychological Bulletin*, *107*, 210–214.

Cialdini, R. B., Kenrick, D. T., & Baumann, D. J. (1982). Effects of mood on prosocial behavior in children and adults. In N. Eisenberg (Ed.), *The development of prosocial behavior* (pp. 339–359). New York: Academic Press.

Clary, E. G., Snyder, M., Ridge, R. D., Copeland, J., Stukas, A. A., Haugen, J., et al. (1998). Understanding and assessing the motivations of volunteers: A functional approach. *Journal of Personality and Social Psychology*, *74*, 1516–1530.

Durkheim, E. (1951/1898). *Suicide*. (Trans. J. Spalding & G. Simpson.) New York: Free Press

Elliott, G. C., Colangelo, M. F., & Gelles, R. J. (2005). Mattering and suicide ideation: Establishing and elaborating a relationship. *Social Psychology Quarterly*, *68*, 223–238.

Ellliott, G. C., Kao, S., & Grant, A. (2004). Mattering: Empirical validation of a social-psychological concept. *Self and Identity*, *3*, 339–354.

Friedland, R. P., Fritsch, T., Smyth, K. A., Koss, E., Lerner, A. J., Chen, C. H., et al. (2001). Patients with Alzheimer's disease have reduced activities in midlife compared with healthy control-group members. *Proceedings of the National Academy of Sciences*, *98*(6), 3440–3445.

Grube, J., & Piliavin, J. A. (2000). Role identity, organizational experiences, and volunteer performance. *Personality and Social Psychology Bulletin*, *26*, 1108–1119.

House, J. S. (1995). *Americans' Changing Lives: Waves I and II, 1986 and 1989*. Ann Arbor, MI: Interuniversity Consortium for Political and Social Research.

Keyes, C. L. (1995). *Social functioning and social well-being: studies of the social nature of personal wellness*. Unpublished PhD dissertation, University of Wisconsin-Madison.

Luoh, M., & Herzog, A. R. (2002). Individual consequences of volunteer and paid work in old age: Health and mortality. *Journal of Health and Social Behavior*, *43*, 490–509.

Marks, S. R. (1977). Multiple roles and role strain: Some notes on human energy, time and commitment. *American Sociological Review*, *42*, 921–936.

McCall, G. J., & Simmons, J L. (1978). *Identities and interactions*, New York: The Free Press.

Mirowsky, J., & Ross, C. E. (1986). Social patterns of distress. *Annual Review of Sociology*, *12*, 23–45

Moen, P., Dempster-McClain, D., & Williams, R. M., Jr. (1989). Social integration and longevity. *American Sociological Review*, *54*, 635–647.

Moen, P., Dempster-McClain, D., & Williams, R. M., Jr. (1992). Successful aging: A life-course perspective on women's multiple roles and health. *American Journal of Sociology*, *97*, 1612–1638.

Musick, M. W., Herzog, A. R., & House, J. S. (1999). Volunteering and mortality among older adults: Findings from a national sample. *The Journals of Gerontology: Psychological Sciences and Social Sciences, 54B*, S173–S180.

Musick, M. W., & Wilson, J. (2003) Volunteering and depression: The role of psychological and social resources in different age groups. *Social Science and Medicine, 56*, 259–269.

Oman, D., Thoresen, C. E., & McMahon, K. (1999). Volunteerism and mortality among the community-dwelling elderly. *Journal of Health Psychology, 4*, 301–316.

Piliavin, I. M., Rodin, J., & Piliavin, J. A. (1969). Good Samaritanism: An underground phenomenon? *Journal of Personality and Social Psychology, 13*, 289–299.

Piliavin, J. A., Dovidio, J. F., Gaertner, S. L., & Clark, R. D. III (1981). *Emergency Intervention*. New York: Academic Press.

Piliavin, J. A., and Siegl, E. (under review). *Health benefits of volunteering in the Wisconsin Longitudinal Study.*

Rosenberg & McCullough (1981) Mattering: Inferred significance and mental health among adolescents. *Research in Community and Mental Health. 2*, 163–182.

Ryff, C. D. (1989). *The parental experience in midlife*. Chicago: University of Chicago Press.

Seeman, M. (1959). On the meaning of *alienation*. *American Sociological Review, 24*, 783–791.

Sewell, W. H., Hauser, R. M., Springer, K. W., & Hauser, T. S. (2004). As we age: The Wisconsin longitudinal study, 1957–2001. In K. T. Leicht (Ed.), *Research in Social Stratification and Mobility*, Vol. 20 (pp. 3–111). London: Elsevier.

Sieber, S. D. (1974). Toward a theory of role accumulation. *American Sociological Review, 39*, 567–578.

Sober, E., & Wilson, D. S. (1999). *Unto others: The evolution and psychology of unselfish behavior*. Cambridge, MA: Harvard University Press.

Stryker, S. (1980). *Symbolic interactionism: A social structural version*. Menlo Park, CA: Benjamin/Cummings.

Tajfel, H. (1970). Experiments in intergroup discrimination. *Scientific American, 223*, 96–102.

Tajfel, H., & Turner, J. (1979). An integrative theory of intergroup conflict. In W. G. Austin & S. Worchel (Eds.), *The social psychology of intergroup relations*. (pp. 33–48). Monterey, CA: Brooks/Cole.

Thoits, P. A. (1986). Social support and psychological well-being: Theoretical possibilities. In I. G. Sarason & B. R. Sarason (Eds.), *Social support: theory, research, and application* (pp. 51–72). Dordrecht, the Netherlands: Martinus Nijhoff Publishers.

Thoits, P. A. (1992). Multiple identities: Examining gender and marital status differences in distress. *Social Psychology Quarterly, 55*, 236–2 56.

Thoits, P. A. (1995). Identity-relevant events and psychological symptoms: A cautionary tale. *Journal of Health and Social Behavior, 36*, 72–82.

Thoits, P. A., & Hewitt, L. N. (2001). Volunteer work and well-being. *Journal of Health and Social Behavior, 42*, 115–131.

Uggen, C., & Janikula, J. (1999). Volunteerism and arrest in the transition to adulthood. *Social Forces, 78*, 331–362.

Van Willigen, M. (1998). *Doing good, feeling better: The effect of voluntary association membership on individual well-being*. Paper presented at the annual meeting of the Society for the Study of Social Problems.

Van Willigen, M. (2000). Differential benefits of volunteering across the life course. *Journal of Gerontology: Social Sciences, 55B*, S1–S11.

Young, F. W., & Glasgow, N. (1998). Voluntary social participation and health. *Research on Aging, 20*, 339–362.

15

Cooperation With and Without Trust

Evidence From Local Settings

WENDY M. RAHN

People value security and prosperity, not just for their own survival, but for the well-being of others too. But wanting and having are not the same thing, as children very soon discover. Grown-ups have political philosophers to remind us that good intentions alone are insufficient for achieving desirable collective outcomes. Hobbes' state of nature arises not because human beings are particularly wicked, but rather because they find themselves in an impossible situation, what we now recognize as a social dilemma. Social dilemmas, of which the prisoner's dilemma is but one well-known example, do not get resolved simply because people wish it so. Even if everyone recognizes the advantages of cooperation, more primitive motives, namely self-preservation and self-aggrandizement, or fear and greed, get in the way of realizing common objectives (see Hanley, Hartwig, Orbell, & Morikawa, this volume).

How to temper fear and greed so that the gains of cooperation can be realized is the key question of social order, and social theorists from Hobbes to Freud to Durkheim have proposed a number of different solutions: Leviathan, the superego, and social norms, respectively (Wrong, 1994). More recently, social scientists from a variety of different disciplines have studied the problem of cooperation, researching the ways in which repeated interaction, reputational concerns, group identity, prosocial orientations, framing, conscience, the design of institutions, and a whole host of other factors can affect the likelihood of cooperation in social dilemma settings (Kollack, 1998; Ostrom, 2003). Psychologists are naturally drawn to explanations that focus on individual differences in orientations to others (see, e.g., Van Lange, this volume) or to group identity considerations (Tyler, this volume). In some places the "war of all against all" is much less destructive than in others because their denizens are kinder, gentler, and more group- than self-oriented. Political scientists and sociologists, on the other hand, are much more likely to conclude that even saints will become sinners given the right circumstances.

Fortunately, as this volume indicates, an interdisciplinary perspective on cooperation has emerged in which person and situation are no longer seen as rivals for influence. What is less appreciated, perhaps, is that integrative explanations require that we have adequate variation in both persons and situations. Researchers have developed an impressive number of scales to measure individual differences in dispositions that incline people toward helping behaviors and cooperation (Eisenberg & Eggum, this volume; Penner, Dovidio, Piliavin, & Schroeder, 2005; Van Lange, this volume; more generally, see Weber, Kopelman, & Messick, 2004), but place-based variation is either artificially created in the laboratory, as in most social psychological experiments using a social dilemma paradigm, or is measured perceptually in surveys without regard to the real variation that presumably underlies it, introducing hopeless problems of endogeneity. In this chapter, I make use of multi-level data in which both people and places vary in the amount of cooperation they exhibit. While the research design does not permit problem-free inferences about either people or places, it does allow me to disentangle individual cooperation from community-level trust.

The relationship between trust and cooperation is a complex one. Some researchers treat them as so hopelessly intertwined that they are best viewed as different indicators of the same underlying concept, frequently referred to as social capital (e.g., Putnam, 2000). Others prefer to keep trust and cooperation analytically and empirically distinct (e.g., Brehm & Rahn, 1997; Buchan, Croson, & Dawes, 2002; Ostrom, 2003; Yamagishi, Kanazawa, Mashima, & Terai, 2005). If they are related but not completely overlapping concepts, the question naturally arises about their causal ordering and the mechanisms that produce their co-variation. On one side are those, such as Uslaner (2002) and Stolle (1998), who believe that the dominant mechanism is self-selection: people who already trust others select themselves into cooperative arrangements; trust breeds cooperation. Others (e.g., Brehm & Rahn, 1997) believe that there can be genuine *socialization* effects of participation, that the experience of successful cooperation itself can help reduce doubt and uncertainty about (unknown) others' intentions.

In my home discipline of political science, researchers have used simultaneous equation models (Brehm & Rahn, 1997; Shah, 1998; Uslaner, 2002), panel data (Claibourn & Martin, 2000; Rahn, Brehm, & Carlson, 1999) and time series models (Keele, 2005) to unravel the linkages, and predictably, no consensus has emerged about causal priority. One reason for this mixed state of knowledge, I argue, is that these empirical tests have been conducted at very high levels of aggregation, typically at the national level. We can make more conceptual and empirical progress, I believe, by taking advantage of the fact that there is substantial heterogeneity across localities, variation that can be leveraged to better understand these complex relationships. It is very likely the case that in some places, trust produces cooperation whereas in other locations, the relationship is the reverse. In the first scenario, cooperation is *confirmatory*; in the second, it is *revelatory*. Below I elaborate on the importance of this distinction.

In either scenario, however, cooperation is contingent. Human nature is neither angelic nor depraved, but some combination (Alford & Hibbing, 2004). Social dilemmas get resolved—cooperation does happen—but for different reasons in different circumstances (de Hart & Dekker, 2003). Trust in others and cooperating with them to further group goals reinforce each other, but they are not the same thing. This chapter seeks to explore the relationship between trust and cooperation across different kinds of communities, asking, in particular, two questions: Where do people trust? And who cooperates even in the absence of trust?

I Trust, Therefore, I Cooperate: The Logic of Confirmatory Cooperation

Cooperation takes many forms. Sometimes it involves working with others in horizontal relationships to achieve a group task. At other times, the relationships are more vertical in which people are asked to comply with the decisions, demands, and exhortations of group authorities, from paying taxes to accepting political outcomes that are not in one's interest (see Hibbing & Theiss-Morse, this volume; Tyler, this volume). In either case, theoretical and empirical work suggests that people's perceptions of what other group members are likely to do in the same situation bear heavily on individuals' own decisions about whether it is worthwhile for them to cooperate (Chong, 1991; Pruitt & Kimmel, 1977). In these cases, the social dilemma is not based on the structure of the prisoner's dilemma (PD) discussed above, but rather, takes the form of an assurance game (Chong, 1991; Kollack, 1998; Levi, 1997). In assurance games, unlike PD, defection is not the dominant choice, and the main obstacle to cooperation is fear that one's cooperation will be exploited by others rather than avarice (see Chong, 1991; Hayashi, Ostrom, Walker & Yamagishi, 1999; Heckathorn, 1996; Kollock, 1998; Pruitt & Kimmel, 1977; Simpson, 2004).[1]

Consider two situations of the "vertical" sort in which assurance can be the predominant form of the social dilemma: military drafts and paying taxes. Margaret Levi (1997) argues that people comply in these situations for reasons that are often "quasi-voluntary" rather than legally compelled. People cooperate because they believe others will do the same, beliefs that reduce concerns that one's contribution to the collective good will be wasted (because not enough others also cooperate) or that one's own cooperation will be exploited (Chong, 1991).

An empirical study on desertion from the Union Army during the American Civil War by the economists Dora Costa and Matthew Kahn (2003) provides gripping evidence that governmental coercion is an insufficient explanation for compliance. Although the probability of a Union soldier dying was exceedingly high (nearly 1 in 5, mostly from disease) and the chances that a deserter would be caught and punished miniscule, overall desertion rates were quite modest, about 1 in 10, with another 3% absent without leave. Interestingly, desertion and AWOL rates varied enormously across the different states that were obliged to muster the companies comprising the Union Army. In Connecticut, nearly 20% of soldiers in Costa and Kahn's sample deserted. Yet in Iowa, Minnesota, and Wisconsin, desertion rates were less than 4%.

Studies of tax compliance similarly show that people are honest on their tax returns not simply because they are afraid of an IRS audit, but because they believe that other citizens can be trusted to do their duty (Scholz & Lubell, 1998). As Tyler (this volume) points out, deterrence, such as heavy penalties for tax cheating, may even backfire by undermining individuals' internalized moral sense of obligation to comply. The overzealous application of punishment when none is really needed in the first place may be counterproductive to societal levels of cooperation in the long run (Lubell & Scholz, 2001).

I Cooperate, Therefore, I Trust: The Logic of Revelatory Cooperation

However, as Hobbes recognized long ago, when trust in others in lacking, enforcement mechanisms and sanctions for noncompliance may be necessary to get cooperation started (Lubell & Scholz, 2001)—one reason why groups facing collective action problems can rationally decide to empower a group authority to make decisions and mete out punishment (Samuelson & Messick, 1995; Tyler & Degoey, 1995; Van Vugt, 2002). Cooperation, in other words, can be achieved without trust, provided that there are guarantees, in the form of credible sanctioning systems, that potential non-cooperators can be extrinsically motivated to do the right thing (Anthony, 2005; Fehr & Fischbacher, 2004; Lubell & Scholz, 2001; Ostrom, 1990) or in other ways, individuals are publicly accountable for their behavior (Andreoni, & Petrie 2004; De Cremer, Snyder, & DeWitte 2001; Ostrom, 1990).

Are there other ways to induce cooperation in the absence of trust that do not depend on Leviathan or concerns about one's reputation? A variety of solutions to social dilemmas depend on so-called "internal" motives for cooperation rather than on "structural" solutions, such as externally provided selective incentives like punishment for non-cooperation or private rewards that can exclude free rides (Olson, 1965). These include the previously mentioned prosocial orientations, such as altruism or group identity, factors that are discussed at length in other contributions to this volume.[2]

But there is yet another route to cooperation in the absence of trust, one which does not necessarily require people to be self-sacrificing or other-oriented, but is nevertheless crucial to motivating collective action in situations in which the only thing that is certain is one's own motives, not those of others. Even rational individualists can be motivated to undertake cooperative efforts as long as their efforts are critical to the achievement of the group outcome. Beginning with Olson (1965), social scientists have understood that one of the chief impediments to large-scale collective action is the feeling that one's contribution doesn't matter for the production of the collective good: it's just a drop in very big bucket. However, as Moe (1980) argues, people's calculations of their own efficacy are often overestimated. What is important for participation is the *perception* that one is efficacious, not the objective reality.

Thus, even in the absence of positive expectations of others, it may still make sense to contribute, but participation here is contingent on one's sense, perhaps inflated, that one can be pivotal to the outcome. Feelings of efficacy thus affect cooperation by making one's efforts seem worthwhile (Finkel, Muller, & Opp, 1989; Klandermans, 1984; Moe, 1980; Olson, 1965; Rothenberg, 1992). In addition, they influence one's views about the likelihood that others, too, will join, by inducing a belief, whether real or imagined, that one's own choices influence the behavior of others (Acevedo & Krueger, 2004; Goldberg, Markoczy, & Zahn, 2005; Hayashi et al., 1999; Quattrone & Tversky, 1984). If not me, then who? Note that unlike the assurance game situation, our efficacious cooperator does not necessarily believe that others are, in fact, trustworthy. Rather, she believes that she can *make* them so through her own behavioral choice to cooperate.

For example, a local denizen might not have a reliable conjecture about how many of her neighbors will show up to tend the community garden. What she does know, however, is that if she gets her hands dirty, the job is more likely to get done. It is especially important, therefore, that she makes the effort because she can improve the looks of the place at least to some degree by herself. Moreover, she may just possibly inspire others to do the same. She may reason, however illogically, that if she doesn't pull the weeds, no one else will either.

To put it another way, the cooperation with others in joint efforts may come as something of a "surprise" in settings in which the trustworthiness of others is in doubt. This revelation perhaps prompts our efficacious (or other internally motivated) cooperator to revise her expectations about what her neighbors are like. She wasn't sure anyone else would show up, but by gum, some did. Under this scenario, therefore, cooperation can lead to trust because one's own cooperation is reciprocated even though, going in, this was not expected to happen.

Data: Social Indicators Survey

The data for my study are drawn from a survey conducted in the fall of 2003. Nineteen hundred adults in eight states in the Midwest and Northwest were queried by trained interviewers at the Oregon Survey Research Laboratory about their own personal situation and about conditions in their community, defined in geographic terms by mailing address. In their estimate, for example, how many people in the place care what it looks like? Are local political leaders trustworthy, or do they "play favorites?" Is the community a good place for young people, or do they move away for better opportunities? I drew from this survey the set of respondents who lived in communities with at least 15,000 people, according to the 2000 US Census. I wanted mid- to large-sized places for two reasons: (1) to insure that the communities were big enough so that people would not know most community residents personally;[3] (2) so that administrative sources of contextual information were available for those places. From this set, I further reduced the number of communities to those for

Table 15.1 Communities in the study

City	Population	City	Population
Aberdeen, SD	24,658	Lake Oswego, OR	35,278
Beaverton, OR	76,129	Lewiston, ID	30,904
Bellevue, WA	109,569	Meridian, ID	34,919
Billings, MT	89,847	Minneapolis, MN	382,618
Bismarck, ND	55,532	Minot, ND	36,567
Boise, ID	185,787	Missoula, MT	57,053
Bozeman, MT	27,509	Moscow, ID	21,291
Caldwell, ID	26,967	Nampa, ID	51,867
Cedar Rapids, IA	120,758	Olympia, WA	42,514
Coeur d'Alene, ID	35,514	Oregon City, OR	25,754
Davenport, IA	98,359	Pocatello, ID	51,466
Des Moines, IA	198,682	Portland, OR	529,121
Duluth, MN	86,918	Rapid City, SD	59,607
Eugene, OR	137,893	Rochester, MN	85,806
Everett, WA	91,488	Salem, OR	136,924
Fargo, ND	90,599	Seattle, WA	563,374
Grand Forks, ND	49,321	Sioux City, IA	85,013
Great Falls, MT	56,690	Sioux Falls, SD	123,975
Gresham, OR	90,205	Spokane, WA	195,629
Helena, MT	25,780	St Cloud, MN	59,107
Hillsboro, OR	70,186	St Paul, MN	287,151
Idaho Falls, ID	50,730	Tacoma, WA	193,556
Iowa City, IA	62,220	Watertown, SD	20,237
Jamestown, ND	15,527		

which at least five interviews were completed with community residents.[4] My selection rules resulted in a data set with 730 respondents from 47 different communities. These places and their associated population sizes are listed in Table 15.1.

Measures: Dependent Variables

Perceptions of the community cooperative context

In this chapter, I prefer to use perceptions of the community cooperative context (PCCC) to describe residents' expectations of others rather than the concept of social, or generalized trust that I have used in previous work in order to indicate that respondents in this particular survey were asked about people *in their communities* rather than their more general views about "most people." PCCC, in other words, is a slightly more bounded, or parochial, form of trust. Another reason for using a more specific construct is that the measures of participation I will be using, described more fully below, typically refer to involvement in local or community-oriented activities.

Respondents in the survey were asked for their estimates of how many people in their community would perform certain cooperative acts, such as returning a lost wallet, or possessed community-supportive dispositions, such as caring about the upkeep of the place. People were given the response options of "all, most, some, or just a few," although in response to a question about returning a lost wallet, nearly 5% also volunteered the response, "none." The five items were averaged, resulting in a scale that achieved respectable reliability of .7. Its range is 1 to 5, with a score of 5 meaning that respondent believed that all of her fellow citizens were trustworthy.

Individual cooperation

People are drawn to different kinds of activities for different reasons. When your kids are in school, participation in the PTA might seem more appealing than, say, attending meetings of the garden club or volunteering to work on the campaign of a city council representative. There are also differences in preferences for styles of participation. Some people enjoy the rough and tumble of political campaigns, whereas others prefer collective activity that is more communally oriented (Campbell, 2006; Verba & Nie, 1972).

The survey upon which I draw contained a long series of questions asking respondents whether they had engaged in a number of different activities or had been involved with certain kinds of organizations "in the last 12 months." Based on a factor analysis, I designated two general forms of cooperation: political engagement and civic engagement. The former is best exemplified by attendance at political party meetings, contacting local public officials, attending local government meetings, and being involved in political or civic groups. Civic engagement, on the other hand, is indicated by displaying a community symbol, performing volunteer work, involvement in service clubs, attending local cultural events, and involvement in recreational, sports, and hobby clubs.

I created a simple scale for each form of cooperation by counting the number of times respondents reported yes to participating in these activities. Not surprisingly, political engagement is much less widespread than community involvement. On average respondents reported engaging in only one of the four political activities compared to over two and half of the less conflictual sort.

Measures: Independent Variables

Efficacy

In the Social Indicators Survey, respondents were asked how often they believed that "people like you" can have an impact on making the community a better place. The provided responses ranged from "always" to "rarely." In addition, a few respondents (about 2.5%) volunteered the response "never." Nearly half of the respondents replied that they "always" (18%) or "most of the time" (33%) could have an impact.

Reality, or the true level of community trustworthiness

The most novel aspect of this chapter is that in contrast to many other studies of trust, I have both subjective estimates of community trustworthiness (defined above as PCCC) and *objective* measures of community cooperation, or "real" trustworthiness. It is possible, therefore, to empirically ascertain the correspondence between perception and reality. Two indicators of community-level cooperation were obtained for each place in my sample, one designed to represent horizontal cooperation, the other, its vertical dimension. The first, the community-level response rate to the 2000 US Census, is viewed by both the Census Bureau and social scientists (e.g., Knack & Kropf, 1998) as a "measure of cooperation by the US public."[5] On average, the communities in Table 15.1 achieved a 73% response rate, considerably higher than the national average of 67%. The range, however, was quite broad. Eighty-one percent of Rochester, MN, households responded to the US Census by mail, postcard, telephone, or internet. In contrast, the Census Bureau posted a 63% response rate for Caldwell, ID.

My second indicator is designed to assess compliance with legal authorities. It is the crime rate per 100,000 population in 2000 as reported in the Uniform Crime Report of the Federal Bureau of Investigation, available on-line from the Bureau of Justice's website.[6] Again, there is considerable variation across the 47 communities. For examples, residents of Sioux Falls, SD, have much less to fear than the inhabitants of Sioux City, IA. Although Sioux City is only two-thirds the size of Sioux Falls, normally an advantage in crime control, its crime rate, at 6,700 per 100,000 inhabitants, was nearly twice that of the larger city of Sioux Falls.

The correlation between the two measures of community-level cooperation is –.51; that is, places with higher Census response rates also had lower crime rates. Each community was assigned a factor score based on a factor analysis of the two measures of actual cooperation. This produced a rank order of communities, from most to least trustworthy. I then classified the towns and cities in my sample into three categories, "low," "medium," and "high" trustworthiness.

Test of Mean Differences in Dependent Variables

I examined mean differences in PCCC, civic, and political engagement across the three levels of community trustworthiness. Neither civic nor political engagement levels differed significantly across the three types of communities ($F = .96$, $p > .38$; $F = .30$, $p > .75$, respectively). The PCCC variable, on the other hand, was highly responsive to "real" measures of community cooperation ($F = 20.68$, $p < .000$).

Discussion

What do we make of these simple findings? First, they reinforce earlier claims (e.g., Brehm & Rahn, 1997) that trust and cooperation need to be theorized in their own rights and, therefore, it is a mistake to combine them into a unitary measure of social capital even though empirically they might be related. By combining both individual- and community-level variables I have demonstrated that expectations for others' behavior and one's own behavioral choices are not necessarily mirror images. Even when the trustworthiness of others is, for well-founded reasons, in doubt, individuals appear ready to cooperate on common objectives.

But as my earlier discussion implied, cooperation by individuals may be differently motivated depending on circumstances. If one is fairly confident about what others will do, then one's cooperation is confirmatory and thus permits the *maintenance* of benign social beliefs. If there is some doubt, on the other hand, about others, then one's cooperation has the potential to be revelatory. Pessimistic social beliefs, therefore, may be revised in a more hopeful direction. To put it another way, *perceptions* of whether others are cooperative (can be trusted) depend *less* on one's own level of cooperation or feelings of efficacy in settings of high trustworthiness. The origins of perceived trustworthiness in low-trust settings, on the other hand, are more *dependent* on individual- rather than community-oriented characteristics.

Analysis of Moderation

My data are nested—respondents within communities—and therefore, it is necessary to modify basic linear modeling techniques in order to handle the particular statistical problems that arise with multi-level data structure (see Luke, 2004; Raudenbush & Bryk, 2002; Steenbergen & Jones, 2002). In practice, this means explaining *perceived* community trustworthiness as a function both of individual-level variables, namely efficacy and the two measures of cooperation, and the "real" measure of community cooperation, which is measured at the community level. My hypothesis of moderation is then tested by a *cross-level* interaction between the individual-level variables and the contextual variable. Stated simply, I expect that personal efficacy or individual cooperation (or both) is *more* important for perceived trustworthiness of others in settings of *less* actual trustworthiness.

Table 15.2 presents the estimates obtained using HLM, a statistical program developed to work with multi-level data structures. In this analysis, PCCC is the dependent variable, and "reality," efficacy, and both forms of cooperation are my independent variables. In addition, three cross-level interactions between "reality" and the three other independent variables are also part of the specification.

Looking first at main effects, the significant positive coefficients for reality, efficacy, civic, and political engagement mean that *perceptions* of community trustworthiness

Table 15.2 Perceptions of the community cooperative context: individual and contextual origins

	Perceptions of the community cooperative context
Individual-level variables	
Personal efficacy	.11*** (.02)
Civic engagement	.02* (.01)
Political engagement	.03* (.02)
Contextual variable	
Real trustworthiness (reality)	.25*** (.06)
Cross-level interactions	
Efficacy x reality	−.035** (.017)
Civic engagement x reality	−.015 (.013)
Political engagement x reality	−.002 (.016)
Constant	2.3***
Number of communities	46[§]
Number of respondents	720[§§]
Percent of individual-level variance explained over null	13%
Percent of between-community variance explained over null	84%

Note: Table entries are multilevel estimates with standard errors in parentheses.

* $p <.10$, ** $p <.05$, *** $p <.01$

[§] One community was deleted from the final analysis because it was missing data on one of the community-level variables.

[§§] 10 respondents were deleted because they had missing values on one or more independent variables.

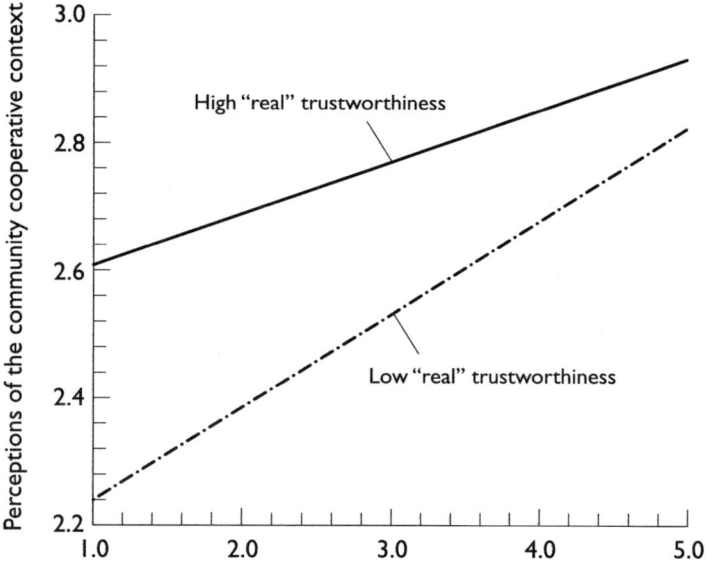

Figure 15.1 The conditional impact of efficacy on PCCC.

are influenced by reality to quite a significant degree (confirming the earlier differ-
ence-of-means test) as well as by individual feelings of efficacy and past cooperative
behavior. Given the scaling of the reality variable, the differences in perceived trustworthiness between communities at two standard deviations in either direction of
the mean community (approximately the difference between Spokane, WA, and
Rocheter, MN) is roughly the difference between believing that "just a few people"
in the community can be trusted to believing that at least "some" of them can be
trusted.

Looking next at the main effects of the individual-level variables, feelings of efficacy emerge from the analysis as more important than either form of cooperation.
Going from least efficacious to most efficacious results in over half a scale point
difference (on a five-point scale) for PCCC. The impact of particular cooperative activities is less dramatic. However, to the extent that cooperation itself feeds
feelings of efficacy, the total impact of cooperation may be larger than either of its
direct effects suggest.

Of most interest are the results for the cross-level interactions. Each is estimated
to have a negative sign, as predicted. In other words, efficacy, civic engagement,
and political engagement are less consequential for shaping perceptions of community cooperation in communities that are characterized by higher levels of "real"
trustworthiness.

In the case of efficacy, the cross-level interaction is statistically reliable. A visual
representation, seen in Figure 15.1, helps to clarify the differences in slopes. In
both low- and high-trust contexts, the slope for efficacy is positive. However, it

is far steeper in contexts characterized by less actual trustworthiness. It appears that high levels of personal efficacy to some degree "buffer" the individual from the effects of less congenial circumstances. In fact, at high levels of efficacy, individuals in low-trust environments perceive their environments to be a little bit more trustworthy than individuals at low levels of efficacy in contexts of "real" trustworthiness.

Implications

The conditional effects reported in Table 15.2 have important implications for the character of cooperation in places typified by different levels of trustworthiness. Because personal efficacy is dependent on resources, especially education (Ross, Mirowsky, & Pribesh, 2001), and personality factors such as dispositional optimism, certain kinds of community residents will be more socially marginalized in places with lower levels of overall trustworthiness. To put it another way, as the actual trustworthiness of a community declines, we should expect to see growing inequalities in civic and political engagement, precisely the pattern that has been observed in the US (Putnam, 2000) and the UK (Warde et al., 2003). Another interesting implication is that the same kind of activity, say, volunteering, may take on a different "flavor" in different places, not necessarily because fewer people do it (although that might also be true), but because the participants have a different mix of qualities.

My findings here mean that it is probably a mistake to make claims about the relationship between trust and cooperation *as a general matter*. In low-trust settings, people may engage in collective action because they feel efficacious enough to bring about the collective good, not because they expect others to do their part. If this cooperation is reciprocated, participants may be "surprised" by each other's behavior, learning that trust may, in fact, be warranted, thus reducing their uncertainty about the likelihood of reciprocity in future interactions.

In communities characterized by high levels of cooperation, on the other hand, the trustworthiness of others is "common knowledge." That others show up is not unexpected, and, as we have seen, there are good reasons for these beliefs. Individual cooperation happens because "it's what everyone does" (Cook & Hardin, 2001), not because one is crucial. The problem in these settings is one of coordination, not cooperation (Hardin, 1982; Chong, 1991), and communities may develop "focal points" as a means of coordinating members' actions (Chwe, 2001). A variety of things could serve this purpose, including group leaders, well-known hangouts, community newspapers, or collective memories, myths, and group rituals.

If cooperation has different motivations in different settings, then it is likely the case that the kinds of self-inferences people draw from their own behavior will also be different. Normative cooperators and efficacious cooperators, for example, may make different attributions for their own cooperative behavior, the former focusing more on external reasons; the latter group, internal. Cooperation, therefore, is "overly justified" in one case; "insufficiently justified" in another. To resolve the tension generated in these situations, people may adjust their beliefs about the worthiness of the collective goal that is the object of their cooperation. Efficacious cooperators may become even more committed to the public good as a result of their cooperation and step-up their efforts on behalf of it; for normative cooperators the reverse is possible.

Acknowledgment

I gratefully acknowledge the generosity of the Northwest Area Foundation in sharing their data with me.

Notes

1 Individual differences may affect whether people "see" the dilemma structure as one of PD or assurance (Simpson, 2004).
2 It is important to note that altruism and group identity "work" for different reasons as solutions to social dilemmas. In the case of altruism, the social dilemma gets solved because one is motivated to secure good outcomes for others, even at cost to oneself. Group identity, on the other hand, seems to facilitate cooperation not necessarily by making a person more concerned about group-level outcomes, but rather because group identity enhances beliefs that other group members are trustworthy (Kollack, 1998; Kramer, Brewer, & Hanna, 1996). Group identifiers transform the prisoner's dilemma into an assurance game, the logic of which is discussed above.
3 Cooperation usually becomes more problematic as group size increases because potential participants do not have the same reputational incentives for cooperation that repeated interaction induces in dyadic and small-group situations (see Sullivan, Snyder, & Sullivan, this volume).
4 The sample is representative at the state-level, but not at the local level. However, my interest in this chapter is in the effects of community-level characteristics on individual beliefs and behaviors, and therefore, representativeness at the individual-level of analysis is less crucial for my purposes than having a sufficient number of places sampled at the community-level of analysis in order to achieve adequate statistical power at this level.
5 http://www.census.gov/dmd/www/response/2000response.html
6 The crime rate is determined by adding the number of violent and property crime offenses reported by local reporting agencies divided by the total population, and then turning this per capita measure into a rate per 100,000. I also calculated separate rates for violent and property crimes. They were so highly correlated ($r = .7$) that I did not see a need to separate them.

References

Acevedo, M., & Krueger, J. I. (2004). The egocentric sources of the decision to vote: The voters' illusion and the belief in personal relevance. *Political Psychology, 25*, 115–134.

Alford, J. R., & Hibbing, J. R. (2004). The origin of politics: An evolutionary theory of political behavior. *Perspectives on Politics, 2*(4), 707–723.

Andreoni, J, & Petrie, R. (2004). Public goods experiments without confidentiality: A glimpse into fund-raising. *Journal of Public Economics, 88*, 1605–1623.

Anthony, D. (2005). Cooperation in microcredit borrowing groups: Identity, sanctions, and reciprocity in the provision of collective goods. *American Sociological Review, 70*(3), 496–515.

Brehm, J., & Rahn, W. M. (1997). Individual-level evidence for the causes and consequences of social capital. *American Journal of Political Science, 41*, 999–1023.

Buchan, N. R., Croson, R. T. A., & Dawes, R. M. (2002). Swift neighbors and persistent strangers: A cross-cultural investigation of trust and reciprocity in social exchange. *American Journal of Sociology, 108*(10), 168–206.

Campbell, D. (2006). *Why we vote: How schools and communities shape our civic life.* Princeton, NJ: Princeton University Press.

Chong, D. (1991). *Collective action and the civil rights movement.* Chicago: University of Chicago Press.

Chwe, M. S. (2001). *Rational ritual.* Princeton, NJ: Princeton University Press.

Claibourn, M. P., & Martin, P. S. (2000). Trust and joining? An empirical test of the reciprocal nature of social capital. *Political Behavior, 22*(4), 267–283.

Costa, D. L., & Kahn, M. E. (2003). Cowards and heroes: Group loyalty in the American Civil War. *Quarterly Journal of Economics, 118*(2), 519–548.

Cook, K. S., & Hardin, R. (2001). Norms of cooperativeness and networks of trust. In M. Hechter and K. Opp (Eds.), *Social norms* (pp. 327–347). New York: Russell Sage Foundation.

Curtis, J. E., Baer, D. E., & Grabb, E. D. (2001). Nations of joiners: explaining voluntary association membership in democratic societies. *American Sociological Review, 66*, 783–805.

De Cremer, D., Snyder, M., & DeWitte, S. (2001). The less I trust, the less I contribute (or not?): The effects of trust, accountability, and self-monitoring in social dilemmas. *European Journal of Social Psychology, 31*, 93–107.

de Hart, J., & Dekker, P. (2003). A tale of two cities: local patterns of social capital. In M. Hooghe & D. Stolle (Eds.), *Generating social capital: Civil society and institutions in comparative perspective* (pp. 153–169). New York: Palgrave Macmillan.

Fehr, E., & Fischbacher, U. (2004). Social norms and human cooperation. *Trends in Cognitive Science, 8*(4), 185–190.

Finkel, S. E., Muller, E. N., & Opp, K.-D. (1989). Personal influence, collective rationality and mass political action. *American Political Science Review, 83*(3), 885–903.

Goldberg, J., Markóczy, L., & Zahn, G. L. (2005). Symmetry and the illusion of control as bases for cooperative behavior. *Rationality and Society, 17*(2), 243–270.

Hardin, R. (1982). *Collective action.* Baltimore, MD: Johns Hopkins University Press.

Hayashi, N., Ostrom, E., Walker, J., & Yamagishi, T. (1999). Reciprocity, trust, and the sense of control: A cross-societal study. *Rationality and Society, 11*(1), 27–46.

Heckathorn, D. D. (1996). The dynamics and dilemmas of collective action. *American Sociological Review, 61*, 250–277.

Keele, L. (2005). Macro measures and mechanics of social capital. *Political Analysis, 13*(2), 139–156.

Klandermans, B. (1984). Mobilization and participation: Social-psychological expansions of resource mobilization theory. *American Sociological Review, 49,* 583–600.

Knack, S., & Kropf, M. E. (1998). For shame! The effect of community cooperative context on the probability of voting. *Political Psychology, 19*(3), 585–600.

Kollack, P. (1998). Social dilemmas: The anatomy of cooperation. *Annual Review of Sociology, 24,* 183–214.

Kramer, R. M., Brewer, M., & Hanna, B. A. (1996). Collective trust and collective action. In R. M. Kramer & T. R. Tyler (Eds.), *Trust in organizations: Frontiers of theory and research* (pp. 357–389). Thousand Oaks, CA: Sage publications.

Levi, M. (1997). *Consent, dissent, and patriotism.* Cambridge, UK: Cambridge University Press.

Lubell, M., & Scholz, J. T. (2001). Cooperation, reciprocity, and the collective-action heuristic. *American Journal of Political Science, 45*(1), 160–178.

Luke, D. A. (2004). *Multilevel modeling.* Thousand Oaks, CA: Sage Publications.

Moe, T. M. (1980). *The organization of interests.* Chicago: University of Chicago Press.

Olson, M. (1965). *The logic of collective action.* Cambridge, MA: Harvard University Press.

Ostrom, E. (1990). *Governing the commons: The evolution of institutions for collective action.* Cambridge, UK: Cambridge University Press.

Ostrom, E. (2003). Toward a behavioral theory linking trust, reciprocity, and reputation. In E. Ostrom & J. Walker (Eds.), *Trust and reciprocity: Interdisciplinary lessons from experimental research* (pp. 19–79). New York: Russell Sage.

Penner, L. A., Dovidio, J. E., Piliavin, J. A., & Schroeder, D. A. (2005). Pro-social behavior: multilevel perspectives. *Annual Review of Psychology 56,* 365–392.

Pruitt, D. G., & Kimmel, M. J. (1977). Twenty years of experimental gaming: Critique, synthesis, and suggestions for the future. *Annual Review of Psychology, 28,* 363–392.

Putnam, R. (2000). *Bowling alone: The collapse and revival of American community.* New York: Simon and Schuster.

Quattrone, G. A. & Tversky, A. (1984). Causal versus diagnostic contingencies: On self-deception and the voter's illusion. *Journal of Personality and Social Psychology, 46,* 237–248.

Rahn, W. M., Brehm, J., & Carlson, N. (1999). Elections as institutions for building social capital. In M. Fiorina & T. Skocpol (Eds.), *Civic engagement in American democracy* (pp. 111–160). Washington, DC: Brookings Institution Press.

Raudenbush, S. W., & Bryk, A. T. (2002). *Hierarchical linear models* (2nd ed.). Thousand Oaks, CA: Sage Publications.

Rothenberg, L. S. (1992). *Linking citizens to government: Interest group politics at common cause.* Cambridge, UK: Cambridge University Press.

Ross, C. E., Mirowsky, J., & Pribesh, S. (2001). Powerlessness and the amplification of threat: neighborhood disadvantage, disorder and distrust. *American Sociological Review, 66,* 568–591.

Samuelson, C. D., & Messick, D. M. (1995). When do people want to change the rules for allocating shared resources? In D. A. Schroeder (Ed.), *Social dilemmas: Perspectives on individuals and groups* (pp. 143–162). Westport, CT: Praeger.

Schofer, E., & Fourcade-Gourinchas, M. (2001). The structural contexts of civic engagement: Voluntary association membership in comparative perspective. *American Sociological Review, 66,* 806–828.

Scholz, J. T., & Lubell, M. (1998). Trust and taxpaying: Testing the heuristic approach to taxpaying. *American Journal of Political Science, 42*, 398–417.

Shah, D. V. (1998). Civic engagement, interpersonal trust, and television use: An individual-level assessment of social capital. *Political Psychology, 19*(3), 469–498.

Simpson, B. (2004). Social values, subjective transformations, and cooperation in social dilemmas. *Social Psychology Quarterly, 47*, 385–395.

Steenbergen, M. R. & Jones, B. S. (2002). Modeling multilevel data structures. *American Journal of Political Science, 46*(1), 218–237.

Stolle, D. (1998). Bowling together, bowling alone: The development of generalized trust in voluntary organizations. *Political Psychology, 19*(3), 497–525.

Tyler, T. R. & Degoey, P. (1995). Collective restraint in social dilemmas: Procedural justice and social identification effects on support for authorities. *Journal of Personality and Social Psychology, 69*, 482–497.

Uslaner, E. (2002). *The moral foundations of trust.* Cambridge, UK: Cambridge University Press.

Van Vugt, M. (2002). Central, individual, or collective control? Social dilemma strategies for natural resource management. *American Behavioral Scientist, 45*(5), 783–800.

Verba, S., & Nie, N. (1972). *Participation in America.* Chicago: University of Chicago Press.

Warde, A., Tampubolon, G., Longhurst, B., Ray, K., Savage, M., & Tomlinson, M. (2003). Trends in social capital: Membership of associations in Great Britain, 1991–1998. *British Journal of Political Science, 33*, 515–534.

Weber, J. M., Kopelman, S., & Messick, D. M. (2004). A conceptual review of decision making in social dilemmas: Applying a logic of appropriateness. *Personality and Social Psychology Review, 8*(3), 281–307.

Wrong, D. H. (1994). *The problem of order: What unites and divides society.* Cambridge, MA: Harvard University Press.

Yamigishi, T., Kanazawa, S., Mashima, R., & Terai, S. (2005). Separating trust from cooperation in a dynamic relationship. *Rationality and Society, 17*(3), 275–308.

16

Cooperation in Negotiation and Conflict Resolution

KATHLEEN M. O'CONNOR

In this chapter I provide a short, selective review of theory and experimental research on the role cooperation plays among negotiators seated at the bargaining table. Following the review, I describe work I have done on negotiators' reputations. I highlight the ways in which parties' reputations affect their partners, shape their interactions, and influence the quality of agreements they reach. I conclude with suggestions for integrating experimental psychological research on negotiation with political scientists' work on civil war and interstate conflict.

Cooperation in Negotiation and Conflict Resolution

Negotiation is the process by which people attempt to resolve perceived incompatible goals (Carnevale & Pruitt, 1992). Nearly all of the empirical psychological work on negotiation over the past three decades has attempted to understand and predict how negotiators can reach high-quality deals (for review, see Bazerman, Curhan, Moore, & Valley, 2000). To answer these questions, scholars have focused on a number of likely factors, including the role played by negotiators' cognitions (Neale & Bazerman, 1985), their emotions (Allred, Mallozzi, Matsui, & Raia, 1997; Carnevale & Isen, 1986; Van Kleef, De Dreu, & Manstead, 2004), and their cultural backgrounds (Adair & Brett, 2005; Gelfand & Christakopoulou, 1999), to name a few. One of the best studied streams of work has focused on the effects of negotiators' motives—cooperative or competitive—on the tactics negotiators use and the quality of deals they reach (De Dreu & Van Lange, 1995; Olekalns & Smith, 2003; Pruitt & Lewis, 1975).

What follows is a short review of theory and experimental research on cooperation's role at the negotiating table. Once the stage is set, I describe research that I have done that extends this line of work to consider how negotiators' reputations as cooperators or not affect them at the bargaining table. In particular, I describe two kinds of reputations—a reputation for cooperativeness and value creation (i.e., an integrative reputation), and a reputation for competitiveness and value claiming (i.e., a distributive reputation)—and report on experimental research that shows how they shape the bargaining exchange, and the quality of deals negotiators reach. I conclude with suggestions for integrating psychological studies of negotiation with political scientists' research on civil war and interstate conflict.

Studying Cooperation in Experimental Negotiation Settings

To understand the findings of experimental negotiation research, it might be helpful to describe how the data are gathered. Most experimental studies in this domain follow the same procedure: university students take part in an hour-long study that requires them to negotiate a predetermined set of issues with a person they have never met before and will not work with again in the future (Carnevale & Pruitt, 1992). Very often, the negotiation centers on a business transaction, for instance, the purchase of a house or working out the details of an employment contract. Depending on the researchers' question, written instructions to participants might contain a manipulation of some key independent variable. For instance, a study of time pressure might include a note on how much time parties have to negotiate, with those in the high time pressure condition given 15 minutes, whereas in the low time pressure condition, participants are told they will have 30 minutes. Before and after the negotiation, participants commonly complete questionnaires that contain measures of participants' motives or attitudes or emotions or intentions, for instance. Researchers with an interest in negotiators' behaviors or choice of tactics can choose to tape and transcribe the conversations. The statements, offers, queries can be coded according to some system and then quantified and included in the analyses.

Negotiation experiments typically include a mix of issues. Drawing on a distinction made by Walton and McKersie (1965), scholars differentiate between fixed-sum issues—known as distributive issues—and variable-sum issues—known as integrative. For distributive issues, gains for one party translate into losses for the other side. Thus, the task for negotiators is to determine how to split the resource at hand. Consider Mary Follet's (1940) classic example of two sisters and an orange. The sisters each want the orange and must decide how to share it. If they see the orange as a single distributive issue, then no matter how the orange is split, more of the orange for one sister, gives the other sister less. For integrative issues, the gains for one also translate into losses, but they are not equivalent. Rather than see the orange as a single resource, the sisters could view the orange as consisting of three parts—juice, rind, and pulp. With more "issues" to negotiate, the sisters have more options for allocating the resources. In fact, depending on each sister's plan for the orange, there might be a difference in the value each sister gives to the parts of the orange, with one sister wanting more juice than rind and the other preferring rind to juice. Such differences create opportunities for the sisters to trade what they do not want in return for more of what they do want.

The distinction between integrative and distributive negotiations also refers to two kinds of strategies (and associated tactics) negotiators can choose to pursue. Negotiators who pursue a distributive strategy try to leverage what power they have to force the other side to make deep concessions. To do this, they can make threats, exaggerate their claims, commit to their positions, and bluff (Pruitt, 1981). These tactics can be successful in extracting concessions, but they also can backfire and increase the likelihood of impasse, particularly if negotiators miscalculate their relative power.

When the negotiation contains integrative potential, negotiators can pursue the kind of distributive strategy I just described, or they can choose an integrative path (O'Connor, 1997). This typically involves cooperative tactics, such as creating a collaborative, trusting climate in which honest information can be exchanged, and reciprocating one another's concessions (Pruitt, 1981). Let us return to the sisters with the orange. Although the orange has three parts, they may fail to recognize this, or choose to rely on distributive tactics to determine who should get the bigger slice of the orange. Alternatively, the sisters can pursue an integrative strategy, with each sister describing why she wants the orange, and then finding ways for each to get what she needs. One sister might explain that she needs the rind to bake a cake, whereas the other admits that she would like the juice for drinking. If they trade these issues so as to provide the first sister all the rind and the second sister with all the juice, their outcomes look much different than they would have had they sliced the orange in half, with each side getting only half of what she really wanted and half of what she did not. In economic terms, once the sisters make the trade-off between the two issues, they push out the economic frontier, creating value for both sides.

Whether a negotiator pursues a more integrative or a more distributive strategy depends, in part, on the negotiators' motives. Three motives figure prominently in negotiation scholarship: cooperative (prosocial), which is an interest in maximizing both parties' gains; individualistic (egoistic or proself), which is an interest in maximizing one's own gains; and, competitive, which is an interest in maximizing the difference between parties' outcomes (Messick & McClintock, 1968). Negotiators with individualistic motives are likely to rely on distributive tactics to maximize their own gains. Because negotiators with cooperative motives focus on delivering good outcomes to both sides, they typically reach for integrative tactics (De Dreu, Weingart, & Kwon, 2000; O'Connor, 1997).

Motives can be considered as individual differences (i.e., traits) or as factors that can be shifted by the demands of the situation or the incentives provided. When scholars study motives as traits, they measure them prior to an experiment (e.g., McClintock, Messick, Kuhlman, & Campos, 1973). Typically, participants engage in decomposed prisoner's dilemma games to determine whether they show more cooperation or more individualistic behavior (McClintock et al., 1973). It also is possible to manipulate motives through the instructions that participants receive (Deutsch, 1958) or by varying their incentives for maximizing their own or the dyad's outcomes (e.g., Deutsch, 1973). Findings are consistent for both methods.

Experimental evidence shows that cooperative relations between negotiators yield a wealth of positive outcomes, from high-value deals to continued interest in working together in the future (De Dreu et al., 2000). Negotiators with cooperative motives tend to place more trust in the other side, encouraging them to divulge potentially sensitive information (O'Connor, 1997). Knowledge of both sides' interests allows negotiators to package issues in ways that create value (Thompson, 1991), making cooperation very important to the quality of deals negotiators reach. Once negotiations have ended, cooperative bargainers tend to be more satisfied with their deals, and leave the table with more positive feelings about their partners and the negotiation process itself.

In a meta-analysis of 28 experimental studies published between 1975 and 1998, De Dreu and his colleagues (2000) concluded that cooperative motives are beneficial in negotiation. According to their findings, negotiators with cooperative motives shared critical information and made profitable trades. They also were less likely to use contentious tactics. Their deals were better than those reached by negotiators with more individualistic motives. The analysis supported Pruitt's Dual Concern Model: cooperative motives led to good outcomes only when negotiators were able to resist capitulating to their partners.

Much of the work I have reviewed relies on the traditional paradigm for experimental negotiation research: one-shot negotiations between strangers (Carnevale & Pruitt, 1992). This paradigm has its limits and, increasingly, scholars are broadening it. Some focus on how negotiators' prior relationships affect their bargaining behavior and the deals they reach (Greenhalgh & Chapman, 1998; Valley, Neale, & Mannix, 1995), finding that close, cohesive relationships between parties can help them achieve greater gains. Others have shown that negotiators' expectations of cooperative future interaction with one another shape the tenor of their negotiations, making them more cooperative (Ben-Yoav & Pruitt, 1984).

Extending this work, my co-authors and I have explored how past negotiation experiences affect negotiators' subsequent bargaining behavior and outcomes (O'Connor & Arnold, 2001; O'Connor, Arnold, & Burris, 2005). We find that when negotiators have had unproductive negotiations in the past—that is, when they have failed to reach agreements—their subsequent deals suffer compared to those brokered by negotiators who have had prior successes. This is true even when negotiators change partners the next time.

Past experiences can haunt the negotiator by influencing his/her subsequent behavior, and if these experiences are passed along as stories from one person to another, they can take the form of a reputation that can affect their future partners. Very little experimental work has examined how reputations matter in negotiation. Catherine Tinsley and I have been studying reputations, focusing on how they shape their partners' motives, and consequently, their expectations, behavior, and outcomes. Below I review our empirical work, focusing on cooperative behaviors.

Reputations

Stories of a counterpart's past exploits are likely to precede him/her to the bargaining table. Consider the vendor who routinely phones at the last minute to tack on additional costs. As accounts of these practices are passed across departments, the vendor develops a reputation for eleventh-hour tactics, for sneakiness, for trying to squeeze just a little bit extra out of the deal. As future partners learn about these behaviors, they are alert to them, wary about what the vendor will spring on them. In this way, the reputation the vendor has developed affects the expectations and behaviors of her future partners. Distortion is likely to accompany the tales that are told, making them unreliable. Or they may be unreliable because the unseemly behavior was particular to a past negotiation, perhaps in response to a partner's behavior, not likely to be seen again. Still, the stories can create a vivid picture of a negotiator that can be difficult to change once word gets out. The empirical question is how these stories will influence those who hear them, most especially future partners.

Relying on reputation information can be seen as a perfectly rational attempt to reduce uncertainty about the other party and what to expect from them in the negotiation to follow (Kreps & Wilson, 1982). Catherine Tinsley, Brandon Sullivan and I define reputations as schema (Tinsley, O'Connor, & Sullivan, 2001). That is, they are mental representations one party has of another party that may be based on prior exposure to the second party's behavior, as well as on credible third-party information about that second party's behavior (Fiske & Taylor, 1991). These cognitive representations are cobbled together from information gained from first-hand experience or second-hand stories. They are not simply a summary of a random collection of traits, but, we argue, an amalgamation of related characteristics that form a coherent image. Like any schema, another party's reputation provides a future partner with information about the character of that other party, helping the partner sketch out the party's likely moves.

Negotiations are rife with uncertainty. Ahead of time, neither side knows for sure what the other really cares about, or what the other side's outside options are, or whether the other side has more cooperative or more individualistic motives. Even close attention to the other side's demands, queries, and responses does not necessarily make it any easier for a negotiator to assess his/her partner' interests, motives, goals. To illustrate the point, consider two negotiators, Fiona and Bill. Fiona runs a local ice creamery and Bill is a buyer for an independent grocery store. Bill opens the negotiation by asking Fiona what she cares about, what her interests are, what is most important to her. But what are Bill's intentions? Bill might be digging to uncover Fiona's priorities so he can help the two of them reach a deal for the sale of ice cream that fits both their interests. Or Bill may be looking for a way to get information that he can use to improve his store's outcomes at Fiona's expense. If Fiona tells Bill that she cares about frequent shipments of ice cream to the store, is Fiona trying to create value by revealing a truly important priority that she is willing to make a concession to get? Or is Fiona feigning interest on shipments because she knows that this is critical to Bill, thereby putting pressure on Bill to make a concession on another issue? As the example illustrates, negotiators, even those who have done their homework, cannot be entirely sure about their partners' interests, motives, and outside options, and gaining insight into clearcut information is difficult. Thus, Fiona and Bill must make judgment calls about what to assume, how much to divulge, and which arguments and facts to believe.

Divulging honest information, although potentially very useful in negotiation, is risky, particularly in situations marked by competing motives. Sharing information makes one vulnerable to being exploited by the partner who is looking for leverage. This possibility makes the judgment calls Fiona and Bill must make very important indeed.

Given these kinds of perils, reputations are likely to figure quite prominently in the minds of negotiators, giving them some bit of information to anchor on, helping them anticipate and interpret their partners' behavior. Theoretical and empirical work in economics supports this claim. According to Wilson (1985), a reputation can be thought of as "a characteristic or attribute ascribed to one person . . . by another" (p. 27). Economists consider reputation to be past behavior, which influences future partners' decision to cooperate. Reliable past performance promotes repeated exchange and trust by signaling reliable future performance (Axelrod, 1984). Relying on formal economic models, Kreps and Wilson (1982) showed the power of reputations by demonstrating the important role they play in multistage games that are characterized by uncertainty.

Despite the power that reputations might have in negotiation, their effects are far from clear because experimental scholars have been slow to document their impact. In what we believe to be the first experimental study of negotiator reputations, my colleagues and I traced the impact of reputations on negotiators' perceptions, behaviors, and outcomes in a controlled laboratory environment. At the heart of our investigation were the questions of whether and how reputations matter in negotiation.

A Reputation for Distributive Bargaining, aka Toughness

Novice negotiators often believe that they must demonstrate toughness at the bargaining table (O'Connor & Adams, 1999), pounding on the table, demanding that the other side accept deep concessions. Novices' intuitions are not entirely incorrect; tough, distributive tactics can be quite effective in getting the other side to make deep concessions. However, their effectiveness is limited if the other side has the power and the wherewithal to reciprocate or walk away. If the other side reciprocates, both parties will find themselves in a conflict spiral, which risks leaving them with no deal at all (Brett, Shapiro, & Lytle, 1998). A clever negotiator might recognize these risks and opt instead to engage selected tactics in small ways that would help cultivate a reputation for toughness without all the accompanying risks of toughness.

Given our review of cooperation research, even a reputation for toughness could carry some risks. Imagine a negotiator who is about to face a partner with a tough, distributive reputation. We anticipate that negotiators will anticipate a non-cooperative partner, and these expectations will affect how they interpret the meaning behind the partner's offers, comments, and queries. We test this idea of reputation as a schema below.

The Experiment

We paired MBA students from one school with MBAs from another and had them negotiate over email, allowing us to collect a transcript of their conversation. Negotiators from both schools were drawn from an elective course in negotiations, but they had had different amounts of training. Negotiators from School A were relatively less experienced, having had just three weeks of training, whereas those from School B were more experienced, having had ten weeks of in-class training. All parties were aware of the experience differences. Presumably, the advantage of extended training is that negotiators from School B have learned a greater range of tactics, have had greater opportunity to put these new tactics into practice, and have developed a greater sense of confidence in their ability to use the tactics effectively. Thus, we hypothesized that negotiators from School B would outperform those from School A in terms of the amount of value each would be able to create and claim from the deal.

We randomly assigned reputations to partners; half the negotiators from School B, the relative experts, were described as having a reputation for distributive bargaining, being especially adept at using tough tactics. Put differently, half of those from School A believed that their partners, in addition to having had more training, also were especially good at getting deals that benefited themselves.

Those to whom such a reputation had been assigned were unaware of it, making it impossible for them either to deny or to exploit their fictitious reputation. Because the reputation information was not rooted in any real behaviors of School B negotiators, any differences in behaviors and outcomes could not be attributed to actual differences in distributive skills. The real expertise differential between parties from the two schools allowed us to compare reputation effects to a baseline condition of enhanced experience.

The Hypotheses

In line with our premise that reputations would guide negotiators' expectations of their partners, we hypothesized that negotiators with reputation information about their partners would anticipate comparatively less cooperative partners. These perceptions should shape negotiators' behaviors; negotiators with partners who carry a distributive reputation should be less likely to divulge sensitive issue-specific information, opting instead to discuss more general information that is far less likely to provide insight into the structure of issues. As a consequence, the deals that these pairs reach should be worth less than the deals negotiated by pairs in which neither party knows about the other's reputation.

We hypothesized that a distributive reputation would sabotage individual outcomes, too. In the baseline (i.e., control) condition, we expected relative experts to outperform their novice partners (cf. Thompson, 1990). With greater experience should come greater skill in using the other party's disclosures both to create value for the dyad and to claim value for oneself. Experts, for example, have learned how to package issues to deliver mutual benefit. When expert partners also carry a distributive reputation, the novices with whom they negotiate will be wary of them, and reluctant to share information about their interests and preferences. By withholding such information, novices will block their more expert partners from both creating and claiming value. Put differently, a distributive reputation will prevent experts from capitalizing on their advantage, keeping them from achieving the same lopsided gains as the experts in the no-reputation (i.e., control) condition.

The Results

Before the negotiation, participants rated their partners' likely behavior, focusing on the extent to which their partners would be reasonable, cooperative, trustworthy, willing to compromise, stubborn, and deceptive. Novice negotiators' expectations showed a clear effect for reputation: compared to novices who learned nothing of their partners' reputations, those who had expected partners who would be comparatively less reasonable, less cooperative, less trustworthy, less willing to compromise, more stubborn, and more deceptive.

Transcript analysis allowed us to dig deeper into the kinds of behaviors negotiators were enacting during their bargaining sessions, enabling us to trace the effects of reputations over the course of negotiation. Compared to novices who knew nothing of their counterparts' reputations, novices who learned of their counterparts' distributive reputations (1) provided less specific issue-related information to their partners, (2) offered significantly more general information, and (3) engaged in more small talk. Partners' reputations discouraged negotiators from revealing the kind of information that would make them vulnerable to exploitation. Without access to important issue-related information, experts with a distributive reputation should find it difficult to capitalize on their advantage.

Overall, pairs that included a partner with a distributive reputation reached agreements that delivered less value to the pair of bargainers. That is, their deals were worth less than those reached by pairs in which no reputation information was available. A closer look revealed the expertise advantage we hypothesized:

looking at how much the deal was worth to each side, experts outperformed novices. However, when the expert also had a distributive reputation, the experience advantage vanished. Saddled with a distributive reputation, experts could not capitalize on their expertise advantage, and their deals gave them far less value compared to experts without a reputation. Whether the focus is on how well the individual does or how well the pair does, distributive reputations hurt those who had them, and their partners.

We further investigated the question of what prevents an expert with a distributive reputation from achieving what he or she otherwise might have. Despite the fact that experts were unaware of their assigned reputation, and did not know of their partners' uncharitable judgments of them, the other sides' defensive behavior may have led these experts themselves to behave in a tougher, more distributive way. In other words, a reputation for distributive behavior may become a self-fulfilling prophecy. Returning to our earlier example, if Bill has a distributive reputation and Fiona learns it, Fiona may very well adopt more distributive tactics from the get-go. Or Fiona may come to interpret Bill's ambiguous behavior in ways that are consistent with her expectations for his behavior. If she expects distributive behavior, and acts to pre-empt it, or simply match it, she is likely to trigger the same actions in Bill. Thus, schematic interpretations and reciprocity—which occur commonly in negotiations (Putnam & Jones, 1982; Beriker & Druckman, 1991)—might create a "Pygmalion" effect. Indeed, results showed that, compared to experts unencumbered by a reputation, those with a distributive reputation divulged less specific information of their own, offered more general information, and engaged in more small talk, a pattern that mirrors the behaviors of their partners. They suggest that reputations do create self-fulfilling prophesies.

Thus, having a distributive reputation—even one that is unjustified—hobbles negotiators whose reputation precedes them to the table, and undermines the other sides' outcomes as well. The real advantage that the more experienced negotiators had over their novice counterparts disappeared for those with a distributive reputation. Transcript analyses shed light on why that is—negotiators, wary of their tough counterparts, were unwilling to engage in a candid discussion of issues and interests of the kind important for crafting deals that afford value to both parties. Although the partner had no knowledge of his/her reputation, he/she lived up (or down) to the reputation, making it a self-fulfilling prophecy.

Cooperative Reputations

If distributive reputation hurt negotiators, what effects might more cooperative reputation have? In a follow-up experiment, Tinsley and I focused on what we called integrative reputations on negotiators' behaviors and outcomes. In light of our prior findings, one could argue that a reputation for using integrative tactics—that is, cooperative tactics aimed at delivering good deals to both parties—is beneficial to negotiators, signaling that it is safe to trust and share. Yet, empirical decision-making research finds that positive and negative reputations have an asymmetric effect on people's judgments and behaviors, raising questions about how integrative reputations might operate.

Using data drawn from winning bids on eBay, Standifird (2001) found that the negative effects of negative reputation hurt sellers' prices more than positive reputations helped prices. These findings are consistent with other work on negativity bias (Fiske, 1980). Negative information is thought of as more diagnostic of an actor's true character than positive information (Skowronski & Carlston, 1989). Unfavorable information appears to indicate a manner in which the actor deviates from social norms, thereby signaling something unique about him or her as an individual. Favorable information, in contrast, reveals nothing distinctive, and thus, has much less impact on judgments (Yaniv & Kleinberger, 2000). In our study, this could mean that a partner's integrative reputation is not especially meaningful and has little effect on negotiators' judgments, behaviors, and outcomes.

To help sort through the predictions, we returned to schema theory. Just as distributive skill implies a singular concern for the self, integrative skill implies concern for both oneself and the other party (Pruitt & Rubin, 1986). Learning that a counterpart has a reputation for crafting deals that create value for both parties ought to trigger in a partner's mind the schema of a negotiator concerned with the other side's needs and interests. This should lead those whose partners have an integrative reputation to expect a partner who will engage in more cooperative behaviors, encouraging the negotiator to view the partner's behavior as more cooperative, and fostering greater cooperativeness on the part of the negotiator. We expect relatively more candid discussions of sensitive, critical information during the negotiation among those whose partners have an integrative reputation. We tested these ideas using an experimental procedure nearly identical that used to study distributive reputations.

Negotiators who faced a partner with an integrative reputation were more optimistic that they would reach deals that afforded each side high value compared to those who learned nothing of their partners' reputation. Predictions about the partners' likely behaviors revealed that integrative reputations do not signal greater trustworthiness, which might encourage negotiators to divulge too much. Partners with an integrative reputation were expected to be more willing to compromise, which is likely to encourage negotiators to push harder for their own interests. Because negotiators who learn of partners' reputation do not expect the partners to be more naïve or more easily persuadable, reputation does not appear to convey an image of the other as soft.

As we predicted, expectations about the other side translated into tactics at the table. Compared to negotiators who knew nothing of their partners' reputations, those who had such information were more likely to discuss specific interests with their counterparts. However, closer inspection showed that these negotiators were asking for more information than their counterparts who had no information about partners' reputation. Moreover, when partners' reputation was described, negotiators were more likely to make multiple package offers, an integrative tactic, but one that does not require any trust. Taken together, the pre-negotiation predictions, and negotiators' behaviors reveal a negotiator who believes the partner is going to be focused on making mutually beneficial deals, but not one who is especially trustworthy. Hence, the negotiator uses relatively more integrative tactics, but these are the kind of tactics that do not require the negotiator to make herself/himself vulnerable to exploitation.

Given their choice of tactics, we expected pairs in which one side learned of the other's distributive reputation to reach higher-quality deals. Indeed, pairs in the reputation condition reached deals that gave each side more value than did those pairs who did not have reputation information. Inspection of issues revealed that pairs in the reputation condition also made trades among the issues that allowed each side to collect more value than did pairs in the no-reputation condition.

Both studies show that the substance of a reputation carries important information that negotiators attend to and rely on during their negotiations. In other words, whether a reputation is for tough behavior or cooperative behavior, negotiators' expectations change, putting into motion a strategy that conforms to those expectations. In this way, reputations become self-fulfilling for those who have them, even if they are unjustified.

The significant influence of integrative reputations indicates that the negativity bias did not hold for these negotiators. Cooperative reputations signaled that good deals were likely, and negotiators responded by using more integrative tactics. The findings speak to the power of reputations at the table, and show how they operate. They also underscore the importance of cooperation at the table.

Integrating Negotiation Research Across the Disciplinary Divide

For many who do experimental studies of negotiations, the focus is on understanding what enables or inhibits parties from reaching high-quality deals. Analyses often center on the give and take between negotiators at the table (i.e., the process of the negotiation). Political scientists who study conflict and its resolution are rarely privy to the exchange between representatives on different sides of an armed conflict, and so cannot make these data part of their analyses. Instead, they focus on explaining the success or failure of negotiation and the features that shape them. Typically, these efforts highlight structural variables, such as parties' capabilities, numbers of people killed, and so on. On its face, differences in approach and data would present considerable obstacles to those interested in integrating work across disciplinary boundaries. A deeper look, however, reveals some common ground for experimentalists and those who rely on archival evidence to work together to improve success rates for negotiated settlements.

Changing the nature of the transaction that negotiation experimentalists study is one way to integrate theory and empirical findings. Most negotiation experiments center around an economic transaction—e.g., the price paid to a business unit for a piece of technology, the terms of the sale of a firm, the details of an employment contract. Rarely do laboratory researchers model negotiations that seek to resolve an ongoing and costly conflict. Yet, here, too, there are lessons to be learned. Testing current theories on negotiations that follow interpersonal or intergroup conflict would go further to demonstrate the robustness of the theories. Also, this work would highlight the unique features of different sorts of negotiations, possibly suggesting variables that have not been considered by experimental researchers.

As Regan (this volume) has noted, negotiations that follow military conflict are typically held behind closed doors with non-participants rarely allowed a glimpse inside. This makes it difficult to get anything like a precise accounting of the parties, or their interests and demands, or the way they talk about the conflict and issues. It is not surprising then that work by political scientists on armed conflicts and their resolution focuses on the context of the conflict. Regan mentions factors like the intensity of the violence that precedes the talks, cultural similarities between the parties, and whether there exist power imbalances between the sides. These factors have some nice properties; they can be measured and their impact can be assessed without having much information about the talks themselves. Experimentalists have little to say about how intensity of the conflict, for instance, affects negotiations. Isolating a factor like this would enrich current theory and provide a point of connection between scholars in the two camps.

To be sure, the considerable toll that armed conflicts take cannot be captured in the laboratory. At the same time, it is possible to model the effects of a pre-negotiation conflict for would-be negotiators. Linking negotiation more explicitly to a just-experienced dispute would enable scholars to consider a host of conflict-related cognitions and emotions whose impact on negotiation remains unknown. Interpersonal and intergroup conflicts are likely to result in injury to one's feelings of pride, violations to one's sense of respect, a perception that one's identity is threatened. These are important consequences of conflict that could affect the tone, pace, and course of negotiation, but have yet to be accounted for in experimental research.

When thinking about possible links between experimental and archival research on negotiation, one must consider how to create appropriate conditions in the laboratory. Psychologists who study questions around aggression and violence offer suggestions for starting points. For instance, Cohen, Bowdle, Nisbett, & Schwarz (1996) studied what anthropologists have termed the "culture of honor" among white men from the southern US. The researchers created scenarios in their laboratory in which participants were insulted. They then measured participants' cortisol levels, testosterone levels, attitudes, intentions, and behaviors to test their ideas about how insults trigger aggressive behavior. Protocols like this could be used to create a conflict that would activate real feelings of insult, threats to face and identity, for instance. If followed by a negotiation that is relevant to the conflict, the effects of these factors could be identified. This line of research could shed light on how dispute-based negotiations evolve, and what allows them to be settled most effectively.

Regan's chapter reminds negotiation researchers that we have adopted a rather narrow view of when and in what settings negotiations occur, emphasizing economic transactions between strangers. While this substantive focus is a good match to the current paradigm, it means that our insights into how negotiation can help end ongoing conflicts are limited. By broadening the types of negotiations we examine and expanding the variety of variables we consider, experimental researchers are well equipped to contribute significantly to what we know about interstate and civil conflict.

References

Adair, W. L., & Brett, J. M. (2005). The negotiation dance: Time, culture, and behavioral sequences in negotiation. *Organization Science, 16,* 33–51.

Allred, K. G., Mallozzi, J. S., Matsui, F., & Raia, C. P. (1997). The influence of anger and compassion on negotiation performance. *Organizational Behavior and Human Decision Processes, 70,* 175–187.

Axelrod, R. M. (1984). *The evolution of cooperation.* New York: Basic Books.

Bazerman, M. H., Curhan, J. R., Moore, D. A., & Valley, K. L. (2000). Negotiation. *Annual Review of Psychology, 51,* 279–314.

Ben-Yoav, O., & Pruitt, D. G. (1984). Resistance to yielding and the expectation of cooperative future interaction. *Journal of Experimental Social Psychology, 20,* 323–335.

Beriker, N., & Druckman, D. (1991). Models of responsiveness: The Lausanne Peace Negotiations (1922–1923). *Journal of Social Psychology, 131,* 297–300.

Brett, J. M., Shapiro, D. L., & Lytle, A. L. (1998). Breaking the bonds of reciprocity in negotiations. *Academy of Management Journal, 41,* 410–424.

Carnevale, P. J. D., & Isen, A. M. (1986). The influence of positive affect and visual access on the discovery of integrative solutions in bilateral negotiations. *Organizational Behavior and Human Decision Processes, 37,* 1–13.

Carnevale, P. J., & Pruitt, D. G. (1992). Negotiation and mediation. *Annual Review of Psychology, 43,* 531–582.

Cohen, D., Bowdle, B. F., Nisbett, R. E., & Schwartz, N. (1996). Insult, aggression, and the southern culture of honor: An "experimental ethnography." *Journal of Personality and Social Psychology, 70,* 945–960.

De Dreu, C. K. W., & Van Lange, P. A. M. (1995). The impact of social value orientation on negotiator cognition and behavior. *Personality and Social Psychology Bulletin, 21,* 1178–1188.

De Dreu, C. K. W., Weingart, L. R., & Kwon, S. (2000). Influence of social motives on integrative negotiation: A meta-analytic review and test of two theories. *Journal of Personality and Social Psychology, 78,* 889–905.

Deutsch, M. (1958). Trust and suspicion. *Journal of Conflict Resolution, 2,* 265–279.

Deutsch, M. (1973). *The resolution of conflict: Constructive and destructive processes.* New Haven, CT: Yale University Press.

Fiske, S. T. (1980). Attention and weight in person perception: The impact of negative and extreme behavior. *Journal of Personality and Social Psychology, 38*, 889–906.

Fiske, S. T., & Taylor, S. E. (1991). *Social cognition* (2nd ed.). New York: McGraw-Hill.

Follett, M. P. (1940). Constructive conflict. In H. C. Metcalf & L. Urwick (Eds.), *Dynamic administration: The collected papers of Mary Parker Follett* (pp. 30–49). New York: Harper.

Gelfand, M. J., & Christakopoulou, S. (1999). Culture and negotiator cognition: Judgment accuracy and negotiation processes in individualistic and collectivist cultures. *Organizational Behavior and Human Decision Processes, 79*, 248–269.

Greenhalgh, L., & Chapman, D. I. (1998). Negotiator relationships, construct measurement, and demonstration of their impact on the process and outcomes of negotiation. *Group Decision and Negotiation, 7*, 465–489.

Kreps, D. M., & Wilson, R. (1982). Reputation and imperfect information. *Journal of Economic Theory, 27*, 253–279.

McClintock, C. G., Messick, D. M., Kuhlman, D. M., & Campos, F. T. (1973). Motivational bases of choice in three-choice decomposed games. *Journal of Experimental Social Psychology, 9*, 572–590.

Messick, D. M, & McClintock, C. G. (1968). Motivational bases of choice in experimental games. *Journal of Experimental Social Psychology, 4*, 1–25.

Neale, M. A., & Bazerman, M. H. (1985). The effects of framing and negotiator overconfidence on bargaining behaviors and outcomes. *Academy of Management Journal, 28*, 34–49.

O'Connor, K. M. (1997). Motives and cognitions in negotiation: A theoretical integration and an empirical test. *International Journal of Conflict Management, 8*, 114–131.

O'Connor, K. M., & Adams, A. A. (1999). What novices think about negotiation: A content analysis of scripts. *Negotiation Journal, 15*, 135–147.

O'Connor, K. M., & Arnold, J. A. (2001). Distributive spirals: Negotiation impasses and the moderating effects of disputant self-efficacy. *Organizational Behavior and Human Decision Processes, 84*, 148–176.

O'Connor, K. M., Arnold, J. A., & Burris, E. R. (2005). Negotiators' bargaining experiences over time and their effects on future negotiations. *Journal of Applied Psychology, 90*, 350–362.

Olekalns, M., & Smith, P. L. (2003). Testing the relationships among negotiators' motivational orientations, strategy choices, and outcomes. *Journal of Experimental Social Psychology, 39*, 101–117.

Pruitt, D. G. (1981). *Negotiation behavior*. New York: Academic Press.

Pruitt, D. G., & Lewis, S. A. (1975). Development of integrative solutions in bilateral negotiation. *Journal of Personality and Social Psychology, 31*, 621–633.

Pruitt, D. G., & Rubin, J. Z. (1986). *Social conflict: Escalation, stalemate, and settlement*. New York: Random House.

Putnam, L. L., & Jones, T. S. (1981). Reciprocity in negotiations: An analysis of bargaining interaction. *Communication Monographs, 49*, 171–191.

Skowronski, J. J., & Carlston, D. E. (1989). Negativity and extremity biases in impression formation: A review of explanations. *Psychological Bulletin, 105*, 131–142.

Standifird, S. S. (2001). Reputation and e-commerce: eBay auctions and the asymmetrical impact of positive and negative ratings. *Journal of Management, 27*, 279–295.

Thompson, L. (1990). An examination of naïve and experienced negotiators. *Journal of Personality and Social Psychology, 59*, 82–90.

Thompson, L. L. (1991). Information exchange in negotiation. *Journal of Experimental Social Psychology, 27,* 161–179.

Tinsley, C. H., O'Connor, K. M., & Sullivan, B. A. (2001). Tough guys finish last: The perils of a distributive reputation. *Organizational Behavior and Human Decision Processes, 88,* 621–642.

Valley, K. L., Neale, M. A., & Mannix, E. A. (1995). Friends, lovers, and strangers: The effects of relationships on the process and outcome of dyadic negotiation. In R. Bies, R. Lewicki, & B. Sheppard (Eds.), *Research in negotiation in organizations, 5* (pp. 65–94). Greenwich, CT: JAI Press.

Van Kleef, G. A., De Dreu, C. K. W., & Manstead, A. S. R. (2004). The interpersonal effects of anger and happiness in negotiations. *Journal of Personality and Social Psychology, 86,* 57–76.

Walton, R. E., & McKersie, R. B. (1965). *A behavioral theory of labor negotiations: An analysis of a social interaction system.* New York: McGraw-Hill.

Wilson, R. (1985). Reputations in games and markets. In A. Roth (Ed.), *Game-theoretic models of bargaining* (pp. 27–62). Cambridge, UK: Cambridge University Press.

Yaniv, I, & Kleinberger, E. (2000). Advice taking in decision making: Egocentric discounting and reputation formation. *Organizational Behavior and Human Decision Processes, 83,* 260–281.

17

Structural and Contextual Conditions and Negotiation Outcomes in Violent Armed Conflicts

PATRICK M. REGAN

Introduction

Violent armed conflicts within and between states pose a serious problem for regional and global stability, and as such it is often in the interest of members of the world community to actively work to resolve these military contests. And while it is generally easy to see why trying to manage violent armed conflict is important, it is less clear how best to do so. For the past couple of decades scholars have been studying the conditions that lead to successful bilateral negotiations or third-party mediation within the context of violent armed conflicts. Most of these broadly cross-national studies rely on models that account for the role of structure, context, and strategy in the success or failure of negotiations.

While intuition would point to a critical role for negotiations in resolving inter-state and civil wars, evidence describes a rather different situation. In fact if you consider each negotiation or mediation attempt in the context of violent armed conflict, most such attempts at conflict resolution fail to reach a peace agreement. For instance data on the success of third-party mediation generally show that at best only 30% of the attempts reach a full or partial settlement of the issues under contention (Bercovitch & Diehl, 1997). One inference might be that negotiations are inefficient, that military capability will determine outcomes, and that conflict management efforts are futile. That set of inferences would not be entirely correct. What might be more correct is to suggest that context can account for only 30% of the successful outcomes. For a fuller explanation we have to look more closely at what goes on within the negotiations.

So there is a conundrum that confronts researchers trying to develop an understanding of how best to manage armed conflicts. On the one hand most things about the study of negotiation suggest that they should work to bring about an acceptable resolution of a conflict, on the other we know that they are not as effective as we would expect. The answers to this puzzle might be found in the different approaches to studying negotiation, not in the role of negotiations themselves. In this chapter I will summarize the state of our knowledge about negotiation and mediation in violent armed conflicts between or within states. The primary focus will be on how contextual and structural factors influence the likelihood of observing negotiations and the success of those that do take place. Ending at that point would, however, be incomplete. Rather, I will follow this discussion by focusing on how attention to the process of negotiation may increase our ability to articulate models that account for success or failure of negotiations to end armed conflicts. This latter emphasis becomes more complicated when we think about units of observation at the level of the state or armed rebellious groups, in part because secrecy, national security, and group processes generally hold sway. But what we know from studies in psychology is that the ideas and expectations that negotiators bring to the table can have an important influence on how they walk away (O'Connor, this volume). Combining insights from these different levels of observation with different theoretical orientations and with different methodological approaches to testing ideas may enhance our ability to understand the management of violent armed conflicts.

Literature Review

Context and structure provide an invaluable tool for understanding the success or failure of negotiations, whether those negotiations take place between armed opponents or married couples. In the realm of international politics the context and structure often exist at the level of mantra. Power relationships purportedly determine who concedes and how much. The strong make demands; the weak take what they can get. If information is symmetric among those involved in the conflict then the military balance should provide the mechanism for understanding the outcome. It is when information is asymmetric—when the structure of the relationship creates uncertainty—that power holds less sway over outcomes.

Studies of negotiation attempts to resolve conflicts between states generally focus on a range of factors that include power disparity, mediator status, cultural similarity, and the intensity of violence. For example, during the Cold War the United States and the Soviet Union were involved in many militarized disputes with each other, but in very few cases did they agree to the use of third-party mediation to resolve the issues at hand. Two superpowers, apparently, were loath to use the services of a "lesser" international actor. They did, on the other hand, engage in numerous bilateral negotiations, and in fact at times these negotiations lasted years and continued in spite of the military hostilities taking place in the background. Without the ability to get into the minds of the various leaders, the structure of the relationship appears to have driven their use of conflict management techniques.

In a study of mediation in interstate armed conflict Bercovitch and Langly (1993) demonstrate that the complexity of the dispute and the number of fatalities have a negative effect on the likely success of the mediation effort. This should not come as a great surprise, even though some think that complexity and intensity can lead to ripe conditions that make way for a negotiated outcome. Regan and Stam (2000) and Regan and Leng (2003) also find that the level of fatalities and the existence of ongoing hostilities decrease the chances that mediation or negotiations will lead to a settlement of a conflict. One of the theoretical keys that drive these empirical studies is whether hostilities generate negative feedbacks, where violence leads to more violence, in part because of the attitudes of the combatants. From a structural perspective this can be thought of in terms of sunk costs and expectations for future costs. Those who argue that early negotiations are most effective see sunk costs as something that increases animosity and therefore decreases the willingness to reach a cooperative outcome. The alternative is that when the costs get too high decision makers have to find a way out. Information about current and expected conditions can be gleaned from the battlefield.

Regan and Leng (2003) also demonstrate that cultural similarities can have an effect on negotiations and their outcomes. Culture provides one mechanism by which signals and cues are delivered and understood. We might expect, therefore, that negotiations within militarized conflicts between groups of similar cultures would have a greater success rate than those that have to bridge a cultural divide. There are fewer avenues for miscommunication, a reduced need to translate signals, and a greater awareness of subtle cues when the parties in conflict share a common language, religion, or ethnic heritage. Culture is undoubtedly a complex contextual variable, but our results suggest that cultural similarity does lead to higher success rates of negotiations and mediation. In fact the results point to culture as a significant factor in determining which pairs of states get into militarized disputes, and ultimately how they resolve the issues at hand. In short, context seems to matter in the ability of negotiators to reach a settlement.

Context would be tempered by two (at least) other considerations. The psychological conditions, perspectives, or orientations of the participants to the negotiations should be important, as would be the strategy or acumen of any outside mediator. While I am less capable of speaking to the issues of psychology, O'Connor (this volume) and Ronson and Peterson (this volume), among others, draw linkages between cognitive conditions and negotiation outcomes. For example, reputation of the negotiators can apparently influence the tactics within negotiation settings, just as trust might be an important determinant in generating cooperation. There is, however, some evidence in the political science literature on the role of the strategy of a mediator in shaping the outcome of negotiations.

When studying armed conflict between or within states, strategy generally gets defined in terms of who mediates, how often, with what type of involvement, and when in the life cycle of the conflict. What we almost never know from the broadly cross-national studies is what they say, how they say it, and who makes what types of concessions. If we think of strategy in terms of the depth of involvement of the mediator, then studies tend to show that a directive strategy is more effective than, say, a simple communicative one. Evidence suggests that the more direct, force-ful, and proactive the outside party, the more likely that the mediation effort will achieve at least a partial settlement. This seems to hold regardless of whether the militarized disputes are between pairs of states that are in recurrent conflict (rivalries) or those that are less frequent or recurring within the same dyad (e.g., Bercovitch & Regan, 1997; Bercovitch & Diehl, 1997). There is comparably little systematic knowledge of the strategy of the negotiators involved in direct bilateral talks, at least those associated with armed violence. That is, studies that focus on the behavior of the parties to the negotiations generally restrict their research to those cases in which an outside party served as a mediator.

Strategy can also be a function of timing and/or sequencing. One area where knowledge is sparse, intuition strong, and evidence lacking is in the link between timing, sequencing, recurrence, and outcomes. For example, the argument has been made that negotiations—including mediation—should be most effective early, before the parties become overly entrenched (Northridge & Donelan, 1971). Alter-natively, if armed conflict is a result of uncertainty over the military balance, then letting warfare sort out expectations of victory will help with future negotiations. Negotiations somewhere in the middle of the conflict should be most effective. Finally, once both sides reach a point of a stalemate after an extended period of armed conflict, negotiations should be more likely to produce a positive result. Theoretically an argument can be made for the adroit timing of any negotiation attempt, but empirically all times cannot be equally conducive to successful out-comes. There are difficulties to thinking about timing, but if warfare reflects a form of bargaining, then intuition tells us that timing must be an important component of any negotiating strategy.

Regan and Stam (2000) attempted to test empirically the relationship between the timing of mediation attempts and the expected duration of the dispute. Their results suggest that there is a curvilinear relationship with the optimal times to ini-tiate mediation right at the beginning, and then again after a period of conflict. The results of their analysis also point to continuity among the mediators being more conducive to success than changing mediators across subsequent media-tion attempts. Put differently, if there are recurring efforts within the same conflict, sticking with the same mediators is better than the alternative of sending in a new team to build on earlier attempts. One explanation for the constructive influence of continuity among negotiating teams might be tied to the role of trust and/or rep-utation (Ronson & Peterson, this volume; O'Connor, this volume). This begs the question of whether or not negotiation or mediation attempts are cumulative, in the sense that small successes or abject failures both contribute to the longer-term efforts to manage a conflict. One could readily imagine that the initial attempts to reach a resolution falter, but with each effort a little more information is conveyed that helps clarify positions and reduce uncertainty and information asymmetries. By the tenth (or whatever) meeting the parties reach a tipping point whereby further concessions begin to fall into place (Schelling, 1972; Pillar, 1983). Underpinning this concept is the idea that full settlements are the result of numerous individual concessions that transpire over a sequence of negotiations. Put differently, the effect of concessions might be cumulative even though each concession is by itself insufficient to lead to a resolution.

The question of strategy, context, and structure in intrastate armed conflict can be more problematic. One of the key elements of resolving intrastate—or civil—wars is overcoming the problem of neither side being able to easily commit to a negotiated outcome. When the armed conflict is between two states each side has sanctuary to which it can retreat. But armed conflicts between members of the same country leave neither side completely secure, and therefore neither side has a strong incentive to abide by the terms of an agreement. This can be seen most readily in issues of demobilization.

Negotiations to end civil wars can come to a successful agreement but getting that agreement implemented is often problematic. Because no one country can accommodate two competing centers of authority, at least one side to the conflict must disarm and let the other reserve the right to use force. This appears to be an incredibly difficult condition to meet, and one for which trust becomes incredibly important. The problem is less in the process of negotiations than in the process of getting the outcome to hold, but the negotiation process has to take this problem into account. To put this back into the realm of context, structure, or strategy, the overall environment in which the negotiations take place portend to be important elements in the ultimate resolution of internal armed conflicts. Neither side will sign an agreement unless they have enough guarantees that their opponent will abide by the terms of the agreement. The minute one side lays down its arms the other side has the military capability to renege. The military balance—or fears about its future condition—affects the ability to negotiate in good faith. External guarantees appear to facilitate successful negotiations, if they are not a necessary condition (Walter, 2002).

Although evidence is not overwhelming, contemporary research generally suggests that military capability matters; the weak more often have to succumb to the strong. Most civil wars end in some form of military defeat, and only about 40% of all civil wars try to reach a negotiated settlement with the help of a mediator. Presumably more use direct bilateral negotiations, but currently we do not have data on these instances. Furthermore, given the problems associated with the instability of negotiated agreements, it must be difficult for bilateral negotiations to take root in civil wars. The process of getting internal opponents to choose a negotiated outcome over a military one involves changing the incentive structures, and this is partially achieved through removing the uncertainty that each holds about the intentions and capability of the other. Uncertainty in this instance is borne of asymmetric information, much like it is in interstate armed conflicts.

Because the structure of the relationship—that is the military balance—plays such a critical role in thinking about the outcome of civil wars, neither side has a unilateral incentive to reveal their true expectations or capabilities. And because of the difficulty of betraying this information in a bilateral setting, outside mediators may prove to be critical in resolving civil wars. Negotiations necessarily involve transferring information, information about possible deals, acceptable outcomes, and military capabilities, all the while knowing that mistakes, when there is no sanctuary, can be fatal. Beyond the ability to manipulate information, outside mediators must also attempt to influence the incentives, incentives that affect both the structure and the context. By combining economic and military inducements or sanctions with information that betrays an objective version of the current battlefield conditions a mediator should be able to move parties toward positions that represent open bargaining space—or positions that have some probability of being accepted by both sides. Presumably military, economic, or diplomatic interventions alone could achieve similar outcomes, but the question is whether different strategies or sequences are more or less effective. Ideas developed from game theoretic models of bargaining help to generate expectations, where for instance we can think of the strategic choices resulting in outcomes from stable conflict to stable cooperation. In terms of an approach for mediation and other forms of material interventions, the key is to generate this movement through the bargaining process and then lock in the cooperative outcome with material support. This is likely to require a sequence to the strategy of intervention that manipulates information and structure in a defined order. The notion of sequencing interventions forms part of the recommendation of a World Bank report on ending civil wars.

The empirical evidence is generally supportive of the idea that a strategy which combines mediation with material interventions is more effective than either component alone, even if it is sparse. That is, mediation reduces considerably the expected duration of a civil war, and in fact an early mediation effort can contribute to considerably shorter civil wars. Most of the evidence suggests that military or economic interventions tend to lengthen civil wars, but mediation can at least offset the deleterious consequences of economic interventions and lead to conflict of somewhat shorter duration. This supports the idea of finding a stable equilibrium and then locking in the parties with material incentives to remain there (Regan & Aydin, 2006). Without the explicit focus on mediation or negotiation, research by Walter (2002) contributes to the inference that outside contributions to the negotiating process, including guarantees of security, have an important influence on the success of negotiations and the ability of the parties to fully implement a peace agreement (see also Doyle & Sambanis, 2000).

To recapitulate, the evidence clearly suggests that the structure of the relationship between the combatants matters considerably. One of the more enduring empirical relationships in world politics is that between military capability and armed conflict. It explains a significant amount of the variation in which countries get into armed conflicts and how they get out of it. The context that describes the conflict also contributes to our understanding of negotiation success and failure. Most arguments and evidence that point toward a breaking point—tipping point, hurting stalemate, or a precipice—do so in terms of the intensity of the conflict. Military or economic interventions into civil wars have a higher probability of leading to the end of the conflict when the level of killing is rather high, but negotiations are more likely to fail when the number of fatalities is high, at least in interstate conflicts. The difference might be in tipping the outcome toward victory versus negotiations, negotiations fraught with negative attitudes about the enemy that comes from intensive combat. This might point to the role of psychological processes driving the negotiation process between states, while the dictates of the military balance can drive the outcome within them. And finally, most evidence will support the notion that the approach—or strategy—adopted by mediators has an impact on the outcome of negotiations. The more direct and participatory the mediator, the better the odds for a successful outcome, while the more multifaceted an outside intervention into civil wars, the higher the chances of a successful resolution.

There is, additionally, some evidence to suggest that direct bilateral negotiations are more successful than third-party mediation, at least when the parties in conflict have a long history of militarized disputes (Bercovitch & Regan, 1999). Druckman (2001), moreover, begins to turn the page and suggest that processes and context interact in ways that may make the whole greater than the sum of the parts. To many who study armed conflict involving state actors, interstate or intrastate violence is part of a bargaining process. Information that cannot be—or is not—revealed before the onset of military hostilities is often clarified by the resort to arms. Negotiations play into this process, but the actors still must confront the influence of the structure and the context in which they take.

Moving Beyond Context

Given that context tells us some things about the conditions that lead to successful negotiation outcomes, what are we missing and how can we advance our knowledge on negotiations to end armed conflicts? At the level of business, interpersonal, or community negotiations there is considerably more emphasis on the role of negotiation processes. Some of the central concepts involve turning points, impasses, negative emotions, and the skill of the negotiators, all things that are quite difficult to capture in broadly cross-national studies at the level of the state—or interstate relations. In effect, focusing on the context under which negotiations attempt to resolve armed conflicts neglects the finer details of just how negotiators work to do so. The more broadly contextual studies of negotiations could benefit from an inclusion of some of the "micro" aspects of the negotiation process. The road to that point is, however, littered with a multitude of difficult hurdles to overcome.

The main obstacle to an inclusion of process conditions is in the sheer number of cases of negotiation that would have to be examined. For example, Bercovitch and Houston (2000) describe data on over 2,600 conflict management attempts in 295 individual militarized disputes from 1945 to 1995. These 2,600 instances include cases of mediation, arbitration, bilateral negotiation, and multilateral conferences. Regan and Aydin (2006) furthermore, record nearly 400 instances of mediation alone in the 153 civil wars since 1945. In short, the task of generating the data at the level of the negotiation is monumental, and this leads to one of two strategies: (1) neglect process conditions and remain focused on contextual ones, or (2) reduce the size of the sample used in the analysis to a number that will permit the inclusion of process conditions. Druckman (2001) provides a window into how different sample sizes can influence the way we think about negotiation outcomes.

Some of the important aspects of the process of reaching a compromise that elude those who engage in cross-national studies of armed conflict include the role of bargaining positions and concessions (Regan, 2002). Understanding the initial demands, the acceptable range of outcomes, and the timing and significance of concessions does not get us directly to the intricacies of the process, but they do provide indicators that would betray elements of the process. These types of data, however, prove to be difficult to code with any degree of reliability (Regan & Leng, 2003).

At issue is not how difficult the data are to generate, but how ideas and evidence at one level of observation can inform our understanding of negotiations from another level. If we leave broadly cross-national issues of data aside, the implications for combining contextual factors with process ones portend to advance both types of research. It should be clear that there are those who toe the fine line between these relatively distinct genres of research, and those that do so generally come from the field of political psychology. Daniel Druckman (e.g. 2001) and William Zartman (1995), for example, incorporate process and contextual conditions into their analyses, but when they do the large-N cross-national analyses of procedural aspects give way to context conditions (e.g. Druckman, 2001).

One of the key factors in understanding negotiation outcomes involves concessions. Bargaining models implicitly or explicitly put the onus for success on the two parties finding issue space that holds a mutually agreeable set of conditions that will resolve the conflict, even if the probability of finding this issue space is rather low. Bargaining models also tend to assume that if there is overlapping issue space—that is conditions that both sides can agree to a settlement—then they will find it. Bargaining models, moreover, influence considerably the development of contextual analyses in political science.

Scholars who emphasize processes are looking for the set of events, conditions, characteristics, or behaviors that facilitate the search for the overlapping issue space. One might think, for instance, that two parties are close to finding an agreement but for the lack of diplomatic acumen, the missing of a cue, or prior reputations, neither side will agree. In effect the process of negotiating itself can serve as an impediment or facilitator of a negotiated outcome, in spite of or in compliment to the contextual conditions.

Daniel Druckman emphasizes turning points within a negotiation that are critically important for understanding successful outcomes (2001). A turning point represents a juncture where the flow of events turns more toward cooperation from conflict. Turning points might be represented by the breaking of an impasse, the signing of an interim framework, or by the recognition of changing events external to the negotiations. Such turning points signal the change in phases of the conflict. Since contextual factors tend to change slowly if at all during the course of negotiations, we might productively think of these transitions as resulting from aspects of the process. But what is it that propels one event to be a turning point and another an impasse? Or better put, is there something about the acumen or reputation of the negotiators that accounts for differences in outcomes?

Tinsley, O'Connor, and Sullivan (2002) demonstrate that in controlled settings reputation can influence the opponents' negotiation tactics and the outcome of the negotiations. Reputation has at least two dimensions. On the one hand reputation may inform an opponent's idea about the skill of the person sitting across the table; on the other it can contribute to expectations as to whether the opponent will seek distributive or integrative outcomes. The logic behind this approach to thinking about the process of negotiation is built on schema theory. That is, individuals will hold preconceived ideas about their opponent and hold expectations based on these preconceived notions. To use their terms, a "schema provides a negotiator with information about the counterpart's character, which helps the negotiator anticipate" future actions and intent (p. 622). One of the key dimensions of this psychological evaluation is whether the negotiator's counterpart is a value creator or someone who is adroit at claiming value for herself. As a negotiator you might approach a negotiating session with these expectations and adopt your strategy accordingly. Presumably the expectations that one brings to the negotiations can affect the ability to recognize and accept cues and signals for what they are, directly influencing tactical choices. These tactical choices might include the willingness or ability to recognize and act on turning points.

There are many significant advantages to focusing at the individual level of analysis, even within the context of international armed conflict. The task, however, is quite complicated. The notion of reputation and other types of priors with which negotiators go into a negotiation are predicated to some degree on the condition of multiple or repeated interactions between the same pair of actors. If armed conflict was a "one-shot" game devoid of memory or future expectations, then reputation or acumen would not be important. But world politics often involves repeated interactions, repeated military disputes, and repeated efforts to negotiate solutions between or among the same actors.

The key element to thinking about reputation, skill, or tactics is really one of information. What types of information does each side hold about the other, how symmetrical is that information, and how does information inform expectations? Bargaining models of armed conflict generally rely on concepts of ideal points, reservation points, relative capabilities, and other contextual characteristics. Each of these factors reflects either privately held information or subjective estimates by the opposing sides, and neither side is generally willing to come to the table prepared to create an environment of complete information. Uncertainty, incomplete information, and information asymmetries are the norm. The difficulties associated with revealing your true military capabilities, reservation points, or possible concessions are part of the entire aura of risks to national or group security in the face of an armed adversary. The psychological literature on negotiations suggests that reputation can help overcome information asymmetries and uncertainties, in effect by using prior information on past performance to develop an understanding of the likely tactics in the current negotiations.

This leap from individual psychology to representatives of a state or armed groups fighting a state is not straightforward, particularly when you consider the challenges to generating empirical evidence. It is one thing to design a controlled experiment where information and reputation are manipulated, yet quite another to find traces of reputation, tactics, and strategy within the context of negotiations to end armed conflicts. We generally don't know, for instance, whether a particular negotiator seeks integrative or distributive outcomes, nor what the opposing side thinks about reputation or prior performance. The linkage, however, provides a potentially important step forward.

Linking Basic Negotiation Research to Contemporary Work on Armed Conflict

Without recourse to controlled experiments, but accepting the importance of variables specific to the individual in understanding the outcome of negotiations to stop armed violence, scholars of armed violence involving state actors face difficult choices. Primarily, combining these two research traditions requires the ability to: (a) capture the effects of repeated interactions; (b) develop indicators of reputation, status, tactics and the like; and (c) have at least a quasi-control group that allows analytical comparisons. As mentioned before, as you increase the numbers of observations and diversity of participants this becomes a more difficult task.

There is, however, a set of armed conflicts that provides the potential to integrate these two research paradigms. In the study of interstate armed conflict they are referred to as enduring rivalries (Goertz & Diehl, 1995). Enduring rivalries represent a condition where members of a dyad engage in repeated threats to use or the direct use of force against each other over an extended period of time. In many instances these parties also engage in negotiations to resolve or moderate the issues at stake. If the psychological literature provides a key to understanding how expectations based on prior interactions influence outcome, then this should show up in the empirical record of repeated negotiations between parties to an enduring rivalry. These types of studies are at an early stage, but Regan and Leng (2006) have generated data on negotiations that take place between militarized disputes within rival dyads. That is, the data present a snapshot of the negotiations that take place during periods of military hostilities as well as between them, among pairs of states involved in repeated hostile interactions.

The data on negotiations within and between armed interstate rivalries consist of a number of contextual conditions associated with the conflict, the culture of the parties, and the international system. Importantly, we also record where possible the specific identity of the negotiators, including any outside mediators. This provides the opportunity to examine the effect of repeated participation by the same negotiators within the context of repeated "plays" of the same or similar conflicts. There also exist data on what might be considered a control group of interstate conflicts that are not part of a recurring rivalry. In these cases we have something much more akin to a single play of the conflict game, with few or no opportunities for prior reputation to influence outcomes. The combination provides for an empirical integration of the complementary theoretical foci of negotiation processes and context. While the data we have do not directly tap into the notion of integrative or distributive reputation, in a small way they can give a clue as to the reputation, at least the reputation for success or failure in prior negotiations. Early evidence points to the positive effects of previous negotiations on future ones, and the influence of negotiations between military hostilities on negotiations that take place during militarized disputes (Regan & Leng, 2006).

To give some sense of the range of data, there have been 35 enduring rivalries in the post-World War II period for which we know quite a bit about the contextual conditions. These rivalries are those pairs of states that have had at least six militarized disputes over a span of at least 20 years. Rivalries account for about 40% of all militarized disputes since 1816, and we know from prior research that these pairs of states are somewhat intractable to the efforts of outside mediation (Bercovitch & Regan, 1999). Since 1945 these 35 rivalries have been engaged in roughly 400 militarized disputes. The Pakistan–India rivalry, for instance, spans more than 55 years, has involved over 30 militarized disputes and four wars. This pattern of interaction also provides 31 intervals between militarized disputes or wars for which we code data on negotiations. There are, moreover, tens of individual negotiations between India and Pakistan throughout the course of this rivalry, and in each instance we record characteristics of the negotiators and mediators, if any. Not all rivalries are as intense, as long, and as violent as the Indo-Pakistani one, but data on negotiations within all rivalries will provide an opportunity to evaluate questions of negotiation processes in conjunction with those of the context.

The project that spawns the data on negotiations within rivalries involves trying to develop an understanding of how—and what—states learn from their cooperative and conflictual interactions. Much of the prior research on learning in a violent international context points to the dominating influence of realpolitik, or power politics, in future interactions. That is, states seem to learn that increasing levels of violence against the same actor is the best strategy (cf., Leng, 1983; 2000). Most of this evidence, however, is predicated on a close reading of conflictual events almost to the exclusions of cooperative efforts to diffuse the conflict. Because violence is costly, and increasingly high levels of violence are increasingly costly, political decision makers have an interest in finding cooperative ways out of militarized disputes. There is some reason to believe that states learn from the cooperative efforts in a way that tempers the resort to arms that is driven by the dictates of realpolitik pressures. Advancing this line of research could make productive use of some of the ideas from psychology about trust, reputation, or altruism discussed in the other chapters in this volume.

Conclusion

The outcome of negotiations is a result of a complex process, but importantly it is a process that takes place at multiple levels of aggregation, from interpersonal to interstate relations. Research at different levels of aggregation, moreover, tends to focus on different explanations for the observed outcomes. Those who study negotiations to manage armed interstate conflict generally rely on contextual variables measured at the level of the state, or variables that describe the structure of the relationship among the combatants. Relative military capabilities, the number or rate of fatalities—as a proxy for sunk costs—and the like provide some window into when negotiations succeed or fail. Understanding the link between structure or context and outcomes of negotiations can take us along a path to policy, but quite often the factors studied cannot be readily manipulated and therefore do not lead to immediate policy advice.

Social psychologists, on the other hand, tend to focus their attention on lower levels of social aggregation—business negotiations, divorce—and in doing so are able to observe aspects of the behavior or strategy of the negotiators. There are important questions to be answered in the realm of "how to" negotiate, how prior knowledge affects current strategies, and under what conditions do different approaches to negotiation succeed or fail. There are many ways to think of the outcome of negotiations being linked to both the structural conditions under which they occur and the reputation, acumen, or strategy of the participants. Scholarship, however, has not traveled very far down that path.

References

Bercovitch, J., & Diehl, P. F. (1997). Conflict management of enduring rivalries: Frequency, timing, and short-term impact of mediation. *International Interactions, 22*, 299–320.

Bercovitch, J. & Houston, A. (2000). Why do they do it like this? An analysis of the factors influencing mediation behavior in international conflicts. *Journal of Conflict Resolution, 44*(2), 170–202.

Bercovitch, J., & Langley, J. (1993). The nature of dispute and the effectiveness of international mediation. *Journal of Conflict Resolution, 37*, 670–691.

Bercovitch, J., & Regan, P. M. (1999). The structure of international conflict management: An analysis of the effects on intractability and mediation. *International Journal of Peace Studies, 4*(1), 1–20.

Doyle, M. W. & Sambanis, N. (2000). International peacebuilding: A theoretical and quantitative analysis *American Political Science Review, 94*(4), 779–801.

Druckman, D. (2001). Turning points in international negotiation: A comparative analysis. *Journal of Conflict Resolution, 45*(4), 519–544.

Filson, D., & Werner, S. (2002). A bargaining model of war and peace: Anticipating the onset, duration, and the outcome of war. *American Journal of Political Science, 46,* 819–837.

Goertz, G., & Diehl, P. F. (1995). The initiation and termination of enduring rivalries: The impact of political shocks. *American Journal of Political Science, 39*(1), 30–52.

Leng, R. J. (1983). Will they ever learn? Coercive bargaining in recurrent crises. *Journal of Conflict Resolution, 27*(3), 379–419.

Leng, R. J. (2000). *Bargaining and learning in recurring crises: The Soviet–American, Egyptian–Israeli, and Indo-Pakistani rivalries.* Ann Arbor, MI: University of Michigan Press.

Northedge, F. S., & Donelan, M. D. (1971). *International disputes: The political aspects.* London: Europa Publications.

Pillar, P. R. (1983). *Negotiating peace: War termination as a bargaining process.* Princeton, NJ: Princeton University Press.

Regan, P. M. (2002). Thoughts on how to organize a data set on diplomatic methods of conflict management. *International Negotiation, 7*(1).

Regan, P. M., & Aydin, A. (2006) Diplomacy and other forms of intervention in civil war. *Journal of Conflict Resolution, 50*(5), 736–756.

Regan, P. M., & Leng, R. J. (2003). Culture and negotiation in militarized interstate disputes. *Conflict Management and Peace Science, 20*(2), 111–132.

Regan, P. M., & Leng, R. J. (2006, November 11–13). *Negotiations within enduring rivalries: what do they learn and how much?* Paper delivered to the annual meetings of the Peace Science Society International, Columbus, OH.

Regan, P. M., & Stam III, A. C. (2000). In the nick of time: Conflict management, mediation timing, and the duration of interstate disputes. *International Studies Quarterly, 44,* 239–260.

Schelling, T. C. (1972). The process of residential segregation: Neighborhood tipping. In A. H. Pascal (Ed.), *Racial discrimination in economic* life (pp. 157–185) Lexington, MA: Lexington Books.

Tinsley, C. H., O'Connnor, K. M. & Sullivan, B. A. (2002). Tough guys finish last: the perils of a distribute reputation. *Organizational Behavior and Human Decision Processes, 88,* 621–642.

Walter, B. F. (2002). *Committing to peace.* Princeton, NJ: Princeton University Press.

Zartman, I. W. (1995). Dynamics and constraints in negotiations in internal conflicts. In Zartman, I. W. (Ed.), *Elusive peace: Negotiating and end to civil wars.* Washington, DC: Brookings.

18

The Politics of Human Happiness

BENJAMIN RADCLIFF

Introduction

If politics matters for the lives of ordinary people, we should expect the subjective quality of life that individuals experience to vary in response to differences in what kinds of policies elected governments pursue. This chapter attempts to establish that such relationships exist by demonstrating that national levels of well-being are determined by the extent to which a nation's public policy regime can be characterized as social democratic. Specifically, the degree to which citizens find their lives satisfying is heavily influenced by the two institutions that are emblematic of the social democratic project: the size or generosity of the welfare state, and the organization of works for collective action in the form of labor unions. Each in turn can be conceived of as manifestations of cooperation.

As the various chapters of this volume illustrate, cooperation is an elastic concept. As it of necessity involves individual human beings, there are strong incentives to conceive of it as an individual level phenomenon. In this sense, cooperation can be profitably (if not very precisely) thought of as a set of interpersonal relationships characterized by norms of reciprocity. The utility of this interpretation as a basis to approach the connection between cooperation and happiness is apparent in the large body of evidence suggesting that individuals embedded within cooperative networks exhibit greater satisfaction with life than others. In simple terms, as Robert Lane (2000) has so persuasively argued, those who are more socially connected with others appear to evaluate their lives much more positively than those who are not. Thus, in the phrase made justly famous by Robert Putnam (2000), "bowling alone" provides people with less emotional and psychological rewards than bowling in leagues or with friends. More generally, of course, the metaphor speaks to a wider phenomenon: The cooperation implicit in social connections benefits individuals who participate, i.e. those who cooperate.

As important as this conjecture is, its relevance to social science is limited. In discussing the implications of his work, Lane (2000) laments that creating "supportive relationships" (the "heart" of his thesis on what really creates happiness) is not especially "amenable to government action." Similarly, while Putnam and his followers have carefully traced some ways in which public policies might be structured so as to foster more social connection, they too ultimately draw our attention away from politics for the very same reason: "social connections" are not something that states efficiently produce. To be more precise, as important as the work of Lane and Putnam is, they draw our attention away from the political or the macro-social insofar as we remain fixated on individuals or the small groups that provide their social connections.

Thus, for instance, while Putnam makes a series of perfectly reasonable and commendable suggestions for increasing social capital, and thus social well-being, these remain vague, difficult to realize, and above all, only marginally related to public policy. He wishes to see more "participation and deliberation" in things like "team sports and choirs," more people involved in voluntary community service programs, more extracurricular activities in schools, more "family-oriented workplace practices," more "pedestrian-friendly" areas in our city planning, and tapping more seriously into the "crucial reservoir" of social capital in "faith-based communities." To be fair, Putnam takes notice of things like declining voter turnout, but in the end his focus, like that of most of his followers, is fixed on practices beyond or only tangentially related to the political. Thus, in the end, he puts his hopes on a "Great Awakening" of a "spiritual community of meaning."

There is, if not an alternative, at least a complimentary approach, alluded to in the introduction to this volume: cooperation can be thought of as a collective or "emergent" property of human communities. This powerful idea can be pushed, or ushered, toward the more specific suggestion that we think of cooperation as an institutional phenomenon. It is here that the political emerges from background to center. Insofar as political power can at least potentially be harnessed by human communities for the benefit of the community, there is the real possibility that institutions can be structured in ways that facilitate cooperation and thus well-being.

Cooperation might find expression in institutional forms in at least two (not mutually exclusive) ways. First, we can look to institutions that nurture cooperative behaviors and outlooks. In this interpretation, institutions can be the cause of cooperation. Alternatively, we can think of institutional structures as expressions of cooperative or even solidaristic norms. Thus, institutions can also embody or reflect cooperation. The two functions are likely to overlap, of course, so that, for instance, institutions that express cooperation are also likely to reinforce it.

From the point of view of subjective well-being, there are two board cooperative institutions that command our attention. One, of the first type discussed above, is the labor union. Another, of the second type, is the welfare state. I argue that concentrating on these institutions provides greater leverage than hoping for a "Great Awakening" of communal aspiration, in that it directs our attention toward political arrangements that we are capable of modifying. We certainly know how to increase or decrease public spending on welfare. Similarly, we know perfectly well how to structure the laws on organizing so as to make unions represent more or fewer workers. It is far less obvious how we see to it, to take another (and highly illustrative) example of Putnam's (2000) suggestions, that "Americans spend less leisure time sitting passively alone in front of glowing [computer] screens and more time in active connection with our fellow citizens." Rather than awaiting the "Great Awakening" of the American spirit, the institutional approach to cooperation points us toward changes in tangible and obvious macro-social institutions that are under our political control. If the welfare state and the labor union have profound consequences on well-being, as I argue presently, then their manipulation is a surer route to social betterment.

The Welfare State

It is widely agreed that the two social mechanisms available for the distribution and generation of well-being are markets and politics (e.g. Lindblom, 1977). In the liberal democracies, the conflict between these systems of allocation typically manifests itself in the struggle to replace or supplement the perceived inequalities of market distribution with the presumed equality of citizenship rights, i.e. to make "citizen entitlements . . . rather than the market contract" the basis of the allocation of well-being (Esping-Andersen, 1985, p. 159). Those favoring political "entitlements" in place of the market may do so for a variety of reasons, but all ultimately reduce to the fact that markets are "indifferent to the fate of individuals" (Lane, 1978). As I argue presently, there are ample reasons to believe that citizenship rights will tend to produce greater average satisfaction than market distribution.

The mechanisms by which markets contribute to unhappiness are sometimes tied to the generalized effects of capitalism on the human personality (e.g. Lane, 1978), but are more commonly argued to result from the economic insecurity and personal loss of autonomy that accompany market economies. Echoing Marx and Lindblom (1977), among others, Esping-Andersen observes that, whatever the many positive and commendable aspects of a capitalist economy, "the market becomes to the worker a prison within which it is imperative to behave as a commodity in order to survive" (1990, p. 36). It is hardly surprising or even controversial to suggest that human beings do not enjoy being reduced to a commodity to be bought and sold, and that their lives are likely to be less rewarding the more this metaphor approaches literalness. In that regard, it is certainly the case that the great mass of citizens in the industrial world depend for their livelihood on the sale of their labor power as a commodity. The market for that commodity is by its very nature characterized by uncertainty. Thus, as Lindblom notes, "a pertinent objection to markets is that they foist insecurities on the population" which become "all the more a problem when [one's] livelihood is at stake" (1977, p. 82). Thus so long as individuals depend upon the sale of their labor power in conditions of uncertainty "they are captive to powers beyond their control" such as business cycles, globalization, technological innovation, or other market vagaries (Esping-Andersen, 1990, p. 37).

Accordingly, I argue that it is the extent to which a program of "emancipation" from the market has been institutionalized within a given state that is the principal political determinant of subjective well-being. Put differently, life satisfaction should increase as we move from less to more social democratic welfare states.

Even the most ardent defenders of capitalism concede that insecurity is endemic in market economies. Economic insecurity translates into chronic psychological stress, which is clearly inimical to life satisfaction. To the extent that a society insulates its citizens against market dependence, it also insulates them from the stress and anxiety of the market—which is to say, from being a commodity themselves. Furthermore, markets, as economists since Adam Smith have recognized, contribute to inequality. The social democratic project again facilitates well-being by mitigating the worst effects of inequality through the idea of social citizenship: society, through the redistributive power of the state, guarantees a basic, and ideally middle-class, level of need-satisfaction. In sum, the political program of the left attempts to "marginalize the market as the principal agent of distribution and the chief determinant of peoples' life chances" (Esping-Andersen, 1985, p. 245).

The alternative to the market, as classically articulated by Marshall (1950), is to establish that individuals have claims on the product of society because they are citizens. It is thus one's status as a citizen, rather than one's class position or one's income, that becomes a principle guiding the distribution of well-being. Just as individuals in the modern liberal state reasonably expect police protection without having to purchase it, they similarly might expect access to other social goods, such as housing, medical care, and a minimal income when unable to work. The state of necessity intervenes to limit the importance of markets in providing some of the things that most people find necessary for enjoying a high quality of life. Physical security in their person and property against violence or theft is, again, perhaps the most basic. The social democratic project aims to extend the range of goods that are provided publicly, so as to reduce dependence on the market, and thus improve quality of life.

To the extent that social rights have evolved, then, the happier individuals should be, on average. Put another way, if, as argued, market independence contributes to subjective well-being, then the expansive "emancipating" welfare state associated with the social democratic model should produce a higher general level of life satisfaction.

I substantiate these theoretical expectations in two primary ways. First, by reviewing (in a non-technical fashion) the reasonably elaborate econometric models reported in Radcliff (2001) and Pacek and Radcliff (n.d.). Second, by providing some original data analysis that confirms their findings. Before turning to that discussion, however, it may be instructive to consider some simple visual evidence of the core relationship. Figure 18.1 provides a plot of mean happiness (using data from the 1990 wave of the World Values Survey [WVS]) and a measure of welfare state

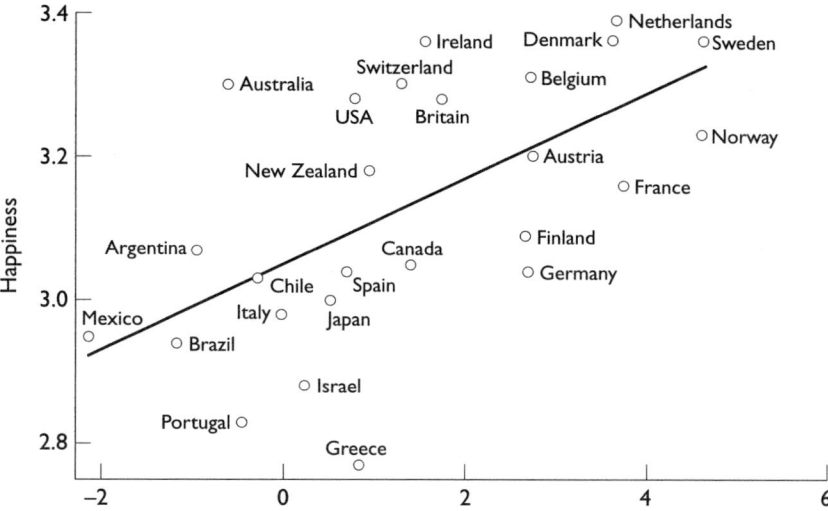

Figure 18.1 Happiness and the welfare state

generosity provided by Messner and Rosenfeld (1997).[1] The former is the national mean (measured on a 1–4 scale with higher values indicating greater happiness) to the standard question which asks respondents how happy they are "all in all." The latter is a measure of the amount of "decommodification" of labor (a concept to be discussed in more detail below) provided by the welfare state; higher scores indicate higher levels of decommodification.

While the bivariate pattern is not perfect (reflecting in part that there are more determinants of subjective well-being (SWB) than the welfare state alone), the graph clearly illustrates the basic contention: the less workers are confined to the "market as prison" the better the quality of their lives.[2]

I have examined this pattern more rigorously in an article in the *American Political Science Review* (Radcliff, 2001). There I rely primarily upon a measure of life satisfaction, again taken from the 1990 wave of the WVS: "All things considered, how satisfied or dissatisfied are you with your life now?" There are ten response categories, with higher values indicating greater satisfaction. I analyze these data in two ways. First, following the convention of the literature, satisfaction is aggregated to the level of national means; the purpose here is of course to identify those country-level factors that affect average happiness. Second, I turn to the individual survey data themselves, explicitly modeling satisfaction as a function of both individual- and national-level variables.

In each instance, I rely upon multivariate methods, modeling satisfaction as a function of various indicators of the welfare state and a set of control variables designed to isolate the impact of the political. Using the conventional aggregate data, I utilize the three controls common to the literature. Two are economic: the unemployment rate (average 1955–1990, data from Hall & Franzese, 1998) and real per capita GDP in 1990 purchasing power parity (from the Penn World Table, version 5.6, http://pwt.econ.upenn.edu/). The third is a measure of the "invidualism" of national cultures devised by Triandis (1989, 1995); data are reported in Diener, Diener, and Diener (1995).

This leaves the extent to which social rights have replaced markets to be explained. I utilize two different operationalizations of this concept. It may be instructive to review these measures briefly, in that such details may clarify the mechanisms by which the welfare state can contribute to a higher quality of life.

Perhaps the best, and certainly the best known, indicators of the extent to which states protect citizens against market dependence are suggested by Esping-Andersen (1990). He provides, first, a set of three interval level variables tapping how much a nation's welfare system embodies elements of his three ideal types of welfare regimes: liberal, conservative, and socialist. The liberal "effectively contains the realm of social rights" with modest and typically means-tested programs. The conservative may provide more generous benefits, but in the end still has a "negligible" redistributive impact, reflecting its emphasis on "the preservation of status differentials." The socialist is, of course, predicated explicitly upon the substitution of citizenship rights for markets. As Esping-Andersen (1990, p. 27) puts it, this vision of the welfare state is one that "would promote an equality of the highest standards . . . by guaranteeing . . . [everyone] full participation in the quality of rights enjoyed by the better-off." This approach "crowds out the market" in favor of state-provided social rights.

As these are ideal types, countries naturally do not fit neatly into any one single category. Actually existing welfare states combine elements from each. For that reason, Esping-Andersen (1990, table 3.3) provides, and I utilize, three indices accessing the amount of socialist, conservative, and liberal elements in a given nation's policy regime. Each country is scored on each variable, the three together representing the particular mix of the three attributes in its policy regime. As social democratic attributes are clearly those most conducive to ending market dependence, I expect that subjective quality of life will vary directly with the extent to which socialist elements are present. As the liberal welfare state depends most strongly on the market, it should be negatively associated with subjective well-being. The direction of any possible conservative regime effect is difficult to predict, but the net effect should be small whatever its direction.

Esping-Andersen also (1990, table 2.2) provides an alternative operationalization of what he explicitly refers to as "market independence" in the form of his index of the decommodification of labor. We have already encountered the idea of commodification and its negative consequences for well-being. It is clear then that labor is decommodified to "the degree to which individuals, or families, can uphold a socially acceptable standard of living independent of market participation" (Esping-Andersen, 1990, p. 37). The actual numeric index is a summary assessing the amount "emancipation from market dependency" in three specific domains: pensions, income maintenance for the ill or disabled, and unemployment benefits.

For reasons developed previously, the extent of decommodification should obviously contribute to quality of life.

The empirical analysis confirms our expectations: in each of the operationalizations of market independence (analyzed separately in consecutive models) the relevant coefficients are significant and correctly signed. In the first model considering regime attributes, socialist regimes appear to have positive consequences for well-being, while liberal welfare state regimes have a negative impact; center regimes prove to have no significance. The obvious implication is that the more socialist, and the less liberal, a welfare state regime, the more satisfied with their lives citizens tend to be. Similarly, we find that the greater the decommodification accomplished by state policy, the greater is the social level of satisfaction. Finally, the greater the time in power of the left and the less the time in power of the right, the happier are citizens; center-party control of government appears to have little effect.

These relationships are significant in a practical as well as a statistical sense, meaning that the magnitude of the relationships are quite pronounced. This can be seen by computing the predicted change in satisfaction across the range of each of the political variables, expressed as standard deviations of life satisfaction: 1.6 for the social democratic variable, −1.1 for the liberal regime variable, 2.3 for decommodification, and 1.4 for left-dominance. The implication is clear: the nature and extent of the welfare state makes an enormous difference in quality of life. Those who live in social democratic countries are more satisfied with their lives than those who do not, net of cultural and economic factors.

Much the same conclusion emerges from an analysis of individual rather than aggregate level data. Prior research at this level of analysis consistently shows that the same basic characteristics tend to affect individuals similarly across industrialized countries (see especially, Di Tella, MacCulloch & Oswald, 1997). The basic determinants are those that relate to simple demographics, such as gender, age, income, education, and social connectedness (e.g. Lane, 2000). Using appropriate variables from the World Values Study, I thus provisionally treat life satisfaction as a function of gender, age, household income, education, whether the chief wage earner is unemployed, whether the respondent is married (or living as married), the number of children, the respondent's appraisal of the quality of their home life, and frequency of church attendance. I also control for the same national-level variables as above: per capita GDP, aggregate unemployment, individualism, and political factors.

Results are much as before: each of the different operationalizations of market independence proves to be significant and of the expected sign in their respective equations. The substantive implication is, of course, once again citizens tend to be happier, controlling for other factors, when they live in expansive, decommodifying, social democratic societies.

They also allow us to ask a different question: Does the welfare state contribute positively only to the lives of the less affluent or does it benefit society in general? The simplest and most intuitive way to test is to divide the sample into high- and low-income groups and repeat analysis on each group. When doing so I find that decommodification is significant for both income categories, though its magnitude is about 50% greater for those with lower incomes. Left-dominance is twice the magnitude for those with lower compared to higher incomes (though only marginally significant in the latter case). Socialist regime attributes are significant and large for the lower-income group, while for the upper they are somewhat smaller in magnitude (and again only marginally significant). The liberal variable, negative and significant as expected for those with smaller incomes, is halved in magnitude and reduced to insignificance for the higher-income group, suggesting that the deleterious effects of liberal welfare state regimes are concentrated on those of lower status. In sum, this evidence suggests that those of modest incomes are most affected by all the measures of welfare dependence. There is also reason to believe (though admittedly with less certainty) that higher-status citizens also benefit, if somewhat less, from social democracy.

One shortcoming of the analyses described above is that they rely entirely upon cross-sectional data. They suggest that changes in the welfare state over space (i.e. across countries) appear to be associated with changes in the level of satisfaction over space. It would be more compelling still to be able to show that changes in the welfare state across both space and time (i.e. across both countries and years) produce changes in SWB in those country-years. In an effort to provide such evidence, I examine national levels of satisfaction across the industrial democracies using all waves of the WVS from 1981 to 2000. The number of observations varies by country but averages 3.1.

The dependent variable is mean life satisfaction (using the same indicator as before). Market independence is operationalized using decommodification scores from Scruggs (n.d.), which follow Esping-Andersen's original formulation. The sample includes the 13 western European countries plus the United States, Canada, Australia, New Zealand, and Japan. Control variables are as above: the Triandis measure of the individualism of cultures, plus GDP and unemployment. To control for the pooled structure of the data, I utilize a random effects model, which is appropriate given the number of time points relative to the number of countries.

Results are in Table 18.1. As is apparent, theoretical expectations are once again confirmed: The coefficient of decommodification is significant and of the correct sign. This confirms using pooled time-series data, what the cross-sectional models discussed previously suggested: The less people are forced "to behave as commodities in order to survive" the greater their satisfaction with life.

Pacek and Radcliff (n.d.) provide additional time-series evidence for this conclusion. In particular, they consider the one set of countries for which high-quality, yearly satisfaction data exist: the 11 core states of the European Union, courtesy of the Eurobarometer surveys (http://ec.europa.eu/public_opinion/index_en.htm). Using a fixed-effect model (a highly demanding statistical technique that fits a constant effect for each nation, thus capturing long-term factors such as culture which might cause satisfaction to differ across countries) along with economic control

Table 18.1 Life satisfaction and the welfare state

Decommodification	.033*
	(.015)
Culture	.144*
	(.061)
GDP	.000
	(.000)
Unemployment	−.010
	(.013)
Constant	5.50**
N	55
R-square	.359

Note: Dependent variable is mean life satisfaction. Estimation is with a GLS random effects model.

* sig. at .05 level, ** sig. at .001 level.

variables, they find that decommodification and party control show the same positive impact on satisfaction we have repeatedly encountered above. Thus, while not everyone agrees (see, in particular, Veenhoven, 2000 for a dissenting voice), there is a huge preponderance of evidence to suggest that the welfare state does indeed contribute to improving the human condition, at least insofar as we use human happiness as a metric of that concept.

Labor Organization

Unionization contributes to happiness through a variety of mechanisms. Some are direct, in the sense that they affect organized workers as individuals per se; in this way, a society is happier as union membership increases because the benefits of organization apply to a larger share of society's members. Others are indirect, affecting both the organized and unorganized; aggregate levels of well-being thus increase with membership because greater organization alters social arrangements such that they better contribute to a generalized improvement in living conditions. All are ultimately political in that union strength itself is universally agreed to be substantially (though of course not entirely) determined by governmental policy (e.g. Western, 1997).

Let us begin with direct effects. While it is often argued that the main sources of happiness come from outside work (e.g. Lane, 2000), it remains the case that work is one of the central focuses (perhaps the only focus) of most people's lives (e.g. Seeman & Anderson, 1983). The workplace is certainly one in which labor market participants spend a large portion of their waking lives. To the extent that the work experience is an agreeable one, people surely ought to be happier over all. Empirical evidence confirms that intuition: Job satisfaction is one the most important determinants of overall life satisfaction (see Sousa-Poza, 2000, for a discussion). Belonging to a labor union may tend, in turn, to increase job satisfaction (e.g. Pfeffer & Davis-Blake, 1990). The mechanisms are many, but the core relationships are clear enough: Job security, and a good work environment, nurture satisfaction with one's job (e.g. Sousa-Poza, 2000). Unions, of course, tend to increase the production of those goods. Through collective bargaining, the ways in which the workplace is organized and governed are negotiated, and thus are likely to be more conducive to the preferences of workers. Job security is similarly increased through contracts that provide protection from arbitrary dismissal. Members may also feel empowered by the existence of grievance procedures that give them the ability to appeal decisions made by employers. In all of these ways, labor unions facilitate the creation of a workplace that functions through "due process," with felicitous consequences (see Sutton, 1990). If unions contribute to job satisfaction, and if job satisfaction contributes to life satisfaction, then union members should demonstrate higher life satisfaction.

A closely related argument relates to the fact that unions may help reduce alienation by giving individuals a collective say in how the enterprise at which they work is managed. Individuals who are less alienated are in turn likely to be happier with their jobs, and thus their lives. Alienating work imposes psychological costs on individuals that contribute to depression and job dissatisfaction (see Greenberg & Grunberg, 1995), and a general decline in life satisfaction (Loscocco & Spitze, 1990). Similarly, it is widely agreed that autonomy on the job is vital for well-being. As Kohn, Naoi, Shoenbach, Schooler, and Slomczynski (1990, p. 964) put it, "occupational self-direction . . . affects values, orientations, and cognitive functioning" in exactly the way one would imagine: Those who lack self-direction are more prone to psychological "distress" (e.g. anxiety, lack of self-confidence). To be sure, alienation, and especially autonomy, are largely determined by occupation, but there are reasons to expect those represented by unions to evidence these pathologies to a lesser degree for any given type of occupation. While the union workplace may, of course, actually reduce autonomy in the abstract (given that union rules are indeed more rules that must be adhered to), unions are also contextually more supportive of self-determination in two respects. First, they establish a degree of autonomy for their members through collective bargaining at a level that is almost by definition higher than in non-union workplaces. Workers thus rightly interpret autonomy as something collectively achieved, i.e. as a benefit of organization. Further, as Fenwick and Olson (1986) observe, the experience of union membership fosters cognitive changes that encourage exactly the workplace participation that unionization allows, which may in turn foster more self-direction. To the extent that unions lessen alienation, then, we should again see a positive relationship between membership and well-being, net of other factors.

Unions also contribute to happiness through their effect on another variant of connectedness. A large literature in social psychology has demonstrated that individuals are afforded some protection against the deleterious consequences of stress, and especially job-related stress, through social support networks (e.g. Cohen & Wills, 1985). Work, even enjoyable work, can be a major source of stress, particularly when performance affects one's livelihood. While support from all quarters is surely helpful, evidence suggests that buffering is most effective when the source of support is from the same domain as the source of stress. Work-related stress, then, is best buffered by having sources of emotional support at work. Common sense would suggest that unions facilitate such support, in that they help build not only connections, but a sense of solidarity among coworkers. Indeed, Uehara (1990) goes so far as to specify "solidarity" as a critical agent in effective social support networks. By nurturing solidarity, unions thus provide an ideal context in which to find the type of social support that helps insulate against work-related stress.

There are few rigorous empirical studies of the general role of unions, social connection, and stress, but the extant literature does offer some evidence suggesting that unions facilitate both general social support (e.g. Lowe & Northcott, 1988) and protection against job-related stress per se. The evidence in regard to the effect of job stress on happiness is clearer still. Loscocco and Spitze (1990) demonstrate that precisely the negative consequences for happiness that one would expect do in fact obtain. Clearly, then, unions should again contribute to higher quality of life among their members.

The arguments above bring us to social capital (e.g. Putnam, 1993, 2000). At its core, "social capital refers to connections among individuals—social networks and the norms of reciprocity and trustworthiness that arise from them" (Putnam, 2000, p. 19). Generalizing slightly, the implicit idea at its most simple is that social networks facilitate positive psychological and cognitive changes in individuals that are not only politically desirable but also conducive to greater personal well-being (Putnam, 2000, p. 333–334). The literature, indeed, is unanimous in suggesting that social connectedness fosters greater subjective well-being. This argument is made most persuasively by Robert Lane (1978, 2000), who places the blame for declining levels of happiness in the United States and western Europe on a growing "famine" of "interpersonal relationships" (2000, p. 9). A variety of other studies have documented the importance of social connection (e.g. Myers & Diener, 1995; Veenhoven, 1996).

That unions as organizations facilitate the building of social networks requires no elaboration. That they are likely as fraternal organizations to foster norms of reciprocity and solidarity is equally clear. We have already noted the positive effect of union membership on social connections in the workplace. We thus have reasons to hypothesize further that union members, given that they tend to enjoy their jobs more and to suffer from less work-related stress, to say nothing of having more social connections (and indeed more social capital), are likely to be better able to build and maintain intimate and rewarding relationships. Labor organization can thus affect the quantity and quality of personal connections between human beings. Few things contribute to happiness as much as fulfilling relationships with one's friends, domestic partners, and children (e.g. Lane, 2000). Those who are more secure in and satisfied with their jobs, as members of labor unions tend to be, are thus more likely, other things being equal, to lead fulfilling personal lives. They in turn are likely to be better mothers and fathers, better daughters and sons, better domestic partners, and better friends—and thus make both their lives and those of their children, spouses, and friends better as well. To the extent that social capital and social connectedness contribute to a better quality of life, we consequently return again to the centrality of labor organization in promoting human happiness.

The social level of unionization should also contribute indirectly to people in general, rather than just union members, enjoying better lives. There are two mechanisms, neither of which requires extensive elaboration. One is a simple contagion effect: If one's personal happiness is to some extent determined by interactions with others, such that we are likely to be more happy ourselves the more we interact with other happy people, then people in countries with a higher proportion of happier-than-otherwise union members are likely to be more happy, on average, than those in countries with fewer proportional members. This effect will be certainly apparent in the intimate relationships discussed above, but the logic extends to all forms of social interaction.

A more immediate argument relates to the political consequences of having a strong labor movement. One of the best-documented relationships in social science is that between the strength of labor on the one hand, and the fortunes of political parties of the left and the generous social democratic welfare states they ideologically favor on the other (e.g. Esping-Andersen, 1990). We have already examined the connection between the welfare state and SWB. Thus, if strong union movements are, as is widely agreed, among the most important causal mechanisms in the development of such welfare states, then surely unions themselves contribute indirectly to happiness in this way.

As before, I attempt to document empirically the theoretical arguments for labor organization facilitating well-being by reviewing elaborate econometric evidence (see Radcliff, forthcoming) in a more accessible fashion. Before turning to that analysis, it may again be instructive to illustrate the basic empirical pattern in the simplest way possible: by showing the bivariate relationship between happiness and the extent of organizational "density" (that is, the percentage of workers organized). Results are in Figure 18.2.[3] While the pattern is far from perfect, it does clearly confirm the basic contention that quality of life improves the greater the share of workers represented by unions.

As with the welfare state, the empirical analysis is conducted at both the level of national means and the level of the individual. For the sake of brevity, I will concentrate on the latter, noting only that the aggregate analysis is consistent with the findings reported below. Data are again from the 1990 wave of the WVS. The sample includes the 15 western European countries, plus the United States, Canada,

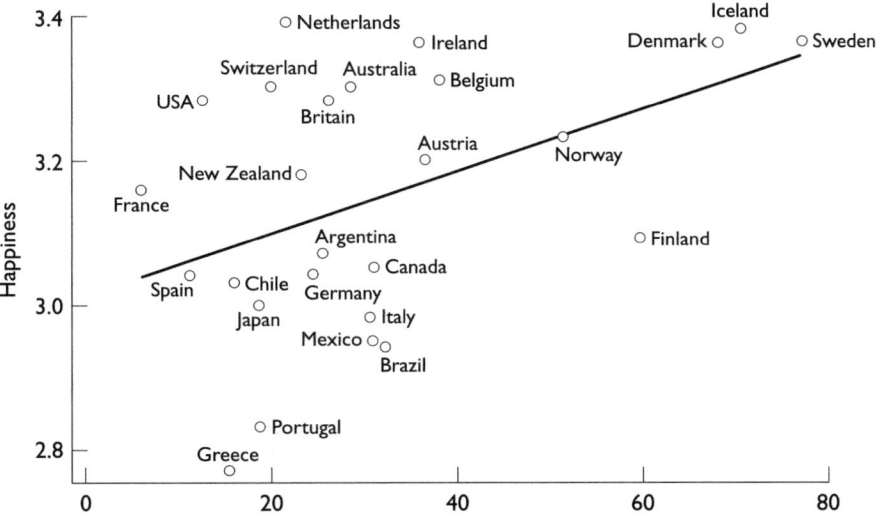

Figure 18.2 Happiness and union density

and Japan. The dependent variable is life satisfaction, with controls as before. The independent variables are individual-level union membership and the aggregate, national level of union density (from Visser, 1996).

The initial results confirm our expectations: Both individual union membership and the aggregate level of labor union density are significant and positively signed. The implication is that members of unions are more satisfied with their lives than others, and that all citizens are more satisfied as the general level of labor organization increases. Importantly, these results also obtain when simultaneously considering a measure of social democracy (from Esping-Andersen, 1990, table 3.3 as discussed previously). When considering both the union variables and the social democracy indicator in the model the social democracy is itself significant and of the expected sign, as are both the unionization terms. Thus, *both* labor organization and the welfare state affect subjective well-being. Further, both individual membership and aggregate density have independent effects. People who belong to unions are happier than those who do not, and all individuals tend to be happier in countries with greater levels of labor organization, irrespective of their own membership status.

It is also possible to further substantiate the claim that the national, aggregate level of labor organization improves the quality of life for both the organized and the unorganized by estimating the basic results when removing union members (and thus the individual union-membership variable) from the sample. Results are as before: Higher levels of aggregate union density do indeed appear to affect the life satisfaction of non-members, net of other factors.

In sum, then, the data suggest that (a) unions contribute to the well-being of their members, (b) unions contribute to the well-being of society as a whole, including non-members, and (c) these effects are net of the positive effects on well-being that unions might produce through their political support for the welfare state or parties of the left (or, indeed, on their potential impact on wages or salaries).

Discussion

In 1949, Albert Einstein contributed an article to the *Monthly Review* entitled "Why Socialism?" The answer, as he saw it, was that only socialism offered practical advice as to "how the structure of society . . . should be changed in order to make human life as satisfying as possible." Much of Einstein's reasoning followed the conventional class-analytical critique of capitalism as a means of production: "workers" (in the most expansive sense of "those who not share in the ownership of the means of production") become prisoners—commodities—within that system of production, such that their lives are characterized not only by "exploitation" but by insecurity. Further, the competitive individualism that such insecurity fosters is inimical to well-being, given that it reduces the ability of humans to cooperate, which, as social animals, further reduces their happiness. If capitalism is thus, as Einstein argued, inimical to happiness, the only solution that presents itself is socialism.

The evidence presented here thus echoes Einstein in concluding that socialism (as least in its social democratic incarnation) provides what is perhaps our best hope for improving the human condition, insofar as we agree that making "human life as satisfying as possible" is indeed the appropriate standard of evaluation. The reasons for this are clear: The welfare state, and the organization of workers into labor unions, do indeed lead to greater satisfaction with life, net of other factors. Thus, to the extent that the welfare state and the labor union are the emblematic institutions of the socialist enterprise, the findings presented in this chapter would seem to vindicate Einstein's judgment. Whatever else we might say about them, welfare states and unions do indeed seem to make important contributions in the project of making "human life as satisfying as possible."

This is not the most hopeful conclusion to draw, given current ideological trends. Both unions and the welfare state appear to be everywhere in retreat. Across Europe, from Sweden to Germany to the UK, the social commitment to the welfare state in general, and to the idea of "decommodification" in particular, has eroded, often at behest of the very social democratic and labour parties that had been their traditional champions. In the United States, these pressures are more keenly felt than ever. With organized labor nearly everywhere in either in a freefall of declining membership (as in the US or France) or waning political power (most everywhere else), the prospects for arresting or reversing these trends do not seem bright. Indeed, the neo-liberal agenda of unfettered markets, privatization, "flexible" labor laws, and lower social spending appears to be advancing nearly unopposed everywhere from

Scandinavia to "communist" China. Barring some massive and unforeseen effective resistance (for which only Latin America seems to offer glimpses of success), pro-market forces seem poised to instill an ideological hegemony (the "Washington Consensus") unknown since capitalism's inception. If the contentions advanced in this chapter carry any validity at all, it takes no great insight to deduce the implications for the human condition.

The question of the ideology takes us full circle back to Robert Lane and the social capitalists. Both stressed in their ways the importance of human connections, of supportive and nurturing relationships among human beings, as the key to human happiness. If "socialism" is not a viable political alternative, can we find in this other approach any basis for a more sanguine view of the future? Einstein speaks to this question as well.

He suggests, familiarly, that humans have two primary "drives." One is "private" or "egoistical"; it encourages one to "to protect his own existence" and "to satisfy his personal desires." The other is "social"; it suggests instead seeking "to gain the recognition and affection of [one's] fellow human beings, to share in their pleasures, to comfort them in their sorrows." Both are always present and necessary, of course, and it is "their specific combination [that] determines the extent to which an individual can achieve an inner equilibrium" in which he or she lives life to its fullest. The "relative strength" of these two drives in most persons is in turn determined "by the structure of society" in which people live. Some institutional arrangements push one of the drives to dominate the other in an unhealthy way. Thus, the extent to which people find the correct "inner equilibrium" necessary for a good life is greatly influenced "by the types of organizations that predominate in society."

Here we come to the central problem with capitalism: As an institution, it encourages individuals to see society as not "as a positive asset, as an organic tie, as a protective force, but rather as a threat to his natural rights . . . such that the egotistical drives . . . are constantly being accentuated, while his social drives, which are by nature weaker, progressively deteriorate." This, then, is the diagnosis of "the real source of evil" in contemporary society: capitalism makes individuals "prisoners of their own egotism," so that "they feel insecure, lonely and deprived of the naïve, simple, and unsophisticated enjoyment of life."

This is, of course, precisely Lane's (2000) point: What makes people happy is ultimately freedom from the "loneliness" that he sees as responsible for the decline in happiness in capitalist societies. Similarly, Einstein's conclusion, "Man can find meaning in life . . . only through devoting himself to society," would please Putnam (2000). By this Einstein does not, of course, mean that one must become a Mother Teresa. His "devotion to society" implies simply an emphasis on the "social drive" so as to build connections and relationships of trust and reciprocity with others, in order to escape being "a prisoner of egotism."

The circle loses itself another way, further, when we consider Einstein's suggested cure. Given that our problems stem from the structural conditions of the market system, the only solution is to replace that system with another—or, at a minimum, to supplement the institution of capitalism with other countervailing institutions that limit its potential for dehumanization. We thus return to where we began: with the necessity for organizational structures like the union and the welfare state.

All roads, thus, would seem to lead to socialism—which is to say, to human cooperation toward socially defined collective goals. To avoid the unpleasant prognosis of an extended and painful decline in the quality of human life that is the logical result of the emerging neo-liberal hegemony, we must find a way back to the social democratic model as a basis for a genuinely *human* society.

Notes

1 The happiness data are taken from the "States of Nations" data set (version p), compiled by Professor Ruut Veenhoveen (2004). Available publicly at http://www1.eur.nl/fsw/happiness (accessed 16 April 2004). The y-axis is the variable hap490. The Messner and Rosenfeld data are standardized (z) scores.
2 The welfare state variable is significant at the .001 level (two-tailed).
3 Happiness data are from Veenhoven (2004). Union data are for the percentage of the of non-agricultural labor force unionized in early–mid-1990s from the International Labour Organization (ILO, 1997). The density variable is significant at .05 level (two-tailed).

References

Cohen, S., & Wills, T. A. (1985). Stress, social support, and the buffering hypothesis. *Psychological Bulletin, 98*, 310–357.

Diener, E., Diener, M., & Diener, C. (1995). Factors predicting the subjective well-being of nations. *Journal of Personality and Social Psychology, 69 (May)*, 851–864.

Di Tella, R., MacCulloch, R., & Oswald, A. (1997). *The macroeconomics of happiness.* The Labour Market Consequences of Technical and Structural Change Discussion Paper Series, number 19. Centre for Economic Performance, Oxford University.

Einstein, A. (1949/2000). Why socialism? Reprinted in *Monthly Review, 52*(1), 36–44.

Esping-Andersen, G. (1985). *Politics against markets.* Princeton, NJ: Princeton University Press.

Esping-Andersen, G. (1990). *The three worlds of welfare capitalism.* Princeton, NJ: Princeton University Press.

Fenwick, R., & Olson, J. (1986). Support for worker participation. *American Sociological Review, 41*(4), 505–522.

Greenberg, E., & Grunberg, L. (1995). Work alienation and problem alcohol behavior. *Journal of Health and Social Behavior, 36 (March)*, 83–102.

Hall, P. A., & Franzese, R. J. (1998). Mixed signals: Central bank independence, coordinated wage bargaining, and European monetary union. *International Organization, 52 (Summer)*, 505–535.

International Labour Organization (1997). *World Labour Report 1997–1998.* Geneva: International Labour Organization.

Kohn, M., Naoi, A., Schoenbach, C., Schooler, C., & Slomczynski, K. M. (1990). Position in the class structure and psychological functioning in the United States, Japan, and Poland. *American Journal of Sociology*, *95*(4), 964–1008.

Lane, R. (1978). Autonomy, felicity, futility. *Journal of Politics*, *40 (Winter)*, 1–24.

Lane, R. (2000). *The loss of happiness in market democracies*. New Haven, CT: Yale University Press.

Lindblom, C. (1977). *Politics and markets*. New York: Basic Books.

Loscocco, K., & Spitze, G. (1990). Working conditions, social support, and the well-being of female and male factory workers. *Journal of Health and Social Behavior*, *31*(4), 313–327.

Lowe, G. S., & Northcott, H. C. (1988). The impact of working conditions, social roles, and personal characteristics on gender differences in distress. *Work and Occupations*, *15*, 55–77.

Marshall, T. H. (1950). *Citizenship and social class*. Cambridge, UK: Cambridge University Press.

Messner, S., & Rosenfeld, R. (1997). Political restraint of the market and levels of criminal homicide. *Social Forces*, *75 (June)*, 1939–1416.

Myers, D., & Diener, E. (1995). Who is happy? *Psychological Science*, *6 (January)*, 10–19.

Pacek, A., & Radcliff, B. (n.d.). *Assessing the welfare state*. Mimeo, Department of Political Science, University of Notre Dame.

Pfeffer, J., & Davis-Blake, A. (1990). Unions and job satisfaction. *Work and Occupations*, *17*(3), 259–284.

Putnam, R. (1993). *Making democracy work*. Princeton, NJ: Princeton University Press.

Putnam, R. (2000). *Bowling alone*. New York: Simon & Schuster.

Radcliff, B. (2001). Politics, markets, and life satisfaction. *American Political Science Review*, *95*(4), 939–952.

Radcliff, B. (forthcoming). Class organization and subjective well-being. *Social Forces*.

Scruggs, L. (n.d.) *Comparative welfare entitlements dataset*. Available publicly at http://sp.uconn.edu/~scruggs/wp.htm

Seeman, M., & Anderson, C. S. (1983). Alienation and alcohol: The role of work, mastery, and community in drinking behavior. *American Sociological Review*, *48*(1), 60–77.

Sousa-Poza, A. (2000). Well-being at work. *Journal of Socio-Economics*, *29*(6), 517–539.

Sutton, J. (1990). Bureaucrats and entrepreneurs: Institutional responses to deviant children in the United States. *American Journal of Sociology*, *95*(6), 1367–1400.

Triandis, H. C. (1989). The self and social behavior in differing cultural contexts. *Psychological Review*, *96 (July)*, 506–520.

Triandis, H. C. (1995). *Individualism and collectivism*. Boulder, CO: Westview Press.

Uehara, E. (1990). Dual exchange theory, social networks, and informal social support. *American Journal of Sociology*, *96*(3), 521–557.

Veenhoven, R. (1996). Developments in satisfaction research. *Social Indicators Research*, *37 (January)*, 1–46.

Veenhoven, R. (2000). Well-being in the welfare state: Level not higher, distribution not more equitable. *Journal of Comparative Policy Analysis*, *2*, 91–125.

Veenhoven, R. (2004). *States of nations, world database of happiness*. Erasmus University Rotterdam (version p). Available at: www.worlddatabaseofhappiness.eur.nl/statnat

Visser, J. (1996). *Unionization trends revisited*. Mimeo, University of Amsterdam, the Netherlands.

Western, B. (1997). *Between class and market*. Princeton, NJ: Princeton University Press.

19

The Well-Being of Nations

Linking Together Trust, Cooperation, and Democracy

WILLIAM TOV AND ED DIENER

In his book, *Nonzero*, Robert Wright (2000) argues that the basic direction of human history is towards greater social and technological complexity and an increasing realization that all people are linked in a fundamental web of interdependence. That is, across every province and nation, the fact remains that we all live in the same world, navigating the course of humanity in the same proverbial boat. This basic fact of interdependence comes with an important implication: that the ultimate survival of all societies rests on finding solutions to social, political, and economic issues that are *non-zero-sum*.

In game theory, a zero-sum approach is one in which winning comes at the expense of others. In contrast, a non-zero-sum solution is one in which all parties gain something so that everyone is better off than before. For example, in the *tragedy of the commons*, a public resource is only sustainable to the extent that everyone uses it responsibly. If several individuals exploit too much of the resource for their own benefit, it is lost and *everyone* suffers. If individuals take only what they need, the resource is replenishable and in the long run, everyone benefits. Non-zero-sum solutions call for cooperation and trust among all parties. To preserve the resource for future use, people must be cooperative in fulfilling their needs. At the same time, in order to curb the impulse to hoard, individuals must trust that others will not hoard for themselves. The benefits are not only material resources as implied by the tragedy of the commons; there are also consequences for the happiness and contentment of individuals and entire communities. Wright's central thesis is that long-term *global* well-being depends heavily on cooperation and trust at the supranational level. There is a utilitarian ethic that undergirds the appeal of non-zero-sumness. That is, by regulating impulsive self-interest, the happiness of all people can be maximized. Although scholars debate how well people are able to follow this principle, the logic is intuitive: a society in which people can trust and cooperate with each other is likely to be happier and more productive than a society paralyzed by rampant distrust and fear. The implication is that trust and cooperation provide the conditions for subjective well-being. Slightly less intuitive is the

possibility that happiness causes and facilitates interpersonal trust and cooperation. In this chapter, we argue that subjective well-being both influences and is
influenced by cooperation and trust. This bi-directional relationship is supported
by empirical research. After reviewing this literature, we explore the association
between national levels of subjective well-being and cooperation in our analyses of
the World Values Survey. First, we briefly discuss the concepts of cooperation, trust,
and subjective well-being.

Cooperation and Trust

Cooperation involves working together toward a common goal. As we discuss later,
cooperation is not necessarily opposed to competition. In competitive contexts
such as sports, the interaction between competing teams requires that everyone
observe the rules governing fair play. Thus, cooperation and competition can function together in a single activity. As Wright (2000) notes, zero-sumness on one level
can even foster non-zero-sumness on another level. Competition between teams
necessitates cooperation among members *within* a team. Cooperation is not inherently good or bad; people can work together to accomplish harmful, antisocial acts.
However, any well-functioning society requires cooperation among its citizens.

What sort of factors facilitate cooperation in society? How do people decide to
cooperate with others—especially those they do not know well? Wright (2000)
points to two critical factors: communication and trust. Communication enables
people to reach an understanding of common goals and an agreed-upon means of
attaining those goals. Trust provides people with assurance that their cooperation
will not be exploited. Both communication and trust are more likely in enduring
social relationships so that people are more likely to trust and cooperate with close
friends and relatives than a stranger. Putnam (2000) draws a distinction between
the *thick* trust that exists among close associates, and the *thin* trust that may be
felt for most people in general. He argues that greater community involvement
can increase social capital, thereby fostering trust in one's fellow citizens. However,
there are two forms of social capital that Putnam (2000) refers to as *bonding* and
bridging. Bonding social capital refers to exclusive forms of relationships such as
when people associate with each other to reinforce shared identities (e.g., support
groups based on gender or ethnicity). In contrast, bridging social capital refers
to more inclusive relationships based on certain causes (e.g., civil rights) or professional networks that emphasize broader identities. Bridging social capital can
broaden one's social networks and expand one's sources of information, but the
social ties are often weak. On the other hand, bonding social capital can provide
emotional support and foster solidarity, but strong in-group loyalty can be accompanied by more hostility toward outgroups.

Thus, bonding and bridging both have advantages and disadvantages. Based
on this distinction, one might expect bridging but not bonding social capital to

increase generalized trust. However, Uslaner (2002) argues that voluntary associations may not always foster generalized trust because they often bring together people with similar interests and perspectives. Such groupings seem to provide little basis for generalizing trust to anonymous others who are more likely to be different from ourselves. Instead, Uslaner proposes that generalized trust reflects an optimistic worldview. Optimistic people are less concerned with being exploited and are more resilient in their efforts to trust and cooperate with others. Optimism also remains positively associated with well-being, even after controlling for education and income (Uslaner, 1998). Whether cooperation and trust are fostered by social connections or optimism, it is important to note that the latter two are both associated with subjective well-being.

Subjective Well-Being

The field of subjective well-being (SWB) refers to the scientific study of happiness and life satisfaction. SWB consists of emotional and cognitive components (Diener, Suh, Lucas, & Smith, 1999). Emotional well-being is reflected in frequent experiences of pleasant emotions and infrequent experiences of unpleasant emotions. The cognitive component of SWB refers to a global evaluation of one's life, often assessed as life satisfaction. The cognitive and emotional components are often correlated so that people with high life satisfaction tend to report more frequent pleasant emotions than those with low life satisfaction (Diener & Fujita, 1995).

SWB is an important value for many societies and is not limited to Western or industrialized nations (Diener, 2000). Over the past two decades, research has illuminated a number of important determinants of SWB. These include differences among individuals in their personalities or emotional predispositions. For example, extraversion is frequently associated with pleasant affect, and neuroticism with unpleasant affect (Costa & McCrae, 1980). Some people are simply more likely to experience pleasant or unpleasant emotions in part because they pay more attention to pleasant or unpleasant stimuli (Derryberry & Reed, 1994). SWB is also affected by the fulfillment of basic needs. When basic needs are not met, the well-being of individuals and societies tends to decrease (Diener, Diener, & Diener, 1995). However, once basic needs are regularly met, other factors become important such as self-development and social relationships. This might explain why income leads to stronger increases in SWB in poorer countries, but has a smaller impact on well-being as the wealth of a nation increases (Diener & Diener, 1995; Oishi, Diener, Lucas, & Suh, 1999). Money and material resources *do* increase SWB—even beyond the level required for basic subsistence (Diener et al., 1995). After a yearly income of roughly $10,000, however, increases in SWB begin to level off.

Aside from personality and material resources, one of the most important determinants of SWB is having social relationships. Diener and Seligman (2002) compared the happiest (top 10%) of a college student sample with the unhappiest individuals (bottom 10%). The happiest individuals reported stronger relationships with friends, family, and romantic partners than those who were unhappy. Even more telling, the unhappiest 10% reported spending more time alone and less time with friends and family. Experience sampling studies in which participants provide reports of their emotions at random moments during the day reveal that people tend to experience more pleasant emotions when they are with others than when they are alone (Oishi, Diener, Scollon, & Biswas-Diener, 2003). Close relationships provide us with opportunities to experience love, joy, and affection, and married individuals consistently report being happier than those who are not married (Myers, 2000). In contrast, the experience of widowhood has a lasting negative impact on happiness. In a 15-year longitudinal study, those who were widowed did not return to prior levels of happiness until eight years later, on average (Lucas, Clark, Georgellis, & Diener, 2003). There is also some evidence that social isolation and loneliness are detrimental to long-term health, and some of these effects have been measured physiologically. Compared to socially integrated individuals, lonely individuals possess higher levels of cortisol (a sign of stress) and poorer immune system functioning (Cacioppo et al., 2000).

In sum, personality, material resources, and social relationships all are critical determinants of SWB. The last finding is of special relevance for our discussion because it highlights the relation between social capital and SWB. According to Putnam (2000), another reason why social capital might increase volunteerism is that individuals with rich social networks are more likely to be *asked for help* by others in their network. If this is correct, an association between SWB and increased sociability would have important implications for cooperation and trust. Indeed, previous researchers found SWB to be a strong correlate of generalized trust, even after controlling for demographic factors (Brehm & Rahn, 1997; Rahn & Transue, 1998). Next, we review evidence of mutual influence between SWB on the one hand, and cooperation and trust on the other.

The Effects of Cooperation and Trust on SWB

Cooperation and trust can have both short-term and long-term effects on SWB. Cooperative interactions may have short-term effects by evoking positive affect and attitudes. When participants engaged in a structured cooperative activity with a member of a stigmatized social group (former mental patients), they developed more positive attitudes toward the group in general than when they worked individually in the presence of the stigmatized person (Desforges et al., 1991). Tasks that are performed within cooperative contexts rather than competitive or individualistic contexts result in better performance as well as increased self-esteem (Stanne, Johnson, & Johnson, 1999). However, the way competition is structured is also important. For instance, Tauer and Harackiewicz (2004) found that youth enjoyed shooting free throws in the context of *intergroup* competition more than they did in an individually competitive context. Intergroup competition involves elements of both cooperation and competition: *cooperation with* team members to shoot a joint number of free throws *in competition with* the performance of an opposing team. Thus, cooperation and competition can be combined to enhance task enjoyment.

Cooperation and trust also have long-term implications for well-being. Compared to individualistic efforts, cooperative tasks more effectively increase social support (Stanne, et al., 1999). Such cooperative efforts may promote positive relationships with others in working toward common goals and help individuals to build upon their social resources, which are among the strongest correlates of SWB (Diener & Fujita, 1995). By facilitating the development of social relationships, then, trust and cooperation can contribute to SWB. In contrast, *pervasive* distrust of others can interfere with the development of rewarding relationships. Consistent with this argument, female college students who had been taught not to trust strangers in their childhood also reported greater loneliness and fear of intimacy than students who had not been taught to be distrustful (Terrell, Terrell, & Von Drashek, 2000). Loneliness, in turn, is associated with stress (Cacioppo et al., 2000). Although more research is needed, these findings support the possibility of a causal relation from trusting attitudes to reduced loneliness and greater SWB.

Trust also facilitates cooperation with others. High trusters were more responsive to cooperative messages than competitive messages from other participants in a social dilemma (Parks, Henager, & Scamahorn, 1996). Trust may encourage cooperation by reducing the fear of being taken advantage of. However, even when one experiences fear, strong trust may override it. For example, Yamagishi and Sato (1986) operationalized trust by comparing friends with strangers in a public goods dilemma. Among strangers, contributions to public goods were reduced when participants either feared exploitation or were motivated by greed. However, among friends, fear and greed were less predictive of contributions. The researchers proposed that even when fear and greed are experienced among friends, people are more likely to retain their mutual trust or decide not to free ride on their friends.

Organizational research attests to the importance of a trusting, cooperative work environment for productivity and job satisfaction. By relying on a tacit understanding that employees and supervisors operate in a trustworthy manner, organizations can avoid the costs of monitoring the behaviors of all employees (Kramer, 1999). Such measures not only cost time and money, but they may lead employees to feel distrusted and to infer that their co-workers must be untrustworthy as well. Feeling distrusted, in turn, can undermine intrinsic motivation, with negative implications for job satisfaction and performance. Enzle and Anderson (1993) found that when participants were surveilled for controlling reasons (e.g, to make sure they followed instructions), they were less engaged with a free-play activity. Not only is it important for employees to feel that they are trusted, it is also important for them to trust their employers. Positive emotions are enhanced when people feel they are being evaluated by a trustworthy authority figure who is using accurate methods (De Cremer, 2004). When an authority is perceived as untrustworthy, people report lower positive emotions regardless of accuracy.

Finally, Lu and Argyle (1991) found that positive attitudes toward group leisure activities predicted greater happiness six months later, even after controlling for prior levels of extraversion and happiness. These findings suggest that attitudes that support positive social interactions like cooperation may also promote and sustain happiness over time.

The Effects of SWB on Cooperation and Trust

A consistent finding in psychological research is that positive moods promote helping behavior and cooperation (Eisenberg, 1991). Much of the evidence relies on experiments that manipulate mood, suggesting that positive moods lead to prosocial behavior. However, *dispositional* positive affect also exhibits similar effects (for a review see Lyubomirsky, King, & Diener, 2005). We review the effects of positive mood and positive affectivity at the individual and group level, and then consider the potential benefits of happiness at the societal level.

Individual level effects

In a classic study, Isen and Levin (1972) induced positive mood by leaving a dime in a phone booth. People who found the dime after using the phone were more likely than those who did not to help a nearby confederate who dropped papers on the ground. People in a positive mood were also more willing to help co-workers (Baron & Bronfen, 1994), more likely to volunteer for future experiments (Aderman, 1972; Isen & Levin, 1972), and more likely to prefer cooperation over competition (Aderman, 1972; Barsade, 2002; Forgas, 1998) than people in neutral or negative moods. Although, negative moods occasionally induce helping, the findings are more consistent for positive mood (Eisenberg, 1991; however, see Eisenberg & Eggum, this volume, for an analysis of how sympathy contributes to helping behavior). Dispositional happiness (or trait positive affectivity) is also associated with greater helping. Happy people report more helping behavior in the past (Krueger, Hicks, & McGue, 2001), as well as greater willingness and intention to help others (Williams & Shiaw, 1999).

Why might positive mood facilitate helping and cooperation? One possibility is that positive mood increases positive thoughts, which may lead to more favorable evaluations of others. Participants who were exposed to a positive newscast were not only more cooperative in a subsequent task, they also *expected* others in the group to cooperate compared to participants who watched a negative newscast (Hornstein, LaKind, Frankel, & Manne, 1975). Positive mood also enhances interest in social and prosocial activities (Cunningham, 1988b), increases liking for other people, and leads to more intimate self-disclosures in social interactions (Cunningham, 1988a). These findings suggest that individuals who experience positive affect are more inclined to trust others, and this is supported by research (Dunn & Schweitzer, 2005).

However, not only might happy people be more trusting, but others might be more likely to trust *them*. Dispositionally happy people tend to be more likeable than depressed individuals (Lyubomirsky et al., 2005). Women who smiled in their yearbook photo were rated as more affiliative and less hostile by observers who interacted with them, as well as by coders who only saw their photos (Harker & Keltner, 2001). Compared to unhappy people, happy people were rated as morally good and more likely to go to Heaven (King & Napa, 1998). When negotiating, people in positive moods were more likely not only to make deals, but to *honor* those deals in an interpersonal setting (Forgas, 1998). Thus, happy people may behave in ways that communicate their trustworthiness, and this can encourage others to be more cooperative with them.

Organizational and group level effects

The relations between happiness, trust, and cooperation may yield important benefits in the workplace. Diener, Nickerson, Lucas, and Sandvik (2002) found that cheerfulness in college predicted job satisfaction and income nineteen years later. The helpfulness of happy people also appears to generalize to the workplace. Reviews of organizational citizenship behaviors (OCB) find a modest correlation between positive affectivity and altruistic behaviors at work (Borman, Penner, Allen, & Motowidlo, 2001; Organ and Ryan, 1995), and both trait and mood measures of positive affect separately predict intentions to engage in OCB (Williams & Shiaw, 1999).

However, happy people do not blindly and invariably trust and cooperate with others. Rather, the effects of positive mood on cooperation may depend on contextual factors such as current goals (Sanna, Parks, & Chang, 2003) or perceived social norms (Hertel, Neuhof, Theuer, & Kerr, 2000). For example, in a public goods game, Hertel et al. (2000) manipulated participants' expectancies about the average contribution of other players so that perceived norms were either cooperative (high average contribution) or uncooperative (low average contribution). In the cooperative norm condition, positive mood led to greater cooperation than negative mood after the first block of trials. In contrast, no effect of mood was found in the *uncooperative* norm condition. Hertel et al. suggested that in a positive mood, people might rely on social heuristics (such as group norms) to guide their behavior.

Thus, happy individuals do not function in a bubble; the surrounding work environment can facilitate or reduce mood effects. Consistent with this idea, Forgas (1998) found that negotiation was most cooperative when two bargaining groups were *both* in a positive mood. In contrast, a happy group that negotiates with a sad group tends to cooperate less. This trend may be due to the strong preference of sad groups for competition over cooperation. However, sad groups were still more likely to cooperate with happy groups than with another sad group—another indication that happy people may invite trust and cooperation from others.

The above research suggests that a positive work environment may be just as important as individual happiness. Management teams with high average trait positive affect reported greater cooperativeness and less conflict on group projects (Barsade, Ward, Turner, & Sonnenfeld, 2000). Greater cooperation among happy work groups might explain the greater productivity and lower turnover rates in such groups (see Diener & Seligman, 2004).

Implications for Society

Inglehart and colleagues (Inglehart, 2000; Inglehart & Klingemann, 2000) have argued that life satisfaction may be necessary (though not sufficient) for the sustainability of democracies. Although democratic countries generally exhibit a higher quality of life, it is also important to consider that no society can function well when most of its citizens are discontented. High life satisfaction may not only indicate that people's needs are fulfilled, it might also help legitimize the government in the eyes of its citizens. Indeed, life satisfaction has been associated with greater confidence in the government (Brehm & Rahn, 1997).

However, the benefits of a happy citizenry might extend beyond the mere fact of stability to the *flourishing* of entire communities. Thoits and Hewitt (2001) suggested that high well-being may be an important resource for individuals to draw upon, enabling them to contribute more time to volunteering. They found that well-being predicted the amount of volunteer work three years later, and that this relation was fully mediated by involvement with community organizations. The authors suggested that well-being may facilitate social integration, which in turn provides individuals with greater opportunities for volunteering. The reciprocal relation was also found. That is, volunteer work at Time 1 predicted well-being three years later. Thus, the relation between well-being and volunteerism may be bidirectional (cf. Piliavin, this volume).

Analyses From the World Value Survey

Using data from the second (1990–1991) and third (1995–1997) waves of the World Value Survey (WVS; Inglehart et al., 2003), we examined the relation among subjective well-being, trust, and cooperation at the nation level. Our analyses include 13 nations from the second wave, and 45 nations from the third wave of the WVS (see Appendix).

Main variables

All items were averaged across participants within each nation. We computed SWB by averaging two items measuring happiness and life satisfaction; scores range from 1 (dissatisfied and not at all happy) to 7 (satisfied and very happy). *Trust* scores reflect the percentage of respondents within a nation who believe that most people can be trusted. Previous analyses of the WVS have included trust and life satisfaction in a composite measure of "self-expression values" (Inglehart & Welzel, 2003). Values such as life satisfaction, trust, and tolerance reflect a regard for individual integrity. In our analyses, we dissect these self-expression values in order to more fully explore the relation of SWB and trust to cooperation.

We examined cooperation at the nation level in two ways. First, we examined mean levels of *volunteerism* (both the level of involvement and the number of voluntary associations). Second, we examined democratic attitudes and beliefs because such attitudes may reflect a cooperative orientation towards governance, political participation, and civic life. These measures included two indices of tolerance. The first is the percentage of respondents in a nation who believe that *tolerance* is an important quality for their children to possess. The WVS also presented respondents with a list of commonly stigmatized groups (e.g., homosexuals, people of different race, etc.) and asked them to indicate which, if any, they would not like to have as a neighbor. Thus, our second measure was an index of *intolerance* created by summing up the number of groups that were mentioned as undesirable neighbors.

We also created two overall measures of positive and negative attitudes towards democratic systems. *Positive attitudes* were the average of two items: the extent to which democracy was viewed as a "good way of governing" one's country, and the belief that democracy is "better than any other form of government." *Negative attitudes* were the average of three items assessing the belief that democracies have poor economic systems, are characterized by indecision and squabbling, and are not good at maintaining order. Other items we examined concerned attitudes toward *competition*, *autocracy* (government by a strong leader with no elections), *preference for a cooperative leader*, and *perceived democracy* (the percentage of respondents who believe the country is run for all people instead of just a "few big interests").

Respondents were also asked to prioritize a list of goals for their nation (e.g., fighting crime). These items have been used previously to measure postmaterialist values. According to Inglehart (2000), as wealth increases in a society, the emphasis shifts from economic growth to quality of life concerns. In our analyses, we concentrate on three of these goals: building a more humane society, giving people more say in their jobs and communities, and giving people more say on important government issues. Scores on these items reflect the percentage of respondents who selected the item as a major priority for their country for the next ten years.

Finally, we included three variables as economic, political, and cultural indicators. For each nation, we obtained data on real GDP *per capita* in constant 1996

Table 19.1 Intercorrelations among SWB, volunteering, attitudes, and societal variables

Variable	1	2	3	4	5	6	7	8	9	10
1 SWB	—									
2 Trust	.39**	—								
3 Vol. inv.[a]	.46***	.16	—							
4 Vol. no.[a]	.37**	.20	.96***	—						
5 Tolerance imp.	.53***	.39**	.24†	.25†	—					
6 Intolerance	−.61***	−.37**	−.10	−.11	−.63***	—				
7 Competition	−.07	−.03	.16	.18	−.06	.36**	—			
8 GDP/capita[a]	.50***	.49***	−.04	−.03	.65***	−.71***	−.32*	—		
9 Freedom	.43**	.38**	.01	.00	.58***	−.57***	−.30*	.79***	—	
10 Filial piety	−.42**	−.72***	−.04	−.10	−.64***	.52***	−.01	−.69***	−.50***	—

Note: N = 58. SWB = average of life satisfaction and happiness; Vol. inv. = level of volunteer involvement; Vol. no. = number of voluntary memberships; Tolerance imp. = importance of one's child possessing tolerance.

[a] Data were transformed via natural log.

† $p < .10$. *$p < .05$. **$p < .01$. ***$p < .001$.

dollars from the Penn World Tables (Heston, Summers, & Aten, 2002). We also obtained ratings of civil liberties and political rights for each nation from the *Freedom in the World* surveys (Freedom House, 2005). These ratings range from 1 (highest level of freedom) to 7 (lowest level of freedom). We reverse scored these ratings and averaged them so that high scores reflect societies with greater *freedom*. As a measure of social culture, we adapted a forced-choice item from the WVS assessing attitudes toward respect for parents. Respondents indicated whether they believed either that one should always love one's parents regardless of their faults, or that one is not obligated to love one's parents if they have not earned it through their attitudes and behaviors. We averaged these responses within nations, and normalized the distribution by applying an inverse transformation so that high scores reflected greater *filial piety*. In societies where filial piety is emphasized, close familial bonds may be highly valued and a stronger distinction might be made between ingroups and outgroups (Triandis, 1989). Thus, filial piety can be seen as a type of bonding social capital (Putnam, 2000) and might be associated with less generalized trust. When appropriate, data were transformed in order to normalize the distribution. For all analyses, we used an alpha level of .05 to evaluate statistical significance.

Results

SWB and trust were positively correlated (r = .39; see Table 19.1) as found in previous analyses of the WVS (Inglehart, 1999). SWB and trust were both associated with greater value placed on tolerance, less intolerance of neighbors, higher GDP per capita, greater freedom, and lower levels of filial piety. Both the level of volunteer involvement and the number of voluntary memberships were positively associated with SWB, but not with trust. However, the *nature* of volunteer involvement may also be important. Putnam (1993) maintained that interpersonal trust is likely to arise from involvement in *horizontal* organizations where members participate as equals. The exact nature of involvement is unclear from the WVS data. We examined specific voluntary memberships and found that the level of trust in a nation correlated with the level of involvement in unions (r = 28, p = .05). To the extent that unions often rely on collective action in the interest of all members, this may support Putnam's arguments (see also Radcliff, this volume). In contrast, memberships in other types of organizations (e.g., church, arts, political parties, etc.) were mostly unrelated to trust.

Interestingly, neither SWB nor trust was associated with attitudes toward competition. Nor were positive attitudes toward competition associated with volunteering or valuing tolerance. Thus, as other researchers have argued (Stanne et al., 1999; Tauer & Harackiewicz, 2004), competition is not inherently opposed to cooperation. The form that competition takes is an important consideration. The WVS asks respondents whether competition is good because it motivates hard work and new ideas, but it does not specify the type of competition. This might explain why societies that value tolerance do not necessarily oppose competition. In contrast, in those societies where intolerance is high, competition tends to be viewed more positively (r = .36). Perhaps in these societies, zero-sum competition is emphasized because it justifies inequities and intolerant attitudes. On the other hand, those countries in which intolerance is high also tend to be less wealthy, and have less freedom and greater filial piety. Thus intolerance and competition might follow from conditions in which resources are scarce, and relationships with one's family or ingroup become tighter as a matter of survival.

Table 19.2 presents the correlations of SWB and trust with various democratic attitudes. Here, trust and SWB show an interesting divergent but supportive pattern of correlations. For instance, SWB is associated with more positive attitudes toward democracy, greater *perceived* democracy, and more importance placed on giving people more say on important government decisions. Trust but not SWB was significantly associated with less negative attitudes toward democracy. Preference

Table 19.2 Correlations of SWB, trust, and GDP/capita with democratic attitudes

Variable	SWB	Trust	GDP/cap.[a]	N
Democracy (positive attitude)	.51**	.26[†]	.05	43
Democracy (negative attitude)	−.23	−.34*	−.04	41
Autocracy	−.52***	−.35*	−.37*	42
Cooperative leader	−.03	.27[†]	.13	42
Perceived democracy	.44**	.28[†]	.14	41
Value more humane society	.42**	.43**	.63***	57
Value more say in job/community	.51***	.43**	.69***	58
Value more say in government[b]	.40**	.14	.59***	58

Notes:

[a] Data were transformed via natural log.

[b] Data were transformed via arcsine of the square root.

[†] $p < .10$. *$p < .05$. **$p < .01$. ***$p < .001$.

for a cooperative leader was not correlated with SWB and had only a weak positive association with trust. Nevertheless, *both* SWB and trust were correlated with less approval of autocratic governance, and greater importance placed on building a more humane society and giving people more say in one's job and community. Taken together these findings suggest that national levels of SWB and trust are associated with a greater preference for participatory and cooperative approaches in government and civic life.

Interestingly, GDP per capita was not associated with either positive or negative attitudes toward democracy. However, several other attitudes do correlate with the wealth of a nation. As GDP per capita also correlates with SWB and trust, it is possible that some of the observed relations among SWB, trust, and cooperative behaviors and attitudes are due to the wealth of a nation, rather than its level of SWB or trust per se. Therefore, we conducted a series of regression analyses predicting volunteering and democratic attitudes from SWB and trust, after controlling for wealth, freedom, and filial piety. These analyses are presented in Table 19.3.

SWB and trust were no longer significant predictors of tolerance after controlling for other variables. For example, valuing tolerance appears to be strongly predicted by filial piety. In societies where filial piety is high and ingroup bonds are presumably stronger, people are less likely to mention tolerance as an important quality for their child to possess. This may mean that tolerance is not a salient value in these

Table 19.3 Regression analyses predicting volunteering and democratic attitudes

Dependent variable	Standardized regression coefficients (β)						
	GDP/cap.[a]	Freedom	Filial piety	Trust	SWB	R^2	N
Vol. inv.[a]	−.46[†]	.09	.14	.22	.62***	.34	54
Vol. no.[a]	−.45[†]	.07	.01	.22	.48**	.24	54
Tolerance imp.	.07	.24	−.52**	−.18	.18	.54	53
Intolerance	−.53**	−.01	−.06	−.05	−.32**	.59	54
Pos. dem	−.72**	.15	−.62**	−.01	.58***	.51	41
Neg. dem	.42	.13	.63*	−.09	−.21	.34	40
Autocracy	.11	−.05	.38	−.01	−.41*	.38	40
Perceived dem.	−.29	.20	.03	.25	.44**	.26	44
Humane soc.	.56*	−.03	.00	.12	.09	.44	55
More say (J/C)	.20	.46**	−.11	−.01	.21*	.69	55
More say (Govt)[b]	.37	.26	−.05	−.25	.18	.40	55

Notes: Vol. inv. = level of volunteer involvement; Vol. no. = number of voluntary memberships; Tolerance imp. = importance of one's child possessing tolerance; Pos. dem. = positive attitudes toward democracy; Neg. dem. = negative attitudes toward democracy; Autocracy = approval of strong leader with no elections; Perceived dem. = perceived democracy; Humane soc. = value more humane society; More say (J/C) = value more say in jobs and community; More say (Govt) = value more say on important government decisions.

[a] Data were transformed via natural log.

[b] Data were transformed via arcsine of the square root.

[†] p < .10. *p < .05. **p < .01. ***p < .001.

societies, rather than that tolerance is negatively regarded. In terms of intolerance, per capita GDP seems to account for much of the variance previously associated with trust and SWB. A number of explanations are possible. Diener et al. (1995) found that wealthier nations tended to have greater equality in terms of income and access to education. Education in turn might reduce stereotypic beliefs about stigmatized groups. Alternatively, intolerance may be a reflection of security needs. In wealthy nations, basic needs are better met and people are more likely to feel safe and secure. As a result, they might also feel less threatened by neighbors who are different from them.

After controlling for filial piety, trust was no longer significantly associated with negative attitudes toward democracy. Societies that value filial piety appear to hold more negative attitudes toward democracy (β = .63, p <.05). However, mean level attitudes for most nations fall between 2 and 3 on a four-point Likert scale. This suggests that countries that are high on filial piety agree only slightly that democracies are flawed and inefficient, while countries that are lower on filial piety only *disagree* slightly with these beliefs. Thus, few countries fully despise democracy. Rather, these associations may be due to greater sense of empowerment among individualistic nations (e.g., the Scandinavian countries), which tend to be lower on filial piety.

After controlling for wealth, freedom, filial piety, and trust, SWB was no longer predictive of the importance placed on either building a more humane society or giving people more say on important government matters. However, SWB continued to show a strong relation with several other variables. For instance, the relation between SWB and volunteering does not appear to be fully accounted for by GDP per capita. These findings are consistent with those of Thoits and Hewitt (2001), who found evidence for a bi-directional relation between well-being and volunteering, even after controlling for family income. Thus, in countries where SWB is high, people may be more likely to possess the psychological resources (e.g., optimism, resilience, sociability) to engage in volunteer work. At the same time, increasing volunteer involvement may also increase social capital and subsequently, well-being.

After controlling for wealth and freedom, countries that are high on SWB continue to have higher mean levels of perceived democracy, positive attitudes toward democracy, greater disapproval of autocratic rule, and less intolerant attitudes. Moreover, wealth and freedom do not fully account for the relation between SWB and the increasing value placed on giving people more say in their job and community, although freedom remained a significant predictor.

Although more research is needed, the findings above generally support our contention that SWB and cooperation have important social implications. In societies where SWB is high, people tend to prefer a government and civic life in which all people can participate. Just as well, in societies where community participation (i.e., volunteerism) is high, people tend to be happier. Although we did not find consistent relations between trust and democratic attitudes after controlling for other variables, it should be noted that many of these variables are intercorrelated. For example, societal levels of generalized trust were strongly linked to the endorsement of filial piety (r = −.72). If societal levels of trust reflect cultural beliefs about human nature or social relations that are strongly embodied in filial attitudes, then the substantive meaning of trust could be lost when controlling for filial piety. Cultural knowledge can have important influences on trust and cooperation (Wong & Hong, 2005; Yuki, Maddux, Brewer, & Takemura, 2005). Thus, in some cases, we may be over-controlling for these variables in the regression models. Given the strong link between GDP per capita and SWB then, it is interesting that

SWB should maintain strong links with several democratic and cooperative attitudes after controlling for wealth. These findings support previous arguments that SWB plays an important role in sustaining and legitimizing participatory forms of government such as democracy (Inglehart & Klingemann, 2000).

Discussion

Recent analyses indicate troubling social trends in the US. According to several researchers, generalized trust has declined over the past few decades among American teenagers and adults (Putnam, 2000; Rahn & Transue, 1998; Uslaner, 2002). Various causes have been proposed from increases in materialistic values (Rahn & Transue, 1998) to decreasing social capital (Putnam, 2000) to greater economic inequality (Uslaner, 2002).

Our analyses indicate that societies that are high on SWB are also higher on trust, volunteerism, and several democratic attitudes—even after controlling for GDP per capita and freedom. Although attitudes are subjective, it is worth pointing out that volunteer involvement is a fairly objective behavioral indicator. It is therefore impressive that national SWB should manifest strong relations to the number of associations that people join in a society. A critical implication of our results is that SWB accompanies both attitudes *and* behaviors that are conducive to building a more trusting, cooperative society. Although our analyses do not speak to causality, both directions of influence are supported by research. Experimental data suggest that positive emotions and greater SWB play a causal role by fostering greater sociability, trust, and cooperation. In positive moods, people tend to view others and be viewed *by* others more positively, show increased preference for cooperation, and are more likely to be active and involved in their communities. At the same time, trust and cooperation are important tools for building social connections, which are key ingredients for sustained happiness.

We do not argue that increasing SWB is the panacea for all our social ills. Positive emotions do not invariably lead to more trust and cooperation; social norms (Hertel et al., 2000) are also important. However, we do contend that SWB is a *necessary* condition for a flourishing society. No society can count on sustaining trust and cooperation when its citizens are discontented. The strong relation between national levels of SWB and cooperation underscore this point.

As nations around the world press on with economic development and establishing political stability, greater cooperation must occur on the international stage. This will entail the recognition and acceptance of common goals that all countries must work toward. Promoting subjective well-being should be one of these goals. If all countries are fundamentally interdependent, then sustaining the well-being of any single nation should be in the interests of all other nations. To the extent that SWB facilitates trust and cooperation, the promotion of SWB through international acts of goodwill is the quintessential non-zero-sum solution.

To this end, it will be necessary to develop national indicators that move beyond economic indices (Diener, 2000; Diener & Seligman, 2004; Diener & Tov, in press). Traditionally, economic measures have been used as a proxy for well-being—and with good reason. Economic development is strongly linked to SWB. Particularly when an economy is developing and the fulfillment of basic needs is at risk, GDP per capita has a clear impact on SWB. However, as societies become wealthier, the utility of objective economic indicators of well-being diminishes. As Radcliff (this volume) shows, other structural aspects of society such as welfare provisions and union organization are also associated with aggregate levels of SWB. We agree with him that social institutions can be structured in ways that optimize cooperation and well-being. In order for this to happen, local and national governments need to be involved, and changes in well-being must be monitored in ways that can inform policy decisions. National measures of trust, community feelings, life satisfaction, pleasant and unpleasant affect need to be developed and implemented over successive periods of time. Consequently, room must be made on national agendas for maximizing well-being in addition to maximizing economic output.

Appendix

Analyses of the World Values Survey includes nations from the 1990–1993 wave (Austria, Belgium, Canada, Czech Republic, Denmark, France, Iceland, Ireland, Italy, Netherlands, Portugal, Romania, Slovakia) and the 1995–1997 wave (Argentina, Armenia, Australia, Azerbaijan, Bangladesh, Belarus, Bosnia and Herzegovina, Brazil, Britain, Bulgaria, Chile, China, Colombia, Croatia, Dominican Republic, Estonia, Finland, Georgia, Germany, Ghana, India, Japan, Latvia, Lithuania, Macedonia, Mexico, Moldova, Nigeria, Norway, Peru, Philippines, Poland, Russia, Serbia and Montenegro, Slovenia, South Africa, Spain, Sweden, Switzerland, Taiwan, Turkey, Ukraine, Uruguay, United States, Venezuela).

Acknowledgement

This work was supported by a National Science Foundation Graduate Fellowship awarded to William Tov.

References

Aderman, D. (1972). Elation, depression, and helping behavior. *Journal of Personality and Social Psychology, 24*, 91–101.

Baron, R. A., & Bronfen, M. I. (1994). A whiff of reality: Empirical evidence concerning the effects of pleasant fragrances on work-related behavior. *Journal of Applied Social Psychology, 24*, 1179–1203.

Barsade, S. G. (2002). The ripple effects: Emotional contagion and its influence on group behavior. *Administrative Science Quarterly, 47*, 644–675.

Barsade, S. G., Ward, A. J., Turner, J. D. F., & Sonnenfeld, J. A. (2000). To your heart's content: A model of affective diversity in top management teams. *Administrative Science Quarterly, 45,* 802–836.

Borman, W. C., Penner, L. A., Allen, T. D., & Motowidlo, S. J. (2001). Personality predictors of citizenship performance. *International Journal of Selection and Assessment, 9,* 52–69.

Brehm, J., & Rahn, W. (1997). Individual-level evidence for the causes and consequences of social capital. *American Journal of Political Science, 41,* 999–1023.

Cacioppo, J. T., Ernst, J. M., Burleson, M. H., McClintock, M. K., Malarkey, W. B., Hawkley, L. C., et al. (2000). Lonely traits and concomitant physiological processes: The MacArthur social neuroscience studies. *International Journal of Psychophysiology, 35,* 143–154.

Costa, P. T., & McCrae, R. R. (1980). Influence of extraversion and neuroticism on subjective well-being: Happy and unhappy people. *Journal of Personality and Social Psychology, 54,* 296–308.

Cunningham, M. R. (1988a). Does happiness mean friendliness? Induced mood and heterosexual self-disclosure. *Personality and Social Psychology Bulletin, 14,* 283–297.

Cunningham, M. R. (1988b). What do you do when you're happy or blue? Mood, expectancies, and behavioral interest. *Motivation & Emotion, 12,* 309–331.

De Cremer, D. (2004). The influence of accuracy as a function of leader's bias: The role of trustworthiness in the psychology of procedural justice. *Personality and Social Psychology Bulletin, 30,* 293–304.

Derryberry, D., & Reed, M. A. (1994). Temperament and attention: Orienting toward and away from positive and negative signals. *Journal of Personality and Social Psychology, 66,* 1128–1139.

Desforges, D. M., Lord, C. G., Ramsey, S. L., Mason, J. A., Van Leeuwen, M. D., West, S. C., et al. (1991). Effects of structured cooperative contact on changing negative attitudes toward stigmatized social groups. *Journal of Personality and Social Psychology, 60,* 531–544.

Diener, E. (2000). Subjective well-being: The science of happiness and a proposal for a national index. *American Psychologist, 55,* 34–43.

Diener, E., & Diener, M. (1995). Cross-cultural correlates of life satisfaction and self-esteem. *Journal of Personality and Social Psychology, 68,* 653–663.

Diener, E., Diener, M., & Diener, C. (1995). Factors predicting the subjective well-being of nations. *Journal of Personality and Social Psychology, 69,* 851–864.

Diener, E., & Fujita, F. (1995). Resources, personal strivings, and subjective well-being: A nomothetic and idiographic approach. *Journal of Personality and Social Psychology, 68,* 926–935.

Diener, E., Nickerson, C., Lucas, R. E., & Sandvik, E. (2002). Dispositional affect and job outcomes. *Social Indicators Research, 59,* 229–259.

Diener, E., & Seligman, M. E. P. (2002). Very happy people. *Psychological Science, 13,* 81–84.

Diener, E., & Seligman, M. E. P. (2004). Beyond money: Toward an economy of well-being. *Psychological Science in the Public Interest, 5,* 1–31.

Diener, E., Suh, E. M., Lucas, R. E., & Smith, H. E. (1999). Subjective well-being: Three decades of progress. *Psychological Bulletin, 125,* 276–302.

Diener, E., & Tov, W. (in press). National accounts of well-being. In K. C. Land (Ed.), *Handbook of social indicators and quality-of-life research.* New York: Springer.

Dunn, J. R., & Schweitzer, M. E. (2005). Feeling and believing: The influence of emotion on trust. *Journal of Personality and Social Psychology, 88,* 736–748.

Eisenberg, N. (1991). Meta-analytic contributions to the literature on prosocial behavior. *Personality and Social Psychology Bulletin, 17,* 273–282.

Enzle, M. E., & Anderson, S. C. (1993). Surveillant intentions and intrinsic motivation. *Journal of Personality and Social Psychology, 2,* 257–266.

Forgas, J. P. (1998). On feeling good and getting your way: Mood effects on negotiator cognition and bargaining strategies. *Journal of Personality and Social Psychology, 74,* 565–577.

Freedom House (2005). *Freedom in the World country ratings.* Retrieved September 6, 2005 from, http://www.freedomhouse.org/ratings/allscores2005.xls.

Harker, L., & Keltner, D. (2001). Expressions of positive emotions in women's college yearbook pictures and their relationship to personality and life outcomes across adulthood. *Journal of Personality and Social Psychology, 80,* 112–124.

Hertel, G., Neuhof, J., Theuer, T., & Kerr, N. L. (2000). Mood effects on cooperation in small groups: Does positive mood simply lead to more cooperation? *Cognition and Emotion, 14,* 441–472.

Heston, A., Summers, R., & Aten, B. (2002). *Penn World Table Version 6.1,* Center for International Comparisons at the University of Pennsylvania.

Hornstein, H. A., LaKind, E., Frankel, G., & Manne, S. (1975). Effects of knowledge about remote social events on prosocial behavior, social conception, and mood. *Journal of Personality and Social Psychology, 32,* 1038–1046.

Inglehart, R. (1999). Trust, well-being, and democracy. In M. E. Warren (Ed.), *Democracy and trust* (pp. 88–120). Cambridge, UK: Cambridge University Press.

Inglehart, R. (2000). Globalization and postmodern values. *Washington Quarterly, 23,* 215–228.

Inglehart, R., Carballo de Cilley, M., Pogosian, G., Klingemann, H.-D., Black, A., Aliev, A., et al. (2003). *World Values Surveys and European Values Surveys, 1981–1984, 1990–1993, and 1995–1997* [Computer file, ICPSR02790-v1]. Ann Arbor, MI: Inter-university Consortium for Political and Social Research.

Inglehart, R., & Klingemann, H.-D. (2000). Genes, culture, democracy, and happiness. In E. Diener & E. M. Suh (Eds.), *Culture and subjective well-being* (pp. 185–218). Cambridge, MA: MIT Press.

Inglehart, R., & Welzel, C. (2003). Political culture and democracy: Analysing cross-level linkages. *Comparative Politics, 36,* 61–79.

Isen, A. M., & Levin, P. F. (1972). Effect of feeling good on helping: Cookies and kindness. *Journal of Personality and Social Psychology, 21,* 384–388.

King, L. A., & Napa, C. K. (1998). What makes a life good? *Journal of Personality and Social Psychology, 75,* 156–165.

Kramer, R. M. (1999). Trust and distrust in organizations: Emerging perspectives, enduring questions. *Annual Review of Psychology, 50,* 569–598.

Krueger, R. F., Hicks, B. M., & McGue, M. (2001). Altruism and antisocial behavior: Independent tendencies, unique personality correlates, distinct etiologies. *Psychological Science, 12,* 397–402.

Lu, L., & Argyle, M. (1991). Happiness and cooperation. *Personality and Individual Differences, 12,* 1019–1030.

Lucas, R. E., Clark, A. E., Georgellis, Y., & Diener, E. (2003). Reexamining adaptation and the set point model of happiness: Reactions to changes in marital status. *Journal of Personality and Social Psychology*, *84*, 527–539.

Lyubomirsky, S., King, L., & Diener, E. (2005). The benefits of frequent positive affect: Does happiness lead to success? *Psychological Bulletin*, *131*, 803–855.

Myers, D. G. (2000). The funds, friends, and faith of happy people. *American Psychologist*, *55*, 56–67.

Oishi, S., Diener, E. F., Lucas, R. E., & Suh, E. M. (1999). Cross-cultural variations in predictors of life satisfaction: Perspectives from needs and values. *Personality and Social Psychology Bulletin*, *25*, 980–990.

Oishi, S., Diener, E., Scollon, C. N., & Biswas-Diener, R. (2003). Cross-situational consistency of affective experiences across cultures. *Journal of Personality and Social Psychology*, *86*, 460–472.

Organ, D. W., & Ryan, K. (1995). A meta-analytic review of attitudinal and dispositional predictors of organizational citizenship behavior. *Personnel Psychology*, *48*, 775–802.

Parks, C. D., Henager, R. F., & Scamahorn, S. D. (1996). Trust and reactions to messages of intent in social dilemmas. *Journal of Conflict Resolution*, *40*, 134–151.

Putnam, R. D. (1993). *Making democracy work: Civic traditions in modern Italy.* Princeton, NJ: Princeton University Press.

Putnam, R. D. (2000). *Bowling alone: The collapse and revival of American community.* New York: Simon & Schuster.

Rahn, W. M., & Transue, J. E. (1998). Social trust and value change: The decline of social capital in American youth, 1976–1995. *Political Psychology*, *19*, 545–565.

Sanna, L. J., Parks, C. D., & Chang, E. C. (2003). Mixed-motive conflict in social dilemmas: Mood as input to competitive and cooperative goals. *Group Dynamics: Theory, Research, and Practice*, *7*, 26–40.

Stanne, M. B., Johnson, D. W., & Johnson, R. T. (1999). Does competition enhance or inhibit motor performance? A meta-analysis. *Psychological Bulletin*, *125*, 133–154.

Tauer, J. M., & Harackiewicz, J. M. (2004). The effects of cooperation and competition on intrinsic motivation and performance. *Journal of Personality and Social Psychology*, *86*, 849–861.

Terrell, F., Terrell, I. S., & Von Drashek, S. R. (2000). Loneliness and fear of intimacy among adolescents who were taught not to trust strangers during childhood. *Adolescence*, *35*, 611–617.

Thoits, P. A., & Hewitt, L. N. (2001). Volunteer work and well-being. *Journal of Health and Social Behavior*, *42*, 115–131.

Triandis, H. C. (1989). The self and social behavior in differing cultural contexts. *Psychological Review*, *96*, 506–520.

Uslaner, E. M. (1998). Social capital, television, and the "mean world": Trust, optimism, and civic participation. *Political Psychology*, *19*, 441–467.

Uslaner, E. M. (2002). *The moral foundations of trust.* Cambridge, UK: Cambridge University Press.

Williams, S., & Shiaw, W. T. (1999). Mood and organizational citizenship behavior: The effects of positive affect on employee organizational citizenship behavior intentions. *Journal of Psychology*, *133*, 656–668.

Wong, R. Y., & Hong, Y. (2005). Dynamic influences of culture on cooperation in the prisoner's dilemma. *Psychological Science*, *16*, 429–434.

Wright, R. (2000). *Nonzero: The logic of human destiny.* New York: Pantheon Books.

Yamagishi, T., & Sato, K. (1986). Motivational bases of the public goods problem. *Journal of Personality and Social Psychology, 50,* 67–73.

Yuki, M., Maddux, W. W., Brewer, M. B., & Takemura, K. (2005). Cross-cultural differences in relationship- and group-based trust. *Personality and Social Psychology Bulletin, 31,* 48–62.

20

The Political Psychology of Cooperation

Synthesis and Prospects

BRANDON A. SULLIVAN, MARK SNYDER,
JOHN L. SULLIVAN, AND CHRISTOPHER CHAPP

The chapters in this book have aimed to make the study of cooperation both more accessible and more approachable. The research presented herein has made enormous strides toward understanding the antecedents and consequences of cooperation, as well as the mechanisms by which it works. Cooperation, we have learned, is not necessarily a straightforward process. Indeed, three chapters in this volume are actually titled with the word "paradox." We take this as evidence of the inherent complexity of cooperative processes, and the necessity of continued research. However, despite the fact that cooperative processes generate paradoxical conclusions, the research in this book has been able to analyze these processes in an extremely sophisticated and systematic manner. This leads to a second general conclusion, that this research on cooperation suggests ways not only to understand cooperation but also to build it. This volume contains concrete implications for how to develop more cooperative dispositions and how to help societies structure more cooperative institutions.

The focus of the chapters in this volume has thus been on "what we know" as opposed to "what we still have to learn," and, while the latter question could certainly frame an entire volume in its own right, we argue that by integrating cross-disciplinary multi-method research, these chapters have greatly advanced our understanding of cooperation. This volume was structured with this integrative framework in mind—chapters were paired across disciplines along the lines of eight important topical questions. This organization emphasized the commonalities across fields. Thus, the authors have presented succinct treatments of cooperation and individual predispositions (chapters 2 and 3), developmental precursors (chapters 4–6), within group cooperation (chapters 7 and 8), cooperation between diverse groups (chapters 9–10), workplace cooperation (chapters 11–13), the health of individuals and communities (chapters 14 and 15), negotiation and conflict resolution (chapters 16 and 17), and the well-being of individuals and nations (18 and 19).

Table 20.1

	Function		
	Individual well-being	*Group viability*	*Guidance for investing in groups*
Effects of cooperation?	Tov and Diener Piliavin	Hanley, Hartwig, Morikawa, and Orbell Hibbing and Theiss-Morse	Greenberg
How and why cooperation effects functioning?	Radcliff Colbert, Bono, and Purvanova Eisenberg and Eggum	Rahn Oliver and Ha Ronson and Peterson	O'Connor Regan
How to facilitate cooperation?	Milburn and Liss	Tyler Dovidio, Gaertner, and Esses Monroe and Etow	Van Lange

In this final chapter, we explore an additional organizational scheme, aimed at answering the three foundational and overarching questions with which this volume began: First, what are the effects of cooperation with regard to individual and group well-being and functioning? Second, how and why does cooperation influence individual and group functioning? Finally, how can institutions, policies, and procedures be designed in order to optimally facilitate cooperation? The answers to these questions come from diverse disciplines. Indeed, a quick look at the chapters' reference sections will reveal that there is little overlap in the research cited by each individual author. Despite this lack of overlap in literatures, however, there exists *remarkable overlap in theoretic perspectives and thematic concerns, and empirical conclusions that are generally compatible.*

Table 20.1 summarizes the chapters along the lines suggested by these foundational questions. While each chapter could appropriately occupy several cells in the table, this organization illustrates how diverse fields approach the scientific study of cooperation with both theoretic and empirical consistency. Accordingly, this chapter revisits each of the foundational questions with which this volume began with respect to three basic cooperative functions: individual well-being, group viability, and guidance for how we invest in groups.

Cooperation and Individual Well-being

Effects of cooperation on individual well-being

Since cooperation is, by definition, an interaction between individuals, the potential certainly exists to overlook how cooperation is related to individual-level outcomes. Tov and Diener's chapter on nations and Piliavin's longitudinal research provide strong evidence that the individual stands to benefit a great deal from cooperative behaviors that bring about greater social connectedness.

Tov and Diener find evidence of a strong reciprocal relationship between subjective well-being (SWB) and cooperation. Individuals who trust and experience positive emotions tend to view others positively, are viewed by others in a positive frame, and subsequently tend to cooperate more. Reciprocally, cooperation itself is essential for building the shared social experience that is necessary for experiencing positive emotions. Numerous studies document how, via cooperation, social support and relationships form the basis of a happy life. Tov and Diener's own analysis supports the existence of this relationship with respect to both cooperative attitudes and cooperative behaviors. Even when controlling for GDP, a strong relationship between volunteer behavior and SWB persists, as well as trust and pro-democratic attitudes. That is to say, holding standard of living constant across countries, SWB "accompanies both attitudes *and* behaviors that are conducive to building a more trusting, cooperative society" (p. 337). If we wish to foster cooperative behavior in society, then, we thus must focus on both the financial and the psychological resources that precede cooperative behaviors.

While Tov and Diener's analysis provides strong evidence that cooperation is related to individual well-being across varied cultures and governmental systems, Piliavin's use of longitudinal survey data speaks directly to the *direction* of this relationship. Piliavin's findings suggest that cooperative behavior (specifically, altruistically oriented volunteer behavior) brings about greater levels of both physical and psychological health in the individual. In addition, more volunteering generally brings about even greater benefits to the individual, and the benefits of cooperative behavior are the greatest for those individuals who are the least well-integrated into society. Volunteering, Piliavin concludes, contributes to the individual's sense of "mattering."

Piliavin's conclusions comport well with Tov and Diener's research on nations. First, it is significant that both chapters find large effects even with controls in place for prior levels of psychological well-being and GDP. Thus, these chapters are an important response to the reasonable suggestion that cooperation's apparent effects on well-being are actually the product of some other factor (like national wealth). Second, despite the fact that both chapters examine cooperation through a very different lens, the effects they observe bear important similarities. Tov and Diener argue that cooperation works as a "tool" for building healthy social connections, and that this, in turn, engenders positive emotions. Likewise, Piliavin's research suggests that volunteer behavior brings about well-being by integrating individuals into society. Cooperation's effects—working through social connectedness, a sense of mattering and identity, and positive emotions—resound throughout this volume as essential features of healthy individuals and groups alike.

Empathy and meaning as key mechanisms in the cooperative process

If cooperation is intertwined with individual well-being in complex yet consistent ways, the mechanisms underlying this process deserve careful attention. Contributions from Radcliff, Colbert, Bono, and Purvanova, and Eisenberg and Eggum use varied approaches to explain how cooperation affects individual well-being. Despite dissimilarity in approach, we find common mechanisms at play in all three chapters—evidence that both comports with and elaborates the contributions from Piliavin and Tov and Diener. While these accounts have important nuances, at each level of analysis we find that empathy and a sense of meaning provide key bridges between cooperation and well-being.

Radcliff argues that the welfare state and the labor union—two organizational structures that foster cooperative interactions—lead individuals to greater life satisfaction. Radcliff's emphasis on these two "macro" organizations, as opposed to "micro" organizations like church groups and sports teams, is, in part, in the interest of practicality. These are organizations we know how to "grow" in societies, through policy making and funding. These cooperative organizational structures are characterized by distinct mechanisms theoretically linked to greater individual happiness.

Radcliff's chapter presents evidence that welfare state policies tend toward greater life satisfaction. This link, Radcliff argues, is caused by the unique effects economic forces exert on individual predispositions. Market capitalism is characterized by high levels of uncertainty and dependence on market forces. Indeed, compared to socialistic market systems, individuals in capitalist countries will be subject to less autonomy and greater economic insecurity. This uncertainty and lack of control, coupled with greater economic inequality, leads toward greater "psychological stress." Accordingly, the greater the "emancipation" from market-generated stresses, the more individuals will experience psychological well-being and a sense of autonomy. Radcliff reviews research and analyzes new evidence that bears out this basic contention—greater levels of decommodification are related to higher levels of life satisfaction.

Unions also work to increase life satisfaction, both directly and indirectly. Directly, unionization increases job satisfaction in straightforward ways (such as creating a safe working environment), which of course extends to overall life satisfaction. Unions also reduce alienation, providing for greater autonomy and self-direction. In addition, unions serve as a social network connecting workers in solidarity, a mechanism which has been widely documented to increase life satisfaction. These mechanisms are consistent with Piliavin's notion of social integration, and Tov and Diener's account of social connectedness. Unions also affect life satisfaction indirectly. Individual happiness is contagious, and thus even non-union members stand to benefit from union members with whom they interact on a regular basis. And, labor unions tend to produce welfare state policies, which in turn reduce various stressors. In short, Radcliff finds strong evidence that cooperative institutional features increase the well-being of the population through a variety of mechanisms.

Colbert, Bono, and Purvanova's chapter provides important points of contrast and comparison with Radcliff's chapter. Unlike Radcliff's research on institutions, research on generative leadership focuses on organizational climate and leadership style. In addition, while subjective well-being is the main dependent variable in Radcliff's work, Colbert and colleagues find that generative leadership has a wide array of benefits, including well-being, but also including worker productivity, the sustainability of business organizations, and so on. Despite differences, however, these chapters have a good deal in common, insofar as they identify similar processes by which cooperation increases human happiness.

Colbert, Bono, and Purvanova's main focus is on generative leadership, a leadership style characterized by focus on long-term organizational sustainability, employee engagement in work, and the growth and development of employees. The authors describe generative leaders as "driven by communal motives," which typically include qualities such as compassion and generosity. Generative leaders enhance workplace cooperation by forming high-quality relationships with employees, and by encouraging high-quality relationships among employees. These relationships tend to be highly cooperative, insofar as they "help a group advance its thinking" and reinforce "a positive social climate within a group."

Leaders, thus, can affect the relative cooperativeness of relationships within an organization. These cooperative relationships fulfill a very basic human need for caring social contact. They help give individuals a sense of meaning in their lives, and increase the perception of connectedness with fellow employees. And, the behavior exhibited by generative leaders tends to be mimicked by others within the organization. In short, Colbert, Bono, and Purvanova treat generative leadership as a sort of exogenous mover, promoting the reciprocal relationship between high-quality (cooperative) relationships and employee well-being.

A number of important connections exist between Radcliff's research on nations and the characteristics of generative workplaces. First, it is significant that the characteristics of union workplaces thought to bring about greater well-being are quite similar to the qualities generative leaders bring to bear on organizations: They exhibit genuine care and concern for the psychological well-being of employees. They create a sense of meaning and attachment to the goals of the organization (as opposed to, say, detachment from the material means of production). And of course, generative leaders create a strong connectedness among workers, with mutual caring, trust, and a sense of shared goals. A second similarity between these chapters is a focus on the practicality of the project. As mentioned, Radcliff researches unions and welfare policy in part because they are institutions we know how to alter. Likewise, there is emerging interest in how to develop generative leaders. Management development may encourage generative leadership, and organizational culture can provide resources to support generative behavior. In addition, management recruitment can be conducted with an eye toward generative qualities.

The chapters by Radcliff and Colbert et al. thus walk the path from institutional and organizational arrangements to psychological well-being, focusing specifically on the macro-level arrangements (like policy and leadership) that encourage cooperation. Eisenberg and Eggum take a more micro-oriented approach, reviewing the specific cognitive and affective mechanisms that make cooperation possible.

Eisenberg and Eggum's chapter focuses on "empathy-related emotions," which serve as a source of prosocial behavior (i.e. voluntary helping), as well as other positive social functions. The authors begin by making an important distinction among empathy, sympathy, and personal distress. The latter, which is a "self-focused, aversive affective reaction to the apprehension of another's emotion" is consistently negatively related or unrelated to prosocial behavior across a wide variety of studies. Empathy and sympathy, in contrast, are consistently related to high levels of prosocial behavior and low levels of antisocial behavior in children.

The authors also review three sociocognitive factors responsible for prosocial tendencies. Inducing "perspective taking," which involves the ability to put one's self in another's place, is related to prosocial behavior under certain conditions. Likewise, the capacity to understand one's own emotions is theorized to create the ability to empathize. Moral reasoning skills are also related to a variety of prosocial behaviors. These sociocognitive skills bear a complex relationship to the ability to sympathize, empathize, and exhibit prosocial behavior. Eisenberg and Eggum conclude that "it is important to foster the capacity for moral affect (such as sympathy) as well as moral values (as reflected in moral reasoning) rather than to merely try to stimulate perspective taking, at least for people with typical levels of sociocognitive skills."

Eisenberg and Eggum contrast with Radcliff and Colbert et al. in terms of how prosocial behavior is induced. In the Eisenberg and Eggum studies, sympathy, empathy, personal distress, and other emotive states are typically induced through some sort of stimulus—a short film, for example—instead of macro-level structural forces. However, while these chapters are dissimilar in focus, the mechanisms responsible for creating healthy societies bear considerable substantive overlap.

For example, Radcliff follows the writings of Albert Einstein to mark distinctions between individuals' "private" drive for self preservation, and a "social" drive, "to gain the recognition and affection of [one's] fellow human beings, to share in their pleasures, to comfort them in their sorrows." This distinction provides an important theoretic rationale for Radcliff's findings: certain institutions tend to satisfy this social drive, facilitating deep connections among individuals in society, generating more cooperation and individual well-being. Colbert and colleagues imply a similar basic need for high-quality interpersonal relationships, necessary to bring about "hedonic" and "eudaemonic" well-being. Eisenberg and Eggum's chapter can be thought of, in many ways, as an empirical examination of these basic human drives. Empathy and sympathy are robustly correlated with cooperation, and are thought to mitigate other social ills, such as prejudice and dehumanization. While Eisenberg and Eggum focus on childhood socialization, it is no stretch to apply the psychological mechanisms identified in their chapter to the socializing effects of institutions. We see great promise for interdisciplinary research exploring the interactions between institutional conditions and the psychological dispositions they nurture.

Facilitating the development of cooperative individuals

The previous sections provide evidence that cooperation can cause greater well-being, and suggest mechanisms that engender this relationship across diverse contexts. Milburn and Liss make an important contribution by demonstrating how to facilitate this linkage, examining the effects of childhood punishment over the course of a lifetime. The authors examine the process of emotional displacement, whereby parties displace an emotion from one situation to another. In particular, Milburn and Liss examine how childhood experiences may manifest in the form of cooperative or conflictive behaviors later in life. "Family experiences," they contend, "are a major source of shame and other personal motives that individuals carry with them and displace onto others, contributing to intractable conflicts." Milburn and Liss find that these experiences—in particular childhood corporal punishment—cause long-term affect displacement, manifested as higher levels of authoritarianism, sexual harassment, etc. In other words, childhood socialization can be a major impediment to the development of cooperative predispositions.

Milburn and Liss thus suggest a somewhat different means to bring about cooperation than the chapters that focus strictly on institutional design. While restructuring a workplace or a government institution may certainly encourage social connectedness, fostering cooperative dispositions begins at a much earlier age. These two schools of thought are not mutually exclusive—as Van Lange notes in his chapter, cooperation is a function of both the person and the situation. Thus, as the authors contend, public policy should not only focus on institutions conducive to cooperation, but it should also promote laws that enhance cooperative orientations.

Group Viability

Chapters discussed in the previous section provide a robust account of cooperation and individual well-being. Cooperating, or even membership in a group that cooperates, produces significantly higher levels of individual well-being. Across levels of analysis, empathy and empathetic relationships are a key mechanism linking cooperation to well-being. In addition, abating personal distress and fostering genuine connections between people tends to increase individual well-being.

Above and beyond this tremendous benefit, it might be asked, how does cooperation affect the success of groups as a whole? Are cooperative groups more successful, or are competitive social arrangements more conducive to the long-term success of the group? This is a fundamental question if we are to design societal arrangements with an eye toward long-term goals and sustained happiness. Indeed, the benefits of cooperation for individual well-being are likely to be lost if cooperative relationships do not also ensure the long-term survival of the group. In this section we find strong evidence, from diverse disciplinary perspectives, that cooperative groups also tend to be flourishing groups.

Evolutionary perspectives on the long-term survival of groups

One recurrent theme in this volume is the notion that "rational choice" models often provide incomplete or insufficient understandings of human behavior. The rational choice model of human decision making posits that individuals are fundamentally rational maximizers of their own utility—all else being equal, humans will make decisions that benefit themselves, even to the detriment of the group. Several authors have noted that this model of human behavior can complicate studies of cooperation, which we define in terms of collective benefit. For example, Tyler distinguishes between "social" and "self-interested" motivations for cooperating. Monroe argues that the "mere existence of altruism challenges the universality" of rational decision making models. Van Lange's chapter reviews several "interpersonal orientations" to the end of developing a more accurate understanding of human nature than that which is explicit in interest-maximizing frameworks.

If cooperation is not a disposition (or behavior) which exists strictly to maximize individual utility, why does cooperation exist in the first place? Or, stated differently, why do cooperative societies exist as opposed to strictly "rational" societies composed of aggregations of self-interested utility maximizers? Evolutionary theories of cooperative groups, presented in several chapters in this volume, provide elegant answers to these basic questions. Cooperative societies are self-sustaining, and have certain adaptive advantages over societies where people act as individuals in a purely selfish manner.

Hanley, Hartwig, Morikawa, and Orbell respond to the rationality paradigm (in their words, "rationality in action") using evolutionary theory. The alternative "rationality in design" perspective is one parsimonious alternative to interest-based accounts of human nature. The research design, unlike any other used in this volume, utilizes computer simulations to explore the trajectory societies would take, given assumptions about human nature that are informed by what we know of actual human behavior. For example, individuals may be predisposed to cooperate or act selfishly, individuals have varied abilities to predict others' behavior, and so on. These qualities combine to produce individuals with varied levels of reproductive fitness. Over the course of generations, inherited traits are passed on, changing the dispositional makeup of the population as a whole.

The chapter finds striking evidence that, given realistic starting parameters, cooperative behavior will naturally emerge in society. The characteristic of "mindreading" is initially selected for (being an advantageous adaptation), which in turn creates conditions for the "upward drift" of cooperative dispositions in society. Eventually, equilibriums emerge characterized by high numbers of individuals with cooperative dispositions. Thus, while the individual is not fully rational, society evolves in a collectively functional manner.

Hibbing and Theiss-Morse propose a related model to account for their findings, suggesting that human society has evolved selecting for individuals who are "wary cooperators." Cooperation is not "socially learned"—it is hardwired. However, much like Hanley et al.'s discussion of "mindreading," individuals don't want to be "played for a sucker." Thus, although humans may naturally have cooperative dispositions, they are also suspicious of potential free riding. Contrary to many rational choice models, individuals cooperate readily when they have reason to trust in future reciprocity. This theory helps explain the mixed results obtained by adding "voice" to the process of decision making.

We see a good deal of promise in evolution-based models of cooperation. These models first provide evidence of the long-term sustainability of cooperative groups—and even their advantages against groups premised on sheer competition. These chapters also demonstrate how behavior that is not narrowly self-interested (in the strictest sense of the term) can emerge naturally in society, and how this behavior is indeed functional for the long-term success of the group.

Group viability across contexts: Cooperation, conflict and trust

In *Democracy in America*, Tocqueville argues that if democratic people do "not learn some habits of acting together in the affairs of daily life, civilization itself would be in peril." The chapters in this volume vindicate much of Tocqueville's concern. Not cooperating has distinct consequences for the functioning of groups. The research presented in this volume also identifies what about cooperation *per se* makes it so important for group success. Cooperation, we have learned, is not merely a habit as Tocqueville suggested, but a complex social phenomenon, dependent on context and trust.

Rahn's chapter explicitly addresses these questions. Rahn finds that cooperation has varied effects on groups depending on context. In high-trust settings, such as corporatist democracies, cooperation is probably the result of pre-existing trust. Rahn theorizes that in such settings, the trustworthiness of others is "common knowledge." In low-trust settings, in contrast, cooperation has the benefit of engendering trust in society. Rahn argues that the initial cooperative act probably stems from individual efficacy—a belief that one can effect collective outcomes by going it alone. When these efforts are reciprocated, trust is learned, and trust and reciprocity become mutually reinforcing. This evidence is important given what is known about civic and political engagement. Communities with low levels of trust-worthiness also have low levels of engagement—a predictable consequence given Rahn's theoretic insight that in such contexts individuals hold the expectation that others will not reciprocate.

The overarching point is that context matters. Cooperative behaviors in and between groups cannot be understood without examining more localized dynamics—a contention that resonates loudly with respect to race and American politics. Oliver and Ha's study of racial composition and cooperation thus examines many of the same dynamics detailed by Rahn, with respect to a very specific social phenomenon.

Oliver and Ha present revealing data on segregation and volunteering in the United States. Whites living in segregated neighborhoods are more likely to volunteer, have high levels of social trust, and have greater attachment to the community. Data on other racial groups, while inconsistent, is no more encouraging. The authors conclude, "Whatever enhanced possibilities ... increased civic involvement provides for people in segregated neighborhoods are undercut by the racial isolation in which it takes place."

Ronson and Peterson present strong evidence for a fundamental connection between cooperation and group viability in a very different context—the workplace. The authors review numerous benefits that the group accrues from cooperative workplaces, from decision acceptance to novel approaches to problem solving. Interestingly, conflict, when properly resolved, can be a foundation for "deep-level cooperation" in the group. This cooperation, they find, serves as the basis for improved group performance.

Conflict brings about better group performance in several ways. For example, disagreement "communicates valuable information about [co-workers'] motivations." This allows work groups to develop integrative solutions to problems. Conflict can aid in the development of trust. When individuals voice a (potentially disagreeable) opinion, they communicate to others the expectation that their opinion matters—that respect is warranted. Ronson and Peterson argue that this form of communication carries with it an implicit and perhaps unconscious sense of trust. Norms of trust are likely to develop if group members act as if they expect a certain level of respect. Conflict can also build trust by generating better decisions through debate that considers multiple opinions. Better decisions, in turn, create positive feedback and build trust among group members.

In examining cooperation and group viability from these three different vantages—the community, the racially diverse neighborhood, and the workplace, we find a highly suggestive set of common denominators about why cooperation is important to group viability. For example, in low-trust workplaces, conflict can tear groups apart. In such environments, individuals have little real understanding of each others' perspectives, and little reason to expect others to reciprocate. This same dynamic may very well explain Oliver and Ha's findings about racial diversity. If race presents a barrier to trust formation, cooperation may be hard to come by. In contrast, in high-trust settings, conflict can actually lead to cooperative and effective groups. Ronson and Peterson's chapter argues that properly channeled conflict (often with the help of group leadership) allows individuals to communicate their motivations and allows others to learn their perspectives. It generates reciprocity, a building block of long-term, meaningful cooperation.

Hibbing and Theiss-Morse's conclusion—that voice in and of itself does not necessarily bring about cooperation—fits with this overall account. Interpersonal interactions become a basis for healthy group functioning insofar as they teach group members about others' perspectives. Meaningless voice in a conflict-laden environment is unlikely to bring about cooperation. However, when group leaders treat all opinions as valued and important parts of the decision-making process, voice can work as a building block for future cooperation.

Facilitating cooperation: the role of identity

Tyler begins his chapter with an important clarification, often overlooked in cooperation research. While cooperative behavior can be voluntary and motivated by social concerns, it can also be entirely self-interested, motivated by incentives or the threat of sanctions. While it is possible to motivate behavior with rewards and punishments, however, cooperation of the Hobbesian ilk often undermines the "intrinsic" motivations that represent the better part of research in this volume. Societies and governments using instrumental methods to bring about cooperation will find themselves spending huge sums of money on ever-increasing incentives, monitoring for non-compliance, etc.

For this reason, identifying methods to bring about social, self-regulatory cooperation is extremely important. Tyler proposes the Group Engagement Model as one means to bring about voluntary cooperation in society. The model has three parts. First, attitudes and values can shape voluntary cooperative behavior in society. Viewing decisions as legitimate, for example, is associated with increased compliance. Second, "procedural justice" brings about these necessary attitudes and values. When people see procedures as just (for example, when they have "voice" or when they are treated with dignity) voluntary cooperation is more likely. Finally, identity plays an important role in this process, as an eventual "merger of the self with the group" is what makes people willing to comply without incentive or threat of sanction. Identity can moderate the effects of procedural justice, as people "care more about whether or not they receive just treatment when their identity is more heavily intertwined with that of the group." Identity can also mediate these effects, insofar as "the procedural justice that people experience and the outcomes that they receive influence people's engagement in the group to the degree that they communicate identity relevant information to the people within groups."

Tyler's chapter, significantly, articulates the importance of a fair and just society in order to bring about greater voluntary cooperation. Interestingly, Tyler frames the argument by comparing voluntary cooperation with instrumental cooperation.

The former is not only normatively appealing, but by being "self-regulatory," it is also more expedient. This contention substantiates much of the research in this volume, which seeks to motivate cooperation by instilling healthy attitudes, not by making it the sole alternative to punishment.

While identity plays an important role in facilitating cooperation in Tyler's model, identity is itself a complex construct. It may, as Oliver and Ha's chapter suggest, paradoxically stand in the way of cooperation. Clarifying the relationship between identity and cooperation, Dovidio, Gaertner, and Esses' chapter provides a nuanced look at precisely which identities can engender cooperation. Dovidio and colleagues begin with Social Identity Theory, which posits that "a person's need for positive self-identity can be satisfied by membership in prestigious social groups." Social identity colors how one sees the world, including ingroup favoritisms and outgroup hostilities. While these categorizations are an important part of the self, they present challenges for fostering cooperation across group lines (a contention that is evident in Oliver and Ha's chapter).

Dovidio, Gaertner, and Esses propose the Common Ingroup Identity Model as one effective solution for this dilemma. This model mitigates conflict between groups though a process of recategorization into a single superordinate group. The process of recategorization often still allows for the development of coexisting subgroup identities. Through an inclusive "recognition of the unique contributions of members of different groups," both intragroup and intergroup cooperation can be enhanced.

The Common Ingroup Identity Model provides for a psychological account of how to alleviate hostile conflict and engender cooperation. Rather than attempt to erase or ignore social identity—which decades of scholarship has established as an enduring part of the human condition—this model molds identity into something that can bring about greater cooperation. This model has numerous implications and applications. For example, consider the Contact Hypothesis discussed by Oliver and Ha in this volume. Contact alone will not, as Oliver and Ha conclude, abate interracial competition and suspicion. However, Dovidio, Gaertner, and Esses suggest that a common ingroup identity can work as a mediating factor between contact and cooperation. Thus, in addition to looking at the racial composition of neighborhoods, we ought to consider the identities of residents. Do individuals identify as whites, African Americans, Latinos, and Asians, or are superordinate identities being developed around the neighborhood itself, the local high school, or even as "Americans"? Dovidio, Gaertner, and Esses' research suggests that the development of common identities is an important prerequisite for cooperation.

The implications of identity go beyond intergroup conflict and cooperation. Monroe and Etow's chapter investigates the impact of identity on altruism. While altruism is related to cooperation insofar as they "may tap into the same emotions," Monroe distinguishes the two concepts. Cooperation, as Monroe and Etow define it, may be motivated by "selfish concerns" or "the desire to receive reciprocity," while altruism may be undertaken with great cost and/or risk. Thus, these two types of behavior may be motivated by different factors.

Like Dovidio, Gaertner, and Esses, Monroe and Etow's research on altruism also stems from research on Social Identity Theory, which, to repeat, involves the construction of social categories. Monroe emphasizes that individuals "accord moral salience" to these categories in different ways. In her own research on Holocaust survivors and rescuers, Monroe finds that, while rescuers did draw distinctions between Jews and Nazis, "they did not accord moral salience to these categories." Rather, rescuers found the category of "human race" to be ethically relevant, a "perspective" that motivated altruistic behavior.

The construction of a broader ethically relevant category which supersedes ethnic distinctions has tremendous theoretic overlap with the Common Ingroup Identity Model. While the models are distinguished both by the type of behavior they predict and in how they conceive broader category membership, both models see redefining group boundaries as an essential part of developing prosocial behavior.

Guidance for Investing in Group Cooperation

Previous discussion has focused on the effects of cooperation on individual well-being and group viability, the mechanisms behind this process, and how to facilitate the relationship. In this final section, we discuss four chapters that provide specific guidance for how to invest in groups, and what strategies groups should employ.

When will the effects of cooperative behavior take place?

Most of the research in this volume has emphasized the positive effects cooperation can have on both individual well-being and the well-being of the group as a whole. Greenberg's chapter, significantly, suggests that these effects have limitations. The benefits of cooperation are context-dependent.

Greenberg's chapter investigates the extent to which democratic and cooperative decision making in workplaces "spills over" into the community at large. That is to say, do individuals in cooperative and/or democratic workplaces also make more cooperative and democratically inclined citizens? While Greenberg finds substantial evidence that cooperative workplaces produce healthier, happier employees and better organizational performance, he finds little evidence that progressive workplaces bring significant "spill over" benefits to the community. Greenberg speculates that, among other things, the cooperative features of a workplace might not be powerful enough to have effects beyond company walls.

Greenberg's finding may be informed by the research of the other authors in this volume. Cooperation creates optimally functioning groups by building a deeper understanding of group members (Ronson & Peterson) and their trustworthiness (Rahn). Thus, while one might develop a mutually cooperative relationship with one's co-workers, this relationship may not be fully transferable to one's non-work relationships. Cooperation's effects are developed over time, and may be limited only to those contexts in which we develop the requisite levels of trust and understanding.

From conflict to cooperation: Negotiation strategies

Several of the mechanisms by which cooperation works to bring about benefits to individuals and groups involve the presence of leadership. In the Hibbing and Theiss-Morse chapter, for example, how the leader treats members of the group is vitally important for whether or not voice will have a positive effect. Likewise, Ronson and Peterson find that how team leaders handle a group is essential to developing cooperative workplaces. O'Connor and Regan focus on a particular type of leadership behavior—negotiation. Negotiation research across diverse contexts provides specific guidance for how leadership can bring about cooperative outcomes.

O'Connor makes a useful distinction between two types of negotiation strategies. Distributive negotiations are zero sum—one's loss is another's corresponding gain—and usually involve leveraging one's power for maximum benefit. Integrative strategies, in contrast, typically involve cooperation, building trust, and reciprocating. In an experimental analysis, O'Connor and colleagues manipulated negotiator's reputations to create different bargaining climates. A distributive reputation "hobbles negotiators whose reputations precede them to the table, and undermines the other sides' outcomes as well." Upon hearing about a tough, distributive reputation, negotiators were unwilling to engage in conversation that could lead to mutual benefit. In contrast, with all else being equal, prior integrative reputations lead to outcomes of greater mutual benefit. O'Connor concludes that reputations often work as a "self-fulfilling prophesy." When bargaining partners are aware of a reputation for cooperation, or if they expect to be bullied, they behave accordingly.

Regan's chapter examines negotiation tactics in interstate rivalries. Research on interstate conflict has typically focused on structural precursors of violence, a method that largely ignores the accumulated research on negotiations in other contexts as described by O'Connor. As Regan shows, this is in part because understanding the effects of individual-level factors like those O'Connor examines pose several unique challenges when the units of analysis are states. Regan's innovative theoretic framework for grappling with these challenges is an excellent example of the potential of integrative research in the social sciences. Substantively, Regan proposes a model that uses indicators of reputation and status to compare states engaged in enduring rivalries with "one-shot" conflict situations. This method thus examines reputational factors without an experimental design, and applies an already robust literature on reputation to the study of interstate conflict. Regan's work, like O'Connor's, thus provides guidance for how to bring about cooperative outcomes by examining the reputational priors negotiators bring to the table.

*Guidance for investing in groups: Individual predispositions
and aggregate effects*

Van Lange's chapter provides a conceptual framework for how to think about cooperation at multiple levels of analysis. Van Lange reviews evidence of six significant interpersonal orientations: altruism, cooperation, equality, individualism, competition, and aggression. Van Lange presents evidence on behalf of both "logical" and "paradoxical" effects. That is, orientations such as "altruism" will exert logical and even predictable effects on collective outcomes. However, Van Lange argues, these same individually desirable orientations may also undermine collectively desirable goals.

This second premise—that individual orientation can undermine collective outcomes—deserves careful attention. Altruism is one excellent example. As Monroe's chapter details, altruistic individuals have performed countless acts of good, often at their own peril. However, calling attention to the empathetic components of altruistic acts, Van Lange points out that an affective connection with a single individual may lead to tunnel vision, whereby the altruist loses sight of the collective.

For example, an altruist in a corporate situation may retain a poor employee out of compassion, even when the employee is hurting the company as a whole. This altruistic act could, potentially, hurt the company's competitive advantage. It might be objected that this contention is at odds with research on generative leadership, since generative leaders have a deep empathetic connection with their employees. However, as articulated by Colbert et al., generative leaders also retain focus on the long-term goals of the organization. This is thus an illustrative example of how multiple orientations aggregate into collective outcomes. Altruism, in this case, could have paradoxical effects, while the more specified "generative leader" is good for the long-term success of business organizations.

This example also highlights the necessity of integrated research in the social sciences. Van Lange's chapter promotes a healthy awareness of the challenges of fostering cooperation in society. Attaining mutually desirable outcomes may often involve "the usual suspects"—building trust, encouraging egalitarian norms, etc. However, cooperation can also be built through non-intuitive means. Even aggression, properly channeled into the exclusion of non-cooperators, may work to build long-term cooperation. Indeed, this is almost precisely the mechanism at play in Hanley et al.'s chapter, whereby non-cooperators are "punished" with lower reproductive fitness via some form of exclusion. Studies of cooperation must thus be nuanced, examining consequences at multiple levels of analysis.

Integrating Research on Cooperation in the Social Sciences

This chapter has summarized evidence from a wide range of perspectives in an effort to answer three foundational questions about the nature of cooperation. It is important to note that the conclusions derived from the chapters in this book have *not* come *in spite of* these broad and varied perspectives. Rather, we would contend that it is *only* possible to understand cooperation's effects, its mechanisms, and how it is facilitated, by taking an integrative approach. For example, we begin to see a complete picture of how cooperation operates within and between contexts only when considering Greenberg's chapter together with the work of Rahn and Ronson and Peterson. Likewise, the Common Ingroup Identity Model is infused with interesting implications for the relationship between neighborhood homogeneity and cooperation, as articulated in Oliver and Ha. Integrated research on cooperation is thus a necessary precondition for truly understanding the phenomenon. The questions with which we frame this chapter are, we believe, foundational in the true sense of the word. Answers to these questions can be groundwork for both further integrated research on cooperation and more cooperative societies.

Index

the joists. *See also* tongued and grooved boards.

floor finish

A material applied to ground and upper floors to provide a decorative, hardwearing surface and includes carpets, tiles and sheet materials.

floor joist

A timber beam used to support a floor above and may be required to support a ceiling below. *See also* joist, common joist, trimmed joist, trimmer joist, trimming joist, trussed joist.

floor plan

A plan indicating the layout of buildings showing, in particular, the size and disposition of rooms for existing, or potential, use.

floor screed

See screed.

floor space index

A procedure used to assist a local planning authority in the control of the density of new development. It is the ratio of gross floor area to site area, plus half the width of any roads which border the property.

floor strutting

See strutting.

floor tiles

A covering for a solid floor which includes clay, terrazzo, and PVC.

flow pipe

A pipe carrying hot water from a boiler to a cylinder or radiator. *See also* return pipe.

flue

A pipe, or duct, connected to a burning appliance to allow burnt gases and smoke to escape. *See also* flue blocks, flue liner, chimney.

flue blocks

Special lining blocks, built into a brick chimney stack, which are resistant to sulphur attack from coal-burning appliances.

flue liner

A pipe or duct incorporated in an existing chimney stack to allow exhaust fumes to escape from a gas-burning appliance.

flush door

One that has a smooth finish to both faces and may be an internal, external or fire door.

water and direct it to a discharge point such as an open ditch. *See also* land drain.

French window
See French casement.

friction pile
An in situ concrete pile which supports and transfers the load from a building to the ground by virtue of its shape and frictional resistance, and is not supported by a load-bearing stratum. *See also* bored pile.

friendly societies
Organisations registered under the Friendly Societies Act 1977, as amended, to provide, by means of voluntary contributions, for the relief of members and their families during times of sickness, old age etc. They are incorporated mutual insurance associations which possess mortgage lending powers.

size
The part of the wall below a cornice.

frontage
The length of a plot of land, or building, measured along the line to which the plot of land or building fronts.

frontager
Owner or occupier of land which abuts a highway, seashore or river.

front money
Sums of money made available usually as initial short-term finance for the development of land. Often the short-term finance involves the interest being rolled up during the construction period of the development project.

frost action
The effect of absorbed water expanding upon freezing and exerting pressure within a material, such as bricks and concrete, resulting in cracking and flaking at the surface. *See also* durability.

frost heave
The effect of ground water freezing and exerting pressure on external walls due to the expansion of the frozen water.

full management
A situation where all aspects of property management are the responsibility of a managing agent.

flushing cistern
A water tank positioned above a WC that is operated by a lever or chain that allows an amount of water to be discharged into the WC pan to clear the waste. *See also* automatic flushing cistern, low level flushing cistern, water closet.

flush pointing
See mortar joint.

flying shore
A temporary support system to an existing wall that requires strengthening, which is attached to the walls of opposite buildings above ground level while maintaining access below. It consists of a main horizontal member (flying shore) with inclined members attached to the wall at one end and the horizontal member at the other, fixed each side above and below. *See also* dead shore, raking shore, shore.

foil-backed plasterboard
Plasterboard sheets with aluminium foil bonded on one side to act as a vapour barrier. *See also* aluminium foil.

footing
The widening of a solid brick wall at the base to spread the load on the foundation upon which it is supported by creating a series of steps.

force
The effect of load that causes the fibres of a material to be in a state of compression or tension. *See also* compression, tension.

forced sale value
The Royal Institution of Chartered Surveyors *Guidance Notes on the Valuation of Assets* define it as 'open market value, but with the proviso that the vendor has imposed a time limit for completion, which cannot be regarded as a reasonable period in which to negotiate the sale, taking into account the nature of the property and the state of the market'.

foreclosure
The situation under the Law of Property Act 1925 where a mortgagee has restricted power to extinguish the mortgagor's right of redemption by transfer of the mortgagor's interest in the property to himself, provided the mortgagor defaults in payment of dues, or in comply-

ing with any other terms of the mortgage deed.

foreshore
Part of the seashore lying between mean high and mean low tide lines. It is normally held that the foreshore is owned by the Crown.

forfeiture
The process whereby a landlord exercises his right to retake physical possession of premises and thus extinguish a lease following the tenant's failure to remedy a breach of the terms of that lease.

formal tender
A formal bid made by a tenderer. *See also* tender, tendering process.

formation level
The level produced after stripping off the vegetable layer from the ground to expose the subsoil which is the layer upon which the building is constructed. *See also* subsoil, vegetable layer.

Formica
A laminated plastic sheet used for facing surfaces such as kitchen fittings.

formwork
Temporary support for in situ reinforced concrete work such as foundations, and which is removed when the concrete has hardened.

forward finance
The forward commitment where an amount of money is made available and is repaid relatively quickly thereafter from the proceeds of a sale.

forward letting/sale
An arrangement where agreement is entered into for the taking of a lease or purchase of property in advance of completion of the development.

foul drain
A pipe situated below ground level which is used for disposing foul water from a building(s) within the boundary of a property and maintained by the owner(s).

foul sewer
A pipe situated below ground level used for disposing of foul water from foul drains and transferring it to a sewage treatment plant and which is the responsibility of the water authority.

foul water
The waste water flow from soil and waste fittings such as WCs, baths and sinks.

foundation
That part of the building which supports the total load and transfers it to the subsoil. *See also* strip foundation, wide strip foundation, wild strip foundation, raft foundation, beam and pile foundation, ground beam.

frail elderly housing
In the housing association context, housing for frail elderly people. It includes housing which provides personal care and support for this category of person. *See also* elderly persons' dwellings, mobility housing.

frame
An arrangement of metal or timber which forms a basis for fixing a sheet covering to form a structure such as a partition.

framed door
See battened door, panelled door.

framed partition
See stud partition.

frank-fee
Freehold land.

frank tenement
Freehold.

fraudulent conveyan
A transfer of land wit
sideration and with
defraud a subsequ
chaser. Such actions
able by the purchaser
Law of Property Act 1

freedom from encu
Land and property
any binding rights
other than the owne

freehold
The most complete
ership of land. A le
fee simple.

French casement
A combination of
doors as one unit r
prising a pair of
with casement
side.

French drain
A trench filled w
ilar rubble used

full rental value
The best possible rental that could be expected on the open market.

full repairing and insuring lease
A lease where the lessee is responsible for the full cost of repairing, maintaining and insuring the property.

funding
The situation where a lender advances part, or the whole, of the development costs of land, or where a potential purchaser similarly advances part, or the whole, of the full development costs and, on completion, acquires the property at a price normally calculated with regard to a formula, as embodied in the agreement.

fungus
A plant whose growth is formed by warm and humid conditions and can destroy timber. *See also* dry rot.

furniture beetle
An insect that bores into the wood of furniture, leaving a hole approximately 1.5mm in diameter.

G

gable
The side wall of a building where the edge of a pitched roof forms a triangle. *See also* hip, valley.

gable board
See bargeboard.

gable roof
A pitched roof which forms a gable wall at each end. *See also* pitched roof, gable, hipped roof.

gable wall
See gable.

galleting
Small pieces of tile which are bedded in mortar to fill in the ends of pan tiles at the eaves, or set in walls for decoration.

gallets
Small pieces of rock, stone or tile.

galvanised nails
Nails with a protective layer of zinc. *See also* galvanising.

galvanising
Protective coating on steel, usually zinc, to prevent corrosion.

ganger
Person in charge of a group of non-skilled operatives, such as those carrying out general building work (e.g. excavating).

garden wall bond
A brick bond where the majority of courses consist of stretchers but incorporating an occasional row of bricks in either English or Flemish bond. *See also* header, stretcher, English bond, English garden wall bond, Flemish bond.

gargoyle
A stone projection situated near

to the eaves which acts as a main water spout and is usually shaped in the form of a grotesque face.

gas-fired boiler
See boiler.

gasket
A thin strip or ring of flexible material used to seal joints between components.

gauge
1. A method used to proportion materials for mortar and plaster mixes.
2. The distance between the centres of roof slates and tile battens. In this case, the gauge is the same as the exposed distance between the edge of the slates or tiles, which is known as the margin and is also used to determine the lap. *See also* lap, roof slates, roof tiles.

gauged arch
See arch.

gauged mortar
Sand and cement mortar to which a portion of lime is added to produce a workable mix.

gazebo
A summer house in a garden,

often of a lightweight construction.

gazumping
A vendor withdrawing from an agreed sale of land before a legally enforceable contract exists with a view to securing a higher price from another purchaser. *See also* reverse gazumping.

geared rent
A situation in which rent is determined as a proportion of: first, the rental value of, or the actual rent received from, the subject property; or, second, the rental value of a similar property.

General Development Order
A statutory instrument permitting certain classes of development without the necessity of making a formal planning application in accordance with the Town and Country Planning Acts. *See also* deemed planning permission, permitted development, permitted use.

general improvement area
An area – usually an older, residential area – designated by a local housing authority with a

view to improving the houses and amenities. *See also* Housing Act 1985.

General Needs Index
In housing association terms, a statistical index of relative housing needs used by the Department of the Environment to assist it in making housing investment programme capital allocations to local authorities.

gentrification
The rehabilitation of a residential area which was formerly run-down, resulting in the influx of wealthier, often younger, professional people into the area.

Georgian wired glass
See reinforced glass.

girder
A steel beam. *See also* beam.

glare
The effect of sunlight on a surface which may cause discomfort. *See also* solar glass.

glass
A hard, non-crystalline, brittle substance made by fusing together one or more of the oxides of silicon, borax or phosphorous with certain basic oxides (e.g. sodium, magnesium, calcium, potassium) and cooling the product rapidly to prevent crystallisation or denitrification. *See also* plate glass, float glass, laminated glass, sheet glass, heat-resistant glass, plate glass, toughened glass, reinforced glass, solar glass.

glass block
Hollow glass blocks used to construct internal translucent partition walls or translucent panels within partition walls.

glass fibre
See glass wool.

glasspaper
A cloth or paper, with an abrasive surface on one side, which is used for smoothing rough surfaces. Various textures from coarse to fine are available. *See also* sandpaper.

glass-reinforced concrete (GRC)
Concrete which is reinforced with glass fibres and generally used to produce thin section components, such as external cladding panels.

glass-reinforced plastic (GRP)
Glass fibres mixed with synthetic resins to produce such components as panels used for external cladding.

glass wool
Fibres of glass used to produce a thermal insulation quilt or used to reinforce such materials as plastics. *See also* mineral wool, insulation quilt.

glazing bar
A rebated timber or metal bar into which a pane of glass is fixed.

glazing bead
A strip of metal, timber or plastic which is used to secure a pane of glass to a glazing bar, casement or frame.

glue
See adhesive.

going
The horizontal distance between the nosing of a tread and face of the riser. *See also* total going, nosing, tread.

good leasehold title
A good leasehold title is granted under the Land Registration Act 1923, as amended, and is equivalent to an absolute title except that it cannot be guaranteed that the landlord will grant a lease. It usually occurs when the deeds showing the title of the landlord have not been registered.

good marketable title
The situation where the title is entirely free of encumbrances.

good title
The situation where the title to land is supported by adequate evidence.

grade
The procedure involved in levelling and clearing a surface, such as the top layer of subsoil, in readiness for setting out the building foundations to commence excavation.

graded aggregate
Coarse and fine aggregate whose particles are in specified proportions to give a dense mix.

gradient
The slope or inclination of a surface from the horizontal generally expressed as a ratio (e.g. 1 in 40 means that the surface is

inclined one unit vertically for every 40 units measured horizontally). *See also* pitch.

granite
An igneous rock formed by cooling from a former molten state under a deep cover of older rocks. It is crystalline in nature and consists of quartz, feldspars and mica.

granolithic concrete
See granolithic screed.

granolithic screed
A floor screed incorporating fine granite chippings which produce a hard, non-slip durable surface. *See also* screed.

grant-aided land
In housing association terms, a phrase used to define property which cannot be disposed of without the consent of the Housing Corporation under section 9 of the Housing Associations Act 1985.

gravel
See coarse aggregate.

grease gulley
A special gulley which incorporates a perforated tray to collect grease from kitchen sink waste and can be removed and cleaned. *See also* gulley.

grease trap
See grease gulley.

green belt
The name given to a town planning concept where an area of rural land surrounding a town, is designated, and development is discouraged from being undertaken there. The object is to protect urban sprawl and to provide recreational opportunities for the residents. *See also* green wedges.

green concrete
A term used to describe concrete that has not fully dried and hardened and which is useful for directly applying as a floor screed to a concrete slab to achieve a good bond. *See also* monolithic screed, screed.

green wedges
A concept, similar to that of a green belt, whereby a planning authority designates areas of woodland, agricultural land or other recreational land for the purpose of separating urban neighbourhoods. *See also* green belt.

grey land

The area of land containing property surrounded by, or adjacent to, a clearance area where acquisition is necessary for the satisfactory development of the cleared area. It attaches a special basis of compensation for compulsory acquisition.

gross external area

The aggregate superficial area of a building, taking each floor into account. The Royal Institution of Chartered Surveyors Code of Measuring Practice includes within this concept: external walls and projections; internal walls and partitions; columns; piers; chimney breasts; stairwells and liftwells; tank and plant rooms; fuel stores, whether or not above the main roof level; open-sided covered areas; enclosed car-parking areas. It excludes: open balconies; open fire escapes; open vehicle parking areas; terraces, etc.; domestic outside WCs; and coalhouses. In calculating the gross external area, party walls are measured to the centre line while areas with a headroom of less than 1.5 metres, are excluded and quoted separately. *See also* gross internal area.

gross income

The income before deduction of any outgoings.

gross internal area

The measurement of a building in the same manner as gross external area, but excluding external wall thicknesses. *See also* gross external area, net internal area.

gross lease

A lease which requires the lessor to meet all, or part of, the expenses of the lease property, such as taxes, maintenance, utilities, and insurance.

gross value

Defined by the General Rate Act 1967 as 'the rent at which a hereditament might reasonably be expected to let from year to year if the tenant undertook to pay all the usual tenant rates and taxes and the landlord undertook to bear the cost of repairs and insurance and other expenses, if any, necessary to maintain the hereditament in a state to command the rent'.

ground

The term used to describe soil or earth. *See also* subsoil, top soil.

ground beam
A reinforced concrete strip placed just below ground level whose purpose is to support a wall. *See also* foundation, beam and pile foundation, strip foundation.

ground floor
Provided at ground level within a building to accommodate the requirements of a floor. It may be either solid or hollow. *See also* floor, solid ground floor, hollow ground floor.

ground lease
A long lease granted at ground rent – i.e. a rental value which disregards the value of any buildings on the land, but reflects the right to develop the land with buildings.

ground rent
The rent payable for vacant land which is suitable for development.

ground water
Water present in the ground and above the water table and varies depending upon the absorption and drying out of surface water. *See also* subsoil water, water table.

group home
A residential dwelling where a group of single people live together as one household.

grout
A neat paste of cement and water which is applied between tiles to seal the joints.

G-rules
The rules provided by the National Federation of Housing Associations for non-charitable housing associations.

guarantee
An agreement to pay a debt in the event of the debt not being paid.

guarantor
A third party to a contractual agreement who guarantees to do certain things under the contractual agreement.

gulley
A drain fitting which is positioned at the beginning of a drain and into which soil, waste and rainwater pipes are connected, and from which the water/waste is discharged. The gulley incorporates a water seal to prevent foul air and matter

coming into contact with the outside. *See also* grease gulley.

gutter
A channel provided in a roof to collect and dispose of surface water. *See also* box gutter, eaves gutter.

gypsum lath
Gypsum plasterboard sheets of various lengths and 406mm wide and 9 or 13mm thick which are used for providing a ceiling to upper timber joisted floors. They require a coat of Class B (retarded hemi-hydrate gypsum) plaster. *See also* gypsum plasterboard, gypsum baseboard.

gypsum baseboard
Gypsum plasterboard sheets, 914mm wide, designed to receive a coat of Class B (retarded hemi-hydrate gypsum) plaster and used for a similar purpose as gypsum lath. *See also* gypsum plasterboard, gypsum lath.

gypsum plank
Gypsum plasterboard sheets manufactured in widths of 457mm or 610mm and 19mm thick and used to produce a

solid core partition wall. *See also* gypsum plasterboard.

gypsum plasterboard
Gypsum plaster, faced on both sides with thick sheets of paper to form a thin board and available in various sizes and thicknesses. *See also* gypsum lath, gypsum baseboard, gypsum plank, insulating plasterboard, gypsum wallboard.

gypsum plasters
Produced by heating calcium sulphate at low temperatures to produce a hemi-hydrate plaster (Class A), sometimes known as Plaster of Paris, which sets rapidly when water is added. A retarder may be added to produce a retarded hemi-hydrate plaster (Class B). Heating at high temperatures produces anhydrous plasters (Class D) which set slowly when water is added. An accelerator may be added to speed setting, producing Keene's or Parian cement (Class E).

gypsum wallboard
Gypsum plasterboard sheets approximately 1220mm wide, 1829 to 3658 long and 9.5mm or 12.7mm thick. One face is ivory-

coloured for direct decoration and the other face is suitable to take a Class B (retarded hemi-hydrate gypsum) plaster. The long edges may be square, recessed, tapered. It is used for dry lining walls. *See also* gypsum plaster, drylining.

H

hair cracks
Fine cracks that usually appear on a plaster surface, caused by shrinking or drying out of new plaster and general movement of the building in existing plaster surfaces.

half bond
The arrangement of bricks so that the bricks in each course overlap the bricks below by a half a brick. Commonly used for cavity walls. *See also* stretcher bond.

half brick wall
A wall which is half a brick in thickness and built in stretcher bond. *See also* stretcher bond.

half landing
A landing between floors extending at least the full width on two flights with a 180° turn and used in the construction of a dog leg stair. *See also* dog leg stair, landing.

halved joint
A method of joining two timber members by cutting out a half thickness of material on each so that, when the timbers are joined, the total thickness is maintained.

handrail
A rounded and moulded timber member which is fixed to the top of the balusters of a stair, or fixed to a wall enclosing a stair.

hanger
A metal or timber structural strap which is used to intermediately support ceiling joists by fixing one end to purlins and the other end to a horizontal timber structural member (runner) which is attached to ceiling joists. *See also* purlin, runner.

hanging stile
The vertical frame of a panelled door to which the hinges are fixed. *See also* stile.

harassment
Under the Protection from Eviction Act 1977, as amended, it is an offence for a landlord of residential property to use or threaten violence to obtain possession. The offence can be committed by interference with the tenant's comfort and enjoyment of his home.

hardboard
A composite sheet compressed during manufacture to give the required density. An economical material used for facing internal doors and lining existing boarded floors before laying carpets or tiles. *See also* fibreboard.

hardcore
A bed of crushed rock or stone which is compacted in layers on top of the subsoil in order to provide a suitable hard level surface upon which to construct a solid concrete floor slab. *See also* solid ground floor.

hardwood
Timber that is produced by deciduous trees (i.e. having broad leaves which are shed in the autumn). It is expensive compared to softwood and is used for high-class joinery work. It includes oak, maple and mahogany, and is left exposed and polished for effect. *See also* oak, mahogany, softwood.

hardwood blocks
Oak or mahogany timber blocks arranged in a pattern, e.g. herringbone.

haunching
A concrete support to a drainpipe.

head
The upper horizontal part of a door, or window opening, or frame.

header
The face of a brick placed so that the full width is seen. *See also* stretcher.

headlease
The principal lease held directly from the freeholder which may be subject to a series of underleases for part, or the whole, of the property.

head rent
The rent payable by the head lessee to the freeholder.

headroom
The uninterrupted minimum space below a ceiling. It is normally measured to the underlying floor below the ceiling.

heads of claim
The categories, or titles, by which claims may be made. Often associated with claims for compensation.

heads of terms
The principal points of agreement which form the basis of a contractual agreement. In a lease they often include the duration of the letting, the initial rent and the rights and obligations of the various parties.

hearth
A concrete slab which forms the bottom part of a fireplace and which projects into a room. The projecting portion is usually covered with a pre-formed slab of tiles or stone for appearance.

heat
A form of energy. *See also* temperature, conduction, convection, radiation.

heat exchanger
A device used for heating water into which it is immersed, e.g. in a cylinder. It is connected to a water pipe which is heated by a boiler giving off surface heat which, in turn, heats the water in which it is immersed. *See also* direct *and* indirect cylinder.

heat gain
Heat energy gained from the sun. *See also* solar heat gain.

heat loss
Heat energy that is lost from the inside of a building through the fabric and through infiltration of cool air. Buildings must be constructed to limit the amount of heat lost from the inside to the outside. *See also* fabric heat loss, infiltration heat loss.

heat-resistant glass
Glass which is capable of resisting heat and flame without breaking. *See also* glass.

heat transfer
The movement of heat energy by conduction, convection or radiation.

hemi-hydrate plaster
A Class A gypsum plaster, com-

monly known as Plaster of Paris, which sets quickly when water is added. *See also* gypsum plasters.

hereditament
A unit of land that was separately assessed for rating purposes. *See also* mixed hereditament.

heritage property
Property of historical value as defined by the Inland Revenue under section 30 of the Inheritance Tax Act 1984, as amended. It includes:

● pictures, works of art, etc. which are of national importance.
● land of outstanding scenic, historic or scientific value.
● buildings needing special steps for preservation because of their outstanding interest.

Transfers of all such property are potentially exempt from inheritance tax.

herringbone
The arrangement of flooring and paving blocks in a diagonal pattern.

herringbone strutting
See strutting

high calcium lime
Lime with a high calcium oxide content which is used for mortars and renders after slaking.

high-rise building
Generally a building of considerable height in relation to the average height of other buildings in the locality. Generally accepted as a block of flats over five storeys in height. *See also* tower block.

high-tech building
A colloquial term meaning modern buildings which have flexible uses and an internal space arrangement which can be easily altered.

highway
Normally understood to mean a main road but, in law, considered as a strip of land over which the public have a right of passage for purposes specified in relation to the particular set of circumstances.

hinge
Metal plates which are connected so that they can open to 180° and which are used for fixing doors and casements to frames to allow them to be in an

open or closed position. *See also* rising butt hinge.

hip
The external angle formed where two pitched roof surfaces meet. *See also* gable, valley.

hip iron
A curved metal bracket which is fixed to the bottom of a hip rafter to prevent the bottom hip tile from slipping.

hipped roof
A pitched roof containing hips at one or both sides. *See also* pitched roof, gable roof.

hip rafter
A roof rafter which is used to form a hip and to which jack rafters are fixed. *See also* rafter, common rafter, jack rafter, hip.

hip tile
A rounded or angular clay or concrete tile, the purpose of which is to cover the joint of the roof covering the full length of a hip. *See also* hip.

holding
Land which is demised to a tenant.

holding over
Continued occupation by a tenant after determination of his lease. If the landlord accepts rent from the tenant a new tenancy is created.

hollow core door
A flush door consisting of a central open timber framework faced both sides with plywood sheets and used internally. *See also* core, internal door.

hollow ground floor
A floor constructed of timber floor joists supported on sleeper walls so that there is a space beneath the floor. It is important that sufficient air circulation is provided to prevent dry rot occurring. *See also* air brick, sleeper wall.

Alternatively pre-cast concrete units are available which are laid on sleeper walls with spaces between which are filled in with a lightweight block. *See also* floor, solid ground floor.

Homeless Families Initiative
A Housing Corporation programme which attempts to provide homes specifically for homeless families.

homelessness
Defined under section 58 of the Housing Act 1985 as a person who has no accommodation in England, Wales or Scotland, or who has accommodation but is unable to occupy it. Local authorities have responsibility for housing people who are homeless and in priority need. *See also* priority need.

homeless person
Under the Housing (Homeless Persons) Act 1977, as amended, a person is considered homeless if he has no living accommodation or he has accommodation to which he is unable to secure access. A local authority has a duty to house an unintentionally homeless person. *See also* homelessness.

honeycombed sleeper wall
See sleeper wall.

hope value
The value of a property above its existing use value, determined by the prospect of an alteration giving a more valuable future use. Often associated with the grant of planning permission for a more beneficial use.

horizontal load
Live load caused by wind pressure acting in a near horizontal direction on the side of the building. *See also* dead load, live load, total load.

hostel
A building providing residential accommodation and either board or facilities for the preparation of food.

hostel deficit grant
In the housing association context, a grant payable towards deficits arising from the running costs of approved hostel projects. Now replaced by the Transitional Special Needs Management Allowance.

hot water cylinder
See cylinder.

hot water pipe
A pipe which carries hot water from a cylinder or boiler.

housed joint
A joint used for connecting two timber members by housing or sinking one member into the other. *See also* housing.

house longhorn beetle
An insect that destroys wood,

usually sapwood, by boring holes in it.

housing

A groove in a timber member to allow another timber member to be joined to it. *See also* housed joint.

Housing Act 1980

This Act introduced the Tenant's Charter and the statutory Right to Buy (i.e. the right given to some tenants to purchase, at a discount, the dwelling in which they are living after a minimum period of residence) to tenants of non-charitable registered housing associations and local authorities. The Act also introduced a statutory form of accounts, which is the form in which statutory housing association accounts must be published. *See also* housing association, Right to Buy, Tennant's Charter.

Housing Act 1985

The main Act to consolidate housing legislation since 1957, when the last previous consolidation took place.

Housing Act 1988

This Act removed housing association tenancies from 'secure tenancy' (i.e. security of tenure), the privileges of the Tenant's Charter (security, the right to sublet and to undertake improvements defined by Part IV of HA 1985) and fair rent (rent fixed by the rent officer for a period of two years), replacing them with 'assured tenancies'. *See also* Housing Action Trust, Tenant's Charter, tenants' choice.

housing action area

An area of residential uses declared by the local housing authority under the Housing Act 1985, as amended. It is designated when the condition of the properties is considered unsatisfactory with regard to their physical state and the social condition of the people living in the area. It allows authorities to acquire land and repair and improve housing accommodation and the environment, with grants supplied by central government.

Housing Action Trust (HAT)

An organisation established under the Housing Act 1988, as amended, which removes housing from local authority control and hands it over to a statutory trust charged with improving the stock. *See also* Housing Act 1988.

Housing and Building Control Act 1984

This Act introduced transferable discounts for tenants of charities and two new rights for secure tenants (i.e. local authority tenants and housing association tenants whose tenancies commenced before 15 January 1989): the right to repair and the right to exchange.

housing association

Under section 1(1) of the Housing Associations Act 1985 and section 5(1) of the Housing Act 1985 defined as 'a society, body of trustees or company, which is established for the purpose of, or amongst whose objects or powers are, including those who are providing, constructing, improving or managing, or facilitating, or encouraging the construction or improvement of, housing accommodation and which does not trade for profit or whose constitution or rule prohibits the issue of capital with interest or dividends exceeding such rate

as may be prescribed by the treasury whether with, or without, differentiation as between share and loan capital'.

housing association grant

The main form of financial subsidy for housing association work paid for by the Housing Corporation.

Housing Associations Act 1985

One of three consolidating Acts passed in this year. This Act contains all the legislation passed to date which relates specifically to housing associations. *See also* housing association.

housing association tenancy

A tenancy where the landlord is a housing association, the Housing Corporation or a housing trust.

housing authority

Under section 4 of the Housing Act 1985, defined as 'a local housing authority, a New Town Corporation, or the Development Board for Rural Wales'.

housing cooperative

Under section 27(2) of the Housing Act 1985 defined as 'a

society, company, or a body of trustees for the time being approved by the Secretary of State for the purposes of this section', which empowers a local housing authority to enter into agreements for cooperatives to undertake any of the housing authority's duties concerning the provision of housing accommodation on land owned by the authority.

Housing Corporation

An organisation, established under the Housing Act 1964, which is responsible for promoting non-profitmaking housing associations, with a view to providing homes for people in need. It maintains the register of housing associations and makes public funds available for such associations to develop appropriate housing developments. *See also* housing association.

Housing Homeless Persons Act 1977

Legislation which made local authorities responsible for providing accommodation for those persons accepted as being homeless. Amended by Part III of the Housing Act 1985.

housing investment programme

The annual programme of capital expenditure on housing for each local authority, agreed by the Department of the Environment.

housing manager

A person who engages in the profession of the management and maintenance of properties.

Housing Needs Indicator

A measure of the relative requirement within each local authority area for new provision of housing by housing associations for people in need. It is used by the Housing Corporation to decide the allocation of capital resources between its regions and gives guidance for expenditure within regions.

Housing Organisations' Mobility and Exchange Scheme

In the housing association context, a national organisation funded by the Department of the Environment and formed in 1990 with the responsibility to streamline exchanges among people living in social housing.

housing repairs account

The local authority's account for repairs purposes.

Housing Revenue Account (HRA)

The landlord's revenue account for local authorities. *See also* Local Government and Housing Act 1989.

Housing Revenue Account Subsidy

The Department of the Environment's subsidy paid to local housing authorities according to an annually determined formula.

housing society

An organisation, registered under the Industrial and Provident Society's Act of 1893, which does not trade for profit and whose primary function is to improve, construct or manage houses.

housing trust

Under section 2 of the Housing Associations Act 1985, and section 6 of the Housing Act 1985, defined as 'a corporation, or a body of persons which (a) is required by the terms of its constitution to use the whole of its funds, including any surplus which may arise from its operation, for the purpose of providing housing accommodation or, (b) is required by the terms of its constitution instrument, to devote the whole, or substantially the whole, of its funds for charitable purposes and in fact, uses the whole, or substantially the whole of its funds, for the purpose of providing housing accommodation'.

humidifier

An appliance which is used to raise the relative humidity in a room by the diffusion of water vapour into the air, often forming part of a heating or air-conditioning system.

humidity

The presence of moisture in the air in the form of water vapour, which can cause unpleasant conditions if not controlled. *See also* dehumidifier, relative humidity.

hydrated lime

See slaked lime.

hydraulic lime

A lime which contains aluminium silicate which hardens when mixed with water.

hydraulic test

A test on foul and surface water drains. Generally carried out on drainage runs between inspection chambers and consists of blocking one end of the drainage run and filling with water from the other via a temporary vertical pipe to give a test head, any variation in water level indicating a leakage. *See also* air test, smoke test.

I

igneous rock
Rock formed by cooling from a former molten state under a deep cover of older rocks. It is crystalline in nature and formed of quartz, felspar and mica.

immersion heater
An electrical device fitted to a hot water cylinder and used for heating water stored in the cylinder either as an independent means or to supplement a boiler. *See also* cylinder.

impact sound
See structure-borne sound.

impermeability
The resistance of a material to liquid passing through it. *See also* permeability.

implied covenant
A covenant which is assumed by the law to exist in a lease even though it may not be so expressly stated.

implied trust
A trust developing from either the unexpressed intention of the settlor, or by the law of equity.

imposed load
A combination of dead and live loads. *See also* dead load, live load, total load.

improved ground rent
A rent which does not exceed the full rental value of land, but is greater than the previously paid ground rent under a lease since the grant of which, land values have increased.

improvement for sale
In the housing association context, a scheme whereby housing associations can buy and modernise an older property for outright sale.

improvement grants

Grants which are means-tested and paid by local authorities to owner occupiers to assist them in improving their property to an agreed standard.

improvement line

The delineation on a plan alongside a street, and some distance from it, where buildings would not be permitted to be erected or extended. The line is normally designated for the purpose of allowing road widening.

improvement notice

Under the Housing Act 1985, a notice issued by the local housing authority requiring a dwelling, which has fallen below set standards, to be brought up to an acceptable standard. The procedure can only be implemented if the residential property is contained within a general improvement area, or housing action area, or has been built or converted before 3 October 1961, and representations have been made by the occupying tenant and the local housing authority in an agreement that it is below the required standard.

immediate landlord

Normally held to be the free-holder, head lessee and/or occupying tenant.

incentive fee

See contingency fee.

inclusive rent

A rent payable where the landlord has an obligation to pay the rates. It may also be applied to a situation where a landlord is responsible for the provision of certain services.

incombustible

See non-combustible.

income support

A benefit designed to supplement low income. It is means-tested and does not include housing benefit. A person is entitled if his or her income is below a specified amount and the person is actively seeking employment.

income tax

A levy on income or profits administered under the Income and Corporation Taxes Act 1988, as amended. The tax is implemented each year under the annual Finance Act. The tax is related to different types of sources of income such as rents, company dividends, etc. The tax year of assessment runs from 6 April to 5 April. The tax is managed by the Commissioners of the Inland Revenue, Inspectors of Taxes being their subordinate local officers. A person who is aggrieved by an assessment made by the Inspector may appeal to the local Commissioner.

incorporation
The merging together into a single whole. It refers principally to the creation of a single legal personality.

Incorporated Association of Architects and Surveyors
A body established in 1925 with a view to register the interests of its members, each of whom was practising as an architect and/ or surveyor. Its members are required to abide by a code of practice and are qualified by professional examinations.

Incorporated Society of Valuers and Auctioneers
An organisation established in 1967 by the amalgamation of the Valuers' Institution and the Incorporated Society of Auctioneers and Landed Property

Agents. Its members have to abide by a code of professional practice and election is by way of professional examinations.

indemnity insurance
Protection resulting from an insurance policy (contract) whereby, on the occurrence of the insured risk, e.g. flood, the insurer will make sufficient payment to meet the financial losses incurred.

indemnity period
The term by which an insurance policy will entitle the holder to receive compensation for loss, injury or damage, arising from the risk defined in the policy document.

independent contractor
An individual who contracts to undertake duties for another and is not under the direct control of the employing party.

independent expert
A professional person with appropriate specialist knowledge appointed to resolve a difference between two parties. He examines the evidence presented by the two parties, and can use his own expert know-

ledge to resolve the dispute. His decision is normally binding on both parties, unless one party can prove negligence. Sometimes referred to as an arbitrator.

independent surveyor
A surveyor who is impartial and appointed with a view to resolving a dispute. The surveyor may be appointed as an arbitrator, or simply to express an independent opinion, either expressly or by implication, depending on the terms of his particular appointment and the circumstances of the dispute.

independent valuer
A surveyor engaged to undertake an impartial valuation. The appointment may be to adjudicate between two parties, or to settle a difference in valuation between two existing valuations.

indexation
The adjustment to a price, rate or payment in accordance with a specific index, e.g. the retail price index.

indicator rents
Guidelines on rents issued to housing associations by the National Federation of Housing Associations. They are revised annually.

indirect construction costs
Costs incurred in building works which are beyond the normal ones of labour, machinery and materials. Normally taken to include the cost of financing, administration, insurance, taxes and loss of interest on money investment, and professional fees.

indirect cylinder
A container for storing hot water that has been heated by a heat exchanger. *See also* direct cylinder, heat exchanger.

industrial and provident societies
Organisations controlled under the auspices of the Registrar of Friendly Societies and must accord with the Industrial and Provident Societies Acts in organising their affairs. The majority of housing associations are industrial and provident societies.

industrial housing associations
Housing associations created

particularly to provide residential accommodation for key workers of the workforce of a particular industry and company.

industrialised building
See system building.

infiltration heat loss
Heat energy that is lost or cooled by virtue of cold air entering a building through windows and doors. *See also* heat loss, fabric heat loss.

informal tender
A tender not containing the characteristics appertaining to a formal tender. *See also* tender, tendering process.

infrastructure
The services which are required for the development and use of land, normally taken to include roads, bridges, railways, gas, water, sewage, electricity and telephone installation.

inherent defect
A defect contained within the structure of a building which was unintentionally built in during the design or construction, or both.

inheritance
Things which are passed on from a man or woman to their heirs.

inheritance tax
Formerly termed capital transfer tax and being a levy charged on transfers made during the lifetime of the taxpayer as well as on his or her death. Lifetime gifts may be exempt if given seven years before the death of the grantor. If given within three to seven years, tax, if payable, is on a sliding scale.

initial return/yield
The net income initially received at the date of purchase and usually expressed as a percentage of the purchase price.

injunction
An order or decree from the court where a party to an action is required to refrain from doing a particular deed or is required to do a particular deed. Injunctions are either mandatory (compulsory) or restrictive (prohibitive).

Injunctions are granted as an interim measure (interlocutory injunction) or permanently (perpetual injunction). They may be granted in divorce and judicial separation proceedings to prevent molestation or the removal of assets.

injurious affection
Reduction in the value of an interest in land, resulting from the implementation of statutory powers.

inner leaf
See cavity wall.

inner sash
The sliding part of a sash window that is fixed into a frame so that it is nearest to the inside of a room. *See also* outer sash, sash window.

in situ
The production of a component placed in the finished position on-site rather than pre-cast in a factory.

in situ concrete
Concrete that is mixed on site or ready mixed and placed in the finished position. *See also* concrete, pre-cast concrete.

in situ concrete pile
See bored pile.

insolvency
The situation where a person is unable to pay his or her debts when they become due.

inspection
In terms of building society valuations, defined by the Royal Institution of Chartered Surveyors as 'a visit to, and examination of a property, for the purpose of obtaining information prior to expressing a professional opinion as to its value, state of repair, or any other aspects'. The extent of the inspection will depend upon its purpose.

inspection chamber
An access provided on a foul or surface water drain for the purpose of inspection, cleansing maintenance and repair. They should be provided at the head of drains, where drains change direction and where branch drains connect into main drains to allow access for cleansing and unblocking drains. They may be constructed of brick, pre-cast concrete sections or pre-formed PVC and are covered with a sealed cover and frame. *See also* back drop manhole.

institutional investors
Normally held to include pension funds, insurance companies, banks, unit trusts, etc.

instrument
A legal document in writing, such as a deed.

insulating plasterboard
Gypsum plasterboard that has one surface faced with aluminium foil which acts as a vapour barrier to prevent interstitial condensation. *See also* gypsum plasterboard, vapour barrier.

insulation
A layer of material incorporated in a building element (eg wall, floor, roof) to reduce noise transmission and heat loss. *See also* insulation block, insulation board, insulation quilt, loose-fill insulation.

insulation block
A concrete block with an insulation layer incorporated on one face, and used for constructing the internal leaf of cavity walls. *See also* concrete blocks.

insulation board
A composite sheet compressed during manufacture to give a light density and used for insulation purposes. *See also* fibreboard.

insulation quilt
A material used to reduce heat loss through a building element such as a wall, ground floor or roof. Also used to absorb sound transmission through walls and floors separating buildings. *See also* insulation.

insurance
The situation whereby a person (the insurer) indemnifies the other person (the insured) against financial losses resulting from a loss caused by way of damage or injury suffered for a situation specified in the insurance policy/contract.

insurance contract
The contractual agreement between the insured and insurer stating the precise terms and conditions of premiums payable and the events against which loss or damage will be compensated.

insurance value
The amount of money estimated that would normally indemnify

the owner and/or occupier of a building if it is destroyed or damaged. It is normally held to be the cost of reinstatement including professional fees and also possibly some form of indexation.

insured
A party which is protected under an insurance policy.

insurer
The party providing protection under an insurance policy.

interest in property
The right of ownership, or some right existing in land owned by another party.

interest on unpaid compensation
The interest that an acquiring authority must pay under compulsory purchase powers on the outstanding compensation from the date of possession until completion of the conveyance.

interim certificate
A certificate issued by an architect or surveyor certifying that work carried out under the terms of the contract during a specified period has been completed and requesting payment from the employer to the contractor.

interlocking piles
See sheet piles.

interlocking tiles
See concrete roofing tiles.

internal door
One that allows access to and from rooms. It generally comprises a lightweight core, such as heavy duty paper, in a box arrangement faced both sides with a sheet material such as plywood or hardboard fixed to a timber edging strip. *See also* core, fire door.

internal repairing lease
The situation where a lease requires that all, or some, of internal repairs, are the responsibility of the tenant. The extent of external repairs to be undertaken by the landlord will be specified in the terms of the lease.

internal valuer
A professional valuer employed within a particular organisation to value the assets of the organisation. *See also* Royal Institution of Chartered Surveyors.

internal wall

A wall used to divide the internal space of a building. *See also* wall, partition wall, division wall, prefabricated partition, stud partition.

interstitial condensation

Moist air that tracks through a building element, such as walls and roofs, and forms water particles within that element. *See also* condensation, vapour barrier, vapour check.

inter vivos

Between living persons.

intestate

A term used to describe a person who dies without having made a will

intestate succession

The Administration of Estates Act 1925, as amended, administers this legal doctrine. The rules are generally that persons who are intestate, had they made a will, would have made provision for certain classes of near relative. For example, children would be provided for equally.

in the market

1. Describes property which is presently for sale or to let.

2. Describes a person seeking to purchase or rent a property.

intimidation

Violence or threats of such, the aim being to compel a person to abstain from, or do, something which he or she has a legal right to do or abstain from doing.

intra vires

Within the powers.

invert

The lowest internal part of a drainpipe or inspection chamber.

invert level

The vertical distance measured between a datum and the lowest internal part of a drainpipe. Used for setting out and positioning pipes to the required gradient.

investment

The application of a capital sum to purchase an asset with a view, hopefully, to increasing the value of the asset upon subsequent disposal.

investment company

Under section 103 of the Taxes Act 1988, defined as 'any company whose business consists wholly, or mainly, in the making of investments and the principal part of whose income is derived therefrom'.

investment file
In the housing association context, it comprises the association's monitoring profile, the association schemework profile and the association investment profile and is prepared and used by the Housing Corporation to establish whether a particular housing association is eligible for further capital funding.

investment method
A method of valuation of an interest in land determined by the capitalisation of estimated or actual net rental income.

investment property
A property purchased with a view of retaining it and enjoying the total return at some future date, i.e. capital appreciation and/or income over the life of the interest acquired.

investment yield
The return, expressed as an annual percentage, which is considered to be appropriate for a particular valuation or investment. It is an estimate of the investor's opinion about the prospects and risks attached to the investment. The better the prospects and lower the risks, the lower the expected yield and greater the capital value.

investor in land
A person acquiring land with the intention of holding it for a return in the form of rent and/or longer term capital appreciation.

ironmongery
See door furniture, window furniture.

isolated foundation
See pad foundation.

isometric projection
A drawing produced to give a three-dimensional view of a building and where all horizontal lines are drawn at an angle of 30°. See also orthographic projection, perspective drawing.

J

jack rafter
A structural pitched roof member one end of which is fixed to a valley or hip rafter and the other end fixed at the eaves. *See also* rafter, common rafter, hip rafter.

jamb
The side of a door or window opening that shows the full width of the wall. *See also* reveal.

JCB
Tradename for an excavating machine.

JCT contract
A standard form of building contract published by the Joint Contracts Tribunal. It is the standard form of contract used in the construction industry, but does not derive from any particular statute. *See also* Joint Contractors Tribunal.

joiner
A craftsman who is responsible for fixing the finishing woodwork to a building such as doors, skirting boards, architraves, windows and stairs. *See also* carpenter.

joinery
The work involved in woodwork finishes to a building. *See also* joiner.

joint
A connection between two members.

joint account
A bank account that can be operated by any or all of the persons concerned, either singly or collectively.

joint agent
1. Two or more agents appointed by the principal to act

on his behalf, for the sale or letting of buildings.

2. Two or more estate agents charged by the owner to secure the sale or letting. *See also* joint sole agent.

joint and several obligations

Where two or more persons enter into an obligation by which each party is liable severally (individually) as well as jointly with the others.

joint board

An organisation representing two or more bodies, e.g. joint planning boards consisting of two or more statutory local planning authorities.

Joint Contracts Tribunal

A forum of people representing contractors, surveyors, architects, etc. in order to publish standard forms of building contract.

joint finance

In the social housing context, finance provided by a district health authority and a social services department of a local authority.

joint funding

In the housing association con-

text, an arrangement in which certain revenue costs are met by some of the statutory charitable sources, before approval for a housing association grant is given.

jointless floor

See composition floor.

joint mortgage

A mortgage taken out by two or more mortgagors.

joint obligation

The situation where two or more parties enter into an obligation so that, in the event of litigation, all must sue or be sued together.

joint sole agent

Describes one of two or more estate agents who are instructed to sell or let property. It is normal custom for the agents to share a commission fee irrespective of whether the property is sold by the other agent. *See also* multiple agency

joint tenancy

Where two or more persons own a tenancy, no one person having a separate share. Four important concepts exist in a joint tenancy:

- Possession: each must be entitled to possession of the whole property.
- Title: each must acquire by virtue of the same instrument.
- Time: each co-owner must acquire the right at the same time.
- Interest: each must acquire the same interest.

joint valuer
Describes one of two or more valuers who are appointed to provide a valuation. See Royal Institution of Chartered Surveyors *Guidance Notes on the Valuation of Assets*.

joint venture
The situation where two or more parties combine to carry on a single business for profit. *See also* participators.

joist
A timber beam used to support a floor or ceiling. *See also* common joist, floor joist, ceiling joist.

joist hanger
A metal bracket which is fixed to a wall and which has provision for supporting the ends of upper timber floor joists. *See also* ceiling joist.

judge
A public officer appointed to adjudicate on causes in a court of justice.

judgement
The decision of the court following legal proceedings.

judgement creditor
A party whom judgement is made in favour of, for a sum of money. *See also* judgement debt.

judgement debtor
A party whom judgement is made against for a sum of money. Such a party may have the judgement enforced by a variety of means if payment is not made, e.g. bankruptcy proceedings, charging order on property etc. *See also* judgement creditor.

judicial trustee
An officer of the court acting as a trustee appointed under the Judicial Trustee Act 1906, as amended.

judicial separation
A petition presented by a husband or wife to the Family Division of the High Court. The granting of a decree means the petitioner is not required to cohabit with the respondent.

junction pipe
A drainpipe incorporated on a main drain with provision for connecting a branch drain which may be of a smaller diameter.

justice of the peace
A lay magistrate appointed by the Crown to act in a quasi-judicial capacity, dealing with minor cases. *See also* magistrate.

K

Keene's cement
A Class D anhydrous gypsum plaster. *See also* gypsum plasters.

keratin
A substance that is added to a hemi-hydrate gypsum plaster (Plaster of Paris) to retard the setting time. *See also* accelerator, gypsum plasters, Plaster of Paris.

key
Provision for achieving a bond between two materials, e.g. applying plaster to a wall surface.

keyed joint
A concave mortar joint between bricks, also referred to as a bucket handle joint.

keying in
The bonding in of new walls to existing walls.

key plan
See location plan.

key property
A property or parcel of land which is crucial to the successful completion of a land assembly programme, e.g. land which would allow access for the development of backland.

keystone
The top stone of an arch which sets into position the remaining bricks or stone forming the arch.

kick plate
A metal plate attached to the bottom of doors on each side to prevent damage.

kiln
A heating chamber used in the manufacture of clay products, such as bricks, and for seasoning (drying) timber.

kilogram (kg)
A metric unit to measure weight. Represents 1000 grammes(g).

kilonewton (kN)
The metric unit to measure force. Represents 1000 newtons.

kilowatt (kW)
The metric unit to measure power. Represents 1000 watts.

king closer
A brick cut to size and larger than a half brick lengthways, which is used to maintain the brick bond at openings and corners. *See also* queen closer.

king post truss
A traditional timber roof truss comprising two principal rafters fixed at the apex with a principal tie at the base to form a triangle incorporating a vertical post (king post) joined at the apex and to the tie with diagonal struts, each side connected to the base of the post and the rafter. This type of truss is made from solid timber, usually hard-wood such as oak, and is left exposed inside the building. *See also* queen post truss, roof truss.

kite winder
A central winder shaped like a kite. *See also* winder.

knacker
A person who purchases older properties for the materials which he can subsequently dispose of at a profit.

knee wall
See attic wall.

knot
A hard area in wood where a branch grew from the main tree stem.

knotting
Coating wood knots with a special sealant to prevent them from discharging resin which would affect paintwork.

K value
See coefficient of thermal conductivity.

L

labourer
A non-skilled construction worker.

lagging
The provision of a thermal insulation material around water pipes and tanks to prevent freezing and to reduce heat loss.

laminate
The process of bonding together materials under compression, usually to form timber and plastic products.

laminated beam
A beam produced by laminating thin strips of timber which can be curved.

laminated glass
Sheet glass containing plastic which, when broken, is held together. *See also* glass.

laminated plastic
Sheet plastic used to cover such items as kitchen fittings and known as Formica or Melamine.

laminboard
A composite timber board consisting of strips of timber sandwiched between two sheets of thin plywood, the whole glued together to form a standard-sized sheet in various thicknesses. Mainly used for internal fittings and fixtures, such as cupboard units. *See also* blockboard.

land
Land of any tenure including the surface, and in respect of any Acts of Parliament passed since 1978 including buildings or parts thereof, any easement, right or privilege, in, over or under it.

land assembly
The process of acquiring indi-

vidual pieces of land to form a larger single unit with a view to its subsequent development or redevelopment.

land availability study

An investigation undertaken to establish land which is available for a particular purpose. It is normally undertaken by surveyors, developers, local planning authorities, etc.

land bank

The stock of land held by a developer with a view to future development or redevelopment.

land charges

Land charges are administered under the Land Charges Act 1972, as amended. They are kept in a register held by the Land Charges Registry.

Land Compensation Act 1973

This legislation allows that compensation can be obtained if intolerable noise cannot be reduced and it reduces property values.

land drain

A system used to drain land by laying perforated or porous pipes into the ground which admit water and direct it to a discharge point, such as an open ditch or stream. See also French drain.

landing

A platform positioned between floors and between flights of stairs for rest purposes and to allow flights to change directions. See also half landing, quarter landing.

Lands Tribunal

A body established by the Lands Tribunal Act 1949, its function being to determine questions relating to compensation for compulsory purchase and the discharge of restrictive covenants. It deals with appeals from local valuation courts.

land registration

The compulsory registration of land on first conveyance of the freehold or grant of a lease greater than 21 years. The record is in three parts:

● the property register describing the land
● the proprietorship register which states the title absolute and any restrictions appertaining to the sale of land

● the charges register which indicates the mortgages, and restrictive covenants.

The registered proprietor is given a land certificate.

landlord and tenant agreement

The contractual relationship between the landlord and tenant. Such formal and informal agreements are controlled by the various Landlord and Tenant Acts.

Landlord and Tenant Act 1985

This Act codifies the general law on landlords and tenants which is not particular to local authority or housing association dwellings, e.g. repairing obligations, service charges and rent books.

land survey

See survey.

land surveyor

1. A professional person who normally works for the Ordnance Survey of Great Britain and is responsible for producing ordnance survey maps.
2. An independent surveyor who produces topographical plans of an area of land.

lantern light

A type of roof light which projects from either a flat roof or the apex of a pitched roof and incorporates its own glazed or solid roof and glazed side panels. *See also* daylight.

lap

Generally refers to the amount by which roof slates or tiles overlap each other. Slates and plain clay tiles are usually fixed to give a double lap of approximately 75mm and gives three layers where the lap occurs. Concrete tiles are fixed single lap to give two layers of tile where the lap occurs. *See also* gauge, margin.

Large Scale Voluntary Transfer Association

In the housing association context, an association sponsored by a local authority to take up local authority housing under a Large Scale Voluntary Transfer Scheme.

latch

A device for opening and closing a door and consisting of a

metal strap which fits into a keeper and is raised or lowered. The door may be secured by providing a deadlock. *See also* deadlock, mortice lock.

latent damage
Damage which exists in a building or structure and which is not known to the purchaser of the property at the time of purchase, but subsequently becomes known to the purchaser. It is generally held not to be identifiable by the normal process of inspection.

latent defect
A concealed or hidden inherent defect in the design or construction of a building which could not normally be identified by the usual process of inspection.

latent value
The potential value accruing to a property on the occurrence of some future event, e.g. the granting of planning permission for a greater beneficial use.

lateral support
A horizontal support member to provide stability, e.g. between timber floor joists. *See also* strutting.

lath
See lathing.

lathing
Thin strips of timber that are fixed to the underside of timber joists or timber frames to provide a key for the application of plaster.

lattice window
A window pane which is divided into small pieces or areas, often diamond-shaped, by strips of lead.

lavatory basin
A washhand basin which forms part of a bathroom suite.

lavatory pan
See water closet.

Law of Property Acts
The statutes concerning land covered by:

● Law of Property Act 1925
● Administration of Estates Act 1925
● Land Charges Act 1925
● Land Registration Act 1925
● Settled Land Act 1925
● Trustee Act 1925
● Universities and Colleges Estates Act 1925.

layboard
A timber board fixed to the bottom of jack rafters of a roof valley to form a valley gutter.

laylight
A rooflight which may be provided to either a flat or pitched roof and is flush with the roof profile. *See also* lantern light.

layout
The internal or external grouping or arrangement of a building or buildings.

lead
A pure metal with good durable properties which has been traditionally used for roofing and plumbing. Although expensive and not now used for pipework for health and safety reasons, it is still available for roofing work, such as flashings, and is incorporated with another material for use as cavity trays. *See also* cavity tray, flashing.

leaded light
See lattice window.

leaf
Part of a building element such as the outer or inner skin of a cavity wall. *See also* cavity wall.

lean concrete
See lean mix.

lean mix
A mortar or concrete mix having a lower than normal proportion of cement. *See also* rich mix.

lean mortar
See lean mix.

lean-to roof
A single sloped pitched roof joined to the wall of a building and at a lower level than the main roof. May be used as a roof to a single-storey extension. *See also* pitched roof.

lease
Agreement for the exclusive possession of property for a term of years in return for a periodic rent. It must specify the term of years. The person granting the lease is called the lessor and the person who rents it the lessee. If the lessee grants the lease it is called a sublease. All leases for a period exceeding three years must be executed by way of deed. See the Law of Property Act 1925, as amended.

leasehold
Land held under a lease and transferrable by assignment.

Leasehold Reform (Housing and Urban Development Act) 1993

This is legislation which gave certain leaseholders the right to enfranchisement. It also set up the Urban Regeneration Agency which has extensive planning and purchase powers and can operate outside urban areas.

ledged and battened door

See battened door.

ledged, braced and battened door

See battened door.

legacy

Personal property gifted by a will.

legal aid

A scheme, governed by the Legal Aid Act 1988, as amended, which provides persons of limited means financial support to progress or defend an action of certain defined types. In civil cases the scheme is administered by the Legal Aid Board and, in criminal cases, usually by magistrates.

lessee

A party to whom a lease is granted. *See also* lease.

lessor

A party who grants a lease. *See also* lease.

letter of comfort

Letter provided by a third party to one particular party in a contract indicating that the third party is likely to provide funds or a service to assist in whole, or in part, on the successful completion of the contract. Often associated with a letter in principle indicating that funding for a building project will be forthcoming from a bank, building society or other institutional lender.

letter of intent

A concept similar to a letter of comfort, but completely different in that it is written by one party to a contract to the other party and not by a third party.

letting value

Rental value.

level

A surveying instrument used for establishing the height and depths of the various parts of the building during its construction using a datum. It is basically a telescope mounted on a tripod. *See also* automatic level, dumpy level, datum, setting out.

levelling
The procedure involved where a level is required.

lever handle
The fitment on a door which is depressed to open or close the door.

lever lock
A type of door lock where a key must be turned a number of times to either release or secure the locking mechanism.

Lewis bolt
See rag bolt.

licence
An authority to occupy land where the occupant has no interest in the land, in contrast to a lease. The existence of exclusive possession is decisive in determination of whether a licence or lease exists. Licenses do not have statutory protection of security of tenure. *See also* lease.

licensee
A party to whom a licence is granted.

lichen
Plant growth on external surfaces, such as walls and roofs that have collected dirt.

lien
The common law right to hold property of another party as security for fulfilment of an obligation, usually associated with the payment of a debt.

life beneficiary
A person receiving payments from a trust for his or her lifetime.

life estate
A mere freehold, not being an inheritance granted to a person for the rest of his or her life. Can only exist in equity or trust.

lifetime homes
Design criteria which allow the development of housing to accessible standards which meet the needs of almost everyone.

lift
A mechanical platform or cage that moves vertically and is used for carrying goods or people between the floors of a building.

lift shaft
An open vertical area provided within a building to accommodate a lift.

light and air easements
Easements which entitle an owner, or occupier of property, to the benefit of adequate light and air.

light, right to
The right acquired under the Prescription Act 1832, as amended, to unobstructed access to light at a person's window. For the right to exist there must be uninterrupted access to the light for 20 years. The Rights of Light Act 1959, as amended, allows the owner of land to prevent the acquisition of a right of light over his land by notice registered in the local Land Charges Register.

lightweight aggregate
A coarse aggregate having a low density such as clinker, pumice, pulverised fuel ash and is used to produce lightweight concrete. *See also* pulverised fuel ash, pumice, clinker.

lightweight concrete
A concrete used to increase thermal insulation and may be aerated or contain a lightweight aggregate to give a low density. *See also* aerated concrete.

lime
See calcium carbonate.

lime mortar
A mixture of lime and sand which is not as strong as cement mortar but remains workable for a longer period.

lime plasters
Produced by heating calcium carbonate to produce calcium oxide (quicklime) to which sufficient water is added to produce calcium hydroxide (hydrated lime), which is used as an additive to mortars thereby reducing shrinkage associated with the setting of Portland cement as well as giving workability to the mix. *See also* ungauged lime plaster.

limestone
A sedimentary rock which is creamy white in colour and characterised by a structure known as oolitic, i.e. made up of minute egg-like grains set in a matrix of calcium carbonate

133

and often containing a high proportion of shells. It is softer than granite and sandstone, and types include Portland stone and Bath stone.

limitation of actions
The period within which actions for legal redress have to be commenced.

limited company
A public or private company registered under the Companies Acts whose financial liability for debts is limited to the value of the shareholding.

limited liability
The degree to which debts of a company are the legal responsibility of the shareholders.

limited liability company
A company with limited liability.

limited owner
Ownership of an interest in property less than freehold.

limited tender
The form of tender where the invitation to submit tenders is limited to a specified class, group, or stated tenderers. *See also* tender, tendering process.

line of credit
The situation where a borrower is entitled to draw a specified sum of money over a given period of time from a bank, on terms agreed at the outset.

lining
A covering to a surface, such as plasterboard sheets, used to provide a ceiling finish to timber joisted floors.

lining paper
A plain paper applied horizontally on to internal wall surfaces to provide a good base for wallpaper or paint.

linoleum
A cheap type of floor covering manufactured from linseed oil compressed on to canvas and available in rolls with various coloured patterns on one side. Now seldom used, having been superceded by vinyl sheet and tiles.

linseed oil
A vegetable oil extract used for mixing with putty and applying to hardwood sills to keep them 'supple'.

lintel
A short beam of steel, timber or

concrete placed above a door or window opening to support the wall above.

lintol
See lintel.

liquidity
The extent to which a party can meet financial commitments.

listed building
A building of special architectural and/or historic interest listed under the Planning (Listed Buildings and Conservation Areas) Act 1990. *See also* buildings of special architectural or historic interest.

listed building consent
The permission required under the Planning (Listed Buildings and Conservation Areas) Act 1990, as amended, from the local planning authority for the demolition, alteration or extension of a building listed as of architectural and/or historic interest.

listing
The process where buildings are placed on a register of buildings of architectural and/or historic

interest maintained under the Planning (Listed Buildings and Conservation Areas) Act 1990. Such buildings are classified as:

● Grade 1: those buildings of exceptional interest.
● Grade II: those buildings which are particularly important and of more than special interest, but not in the outstanding class.
● Grade III: those buildings of special interest, but not sufficiently important to be counted amongst the elite.
See also spot listing.

litigation
The process where parties place a dispute before the courts for settlement.

litre
The metric measure of volume.

live load
The load imposed on a building which is variable in nature and is due to the weight and movement of people occupying the building and the elements such as wind and snow. *See also* load, dead load, horizontal load, imposed load, total load, vertical load.

135

load

The weight or force on a structure. *See also* axial load, horizontal load, imposed load, point load, permissible load, live load, dead load, total load, ultimate load, uniformly distributed load, vertical load.

load-bearing

The term used to describe a building element, such as a wall, that supports load.

load-bearing wall

An external or internal wall that supports upper floors and the roof. *See also* spine wall, wall.

lobby

An enclosed space that separates and acts as an entrance between rooms and to a building.

local authority

An organisation responsible for administering local government: a district or county council; a London borough; a parish council; or similar defined administrative area.

local government

The system whereby the affairs of the community are administered by regional locally elected representatives. They include responsibilities for such matters as education, rating and valuation, refuse collection, town planning etc.

Local Government and Housing Act 1989

This Act introduced changes in local government housing finance including the ring-fenced Housing Revenue Account (the HRA may only contain income and expenditure attributable to local authority tenants, i.e. it cannot be subsidised from other accounts). This Act also restricted the ability of local authorities to use capital receipts (e.g. from the Right to Buy).

local land charge

A binding charge on land, recorded in the local Land Charges Register maintained by local authorities.

local plan

A plan which is prepared by the local planning authority to show how it would like to see the future development of a particular area. In the determination of applications for planning permission they form an important part of the decision-making process, as those applications conforming to the proposals in the local plan are granted permission and those not conforming are refused.

Different types of local plan are prepared for various purposes under different planning statutes; they are variously called development plans, structure plans, local plans, action area plans etc. The current main form of local plan is the Unitary Development Plan prepared under the Planning and Compensation Act 1991. *See also* local planning authority, Planning and Compensation Act 1991.

local planning authority

The statutory planning authority responsible under the Town and Country Planning Acts for preparing statutory local plans and granting or refusing applications for planning permission. The allocation of planning functions between county and district councils is complicated but, generally speaking, county councils are responsible for strategic plan preparation and minerals and district councils are responsible for detailed local

plans and the determination of most types of applications for planning permission. *See also* local plan, Town and Country Planning Act 1947, planning application.

local valuation court

A tribunal established to adjudicate on appeals against existing entries on the valuation list, or proposals to amend it. There is a right of appeal from the local valuation court to the Lands Tribunal.

location plan

A plan showing the location of a particular building, normally drawn on a scale of 1 to 1250 or 1 to 2500.

lock

A mechanism used for securing a door and operated by turning a metal tongue into a keeper. *See also* cylinder lock, deadlock, mortice lock.

lodger

Person who lives as part of a family and normally shares heating, cooking and other facilities and does not have an exclusive right of occupation of a room or rooms. The Housing

Act 1985, as amended, gives secure tenants the right to take in lodgers with the consent of the landlord.

loft

The roof space in a building formed by a pitched roof and into which access is provided by means of a trap door incorporated in the ceiling and usually positioned above the landing.

longhorn beetle

See house longhorn beetle.

loose-fill insulation

A material consisting of separate particles such as expanded mineral chips and plastic beads. It is mainly used for insulating existing cavity walls and roofs since it can be pumped into position without major disturbance to the building.

loss adjuster

A professionally qualified person normally acting for insurers in an independent capacity and responsible for quantifying the losses under an insurance claim.

loss assessor

A professional person, acting for a claimant in an insurance loss, who is responsible for determining the amount of damage incurred and for negotiating the best financial settlement on behalf of the claimant.

lot

A property offered for sale, often by auction.

lotting

A method used at auctions whereby property is divided into parts, each of which is capable of being sold separately with a view to achieving a greater return on the whole than if sold as a whole.

louvre

An inclined slat that can be adjusted to open or close. It is used for ventilation purposes and protects against rain penetration.

louvre window

A window that incorporates glass louvres.

low-cost home ownership

A colloquial generic term for leasehold schemes for the elderly, shared ownership, do-it-yourself shared ownership, and improvement for sale schemes.

low-level flushing cistern

A cistern placed above the WC pan and operated by a lever handle, rather than a chain which is used to operate a cistern placed at a high level. *See also* automatic flushing cistern, flushing cistern, water closet.

lump

The casual workforce employed in the building industry, which is characterised by unique arrangements for the collection of income tax.

lump sum building contract

A building contract in which the contractor agrees to undertake the works for a fixed price. *See also* fixed price contract.

lunar month

A period of 28 days.

lux

A scientific term used to measure the intensity of light at a given point.

Lyctus powder-post beetle

An insect that feeds on the sapwood of hardwood leaving holes 1–2mm in diameter.

M

macadam
A road surface formed by crushed rock or stone compressed by rolling and then coated with bitumen. *See also* Tarmacadam.

made ground
Areas of land, such as old quarries and refuse tips, that have been filled. They are not generally suitable for constructing buildings since they are highly compressible and may contain toxic substances. May require removal and refill with clean, compacted material or the use of piled foundations. Before development such sites will be investigated and soil samples taken.

made land
Land which is reclaimed from the sea, or by drainage from other land.

made up land
Land which initially was unsuitable for building, but has subsequently been made suitable by such measures as levelling, contouring, etc.

magistrate
An officer with judicial powers in matters of a minor criminal or civil nature. *See also* justice of the peace.

magistrates' court
The inferior criminal and civil court. It normally consists of two or more justices of the peace sitting as a court and advised on legal matters by a legally qualified clerk to the justices.

magnesite flooring
A jointless floor finish applied to a solid concrete floor and consists of magnesium oxide, magnesium chloride, plus fillers. *See also* composition floor.

magnesium
A pure metal element which can be combined with aluminium and zinc to produce a light alloy.

mahogany
A hardwood, reddish-brown in colour, originally used for high-class flooring but now seldom used due to cost and scarcity, although imported tropical wood is available as a 'mahogany' substitute.

main
See service main.

main beam
A structural member whose ends are supported by load-bearing walls. *See also* beam, secondary beam, simply supported beam.

main contractor
See contractor.

maintain
A term in a lease covenant meaning to keep substantially in the same condition as when the lease was granted.

maintenance
1. An order following divorce, nullity or judicial separation requiring either party to a marriage to make periodic payments for the maintenance of the other.
2. The necessary periodic work to ensure that a building does not fall into a dilapidated state and involving routine cleaning, painting and decorating and making sure that all mechanical services are in good working order.

maintenance contract
A contract to provide for the inspection and overhaul of servicing. *See also* contract.

maintenance management
The planning and application of maintenance of an item.

maintenance period
Defects liability period.

Maintenance Trust Fund
A fund established for the purposes of maintaining a particular building specified in the Trust Deed. Normally applied to a single building in multi-occupation, to ensure that funds are available when necessary.

maisonette
A dwelling where the living

accommodation is situated on two upper levels of a building.

major interest
1. Freehold or leasehold interest.
2. A term exceeding 21 years, usually applied for value added tax purposes.

making good
Remedial work carried out on existing parts of a building which have been affected by new or additional work.

maladministration
Matters which are investigated by the relevant 'ombudsman' for administration following complaints of injustice in consequence of neglect by a public body.

mala fide
In bad faith.

mal feasance
Undertaking of an unlawful act.

management agreement
In the housing association context, the situation where a housing association wishes to devolve its responsibility for managing a scheme to another agency. A management agree-ment is the legal contract which defines the responsibility of the two parties.

Management and Maintenance Allowances
In the housing association context, notional sums of money which will be spent on managing and maintaining the property. The allowances are used in the calculation of the Rent Surplus Fund and to assess the reasonableness of a claim for a revenue deficit grant.

managing agent
In the housing association context, an organisation, usually a firm of estate agents, which provides housing management services.

managing trustee
A trustee responsible for managing property under the control of a trust.

manganese
A fine metal element contained in steel.

manganese steel
Steel containing more than 1 per cent of manganese, giving extra strength.

manhole
See inspection chamber.

mansard roof
A pitched roof having two slopes on each side, the first having a steep pitch to near vertical and the upper slope a conventional pitch (i.e. 30°, 45°) and used to incorporate the upper part of the building within the roof space. *See also* pitched roof.

map
A drawing which is a scaled representation of the features of a specified area of the earth's surface. It is drawn to a particular scale, e.g. ordnance survey map at a scale of 1–1250.

marble
A metamorphic rock generally used for ornamental purposes and expensive floor finishes, and polished to expose a variety of colours. There are no true marbles to be found in the UK, so most are imported, e.g. white marble (Italy), black marble (Belgium), green marble (Sweden). A pinkish metamorphosed limestone, resembling marble, can be found in Derbyshire.

margin
The exposed distance between the exposed edge of roof slates and tiles and is normally the same distance as the gauge. *See also* lap, gauge.

market price
The price, or the sums, which are realised when a property is sold in a given market.

marl
A soil or rock with a high proportion of lime.

marriage
The voluntary union of one man and one woman for life to the exclusion of all others. The legal requirements concerning a marriage are contained in the Marriage Acts 1949 and 1983, as amended. The Acts require that certain formalities must be complied with to constitute a valid marriage. A void marriage is one where the parties have gone through a ceremony but there is lacking some essential ingredient. A voidable marriage is a valid one subsisting until a decree of nullity is pronounced.

marriage settlement
A conveyance of property for the benefit of the parties to a marriage. Pre- and post-nuptial

settlements can be varied by the court. See Matrimonial Causes Act 1973 section 24(1) and Inheritance (Provision for Family and Dependants) Act 1975 section 2(1)(b), as amended. *See also* settlement.

marriage value
The potential value which can be achieved by the merger of two or more interests in land.

masking
The provision of a special tape to a surface, such as a glazed area, to prevent paint coming into contact with that surface when decorating.

mason
A skilled person who carves stone, especially with regard to building work.

masonry
Bricks or stone used to construct walls.

masonry nail
A special nail that can be driven into brick, stone and concrete.

masonry paint
Paint that can be applied directly to brick, stone or concrete, which usually contains sand and fibres for durability.

mass concrete
Plain or unreinforced concrete. *See also* concrete.

mastic
A waterproof flexible material which is used to seal joints around external door and window frames.

mastic asphalt
See asphalt.

matrimonial causes
Divorce, nullity and judicial separation suits.

matrimonial home
Property where husband and wife have lived together. Under the Matrimonial Homes Act 1983, as amended, a spouse is given protection from eviction of the matrimonial home.

McCarthy rules
The name given to the principles governing the right to compensation for injurious affection where no part of the claimant's land is acquired.

means of escape
Provision, by means of desig-

nated escape routes within the building leading to fire escape stairs, to exit a building in case of fire.

mechanical adhesive
An adhesive material which fills the depressions in a porous surface, and on setting, interlocks them so forming a mechanical key. *See also* adhesive, specific adhesive.

mechanical ventilation
Ventilation provided within a building by mechanical means such as a fan. *See also* natural ventilation, controlled ventilation.

meeting rail
The top and bottom members of a sash window that meet when the windows are closed. *See also* sash window, inner sash, outer sash, sash lock.

melamine
See laminated plastic.

membrane
A thin layer of impervious material generally used as damp-proof membrane and vapour barrier. *See also* damp-proof membrane, vapour barrier.

memorandum of association
A document required under the Companies Acts indicating, amongst other things, the name of the company, its registered address and its objectives. It applies to both incorporated limited and unlimited liability companies.

mental disorder
Defined under the Mental Health Act 1983 as an illness or incomplete development of the mind, psychopathic disorder or other disability of the mind.

merchant bank
A bank which specialises in advising companies on raising capital and on takeovers of other companies. Such lending is usually on a short-term basis.

merger of interests
The process whereby a superior interest with one or more inferior interests in the same property is amalgamated, thereby amalgamating several titles into one.

merulius lacrymans
See dry rot.

mesh reinforcement
Steel bars welded together to

form squares and manufactured in standard-size sheets and used for reinforcing large areas, such as concrete floors.

messuage
A house including gardens, courtyard, orchard and out-buildings.

metal lathing
See expanded metal lathing.

metallic paint
Paint used to prevent rusting and containing small particles of metal such as aluminium, bronze and zinc.

metamorphic rock
Usually a former sedimentary rock which has been altered by great pressure and/or heat in the earth's crust until the constituent minerals have been changed and the structure altered. Marbles and slates are examples. *See also* sedimentary rock.

metre
The metric unit to measure length.

metric brick
See brick.

mezzanine
A floor area that overlooks a ground floor and is positioned between the ground and first floor.

micro-bore heating system
A central heating system using small diameter copper pipes to feed radiators. The pipework is provided in rolls so that long lengths can be installed, thereby reducing the number of joints required. *See also* small bore heating system.

middle rail
The middle member in a panelled door. *See also* panelled door.

mild steel
Steel with a low carbon content, which is used for structural purposes, such as beams.

mineral
A natural material found in the ground, such as rock.

mineral fibre
A material made from the fibres of inorganic materials, such as glass.

mineral wool
Mineral fibres used to produce

insulation materials. *See also* glass wool, rock wool.

minimum lending rate
Introduced in 1972 to replace the bank rate. It is the minimum rate at which the Bank of England would lend on the discount market.

minimum rent
The rent below which a variable rent will not fall.

minor
Defined under the Family Law Reform Act 1969 as someone under the age of 18 years.

minor interest
Third-party rights and interests in land which are not registered on the Land Register.

minor tenancy
Under the Compulsory Purchase (Vesting Declaration) Act 1981, defined as 'a tenancy for a year, or from year to year, or any lesser interest'.

MIRAS
Mortgage interest relief at source. The tax relief deducted by the lender so that the borrower does not have to make a claim direct to the Inland Revenue. Relief is available on most individual households for purchase or improvement not exceeding £30 000.

misrepresentation
A statement which is false or misleading in fact made by, or on behalf of, one party to a contract to another party to the contract which, although not forming part of the contract, induces another party to enter into the contract.

mitigation of loss
The situation required of the plaintiff to take reasonable steps to reduce or avoid loss.

mitre
A 45° joint between two members of the same size which form a right angle.

mix
The proportions of materials used to produce concrete, mortar and plaster.

mixed development
A development involving two or more different uses.

mixed drainage system
See combined sewage system.

mixed hereditament

A hereditament, partly residential, partly commercial, of which the proportion of the rateable value, attributable to the part used as a residential hereditament, exceeds one-eighth. *See also* hereditament.

mobility allowance

Benefit paid to a person with a physical disability, who is unable to walk. Now replaced by the Disability Living Allowance and Disability Working Allowance Act 1991, as amended.

mobility housing

Dwellings designed for occupation by people with a mobility impairment, and who may need to use a wheelchair occasionally. *See also* elderly persons' dwellings, special needs housing.

model rent review clause

A clause concerning rent reviews, published as a standard in the drafting of leases. The Royal Institution of Chartered Surveyors and the Law Society publish a number of model clauses.

modernisation

Changes undertaken to a building, the purposes of which are to reflect contemporary developments of design, function, decoration, etc.

modular brick

See brick.

moisture barrier

Provision within a building element to prevent moisture penetration. *See also* damp-proof course, damp-proof membrane, vapour barrier.

moisture content

The moisture contained within a material, e.g. the amount of moisture in a soil sample can be determined by comparing it to the weight of the dry solid material.

moisture gradient

The change in moisture content of a building element, such as an external wall, which will vary due to absorption and drying out of water.

moisture meter

A device for determining the percentage moisture content of a material.

moisture movement

Movement caused by the

absorption and drying out of water. *See also* expansion joint, temperature movement, settlement.

moneylender
Defined in the Moneylenders Acts 1900 and 1927 (repealed by the Consumer Credit Act 1974) as any person whose business was that of moneylending, or who advertised or announced himself or held himself out in any way as carrying on that business, but not including pawnbrokers, friendly societies, bankers or bodies exempted by the Department of Trade and Industry 1990. Moneylenders are normally regulated by the Consumer Credit Act 1974, as amended.

monitoring
In the context of housing associations, the regular surveillance of the work of each registered housing association by the Housing Corporation.

monolithic
Jointless – as in a jointless construction.

monolithic screed
A cement and sand screed applied to 'green' concrete to achieve a good bond. *See also* green concrete, screed.

mono-pitch roof
A single roof slope having a low pitch (i.e. less than 30°) used for design purposes as an alternative to conventional pitched roofs.

mortar
A mixture of cement, sand and water used to bind bricks and stone together. A plasticiser may be added to produce a workable mix. *See also* mortar joint.

mortar joint
The horizontal and vertical joints between bricks and stone. The joint may be finished flush with the face of the wall (flush-pointed joint) or recessed (recessed joint). *See also* weather-struck joint.

mortgage
An equitable interest in freehold or leasehold property which is conveyed as security for a loan with provision for redemption on repayment of the loan. The mortgagee (lender) has powers of recovery in the event of default by the mortgagor

(borrower). *See also* mortgagee's remedies.

mortgage broker
A person who arranges loans by way of mortgages for borrowers.

mortgagee
The person to whom property is mortgaged; the lender of the mortgage debt.

mortgagee's remedies
If a borrower defaults, the remedies available are as follows: firstly, foreclose; second, exercise the power of sale; third, sue on a personal covenant; fourth, appoint a receiver; and, fifth, take possession of the property.

mortgagor
The person who mortgages his property as security for the mortgage debt, the borrower.

mortice
A slot in timber to form a joint by receiving a tenon formed in an opposite timber member. *See also* tenon, mortice and tenon.

mortice and tenon
A method of joining two members, usually made of wood, by means of a tenon protruding from one member which fits into a slot (mortice) provided in the other. *See also* mortice, tenon.

mortice lock
A door lock and opening mechanism consisting of a deadlock and a brass tongue on a spring which fits into a keeper and is operated by turning a handle which retracts it allowing the door to be opened. *See also* deadlock, latch, lock, cylinder lock.

mortise
See mortice.

mosaic
Small square pieces of coloured glass or marble used for decorative purposes and applied to walls or floors by bedding in cement.

mould
1. Fungal type of growth on a surface which is green/grey in colour and caused by damp, poorly ventilated conditions.
2. A material that has been specially shaped for decorative purposes, such as a cornice.

moulding
A material which has been

specially shaped for decorative purposes, such as a cornice.

movement joint
See expansion joint, contraction joint.

'move on' grant
In the housing association context, a Housing Corporation grant paid per bed space on self-contained units developed under the Housing Act 1988, as amended. The arrangements are for people who have moved out of institutions.

mullion
A vertical member in a window frame which separates glazed areas which may be fixed or opening. *See also* fixed light, opening light, transom.

multiple agency
The appointment of two or more agents to sell or let property. The successful agent is entitled to commission which does not have to be shared with other retained agents. *See also* joint sole agent.

multi-point water heater
A gas appliance which heats cold water instantaneously by opening a hot water tap on an appliance, such as a bath, which causes the unit to fire. It eliminates the need for a hot water cylinder. *See also* combination boiler.

multi-storey
A building of five or more storeys.

municipal law
The laws affecting the administration and implementation of local government.

muntin
A vertical member in a framed door that separates panels. *See also* panelled door.

mutual option
An option available to either party to a contract in the event of a specific happening.

N

nail
A steel spike which is pointed at one end with a head at the other for driving into timber. It is the most common method for fixing and joining timber components.

national assistance
A form of benefit introduced by the National Assistance Act 1948 and superseded by supplementary benefit introduced under the Supplementary Benefit Act 1966, as amended. This, in turn, has been superseded by income support. *See also* income support.

National Association of Estate Agents
An organisation established in 1962 to represent and protect the interests of practising estate agents.

National Federation of Housing Associations
The central organisation representing housing associations in England.

National Health Service
The service introduced by the National Health Service Act 1946, which is responsible for providing comprehensive healthcare to residents of the United Kingdom, irrespective of income.

National Health Trust
A body responsible for the ownership and management of hospitals and other establishments which were previously administered by regional, district or special health authorities.

national insurance
The means by which various social benefits are funded and

supported. Claimants for benefits may appeal against the decision of an adjudication officer to a social security appeal tribunal, or disability appeal tribunal. Further appeal on a point of law is to the Social Security Commissioner.

national loan fund
In the housing association context, the source of government loans to the Housing Corporation.

National Trust
A charitable trust established under the National Trust Act 1907 and responsible for the preservation and conservation of places of historic and/or architectural interest, and natural beauty.

natural asphalt
See asphalt.

natural light
Light obtained from the sky used to illuminate rooms, the degree of illumination being dependent on the amount of glazed area serving the room. *See also* daylight factor.

natural right of support
A right at common law which prevents the owner of an adjoining property from either doing something which endangers the stability of the surface and the substrata of adjoining land, or neglecting to do something which is needed to maintain the stability. No natural right of support to a building exists at law.

natural stone
See igneous rock, metamorphic rock, sedimentary rock.

natural ventilation
Fresh air obtained from the outside of a building through open windows used to ventilate rooms, roofs and floors. *See also* mechanical ventilation, controlled ventilation.

needle
Part of a dead shore. *See also* dead shore.

negative development value
Describes the situation where existing use value is greater than the value of the property following development or redevelopment.

negative value
Describes the situation in which the value of an asset which is a

liability can be disposed of only by means of a payment to the purchaser.

negligence
A breach of a duty of care which results in damage. Actionable in law as a tort.

negotiation
The process whereby two or more parties aim to reach a common agreement. May be verbal or written.

negotiator
A person who undertakes negotiations often as an agent on behalf of the principal.

net internal area
The measured useable space within a building. Measurements are taken to the internal finishes, but exclude toilets, lift and plant room, stairs and lift wells, common entrance halls, lobbies and corridors, internal structural walls and car parking areas. Often referred to as effective floor area. *See also* gross internal area, gross external area.

net rent
Rent less outgoings.

newel
A vertical post situated at the top and bottom of a flight of stairs into which the handrail and outer string is fixed.

newel cap
The top part of a newel which is usually moulded and fixed separately or worked on the solid. *See also* newel.

newel post
See newel.

newton
The metric unit to measure force (100N = 1kN).

new towns
Large settlements newly created by development corporations established under the New Town Act 1946, as amended.

next of kin
The nearest blood relative.

nib
The projecting portions incorporated in a roof tile which are used to hang the tile over roofing battens. *See also* roof tiles.

night latch
See night lock.

night lock
A cylinder lock that is operated by a key from the outside and a handle from the inside. *See also* cylinder lock.

nogging
That part of a timber frame which is fixed horizontally to stabilise vertical members of the frame. *See also* stud partition, stud.

noise
When a noise becomes a nuisance the local authority can issue an abatement notice, contravention of which is an offence. Alternatively, the local authority can issue an injunction under the Control of Pollution Act 1974, as amended.

noise control
See sound insulation.

noise insulation
See sound insulation.

nominated subcontractor
A firm that is nominated by the architect and which the contractor must employ to carry out a specified part of the building work which is usually specialist in nature, such as heating and ventilating. *See also* subcontractor.

nominated supplier
A firm that is nominated by the architect and from whom the contractor must purchase certain building items such as windows, doors and roof tiles. *See also* supplier.

non-cohesive soil
A soil containing granular materials such as sands and gravels and whose strength depends upon density and granular distribution. *See also* subsoil.

non-combustible
Describes a material that will not burn but could alter in state with fire. *See also* fire resistance, non-flammable.

non-conforming use
The use of land and buildings which do not conform with the local planning authorities allocated use for an area. Such uses were normally in existence before statutory planning controls were introduced.

non-ferrous metals
Metals such as copper, lead and aluminium, and alloys of copper such as brass and bronze.

non-fines concrete

A concrete mix that eliminates fine aggregate, resulting in a porous mass with improved thermal insulation properties. *See also* concrete.

non-flammable

A material that will not readily burst into flames due to fire. *See also* fire resistance, non-combustible, spread of flame.

non-load-bearing

An element of a building that does not support a load other than its own weight, e.g. a non-load-bearing wall.

non-load-bearing wall

A wall that does not support upper floors and roof and is usually an internal wall. *See also* partition wall, wall.

non-recourse loan

A loan where the terms provide that the only security to the lender is the property offered as collateral.

non-recurring expense

Expenditure which is usually not repeated, e.g. works required to meet a statutory requirement.

north light roof

One having roof slopes at pitches of different angles, usually 60° and 30°, the steeper slope being glazed and facing the northerly aspect to prevent sunlight and glare affecting the inside of the building.

north point

A sign on a map, often in the form of an arrow, indicating the geographical north.

nosing

The external angle of a step which is the projecting part of the tread over the riser. *See also* tread, riser.

nosing line

See pitchline.

notice to quit

A periodic tenancy runs indefinitely unless either the landlord or tenant serves a notice to quit. It must specify the correct date for termination of the tenancy which has to be an anniversary date.

notice to treat

A notice served on the owners, mortgagees and lessees by a public authority when using its compulsory purchase powers. The notice provides details of the property to be acquired, demands details of ownership and recipients' claim for compensation. It indicates that the acquiring authority is willing to treat for the purchase of the land. *See also* compulsory purchase, compulsory purchase order.

nuisance

Legally there are two types: first, a public or common nuisance; and, second, a private nuisance.

A public or common nuisance is an act which interferes with the enjoyment of a right to which everyone is entitled, such as the right to travel, the right to fresh air, etc. A public nuisance is a crime.

A private nuisance is any wrongful disturbance or interference with a person's use or enjoyment of land or an act allowing the escape of deleterious things on to another's land, e.g. water, smoke, smell, fumes etc.

O

oak
A hardwood used for high-class joinery work, such as block flooring, due to its appearance and durability.

obscured glass
Glass with a roughened, patterned surface on one side and which therefore cannot be seen through. It is used in such situations as glazing bathroom windows. *See also* patterned glass.

occupation
The state of having physical control or possession of land.

occupier's liability
See dangerous premises.

off-site improvements
Works undertaken on land to make other land suitable for development, e.g. access roads, sewers, water mains, etc.

ogee
A type of moulding to a length or strip of timber used for decorative purposes, e.g. as an edging to door panels.

oil-fired boiler
See boiler.

oil paint
A liquid substance, available in a variety of colours and used for applying to metal and wooden surfaces to give a decorative finish, which is formed by the oil oxidising to create a hard film. *See also* paint.

ombudsman
Popular name for the Parliamentary or Local Commissioner who is the public officer responsible for investigating and making recommendations concerning maladministration in central or local government.

on-costs
Additional costs beyond basic costs. They may include professional fees, legal charges, insurance and finance.

one-pipe system
A system that incorporates soil and waste pipes into one common pipe or stack and is used to serve buildings where the soil and waste appliances are identical on each flow. An anti-siphon pipe would also be incorporated within the system. *See also* two-pipe system, single stack system.

open contract
A contract for the sale of land which simply states the names of the parties, the price and a description of the land. It leaves statute and common law to determine any necessary terms.

open eaves
See eaves.

open floor
An upper timber joisted floor where the underside of the joists are exposed by eliminating a ceiling.

opening light
Part of a window that opens to

allow in fresh air. *See also* fixed light, casement window.

open market value
The best price which could potentially be achieved for an interest in property at the valuation date. The Royal Institution of Chartered Surveyors *Guidance Notes on the Valuation of Assets* define it as 'the best price which might reasonably be expected to be obtained for an interest in the property at the date of valuation, assuming firstly a willing seller, secondly a reasonable period in which to negotiate the sale, thirdly that values will remain static during that period, fourthly that the property will be freely exposed to the market, and fifthly that no account will be taken of any higher price that might be paid by a person with a special interest'.

open newel stair
A staircase having a central open well with newels placed at each change of direction, and where the width of the stairwell is generally more than twice the width of the staircase. *See also* newel, stairs.

open riser stair
A staircase where the steps consist of treads only. *See also* stairs.

open roof
Where the roof space and rafters are exposed to the room below by eliminating a ceiling.

open stair
A stairway which has a wall on one side and a bannister on the other. *See also* stairs.

open string
See cut string.

open well stair
Where the flights of stairs are arranged so that a large open area is produced in the centre which is sometimes utilised for incorporating a lift. *See also* stairs.

option
A contractual right enabling one of the parties, if they so wish, and if the circumstances are available under the terms of the contract, to exercise a right to do something, or require the other party to do something in the future.

order
A direction of a court.

ordinary Portland cement
See Portland cement.

Ordnance benchmark
Reference points indicated on an ordnance survey map which indicate the height or depth below sea level. *See also* ordnance datum, benchmark.

ordnance datum
The point at which the heights and depths of Great Britain are established and from which benchmarks are determined. It is derived from mean sea level readings at Newlyn in Cornwall. *See also* Ordnance Survey.

Ordnance Survey
An organisation established in 1791 to produce maps for military purposes. It is now a government agency responsible primarily for producing topographical maps.

orientation
The positioning of a building in relation to north, south, east and west.

orthographic projection
A drawing produced to give a two-dimensional view and in which all lines are drawn

horizontally or vertically. It is used to produce elevations, plans and sections of a building. *See also* isometric projection, perspective drawing.

outbuilding
A small building within the boundary of a main building but not part of it, such as a shed or store.

outer leaf
See cavity wall.

outer sash
The sliding part of a sash window that is fixed into a frame so that it is nearest to the outside. *See also* inner sash, sash window.

outer string
The string that is fixed on the opposite side of the wall string and is exposed. *See also* string.

outfall
The point at which a sewer – usually a surface water sewer – discharges into the sea, river or stream.

outgoings
Sums of money paid by the owner of an interest in property, e.g. rates, insurance, etc. It is normally expressed on a yearly basis.

outhouse
See outbuilding.

outlet
An opening incorporated in a rainwater gutter or drainpipe to provide a means of connecting another pipe.

outline planning application
An application for outline planning permission. *See also* planning application.

outline planning permission
The formal consent granted by a local planning authority in response to an application for outline planning permission, subject to the grant of reserved matters usually concerning design, materials and external appearance. *See also* planning permission.

overflow pipe
A pipe which is connected to a flushing cistern and projects through an external wall and allows water to drain away should it rise above its normal level within the cistern due to a faulty ball valve. *See also* warning pipe.

161

overhand work
Generally used to describe a building element that has been constructed on the opposite side of the natural working position.

overhang
A projecting part of a structure beyond the external face of a supporting wall.

overhanging eaves
The bottom part of a roof that projects over the wall that supports. *See also* eaves.

oversale
A wire or cable crossing land without support on the land.

oversite
The soil that is left exposed after the removal of the vegetable layer (i.e. subsoil). *See also* subsoil.

oversite concrete
A layer of concrete laid on hard-core to prevent rising damp from the ground affecting a hollow timber floor constructed above.

ovolo
A type of moulding to a length or strip of timber which is used for decorative purposes such as on the top edge of a skirting board.

owner
Generally meant to mean the freeholder or leaseholder. The definition varies depending on the statute referred to.

oxidation
The chemical process involved when metal is left exposed and in contact with air, which causes some metals, such as steel, to rust and corrode but leaves a protective skin on other metals, such as a green coating on copper.

P

packing
Small pieces of timber or other materials used to fit between components to obtain a proper fit and alignment.

pad
See padstone.

pad foundation
A square or rectangular slab of plain or reinforced concrete that supports an isolated load such as that from a column. *See also* pile cap.

padstone
A stone or concrete capping placed at the top of a pier to provide a seating for the end of a beam.

paint
A liquid applied to a surface to protect and decorate and consisting of pigments carried in a liquid medium which dries to a hard film after application. *See also* emulsion paint, oil paint, primer, undercoat.

parting agent
See release agent.

paint system
A number of coats of paint applied to a surface, each having a specific function such as a primer, undercoat and final coat.

pallet
A special timber platform used for stacking materials which are moved by a forklift truck.

pane
A glass panel in a door or window.

panel
Timber moulded from the solid to be incorporated in a panelled

door or wall. *See also* pannelled door.

panel absorber

A special sound-absorbent panel used for lining ceilings and walls to absorb sound. *See also* sound insulation, insulation.

panel heater

A thin electric heating panel fixed to walls.

panelled door

A door which is framed and has panels incorporated in the spaces between the framework. *See also* muntin.

panel solicitors

In the housing association context, firms of solicitors approved by the Housing Corporation to act as conveyancers for both the housing association and the Housing Corporation under a common code and scale of fees.

panic bolt

A large bolt which extends the full width of a door and is operated by pushing downwards to unlock and open the door from the inside.

pan tile

A clay roof tile which is curved to give an S shape in cross-section and is laid single lap. *See also* clay roof tiles, Roman tile.

parapet

See parapet wall.

parapet gutter

See box gutter.

parapet wall

The top part of an external wall that is constructed above a flat roof to form a small enclosing wall. *See also* wall.

parcel

A separately identifiable area of land usually in one ownership. The term is often used in association with conveyancing.

parent

Father or mother of a child. See Family Law Reform Act 1987, section 1.

parental responsibility

The rights, duties and responsibilities and authority which, by law, parents have in relation to their children and property. See Children Act 1989, section 3, as amended.

pargetting

1. Cement render applied to the inside of a brick flue to seal it.

2. Patterned plasterwork applied to the outside of buildings.

Parker Morris Standards

Standards for housing associations and local authorities new build schemes established by the government in 1967. They are now superseded by the design criteria published by the Housing Corporation.

parking ratio

The ratio of a number of car parking spaces to the amount of accommodation made available for a particular building or development project.

parquet

Thin hardwood blocks or strips.

parquet floor

A floor consisting of parquet which is normally laid on top of a plywood sub-base.

partial completion certificate

A certificate issued by an architect or surveyor to a building contract where the employer wishes to take possession of a completed part of a building.

participators

Parties to a joint venture who share its risks and profits or losses. The benefits and obligations of the parties to the venture depend on the specific terms of the agreement entered into. *See also* joint venture.

particle board

A composite board manufactured from timber waste that is chipped and bonded with resins and compressed in standard sizes and thicknesses. *See also* composite board.

particulars

Property details pertaining to a building or land which is to be sold or let, often prepared by an agent and distributed to potential purchasers or tenants.

parties

Persons suing or being sued.

parting bead

A narrow strip of timber which is fixed vertically to each side of a box frame to keep separate and allow the two windows in a sash to move up and down independently. *See also* sash window.

parting slip

A narrow strip of timber which

is fixed inside a box frame to keep separate the weights which are used to operate a sash window.

partition

The physical division of land amongst its owners either voluntarily by deed or compulsorily by court order.

partition wall

A non-load bearing internal wall creating a division. *See also* division wall, prefabricated partition, stud partition.

partnership

The relationship that exists between persons carrying on a business together with a view to making a profit. The rights of the partners is governed by a partnership agreement. Every partner is liable for the debts of the partnership to the full extent of his or her property.

part possession

The situation where part of the property is occupied by the owner, or is vacant, with the remainder being subject to one or more tenancies.

Part Three Homes

In the housing association context, residential accommodation for people in need of care and support for reason of age infirmity or physical disability. These homes were first provided under Part 3 of the National Assistance Act 1948 and are now required to be registered under the Registered Homes Act 1984, if they provide board and personal care.

party wall

A wall belonging to more than one owner. Generally tenancy in common of a wall is assumed. Under the Law of Property Act 1925 section 38(1), as amended, a party wall is deemed to be severed vertically between the respective owners, each of whom have the requisite rights of support and use over the rest of the wall.

Party Wall Agreement

An agreement indicating the respective rights of the owners of properties divided by a party wall. It is an agreement enforceable against purchasers when registered as a land charge.

passing rent

Existing rent which is payable under the terms of a lease or tenancy agreement.

patent defect
Plainly visible defect which would be identified by the exercise of reasonable observation.

patent glazing
Standard-size glass panels fixed directly into windows and doors using special fixing beads and sealing strips. The panels are usually double-glazed and the system is usually manufactured in a factory.

patina
A protective film that forms on the surface of certain metals, e.g. copper exposed to air. *See also* oxidation.

patio
A paved area generally positioned at the rear of a house and which is used for the purpose of relaxation.

pattern staining
Dirt that collects on a surface which has an uneven thermal resistance, e.g. where the lines of the joists are shown on the ceiling of a timber joisted floor.

patterned glass
Glass which is textured or patterned on one side and smooth on the other. *See also* obscured glass.

pavement
A pathway provided at the side of a road for the use of pedestrians.

peat
A soil consisting of decayed vegetable matter and high in moisture and acidic content.

pebble dash
See render.

pedestal washbasin
A wash handbasin that is fixed to the wall and the base supported on a shaped matching upright component.

pelmet
A strip of timber or cloth fixed at the top of a window on the inside to conceal a curtain track.

penal rent
A vastly higher payment due during a period of default by a tenant to honour the obligations to pay rent at the proper time.

penthouse
A building, such as an apartment, constructed on the flat roof of a main building for living purposes.

peppercorn rent
A nominal amount of money, or token rent, payable to the landlord. It is often associated with payment of a premium to the landlord by the tenant.

Performance Bond
A guarantee that the provider of goods and services will meet the terms of the contract and will pay compensation. In the housing association context, a Performance Bond may be guaranteed by the Housing Corporation.

performance indicator
In the housing association context, the Housing Corporation requires registered housing associations to use and publish performance indicators and arrange housing management finance and development activities.

performance specification
A detailed description of the required standards of a material or component. *See also* Agrément Board.

perlite
A natural volcanic glass which is used as a lightweight aggregate for lightweight concrete and as a substitute for sand in plasters.

perlite plaster
A lightweight plaster, using perlite instead of sand, which has good thermal insulation properties.

permeability
The property of a material to allow a liquid to pass through it. *See also* impermeability.

permissible load
The maximum load which an element should withstand and for which it has been designed. *See also* load.

permissible stress
The ultimate tensile stress of a material divided by the factor of safety.

permitted development
A colloquial term meaning planning permission which is granted as deemed without the need to make a formal planning application. *See also* deemed planning permission.

permitted use
A colloquial term meaning:
1. The use of land or buildings for which planning permission has been granted.
2. The use of land or buildings

which is deemed to be granted under the General Development Order. *See also* deemed planning permission, General Development Order.

perpend
The corner of a brick wall that is set vertically during construction and from which the remainder of the wall is built.

perpetuity
Without a time limit.

personal representative
Under the Administration of Estates Act 1925, as amended, a personal representative is the executor of a deceased person's property.

perspective drawing
A drawing produced to give a three-dimensional view of a building. It is normally drawn freehand rather than to scale and represents views of the finished building. *See also* isometric projection, orthographic projection.

perspex
A thermoplastic which is transparent and used as a substitute for glass.

pH value
A measure of acidity or alkalinity in a solution which is measured on a scale 0 to 14, 7 being neutral and below acid and above alkaline.

physical factors
Defined under section 1(2) of the Land Compensation Act 1973 as noise, vibration, smell, fumes, smoke, artificial lighting and the discharge on to land of any solid or liquid substance. Compensation may be payable where there is a diminution in value by any of these physical factors created by the use of physical works.

physical life
The term during which it is assumed a building is capable of occupation and is capable of meeting accepted standards and statutory requirements.

picture rail
A length of moulded timber fixed around the upper part of the wall in a room.

pier
The thickening of a wall to form an attached column of brickwork which may be used to strengthen a length of walling or

provide support to a beam. The sizes vary but would generally be a half to one brick projection from the wall and are two bricks wide. *See also* buttress.

pigment
A substance that is added to a material to produce a colour such as that added to paint.

pile
A concrete column placed in the ground to support the foundation of a building in weak soils or soils subject to volume change, e.g. cohesive soils. *See also* bored pile, displacement pile, bearing pile, friction pile, sheet pile, pre-cast concrete pile.

pile cap
1. A protective capping placed at the head of a pile to prevent damage during installation.
2. A slab of concrete placed on top of piles after installation to provide a base in the form of a pad foundation. *See also* pad foundation.

pile driver
A machine used for the installation of piles.

pile shoe
A metal point that is attached to the first pre-cast concrete pile to facilitate driving.

pillar tap
A tap connected to both a water pipe and an appliance, such as a bath or a lavatory basin. *See also* tap.

pilot light
A small flame in gas appliances that is always burning and causes the main gas jets to function when the appliance is operated.

pine
See softwood.

pink hatched yellow land
Land around a clearance area added because it contains badly arranged houses and is indicated on the definitive plan in pink and yellow hatching.

pink land
Land which contains dwellings unfit for human habitation and shown as pink on plans for clearance areas.

pipe
A tube manufactured in a variety of materials and diameters for specific purposes, such as

conveying foul and surface water.

pitch
1. The slope or inclination of a surface from the horizontal, expressed in degrees (of 30°, 45°). *See also* gradient.
2. The residue of tar.

pitch fibre
A woven fibre material impregnated with pitch or bitumen which is used to manufacture chain pipes.

pitch pine
A type of pine. *See also* softwood.

pitched roof
One that is inclined at an angle of 10° or more and is covered with slates or tiles. *See also* flat roof, couple roof, close couple roof, collar roof, hipped roof, lean-to roof, gable roof, mansard roof, double roof.

pitchline
The line produced by joining the nosings of a stair. *See also* nosing.

pitchmastic
A substance containing a fine aggregate and pitch applied in a hot condition to a floor surface to produce a jointless floor finish. *See also* composition floor.

pivot
The provision to a window which allows it to open from the central vertical or horizontal axis.

pivot window
A window consisting of one pane which is fixed to open from the central vertical or horizontal axis, so that, when fully open, one half of the pane is inside the room and the other half outside. *See also* window.

plain concrete
Concrete that does not incorporate steel reinforcement and would generally be used to carry loads where it is supported over its whole area, e.g. as a solid floor slab or strip foundation. *See also* concrete.

plain concrete strip foundation
See strip foundation.

plaintiff
A person who brings an action in law.

plain tiles
See clay roof tile.

plan

A scale drawing of the layout of, and construction of an existing or proposed building, in the horizontal plane. Also a drawing of a relatively small area of land indicating its boundaries, buildings, services, etc. *See also* drawings.

planking and strutting

Temporary timber supports provided to the sides of an excavation to prevent collapse and to allow work to be safely carried out. *See also* waling.

planner

A colloquial term meaning:
1. A town planner – i.e. a professional person who engages in the practice of town and country planning. Usually a Corporate Member of the Royal Town Planning Institute.
2. A person who is engaged in the management of a building project. Sometimes called a planning engineer.

planning

By virtue of the Town and Country Planning Act 1947, as amended, the statutory control of development which includes both buildings and use of land.

Planning and Compensation Act 1991

This Act introduced four significant changes to the planning framework: the first to development control, where a 'plan-led' system was adopted; the second was to make the adoption of district-wide local plans mandatory; the third was to abolish the requirement for central approval of structure plans; and the fourth was to introduce a mandatory requirement for counties to produce mineral plans and waste plans for the whole of their areas. *See also* local plan.

planning appeal

The process whereby a person who has been refused planning permission or an enforcement notice appeals to the Secretary of State for a more favourable outcome. A Planning and Housing Inspector is appointed by the Secretary of State to review the decision of the local planning authority and issues a reasoned letter informing the appellant of his decision.

planning application

The making of an application to

the local planning authority for permission to undertake development. The application can either be for outline or detailed permission. The former is for permission in principal and the latter for permission of the whole scheme. *See also* local planning authority.

planning blight
The diminution in the value of land adversely affected by a development planning proposal which provides for the land's acquisition at some future date by a public authority. Owner-occupiers in certain circumstances may serve notice on the local authority requiring it to purchase the land.

planning brief
Planning policies and guidelines indicating the future development pattern of an area of land. Usually a term referring to a document issued by a local planning authority.

planning consent
A colloquial term meaning that planning permission has been granted.

Planning (Listed Buildings and Conservation Areas Act 1990)
A consolidating Act relating to most of the provisions relevant to heritage properties, although those relating to ancient monuments are still separate in the Ancient Monuments and Archaeological Areas Act 1979.

planning obligation
Replaces the term 'planning agreement'. A person interested in developing a piece of land may, by agreement or otherwise, enter into an obligation:

● restricting the use of the land in a particular way
● requiring specified operations or activities to be carried out
● requiring the land to be used in a specified way
● requiring a sum, or sums, to be paid to the authority.

planning permission
The formal consent of the local planning authority in response to the submission of a planning application. Granted either unconditionally or with conditions attached. Permissions are normally in response to

applications for outline or detailed permission. *See also* outline planning application.

plant
Equipment and machinery used to assist construction methods and techniques and a major building resource.

planted mould
A shaped strip of timber which is attached to a surface for decorative purposes, e.g. around the edge of door panels. *See also* stuck mould.

plastic wood
A substance manufactured from cellulose and resins which hardens when dry and is used for filling in small holes in timber surfaces.

plaster
See gypsum plasters, lime plasters.

plasterboard
See gypsum plasterboard.

Plaster of Paris
A Class A hemi-hydrate gypsum plaster.

plasticiser
See admixture.

plastics
See thermoplastic, thermosetting.

plate glass
Glass manufactured by pouring molten glass on to a table and rolling the required thickness. The surfaces are then ground and polished. *See also* glass.

plinth
The thickening of a wall along the full length of its base to form a projection of bricks or stone.

plot ratio
The ratio of gross floor area of a proposed or existing building to the site area.

plug
A piece of timber or special hollow plastic fixed into a predrilled hole in a surface, such as a wall, into which a component can be screwed.

plumb
To ensure that an element is vertical.

plumb bob
See plumb line.

plumb line
A simple device used to obtain a

vertical line and consisting of a length of string with a pointed weight attached.

plumb rule
A straight-edged board from which a plumb line is suspended. *See also* plumb line.

plywood
A composite timber sheet comprising thin sheets or veneers of timber glued and pressed together in a variety of sizes and thicknesses, having a number of uses, such as linings to floors and roofs, cupboard units, and as a structural component for the manufacture of trussed joists.

pointe gaurde
A concept in the assessment of compensation where land is acquired compulsorily. It means that any increase or decrease in the value of the land taken, resulting from the scheme underlying the acquisition, shall be ignored.

point load
A load that acts on a specific area such as the load from a column. *See also* load, uniformly distributed load.

polarised glass
See solar glass.

polyethylene
A thermoplastic sheet manufactured in various gauges and used for damp-proof membranes and vapour barriers. *See also* thermoplastic, damp-proof membrane, vapour barrier.

polymer
Generally, an artificially produced substance used in the manufacture of plastics.

polypropylene
A thermoplastic rigid material used to produce pipes. *See also* thermoplastic.

polystyrene
A thermoplastic lightweight material used for insulation purposes. *See also* thermoplastic.

polythene
See polyethylene.

polyvinyl chloride (PVC)
A thermoplastic used to produce a variety of materials from flexible sheet materials to rigid materials used for drainpipes.

porosity
The ability of a material to absorb air, water or other fluids.

porous
The nature of a material which has a degree of air space (i.e. voids) within its mass that allow water or air to be absorbed.

portal
A large entrance or gateway.

portal frame
A structural frame incorporating the roof supports and roof members as one complete component producing a rigid structure without the need for the struts and ties associated with roof trusses, thereby allowing the whole internal volume to be utilised. The portal would be spaced at intervals and would incorporate purlins for attaching large sheet covers to the wall and roof. *See also* roof truss.

portfolio
A collection of investment properties held in one ownership.

Portland cement
A mixture of approximately 66 per cent calcium carbonate (pure limestone or chalk) and 20 per cent sand and clay. Rapid hardening Portland cement is similar, but materials are ground more finely during manufacturing process, and hardens more quickly on the addition of water. Sulphate-resisting Portland cement may be used for concrete that has to resist sulphate attack, e.g. for foundations in contact with ground sulphates (salts). *See also* cement.

Portland stone
See limestone.

possessory title
1. An ownership claim to land based on inconclusive or non-existent evidence and which, within a prescribed period, is challengeable by a person who has a stronger claim.
2. With regard to registered land, a title which is subject to some qualification or exception as stated in the Lands Register.

post-tensioned concrete
A method used for prestressing concrete which is done by stressing the reinforcement after the concrete has set. *See also* prestressed concrete.

poundage
The amount payable by a ratepayer for every pound of rateable value.

poverty trap
The situation in which people with low incomes or in receipt of means-tested benefit find that any increase in their income results in similar cuts in benefit.

powder-post beetle
See Lyctus powder-post beetle.

power float
A mechanical device used for obtaining a smooth level surface on wet concrete floors to produce a finish and also used to eliminate a cement and sand screed.

power of attorney
A deed by which a person empowers another to act for them generally or in specific areas. The donor is called the principal and the donee the attorney.

practical completion certificate
A certificate, issued by an architect or surveyor, in relation to a building contract at the time when the building is complete in virtually all respects and ready for occupation. The certificate authorises the release of an agreed sum of money and any retention money.

preamble
An introduction to a section or part of a document, such as a bill of quantities.

pre-cast
See pre-cast component.

pre-cast component
A building component which is manufactured in a factory or on-site ready for assembly and is usually associated with concrete items such as floor units and lintels. *See also* pre-cast concrete, prefabricated component.

pre-cast concrete
Concrete that is manufactured in a factory in a variety of components and delivered to the site ready for assembly, e.g. floor units. *See also* concrete, in situ concrete.

pre-cast concrete pile
Square or circular reinforced concrete sections manufactured in a factory and which are driven into the ground with

each section joined until the required depth is reached. *See also* pile, bored pile.

pre-cast stone
See artificial stone.

precept
The amount of money demanded from rating authorities by a precepting authority, such as a parish council. The amount is normally expressed as part of the rates and is required to cover the cost of running the precepting authority.

precepting authority
The authority which precepts.

pre-contract deposit
An amount of money paid in advance of the contract as an expression of good faith and usually held by a third party, e.g. a solicitor. A deposit normally acts as part-payment on completion of the contract. It does not create a legally binding agreement in the meantime.

pre-emption
The right of first refusal.

prefabricated
See prefabricated component.

prefabricated building
A building constructed of mainly prefabricated components. *See also* prefabricated component.

prefabricated component
A building component which is manufactured in a factory and delivered to site for assembly and is usually associated with carpentry and joinery items such as trussed rafters and windows. *See also* pre-cast component.

prefabricated partition
A lightweight partition wall, manufactured in standard floor-to-ceiling height units, consisting of a lightweight cellular core (e.g. heavy duty cardboard) faced both sides with plasterboard to a finished thickness of approximately 50mm. *See also* partition wall, wall panel.

pre-funding
Finance provided on a long-term basis for a development project arranged before commencement of the building works.

pre-let
An enforceable agreement in

law for a letting which takes effect at a future date.

preliminaries
The introductory section to a bill of quantities.

premium
1. An amount paid by an actual, or prospective, lessee to a lessor. Usually the rent is reduced in return for the consideration.
2. A colloquial term meaning the price paid for the purchase of a leasehold interest.
3. Sums payable to an insurer by the insured.

premium rent
A rent considered to be above a reasonable level that would be expected to be commanded in the open market on normal terms.

pre-mix
A dry mixture of ingredients which produces concrete, mortar and plaster upon the addition of water.

present value
The future worth of property discounted to its present-day equivalent.

preservative
A substance used for treating timber against dry and wet rot and insect attack. It includes copper compounds, creosote and pentachlorophenol.

pressed brick
A brick that is produced by pressing the material into a mould during its manufacture and results in sharp arrises and smooth surfaces with an indent (frog) on one surface. *See also* brick, wirecut brick.

pressed steel
Sheet steel which is shaped by pressing to produce such items as lintels. *See also* lintel.

pressed steel lintel
A lintel manufactured from pressed steel, the most common of which is a CATNIC. *See also* lintel.

prestressed concrete
Pre-cast concrete where stresses have been induced in the steel reinforcement during manufacture so that, when the component is loaded, less cracking occurs. *See also* concrete, pre-cast concrete.

pressure
The concentration of a force acting on a surface, which increases with load.

priced bill
A bill of quantities containing costs.

price payable
The amount paid by the lessee of a dwelling house, who is enfranchised.

primary cooperative
In the housing association movement, a housing cooperative – the term distinguishes the organisation providing housing from a secondary cooperative which supplies services to it. *See also* cooperative housing, secondary cooperative.

prime cost sum
A sum specified in a bill of quantities for materials and work to be carried out by a nominated subcontractor or nominated supplier. *See also* bill of quantities.

prime cost contract
A building contract where the contractor's payment is calculated on the actual cost of materials, labour and plant, etc. plus an agreed amount or percentage for administration, overheads, and profits. *See also* contract, fixed price contract, cost plus contract.

prime property
Best property available when viewed from an individual's perspective.

primer
A type of paint that is initially applied to a surface to seal it and protect it from corrosion in the case of metal surfaces. *See also* paint.

prime tenant
A tenant with a high reputation for meeting their obligations under the terms of a lease. May be an existing or potential tenant.

priming coat
See primer.

primogeniture
The right of succession of the eldest son to an estate on the owner's death. It normally applies to the exclusion of all other claimants.

principal
1. The total sum of money involved in a loan or mortgage, as distinct from the interest payable.
2. The client on whose behalf an agent acts.

principal rafter
The structural rafter in a roof truss which supports purlins which in turn supports common rafters. *See also* roof truss.

principal tie
The structural ceiling joist in a roof truss or trussed rafter. *See also* roof truss.

priority estates project
A project originally sponsored by the Department of the Environment, but now by a private organisation which advises housing associations and local authorities on how to deal with housing estates with a history of management difficulties.

priority investment areas
Rural or urban areas of housing stress which have priority for public investment. They are determined by the regional offices of the Housing Corporation.

priority need
A term used to define the categories of statutory homeless households for which a local authority must provide accommodation, provided they are not intentionally homeless. *See also* homeless person, homelessness.

private sewer
A pipe situated below ground level which is used for disposing of foul and surface water from drains of a group of buildings and is maintained by the owners.

private stair
A stairway to provide access to floors and landings and situated within a dwelling. *See also* stairs.

private tender
A tender restricted to specified named parties. *See also* tender, tendering process.

private treaty
The process for the disposal of real property whereby negotiations are carried out between the vendor and prospective purchaser privately. There is usually no limit on the time within which they must come to an agreement before contracts are exchanged.

probate
Certificate granted by the Family Division of the High Court proving the will of a person. The grant of probate confirms the authority of the executor.

probate duty
Formerly called stamp duty on grant of probate on the value of an estate of a person who died intestate. It has been replaced by estate duty.

probate registry
The office which deals with the issue of grant of probate.

professional indemnity insurance
Insurance taken out by professional advisers, such as architects and surveyors, against actions in negligence, or other relevant matters.

prohibition notice
A notice served by an inspector appointed under the Health and Safety at Work, etc. Act 1974, as amended, which states, in the opinion of the inspector, that certain activities at work involve, or will involve, a risk of serious personal injury. It specifies the matters giving rise to the risk, indicates the alleged contravention of statutory provisions and directs that the activities concerned shall not be carried out unless the matters specified are rectified. The notice is of immediate effect and there is a right of appeal to an Industrial Tribunal.

project management
The management of a building or development project involving the roles of coordinating budgets, taking advice from professionals and generally ensuring that the project is completed in accordance with the client's stated requirements.

projecting scaffold
A temporary platform fixed to, and projecting from, the outer face of a wall to allow work to be carried out.

prop
A temporary support. *See also* acrow prop.

property management
The arrangement of functions including collection of rents, payment of outgoings, maintenance, provision of services, etc. The precise duties between

the landlord and tenant will be specified in the terms of the lease.

property management agreement

The contract between an owner and property manager. The precise terms of the agreement are specified in the contract. *See also* property management.

proper valuation

Under the Insurance Companies Regulations 1981 defined as 'in relation to land a valuation by a qualified valuer, not more than three years before the relevant date, which determines the amount which would be realised at the time of the valuation on an open market sale of the land, free from any mortgage or charge'.

protected opening

Generally a horizontal means of escape route within a building which is compartmented by fire doors to prevent flame spread in the case of fire. *See also* fire protection.

protected shaft

Generally, a vertical means of escape route within a building,

such as a stair which is enclosed by fire-resisting walls and doors. *See also* fire protection.

protected shorthold tenancy

A tenancy where the landlord has an extra ground for claiming possession against a tenant provided it is a shorthold tenancy. *See also* shorthold tenancy.

protected tenancy

By virtue of the Rent Act 1977, as amended, a tenancy which is rent controlled and there is security of tenure.

protective coating

The application of a substance to the surface of a material or the treatment of the surface. Generally associated with steel to prevent corrosion and increase durability.

provisional sum

A sum of money included in a bill of quantities to cover the cost of unexpected work.

P-trap

The bend in a soil or waste appliance shaped in the form of the letter 'P'. *See also* trap, water trap.

public authority
An organisation carrying out functions for the public benefit.

Public Expenditure Survey Committee
A committee of ministers and senior civil servants of the spending departments, which reviews government spending.

public house
Premises licensed for the sale of intoxicating liquor for consumption on the premises.

public nuisance
See nuisance.

public sewer
A pipe situated below ground level, used for disposing of foul and surface water from drains and private sewers of buildings; the responsibility of the water authority.

public stair
A stairway providing access to floors and landings and intended for common use within a building. *See also* stairs.

public tender/open tender
A tender which is open to any member of the public provided their tender meets any terms specified in the tender document.

puffing
In auctions usually meant to mean exaggerating a property's good points.

pugging
A method of sound-insulating upper timber floors and stud partitions by filling in with a dense material such as slag wool. *See also* insulation, sound insulation.

puisne mortgage
A mortgage not protected by the deposit of title deeds. It is a second or subsequent mortgage.

pulley head
The top horizontal part of the box frame of a sash window. *See also* sash window.

pulley stile
The vertical part of the box frame of a sash window. *See also* sash window.

pulley wheel
See sash pulley.

pulverised fuel ash (PFA)
The remains of coal dust burnt

at power stations which is used as a lightweight aggregate.

pumice
Volcanic rock used as a lightweight aggregate.

pump
A mechanical device used for either driving or lifting liquids through pipes. Often used as part of a central heating system for the mechanical circulation of hot water.

purchase
The acquisition of land by a legal voluntary act such as conveyance, as opposed to intestacy or bankruptcy.

purchase notice
Land which has become incapable of reasonable beneficial use can, in certain circumstances, be required to be purchased by service of a notice on the appropriate local authority. See Town and Country Planning Act 1990 Part VI, as amended.

purchaser
A person who acquires land by purchase. Under the Law of Property Act 1925, section 205(1)(xxi) the term 'purchaser' includes a lessee and mortgagee.

purlin
A structural timber roof member which provides intermediate support to rafters and ceiling joists. *See also* hanger, runner.

purlin roof
A roof where the purlins are supported on walls rather than trusses. *See also* roof truss.

purpose-made brick
A brick moulded by hand. *See also* pressed brick, wirecut brick.

push plate
A flat plate fixed to a self-closing door positioned for pushing the door open.

putlog
Part of a scaffold.

putty
A material used for fixing glass panels. It is flexible and waterproof and hardens after a period of time.

PVC
See polyvinyl chloride.

Q

qualified property
Special property.

qualified valuer
1. A professionally qualified person who engages in the valuation of land or buildings.
2. Under the Royal Institution of Chartered Surveyors *Guidance Notes for the Valuation of Assets*, defined as 'a corporate member of the Royal Institution of Chartered Surveyors, or the Incorporated Society of Valuers and Auctioneers, or the Rating and Valuation Association, with appropriate post-qualification experience and with knowledge of valuing land in the location and of the category of the asset'.

qualifying costs
In the context of housing associations, expenditure incurred by a housing association in undertaking a development which contributes to the amount in which entitlement to housing association grant is calculated.

quango
Quasi-autonomous non-governmental organisation.

quantity surveyor
A qualified person who is responsible for producing a bill of quantities and dealing with all financial and contractual matters. He or she is part of the design team and would have regular meetings with the contractor's quantity surveyor to discuss contractual issues and agree monthly and final accounts. *See also* Bill of Quantities, design team, contractor's quantity surveyor, surveyor.

quantum meruit
As much as it is worth. A term often used for the quantification

of time spent by professionals in claiming remuneration by way of fees.

quarter landing
A landing between floors extending the full width of one flight with a 90° angle. *See also* landing, half landing, stairs.

quarter round
A moulding that is curved to a 90° angle.

quartz
A crystalline mineral substance found in rocks.

quartzite tiles
A floor tile manufactured from sandstone containing quartz.

quasi-easement
A right which could amount to an easement if the dominant and servient lands were in separate ownership and occupation. *See also* easement.

queen closer
A brick, cut in half along its length, which is used to maintain the brick bond at openings and corners. *See also* king closer.

queen post truss
A traditional timber roof truss comprising two principal rafters fixed at the open end with a principal tie at the base to form a triangle incorporating two vertical members (queen posts) each side joined to the tie and each rafter. An additional horizontal tie may be incorporated at the top and between the posts. This type of truss was traditionally made from solid timber, usually hardwood such as oak, and would be left exposed inside the building. *See also* king post truss, roof truss.

que estate
A dominant tenement.

quicklime
See calcium oxide.

quiet enjoyment
A covenant for quiet enjoyment is implied into a conveyance for freehold land by virtue of Schedule 2 Part 1, Law of Property Act 1925. A covenant for quiet enjoyment is implied in every lease.

quilt
A layer of material used for insulation purposes. *See also* insulation quilt.

quinquennial
1. Occurring once every five years.
2. Over a period of five years.

quoin
The external corner of a masonry wall.

quoin header
The first brick in a course at the external corner which produces a header on one side of the corner and a stretcher on the other. *See also* header, stretcher.

quorum
The minimum number of members of an organisation who have to be present to make the body legally competent to transact business.

R

race relations
The harmonisation between different nationals. Controlled legally by the Race Relations Act 1976 and administered by the Commission for Racial Equality.

rack-rent
Open and full market annual value at the beginning of a lease.

radial brick
A special tapered brick used for constructing curved brickwork. *See also* brick.

radiant heating
Heat produced by radiation from an appliance, such as an electric fire.

radiation
The transfer of heat energy from a heat source that causes it to be emitted, as in a central heating radiator or electric fire. *See also* conduction, convection.

radiator
A metal panel that emits heat from its surface by virtue of the solution it contains, e.g. hot water, as part of a central heating system. *See also* central heating system.

radon
A radioactive gas produced by some rocks and soils. Adequate provision for the ventilation of buildings constructed in such areas is important for health and safety.

rafter
A structural roof member which spans from the apex to the eaves and supports a pitched roof covering. *See also* common rafter, hip rafter, valley rafter, jack rafter.

rafter filling
A brick infill between the rafters at the eaves.

raft foundation

A solid slab of in situ plain or reinforced concrete provided to the whole area of the building in order to spread the total load over the whole building area. It is used on poor load-bearing subsoils and also serves as a solid ground floor. *See also* foundation, beam and pile foundation, strip foundation.

rag bolt

A short metal bar with a roughened surface at one end which is bedded into a concrete slab, such as a padstone, with the other end, which is threaded to receive a nut, left projecting so that the ends of a steel beam or roof truss can be connected into it. *See also* padstone, roof truss.

rail

A horizontal member of a timber frame.

rainwater

See surface water.

rainwater gutter

See eaves gutter.

rainwater hopper

An open box fitting attached to the top of a rainwater pipe into which surface water from a flat roof gutter discharges.

rainwater pipe

A pipe placed above ground level into which surface water gutters are connected. Its purpose is to convey surface water to a surface water drain into which it is connected.

rainwater shoe

A splayed fitting attached to the bottom of a rainwater pipe to direct surface water into the top of a gulley.

raked joint

See mortar joint.

raking out

Cleaning out mortar from a brick joint to form a recessed joint or for repointing.

raking riser

A riser that slopes inwards from the nosing of the tread above. *See also* riser, nosing.

raking shore

A temporary support to the existing wall of a building which is in danger of collapse and consists of inclined members (rakers) the top end of which is attached to the wall adjacent to an upper floor and the bottom end secured at ground level. *See also* dead shore, flying shore, shore.

ramp
A steady incline joining levels. Often used at the entrance to buildings to provide easy access for wheelchairs.

random rubble
See rubble wall.

rapid-hardening Portland cement
See Portland cement.

rate
A tax set by a local authority on the occupier of property in relation to its value. The rates levied on domestic properties were replaced by the community charge which has since been replaced by council tax.

rateable occupation
Occupation which gives rise to a liability to pay rates.

rateable occupier
The occupier of property who meets the criteria for a rateable occupation.

rateable property
Property on which the occupier is liable to be rated.

rateable value
Defined under section 19 of the General Rate Act 1967, as amended, as a figure upon which rate poundage is charged; 'for those properties assessed direct to net annual value, an amount equal to the rent at which it is estimated, the hereditament might reasonably be expected to let from year to year that tenants undertook to pay all usual tenants' rates and taxes and to bear the cost of the repairs and insurance and the other expenses, if any, necessary to maintain the hereditament in a state to command that rent.'

rate demand
The document issued by the rating authority to a ratepayer requiring payment of rates due.

Rating and Valuation Association
An organisation, established in 1882, whose membership consists of persons engaged in rating assessments, revenue col-

lection, valuation and allied spheres of activity.

rating areas
Defined in section 1(1) of the General Rate Act 1967 as the boroughs and districts of every county, the City of London, the Inner Temple and the Middle Temple.

rating authorities
Section 1(1) of the General Rate Act 1967 defines these as each borough or district council, the common council of the City of London, the sub-Treasurer of the Inner Temple and the under-Treasurer of the Middle Temple.

rating officer
The official responsible for rating matters within a rating authority.

Rating Surveyors Association
An organisation established in 1909 whose membership consists of surveyors specialising in rating.

rating year
A period of twelve months beginning 1 April.

rawlplug
See plug.

ready-mixed concrete
Concrete mixed at a depot rather than on-site. Now used almost exclusively for in situ work due to availability, quality control and elimination of storage and mixing requirements on-site. *See also* concrete.

real property
Land, including things attached to it, minerals, rights appertaining to it, and profits.

realty
Real property.

rebate
A recess cut in timber or other material in order to fit a component, such as a panel.

rebound hammer
See Schmidt hammer.

rebound hammer test
See Schmidt hammer test.

rebuild
The reconstruction of an entire, or part of a, building, restoring it to its original form.

rebuilding clause
The clause in a lease which requires the lessor or lessee to

rebuild the demised properties in certain circumstances.

receiver
A person appointed by a court or mortgagee under statutory powers, to safeguard property at risk and to collect the debts or rents due on behalf of mortgagees, debenture holders or other creditors.

recessed mortar joint
See mortar joint.

recision
The termination or cancellation of a contract.

recitals
Details of relevant earlier events attached to a deed, which explain the background to transactions. Recitals start with the word 'whereas'.

reconveyance
Property subject to a mortgage prior to 1926 when it was conveyed to the mortgagee, who recovered the property on repayment of the loan.

record, conveyances by
Conveyances of land effected by judicial or legislative act, as evidenced by the record, e.g. by Act of Parliament.

recovery
High or county court procedure for the recovery of land from a person in wrongful possession. *See also* tenant in the praecipe.

Reddendum
The clause within a lease specifying the rents to be paid, or the formula for its calculation.

redemption
Repayment of a mortgage debt. If the mortgagee refuses to release the property from the mortgage on repayment of the loan, the mortgagor can bring an action for redemption.

redemption date
A date when a repayable security is due for encashment at its face value.

redemption period
The term during which a mortgagor may, by statute or agreement, redeem a mortgage.

redevelopment clause
A clause in a lease allowing for the redevelopment of property by one or other parties at a certain date.

reduced level
A point above or below a datum. *See also* datum.

re-entry
The lessor's right to reclaim the title to a property where there is a default in rental payments, or other breach of the lease agreement.

reference
The procedure where the Lands Tribunal is formally requested to determine a matter such as: first, compensation, as a result of compulsory purchase of land, injurious affection, revocation orders; and, second, valuations for taxation.

refractory bricks
Bricks manufactured from materials that are resistant to high temperatures, and would be used for lining furnaces. *See also* brick.

refurbishment
The modernisation, or improvement, of a building, falling short of redevelopment or rebuilding.

registered care home
This is a scheme which is registered under the Registered Homes Act 1984, and provides accommodation for elderly people, people with mental health problems, people with learning difficulties and those with a drug or alcohol abuse problem. *See also* Registered Homes Act 1984.

Registered Homes Act 1984
This Act requires many special needs housing projects with four or more residents which provide board and personal care to register with the local social services authority. The authority is required to inspect projects regularly and can insist on improved physical standards or staffing levels. *See also* registered care home.

registered housing association
A housing association registered by the Housing Corporation under the provisions of the Housing Association Act 1985, as amended.

registered property
The person who is registered as the proprietor of registered land. *See also* registered title.

registered title
A title registered under the Land Registration Act 1925. At the Land Registry the following

titles must be recorded; fee simple, lease exceeding 21 years and an assignment of a lease with more than 21 years to run.

Registrar of Friendly Societies and Charity Commissioners

The Registrar who has responsibility for enforcing the provisions of the Industrial and Provident Societies Act. Housing associations that are industrial and provident societies must furnish an annual return to the Registrar. *See also* registration.

registration

In the housing association context, housing associations have to register with at least two government agencies which have a supervisory and regulated powers over them: the Registrar of Friendly Societies and Charity Commissioners and the Registrar of Companies. All must register with the Housing Corporation.

registration of a site

When a housing association identifies a site suitable for a housing project which it wishes to undertake, it registers it with the Housing Corporation, thereby preventing competition or duplication of effort among other associations.

regulated tenancy

A statutory or protected tenancy which is not a controlled tenancy. Residential tenancies created since 1989 are assured tenancies.

reinforced concrete

Concrete which has steel added to give the concrete tensile properties. The steel may be in the form of bars which would be added to a concrete beam or mesh which would be added to a concrete floor slab. *See also* concrete, plain concrete, prestressed concrete.

reinforced glass

Glass incorporating a series of thin metal wires and generally used where fire resistance is required, such as glass panels in fire doors, or large external glazed areas. *See also* glass.

reinforced masonry

Stone or brick walls incorporating steel bars or mesh in the horizontal mortar joints to increase the strength of the wall.

reinforced strip foundation

A concrete strip foundation incorporating steel reinforcement and used where heavy loads have to be supported. *See also* foundation, wide strip foundation.

reinforcement

A material, such as steel bars, incorporated in concrete to resist tensile forces. *See also* reinforced concrete.

reinspection

1. A return visit to a building site to determine that work, deemed to be necessary during an earlier visit, has been carried out during the course of the building contract.
2. A further visit to a property which has previously been inspected. This is often carried out for mortgage valuation purposes to determine if certain loan conditions have been carried out.

reinstatement

The process by which a building is put back into the state it was at some relevant previous date.

reinstatement basis of insurance

A method of loss assessment under an insurance policy where the amount payable is based on the cost of the insured property being repaired if damaged, or rebuilt if destroyed. *See also* reinstatement value.

reinstatement value

The value resulting from applying the reinstatement basis of insurance.

reinsurance

The situation where an insurer insures the risk, or part thereof, with another insurer.

relative density

The density of a substance divided by the density of water.

relative humidity

The amount of water vapour present in the air compared with the maximum the air can hold at that temperature. *See also* humidity.

release agent

An oil or grease which is applied to the inside surfaces of formwork to produce a smooth surface on the finished concrete and to prevent it from adhering to the formwork when it is removed.

relieving arch
A brick arch supporting the internal part of a wall above an opening to reduce the load a lintel has to support.

render
A mixture of sand, cement and water applied in two coats to the external face of a wall. A waterproofing agent may be added, and the surface may be textured and painted and stones thrown on to produce pebble dash. *See also* stucco.

render coat
The first coat of wall plaster consisting of gypsum plaster and sand mixed with water, spread on to the wall surface. *See also* render, float coat.

renovation
Repair work carried out to an existing building to restore it to its original state.

rent
Periodic payment made by the tenant to his or her landlord as compensation for the right to possession of the let property.

rentable area
Floor space for which rent is calculated.

Rent Act 1977
This Act is relevant to the private sector and consolidates earlier legislation relating to security of tenure and rent control. For housing associations, its importance lies in the parts that govern the operation of the fair rent system and rent officer service. Fair rents are regulated under this Act, but since the Housing Act 1988, housing association and private levied tenancies are not subject to fair rents. *See also* Housing Act 1988.

rental value
The open market rent that might reasonably be expected to accrue subject to the terms of the lease.

Rent Assessment Committee
A committee established to assess rents and agree terms of the statutory periodic tenancy under the Housing Act 1988 and to hear appeals from the decision of the rent officer under the Rent Act 1977, as amended.

rent assessment panel
Persons appointed by the Secretary of State for the Environment and Lord Chancellor who are drawn on to be members of

leasehold valuation tribunals, rent assessment committees and rent tribunals.

rent allowance
In housing association context, the amount of money which an individual tenant obtains to help pay the rent to the housing association or private landlord. Since 1993 rent allowances have been included in the housing benefit.

rent book
The book which must be provided to record payments for every residential tenancy and which must contain certain specified information. Under sections 4–7 of the Landlord and Tenant Act 1985, as amended, it is a criminal offence not to provide such a book.

rent control
The rent of private residential tenancies created before 1989 is restricted to a fair rent according to the Rent Act 1977, section 70. After that date, under section 14 of the Housing Act 1988, as amended, the rent of such tenants, including housing association tenants, is restricted to market rent.

rent-free period
The period agreed during which a lessee is allowed occupation without payment of rent.

rent officer
An official appointed by, but independent of, the local authority who, under the Rent Act, determines and registers fair rents following an application by the landlord or the tenant, or both, under a regulated tenancy of a dwelling house.

rent rebates
Rent allowances granted to needy tenants under the Housing Finance Act 1972, the Furnished Lettings (Rent Allowance) Act 1973 and the Rent Act 1974. This scheme is supplemented by housing benefit under the Social Security Act 1986.

rent review
The provision in a lease where the rent is reconsidered at stated intervals. The procedure for reviewing the rent is stated in the terms of the lease.

rent roll
1. The total amount of rent payable under the tenancies of one estate.

2. A method of recording information concerning the details of the rents payable from the tenancies of an estate.

rent to mortgage
A scheme which gives those secured tenants with local authorities and non-charitable housing associations, which have the right to buy, a right to convert their rent into a mortgage payment enabling them to buy a stake in the property.

rent tribunal
A rent assessment committee sitting as a rent tribunal to determine rents for restricted contracts under the Rent Acts, as amended by the Housing Act 1980.

repair
The making good of defects in property which has deteriorated from its original state. Legally, its meaning must fall short of effectively reconstructing or improving buildings.

repairs notice
1. A notice served by a local housing authority under the Housing Act 1985, as amended, requiring the execution of works to make a house fit for human habitation.
2. A notice served by the local planning authority requiring works to be carried out to a listed building for its proper preservation.

replacement cost
The cost of replacing damaged items with new ones, often used in association with insurance contracts.

requisitions on title
Questions raised by a purchaser of land concerning the vendor's title. This could include identity of property, outstanding mortgages, execution of deeds etc.

resettlement units
Hostels run on a direct access basis and usually occupied by homeless single people in need of emergency housing.

residence
The place where a person or persons live.

residence order
An order under section 8 of the Children Act 1989 which settles the arrangements as to the person with whom a child is to live.

residential occupier
An occupier of a residence under statute, giving them the right to remain.

residual stress
Stresses that remain in a material after it has been manufactured, as in some moulded plastics. *See also* stress.

residual method of valuation
A process of valuation of the property which has potential for development or redevelopment. The estimated total cost of the work, taking account of fees, an allowance for interest, and the developer's profit and risk, is deducted from the gross value of the completed project. The resulting amount is then adjusted to the date of valuation, to produce the residual value.

residual value
The value determined by the residual method of valuation.

residuary devisee
The beneficiary entitled under a will to all real property not included in specific gifts in the will.

resin
Generally, a natural substance produced by certain wood saps and used as binders for paints. *See also* synthetic resin.

resin-bonded
Glued together with synthetic resins, e.g. as in plywood.

resistance
See thermal resistance.

rest bend
A curved drainpipe used to connect a soil pipe to a foul drain.

retained agent
An agent retained by the principal with an instruction to sell, let or seek property. The payment of fees is normally on a contingency basis upon successful performance of the service.

retained sum
The agreed percentage under a building contract which is to be retained by the employer for a specified period and paid only as and when specified defects have been satisfactorily remedied.

retaining wall
A wall that retains and supports

a mass of material on one side, such as soil.

retarded hemi-hydrate plaster
A Class B gypsum plaster made by adding a restarter to hemi-hydrate plaster to slow setting time. Used for undercoat work or finishing coat on plasterboard. *See also* gypsum plasters.

retarder
A substance added to a hemi-hydrate gypsum plaster (Plaster of Paris) to slow the setting time. *See also* gypsum plasters, accelerator.

retirement relief
The relief from tax granted under the Capital Gains Tax Act 1979, as amended, for persons over the age of 60 years and who dispose of a business on retirement.

return
A change in direction of a wall at a corner which is normally set at 90°.

return pipe
A pipe carrying cooled water from a radiator back to the boiler for heating. *See also* flow pipe.

revaluation
1. A subsequent valuation.
2. The process of reassessing all heriditaments to a specified date for the purposes of rating, thereby creating a new valuation list.

reveal
That part of a jamb that is visible and not covered by a door or window frame. *See also* jamb.

reverberation
The continuation of sound in a room after the source has stopped. It is controlled by providing acoustic panels, as would be necessary to absorb the sound in such buildings as cinemas.

reverberation period
A measure of reverberation used to design the acoustics of a room.

reversion
Where land is granted by the owner for an interest less than he has, his undisposed interest is called the reversion.

reversionary income
Normally applies following a rent review or renewal of a lease where there is a potential change in income.

reversionary interest
Any right in land which is deferred.

reversionary investment
An investment property where the whole, or a substantial part of the capital value, is attributable to the prospect of a reversionary increase in rent.

revenue deficit grant
A grant which is discretionary and payable to housing associations under the provisions of the Housing Act 1985 to cover the difference between rental income and outgoings on the managing and maintaining of properties and loan charges.

reverse frontage
A site or building's frontage to a side road or footway as distinguished from the main frontage, which is normally situated along the more prominent highway.

reverse gazumping
The situation in which a purchaser breaks his word and fails to enter into a contract which fairly reflects the terms agreed but perhaps is willing to proceed with the original purchaser at a lower price. This situation is more likely to occur in a falling market when the advantage is given to the purchaser to acquire other property on better terms. *See also* gazumping.

revolving door
An entrance consisting of four doors, each of which are connected to a central pole about which they rotate.

rich mix
A mortar or concrete mix having a higher proportion than normal of cement. *See also* lean mix.

ridge
See also ridge board.

ridge board
A timber board to which the ends of rafters are fixed at the apex of a roof. *See also* apex.

ridge course
The course of tiles or slates next to the ridge.

ridge tile
A rounded clay or concrete tile used to cover the joint of the roof covering of a pitched roof at the apex.

right of entry
The right of resuming, or taking, possession of land by entry in a peaceable manner. See the Law of Property Act 1925.

right of way
The right of passage over land owned by someone else. Rights of way are of different kinds and the purpose is often specified, e.g. footpath, bridleway etc.

A private right of way is either an easement or customary right of way.

Right to Buy
A right conferred upon certain tenants of non-charitable housing associations and local authorities to purchase a dwelling in which they are living, at a discount, after a minimum period of residence. *See also* Housing Act 1980.

right to light
See light, right to.

rim deadlock
See deadlock.

rim lock
See mortice lock.

ring main
An electrical system, provided in a building, consisting of two electric wires, the ends of which are connected to the mains supply and from which power outlets are connected to serve electrical appliances.

riparian
Associated with a stream or river, e.g. land abutting a stream.

riser
The vertical part of a step the height of which is the distance between consecutive treads. *See also* nosing, tread.

rising butt hinge
A hinge that causes a door to rise when it is opened and is generally used to ensure that the door clears the top of a carpet. *See also* hinge.

rising damp
Ground water that is absorbed in an upward direction by porous materials such as bricks and concrete and is controlled by the provision of damp-proof

courses in walls and damp-proof membranes in ground floors. *See also* damp-proof course, damp-proof membrane.

rising main

A cold water pipe that supplies water from the main to the cistern. *See also* cold water supply.

rising rent

A rent which increases upwards only by predetermined amounts at stated times during the terms of the lease.

risk

The items in an insurance agreement against which protection is provided.

RMC

See ready-mixed concrete.

rock

See igneous rock, metamorphic rock, sedimentary rock.

rock asphalt

A natural form of bitumen found in some limestones. *See also* asphalt.

rock wool

See mineral wool.

roding eye

An opening on a drain to allow for cleaning. It incorporates a sealed access plate which is removed so that cleaning rods can be inserted.

rolled steel joist

A traditional steel 'I' section beam with a tapered flange manufactured by hot rolling mild steel to produce various sized sections. *See also* universal beam.

roll over relief

The postponement of capital gains tax payments where the proceeds, or part of the proceeds, of disposal of business assets, are used to acquire other assets.

rolled up interest

Interest which is not paid at intervals, but instead is added to the principal amount of a loan as it accrues. Often used in association with a development project, allowing for payment on completion of the project after sales of the building, or buildings.

Roman brick

A thin clay brick approximately 50mm thick laid with thin mortar joints and generally used for internal work such as fireplace surrounds. *See also* brick.

Roman tile

A clay roof tile which has a roll along one edge to give the shape of the letter 'P' in cross-section and is laid single lap. *See also* clay roof tiles, pan tile, lap, gauge.

roof

The top part of a building. *See also* flat roof, pitched roof.

roof boards

Boards fixed to rafters to provide a base for roof coverings.

roof cladding

The waterproof covering to a flat roof and the slate and tile covering to a pitched roof.

roof decking

See decking.

roof felt

See bitumastic felt.

roofing nail

A special non-corrosive nail with a large head used for fixing slates and tiles.

roof light

A glazed area provided in a roof to admit natural light. *See also* lantern light, laylight.

roof slates

Thin sections of slate in a variety of sizes for covering pitched roofs and nailed to battens either at the head or centre and laid double lap. *See also* slate, lap.

roof space

The area beneath the roof rafters and above the ceiling joists.

roof tiles

Covering to a pitched roof. *See also* clay roof tiles, concrete roof tiles, shingles.

roof truss

A structural roof component generally constructed of mild steel tubes or angles comprising rafters, ceiling joists, struts and ties as one complete component and would be used for buildings where large spans are required. The truss would be spaced at intervals and steel purlins incorporated to support large sheet roof coverings, and would be supported on steel columns or load-bearing walls. *See also* trussed rafter, portal frame.

rot
See dry rot, wet rot.

rough bracket
Timber pieces placed beneath a stair fixed to alternate sides of a carriage and to the underside of the treads. *See also* stairs, tread, carriage.

rough cast
A render with large stones on the surface. *See also* render.

rough string
See carriage.

Royal Institution of British Architects
A professional body established in 1834 and granted a Royal Charter in 1837, its purpose being the advancement of civil architecture and facilitating the acquisition of knowledge connected therewith.

Royal Institution of Chartered Surveyors
The professional body established in 1868 concerned with surveying. It was granted a Royal Charter in 1881. The Institution is divided into various divisions, these being building surveyors, general practice surveyors, land agency surveyors and agriculture surveyors, land surveyors, minerals surveyors, planning and development surveyors and quantity surveyors.

Royal Town Planning Institute
The professional body in the United Kingdom, established in 1914 and concerned with town planning.

RSJ
See rolled steel joist.

rubble wall
A wall constructed of various sized stones so there are no regular courses or straight mortar joints. *See also* squared rubble.

runner
A timber structural member which is attached to the top of ceiling joists and to which are fixed vertical supports (hangers) which are attached to purlins to provide a means of intermediate support to ceiling joists. *See also* purlin, runner.

running with land
See covenant

rust
See oxidation.

Ryde's scale
The scale of fees paid to valuers for work carried out in preparing compensation claims and negotiation of their settlement following the compulsory acquisition of land.

S

saddle back coping
A coping that has two sloping surfaces so that water is shed each side of a wall. *See also* coping.

saddle roof
A symmetrical pitched roof.

safety factor
See factor of safety.

safety glass
See toughened glass.

sailing course
See string course.

salamander
A portable fan heater which is used for rapidly drying out a building, usually plaster walls, to allow work to be completed.

sale
Transfer of real property in consideration for a sum of money.

sale, power of
The right to sell the property of another, usually in association with settlement of a debt that is owed and via a statutory procedure, e.g. a charging order.

sale price
The amount realised on the disposal of the property.

salt
A chemical compound which may also exist as a natural mineral such as calcium sulphate, which is used to produce gypsum plasters.

salt glaze
Common salt (sodium chloride) which is added during the manufacturing process of certain clay products such as drainpipes to produce a smooth glazed surface.

salt-glazed stoneware
Clay products such as drain-pipes that have a glazed surface. *See also* salt glaze.

salt-glazed stoneware drainpipes
Pipes manufactured from clay and burnt to high temperatures to produce a hard, vitreous material, with a salt-glazed external surface and spigot and socket ends. *See also* spigot and socket joint, vitrified clayware.

sand
See fine aggregate.

sand blinding
See blinding.

sand-faced brick
A facing brick with a sand facing on one stretcher face and the two header faces. *See also* brick.

sand-lime brick
See calcium silicate bricks.

sandpaper
A paper with sand particles glued to one side to produce an abrasive surface for smoothing wood surfaces. It is available in coarse to fine textures. *See also* glasspaper.

sandstone
A sedimentary rock consisting almost entirely of silica, being made up of grains of quartz (sand) cemented together by a material which may be either siliceous, calcareous or ferruginous in nature. The siliceous cements produce the most durable stones, e.g. York stone – a hard reddish stone.

sandwich panel
A composite panel containing a cellular core of foam material faced both sides with plywood or plasterboard sheet.

sanitary appliance
See soil appliance.

sanitary fitting
See soil appliance.

sarking felt
Bitumastic felt which is fixed to the top of roof rafters and acts as an additional waterproof layer to pitched roofs by preventing any water that may have seeped through slate or tile coverings by capillary action penetrating the roof space. *See also* bitumastic felt.

sash
One of the sliding parts of a sash

window. *See also* sash window, inner sash, outer sash.

sash balance
A spring mechanism used to operate a sash window as an alternative to counterbalancing weights. *See also* sash cord.

sash chain
A chain used as an alternative to a cord. *See also* sash cord.

sash cord
Special waxed cord or rope, one end of which is attached to the top of a sash window and the other end passed over small wheels fixed at the top of a hollow frame to which weights are attached and concealed within the frame to act as a counterbalance during the opening and closing of a sash. *See also* sash window.

sash door
A door which has a glazed upper part.

sash lock
A device used for securing a sash window consisting of a sliding part which is fixed to the meeting rail of the inner sash which slides into a keeper fixed

to the meeting rail of the outer sash. *See also* meeting rail, inner sash, outer sash.

sash pulley
A small wheel fixed at the top of a hollow frame, over which a sash cord is fed, and used as part of the sliding operation of a sash window. *See also* sash window.

sash weight
A metal weight attached to a sash cord and concealed in a hollow frame and used for counterbalancing purposes during the operation of a sash window. *See also* sash window.

sash window
A window in two parts both of which are opened and closed by sliding them vertically. They are fixed into a hollow or box frame at each side and are operated by means of a waxed rope or cord which is attached at each side to the top of each part and is fed over pulley wheels fixed at the top of the hollow frame and to which is attached weights which act as a counterbalance during operation. *See also* inner sash, outer sash.

satin finish
A decorated surface with a fine-textured semi-matt sheen.

saturation coefficient
The ratio between the volume of water absorbed by a material and the volume of its void space such as a brick.

sawn timber
Unplaned wood with a rough surface which is generally used for carpentry work.

sawn wood
See sawn timber.

scaffold
A temporary framework of metal tubes supporting timber platforms used to provide access to the upper part of a building to allow work to progress. *See also* scaffold board, scaffold pole.

scaffold board
A timber plank or board which is horizontally supported on a scaffold and is used to provide a platform for access. *See also* scaffold, scaffold pole.

scaffold pole
A standard metal tube used with special fittings to construct a scaffold. *See also* scaffold, scaffold board.

scale
Units used on a drawing to represent the actual size of a building element, e.g. a scale of 1:5 means that each unit drawn is five times smaller than the actual size.

scaled drawings
See orthographic projection.

scale fees
The charges authorised as appropriate by a professional body for specific types of work. It is no longer possible for such scales to be accepted as minimum fee scales, except in limited cases.

scale rule
A special rule containing a number of scales ranging from 1:1 to 1:2500 for producing or reading dimensions from drawings. *See also* scale.

scarf joint
A joint for connecting timber structural members, such as beams.

scarifying
The process of roughening a concrete surface using a special machine so that a good bond is achieved when another material, such as a screed, is applied to a concrete floor.

scheduled monument
A monument registered in a schedule of monuments maintained by the appropriate Secretary of State under the Ancient Monuments and Archaeological Areas Act 1979, as amended.

schedule of condition
A document indicating the physical state of a building often used in association with the assessment of compensation under a compulsory purchase order. *See also* compulsory purchase, compulsory purchase order.

schedule of dilapidations
A document listing the requirements of repair and maintenance which a tenant or landlord is obliged to make good under the terms of a lease or tenancy.

schedule of prices
A priced specification of works.

schedule of works
See specification of works.

scheme audit
In a housing association context, an analysis by the Housing Corporation of new housing association schemes carried out on a sample basis after their completion, to determine whether an association has performed its procurement function correctly.

scheme performance criteria
In a housing association context, a set of standards to which new publicly funded housing association schemes must conform.

Schmidt hammer
A spring-loaded device used for assessing the strength of hardened concrete.

Schmidt hammer test
A non-destructive test on hardened concrete using a Schmidt hammer.

scotia
A type of moulding which is fitted to a length or strip of timber, such as the edge of a skirting board.

scratch coat
The first plaster coat or under-

coat which is roughened so that a good bond is achieved when the neat coat is applied.

screed
A type of cement mortar approximately 50mm thick applied to the surface of concrete floors in order to give a smooth level surface on which to lay a floor finish. *See also* self-levelling screed, granolithic screed, green concrete, manolithic screed.

screw
A metal fastener used for connecting one component to another or to a surface and comprising a threaded shank and slotted head for turning. *See also* wood screw, self-tapping screw.

scribe
To scratch a line on a material so that it will fit an irregular surface when cut to that line.

scrim
A special fabric or tape that is applied as a reinforcement over joints of plasterboard sheets to prevent the plaster set coat from cracking.

seal
See trap.

sealant
A flexible, waterproof material used to seal a joint between the edge of door and window frames and the wall to prevent water penetrating through from the outside. It is also used to seal around sanitaryware such as baths and sinks.

sealed unit
A glass panel consisting of two or more panes of glass with spaces between which are filled with dry air and the edges sealed. They are used to reduce heat loss and sound transmission. *See also* double glazing, secondary glazing.

sealing compound
See sealant

search
An examination of registers and records to determine encumbrances affecting the title to property. An official search may be made and a certificate of the findings issued under section 3, Land Charges Act 1972, as amended.

seasoning
The process involved in drying timber to a suitable moisture

content by either natural or artificial means.

secondary beam

A structural member supported at each end by main beams. *See also* beam, main beam, simply supported beam

secondary cooperative

In a housing association context, an organisation, normally a registered housing association, supplying development, financial and other services to primary cooperatives. *See also* cooperative housing, primary cooperative.

secondary glazing

Glass panels that are added internally to existing windows to achieve double glazing. *See also* double glazing, sealed unit.

secret nailing

A method of fixing tongue and grooved floor boards by nailing above the tongue diagonally so that the nail head is hidden by the groove of the next board. *See also* tongue and grooved boards, floorboards.

section

A drawing to scale which shows the construction of the various parts of a building from the foundations to the roof. *See also* drawings.

secured loan

Monies advanced by way of a loan but where, on default by the borrower, the lender has a legal right to sell property against which the loan has been secured.

secure tenancy

A tenancy where the tenant has security of tenure by virtue of the Housing Act 1985, as amended.

security of tenure

A statutory right of a tenant to continue occupancy after the completion of a term has expired.

sedimentary rock

Rock formed by the accumulation and consolidation of mineral and organic fragments deposited in water and ice. The most common types are sandstones and limestones.

segregation

The separation of the aggregates in a concrete mix resulting in a porous, non-uniform mix, with a loss of strength. It generally happens when concrete is dropped into position from a height, since concrete requires compaction to achieve density and strength. *See also* compaction.

self-build society
Defined by the Housing Associations Act 1985 as 'a housing association whose objective is to provide for sale to, or occupation by, its members. Dwellings built or improved principally with the use of its members own labour.'

self-levelling screed
A latex material which is poured on to the top of concrete floors to a thickness of approximately 3mm and is used to provide a smooth level surface on which to lay a floor finish. Also used to repair existing concrete floors. *See also* screed.

self-tapping screw
A screw used for connecting metal, which cuts its own thread during the driving process. *See also* screw.

selling price
The amount which a vendor

states that he is willing to accept whether or not it is the price eventually realised.

semi-detached house
Two separate dwellings which are joined by a separating or party wall. *See also* detached house, terraced house.

semi-engineering brick
A brick not as strong as an engineering brick but stronger than a common brick. *See also* brick, engineering brick.

semi-hydraulic lime
A type of lime that hardens upon drying and is similar to high calcium lime with some hydraulic lime properties.

separate sewage system
A system in which foul water and surface water are conveyed in separate sewers – foul water to a sewage treatment plant and surface water to a suitable outfall such as a river, stream or sea. *See also* combined sewage system.

separating wall
See party wall.

separation agreement
An agreement concerning the

disposition of a matrimonial home.

septic tank
An underground chamber into which sewage is discharged from buildings whose foul drains are not connected to public sewers. The sewage is broken down leaving an effluent that can be safely drained away. These now replace cesspools. *See also* cesspool.

serpula lacrymans
See dry rot.

service charge
The sum payable by a tenant for services provided by the landlord.

service contract agreement
In the housing association context, a legal contractual agreement using a partnership scheme to provide special needs housing and defining the responsibilities of the housing association as a voluntary agency.

service main
A cable or pipe, provided by the authority, that conveys gas, water, electricity or other service to a road and to which the service pipe is connected. *See also* service pipe.

service occupancy
An occupancy, normally residential premises granted by an employer to an employee as part of his conditions of employment for the better execution of his duties, which persists only during the period of employment. *See also* service tenancy.

service pipe
A pipe which carries gas or water from the authority's main to the building. *See also* service main.

services
Gas, water, electricity, drains and other provisions serving a building.

service tenancy
A tenancy where the tenant is an employee of the landlord. The employment being the motive for the grant of a tenancy. *See also* service occupancy.

servient tenement
A tenement subject to an easement.

servitude
Easement.

set
See skim coat.

set square
A plastic or metal triangular-shaped drawing instrument used for drawing angles of 30°, 45°, 60° and vertical lines. *See also* T-square, square.

setting coat
See skim coat.

setting out
The procedure involved in positioning the building prior to construction and requiring the use of surveying equipment. *See also* datum, level.

settled land
Land limited to certain persons in succession. Under section 1 Settled Land Act 1925 it is defined as:

● limited in trust for any person by way of succession
● limited in trust for any person in possession (a) for an entitled interest, (b) for an estate subject to an executory limitation over, (c) for a base or determinable fee, (d) being a minor
● limited in trust for a contingent estate

● limited to, or in trust for, a married woman with a restraint on anticipation
● charged with a rent charge for the life of any person.

settlement
1. Movement of the foundations due to compression of the subsoil as a result of load or volume change due to water content. *See also* differential settlement.
2. The instrument or instruments by which land is settled. *See also* compound settlement, marriage settlement, strict settlement, voluntary settlement.

sewage
Waste matter that is discharged into a foul sewer from a foul drain. *See also* foul sewer, foul drain.

sewer
A pipe situated below ground level which is used for disposing of surface and waste water. *See also* surface water sewer, foul sewer.

sewer brick
A type of engineering brick with low absorption, used for the construction of inspection chambers and sewers. *See also* brick, engineering brick.

sex discrimination

The singling out of a person or group because of gender for special favour or disfavour. Discrimination may be direct, indirect or by victimisation. It may be unlawful under the Sex Discrimination Act 1975.

shake

The separation of wood fibres in a piece of timber resulting in a defect.

shale

Compressed layers of soil and silt.

shared housing

Residential accommodation in which two or more individuals live together and share facilities. The term also includes hostels.

shared ownership

In a housing association context, the sharing of the equity in a property between the occupier and housing association. The occupier purchases a property at a proportion of the value and pays rent to cover the share in the equity retained by the housing association. Typically the purchaser acquires 50 per cent equity and pays 50 per cent at normal rent. When the purchaser leaves the property he realises the capital invested.

shear

Forces that, when load is applied, act in such a manner as to cause portions of a material to slide over one another in opposite directions. *See also* compression, tension.

shear force

A force causing the fibres of a material to slide over one another. *See also* shear.

shear strain

Deformation of a material caused by shear. *See also* shear.

shear strength

The maximum amount of shear force a material can withstand before it fails. *See also* shear force.

shear stress

The measure of shear of a material determined by the sheer force divided by the cross-sectional area. *See also* shear, shear force.

sheathing paper

See building paper.

sheet glass
Manufactured by dipping into a tank of molten glass a special blind which extracts a thin sheet of semi-molten glass which is passed between rollers, cooled and cut to size. This type of glass is used for general building work, such as window panes. *See also* glass.

sheet piles
Metal sheets 300mm to 400mm wide and up to approximately 20m long which are driven into the ground and placed side by side so that they interlock. Used for retaining soil and water from deep excavations.

shell
A building under construction where the external walls and roof have been completed but is unfinished internally.

shellac
A substance used to produce French polish and varnish.

shell roof
A curved roof generally constructed of thin reinforced concrete. *See also* reinforced concrete.

Shelter
An organisation, established in 1965 following public concern about the plight of homeless people. It is responsible for campaigning on behalf of the nation's homeless and raises money from various sources to support its campaigning roles, finance a national network of housing aid centres and support individual projects aimed at alleviating homelessness.

sheltered housing
A colloquial term used to mean housing specially designed for elderly people grouped around a range of communal facilities. *See also* category 1 and category 2 housing.

sheradising
A protective coating on iron or steel obtained by heating in a metal container with zinc dust.

shingles
Timber tiles used as roof coverings for external cladding purposes. *See also* roof tiles.

shiplap boards
Timber boards rebated together and used as an external cladding.

shoe
See rainwater shoe.

shore
A temporary support to the existing wall of a building to allow alteration and repair work to be carried out. *See also* dead shore, raking shore, flying shore.

short bored pile
See beam and pile foundation.

shorthold tenancy
A tenancy of a residence under which the landlord has the mandatory ground for obtaining possession. *See also* protected shorthold tenancy.

short lease
For income tax and capital gains tax purposes a lease for a term of 50 years or less. *See also* lease.

short-life housing
Properties which can be used temporarily, e.g. student accommodation or single accommodation.

short tenancy
In relation to compulsory purchase a tenancy for not more than a year. *See also* compulsory purchase.

shower
A waste appliance consisting of a unit which heats water which is emitted as water jets drained in a shower tray, the whole being enclosed by a cubicle. A shower may also be incorporated above a bath and enclosed by a waterproof curtain or screen. *See also* shower tray, shower unit.

shower tray
A square sink-type unit which is strong enough to support a person and is fitted with an outlet which is connected to a trap and waste pipe to dispose of waste water. *See also* shower, shower unit.

shower unit
A unit comprising a heater, control valve and perforated outlet which is fitted to a cold water pipe, heats water when operated and is used for shower purposes. *See also* shower.

shrinkage
A reduction in the size of a material due to the drying out of water which causes warping of timber and cracking of plaster surfaces.

shrinkage joint
See contraction joint.

shutter
Slatted timber or metal doors that are fitted to the outside of windows and close over them for protection and safety at night.

shuttering
See formwork.

side inlet gulley
See back inlet gulley.

sidelight
A glazed panel fixed next to an external door and incorporated in the same frame.

side string
See outer string.

signing date
The date on which a valuation report or certificate is signed.

silica
A constituent part of sand, quartz and flint. The main raw material used in glass manufacture.

silica brick
A brick containing a high portion of silica which is used where high temperatures are present. *See also* brick.

silica gel
A substance that absorbs moisture and can be used to prevent surface condensation occurring on windows by placing a container at the base of the window to absorb moist air.

sill
The bottom portion of a door or window frame that is designed to project beyond the face of the wall to throw rainwater clear.

sill board
See window board.

simply supported beam
A short spanning structural member which is built into, and supported at each end by, load-bearing walls. *See also* beam, main beam, secondary beam.

single bridging
One row of floor strutting. *See also* strutting.

single floor
A timber joisted upper floor comprising joists that are only supported at each end. *See also* double floor.

single glazing
A glass panel incorporated in a door or window, consisting of one sheet of glass.

single hung window
A sash window where one sash moves and the other is fixed.

single lap
See lap.

single lap tiles
See interlocking tiles.

single roof
See couple roof.

single-stack system
A one-pipe system which serves soil and waste appliances from a single house and the connections of which are designed to eliminate the need for an anti-siphon pipe. *See also* one-pipe system, two-pipe system.

sink
A waste appliance used for washing and cleaning purposes. *See also* Belfast sink, slop sink.

siphon
See siphonage.

siphonage
Differences in atmospheric pressure which cause movement of water in pipes. *See also* anti-siphon pipe.

siphonic WC
A WC where the action of flushing causes waste matter to be drawn away from the pan by siphonic action. It is a quiet operation because of its double-trapped system whereby the flushing action on the second trap creates a suction on the first trap causing the waste to be sucked away. *See also* washdown closet.

sirapite plaster
See anhydrous gypsum plaster.

site
An area of land to be used for a building project.

site coverage
The proportion of a site which is covered by buildings, often expressed as a percentage of the area covered by buildings to the total area of a site.

site investigation
A survey carried out to gather facts and information of the building site used for design purposes and, in particular, foundation design.

site lighting
Temporary lights provided on a building site to allow work to be carried out in poor lighting conditions.

site line
A line used on a plan to establish visibility standards at road junctions or access points on to public roads. The basic criterion is that at eye level – i.e. 1.05 metres above road level – there should be a clear view over a given area.

site plan
A drawing in the horizontal plane of an area of land showing boundaries and the physical extent of the land included in a particular parcel.

site value
The value of undeveloped property as a site for future development.

sitting tenant
A tenant who is lawfully in physical possession, or is entitled to immediate physical possession of the demised premises.

sitting tenant value
The price which might reasonably be expected to be secured on the open market at a given time by the tenant currently in possession of the land.

SI units
The international system of metric units used for scientific and technical purposes.

skeleton
A framework prior to providing some form of covering or cladding.

skeleton core
See hollow core door.

skill and care warranty
A warranty stating that proper skill and care has been exercised in carrying out the planning, design and/or construction of the development. It is obtained by a building owner/developer or other party with an interest in a development project but where there is no direct contractual relationship between the builders and architecture engineers.

skim
The process of obtaining a skim coat. *See also* skim coat.

skim coat

A final plaster coat consisting of neat plaster mixed with water and applied to previous plaster coats (i.e. float coat) or to plasterboard sheets. *See also* float coat.

skirting board

A length of timber with one edge rounded or moulded which is fixed around the edge of a floor at the junction with the wall to act as a cover strip.

skylight

See laylight.

slab

1. A thin regular-shaped piece of concrete or stone.
2. A large area of concrete forming a solid ground floor.

slag wool

A mineral wool.

slaked lime

The addition of water to calcium oxide (quicklime) to produce calcium hydroxide (hydrated lime). *See also* lime plasters.

slaking

The procedure involved in producing slaked lime. *See also* slaked lime.

slat

A thin piece of timber included in a louvre. *See also* louvre.

slate

A metamorphic rock. Most slates are known as clay slates, are blue-grey or green in colour, split easily and were traditionally used for damp-proof courses and roof coverings, although cost has now made them an expensive material. The leading types are those from North Wales which are considered to be the finest slates. They are blue/grey in colour and thin in thickness. Cornish slates are thicker, less durable and green/grey in colour, whereas slates obtained from the Lake District are green in colour and thicker, formed from volcanic ash and less durable than the former types. *See also* metamorphic rock.

sleeper wall

A small wall of minimum two courses of brickwork built off a concrete slab and used to support the joists of a hollow ground floor. The bricks are arranged with gaps between to allow air circulation to a timber joisted floor for ventilation purposes to prevent dry rot (i.e. honeycombing). *See also* hollow ground floor.

sliding door
A door which is fixed to a track at the top and slides sideways when opened and closed.

sliding sash
A window that opens and closes by sliding horizontally.

sliding sash window
See sash window.

slipper bath
See bath.

slop sink
A deep, rectangular glazed stoneware sink for disposing of waste water used for cleaning purposes. It is fitted with a hinged grid for placing and supporting a bucket whilst it is filled with clean water. *See also* sink.

slum clearance
The procedure for designating or acquiring and demolishing unfit buildings.

slump test
A test on wet concrete to ensure that the consistency is being maintained and is carried out by placing a sample of mixed concrete in a truncated metal core in compacted layers, removing the core and measuring the amount the concrete has dropped or slumped. This should be consistent for consecutive mixes.

slurry
Water and cement mixed to form a liquid.

small bore heating system
A central heating system using small diameter copper pipes of approximately 15mm diameter and in which the hot water feeding the radiators is circulated by pressure from a pump. *See also* micro-bore heating system.

SMM
See Standard Method of Measurement.

smoke detector
An electronic device, usually fitted to a ceiling, comprising an alarm which is activated when smoke is present.

smoke stop
See fire stop.

smoke test

A test on a foul and surface water drain generally carried out on drainage runs between inspection chambers and consisting of blocking one end of the drainage run and pumping in smoke from the other end via a special smoke machine. Leakages are then detected by escaping smoke through joints. Smoke bombs are now generally used instead of a smoke machine since they are simple to use and are approximately the size of a firework. These are placed in the open end of the blocked-off drain after lighting. *See also* hydraulic test, air test.

snecked rubble

A wall built of various sized square stones.

soakaway

A pit filled with stone or brick rubble into which surface water drains into the ground.

soaker

A piece of lead that is fixed between tiles or slates to a roof that abuts against a wall with an upstand which is covered by a flashing provided in the wall.

See also stepped flashing, lean-to roof.

socket outlet

An electrical fitting connected to a ring main into which plugs attached to electrical appliances can be fixed.

soffit

The underside of a particular building component such as a beam, stairs or eaves of a roof.

soffit board

A timber board fixed to brackets attached to the ends of roof rafters to form the underside of closed eaves. *See also* eaves.

softwood

Timber that is produced by coniferous trees and is used for general carpentry and joinery work, such as flooring, roofing, windows, doors and internal fixtures. It requires painting or staining and varnishing if used for joinery purposes such as in windows and doors. Structural timbers, such as flooring and roofing, would generally be treated with a preservative. *See also* hardwood.

soil

1. A mineral-rich organic sub-

stance forming the top layer of the land surface and composed of disintegrated rock particles, humus, water and air. *See also* subsoil, top soil.

2. Waste matter, usually human waste.

soil and vent pipe
A vertical pipe which acts as both a soil pipe and vent pipe. *See also* soil pipe, vent pipe.

soil appliance
An appliance used for the disposal of human waste, such as a WC. *See also* water closet.

soil drain
See foul drain.

soil pipe
A pipe placed above ground level and into which soil and waste appliances are connected. Its purpose is to convey foul water to a foul drain into which it is connected. *See also* soil and vent pipe, vent pipe.

soil stack
See soil pipe.

solar block
See insulation block.

solar glass
Glass that is tinted and used in situations to resist solar radiation and glare. *See also* glass.

solar heat gain
Heat energy that enters a building through the fabric by direct radiation from the sun. *See also* solar radiation.

solar radiation
Heat energy that is emitted by the sun. *See also* radiation.

soldier
A brick set on end so that the stretcher or header faces vertically, as in a soldier arch or coping. *See also* stretcher, header.

soldier arch
Bricks laid on end above a window or door opening so that the stretchers face vertically.

soldier course
See brick-on-edge coping.

sole agent
A person who is the only agent entitled to represent his principal.

sole plate
The bottom member of a timber frame.

sole selling/letting right

The right affected by an agent when the principal has contracted to convey exclusive rights to sell or let the property, entitling the agent to a commission even if the principal acts on his own behalf.

solicitor

A legal practitioner – one who offers legal advice. For a person to practise as a solicitor, they must:

● be admitted as a solicitor
● have his or her name on the roll of solicitors
● have in force a current certificate issued by the Law Society.

solid bridge

Floor strutting consisting of solid timber sections equal in size to the floor joists. *See also* strutting.

solid core

See solid core door.

solid core door

A flush door comprising vertical timber strips glued together and faced both sides with plywood. *See also* external door, fire door.

solid floor

See solid ground floor.

solid frame

A door frame where a rebate has been incorporated, rather than formed by planting on a separate strip of timber.

solid ground floor

A floor constructed of a solid slab of in situ plain or reinforced concrete laid on a hardcore base with a damp-proof membrane incorporated. *See also* floor, hollow ground floor.

solid wall

A wall consisting of bricks or stone to form a solid construction. *See also* wall.

sound

See airborne sound *and* structure-borne sound.

sound-absorbent panel

See panel absorber.

sound insulation

Provision within a building element to reduce both airborne and structureborne sound. *See also* insulation, pugging, panel absorber.

soundproofing
See sound insulation.

space heating
A method of heating the inside of a building using warm air provided through ducts rather than by hot water feeding radiators. *See also* central heating system.

spacer
A small block of timber, concrete, or a special plastic attachment, fixed to steel reinforcement to produce a space between the reinforcement and formwork so that the reinforcement is fully covered by concrete when it is placed.

spall
The external surface of brick, concrete or stone that flakes off due to general weathering, freezing of absorbed water, efflorescence and knocks.

span
The distance between building elements, e.g. walls. *See also* clear span, effective span.

spandrel
1. The triangular area of a staircase below the string. *See also* stairs.

2. The triangular area of wall surrounding the outer curve of an arch.

spar
See rafter.

special damage
Damage of a kind that must be expressly pleaded and proved before the court.

special needs housing
Residential accommodation provided for people with a special disability or requirement, in addition to their need for a home. It is either self-contained accommodation or shared housing. *See also* elderly persons' dwellings, frail elderly housing, mobility housing.

special needs management allowance
In a housing association context, an allowance paid to registered housing associations to cover the additional cost of special needs schemes established since the Housing Act 1988. *See also* special needs housing.

special projects promotional allowance
In a housing association context,

a special housing association grant allowance to cover some of the additional costs incurred when associations develop special needs schemes. *See also* special needs housing.

specific adhesive
An adhesive which bonds simultaneously to the sides of the pores of the materials to be joined. *See also* adhesive, mechanical adhesive.

specification
A description contained in a specification of works.

specification of works
Part of the design information which describes the work involved in carrying out the various parts of the building work and is either a separate document or used to supplement a bill of quantities. *See also* design information, bill of quantities.

specific gravity
See relative density.

speculative development
The development of a building or buildings where, at the start of the project, there is no known buyer or tenant.

speculative funding
The funding of a future development where there is a risk of not selling or letting at a figure exceeding, or even attaining, the development expenditure.

speculator
A person who undertakes transactions in property with a view to making a profit but with the risk of making a loss.

spigot and socket joint
A rigid joint between drainpipes where one end of the pipe is slightly grooved and fits into a large opening at the other end of a pipe, the joint formed by wrapping a tarred rope around the spigot end and completed by sealing with cement mortar. *See also* salt-glazed stoneware drainpipes.

spine wall
An internal load-bearing wall which runs the whole length or width of a building and is connected into the external load-bearing walls. *See also* load-bearing wall.

spiral stair
A stairway which is curved around a central pole or open-

ing and where all the treads are winders. *See also* stairs, winder.

spirit level
A metal or wooden device containing liquid and a bubble in a glass tube which is used for levelling building components such as brick walls during construction.

splashback
A row of tiles or similar waterproof material attached to a wall above a sink unit.

splay
The edge of an object that is cut at an angle the full width.

spoil
Surplus excavated material, such as soil.

spot listing
The emergency process whereby a building is added to the list of buildings of architectural and/or historic interest. The process is usually initiated by the local planning authority in response to a real or perceived threat to an appropriate class of building. *See also* listed building, listing.

spouse
A husband or wife.

spread of flame
The ability of a material to allow flame to spread across its surface. Materials are classified into five groups, Class 0 having a very low flame spread and Class 4 having a very rapid flame spread. *See also* fire protection, fire resistance, noncombustible, non-flammable.

springer
The first brick or stone at each end of an arch.

sprocketed eaves
Short lengths of timber fixed to the bottom of rafters to produce a smaller angle than the main roof slope and causes the roof slates or tiles to fan out at the base. *See also* eaves.

sprung floor
Comprises metal clips with a rubber bush which are bedded in a concrete floor and into which timber battens are placed for fixing hardwood strips so that the floor 'springs' when load is applied. *See also* floor, strip floor.

square
A large L-shaped timber or metal tool which is used to set out right angles during the construction of a building. *See also* set square, T-square.

squared rubble
A wall built with square stones. *See also* rubble wall.

squatter
Someone who is not a tenant, licensee or otherwise and who occupies land or property without permission from the person who is entitled to occupation.

squatter's title
The title to land acquired by 12 years adverse possession against the person who has lawful possession of the land. *See also* adverse possession.

stable door
A door with separate top and bottom halves which open and close independently.

stabilised soil
Soil that has been treated to increase its strength by techniques such as injection of chemicals, grouting, freezing or compacting.

stability
The capability of a building element or component to resist movement or collapse due to load.

stack
See chimney.

Staffordshire blue
An engineering brick which is dark blue in colour. *See also* engineering brick.

stain
A liquid applied to softwood to penetrate and colour the surface and thereby give a hardwood effect.

stainless steel
An alloy of low carbon steel with an amount of chromium compounds added which form on the surface to give a high resistance to corrosion. *See also* steel.

staircase
A complete construction including steps, bannisters, landing, strings and other associated parts. *See also* stairs.

stairs
A series of steps to provide access between floors and land-

ings within or outside a building and also to provide a means of escape in case of fire. *See also* accommodation stair, fire escape stair, private stair, public stair, open newel stair, open riser stair, open wall stair, open stair, closed stair, spiral stair, straight flight stair.

stairway
See staircase.

stairwell
An opening between flights of stairs and around which a staircase is constructed.

stamp duties
Duties raised by affixing stamps to instruments such as conveyances and leases.

stanchion
See column.

Standard Method of Measurement (SMM)
A document containing the nationally recognised method for measuring quantities from drawings and used to produce a bill of quantities. *See also* bill of quantities.

starter homes
Residential accommodation spe-cifically designed and con-structed for first-time buyers.

statutory form of accounts
In a housing association context, the formula in which the accounts of registered housing associations must be published as set out by statutory instru-ment under the Housing Associ-ations Act 1985.

statutory tenant
A tenant who remains in posses-sion of a residence after the proper term has been completed by virtue of the Rent Act 1977, as amended.

staying put
Colloquial term used to describe agency services which provide assistance to elderly home own-ers with housing repairs, im-provements and adaptations.

steel
An alloy made from iron and carbons and used for producing such items as beams, columns and reinforcement for concrete. *See also* stainless steel.

steel casement
A window manufactured from galvanised steel.

step
1. A component consisting of a tread and riser used to gain access between different levels.
2. A part of a series of steps forming a stair. *See also* tread, riser, stair.

step iron
A metal rung which is built into the side of deep inspection chambers to provide a step for access. *See also* inspection chamber.

stepped flashing
A waterproof covering of sheet lead, provided to a wall to which a pitch roof abuts, dressed over an upstand formed against the wall from soakers. The flashing is fixed into the horizontal mortar joints of the wall and stepped down to follow the pitch of the roof. *See also* flashing soaker, lean-to-roof.

stepped foundation
A strip foundation used to support a wall on sloping ground and constructed at various levels connected by steps to suit the ground slope. *See also* strip foundation.

stile
The vertical frame at each side of a panelled door. *See also* hanging stile.

stone
See rock and artificial stone.

stoneware
Clay products, such as drainpipes, that are burnt to high temperatures to produce a hard, vitreous material. *See also* vitrified stoneware.

stoothed partition
See also stud partition.

stopcock
A device fitted on to a gas or water pipe which stops the flow at that point and is used as a safety device to allow repairs to be carried out.

stop notice
The part of the planning enforcement process defined under the Town and Country Planning Act 1990 as: 'Where the local planning authority consider it expedient that any relevant activity should cease before the expiry of the compliance with an enforcement notice, they may, when they

serve a copy of the enforcement notice or afterwards, serve a stop notice prohibiting the carrying out of that activity on the land to which the enforcement notice relates, or any part of that land specified in the stop notice.'

stop tap
See stopcock.

storage cistern
See cistern.

storage heater
An electrical appliance used to heat individual rooms and containing materials capable of storing heat, such as bricks. The heat is released at certain times of the day, and the device makes use of cheap rate electricity.

storage tank
See cistern.

storey
A floor or level of a building.

storm drain
See surface water drain.

storm water
See surface water.

straight arch
See arch.

straight flight stair
One complete staircase between a floor and landing where all the steps are parallel. *See also* stairs.

strain
The deformation of a material due to imposed load. *See also* imposed load.

strata
See stratum.

stratum
A layer of rock.

street
A term generally meaning to be a made-up road which has houses, or other buildings, on one or both sides. The term, however, has different meanings in different statutory circumstances.

stress
A measure of force on an element and is determined by dividing the force by the cross sectional area of the element upon which it acts. *See also* compressive stress, tensile stress.

stress-graded timber

Timber that has been tested and divided into classes according to its strength.

stretcher

The face of a brick placed so that the full length is seen. *See also* header.

stretcher bond

Arrangement of bricks so that each course within a wall comprises stretchers. *See also* half bond.

strict settlement

A settlement designed to retain landed estates in a particular family. *See also* settlement, compound settlement.

string

An inclined member carrying the treads on the risers of a stair which are housed, wedged and glued into tapered grooves cut into one side. *See also* wall string, outer string, cut string, riser, tread.

string course

A projecting horizontal course of brickwork or stone situated at the upper part of an external wall for decorative purposes and to throw surface wall clear of the wall below.

strip floor

Hardwood strips of maple or mahogany, approximately 100mm wide and 20mm thick, fixed to timber battens incorporated in a concrete solid floor as a high-class floor finish. *See also* floor, sprung floor.

strip foundation

One that supports a load-bearing wall over its whole length. It consists of a plain or reinforced concrete strip, minimum 150mm thick, placed in the bottom of a trench. The Building Regulations give minimum widths for plain concrete strip foundations depending on the subsoil types and loads to be supported. *See also* foundation, deep strip foundation, reinforced strip foundation, wide strip foundation, wild strip foundation, ground beam.

stucco

A smooth render applied to the outside of walls, traditionally made from lime and sand but now usually cement, and generally painted in various colours. *See also* render.

stuck mould
Shaped timber cut from solid material for decorative purposes, such as the moulded edge on a skirting board. *See also* planted mould.

S-trap
The bend in a gulley, soil or waste appliance shaped in the form of a letter 'S'. *See also* trap.

structure-borne sound
Sound that is transmitted through the fabric of a building. *See also* airborne sound, sound insulation.

stud
A vertical timber member in a stud partition. *See also* nogging, stud partition.

stud partition
An internal non load-bearing wall consisting of a timber framework faced both sides with a sheet finish, such as plasterboard. *See also* internal wall.

structural design
The process involved in the designing of the structural parts of the building such as load-bearing walls and beams.

structural engineer
A qualified person who is responsible for structural design.

structural timber
Timber components that support loads, such as floor joists and roof rafters

structure plan
A strategic plan for the future development of an area, usually prepared by a county planning authority. The document does not contain site specific land-use policies. *See also* local plan.

strut
The structural part of a roof truss or trussed rafter which causes forces to act towards the point at which it is jointed under load. *See also* tie, roof truss, trussed rafter.

strutting
Timber or metal strips fixed diagonally between timber floor joists to provide stability to the floor. *See also* lateral support, solid bridge.

subcontractor
A firm employed by a contractor to carry out a certain part of the

building works such as painting and decorating. *See also* nominated subcontractor.

subframe
An initial or secondary timber frame into which a main frame such as a door or window frame is fixed.

subsidence
See settlement.

subsill
The bottom frame of a window that sits on top of a sill. *See also* sill.

subsoil
The earth below the top layer of soil and is variable in nature, the characteristics of which influence the selection and design of an appropriate foundation. *See also* cohesive and non-cohesive soil, vegetable layer.

subsoil water
Water retained in the ground below the water table. *See also* ground water, water table.

substation
An electrical installation used for distributing electricity. *See also* electricity distribution, electricity supply.

substructure
That part of a building below ground level but up to and including the damp-proof course and ground floor. *See also* superstructure.

sulphate
A salt which may be present in the ground and reacts chemically with cement causing it to decay. *See also* sulphate-resisting Portland cement.

sulphate attack
See sulphate.

sulphate-resisting Portland cement
A cement that resists attack from sulphates. *See also* cement.

sum insured
The maximum sum of an insurer's liability in terms of an insurance contract, being determined by adjustment or settled on request of the insured.

sump
A pit that collects water from excavations.

sump pump
A pump that empties water from a sump.

superimposed load
See live load.

superstructure
That part of a building above the damp-proof course and ground floor. *See also* substructure.

supersulphated cement
A cement that has a high resistance to sulphates. *See also* sulphate-resisting Portland cement.

supervision order
An order whereby a minor is placed under the supervision of a local authority or probation office. See Children and Young Persons Act 1969, sections 7 and 11 as amended by the Childrens Act 1989, Criminal Law Act 1977 section 65(4), Powers of Criminal Courts Act 1973, section 26 and Matrimonial Causes Act 1973, section 44, as amended.

supplier
A firm from whom a contractor purchases building items and materials such as drainpipes and timber. *See also* nominated supplier.

supply pipe
A water service pipe. *See also* service pipe.

surety bond
In a housing association context, a guarantee purchased by a housing association to provide cover if a contractor is unable to complete a contract.

surface condensation
Water particles that form on the inside of a cold surface.

surface resistance
The resistance to the passage of heat through a structure, such as an external wall, by the external and internal surface. It is dependent upon the emissivity of the surface and degree of exposure of the structure, and is used in the calculation of 'U' values. *See also* thermal heat transmission coefficient.

surface spread of flame
See spread of flame.

surface tension
The ability of the surface of a liquid to support an object by virtue of it appearing to have a thin surface skin.

surface water
Water which is the result of either rain or thawed snow and which must be drained away so

239

to protect built constructions and their immediately surrounding land from overimmersion or flood.

surface water drain

A pipe situated below ground level which is used for disposing surface water from a building(s) within the boundary of a property and maintained by the owner(s).

surface water gutter

See eaves gutter.

surface water pipe

See rainwater pipe.

surface water sewer

A pipe situated below ground level used for disposing surface water from surface water drains. It is the responsibility of the water authority.

surrender

The yielding of a lease of land. Normally executed by deed.

surrender clause

The clause in a lease obliging the tenant to surrender or offer to surrender the lease.

surrender value

Value of the unexpired portion of a lease if surrendered to the immediate landlord.

survey

A systematic investigation of a problem via measurement and/ or assessment, e.g. building survey, car parking survey etc.

surveyor

A qualified person who would normally be a member of the Royal Institute of Chartered Surveyors and would be involved in one of the surveying disciplines. *See also* quantity surveyor, building surveyor, land surveyor.

suspended ceiling

A ceiling finish which is supported on a framework attached to the underside of the floor above thereby creating a ceiling void (space).

suspended floor

See hollow ground floor.

suspended ground floor

See hollow ground floor.

suspended timber floor

See hollow ground floor.

swan neck

An 'S'-shaped rainwater pipe

fitting which is used to connect an eaves gutter to a rainwater pipe.

synthetic resin
An artificial polymer with similar properties to natural resins.

system building
A building method adopted in the 1960s which consisted of prefabricated components manufactured in a factory and delivered to the site for quick assembly. This method was generally used for building multi-storey blocks of flats for social purposes, and many systems were developed between consortiums of building organisations and local authorities to meet social housing demands much quicker than could be achieved by traditional methods. Due to ensuing social problems, poor design and high maintenance costs, system building is no longer used, and many system-built flats are being demolished to make way for traditional housing.

T

tacking
The determination of the priority of mortgages over the same property by the order in which the mortgages were made. Repealed by the Law of Property Act 1925.

taking off
The measurement and listing of quantities of materials from drawings for the purpose of preparing a bill of quantities in accordance with the Standard Method of Measurement (SMM) of building works, or for estimating, planning and ordering purposes. *See also* bill of quantities, Standard Method of Measurement.

tanalised timber
Wood that has been treated with a preservative and is generally used for carpentry, e.g. roof timbers.

tank
An enclosed water container that may be pressurised.

tanking
A method used for waterproofing basements consisting of a damp-proof membrane incorporated in the walls and coating the floor with asphalt to form a waterproof box. *See also* damp-proof membrane.

tap
A device fitted to the end of a water pipe which is operated by hand to open, close and control the flow of hot and cold water. *See also* pillar tap, bib tap.

tar
A black substance, obtained from the distillation of coal, which has adhesive properties and is used as a binder in road surfaces. *See also* Tarmacadam.

Tarmacadam

Crushed rock or stone mixed with a bitumen and rolled to produce a paved surface. *See also* macadam.

taxation of costs

The process in which the disputed costs of a court action, public inquiry etc., are reviewed by the relevant officer of the court to determine the charges recoverable by one party from the other.

tell tale

A process whereby two metal pins are placed each side of a crack in a wall and the distance between them measured periodically to determine whether the crack is widening. Alternatively, a glass plate may be cemented across the crack so that any movement of the wall will break the glass.

temperature

1. The degree of hotness or coldness of a body, substance or medium, relating to the kinetic energy of the atoms or molecules.
2. A measure of the degree of hotness or coldness indicated on a scale that has one or more fixed reference points. The measurement is usually expressed in degrees Celsius or Fahrenheit.

temperature movement

Movement caused by the expansion and contraction of a material due to temperature differences. *See also* expansion joint, moisture movement, settlement.

template

A full-size temporary component generally made from wood, such as a door or window frame, built into a wall so that, when it is removed, the opening formed will accommodate a window or door frame.

temporary benchmark

A fixed point used to determine the levels of a building during construction. *See also* benchmark.

tenancy in common

Where two or more persons have concurrent ownership, each having a distinct but 'undivided' share in property. No one person is entitled to exclusive use or title, each being entitled to occupy the whole in common with others. Since the Law of

Property Act 1925 tenancy in common only exists as an equitable interest under a trust.

tenant
The holder of land. Applies to freehold and leasehold property but is commonly applied to a person holding a lease.

tenant at sufferance
A person who has originally come into possession of land by a lawful title and continues possession after his interest has determined.

tenant at will
A state of being between tenant and lessee.

tenant for life
A tenancy which expires upon the tenant's death. Since 1925 a life tenant can only exist in equity.

tenant for years
A lessee with a term of years certain.

tenant from year to year
A tenant whose tenancy can only be terminated by a notice to quit on its anniversary. A six months' notice to quit is usually required.

tenant in the praecipe
A tenant against whom a writ is issued in a real action. *See also* recovery.

tenant-right
The right of a tenant after determination of his tenancy.

tenants' association
A voluntary association of tenants who live in a particular area or scheme.

Tenants' Charter
A charter under the Housing Acts which gave tenants new rights – namely the security to sublet and undertake improvements. *See also* Housing Act 1980, Housing Act 1988.

tenants' choice
A colloquial term used to describe the process introduced in the Housing Act 1988 which gives secure local authority tenants in England and Wales, the opportunity to change landlord while staying in their present homes. *See also* Housing Act 1988.

tenant's improvements
Improvements to land or buildings carried out wholly or partly

at the expense of, and to meet the needs of, the tenant.

tenant's repairing lease
A lease where the lessee is under an obligation to maintain and repair the property.

tender
1. An offer of land, goods or services which, if accepted, creates a legally enforceable contract.
2. An offer made by a contractor, and requested by an architect, to carry out the building works in accordance with the design information for a certain sum of money. *See also* formal tender, private tender, public tender.

tendering
The procedure undertaken by a contractor in preparing a tender working from the design information.

tendering process
The process of inviting bids by tender, receiving, considering and usually accepting one. The normal process is:

● preparation of identical tender documents stating details about the subject of the bid
● dispatch of the tender documents to the tenderers, who

may be selected, or to any one who requests and may have to meet certain criteria

The contents of each bid are confidential until a time and date specified at the outset, when the tenders are opened.

No tender is accepted after the date for opening and considering tenders.

tenement
1. Something which is the subject of tenure, e.g. land.
2. A house let as different apartments.

tenon
A protruding portion of timber which is used to fit into a slot provided in an opposite timber member to form a joint. *See also* mortice, mortice and tenon.

tensile strength
The maximum amount of tensile force a material can withstand before it fails.

tensile force
A force causing the fibres of a material to stretch. *See also* tension.

tensile stress
A measure of the force required

to cause a material to be in a state of tension and expressed in N/mm^2 and kN/mm^2. *See also* stress, tension, compressive stress, ultimate tensile strength.

tension
Forces that, when load is applied, act in opposite directions causing the material to stretch apart, such as the bottom portion of a beam when bending occurs. *See also* compression, shear.

tenure
The type of holding of land, as in freehold tenure.

tenure, security of
The right of a tenant or licensee of land to continue possession under a statute after determination.

term of years
An interest in land for a fixed number of years.

terra
Land.

terrace
A large external raised platform from which access is normally gained from the rear of a building. Part of a flat roof area may form a terrace.

terraced house
A dwelling incorporated in a row of three or more dwellings which are joined by separating party walls. *See also* detached house, semi-detached house.

terracotta
A clay block manufactured from burnt clay which has a smoother face than clay bricks and is used as a decorative facing to external walls. *See also* faience.

terrazzo
A floor finish comprising marble chippings mixed in a white cement which is ground and polished when hardened to expose the various coloured chips.

testate
Having made a will.

testator
One who makes a will.

textured finish
A toughened surface to a wall or ceiling incorporated in plaster.

thatch
The oldest type of roof covering, consisting of reed or straw.

theodolite
A surveying instrument consisting of a telescope mounted on a tripod which is used for determining horizontal and vertical angles.

thermal bridge
See cold bridge.

thermal capacity
The ability of a material to store heat energy.

thermal comfort
An acceptable internal building environment in terms of temperature and humidity.

thermal conductivity
See coefficient of thermal conductivity.

thermal heat transmission coefficient ('U' value)
A value specified for parts of a building and used to calculate heat losses from inside a building. Current regulations specify maximum 'U' values for such elements as walls, roof and ground floors.

It is calculated by determining the reciprocal of the sum of the total resistances and expressed in W/m^2 deg C (SI unit).

$$U = \frac{1}{\Sigma R}$$

where R is the total resistance.

See also thermal resistance, surface resistance.

thermal insulation
Provision within a building element to reduce heat losses. See also thermal resistance, insulation.

thermal resistance (R)
The resistance to the passage of heat of a particular material, which is dependent upon the k value (coefficient of thermal conductivity) and the thickness.

It is calculated

$$R = \frac{\text{thickness of material}}{\text{thermal conductivity of material}}$$

and expressed m^2 deg C/W (SI unit). It is used for determining 'U' values. See also coefficient of thermal conductivity.

thermal transmission
See thermal heat transmission coefficient.

thermometer
An instrument, used for measuring temperature, which contains a substance that is capable of expanding and contracting with changes in temperature, e.g. mercury.

thermoplastic
A material that softens when heated and hardens when cool, the process of which is used to produce plastics such as polyethylene, polypropylene and polystyrene. *See also* polyethylene, polypropylene, polystyrene.

thermoplastic tile
A floor tile made from thermoplastic incorporating fibres.

thermosetting
A material that hardens when heated, the process of which is used to produce such plastics as melamine formaldehyde and polyurethane.

thermostat
A device that operates automatically with changes in temperature and is used to control heating equipment such as radiators.

thinner
A liquid, such as white spirit, added to paints to increase their liquidity.

third surveyor
A surveyor appointed to settle a party wall dispute which has already been investigated by two surveyors representing the two parties.

Thistle plaster
A trade name for a retarded semi-hydrate gypsum plaster. *See also* gypsum plasters.

thixotropic
Having stability when left undisturbed and becoming liquid when agitated.

three-coat work
Wall plaster applied in three coats. The first coat is referred to as the render coat, the second the undercoat or float coat and the third the finish or set coat. *See also* two-coat work

threshold
See door sill.

throat
See check throat.

tie
The structural part of a roof truss or trussed rafter which, when under load, causes forces to act away from the point at which it is jointed. *See also* strut.

tie beam
A horizontal tie connecting two structural members, e.g. at the base of roof rafters.

tied cottage
A dwelling house provided to the occupant as part of, and effective only during, his employment. Usually associated with agricultural employment.

tie rods
A steel tie with thread ends. *See also* tie.

tile batten
See batten.

tiled valley
A roof valley formed with special shaped tiles. *See also* valley.

tile hanging
Roof tiles fixed vertically as a covering to a wall.

tiles
See roof tiles and floor tiles.

timber
Natural wood that has been processed for use for building purposes. *See also* sawn timber, wrought timber.

timber frame construction
A structural part of a building, such as a wall constructed of timber framework and supporting upper floors and roof, and is faced with brickwork or other cladding externally and with plasterboard internally.

timbering
See planking and strutting.

timeshare accommodation
Living accommodation used for leisure purposes by a group of people all of whom have rights to its use at intermittent times.

timeshare developers' association
An association of developers of time-share property.

timeshare rights
Rights accrued by a person who is a timeshare user, being rights exercisable during a period of not less than three years.

title
Term signifying a right to property.

title-deeds
The documents proving title to land.

toe board
A board fixed vertically around the edge of a scaffold platform.

toft
Land on which a building which had decayed once stood.

tolerance
An acceptable gap left between components into which another component can be fitted.

ton
An imperial weight used for measuring bulk quantities of building materials, such as cement and aggregates.

tongue
A thin projecting strip incorporated on one edge of a timber board that fits into a groove incorporated on the edge of another board. *See also* tongue and grooved boards.

tongue and grooved boards
Timber boards used to construct battened doors and as a floor covering to timber joisted floors, comprising strips of timber approximately 150mm wide and 20mm thick with tongued and grooved edges which are cramped together for fixing. *See also* floorboards, secret nailing, tongue.

tonne
A metric ton.

toothed connector
See toothed plate.

toothed plate
A circular metal plate with tooth-edges which is placed between two timber members and bite into the timber when bolted together to form a strong joint.

toothing
A method used for connecting masonry walls in which bricks are left projecting at the end of one wall every fourth to sixth course to fit into holes provided in the other wall into which it is to be joined.

top coat
See final coat.

top-hung window
A casement window hinged at the top to open outwards. *See also* casement window.

topography
The natural features of the surface of a building site, e.g. slopes and depressions.

topping out
The completion of a building project to the point when the structure and frame, including the roof are completed. It is usually marked by a celebration and attaching a small tree to the highest point of the building.

top rail
The top member in a panelled door. *See also* panelled door.

top soil
The top layer of earth which is suitable for landscaping and gardening purposes and which may have to be provided after building works have been completed. *See also* subsoil, vegetable layer.

torching
Plaster or cement pointing to the underside of roof slates or tiles. Was generally used before the advent of roofing felt.

tort
A civil wrong, e.g. nuisance, negligence, trespass etc.

Total Cost Indicators
In the housing association context, the value-for-money criteria used by the Housing Corporation for schemes developed under its current funding regime.

total going
The horizontal distance between the faces of the first and last risers in a flight of stairs. *See also* going, riser, tread.

total load
The sum of the dead and live loads imposed on the building. *See also* dead load, horizontal load, imposed load, live load.

toughened glass
Glass manufactured by the rapid cooling of the surface leaving stresses in the material that increase its strength and causing it to break into small pieces upon impact. *See also* glass.

tower block
A tall building, normally flats or offices which are eight storeys or

more in height. *See also* high-rise building.

town and country planning

The statutory process of planning and controlling the future development of an area introduced under the Town and Country Planning Act 1947, as amended. *See also* Town and Country Planning Act 1947.

Town and Country Planning Act 1947

This legislation brought almost all development under control by making it subject to planning permission. Planning changed from being a 'regulatory function' and development plans were prepared for every area of the country. *See also* planning permission, development plan.

Town and Country Planning Act 1990

This Act consolidated all previous planning legislation.

town house

See terraced house.

town planner

A person who engages in the profession of town and country planning. Usually qualified by Corporate Membership of the Royal Town Planning Institute.

TRADA

The Timber Research and Development Association which is responsible for the research and development of timber products and components used for the construction industry.

trade

A skilled occupation, such as a joiner and bricklayer.

traffic generation

The build-up or potential build-up of vehicular traffic resulting from an existing or potential land use.

tranche

An instalment or part of a total sum of money paid or advanced. A term used in association with development funding with each tranche of money paid at various stages of development in accordance with the terms of a contract and on the issue of certificates from an architect or surveyor. *See also* contract, architect's certificate, quantity surveyor.

translucent glass

See obscured glass.

transom
A horizontal member in a window frame which separates glazed areas which may be fixed to an opening. *See also* fixed light, opening light, mullion.

trap
The bend in a gulley, soil or waste appliance that contains water to act as a seal to prevent foul from drains re-entering the building. *See also* P-trap, water trap.

trap door
A small hinged or removable panel allowing access to a roof space.

tread
The horizontal part of a step which is the distance measured from the nosing to the riser of the next step. *See also* going, nosing, riser.

tree preservation order
An order made by the local planning authority under the Town and Country Planning Act 1990, as amended, to preserve individual or groups of trees. Such an order prohibits the cutting down, lopping, topping, uprooting or wilful destruction of the tree without the consent of the local authority.

trench
A narrow excavation provided to receive a foundation.

trespasser
One who goes on land without permission and whose presence is unknown to the proprietor or, if known, is practically objected to.

trial pit
A hole made in the ground to ascertain the nature of the soil.

trigger notice
A colloquial term normally describing a notice by a landlord or tenant setting in motion a rent review procedure.

trimmed joist
A floor joist which is supported at one end by a trimmer or trimming joist used to form an opening such as that to accommodate a stair. *See also* floor joist, trimming joist.

trimmer
See trimmer joist.

trimmer joist
A floor joist used to form an

253

opening such as to accommodate a stair, one end of which is supported by a trimming joist and into which are fixed trimmed joists. *See also* floor joist, trimmed joist, trimming joist.

trimming joist
A full length floor joist used to form an opening such as to accommodate a stair, and which supports one end of a trimmer joist and sometimes the ends of trimmed joists depending upon span. *See also* floor joist, trimmed joist, trimmer joist.

trunking
A metal or plastic pipe or covering used to protect electric wires in a building.

truss
See roof truss, trussed rafter.

trussed floor
An upper floor that is constructed of trussed joists. *See also* trussed joist.

trussed joist
A component comprising a plywood web with timber battens fixed at the top and bottom to act as flanges, with timber

uprights incorporated each side for stability. These components are lighter and capable of spanning greater distances than solid timber joisted floors. *See also* floor joist.

trussed rafter
A structural timber roof component comprising rafters, ceiling joists, struts and ties as one complete component which eliminates the need for traditional double roof construction. *See also* double roof, roof truss.

trust
The practice of holding property on behalf of and for the benefit of another. The holder of the property is the trustee.

trustee
A person who holds property in trust for another.

T-square
A wooden or plastic drawing instrument, used to support a set square, which rests on a drawing board and can be moved up or down. *See also* square, set square.

tuck pointing
Mortar used to fill into a brick

joint that has been recessed and left projecting for decorative purposes. *See also* mortar joint.

turning

The process of purchasing property and reselling it as soon as possible, at an enhanced price. A process often carried out where the purchaser resells the property between the exchange of contracts and completion.

turnkey deal

The process whereby the vendor or lessor provides a building completely fitted out for immediate occupation. Hence the occupier simply turns the key and moves in.

turpentine

A solvent which may be used to thin paint.

tusk tenon

A traditional timber joint used for connecting a trimmer joist to a trimming joist. *See also* trimmer joist, trimming joist.

two-coat work

Wall plaster applied in two coats, the first coat of which is referred to as the undercoat or float coat and the second the finish or set coat. *See also* three-coat work.

two-pipe system

A system consisting of two separate pipes, one into which the waste appliances from each floor are connected, the other serving the soil appliances. The waste and soil appliances would be identical on each floor of the building and anti-siphon pipes would be incorporated within the system. *See also* one-pipe system, single-stack system.

tyrolean finish

A textured finish applied by a machine to a render.

U

ultimate bearing capacity
The maximum load the ground beneath a foundation can withstand before movement occurs.

ultimate load
The maximum load that a material can withstand prior to failing. *See also* load, permissible load.

ultimate tensile strength
The maximum tensile stress that a material can be subject to prior to failing. *See also* tensile stress.

umpire
A third party appointed to adjudicate in a dispute where each party has appointed an arbitrator with whom they subsequently disagree. *See also* third surveyor.

unadopted road
A road for which the highway authority will not accept responsibility as a public highway and which is therefore not maintained at public expense.

undercloak
That portion of a sheet material, such as roofing felt, that is overlapped by an upper sheet.

undercoat
A type of paint that is applied to a surface that has initially been treated with a primer. It is usually applied in two coats to build up the thickness prior to applying the final coat. *See also* paint, primer, final coat.

under eaves course
The bottom course of tiles or slates provided at the eaves of a roof. *See also* eaves course, double eaves course.

underfelt
See underlay.

underlay
A layer of sheet material such as bitumastic felt laid beneath a roof covering. *See also* bitumastic felt.

underlease
A lease granted by a lessee or tenant.

under offer
The situation where a property is subject to an offer which has been accepted in principle but the transaction still has to be completed.

underpinning
A technique used for strengthening an existing foundation.

under tile
A short length of tile used in an under eaves course. *See also* under eaves course.

undisclosed principal
A principal whose identity has not been disclosed and is usually represented by an agent in negotiations to purchase the freehold or leasehold in property.

unencumbered
A title to land which is free of any encumbrances such as a mortgage.

unfit dwelling
A residential property which has been declared unfit by the local authority because of its failure to meet certain minimum standards of fitness for human habitation. See Housing Act 1985, as amended. *See also* unfit for human habitation.

unfit for human habitation
A dwelling in such a condition that it is unfit for habitation because of deficiencies in relation to: repair, stability, freedom from damp, internal arrangement, natural lighting, ventilation, water supply, drainage and sanitary conveniences, facilities for the preparation of food and arrangements for disposal of waste water.

ungauged lime plaster
Lime plaster without the addition of cement or gypsum. *See also* lime plasters.

uniformly distributed load
A load that spreads over the complete length of a component, such as a wall. *See also* load, point load.

universal beam
A steel 'I' section member with

parallel flanges, manufactured by hot rolling mild steel to produce various size sections where the width of the flange is equal to the distance between flanges. They are used for constructing steel-framed buildings. *See also* rolled steel joist.

universal column
See universal beam.

unplasticised polyvinyl chloride (uPVC)
A hard form of polyvinyl chloride used for manufacturing drainpipes and the frames of sealed units for double glazing.

unregistered land
Land the title of which is not registered at the Land Registry.

untrimmed floor
A floor comprising common joists only. *See also* common joist.

unwrought timber
See sawn timber.

up-front funding
A lender's promise to provide finance at the beginning of a development project.

uplift
Additional rent payable when the terms of the lease give the tenant benefits not prevailing in the market.

uplift rent
Rent payable when the lease terms are considered more beneficial to the tenant than the usual commercial terms, e.g. a higher rent to reflect long rent review intervals.

upper floor
Provided at the upper levels within a building to accommodate the requirements of a floor and consists of timber floor joists supported at each end. *See also* single floor, double floor.

upset price
The reserve or lowest acceptable price. Usually applicable to auctions but, in Scotland, a term applied to transactions by private treaty.

upstand
The edge of a waterproof covering, such as that to a flat roof, which is turned up against the side of a wall and over which a flashing is dressed. *See also* flashing.

uPVC
See unplasticised polyvinyl chloride.

upward/downward rent review
A rent review covenant in a lease which requires the payment of rent on due dates, irrespective of whether this is equal to, greater or less than the rent payable immediately before the review.

upward/downward rent review subject to a base
Essentially the same as upward/downward rent review, except that the rent cannot fall below a previously agreed level.

upwards only rent review
A rent review where the rent payable after a rent review is greater than that payable before it.

Urban Aid
A subsidy paid originally through the Home Office, but now through the Department of the Environment, to local authorities for work in urban areas. Housing associations may obtain funds through the local authority under this scheme for the provision of amenities and services to meet special social needs in the area in which they are operating.

Urban Regeneration Agency
A government agency established in 1993 with extensive planning and purchasing powers.

urban renewal
The redevelopment or rehabilitation of obsolete areas of a town, often including the provision of new infrastructure.

urinal
A soil appliance for male use designed to dispose of and wash away urine.

use and occupation action
An action for damages for the use of property where there has been an owner and occupier relationship but no agreement for the payment of rent.

Use Classes Order
A statutory instrument defining which changes of land use need, or do not need, planning permission by virtue of the Town and Country Planning Act 1990. *See also* existing use rights.

user
One who uses, enjoys or has a right to property.

'U' value
See thermal heat transmission coefficient.

V

vacant possession
Empty property which, by law, can be exclusively occupied or disposed of by the owner without any form of encumbrance.

vacant possession search
A search undertaken immediately before completion of a property transaction to determine that there has been compliance with a contractual term requiring that the property will be transferred with vacant possession.

valley
The internal angle formed where two pitched roof surfaces meet. *See also* hip, gable, tiled valley.

valley board
See layboard.

valley gutter
A method used for disposing of surface water from a pitched roof whereby a valley is incorporated by lining with lead to form a gutter. *See also* layboard.

valley rafter
A roof rafter used to form a valley and to which jack rafters are fixed. *See also* rafter, jack rafter.

valley tile
A rounded clay or concrete tile used to cover the joint of the roof covering the full length of a valley and, by so doing, forms a gutter to discharge surface water. *See also* valley.

value
The price property will be expected to bring if sold at a particular time and in given market conditions.

value added tax
A tax introduced under the

valuation

Finance Act 1972 and payable by the ultimate consumer of goods or services. The tax payable is a percentage of the value of the goods or services sold.

valuation
The estimation of the worth of a property for a particular purpose, e.g. a mortgage valuation for potential lender.

valuation certificate
A certificate issued by a valuer stating the valuation of a property.

valuation list
A statutory document prepared under the General Rate Act 1967 listing all the rating assessments of hereditaments in a valuation area. *See also* hereditament.

valuation officer
A public officer responsible for valuing property primarily for rating purposes.

valve
A type of tap which is fixed to a pipe to control the flow of a liquid or gas.

vapour barrier
A membrane used to prevent

the passage of moist air from inside a building into a blinding element such as a wall or roof. *See also* condensation, interstitial condensation, vapour check.

vapour check
A barrier used in the construction of a building element such as a wall or roof to prevent interstitial condensation. *See also* vapour barrier, interstitial condensation.

variable rent
Rent payable under the terms of a lease which provides that it will change at specified dates by reference to a previously agreed formula or other means.

variation
The changes to the previously agreed design/specification made by the employer in a building contract.

variation order
A written instruction from the architect authorising the contractor to alter or modify the building work. *See also* architect's instruction.

varnish
A transparent coating that forms

a hard protective skin on a wood surface that has been stained.

vault
An arched roof or ceiling. *See also* barrel vault.

Vebe consistometer
Apparatus used for testing the workability of fresh concrete.

Vebe consistometer test
A British Standard test for determining the workability of fresh concrete.

vegetable layer
The top surface of soil which is high in organic matter and compressible. It is removed to a depth of approximately 300mm to expose the subsoil. *See also* top soil, subsoil.

vendor
Seller, particularly of land.

veneer
A thin sheet of timber, usually hardwood, used to face a composite sheet such as plywood and blockboard to give a solid timber effect.

venetian blind
A blind provided to the inside of a window, consisting of horizontal or vertical slats which can be adjusted to deflect light.

vent
An outlet provided to allow water or air to escape from the inside to the outside of a building.

ventilation
The supply and circulation of air within a building by natural or artificial means, or a combination of both. *See also* natural ventilation, controlled ventilation, mechanical ventilation.

ventilation brick
See air brick.

ventilation pipe
See vent pipe.

vent light
A small opening light positioned at the top of a window. *See also* casement window.

vent pipe
A vertical pipe which is open at the top and is connected directly to a soil pipe to allow gases to escape. *See also* soil and vent pipe, soil pipe.

verge
The external edge of a roof at the junction with a gable wall.

verge board
See barge board.

verge tile
A special wide tile used to form a verge.

vertical load
Dead or live load acting in a downward or vertical direction. *See also* load, dead load, live load.

vest
To bestow on another some legal right, or ownership of an interest in land or property.

vested interest
An existing right to a present or future interest in land. The interest vested may be 'in possession' or 'in interest'.

vesting assent
An instrument transferring ownership of land from the personal representatives to the beneficiaries under the rules of intestacy or a will.

vesting declaration
When a compulsory purchase order has come into operation, the land may be acquired by a vesting declaration by the acquiring authority. *See also* compulsory purchase, compulsory purchase order.

vesting deed
A deed transferring the legal estate in the settled land to the beneficiaries in a settlement made during the settlor's life.

vesting order
A court order by which property passes as effectively as it would under a conveyance, e.g. vesting property in trustees.

virement
The movement of expenditure from one spread of expenditure to another, or from one financial year to another.

vinyl flooring
A sheet or tile material, based on polyvinyl chloride, used as a popular floor finish for solid floors.

visibility splay
Sight line.

vision splay
The area of land delineated by

two diverging lines at the point of entry on to a road which enable unobstructed visibility for a reasonable distance.

vitreous
A term used to describe the hard, durable, glossy, waterproof properties associated with vitrified clayware.

vitrified clayware
Clay products such as drainpipes burnt to a high temperature to produce a hard, durable, glossy, waterproof material. *See also* salt-glazed stoneware drainpipes.

void
1. Unoccupied, empty, unlet or unusable building or space in a building.
2. An air space within a material. *See also* porous, porosity.

void allowance
Sometimes called vacancy allowance, being a deduction made for the likely non-receipt of rent during a valuation exercise.

void contract
An agreement which has no legal effect.

void relief
Allowance against rates for the period when a property is unoccupied.

voluntary settlement
A settlement made for valuable consideration. *See also* settlement.

voluntary transfer
A colloquial term to describe the transfer of local authority housing stock to another landlord.

voussoir
A special wedge-shaped brick used to construct an arch. *See also* arch stone.

W

waiver
The abandonment or failure to assert a legal right.

Waldram diagram
A diagram for evaluating the adequacy of daylight in a room. The effect of an obstruction to light is recorded on a grid and the proportion of unobstructed light is calculated from the diagram. *See also* daylight factor.

waling
A horizontal timber member used in the construction of planking and strutting. *See also* planking and strutting.

walking distress
A situation whereby a bailiff prepares a list of goods to be distrained during the levying of distress but leaves them on the premises, subject to an enforceable agreement that they must not be removed.

wall
A vertical structure constructed of masonry, concrete, timber and other lightweight materials that is used to form an external enclosure, and divide the internal space of buildings. *See also* external wall, internal wall, load-bearing wall, non-load-bearing wall, cavity wall, solid wall, parapet wall.

wallboard
Sheet material, such as plasterboard, used to line walls and ceilings. *See also* dry lining.

wall panel
A unit used in the construction of a prefabricated partition. *See also* prefabricated partition.

wallpaper
Paper applied to plastered walls for decorative purposes, and also available for lining walls

prior to painting or applying a decorative wallpaper.

wall plate
A solid rectangular section of timber placed on top of walls whose function is to act as a bearing to the end roof and floor joists.

wall string
The string that is fixed to a wall. *See also* string.

wall tie
See cavity tie.

wall tile
A glazed ceramic or plaster tile applied to a wall for decorative purposes and used in situations where a waterproof surface is required for ease of cleaning, such as in kitchens and bathrooms.

warden
A person providing management services to tenants. A term usually applied to sheltered housing and hostels.

warm air heating
See space heating.

warm roof
A flat roof where the thermal insulation layer is placed near the outside usually on top of the decking so that the air inside the roof space is of a similar temperature to the room below and would not be prone to condensation. *See also* cold roof.

warning pipe
An overflow pipe connected to a cistern and projecting through a roof or wall. It is used to detect water continually flowing out. *See also* overflow pipe.

warp
The condition of being twisted out of original shape due to a change in moisture content caused by heating, the distortion of floor boards which creak when walked on.

warranty
An express, or implied, carrying out of the truth of a statement, whereby the warrantor becomes responsible in law in the event of the facts being otherwise than as stated. For example, a vendor may warrant that property is fit for a particular purpose.

wash basin
See lavatory basin.

washdown closet

A WC where water from the flushing cistern is discharged directly into the pan so that the force of the water washes away waste matter. *See also* siphonic WC.

washer

A flat metal ring placed under a bolt head or nut and used to obtain a tight grip and spread the load when the bolt and nut are tightened.

washhand basin

See lavatory basin.

waste

See foul water.

waste appliance

An appliance used for washing and personal hygiene such as a bath, sink, shower, washing machine.

waste pipe

A pipe connected to a waste trap and soil pipe to convey waste water from a waste appliance. *See also* soil pipe, trap.

waste trap

A trap fitted to a waste appliance. *See also* trap.

waste water

See foul water.

wasting assets

Property with a limited existence. Usually refers to leasehold property.

water bar

A metal strip fixed in grooves between the top of a stone or concrete sill and the inside of a timber sill to prevent water seepage.

water–cement ratio

The amount of water specified for a concrete mix, which is determined by dividing its weight by the weight of the cement in the mix which has an effect on workability. *See also* workability.

water closet (WC)

A soil appliance used for disposing of human waste. It consists of a glazed ceramic pan with a seat and cover. Two designs are used – the washdown closet and the siphonic closet. *See also* water trap, soil pipe, flushing cistern, automatic flushing cistern, low-level flushing cistern, washdown closet, siphonic WC.

water hammer
A noise in water pipes caused by a sudden interruption of water flow, such as the rapid operation of a tap.

water main
See service main.

waterproof
See damp-proof course and damp-proof membrane.

waterproof layer
See damp-proof course and damp-proof membrane.

water-repellent
Describes a surface, such as that of external brickwork, that has been treated with a substance which resists water absorption.

water seal
See water trap.

water table
The level of water in the ground which varies depending upon retained ground water. *See also* ground water, subsoil water.

water tank
See cistern.

water test
See hydraulic test.

water trap
A water seal in the trap of a pipe or gulley to prevent foul water from drains re-entering the building. *See also* trap, P-trap.

wayleave
A right of way over another person's land to lay cables, pipes or conduits, on over or under the land. Normally granted to a statutory undertaker.

weather bar
See water bar.

weatherboard
A projecting moulding strip fixed to the bottom of an external door to throw surface water clear of the sill.

weatherboarding
Internal timber cladding. *See also* shiplap boards.

weathering
The change in colour and texture of the external surface of a material after exposure to these elements over a period of time.

weatherstrip
Strips of metal and plastic materials used to seal around the edges of door and window

frames to prevent the passage of heat and water.

weather-struck joint
A mortar joint splayed so that the bottom edge of the bricks above project over the joint. *See also* mortar joint.

wedge
A tapered portion of wood or metal which is forced into a gap in a joint to tighten it.

weep holes
Drainage points placed in the outer leaf of a cavity wall to allow trapped water to escape outside. *See also* cavity wall.

weld
A method used for joining the edges of sheets of metal or plastic by melting the material and allowing it to cool and harden to form a sealed joint.

well maintained payment
Payments made by a local housing authority at its discretion for an unfit house which has nevertheless been well maintained. *See also* the Housing Act 1985, as amended.

welted drip
The edge of a bitumastic felt roof which is folded to form an eaves to discharge surface water. *See also* flat roof, bitumastic felt.

wet construction
The method used for constructing parts of the building in situ using bulk materials mixed with water, e.g. concrete, mortar and plaster. *See also* in situ, concrete, dry construction.

wet rot
The decay of timber caused by a fungus (*coniophora cerebela* and *conisphora puteana*) which grows in alternating wet and dry conditions. *See also* dry rot.

wet trades
The building construction trades involved in using materials, such as concrete, mortar and plaster, where water is required for mixing.

white land
Land which has not been designated for any particular use by a local planning authority. It is normally rural land.

white spirit
A cheap substitute for turpentine which is obtained from

petroleum and used for removing paint.

wheelchair housing
Dwellings designed for occupation by people who need to use a wheelchair.

wide strip foundation
A reinforced concrete foundation where the width is intended to spread the load over a larger area. *See also* strip foundation, foundation.

will
Declaration by a person describing the disposition of their property after death.

willing seller/buyer/lessee/ lessor
An assumption normally associated with valuation purposes that the relevant party to the property transaction is willing to dispose of, or acquire, his interest and that there is at least one genuine person in the marketplace for that interest.

winder
Steps used to change direction of flight and where the tread is fixed into a newel post and is narrow at the side. Used instead of a landing and also to form a spiral stair. *See also* kite winder, spiral stair.

wind load
See horizontal load.

window
A component comprising glass panels fixed into a timber, metal or plastic framework which are incorporated into openings in external walls in order to allow natural light and ventilation into buildings. *See also* casement window, sash window, pivot window.

window bar
See glazing board.

window board
A horizontal board fixed to the bottom of a window frame on the inside.

window frame
A timber, metal or plastic component comprising a surround, mullions and transoms into which fixed and opening lights are incorporated. *See also* casement window, opening light, vent light, fixed light.

window ledge
See sill.

window furniture

The mechanisms required for locking, opening and closing opening lights. *See also* opening light, vent light.

window sill

See sill.

wind pressure

See horizontal load.

wirecut brick

A brick that is produced by intruding the material and cutting into the required size during its manufacture. The material may be intruded through a mould incorporating rods producing bricks with holes through the thickness or one which produces solid uniform bricks. *See also* brick, pressed brick.

wired glass

See reinforced glass.

without reserve

An auction or tender sale where there is no minimum price attached by the vendor.

wood block floor

See block floor.

wood preservative

See preservative.

wood screw

A screw used for connecting timber components. *See also* screw.

woodwool

A mixture of wood shavings and cement to form a composite slab.

woodwool slab

A composite slab, available in various thicknesses and standard sizes, manufactured from woodwool and used for decking flat roofs.

words of purchase

Words which describe the person who is to take an interest in land in his own right.

workability

The degree to which concrete or mortar is mixed to produce a dense well proportioned mass with a low percentage of voids. *See also* admixture, water–cement ratio.

working capital

The capital funds required for

the day to day running of a business.

working day
For financial purposes a weekday excluding bank holidays.

working drawing
A drawing used to construct the building. *See also* drawings.

working stress
See permissible stress.

writ of right
Action to recover land in fee simple unjustly held from the rightful owner.

wrot timber.
See wrought timber.

wrought timber
Wood that has been planed on one or more surfaces and is generally used for joining walls.

Y

Yale lock
A type of cylinder lock. *See also* cylinder lock.

yard
The rear open, enclosed area to a house.

yard gulley
See gulley.

year of assessment
For capital and income tax purposes, a calendar year starting 6 April and ending 5 April.

yoke
A timber or metal strap used to secure formwork to a column.

Z

zax
A traditional tool used for trimming the edges and holing roof slates.

zinc
A non-ferrous metal used as a protective coating on steel (i.e. galvanising, sheradising). Used extensively in the form of sheet or strip for roof coverings, gutters and flashing. Also available in the form of tubes, wires and rods. *See also* galvanising, sheradising.

zinc nails
Steel nails coated in zinc (galvanised) and used for fixing plasterboard sheets to timber.

zinc oxide
A compound of zinc used as a pigment in paint.

zone
A term commonly used in town planning, being an area having a defined homogeneous land use.

Useful addresses

Association of County Councils
66a Eaton Square
London SW1W 9BH
Tel: 0171 235 1200

Association of District Councils
26 Chapter Street
London SW1P 4ND
Tel: 0171 233 6868

Bar Council
3 Bedford Road
London WC1R 4BD
Tel: 0171 242 0082

Benefits Agency Chief
Executive
Mr P. Mathison
Quarry House
Quarry Hill
Leeds LS2 7UA
Tel: 0113 232 4000

British Association of Social
Workers
14 Kent Street

Birmingham B5 6RD
Tel: 0121 622 3911

Building Research
Establishment
Bucknalls Lane
Garston
Watford WD2 7JR
Tel: 01923 894040

Chartered Institute of Building
Englemere
Kings Ride
Ascot
Berkshire SL5 8BJ
Tel: 01344 23355

Chartered Institute of
Environmental Health
Chadwick Court
15 Hatfields
London SE1 8BJ
Tel: 0171 928 6006

Chartered Institute of Housing
Octavia House

Westwood Way
Coventry CB4 8JP
Tel: 01203 694433

Citizens' Advice Bureaux
136 City Road
London EC1V 2NJ
Tel: 0171 251 2000

Housing Corporation
Waverley House
7 Noel Street
London W1V 3PB
Tel: 0171 292 4400

Law Society
113 Chancery Lane
London LC2A 1PL
Tel: 0171 242 1222

Local Government
Ombudsman

England
21 Queen Anne's Gate
London SW1H 9BU
Tel: 0171 9153210

Scotland
23 Walker Street
Edinburgh EH3 7HX
Tel: 0131 225 5300

Wales
Derwen House
Court Road
Bridgend CF31 1BN
Tel: 01656 661325

Northern Ireland
Progressive House
33 Wellington Place
Belfast BT1 6HN
Tel: 01232 233821

National Federation of Housing
Associations
175 Gray's Inn Road
London WC1X 8UP
Tel: 0171 278 6571

Offices of the Social Security
Commissioners

England and Wales
Harp House
83 Farringdon Street
London EC4A 4DH
Tel: 0171 353 5145

Northern Ireland
Lancashire House
5 Linenhall Street
Belfast BT2 8AA
Tel: 01232 332344

Scotland
23 Melville Street
Edinburgh EH3 7PW
Te:l 0131 2252201

The Parliamentary
Ombudsman
Office of the Parliamentary
Commissioner
Church House

Great Smith Street
London SW1P 3BW
Tel: 0171 276 2130

President of the Independent
Tribunal Service

England, Scotland, Wales
HH Judge K. Bassingthwaighte
City Gate House
39–45 Finsbury Square
London EC2A 1PX
Tel: 0171 814 6500

Northern Ireland
Mr G. G. MacLynn
6th Floor
Cleaver House
3 Donegal Square North
Belfast BT1 5GA
Tel: 01232 539900

Royal Institute of British
Architects
66 Portland Place
London W1N 4AD
Tel: 0171 580 5533

Royal Institution of Chartered
Surveyors
Surveyor Court
Westwood Way
Coventry CV4 8JE
Te:l 0171 222 7000

Social Security Appeal
Tribunals

Mr R. Huggins
National Chairperson
City Gate House
39-45 Finsbury Square
London EC2A 1PX
Tel: 0171 814 6500

Measures

Linear measures

12 inches	1 foot
3 feet	1 yard
22 yards	1 chain
10 chains	1 furlong
8 furlongs	1 statute mile

10 millimetres	1 centimetre
100 centimetres	1 metre
1000 metres	1 kilometre

inch	2.54 centimetres
foot	0.3048 metres
yard	0.9144 metres
mile	1.60934 kilometres

millimetre	0.039 inches
centimetre	0.3937 inches
metre	39.37 inches
kilometre	0.621 miles *or* 3280 ft 10 ins

Square measures

square inch	0.452 square centimetres
square foot	0.0929 square metres
square yard	0.8361 square metres
acre	0.405 hectares
square mile	2.59 square kilometres
square centimetre	0.155 square inches
square metre	1.196 square yards *or* 1550 square inches
hectare	2.4711 acres

Cubic measures

cubic inch	16.387 cubic centimetres
cubic foot	0.0283 cubic metres
cubic yard	0.765 cubic yards
cubic centimetre	0.061 cubic inches
cubic metre	35.31 cubic feet *or* 1.308 cubic yards

Refurbishing Offices for People with Disabilities

A Design and Assessment Guide for Owners, Occupiers, Developers and Advisers

Jack Rostron and Murray A Fordham

Many office buildings are being refurbished and there is evidence to suggest that in the future there will be an increasing trend towards this kind of activity both speculatively and on a bespoke basis. At the present time new build design advice for accommodating the needs of the disabled is available in several books. There is however little available concerning refurbishment of offices – this book meets that need.

The book is in two parts. Part one provides design guidance for occupiers, owners and developers of offices to meet the needs of physically disabled employees for which existing property is suitable. The book is aimed at use by in-house staff and non-specialist external advisers.

Part two provides a means of assessing if an existing or alternative office building is suitable to meet the needs of the physically disabled. The survey sheet is developed for use by disabled people themselves, their employers and 'non-specialist' advisers.

1996   128 pages   Hbk   1 85742 345 3   £27.50

Price subject to change without notification

arena

Adapting Housing for People with Disabilities

Jack Rostron and Murray A Fordham

"This is an attractively presented book and, for its size, it is surprisingly comprehensive. It will be appreciated by people who need a concise introduction to a very complex subject area. I feel it would be appropriate for students intending to work with people with disabilities in the community, who are planning careers in Occupational Therapy, Environmental Health and Special Needs Housing. It would also be useful for experienced staff as a guide to all those elements which have to be considered when discussions begin with the tenant, prospective tenant or owner concerning the options available to provided housing that meets their needs." **Registered Homes**

Part one of the book is aimed primarily at housing associations, providing design guidance for converting existing property. It will help in-house staff and non-specialist external advisers of general housing associations, as well as local authority social services and housing departments.

The second part provides a way of assessing, by means of a survey sheet, if a disabled person's current home is suitable for their needs. The survey sheet is developed for use by disabled people themselves, their families and non-specialist local authority advisers.

1996   104 pages   Hbk   1 85742 363 1   £27.50

Price subject to change without notification

Housing the Physically Disabled

An anthology and reader of practice and policy

Jack Rostron

This book offers an anthology of research undertaken by the author during the period following the passage of the Chronically Sick and Disabled Persons Act 1970. These assess the usefulness of existing concepts, policies and procedures developed to meet the special housing needs of the physically disabled.

These previously published papers which form the book, have been chosen due to their particular interest to students and practitioners in social work, occupational therapy, rehabilitation medicine and nursing, welfare law, housing, health and social services management, architecture and building. It is also hoped that it will be of interest and help to people with disabilities and their carers.

Jack Rostron is a chartered surveyor and town planner currently teaching at Liverpool John Moores University and acting as an adviser to the World Health Organizations' Regional Office for Europe.

1995   144 pages   Pbk   1 85742 283 X   £16.95

Price subject to change without notification

arena